THE HISTORY OF ISRAEL

THE
HISTORY OF ISRAEL

MARTIN NOTH

Professor of Old Testament
University of Bonn

SECOND EDITION

HARPER & ROW, PUBLISHERS

NEW YORK, HAGERSTOWN, SAN FRANCISCO, LONDON

PUBLISHER'S NOTE

For this edition the English translation has been revised throughout by Dr. P. R. Ackroyd of Cambridge. An endeavour has been made to correct the many errors of translation and spelling which appeared in the earlier edition, so that the author's meaning is now more clearly and accurately conveyed. The index of names and subjects has been entirely remade.

1959

CONTENTS

PART THREE

ISRAEL UNDER THE RULE OF THE GREAT POWERS OF THE ANCIENT ORIENT

PART FOUR

RESTORATION, DECLINE AND FALL

ABBREVIATIONS

AASOR	= Annual of the American Schools of Oriental Research
AfO	= Archiv für Orientforschung
ANEP	= The Ancient Near East in Pictures Relating to the Old Testament, ed. by J. B. Pritchard (1954)
ANET	= Ancient Near Eastern Texts Relating to the Old Testament, ed. by J. B. Pritchard (1950, 2nd ed. 1956)
AO	= Der Alte Orient. Gemeinverständliche Darstellungen herausgegeben von der Vorderasiatisch-Ägyptischen Gesellschaft
AOB²	= H. Gressmann, Altorientalische Bilder zum Alten Testament, 2. Aufl. 1927
AOT²	= H. Gressmann, Altorientalische Texte zum Alten Testament, 2. Aufl. 1926
BASOR	= Bulletin of the American Schools of Oriental Research
BBLAK	= Beiträge zur biblischen Landes- und Altertumskunde
BHK	= Biblia Hebraica, ed. by R. Kittel
BRL	= K. Galling, Biblisches Reallexikon (Handbuch zum Alten Testament, I, 1) 1937
BWA(N)T	= Beiträge zur Wissenschaft vom Alten (und Neuen) Testament
BZAW	= Beihefte zur Zeitschrift für die alttestamentliche Wissenschaft
DOTT	= Documents from Old Testament Times, ed. by D. Winton Thomas (1958).
EA	= J. A. Knudtzon, Die El-Amarna-Tafeln (1915)
HAT	= Handbuch zum Alten Testament
IEJ	= Israel Exploration Journal
JBL	= Journal of Biblical Literature
JPOS	= Journal of the Palestine Oriental Society
MVA(e)G	= Mitteilungen der Vorderasiatisch(-Ägyptischen) Gesellschaft
NKZ	= Neue Kirchliche Zeitschrift
PJB	= Palästinajahrbuch
RB	= Revue Biblique
TGI	= K. Galling, Textbuch zur Geschichte Israels (1950)
ThLZ	= Theologische Literaturzeitung
WAT	= M. Noth, Die Welt des Alten Testaments (² 1953)
WO	= Die Welt des Orients. Wissenschaftliche Beiträge zur Kunde des Morgenlandes
WZKM	= Wiener Zeitschrift für die Kunde des Morgenlandes
ZAW	= Zeitschrift für die alttestamentliche Wissenschaft
ZDMG	= Zeitschrift der Deutschen Morgenländischen Gesellschaft
ZDPV	= Zeitschrift des Deutschen Palästina-Vereins

INTRODUCTION

1. *'Israel'*

THE question what 'Israel', the subject of a 'History of Israel', actually was, is not so simple and obvious as not to require a few words of explanation at the very outset: and although the evidence on which the answer to the question is based will emerge only in the course of our presentation of the 'History of Israel', the very fact that the problem exists at all must be made clear and a provisional answer given that will enable us to define the object of our enquiry and the magnitude of our task.

All the information at our disposal serves to establish that 'Israel' was a historical reality with its own historical period, during which it was intimately involved in the multifarious life of the surrounding world. It can therefore be adequately understood only by historical research. Knowledge of the sequence of events which constitute the history of Israel within a definite period of time and of their relationship with one another and with the oriental history of the same era, which was so surpassingly rich in personalities and events, is in part readily available since it has come down to us directly; though, as in every other sphere of history, where the evidence is more indirect, the never-ending concatenation of cause and effect must be reconstructed intuitively. In a history of 'Israel' the whole field has to be explored with the utmost thoroughness from every possible angle and by all the methods open to historical scholarship, precisely because 'Israel' is without question a historical reality.

The genuineness of that historical reality is not affected by the circumstance that in its history we also meet an element beyond the range of human understanding, an element that cannot be ascribed to known causes and effects. An element of the inexplicable is in fact present in *all* human history and is bound to be present not merely because it is not even remotely possible to embrace the whole profusion of cause and effect even in the historical present, let alone in the past, and least of all the remote past, but above all because history is not merely a constant repetition of

complicated concatenations of cause and effect if God is really
active in history not simply as a πρῶτον κινοῦν but as the ever
present Lord working within the superficial interplay of cause and
effect[1]. Inevitably, therefore, there is an element of mystery, of the
'unhistorical', in all human history which makes its presence felt
on the frontiers of all historical knowledge.

The history of 'Israel' is no exception to this general rule, yet
in spite of, or possibly just because of, this it remains authentic
history. It would, however, be too easy to assign all the obscure
events in the history of 'Israel' to this 'unhistorical' sphere,
possibly on the basis of some preconception of the true nature of
'Israel', since deeper historical insight and new possibilities of
comparison with events in other areas of world history may easily
throw light on what is at first apparently incomprehensible; and
the historian's task is always to be seeking for possible comparisons
and explanations, though he must also never forget the presence
of the element of the 'unhistorical'.

The study of the history of the Orient, which has been proceeding
for over a century now with such undreamt of success and with so
many unexpected discoveries to its credit, has brilliantly illuminated
the background of the history of 'Israel'. It has revealed how
closely involved the history of 'Israel' was in the varied life and
historical movements of the ancient Orient and it has supplied us
with abundant material with which to compare events in the history
of 'Israel', so that it is no longer possible to expound the history
of 'Israel' as a whole or in detail without a knowledge of the history
of the ancient Orient. There is hardly any event in the history of
'Israel' that is not clearly related to this ancient Oriental background, the roots of which do not have to be sought in the tumultuous history of the ancient Orient and for which parallels cannot be
found in Israel's Oriental environment. These multifarious connections have illuminated the historical reality of 'Israel' with the
utmost clarity and have taught us to understand better the historical
tradition of the Old Testament in its far-reaching context and
reality. They have often opened up surprising possibilities of comparison and sent us back to study the historical information of the
Old Testament with renewed seriousness.

Yet in spite of all these historical connections and possibilities
for comparison, 'Israel' still appears a stranger in the world of its
own time, a stranger wearing the garments and behaving in the

[1] Cf. Karl Barth, *Die kirchliche Dogmatik*. III, 1 (1945), pp. 84 ff. ; E. T. *Church
Dogmatics. The Doctrine of Creation* (1958), pp. 78 ff.

manner of its age, yet separate from the world it lived in, not merely in the sense that every historical reality has its own individual character, and therefore an element of uniqueness, but rather that at the very centre of the history of 'Israel' we encounter phenomena for which there is no parallel at all elsewhere, not because the material for comparison has not yet come to light but because, so far as we know, such things have simply never happened elsewhere. To make this fact clear will be one of the tasks we shall have to face in our presentation of the history of 'Israel'.

From this point of view the question as to what Israel actually was becomes even more urgent. Apart from a more specialised and circumscribed use of the name which arose later in a closely defined historical situation and in circumstances with which we are quite familiar (cf. p. 183), the name 'Israel' is used in the Old Testament tradition only as a collective term for a group of twelve tribes which had a separate history of their own. The name first occurs in the Old Testament where, in the course of a personifying description of prehistorical Israel, the father of the twelve ancestors and *heroes eponymi* of the tribes is called 'Israel' (Gen. xxxii, 29) and after that the name is used for this person or as a collective term. There is not a trace of evidence as to how the group of the twelve tribes acquired it and whether it had had a previous history in the course of which certain changes of meaning led to this collective name. It is, in any case, idle to make conjectures for which there is no real foundation at all. Even the oldest, very early epigraphic occurrence of the name does not help us. It is found in a song of triumph for the Egyptian Pharaoh Merneptah on a stele which was set up in this Pharaoh's mortuary temple in the Pharaonic necropolis in Thebes, and it is now in the Egyptian Museum in Cairo (the so-called 'Israel stele'[1]). In line 27, in connection with the conquest of some Palestinian cities, the Pharaoh is also extolled for destroying 'Israel'[2]. It is, however, impossible to say with any certainty what the 'Israel' referred to here actually was in the Palestine of *circa* 1225 B.C., whether it was already the 'Israel' of the twelve tribes in the form known to Old Testament tradition or some still older entity which bore the name 'Israel' and then for some now obscure historical reason passed it on to the 'Israel' that we know.

[1] Translation of the text AOT², pp. 20-25, ANET, pp. 376-378, DOTT, pp. 137-141; reproduction of the Stele, AOB², No. 109, ANEP, Nos. 342, 343, DOTT, p. 8.
[2] The Egyptian explanatory sign placed behind it indicates that the name is that of a 'foreign people', whilst the other Palestinian names are provided with the explanatory sign denoting 'foreign land'.

Even if it could be established beyond doubt, the etymology of the name would scarcely be any help. All that we know for certain is that, structurally, the name conforms to a type which is fairly common among the oldest personal and tribal names known to us[1]; on the other hand, indisputable place-names of exactly the same structure are also found in Palestine[2], so it is impossible to form any definite conclusion about the original meaning of the name. Further than the data provided by the Old Testament tradition we cannot go, and must rest content with the fact that the earliest known connotation refers to the group of the twelve tribes. This group of tribes therefore forms the subject-matter of a 'History of Israel'.

The question that must now be asked is whether, without detriment to its special character, 'Israel' can, on the basis of its undoubted historical reality and connection with the history of the ancient Orient, be assigned to a particular category. Whenever a definite appellative term is used at all, 'Israel' is normally described as a *nation* in the Old Testament tradition, and thereby reckoned among the many nations of the ancient Orient[3]. It is a description that was bound to suggest itself. The tribes of Israel were bound together by a common language, though, admittedly, they shared it with numerous neighbours. It was one of the Canaanite dialects established in the civilisation of Syria-Palestine[4]. In the period before the taking of the land their forefathers had presumably spoken an ancient Aramaic tongue, in common with the other nomadic, land-seeking groups on the borders of Syria and Palestine. They were also bound together by living in the same restricted area. It is true that they never held it entirely for themselves and their settlements never formed a completely self-contained unit: nevertheless they were united in geographical proximity. Finally—and in the present context this is the most important point of all—they were bound together by a basically similar historical situation and hence by a common historical experience. It has to be admitted, however, that they did lack certain elements which are usually considered essential to the concept of a

[1] Further details about this in M. Noth, *Die israelitischen Personennamen* (1928), pp. 207 ff.

[2] Cf. the place-names Jezreel, Jabneel, Irpeel and the names *jšp'r* (No. 78) and *j'ḳb'r* (No. 102) which occur presumably as place-names in the Palestine List of the Pharaoh Thothmes III.

[3] The Old Testament words for 'people', *'am* and *gōy*, were used in earlier times for both one's own people and for foreign peoples too; it was only later on that the plural of the latter became a special term for foreign peoples, 'heathen peoples'.

[4] For this language, or more precisely, for the later Judaean form of language in which the Old Testament was revised, the term 'Hebrew' has been used since New Testament times on the basis of a secondary meaning of the concept 'Hebrew'.

'nation'. As far as we know, the tribes of Israel hardly ever acted in history as a unit and certainly never for any substantial length of time—apart from the quite temporary phase of the monarchy of Saul, which was, by its nature, obviously incapable of surviving for long. In the period before the rise of the monarchy on Palestinian soil we find only single tribes—evidently organised in the forms of tribal constitution current at the time—and, occasionally small groups of tribes intervening actively in historical events. Nor were the kingdoms which came to be formed really built up on the basis of a combining of the Israelite tribes, as if the latter had here taken on a more clearly defined historical form. When the kingdoms declined, the tribes continued to live as subject groups in various provinces of successive large empires and the later changes in their fortunes also did not permit any combining for joint historical action, so deeply divided were they. If, therefore, following the Old Testament, we apply the rather vague concept of 'nation' to Israel as, in spite of everything, the most appropriate label for the historical reality, it must be borne in mind that the term cannot be used here in exactly the same sense as it is used of other nations; it may even be better to discard it altogether and speak simply of 'Israel', rather than of the 'nation of Israel'.

What united the tribes of Israel and held them together—in other words, what constituted the real nature of this strange reality—can only emerge, in so far as it is demonstrable at all, from a detailed presentation of its history. On the other hand, the fact that 'Israel' was a unique phenomenon in the midst of the other historical nations arises from a quite general consideration. Thoroughly misguided though it would certainly be to regard later Judaism and 'Israel' as one and the same, and to identify these two quite distinct historical phenomena, there is, nevertheless, a direct historical connection between them; and the historically unique element in Judaism must have been present in embryo in the 'Israel' from which it evolved. Recognition of this fact, however, must not tempt us to isolate 'Israel' from the historical world of the ancient Orient and disguise the reality of its total involvement in that world.

As will be shown in detail later on, the tribes which formed the larger entity 'Israel' were only fully united at the occupation of the agricultural land of Palestine, and it is only from that point that the real 'History of Israel' can take its departure. It must be stated emphatically that Old Testament tradition does not recognise any earlier form of 'Israel' than this union of the

twelve tribes domiciled in Palestine. What it reports of the events
before the occupation of the land it also refers to this same 'Israel'
which it recognises only in its later historical form. This 'Israel'
comes on the scene almost abruptly as the descendants of the twelve
heroes eponymi who, with their common father, are, once again,
simply the personification of the historical situation after the occupation of the land. Concerning the historical evolution of 'Israel'
we have no sort of information, only traditions about events in pre-
historical times, the contents of which are admittedly of decisive
importance but, in their present form, presuppose the subsequent
'Israel' of history. We also have no information whatsoever about
earlier forms of social organisation in which a 'primeval Israel'
may have existed, to be replaced later by the 'Israel' of the twelve
Palestinian tribes which did constitute a kind of nation; and even
for pure surmise there is a complete lack of likely clues[1].

If the appropriate starting-point for a presentation of the
'history of Israel' is thereby established, it is not immediately
clear to what point in time the existence of 'Israel' may be said
to have continued and how far an exposition of its history must be
extended. The destruction of political autonomy on the soil of
'Israel' which took place in the events of the years 733/721 B.C. and
587 B.C. no more signified the end of Israel than the development of
political forms of organisation marked the beginning of its life: it
merely meant the end of a particular period of its history; and only
a false conception of the extent of the deportations which followed
those events could lead anyone to conclude that the substance of the
tribes of Israel was, generally speaking, dissolved and destroyed
at that time and that the old 'Israel' really came to an end. In fact,
the tribes and 'Israel' itself survived. To pursue the history of
'Israel' beyond the decline of its political autonomy is desirable
not only on practical grounds and with reference to the historical
background of the later and latest strata of Old Testament literature, but also for purely objective reasons. Even the historically
significant decline of the ancient Orient which set in with the
emergence of Alexander the Great and the beginning of the
Hellenisation of the Orient, though bringing significant changes
for Israel, had no decisive effect on its situation; there is no reason
to cut the thread of the history of 'Israel' at that point. The end

---

[1] I have fundamental doubts about the validity of W. Caspari's attempt to discover
a 'pre-national organisation' of the 'subsequent people of Israel' in *Die Gottesgemeinde
vom Sinai und das nachmalige Volk Israel* (1922), in which he discusses M. Weber's
Das antike Judentum (Gesammelte Aufsätze zur Religionssoziologie, III (1923)), though
in itself his attempt is full of interest and remarkable detail.

of the historical existence of 'Israel' and the scattering of Jewry among the nations were brought about only by events that took place in the Roman era. In this period we find the tribes of Israel once more domiciled in their own land and conscious of their common inheritance[1]; at the same time, however, there was carried through that process of inner and outer dissolution which becomes apparent and reaches its climax in the unfortunate and disastrous insurrections against Roman rule. It is these revolts which may be said to have brought the history of 'Israel' to its close, and the treatment of the insurrections of A.D. 66–70 and 132–135 may therefore form the appropriate conclusion for a presentation of the history of 'Israel'.

What sprang from this decline of 'Israel' was the phenomenon which we usually call 'Judaism'. Admittedly, it had its roots in the history of 'Israel' and was related to developments which had emerged in the later period of the history of 'Israel' and it has always applied the name 'Israel' to itself; but as the centre of worship had been abolished and there was no homeland and therefore no chance of united historical action it was in fact something substantially new, so that we do well to use the special term 'Judaism' rather than the old name 'Israel'. It is true, of course, that from the womb of 'Judaism' there has emerged in most recent times a new historical entity named 'Israel' which has sought its homeland again in the ancient land of Israel under the auspices of the Zionist movement and has established a new State of 'Israel'. In spite of the historical connections which undoubtedly exist, this new 'Israel' is separated from the Israel of old not only by the long period of almost 2000 years but also by a long history full of vicissitudes and it has come into being in the midst of entirely different historical conditions. It would therefore be improper to extend our historical enquiry from the end of the 'Israel' of old to the 'Israel' of the present day.

2. The Land of Israel

From its beginning to its end, taking both terms in the sense we have just defined, the history of Israel took place in a narrowly confined space, in a land which may, for the period in question, be appropriately described as the 'land of Israel', to use an expression that occurs once in the Old Testament (1 Sam. xiii, 19). A proper

[1] Josephus still speaks of the Israelite tribes in the land as a unit, employing the term 'the people' (τὸ ἔθνος).

and original name for this land as a whole has not come down to
us from Old Testament times[1], and presumably no such name
ever existed; since as a natural phenomenon it was never a homogeneous, self-contained entity and was never occupied by a homogeneous population, and it was hardly at any time the scene of a
political organisation which substantially coincided with its actual
area. So the expression 'the land of Israel' may serve as a somewhat flexible description of the area within which the Israelite
tribes had their settlements. This region is constituted by the
southern third of the extensive mountain country between the
eastern border of the Mediterranean and the Syrian desert, which
is divided into a western and eastern half by a deep valley which
traverses it longitudinally. To the north the land of Israel extended
approximately as far as the southern extremities of the high mountains of Lebanon and Anti-Lebanon, and to the south as far as the
transition from agricultural land to the steppe and desert of the
so-called Sinaitic peninsula, roughly on the latitude of the southern
extremity of the Dead Sea.

It is usual to call the land of Israel 'Palestine', a name that
arose in early Christian literature to describe the setting of the
Bible story, following the official language of the period. When
after the various Jewish insurrections, the provincial name of Judaea
which had been used hitherto and was now no longer suitable, had
to be avoided, the earlier name of Palestine ('Land of the Philistines')[2] was chosen to describe the Roman province which more or
less coincided with the land of Israel, though, to begin with, the
term had been applied to a more limited area; and ever since then
this name has remained in use, officially and unofficially, in the
Christian church and its basic connotation has remained unaltered,
though the lines of demarcation have varied slightly from time to time.

As real and authentic history the history of Israel was always
profoundly conditioned by the nature of the soil on which it took
place. A knowledge of the geography of Palestine is therefore
one of the preconditions for a proper understanding of the history
of Israel; and an exposition of the history of Israel must be preceded
by a brief survey of the basic characteristics of the land itself.[3]

[1] More precise details on this in WAT, pp. 42 ff.
[2] More precise details in M. Noth, ZDPV, 62 (1939), pp. 125-144.
[3] We cannot offer even the outlines of a real geography of Palestine here. Cf., above
all, H. Guthe, *Palaestina* (Monographien zur Erdkunde, 21) ([2] 1927), and also H. Guthe,
·*Bibelatlas* ([2] 1926), G. E. Wright and F. V. Filson, *The Westminster Historical Atlas
to the Bible* (1945, new ed. 1958), and L. H. Grollenberg, *Atlas of the Bible* (1956). In
WAT, pp. 1-82, may be found a discussion of the natural and historical geography of
Palestine, which will not be repeated here.

The heart of the country is formed by a chain of limestone mountains, the strata of which were originally horizontal but disintegrated owing to various tectonic disturbances on the eastern border of the Mediterranean. Whilst, therefore, the original table-land character of the country is still apparent in the eastern part, on the side bordering the Syrian desert, in the western part the limestone plateau has been broken up into a mass of smaller pieces. The great cleft of the valley which traverses the whole land from north to south and continues further at each end, is particularly striking. In it the bed of the Jordan winds to and fro, having its source at the northern extremity of the land at the foot of the Anti-Lebanon: it flows into the Dead Sea which fills the bottom of the deep valley on the southern frontier. It is therefore usually called the Jordan Valley and the whole country is divided into the land east and west of the Jordan. The plateau east of the Jordan, which survives substantially in its original form, and into the edge of which numerous rivers and rivulets have cut their beds, is confronted on the other side of the Jordan Valley by the mountains west of the Jordan which are broken up in many places and which are separated from the Mediterranean coast by a maritime plain. Thus, within its narrow confines, the land embraces the greatest possible differences and contrasts of landscape and climate, and conditions of life varied greatly in the different parts of the country.

Life was different on the (roughly 2000-2500 ft. high) fertile plains in the southern and northern parts of the land east of the Jordan —which gradually pass into the steppe and desert as the rainfall decreases—from life in the mountainous central part of the land east of the Jordan which is wooded even today; and it was different again on the hot, desert-like soil of the ravine-like Jordan Valley, in which water, issuing at various points at the foot of the steep mountains, has produced oases with luxuriant vegetation, from life on the airy heights of the mountains; and life was different on the broad, fertile plain of Jezreel—which interrupts the mountains west of the Jordan and which is drained into the Mediterranean by the Kishon which constantly carries water in its lower course—from life on the heights west of the Jordan which are intersected by streams that are dry in summer; and different again on the less hilly, milder middle sections of the mountains west of the Jordan and north and south of the plain of Jezreel—which are interspersed with pleasant plains of varying sizes—from life in the more precipitous, intensely rugged, rather barren parts of the mountains further to

the north and south, which are very inaccessible; and different
again on the western sides of the mountains west and east of the
Jordan—which are well soaked with winter rains—from life on the
often desert-like eastern slopes of the land west of the Jordan with
its low rainfall; and different again on the warm, productive
maritime plain with its relatively high humidity—which is separated
from the coast by an almost uninterrupted line of dunes—from life
on the wooded ridge of Carmel, which cuts through them and
projects into the sea; different again on the southern declivity of
the mountains west of the Jordan, with their meagre pastures and
poor soils, from life in the adjacent desert to the south in which
shepherds and flocks depend on the few available springs.

It is not surprising that this land was able to contribute little to
a uniform settlement by a uniform population or to combine its
existing inhabitants into a unity. The parts of the country where
conditions were more favourable, above all, the maritime plain
and the plain of Jezreel, the oases of the Jordan Valley and also
the high plains of the northern and southern lands east of the
Jordan, were inevitably the most inviting from the point of view
of permanent settlement and cultivation; and the poorer hilly
districts only attracted settlers when the other parts of the country
were already well and truly occupied and newcomers had to make
do with more modest settlements. Thus the very nature of the land
led, from the very outset, to a great lack of uniformity in the
settlement. Nor was it especially favourable to the subsequent
amalgamation of the whole of its inhabitants. The different conditions in the various parts of the country led to differences in the
way of life of the people and this tended to estrange them from one
another. And the mountains which traverse the land, which are
everywhere furrowed by deep, precipitous valleys, made communications difficult; more or less unrestricted communications
were possible only in the great plains, whilst in the mountains
difficulties of communication promoted small isolated groups.

Nevertheless, in very important matters all the inhabitants did
share certain presuppositions, including, above all, the climatic
conditions. Palestine shares the subtropical climate of the Mediterranean world and the particular consequences which this climate
has in the limestone mountain regions of that world. This climate is
characterised by the alternation of a winter rain period and a rainless summer. The winter rain does not fall continuously throughout
the country: it falls rather in isolated, brief, violent downpours,
often separated by whole days, and these downpours produce

torrents of often dangerous ferocity in the mountain valleys not
merely in the periods of the early rain (above all in October), of the
main rain (mostly in January) and the late rain (roughly in April),
but also between these periods. Since, moreover, the calcareous soil
is very porous and real forests are almost entirely lacking and have
probably been lacking from the earliest historical times—what is
usually described as 'forest' really represents merely a rather low-
lying undergrowth—the land dries up to an extraordinary degree
in the summer months; the springs—which are in any case far from
numerous in the mountainous parts of the country and limited
in number even on the plains at the foot of the mountains—flow
more sparsely and to some extent they dry up completely, and only
a few valleys, above all in the plains and especially in the vicinity
of the Mediterranean coast, still contain water. Only the Jordan
which is fed by the underground reservoir of the high mountains
on the northern border of Palestine, constantly carries an abundance of water to the Dead Sea; but this water-course which
meanders through the desert region of the deep Jordan Valley,
has little practical significance for life in the land.

   The water supply has always been the most vital problem of all
for the inhabitants of Palestine. In contrast to the great river valleys,
Egypt and Babylon, in which the great floods regularly inundate
the land and the river water can constantly be made available for
the use of human beings and animals, Palestine and the whole of
Syria too are dependent on rain for the needs of plants, animals and
human beings. If the rain comes too meagrely at the times when it
is due or fails to come altogether, it means a great catastrophe for
the whole life of the country. And whilst the vegetation of the
annual herbaceous plants is limited to the months of winter
rain, human beings and animals can only live permanently where
even in the summer something of the blessing of the previous
winter's rain is still available, that is to say, where springs are fed
by an underground water supply all the year round, or where the
winter's rain has been collected in adequate quantities in storage-
containers of human construction, the so-called cisterns. This latter
invention, which had already been made when the Israelite tribes
settled in the land[1], made permanent settlement possible even in
those areas where the springs were insufficient or where it was not
at any rate possible to gain access to a subterranean supply of
of water by boring wells in the ground. Admittedly, the cistern
water was not equal to the 'living water' of the springs; and in

   [1] Cf. W. F. Albright in *Studies in the History of Culture* (1942), p. 33.

some districts, as in parts of the eastern slopes of the mountains
west of the Jordan, there is such a meagre rainfall that it is not
even enough to fill the cisterns, and in such places it is impossible
for men and animals to settle permanently.

Thus the water situation had a decisive influence on the distribution of the human settlements in the land and on the life and
economy of the people in the different parts of the country. Every
spring of water inevitably attracted people to settle in its immediate
vicinity; and as springs rise above all at the foot of mountains the
borders of the plains were colonised particularly early on and
particularly densely. Wherever springs and wells were sparse and
unproductive, where there was no space for an accumulation of
people, easily satisfied flocks of small cattle, sheep and goats,
were able at any rate to live with their shepherds; from the very
beginning the eastern side of the mountains west of the Jordan
and the borders of the land on the eastern and southern sides have
been grazing country for such flocks of sheep, goats and pigs.

The peculiarities of the climate have always had a basic influence
on the seasons of human life and work[1]. It is easy to understand
why the springing up of the vegetation in the autumn which
resulted from the increasing dew and early rain was considered the
beginning of a new year. For the indigenous, agricultural population there followed the season of ploughing, sowing and—once the
rainy period had ended—of harvesting and the celebration of the
ancient traditional religious festivals of the beginning and end of
the harvest, the feast of unleavened bread and the feast of harvest
(Exod. xxiii, 15, 16); and in high summer and autumn there
followed the ripening of the tree fruits, especially the grapes, figs
and olives and the joyful season of their harvesting, and finally
the 'feast of ingathering' (Exod. xxiii, 16). But for the owner of
a flock of sheep and goats the year's events included a regular
migration, the so-called change of pasture[2]; whilst the rainy
period in the winter offered their flocks adequate opportunities
for grazing even in areas of steppe and desert, in the dry summer
they were forced to take them to the climatically more favourable
agricultural land, where they found sufficient fodder in the fields
that had been harvested, just as today the Arab tribes still have
their definite winter and summer pastures[3].

---

[1] For a wealth of details on this subject see G. Dalman, *Arbeit und Sitte in Palaestina*, especially Vol. I, i, 2 (1928): Jahreslauf und Tageslauf.
[2] Cf. most recently L. Rost, ZDPV, 66 (1943), pp. 205 ff.
[3] Cf. M. v. Oppenheim, *Die Beduinen*, I (1939), II (1943), III (1952).

All this meant that there was continual intercourse between the agricultural countryside and the neighbouring steppe and desert country; and it is one of the historically significant characteristics of the geography of Palestine that the land is enclosed by natural frontiers on some sides and open on others. On the whole of its western side Palestine is bordered by the Mediterranean, which means that its coast is very long in relation to its total area. Yet, in spite of that, it has no very positive relationship to the sea, and on the whole its inhabitants have taken little interest in seafaring and maritime trade. In contrast to the adjacent Phoenician coast to the north at the foot of Mount Lebanon, with its old and famous Phoenician sea-ports and commercial cities, the coast of Palestine, which is accompanied by a straight line of low-lying dunes, is almost entirely lacking in natural harbours which might have tempted the inhabitants to go in for seafaring and might have attracted foreign sailors. From time immemorial the Egyptians traded by coastal routes with the more distant Phoenician cities, but hardly at all with Palestine, in spite of the fact that it was so much nearer to Egypt. The straight line of the flat coast is only at a few places relieved by rocks which jut out to sea and by cliffs which tower up from the sea, and even at these points there were no really practicable natural harbours, at *yāfa*, the Old Testament Joppa (Japho), *kēsārye*, the later Herodian-Roman Caesarea on Sea, *'athlit*, the Castellum Peregrinorum of the crusaders. The straight line of the coast is only interrupted by Mount Carmel, and in its shelter there arose a great bay, though the coast is still flat and sandy, and at the northern end of the bay there was an old coastal city which is called Acco in the Old Testament and which, apart from Joppa, was the only settlement by the sea in ancient oriental times worth mentioning.

The fact that the land was shut off from the neighbouring sea explains why seafaring and sea-trading played no part at all in Israel and why, in spite of its proximity, the sea plays a purely marginal part in Israel's outlook on life and why it was possible for Israel to formulate a story of Creation which completely ignores the very existence of the sea[1]; and where the sea is mentioned in the Old Testament it hardly ever appears as a means of communication between different countries but rather as a menace on the edge of the inhabited earth, whose uncanny and dangerous power is broken only when it meets dry land[2].

---

[1] Thus the Yahwistic narrative, Gen. ii, 4b ff. [2] Cf. *e.g.* Job xxxviii, 8-11.

On the northern side, too, the land of Palestine is shut off by a natural barrier. The high mountains of Lebanon and Anti-Lebanon hem the country in on this side; and the most northerly part of the land west of the Jordan, the Mountains of Upper Galilee, which contains the highest elevations of the whole country[1], is already a far from accessible region. The country also has no natural outlets to the north either along the coast on which the foothills between Acco and Tyre come right down to the sea, offering an almost insuperable obstacle to the road leading to Phoenicia, or in the Jordan Valley whose corridor into the low land between Lebanon and Anti-Lebanon is also very difficult to pass. Only in a north-easterly direction, on the eastern side of the Anti-Lebanon from the northern land east of the Jordan, is there an outlet in the direction of Damascus.

On the other hand, however, Palestine is all the more open to the east and south, to the steppes and desert which form the frontier. The transition takes place quite gradually as the land moves away from the rain-bringing Mediterranean and rainfall decreases. There are hardly any difficult natural obstacles here to bar the way. On the border of the land east of the Jordan as on the southern border of the land west of the Jordan it is impossible to fix an exact frontier at all; and the area of human settlement has varied in these parts from time to time according to the extent to which artificial devices made it possible to settle in the marginal areas by fully exploiting the winter rainfall[2]: when husbandry was neglected these areas lapsed into desert again. It is therefore easy to realise that there was constant intercourse between the agricultural land and the neighbouring steppe and desert land on the east and south, since the inhabitants of the latter regions always had their eye on the coveted agricultural land and tried to gain a footing in it at every favourable opportunity. The change of pasture made many herdsmen with their flocks regularly seek out the summer pastures for their flocks in the agricultural land and this resulted in a constant movement to and fro between both sides of the frontier. This openness of the land to the east and south was of basic importance for its history in many ways. In addition to the constant infiltration of smaller groups, large-scale immigrations from these areas had a decisive influence on the history of Palestine.

[1] If the volcanic mountian of *jebel ed-drūz* far beyond in the east, which rises even higher, is not included in Palestine.

[2] On the definition of the concepts steppe and desert, and their distribution in the vicinity of Palestine, cf. R. Gradmann, ZDPV, 57 (1934), pp. 161 ff. and especially Plan 1.

At the same time natural conditions brought Palestine in touch
to some extent with the great long-distance trade routes in the
ancient Orient. Like the greater unit of Syria as a whole, it was
a transit area and was therefore repeatedly involved in the intercourse and conflicts of the great powers of the ancient Orient.
After passing the northern part of the Sinaitic Peninsula, the
route from Egypt to the Near East inevitably led first of all on
Asiatic soil to the maritime plain of Palestine; and, as the coast
road to Phoenicia on the northern border of the country was almost
impracticable, the route across Palestine was often preferred: the
plain of Jezreel being reached by passing along the back of Mount
Carmel and then crossing the Jordan Valley south or north of the
Sea of Tiberias and then making for Damascus in the land east of
the Jordan, whence it was possible to go further into northern
Syria or to reach the Middle Euphrates by caravan routes through
the Syrian desert. The routes from southern Arabia to the Mediterranean area which were important for commercial traffic also
touched the border of Palestine; the route passed either along the
edge of the land east of the Jordan and then northwards towards
Damascus or from the northern extremity of the gulf of *el-ʿaḳaba*
to the south Palestinian coast; and thus Palestine also shared in
the exchange of the products of the civilisation of the ancient
Orient. The nature and situation of the land conferred on its inhabitants an extremely varied life with many different interests,
enriched by all kinds of contacts with the outside world.

Palestine has never been a rich country and its inhabitants have
always had to eat their bread 'in the sweat of their brow'. The land
has never been able to feed a population of more than limited
density. Even in the more favoured and fertile parts of the country
the people have always had to slave on their fields and plantations
to wrest a living from the soil, and vegetation of any luxuriance is
found only in the few oases of the Jordan Valley. In the mountains,
however, life was even harder if anything at all was to grow in the
stony fields or, where even that was impossible, if the flocks were
to find enough food in the scanty pastures and watering-places.
And even this meagre subsistence depended on rain falling after
the dry and hot summers both in sufficient quantity and spread
over the normal period. But this could never be relied on and
there was inevitably always an anxious awareness of the fact that
an absence or insufficiency of rain would bring drought and thirst
and the disastrous threat of a bad harvest and starvation. And, even
if everything had grown satisfactorily, one of the recurrent plagues

of locusts could always destroy the whole bounty of the land in no
time and condemn men and beasts to starvation. In addition, the
human settlements were constantly menaced by the earthquakes
which are not unusual in this country.

Until even the most recent times men have led a very modest life
in this country and it will always have been the same. As the
inhabitants' livelihood depended on a combination of agriculture
and small cattle breeding, varying according to local conditions,
home-baked bread and a variety of milk products, with various
seasonal fruits, represented the main foods. Meat eating was always
exceptional and limited to certain special occasions and feast days
—in the old days, religious festivals with animal sacrifices and the
sacrificial meals associated with them—or special visits by guests
who were entertained with typical Oriental generosity, and similar
occasions; more frequent consumption of meat was regarded as
the sign of an unusually luxurious life[1]. Probably a moderate
consumption of wine was customary, varying according to the
income of the individual, until Islam forbade its followers to drink
it. Probably there were more wild game and beasts of prey than
there are today, especially in the wooded hill-country. Apart from
the Mediterranean coast, fishing was a rewarding occupation,
above all on the Sea of Tiberias, though the largest inland lake in
the country, the Dead Sea, has such a strong mineral content that
organic life in and around it is impossible. When in the Old Testament—especially in the deuteronomic-deuteronomistic literature
—Palestine is praised as a 'good land' 'flowing with milk and
honey', the reference is primarily to the contrast between the
blessings of the agricultural land as such and the steppe and
desert. 'Flowing with milk and honey' is moreover apparently a
stereotyped term for a paradisal region, which was current in
the ancient world and which was not coined with any special
reference to Palestine at all, but was used by Israel to praise its
own land in comparison with the immediately adjacent and accessible steppe and desert, not the more remote and unfamiliar
river valley lands of the ancient Orient. The reference to 'milk and
honey' must therefore not be regarded as having arisen from
specifically Palestinian conditions; the people that first adopted
the expression in Israel certainly had in mind the fine pastures
which existed in some parts and which increased the milk produc-
tion of the herds of small cattle, and also the vineyards which
supplied the grape honey (this was what they had in mind—not

---

[1] Cf. *e.g.* Amos vi, 4b.

bee-honey)[1]. For the inhabitants of the steppes and deserts even
the miserable agricultural soil of Palestine inevitably seemed an
alluring and desirable object, and there was a time when the
Israelite tribes had also seen the land in that light, when they were
preparing to establish themselves there, and they rejoiced in its
fruits, and learnt to value them again, especially when their sojourn
in the land was threatened.

It is more curious that in Deut. viii, 9 Palestine is praised because
its stones contain iron and because brass could be dug out of its
hills. There is some exaggeration here. It is true that in the land
east of the Jordan iron does occur at one or two places on the
northern side of the Valley of Jabbok and it is possible that they
were exploited in ancient times like the iron mine of *mghāret
warde* not far from *tulūl ed-dahab*, the ancient Penuel[2]. But these
occurrences of iron can hardly have been of much importance and
in general all necessary metals had to be obtained from abroad,
from the *wādi el-'araba* (between the Dead Sea and the Red Sea)
and from the Lebanon region. The land did not have any other
mineral wealth of importance[3]. Nevertheless it could be said that
in contrast to the steppe and desert it did have at least something
of that kind to offer to its inhabitants.

Palestine had no surplus products of any potential importance
in the commerce of the ancient Orient. At the most it could only
part with some of the produce of its fields and orchards in order
to pay for urgently needed imports[4], perhaps it was also able to
sell some of its small cattle. It was probably possible to meet
the immediate need for foreign products—especially metals—in
this way. But it can scarcely have been feasible to carry on any
large-scale trade with Palestine's modest products. In this respect
the country gave its inhabitants no chance of entering into active
relations with the great world of the ancient Orient. Apart from its
situation in the midst of important long-distance trade routes, its
natural conditions were more calculated to isolate the people of
Palestine from the greater world beyond the steppes and deserts,
just as the nature of the land itself was more apt to separate the
inhabitants from one another than to unite them.

[1] More details in A. Bertholet, *Kulturgeschichte Israels* (1919), pp. 4 ff.

[2] Cf. C. Steuernagel, *Der 'Adschlün* (1927), p. 286.

[3] In ancient times the mineral treasures of the Dead Sea were hardly exploited
at all; there is no evidence that such exploitation began before the Hellenistic period
(cf. Hieronymus of Cardia in Diodorus Siculus, XIX, 98, 1–99, 3), and large-scale
exploitation has only begun in the most recent times.

[4] According to 1 Kings v, 24 f. Solomon gave wheat and olive oil in exchange for
King Hiram of Tyre's timber supplies.

3. *The Historical Situation in Palestine* circa *1200 B.C.*

When the Israelite tribes entered the land it could already look back on a long and eventful history which had given rise to a particular situation in regard to human settlement and civilisation, which was bound to be of direct and substantial importance for the early development of Israel. It must therefore be carefully examined; and we are in a position to describe it fairly concretely and accurately, since the tradition of the Old Testament is not our sole source of information about the conditions which confronted the Israelite tribes when they entered Palestine. Thanks to some fortunate discoveries, we possess a whole series of documents about the history of Syria and Palestine in the course of the second millennium B.C. and we also have at our disposal the results of the archaeological investigations, carried on intensively and successfully especially in the last thirty years, into the material remains which the various historical periods have left behind in Palestine[1].

The first of the documents which must be mentioned are the so-called Egyptian execration texts from the final period of the Egyptian 12th Dynasty *circa* 1800 B.C.[2] written on potsherds, which were used for a special magic rite[3]. In these texts all manner of enemies of Egypt and its royal house are enumerated, including some from the neighbouring Asiatic lands of Palestine and Phoenicia. In this connection we learn all kinds of names of princes and places. The way the rulers' names are formed provides some clue to the ethnic origins of those who bear them and sheds some light on the ethnic structure of the population. The place-names also shed a little, though not much, light on the nature of the settlement. The so-called Mari texts[4] are more or less contemporaneous—only slightly later; they represent the very extensive archives of the Kings of Mari, an old city on the middle Euphrates (the modern

---

[1] On the work and results of the archaeology of Palestine cf. WAT, pp. 83-143.

[2] On the division of Egyptian history into 'Dynasties' cf. WAT, pp. 195 ff. For full details on the most important phenomena of ancient Oriental history and the main concepts of the terminology which has become customary in the study of the ancient Orient, the reader may be referred, once and for all, to WAT, pp. 144-236.

[3] The texts have been published by K. Sethe in *Die Ächtung feindlicher Fürsten, Völker und Dinge auf altägyptischen Tongefässscherben des Mittleren Reiches* (Abh. d. Preuss. Ak. d. Wiss., 1926, phil.-hist. Kl., No. 5), and G. Posener, *Princes et pays d'Asie et de Nubie. Textes hiératiques sur des figurines d'envoûtement du Moyen-Empire* (1940). On the subject cf. A. Alt, ZDPV, 64 (1941), pp. 21 ff.

[4] In combination with a few other texts which have recently become known, the Mari texts have made possible a rectification of the chronology of Mesopotamia that used to be accepted. Cf. E. F. Weidner, AfO, 15 (1945-1951), pp. 85-105 and also a brief reference in WAT, p. 214.

tell ḥarīri near *abu'l-kemāl*) and beside legal and economic texts they contain the wide-ranging political correspondence of the kings, with various information about contemporary Syria as well. They can, however, hardly be expected to contain any specific details about Palestine.[1]

The documents from the 14th century B.C. are more fruitful and come nearer in time to Israelite history. The so-called Amarna tablets must be considered first of all. They consist of about four hundred clay tablets, the first of which were found *in situ* in 1887 and all of which come from an upper Egyptian ruin mound (*tell*) which is situated in the area now inhabited by the Bedouin tribe of *el-'amārina*. This mound contains the remains of the newly established and soon-abandoned residence of the Pharaoh Amenhotep IV (1377–1360 B.C.) and the Amarna tablets form a part of this Pharaoh's political archives that contained his predecessor's and his own foreign correspondence with the States of the Near East, and, above all, with the dependent petty rulers of Palestine and Syria from a period in which Palestine and Syria were, at any rate nominally, under Egyptian sovereignty. This correspondence is written in Babylonian script and language on the clay tablets in common use in Mesopotamia, as was apparently the custom at the time in international correspondence in the ancient Orient, and it offers a wealth of detailed information about political conditions, the historical events of the time, and life in Palestine and Syria. The Amarna tablets were the first document to reveal clearly the historical background of the beginnings of Israel in Palestine and they are thus one of the direct sources for the history of Israel[2].

The so-called Ras-Shamra texts which were only discovered quite recently also date from the same period as the Amarna tablets. They were found during the French excavations which, stimulated by a chance discovery made in 1929, were carried out until 1939 on a mound on the North Syrian coast—opposite the outstretched finger of the island of Cyprus—and were resumed in 1949. In this mound, now called *rās esh-shamra*, are

[1] The Mari texts which were found from 1934/1935 onwards during the French excavations in Mari, have so far only been published in part in *Textes cunéiformes du Musée du Louvre*, Vol. XXII (1946), XXIII (1941), XXIV (1948), XXV (1951), XXVI (1951); cf. the corresponding transcriptions and translations (into French) in the series *Archives royales de Mari* I (1950), II (1950), III (1950), IV (1951), V (1952). Provisional information about the contents of the political correspondence will be found in G. Dossin, *Syria*, 19 (1938), pp. 105-126, and in W. v. Soden, WO, I, 3 (1948), pp. 187-204. Cf. ANET, pp. 482-483.

[2] A transliteration and German translation of the Amarna tablets with explanatory notes will be found in J. A. Knudtzon, *Die El-Amarna-Tafeln* (Vorderasiatische Bibl. 2), 1915. Cf. ANET, pp. 483-490, DOTT, pp. 38-45.

buried the remains of the ancient city of Ugarit which we also
know from the Amarna tablets and Egyptian texts. Every year
from 1930 onwards numerous clay tablets were found here
which display the well-known technique of cuneiform writing on
clay tablets, but are written for the most part in a hitherto
entirely unknown cuneiform alphabet of thirty characters which
was deciphered surprisingly quickly. This is the first extensive
discovery of written documents in Syria-Palestine dating from
pre-Hellenistic times. They contain numerous religious and mythological texts, great and small, and are the first and so far the
only original documents on the religious history of Syria-Palestine
in ancient times, though some of them are very difficult to understand. They also contain governmental texts of great variety from
the royal archives which contain comparatively little historical
information, but, among other things, a wealth of personal names
which shed light on the ethnic structure of the population. It is
true that the *rās esh-shamra* is a good distance from the land of
Israel and it is the site of an old coastal town and port with a
fine natural harbour (now called *mīnet el-bēḍa*, 'the white harbour') and to that extent the scene of a life quite different from life
in Palestine. But nevertheless it was part of the greater entity of
Syria-Palestine, which, in the period before the appearance of the
Israelite tribes, had lived a richly varied but basically uniform
life, and so the Ras-Shamra texts do help to illuminate the
situation which the Israelite tribes found on their arrival in
Palestine[1].

Apart from the groups of texts already mentioned, the Egyptian
reports on the campaigns of the Pharaohs of the New Kingdom
in Palestine and Syria also provide some material about pre-
Israelite Palestine. For a time, these Pharaohs did in fact or at
least in name enjoy sovereign rights over Palestine and Syria and
between the 16th and 13th centuries B.C. the country saw the
Egyptian kings or at any rate their armies on its soil time and
again. So far as we know, Pharaoh Thothmes III, in the first half
of the 15th century, was the first to have lists made of his campaigns
and to have them displayed to his greater glory on the walls of the

---

[1] Most of the Ras-Shamra texts have been published in the journal *Syria* from
Volume 10 (1929) onwards. O. Eissfeldt, ZDMG, N.F. 21 (1942), pp. 507-539, reviewed
the whole body of texts known up to that date. The grammar, transcriptions of the text
and a glossary will be found in C. H. Gordon, *Ugaritic Handbook* (Analecta Orientalia,
25 [1947, new ed. 1955]). C. H. Gordon provides an English translation of the texts in
Ugaritic Literature (Scripta Pontificii Instituti Biblici, 98 [1949]) and G. R. Driver in
Canaanite Myths and Legends (1956); a selection will be found in ANET, pp. 129-155
(H. L. Ginsberg) and in DOTT, pp. 118-133 (J. Gray).

great Imperial temple of the god, Amon-Re, in Egyptian Thebes. One of them is the so-called 'Palestine List' of Thothmes III, which originally contained 117 Palestinian place-names and place-descriptions indicating where his troops were stationed on his first campaign in Palestine[1]. It is true that this list cannot, by its very purpose and nature, provide a survey of the settlements in Palestine at that time; but the names it mentions do testify to the existence of numerous places in Palestine.

Circa 1200 B.C., that is, about the time when the Israelite tribes settled in the land, a period of civilisation was drawing to its close in Palestine, the 'Bronze Age' which was now being superseded by the Iron Age. Though the knowledge and use of these metals (bronze and iron) may not be a very substantial or safe and clear criterion for demarcating the two ages, it is customary to use these conventional terms to describe the great periods of civilisation which can be classified archaeologically on the basis of their cultural remains. In particular, the kinds and forms of their pottery, the fragments and remains of which have survived in great quantities on all the sites of ancient settlements and have lasted thousands of years, and also the characteristics of their jewellery, of which only scanty relics have survived, and their methods of building houses and city walls, are typical of these periods of civilisation and their subdivisions. Excavations in Palestine have given us a fairly clear picture of the Bronze Age civilisation in that country, which evolved in various stages: an early Bronze Age in the third millennium B.C.; a middle Bronze Age in the first four centuries of the second millennium and a late Bronze Age between about 1550 and 1200 B.C. In this period, living in fixed settlements, in cities, developed intensely, and the knowledge we have of the civilisation of the Bronze Age is based on the manifestations of its urban culture. These cities were—and this remains true right up to the beginning of the Hellenistic period—in fact not really cities for living in but walled-in strongholds and storehouses of small size with a rather rambling jumble of small houses and an irregular mass of narrow alleys and, usually, only one fair-sized square immediately inside the city gate which was the scene of public life. But the everyday life of the inhabitants took place mainly outside the city, in the fields and plantations, where it was no doubt the custom to spend the night in the summer time and during the harvest. The

---

[1] Published in W. M. Müller, *Die Palästinaliste Thutmosis' III* (MVAG), 12, 1, 1907 and J. Simons, *Handbook for the Study of Egyptian Topographical Lists relating to Western Asia* (1937), No. 1; for detailed explanations cf. M. Noth, ZDPV, 61 (1938), pp. 26-65. Cf. ANET, pp. 244.

number of permanent cities in the country gradually increased in the course of the Bronze Age. So far as we can infer from archaeological discoveries, new cities were founded in the middle Bronze Age and again in the late Bronze Age; and even if, occasionally, older settlements were abandoned to make way for these new cities, it still meant that the number of Bronze Age cities was constantly growing. This is in exact accordance with the fact that, according to Old Testament tradition, the Israelite tribes found 'Canaanites' dwelling in permanent cities when they occupied the land (cf., for example, Num. xiii, 28). The technique of wall-building, which was the prime concern in the construction of these cities, also made constant progress in the Bronze Age. The middle Bronze Age already knew how to build imposing, escarped city walls in the so-called 'cyclopian' technique[1] (using huge stones without mortar), and the late Bronze Age took over these walls and the technique of building them.

These cities provided the preconditions for the rise and growth of a simple urban civilisation in so far as the urban concentration of population inevitably promoted the development of specialised occupations and the transmission of particular skills. It is true that the normal type of farmer and small cattle breeder predominated in the Bronze Age cities of Palestine; but as the local products of an already advanced pottery and metal work trade show, there were clearly professional trades and even arts and crafts in these cities, and these usually mean the beginning of a commerce which consisted to begin with of barter and then, as trade widened and developed, money was introduced as the means of payment. Thus there is evidence that a simple money economy with different weights of metal as the means of payment was in force at any rate in the cities of the Late Bronze Age in Palestine[2].

This is also confirmed by the fact that in the Old Testament the name 'Canaanite', with which it was customary to describe the whole of the old non-Israelite and pre-Israelite population, whose ancestors had maintained the civilisation of the Bronze Age, occasionally assumed the special meaning of 'merchant' and 'trader' (Isa. xxiii, 8 and elsewhere)[3]. Archaeological discoveries

---

[1] For more precise details on this technique see WAT, pp. 114 ff. and illustration 5A.
[2] Cf. K. Galling, BRL, 174 ff.
[3] The word 'Canaanite' was probably originally simply a term for 'purple manufacturers', 'purple traders', of whom there were many, especially in the coastal towns of Phoenicia, and from that specific meaning the name 'Canaan' developed into a more or less vague term for the country itself (cf. B. Maisler. BASOR, 102 [1946], pp. 7-12). The Old Testament can hardly have been familiar with the original meaning of the

show that commercial relationships and cultural exchanges in the urban civilisation of the Bronze Age extended far and wide on every side, as was only to be expected in Syria-Palestine, which was so markedly a land of transit. In the Bronze Age strata of the cities, Mesopotamia and Egypt are represented by all kinds of imported articles of pottery and jewellery and to these purely imported goods there were added native imitations of foreign industrial products. The welcome given to imports and cultural influences from the Mediterranean world is also characteristic of the late Bronze Age. These influences emanated particularly from the islands of Cyprus and Crete, and Palestine, itself so little open to the sea, probably shared in these imports through the intermediary of the Phoenician coastal towns[1].

This cultural area was inhabited by a rich and ever-changing variety of population, whose movements are to some extent revealed by the literary sources from the second millennium[2], though nothing like a complete insight into the whole complicated situation is available. No doubt the various groups which settled in the land each brought their own traditions and cultural possessions with them, which were then absorbed into the larger complex of the civilisation of the land. For according to the evidence of archaeological discoveries this civilisation was in fact fairly homogeneous in the Bronze Age, not only in Palestine but throughout Syria, including Palestine. In spite of their different origins and character and the difficulty they found in combining into a single larger political unit, the inhabitants of the urban settlements all shared in this civilisation, the products of which were distributed by exchange and commerce over the whole land. The urban system of the Bronze Age in Syria-Palestine was a civilisation belonging.to the land itself, which gradually developed and changed until it finally expired around 1200 B.C., though it is difficult to discern any definite causes for its decline and fall.

As far as our knowledge extends, *i.e.* from the early Bronze Age in the third millennium B.C., men of Semitic language formed the main mass of the population of the country. Old Testament usage describes the whole of the older population as 'Canaanites' regardless of their origins and language. Modern scholarship does not

word, it only uses the term in its secondary sense as the description of a country or a people.

[1] P. Thomsen, *Palästina und seine Kultur in fünf Jahrtausenden*, 3rd edition (AO, 30 [1932], pp. 33-61), gives a short review of the Bronze Age in Palestine.

[2] More details will be found in M. Noth, ZDPV, 65 (1942), pp. 9-67 where the references for the following account will also be found.

follow this usage, though its description is linked to it, but usually describes the basic stock of the population, with its different Semitic dialects, as 'Canaanite'. The reference is not to *original* inhabitants or to the earliest inhabitants of the country. The numerous old, and, to some extent very old, non-Semitic place-names prove that people of different origin occupied the country previously. But we still know nothing for certain[1] about these people, and in any case they are of no significance so far as the history of Israel is concerned. When the Israelite tribes arrived, however, they found that the language spoken was still the Semitic 'Canaanite', and, like many earlier immigrants, they and their kinsfolk adopted this language in place of the probably Aramaic dialect they had spoken previously. We know nothing about the period and the nature of the occupation of the land by the 'Canaanites' and their conflict with the inhabitants they found already living there. They established themselves in the older settlements and also founded new ones alongside them. They appear to have been the first to have occupied the Phoenician coastal centres with their natural harbours which later became so important: for the names of these are in fact thoroughly Semitic[2]. The Phoenician section of the coast was cut off from the interior of the land by the mighty wall of Lebanon and was therefore only opened up for settlement relatively late. The 'Canaanite' immigration must have been so tremendous that the older population was absorbed by it, and, from that time on, their language was spoken in the country, until it was displaced, very much later, at first partially, and then entirely, by Aramaic.

In the 19th/18th century B.C. a new, likewise Semitic, ruling class imposed itself on Syria-Palestine. According to the evidence of the typical personal names that occur in the Egyptian execration texts and the Mari texts, they were elements of the stratum which about the same time seized the reins of government on the middle Euphrates and in Southern Mesopotamia and there established the 1st Dynasty of Babylon and the ancient Babylonian Empire. The historical significance of this movement for Syria-Palestine is not yet really clear nor has any appropriate name been found for this ruling class; they are often wrongly described as 'Amorites'.

[1] Periods of civilisation preceding even the Bronze Age have been proved to exist by archaeological discoveries, and the pre-Canaanite inhabitants probably belonged to these earlier ages. But the lack of any literary information precludes us from any more precise knowledge about this early period.
[2] Cf. M. Noth, WO, I, 1 (1947) pp. 21-28.

The documents of the 14th century B.C. which bring us quite close to the beginning of the history of Israel, reveal a great alteration in the make-up of the population. Here, too, the number of personal names from this period known to us is remarkable. The new constituent which they reveal is a non-semitic element, particularly in the urban centres. It is clear that in the intervening period movements of population had changed the ethnic structure of the country. People with names which may, following the cuneiform record, be called 'Hurrian' appear in especially large numbers among these newcomers. According to cuneiform sources these 'Hurri'[1] were also found at the same time in Mesopotamia, that is in the region between the middle Euphrates and the Tigris, as well as east of the middle Tigris, and their language, which is neither Semitic nor Indo-Germanic, has been proved to be cognate with the language of the Urartians, the inhabitants of the Armenian mountains, who are known to us from the first half of the first millennium. According to this the Hurrians appear to have come from a north-easterly direction into the area of the ancient Orient and to Syria-Palestine, to have settled especially in Mesopotamia but to have spread also in great numbers to Syria-Palestine[2] as a new ruling class which seized possession above all of the cities. But simultaneously with the Hurrians other elements of non-Semitic origin also appeared, of Indo-Iranian descent, Indo-Germans from the region where the group of so-called Satem languages was spoken[3], few in numbers but clearly identifiable from their names. They appear in the Amarna tablets among the minor rulers in various parts of Syria-Palestine, and there is also evidence that they were rulers in Mesopotamia. There is evidence of all kinds of other personal names from the late Bronze Age in Syria-Palestine, which are difficult to interpret, obviously non-Semitic but difficult to classify more accurately. These names indicate, however, how heterogeneous the population was. Factually the Old Testament tradition is thus quite right when, alongside all-inclusive designations of the whole of the pre-Israelite population of the urban civilisation of the Bronze Age[4], it very often enumerates, in varying combinations and sequences, a

[1] This name still occurs in the Old Testament ('Horites') but without any concrete connotation.
[2] On the *rās esh-shamra* some texts have even been found in the Hurrian language.
[3] Since the word for 'hundred' is characteristic, the Indo-Germanic languages are usually divided into the two big groups of *centum* and *satem* languages.
[4] The name 'Canaanite' is mostly used in this sense; but in certain parts of the Old Testament literature the names 'Amorite' and 'Hittite' are used in the same sense. Cf. WAT, p. 67.

whole series of ethnic names, most of which mean nothing to us, to indicate the variety of the population which the Israelite tribes found when they occupied the land (Gen. x, 16-18; xv, 19-21 and elsewhere).

The influx of non-Semitic elements which imposed themselves on Syria-Palestine as a new ruling class and established themselves in the cities, must have taken place as part of a wider historical movement of which we have no direct information though we can see its after-effects. It is almost impossible not to connect this movement with events which took place in Egypt in the period in question, about which Egyptian sources of information are unfortunately scanty and far from coherent. Between the Egyptian Middle and New Kingdoms, Egypt was subject from about the end of the 18th to the beginning of the 16th century to foreign rule which resulted from conquest by an enemy who came from the direction of the adjacent Asiatic land of Palestine-Syria. The conquerors made themselves kings over Egypt and, as a ruling class, subjugated the land and its inhabitants. Their kings resided in the city of Avaris in the eastern delta of the Nile near the Egyptian-Asiatic frontier; and the very situation of this residence indicates that their kingdom included a part of the Near East, at any rate, Palestine-Syria, as well as Egypt. These kings proudly called themselves 'rulers of the foreign lands', *i.e.* $ḥk\}.w\ ḥ\}s.wt$ in the Egyptian language officially used by them as Kings of Egypt, which later developed, in Greek transliteration, into the word Hyksos[1], which it is customary to use today, rather inaccurately, as a general term for this whole historical phenomenon. When the first Pharaohs of the New Kingdom liberated Egypt from the rule of these conquerors, they drove them back into Palestine and then subjugated Palestine-Syria, evidently in order to take possession of the inheritance of the Hyksos kings.

It is hardly possible to avoid the conclusion that the rule of the Hyksos, which possibly extended as far as Mesopotamia[2], and certainly included Syria-Palestine and, finally, Egypt, was the result of a great migration which evidently came from a north-easterly or easterly direction and introduced a powerful new ruling class into the ancient Orient. In connection with this, there came

---

[1] This word is well known from the extensive quotation preserved in Josephus, *Contra Apionem*, I, 14, § 75 ff. Niese, about the Hyksos from the Αἰγυπτιακά of the late Egyptian priest Manetho, who gives a false explanation of the word Hyksos.

[2] In the course of driving out the Hyksos the Pharaohs thrust forward at various times right through Syria-Palestine to the Euphrates, *i.e.* as far as Mesopotamia, where we also find Hurrians and Indo-Iranians.

to Syria-Palestine the Hurrian and Indo-Iranian and possibly other foreign, non-Semitic elements which appear in such great numbers in the documents of the 14th century B.C. Such a powerful historical movement, however, does not usually make merely a contribution to the structure of the population, but changes the historical situation so that its effects extend beyond the period of its immediate influence. Thus the complexion of Syria-Palestine in the 14th century, with which we are comparatively familiar, was influenced in many ways by the preceding rule of the Hyksos, though it is difficult to define the influence at all concretely, since not only have we no direct information at all about the Hyksos period but we have so few details about conditions in Syria-Palestine before the Hyksos came that it is impossible to establish precisely what changes occurred in that period. A few points may nevertheless be established with considerable probability.

The first thing of general importance was that, as far as we can see, it was through the Hyksos that Syria-Palestine was drawn into immediate involvement in the great world of events in the ancient Orient. Up till then the Egyptians had been interested in the ore deposits in the Sinaitic Peninsula and in the commercial ports of Phoenicia and the timber of the forests of Lebanon. The powers of Mesopotamia had been interested in the timber in the Amanus mountains and in the possible access to the 'upper sea' (the Mediterranean) through Northern Syria and to Asia Minor with its rich ore deposits, but Syria-Palestine as a whole had meant little in the history of the ancient Orient. It was only when the Hyksos established themselves in the country, from which they finally conquered Egypt, that Syria-Palestine began to play the part which was prescribed by its geographical position, namely to act as a bridge between the ancient civilisations on the Euphrates-Tigris and on the Nile. Through the mediacy of Syria-Palestine there developed a lively intercourse between the two civilisations. When the Amarna tablets reveal intensive diplomatic relationships between the numerous States of the Near East and the Egyptian Pharaohs, that was probably an after-effect of the Hyksos rule, in which the Pharaohs continued to play the role of the former Hyksos kings. It is permissible to surmise in this connection that the use of Babylonian writing and language which was customary in the Amarna period for diplomatic intercourse and for which there is evidence in a more restricted sphere for the period of the Mari texts, was promoted and extended as far as Egypt, above all by the Hyksos who, in their movements in the ancient Orient, first

traversed areas with an old tradition of cuneiform writing. The
fact that in Syria-Palestine in the late Bronze Age this method of
writing was used not merely within the country itself[1] but also in
correspondence with the Egyptian overlord who himself lived in a
land with its own ancient and highly developed tradition of writing,
can hardly be explained except as the result of a standardisation of
international correspondence which was imposed by force to begin
with and then retained.

In addition, the Hyksos also introduced a new technique of war
which resulted in a new social order in the ancient Orient. The
Hyksos introduced the horse-driven war chariot into the ancient
Orient evidently from the steppes of the Asian interior; and henceforth the kings and rulers of the ancient Orient used this aristocratic weapon of war. It is true that the horse had not been entirely
unknown in the ancient Orient before this: but it only acquired importance and general diffusion in connection with the war chariot.
As a riding animal, also for use in war, it was gradually introduced into the ancient Orient only later on—towards the end of the
2nd millennium B.C.—as a result of incursions into the marginal
areas of the north-east by horsemen, from the interior of Asia; and
as a working animal it is still uncommon in this area even today.
But the war chariot played an outstanding part in warfare in the
ancient Orient from the days of the Hyksos. It is clear that it could
not become a weapon to be used by every member of a people's
army: it called not only for skill and practice but for a high social
position and corresponding affluence[2]. Only knights were able to
fight with chariots, and so the Hyksos ruling class presumably
represented a kind of knighthood. The Hyksos knights established
themselves as minor rulers and lieges of the Hyksos king in the
many old cities and in those newly founded in the Middle Bronze
Age in Syria-Palestine. If we find such rulers in almost all the
cities of Syria-Palestine in the Amarna period, describing themselves as 'men of the city' (as opposed to the Pharaoh)[3] and
exercising hereditary rule, they were in fact identical with these
Hyksos knights who went to war in chariots; and it is precisely

[1] This is shown by the cuneiform tablets found on the *tell ta'annek* (cf. the examples
AOT[2], p. 371), some letters from *rās esh-shamra*, clay tablets from Alalakh in northern
Syria (the modern *tell el-'aṭshane* near Antioch).
[2] It was only later that the State provided the warrior with the necessary weapons
and equipment; in early times the soldier had to be responsible for them himself.
[3] The word 'man' (*amēlu*) which already describes the legal and social position of
the 'free man' in the statute-book of the ancient Babylonian king Hammurabi,
must be a technical term in the above context and may be translated perhaps by
'vassal', 'liege'.

among these men that we meet Hurrian and Indo-Iranian personal names alongside numerous local Semitic names. Whatever the social order may have been like in the Bronze Age cities before the appearance of the Hyksos rulers, at any rate from the Hyksos period onwards we have to reckon with a feudal order, *i.e.* with the contrast between a ruling class and a subject population lacking freedom and presumably subject to taxation and compulsory service. Syria-Palestine, which was perhaps the heart of the Hyksos dominion and, unlike the civilised regions in Egypt and Meso-potamia, did not possess a political and social order with deep historical roots, provided a suitable soil for the growth of such a feudal order. But, once again, the Old Testament tradition is right when it makes the Israelite tribes fear the city-dwelling 'Canaanites' with their 'chariots of iron' at the time of the occu-pation of the land and after (Jos. xvii, 16; Judges i, 19; iv, 3)[1].

We have no direct knowledge of the Hyksos rule, but know of it only from its remains and after-effects. From 1580 B.C. onwards the inheritance of the Hyksos rule in Egypt itself and in Palestine-Syria was taken over by the Pharaohs of the 18th Dynasty who in numerous campaigns subjugated Palestine-Syria as far as the Euphrates, and repeatedly reduced it to submission. On the whole they appear to have retained the Hyksos system of government, inasmuch as they based their sovereignty on the acknowledgement of feudal dependency on the part of the minor rulers who resided in the cities; and they appear, at any rate partly, to have left the old families of Hyksos rulers on their thrones so long as they sub-mitted to the new sovereign, as is indicated by the fact that the rulers still to some extent have Hurrian and Indo-Iranian names. They also maintained a few fortresses as strong points, with numerically probably very small garrisons; in some coastal towns they established supply depots to meet the needs of their cam-paigns; here and there they erected Egyptian temples and made over some landed properties to Egyptian gods, *i.e.* to their shrines and priests[2]. But on the whole they merely claimed the feudal loyalty of the many city rulers; and this loyalty could only be depended on so long as the Pharaohs displayed their superior power in repeated campaigns. When, towards the end of the 18th Dynasty, the Pharaohs Amenhotep III (1413–1377 B.C.) and Amenhotep IV (1377–1360 B.C.) no longer maintained these

---

[1] These chariots were naturally not made entirely of iron, but of wood. The above expression refers to the metal fittings.

[2] Cf. A. Alt, ZDPV, 67 (1944–1945), pp. 1 ff.; BBLAK, 68 (1946–1951), pp. 97 ff.

campaigns, real Egyptian control over Syria-Palestine dwindled rapidly. The Amarna Tablets, which derive from the period of these two Pharaohs, show Egyptian rule in a state of complete dissolution; only a few vassals, such as the ruler of the city of Gebal (Byblos, the modern *jebēl*, north of Beirut) which flourishing commercial relationships had linked to Egypt from the earliest times, still remained loyal to the Pharaoh, whilst most of the others behaved as independent rulers and tried to extend their modest power as far as possible.

The most important Pharaohs of the 19th Dynasty, particularly Seti I (1308–1290 B.C.) and also Rameses II (1290–1223 B.C.), restored Egyptian sovereignty again in Syria-Palestine, though not to the same extent as before. For in the meantime, from their centre in Asia Minor, the Hittites had acquired dominion over Northern Syria; in the Battle of Kadesh on the Orontes (the modern *tell nebi mend*) in the fifth year of Rameses II's reign they were strong enough to thwart the Pharaoh's attempt to invade the Hittite sphere of influence and were therefore able to maintain their position throughout the northern half of Syria. On the basis of the *status quo* which thus came into being, a treaty of reciprocity between Rameses II and the Hittite King Hattusilis was concluded in the 21st year of Rameses II[1]. The Pharaohs of the 19th Dynasty thereby established Egyptian sovereignty once again in Palestine. But *circa* 1200 B.C., with the final decline of the power of the Egyptian New Kingdom, the rule of the Pharaohs came to an end in Palestine, which was their closest neighbour, and henceforth they only maintained a theoretical claim to this land. The fragment of a stele of Rameses IV (*circa* 1150 B.C.) which was found during the excavations in Megiddo, is the last tangible evidence of Egyptian rule in Palestine, which had, by that time, disappeared to all intents and purposes. Henceforward the country was left to its own fate.

But the fact that the occupation of the land by the Israelite tribes was immediately preceded by the century-long Egyptian rule has supplied us with a wealth of Egyptian information about the situation in Palestine in the Late Bronze Age. The Amarna Tablets are the most fruitful group of documents in this connection. From them, and from the Palestine List of Thothmes III, we can

---

[1] Cf. G. Roeder, *Ägypter und Hethiter* (AO, 20 [1919]) and pp. 36 ff. for the text of the treaty. Cf. ANET, pp. 199-203. On the historical background of the Battle of Kadesh cf. J. Sturm, *Der Hettiterkrieg Ramses' II* (Beihefte zur 'Wiener Zeitschrift für die Kunde des Morgenlandes', 4. Heft [1939], pp. 1 ff.).

obtain a very precise picture of the population if we combine this information with the discoveries of the archaeologists[1].

Those urban settlements in which the native Canaanite subject population lived under the knightly rulers, were situated, according to these archaeological discoveries, almost exclusively in the parts of the country most favoured by nature, *i.e.* above all in the plains. But here they were packed tightly together and often only a few miles apart from one another. First and foremost the coastal plain south and north of Carmel, with its relatively abundant water-supply and fertile alluvial soil, was crowded with these 'cities'. The inner edge of this plain, at the foot of the mountains west of the Jordan, with its numerous springs, was most densely popu-lated of all. But the settlements extended out into the plain as far as the line of dunes which ran parallel to the coast, whilst the almost harbourless coast itself had very few settlements. In the great fertile plain of Jezreel which was easily accessible north of Carmel from the coast through the Kishon Valley and from the southern coastal plain across the low hill country between Carmel and the central Palestinian mountains, numerous cities lay along the south-western edge. As for the Jordan valley, the northern half, between the sources of the Jordan and that broad western salient which is traversed by a watercourse (now called *nahr jālūd*) coming from the plain of Jezreel, contained a series of settlements, whilst the desert-like southern half had settlements only in the few oases north of the Dead Sea. East of the Jordan Valley on the further side of the wooded mountain edge there was the great fertile plain of the northern land east of the Jordan on both sides of the Yarmuk, the most northerly tributary of the Jordan, an area dense with urban settle-ments. The table land of the southern land east of the Jordan, on the other hand, an area equally well suited for agriculture, had been filled with cities in the Early Bronze Age, according to the archaeological evidence, but in the first phase of the Middle Bronze Age these settle-ments had been abandoned, for reasons unknown to us, so that at the time of Egyptian rule, there was scarcely any urban life here at all. Not until approximately the 13th century B.C. were any new permanent settlements initiated here, and this, curiously enough, in an area so far distant from the coast, by people who had at least some connections with Mediterranean civilisation[2].

[1] On the following, cf. above all A. Alt, *Die Landnahme der Israeliten in Palästina* (Reformationsprogramm der Universität Leipzig, 1925); reprinted in *Kleine Schriften zur Geschichte des Volkes Israel*, I (1953), pp. 89-125.
[2] There is evidence for this in a stele found in *el-bālū'a* south of the Arnon which bears an inscription in Cretan linear B (cf. A. Alt, PJB, 36 [1940], pp. 34 ff.).

Even in the Late Bronze Age the mountainous parts of Palestine were still only very sparsely populated. In the wooded central part of the land east of the Jordan on both sides of the Jabbok, a tributary of the Jordan, there was an almost complete lack of permanent settlements and there were only a few in the valley of the Jabbok itself. The same applies to the most northerly part of the mountains west of the Jordan north of the plain of Jezreel. The middle section of these mountains was occupied above all by the ancient city of Shechem, situated on the western border of a plain sunk deep into the mountains and accessible from the western maritime plain by a convenient valley. It is mentioned in an Egyptian inscription in a reference to the period of Sesostris III, one of the Pharaohs of the 12th Dynasty in the 19th century B.C.[1], and appears in the Amarna Tablets as the seat of a ruler who was able to extend his sphere of influence widely in various directions because there were hardly any competitors in the vicinity of Shechem. Further south, in the mountains, it is striking that in spite of its uninviting situation on an inaccessible and not very productive part of the mountains the area around Jerusalem was filled with a series of cities. Jerusalem itself, which the Egyptian execration texts prove to have been in existence at the beginning of the second millennium, was in the Amarna period the seat of a ruler who is represented in the Amarna archives by a series of letters to the Pharaoh. To the south he had some freedom of movement: at that time Bethlehem, 5 miles away on this side, was 'a city of the land of Jerusalem'[2], i.e. a place subject to the rule of Jerusalem, and we have no knowledge of any other Bronze Age city in the mountains to the south. But in the north, north-west and west, Jerusalem had various Bronze Age neighbours of whom we know, not from literary tradition, but from archaeological discoveries *in situ*: on the road leading to the north from Jerusalem there was, ten miles away, the town of Luz[3] (the modern *bētīn*), which had been inhabited since the Middle Bronze Age; to the north-west, about 6 miles away, there was the Bronze Age *ed-jīb*, and 8 miles west of Jerusalem there was the city of Kiriath-Jearim, which was known to the Old Testament. Here, then, the whole summit of the mountain between the 'wilderness of Judah' (which is what this uninhabited region was called later on in the Old Testament) sloping down to the Jordan Valley in the east and the

[1] Cf. AOT², pp. 81 f.
[2] EA, 290, 15 f. (from a letter of the ruler Abdiheba of Jerusalem). Cf. ANET, p. 489.
[3] This was the original name of the place which was later given the name of Bethel after the famous sanctuary which was situated on its eastern side.

western slope of the mountain was occupied by a fairly coherent group of city state territories, which prevented one another from extending their respective spheres of influence. In its out-of-the-way position this group admittedly had no great historical significance; and it is therefore not surprising that the Egyptian sources of information say nothing about it, except for Jerusalem. The same is true of Hebron (*el-khalīl*) which is situated in the mountains 25 miles south of Jerusalem—a district as famous for its wealth of grapes in olden days as it still is today. To judge from Num. xiii. 22 Hebron already existed in the Bronze Age; and that is probably the case, though Hebron is not mentioned at all in the Egyptian sources, just because, as a Bronze Age city, its situation was rather isolated[1].

So at the time of the Israelite occupation the mountains were as yet in general little occupied by settlements, and only here and there were there isolated towns or groups of towns. Political and economic life took place in the plains and on the high plateaus where communications were comparatively favourable. After the cessation of Egyptian sovereignty there was a lack of political cohesion between the numerous, usually anything but extensive, city states. Their rulers, once liegemen of the Hyksos kings and then of the Pharaohs, now called themselves 'kings'; at any rate that is how the 'Canaanite' city rulers are described in the Old Testament. No doubt even after the Amarna period there were various contacts between these city kings, friendly and hostile, and innumerable conflicts took place; but about all that we now know practically nothing.

As in the Amarna period, so too afterwards there was yet another element which played a part in the country, belonging neither to the ruling class nor to the old indigenous urban population. According to the Amarna tablets it performed military service, above all for the anti-Egyptian, disloyal city rulers. In the cuneiform writing of the

[1] The case of the town of Debir which is mentioned in connection with Hebron in Jos. xv, 13-19 = Judges i, 10-15, and also Jos. x, 36 ff.; xi, 21, which is said to have been previously called Kiriath-Sepher, remains open to doubt. It is certainly an error to assume that this Kiriath-Sepher was already mentioned in the Egyptian Pap. Anastasi, I, 22, 5 from the time of Rameses (cf. M. Noth, ZDPV, 60 [1937], p. 224, Note 2). But judging from the Old Testament references one is inclined to regard Debir as a Bronze Age city. If, following W. F. Albright, *The Archaeology of Palestine and the Bible* (1932), pp. 77 ff. and elsewhere. Debir is to be located at *tell bēt mirsim*, then it would have been situated at the foot of the mountains 12 miles west-south-west of Hebron and would not fit into the above context. But if, following the statements made in the Old Testament, one prefers to seek for Debir much nearer to Hebron in the mountains (a proposal for the placing of Debir will be found in M. Noth, JPOS, 15 [1935], pp. 48 ff.) then Debir must also be presumed to have been a Bronze Age city in the most southerly part of the mountains west of the Jordan.

Amarna tablets it is usually depicted by a verbal symbol consisting of the two syllables SA. GAZ; and this term appears in phonetic syllabic script as Ḫabiru[1] only in the writings of the city ruler Abdiheba of Jerusalem. There can hardly be any doubt that this is the same word as the Old Testament word 'Hebrew'[2]. We are now familiar with such 'Hebrews' from the whole world of the ancient Orient—they usually had to undertake or perform services of various kinds. We know them from the ancient Babylonian Empire and the Mari texts[3], from the records of the city of Nuzu in the land east of the Tigris of the 15th century B.C., from Hittite Asia Minor of approximately the 14th century B.C., from Syria-Palestine of the same period and, finally, in the form ʿpr from Egypt of the 19th and 20th Dynasty.[4] That it was the name of a people is out of the question, or that there was a people of Hebrews, especially since, wherever the personal names of such 'Hebrews' are mentioned, we find they are of very varied origin. It was more a particular term for a special legal and social status; and we occasionally find the word used in this way in the Books of the Law in the Old Testament (Exod. xxi, 2; Deut. xv, 12)[5]. People or groups of people with inferior legal rights and small financial means appear under the name 'Hebrews' in the civilised lands of the ancient Orient: they perform services as and where they are required. They did not belong or perhaps no longer belonged to the various strata of the old-established population but represented certain restless nomadic elements who had no roots in the soil. The sources to which we have access do not enable us to define their character exactly and possibly their position varied according to time and place and historical circumstances. Even the meaning[6] and origin of the widespread

[1] The equating of SA. GAZ with Ḫabiru has now been established above all by the cuneiform texts from the capital of the Hittite Kingdom (the modern *boghazköi*).

[2] The rendering of SAG. GAZ by ʿprm which has recently been attested in texts from *rās esh-shamra* does not make the equating with the word 'Hebrew' impossible; cf. W. F. Albright, BASOR, 77 (1940), pp. 32 f. (against E. G. Kraeling, *ibid*. p. 32).

[3] *Textes cunéiformes du Louvre*, XXII (1941), No. 131, 13.

[4] The material that has been known for a good time will be mostly found in A. Jirku, *Die Wanderungen der Hebräer im 3. und 2. Jahrtausend v. Chr.* (AO, 24, 2 [1924], pp. 13 ff.). The new material includes the occurrence of ʿpr on a stele of the Pharaoh Amenhotep II (1448–1420 B.C.), l. 30 (A. M. Badawi, *Annales du Services des Antiquités de l'Égypte*, 42 [1943], pp. 1 ff.) found in Memphis, where 'Hebrews' occur among the prisoners of war brought in by the Pharaoh from Palestine-Syria. The ʿpr which are mentioned on a stele of the Pharaoh Seti I (cf. AOB², No. 97) found in the Palestinian town of Beth-shan, establish the connection between the Egyptian ʿpr and the Ḫabiru of the Near East.

[5] But cf. also A. Jepsen, AfO, 15 (1945–1951), pp. 54 ff.

[6] A surmise on this point will be found in W. F. Albright, *The Biblical Period* (in L. Finkelstein, *The Jews* [1949]), p. 57, note 39.

term 'Hebrew' is still somewhat obscure. But the fact that it was widespread means that there is no reason to see any material connection between the Ḥabiru of the Amarna tablets and the Israelite tribes, and there is no mention in the Amarna tablets that they came into Syria-Palestine from the desert or that they had come recently.

About the time the Israelite tribes established themselves in Palestine, an important movement affected the city state territories from another direction. About 1200 B.C. there was an influx of land-seeking groups from the Mediterranean region by sea and land into the civilised areas of the ancient East. We are familiar with this movement from Egyptian sources, since the immigrants also attacked Egypt and the Pharaohs Merneptah and, above all, Rameses III had to ward off these 'Sea Peoples' from their land. They succeeded in doing so and they described their victories in words and pictures[1]. This assault by the 'Sea Peoples' was merely the tail-end of a comprehensive ethnic movement which came over the eastern Mediterranean world from the north and of which the so-called Dorian migration in Greece was a part. With bag and baggage these immigrants apparently came along the coasts to some extent in ox-carts, and partly on ships from island to island or along the eastern border of the Mediterranean. They travelled through Asia Minor and attacked and destroyed the kingdom of the Hittites. On the coast of Syria-Palestine they moved to the south. They also appear to have crossed from Greece and the Greek islands to the Libyan coast of North Africa and to have threatened Egypt from this side. But the final waves of the movement broke on the frontier of Egypt. The Egyptians had all kinds of names for the 'Sea Peoples' who came into their purview, including *prst* and *ṯkr* which are important for us, since we know that the 'Sea Peoples' who were called by these names settled in Palestine at this period. *Prst* is the Egyptian version of the name 'Philistine'; and in the report of the Egyptian official Wen-Amon we hear that around 1100 B.C. the *ṯkr* occupied one of the few Palestinian coastal towns, the town of Dor (the modern *el-burj* near *et-ṭanṭūra*) south of the Carmel salient[2].

The settlement of the Philistines in Palestine had particularly

---

[1] The illustrations and inscriptions in the Palace of Rameses III in *medīnet habu* (on the west side of Egyptian Thebes), are particularly relevant; cf. J. H. Breasted, *Ancient Records of Egypt*, IV (1906), pp. 59-82; AOB², No. 111, 112. ANEP, No. 341.

[2] A translation of this travel report will be found in AOT², pp. 71 ff. and TGI, pp. 36 ff.; the passage in question will be found at I, 8 f., *ibid.* p. 71 or p. 36. Cf. ANET, pp. 25-9.

important consequences for the history of Israel. According to the Old Testament tradition the Philistines had occupied the southern part of the coastal plain of Palestine to the north as far as *nahr el-ʿauja* and lived there in five fairly small states each containing one town—in most cases the evidence suggests that they were ancient Bronze Age cities—as the seat of government. These cities were Gaza (modern *ghuzzeh*), Askalon (modern *ʿaskalān*), Ashdod (modern *esdūd*), Akkaron[1] (modern *ʿākir*) and Gath (situated the furthest inland on the coastal plain at a spot which has not yet been identified). In these states the Philistines lived, in all probability, as a fairly compact, warlike[2] class, ruling over the old Canaanite inhabitants of the region, under five rulers[3] who united in a common alliance, at any rate when military necessity demanded, led by one of the five rulers as the *primus inter pares*. When one remembers that *circa* 1200 B.C. the Pharaohs still maintained their claim to supremacy in Palestine and that as the part of the land nearest to Egypt this southern coastal plain had particularly close ties with Egypt by reason of its Egyptian administration and Egyptian temples, it may easily be surmised that the occupation of the land by the Philistines in this area did not take place without the tacit or even explicit consent of the Pharaohs who thus kept the 'Sea Peoples' out of Egypt itself by encouraging them to settle in neighbouring Palestine.[4] However much the Philistines developed a vigorously expansive military dominion in Palestine, so far as we know they never threatened Egypt again.

The Philistines entered the world of Palestine as a foreign element. The Israelites liked to call them simply the 'uncircumcised' since they did not know and did not adopt the custom of circumcision which was evidently a very old tradition in Syria-Palestine as well as in Egypt and had probably been adopted by the earlier immigrants as well. According to Amos ix, 7, Jer. xlvii, 4 they had come from Caphtor, *i.e.* Crete. But they were not natives of Crete, not the upholders of the Minoan civilisation, whom the Egyptians described quite differently. It may be that Crete was the last stopping-place on their

---

[1] In the Old Testament this name was wrongly vocalised as 'Ekron'; the correct pronunciation can be deduced from the later Assyrian rendering Amkarruna.

[2] Compare the description of the arming of a Philistine hoplite in 1 Sam. xvii, 5-7, which is given with obvious admiration and awe.

[3] According to the Old Testament these Philistine rulers bore the specific title of *seranim*, possibly a Philistinian word, which has been presumed to be connected with the word τύραννος.

[4] Thus A. Alt, ZDPV, 67 (1944–1945), pp. 15 ff.

journey before they settled in Palestine. Their starting-point had certainly been far distant, and the few Philistine personal names known to us suggest the possibility of Illyrian descent[1]. As they probably settled in fairly large numbers in a single self-contained area in Palestine they were able to preserve their own characteristics and their native warlike vigour for several centuries until finally they too succumbed to the fate of every ruling class and were absorbed more and more by the native subject population.

The Philistines were, if not the greatest, certainly the most important 'Sea People' element and the one best known to us, that appeared *circa* 1200 in Palestine, but they were not the only one. Further north, in the coastal plain of Palestine and apparently separate from the Philistines, the above-mentioned *ṭkr* settled in Dor and established there a probably small 'Sea People' domain. Such elements of the 'Sea Peoples' seem to have penetrated into the coastal plain north of Carmel and also into the plain of Jezreel. King Sisera, whom we know from Judges iv and v, and who resided in the region of the route between the northern coastal plain and the plain of Jezreel, also appears to have an Illyrian name[2]. During excavations in *'affūla* in the centre of the plain of Jezreel 'Philistine ceramics' were found[3] and on the site of the city of Beth-shan (the modern *tell el-ḥuṣn* near *bēsān*) on the *nahr jālūd* (which flows from the plain of Jezreel to the Jordan Valley) the excavations have revealed remains dating from the beginning of the Iron Age, which provide evidence of specific contacts with the Mediterranean world[4]. As the information about the *ṭkr* in Dor is merely accidental and incidental, we may assume that the same *ṭkr* or other groups of 'Sea Peoples' gained a foothold in other places in the immediate vicinity of Dor, or further afield. As regards this more remote area, it is doubtful whether the occupation of the land by these strangers also took place with the consent of the Egyptians, as was probably the case when the Philistines settled in Palestine, or whether it was simply a matter of unauthorised conquest by force of arms. Remembering, however, that the excavations have established that at any rate the city of Beth-shan was a special stronghold of Egyptian power and the site of Egyptian temples, one is bound to reckon with the possibility that in this area of

[1] Cf. G. Herbig, *Jahrb. d. Dtsch. Arch. Instituts*, 55 (1940), pp. 58 ff.; A. Jirku, WZKM, 49 (1943), pp. 13 f.

[2] Cf. A. Alt, ZAW, N.F. 19 (1944), p. 78, note 3.

[3] Cf. M. Maisler, *Biblical Archaeologist*, 15 (1952), p. 22.

[4] Cf. AOB², No. 675 with 671 and No. 676 with No. 674. On this whole complex of problems cf. J. Hempel, PJB, 23 (1927), pp. 52-92.

central Palestine too Egyptian territory was made available by the
Pharaohs to land-seeking groups of 'Sea Peoples' after they had
been repelled from Egypt.

But even if they first gained a footing in Palestine by being
assigned land by the Egyptians the 'Sea People' elements did
not rest content with their initial possessions but strove to consolidate their position. From a somewhat later period we know
of the powerful expansionism of the Philistines and their successful attempt to obtain dominion over at any rate the whole
of the land west of the Jordan, and we shall hardly be on the
wrong track if we assume that this was merely the continuation and consummation of an urge to expand which had goaded
them on in Palestine from the very beginning. And if the Sisera
mentioned in Judges iv and v came from the 'Sea Peoples', this
warlike lord may also be regarded as typifying the development of the power of the 'Sea Peoples' in Palestine. It follows
that the appearance of these peoples may have introduced
more unrest and movement into the land than is immediately
obvious from the historical tradition that has come down to us.
For with the actual cessation of Egyptian rule in Palestine the
Egyptian information about conditions and events in the land
breaks off, and the 'Sea Peoples' left no historical tradition of
their own in writing, or, at any rate, none has come down to us.
As the events in question took place in areas with which the
Israelite tribes had little to do at first, we cannot expect the Old
Testament to contain any information on the subject. For the
'Sea Peoples', coming from the coast, entered the Canaanite city-
state territories and settled in those regions. The old Canaanite
city states on the plains of the land west of the Jordan were the
first and, to begin with, the sole territories to be affected by the
aggressive 'Sea Peoples', and had to try to defend themselves
against their dominance. This no doubt led, during the 12th and
11th centuries B.C., to an eventful period in the coastal plain and
the plain of Jezreel, the details of which are completely unknown
to us and only scattered traces of which remain[1]. Since archaeological research has discovered for the period in question numerous
traces of military actions, conquests and cremations in the ruins
of the cities in the area covered by these plains, we are bound to
seek for an explanation above all in conflicts which took place with
the 'Sea Peoples'.

Thus the Israelite tribes at the conquest entered into a land which

[1] An example of this will be found in A. Alt, ZAW, N.F. 19 (1944), pp. 67-85.

in certain areas was crowded with cities which, owing to a stormy
past, were inhabited by a far from uniform population, made up of
the most diverse elements living in a highly differentiated society,
and which, after the cessation of Egyptian rule and the emergence
of the new ruling class of the 'Sea Peoples', were moving into a
period of tumultuous military conflicts with one another. At the
same time, however, these cities had, from the Bronze Age onwards,
been centres not merely of an advanced material civilisation but of
a certain intellectual life which is bound to have been as varied as
the character and origins of the population. We know very little
about this and have at the most some information—above all from
the Ras-Shamra texts—about the religious system in which the
powers of growth and fertility played the dominant role. With the
Babylonian writing and language, which was possibly introduced
by the Hyksos for diplomatic correspondence but may have been
familiar previously, Babylonian traditions and outlook had also
gained a foothold; since even to learn and practise this difficult
mode of writing samples of Babylonian literature were needed
and their contents thereby became familiar.[1] All kinds of elements
of Babylonian tradition and ideas which, as we may see from the
Old Testament, became known to the Israelites certainly reached
them through the mediation of the Bronze Age cities. In the field
of law, too, especially in the documentation of legal business,
Babylonian influence predominated in Syria-Palestine.[2] On the
other hand, the century-long Egyptian rule in Palestine, with the
Egyptian institutions and Egyptian temples which it had introduced, was bound to influence the intellectual life of the towns.
If Psalm civ reveals unmistakably a knowledge of the Hymn
to the Sun composed by the Pharaoh Amenhotep IV, who
called himself Akhenaten[3], it was once again no doubt through
the mediation of the Bronze Age cities that the Israelites acquired
this knowledge.

The world into which the Israelite tribes came possessed a very
important intellectual tool and an important precondition for the
transmission and diffusion of its intellectual life: namely, an alphabet. In fact, Syria-Palestine in the Late Bronze Age appears to
have been the place where this supremely significant and infinitely
momentous discovery of a purely phonetic script was developed

[1] For example, a copy of the Babylonian Adapa myth has been found in the Amarna
archives which had obviously been used for the training of scribes.
[2] Cf. A. Alt, WO, I, 2 (1947), pp. 78 ff.
[3] Translation of this Hymn to the Sun in AOT², pp. 15-18, ANET, pp. 369-371;
DOTT, pp. 142-150.

for the first time. The older systems of writing of the ancient East, the originally Sumerian cuneiform script (which spread over the whole of Mesopotamia and the neighbouring regions) and Egyptian hieroglyphs, were extremely complicated combinations of original systems of word-signs and syllabic scripts with several hundred signs developed from them, which could be written and read only by a handful of specialists, scribes, who thereby not only occupied extremely important and influential positions in politics and government, but, as the 'learned', became the guardians and mediators of intellectual traditions. It was the invention of an alphabetical phonetic spelling, which was able to make do with some twenty different characters, that made the universal dissemination of the art of reading and writing possible, since it was now possible for anyone to learn who wished to do so. This invention had already been made in Syria-Palestine before 1200 B.C., and the Israelite tribes were able to learn and adopt it at once.

The Ras-Shamra script, in which most of the Ras-Shamra texts are written, is an alphabetic script which uses the technique of Babylonian cuneiform and therefore presupposes a knowledge of this system in the land. It was used in the 14th century B.C. in ancient Ugarit (the modern *rās esh-shamra*), but was not entirely unknown outside Ugarit in Syria-Palestine. Two small traces of it have actually been discovered in Palestine, namely a clay tablet from the Late Bronze Age Beth-shemesh on the inland edge of the southern coastal plain[1] and a bronze knife-blade from the district east of Mount Tabor (dating from approximately 1350–1250 B.C.[2]); both examples have the writing from right to left as on one clay tablet from *rās esh-shamra*, whilst usually in Ugarit this writing was written in the opposite direction. This script does not, however, appear to have been very widespread or to have been used for very long, since it yielded to a probably even older and at any rate more serviceable application of the alphabetic principle which did not derive from Babylonian cuneiform, but linked up with Egyptian hieroglyphs, even in its technique: for it was not impressed on to the soft clay of a clay tablet like cuneiform writing, but, except in the case of inscriptions on stone, was written in ink of one kind or other on potsherds or papyrus.

This writing, the mother of all the alphabetic scripts in use in the world today, is known to us above all from a series of stone inscriptions from Byblos, which probably date from the 10th

---

[1] Cf. WAT, p. 168.
[2] Thus Yeivin, *Kedem*, 2 (1945), pp. 32-41, cf. BASOR, 99 (1945), p. 21.

century B.C.[1]. But it is evidently older than that and had various precursors in a number of alphabetic experiments which were carried out in the Middle and Late Bronze Ages, beginning with the so-called Sinaitic inscriptions from the region of the Egyptian mines of *serābīṭ el-khādem* on the Sinaitic Peninsula which have become so famous, but are still not entirely satisfactorily elucidated.[2]

As early as *circa* 1100 B.C. papyrus was being much used as writing material in Phoenicia. According to the travel-diary of Wen-Amon which we have already mentioned, the timber of Lebanon was paid for by the Egyptians in Byblos and elsewhere with 500 rolls of papyrus[3]. In Syria-Palestine these rolls of papyrus will scarcely have been used for writing Egyptian hieroglyphs but probably for writing in alphabetic script. *Circa* 1100 B.C. the writing of this script may well have been quite common, and its development—as a result of numerous very clumsy experiments—no doubt took place in Syria-Palestine as early as the Late Bronze Age. That it spread further in time and space than is explicitly attested by the documents that have been preserved, is only to be expected. The everyday writing material of cuneiform, the dried or even burnt clay tablet on which the characters were impressed, could in tolerably favourable circumstances survive for thousands of years comparatively easily. But the ink with which potsherds were inscribed in the alphabetic script could survive only very rarely; and though the precious papyrus which was used as writing material was durable in the rainless climate of Egypt, it could not last long in Syria-Palestine. So the only evidence of the earliest use of this letter script that has survived consists of stone inscriptions; but in Syria-Palestine stone inscriptions were evidently always few and far between.

It is difficult to over-estimate what the possibility of the wide diffusion of the art of reading and writing meant for government, for trade and commerce, for the law and for intellectual and cultural life in general. In Syria-Palestine the Israelite tribes encountered a world which was no match for the ancient civilisation of Egypt and the lower valley of the Euphrates-Tigris in

[1] Cf. WAT, pp. 168 f. Possibly the Ahiram inscription, though the oldest, only belongs to the 10th century.

[2] Cf. WAT, pp. 169 ff. W. F. Albright, BASOR, 110 (1948), pp. 6 ff. has substantially promoted the deciphering of the Sinaitic inscriptions; he places them in the 15th century B.C. A new fragmentary archaic inscription of the Late Bronze Age has been found on the *tell es-sarem* (south of Beth-shan); cf. R. Brandstetter-Kallner, *Kedem*, 2 (1945), pp. 11 ff. according to BASOR, 99 (1945), p. 21.

[3] Cf. AOT², p. 75; TGI, p. 41 (II, 41).

respect of the originality of its cultural achievements but which led
a richly varied life, fertilised from many sides, and which possessed
in the invention and first application of the alphabetic script a
cultural asset of its own which was of supreme importance and with
which it made a decisive contribution to human civilisation.

4. *The Sources for the History of Israel*

History can only be described on the basis of literary traditions,
which record events and specify persons and places. Even archaeological discoveries can only be understood and appreciated in
relation to information from literary sources. A description of the
development of ancient cultures based merely on archaeology does
not result in history but at the most in pre-history. On the other
hand, the investigation of the material remains of the periods under
review often gives colour and life to the literary traditions and
greatly assists our understanding of them. It is no longer feasible
to describe the 'history of Israel' on the basis simply of the written
records that have come down to us, ignoring the abundant and,
to a very large extent well authenticated, results of Palestinian
archaeology.

If we begin by enquiring about the source of the information
which enables us to establish the outward course of the history of
Israel as a whole and in many of its details, we must refer, in the
first place, to the Old Testament with its wealth of historical
material, but also to a great mass of sources outside the Old
Testament. In the Old Testament one must mention first of all the
great historical work which comprises the books of Deuteronomy,
Joshua, Judges, Samuel, Kings, which we call 'deuteronomistic'[1]
by reason of its language and spirit, and which offers the very first
exposition of the 'history of Israel' up to the events of the year
587 B.C. The author of this compilation passed on numerous
sources from different periods, of different extent and different
origin and nature, partly *in extenso*, partly in extracts, and
developed the whole work from these sources[2]. He thereby conveyed to posterity a mass of valuable traditional material and without his work we should know very little about the earlier phases of
the history of Israel. For the other great historical work in the Old

---

[1] It will be indicated by the abbreviation Deut.
[2] Cf. for further details M. Noth, *Überlieferungsgeschichtliche Studien*, I (Schriften
der Königsberg. Gel. Ges., geisteswiss. Kl. XVIII, 2 (1943)), p. 3-110.

Testament, the 'chronistic' work[1], made use of the deuteronomistic work as the only, or at least the principal, source for these earlier stages, in so far as it dealt with them at all, and only added new material for the period following 587 B.C. derived from a few other sources. For the history of Israel right down to the 5th century B.C. our main source of information is therefore the Old Testament, which offers a great deal of historical material even outside the two above-mentioned historical works.

A more difficult question in this connection is in what sense the Pentateuch can be called a historical work. There can be no doubt that it sets out to relate events that have happened and that it contains a good deal of material relating to historical traditions. On the other hand, however, it is certain that it did not originate and was not planned, at any rate from the outset, as a historical work at all, but has its source in the successive coalescing of sacred traditions which in their turn presuppose and are based on particular historical events[2]. It is a great collective work which conveys historical information but—at the stage of oral transmission in which it acquired its pattern—was not designed and drafted as a coherent historical narrative. The question as to how far it may be drawn on in an exposition of the course of the history of Israel is therefore especially problematical: it can only be used with many provisos.

The close and constant connection of the history of Israel with the history of the ancient oriental world means that many of the historical documents of the ancient Orient—above all, royal inscriptions and other official records—are indirectly, or even directly, relevant to the history of Israel. Apart from all kinds of sporadic information from Egyptian sources, the inscriptions of the later Assyrian kings are the main source for the earlier period. Some of these kings intervened in Israelite history without provocation and decisively. Unfortunately the Neo-Babylonian and Persian kings of whom the same is true, left behind only slight historical information in their inscriptions[3].

Where the real historical tradition of the Old Testament comes to an end, there is, to begin with, a painful gap in the sources

---

[1] Abbreviation: Chr.; on this matter cf. M. Noth, *op. cit.* pp. 110-180.

[2] Further details in M. Noth, *Überlieferungsgeschichte des Pentateuch* (1948).

[3] The most important of these records will be found in translation in ANET and AOT[2], where, admittedly, the sections with the historical texts are rather scanty. The historical tradition of the Egyptians will be found in translation in J. H. Breasted, *Ancient Records of Egypt*, I-V (1906–1907), that of the Assyrians in D. D. Luckenbill, *Ancient Records of Assyria and Babylonia*, I/II (1927). A good selection of texts will be found in TGI. Cf. also DOTT, pp. 46-94.

of the history of Israel. It is only when we reach the second and third quarter of the 2nd century B.C. that a detailed historical tradition becomes available once more in the two books of Maccabees which have come down to us in the Hellenistic form of the Old Testament, that is, the Greek Septuagint. It is true that they also present some problems, above all concerning the relation of the two books of Maccabees to one another, but they do contain so much concrete historical information that the period they describe is one of the best known in the history of Israel. For the subsequent period the Jewish historian Josephus is the main source[1], with his large-scale work on the history of Israel, ἱστορίαι τῆς Ἰουδαϊκῆς ἀρχαιολογίας composed under the Emperor Domitian, for the first half of which he depended almost entirely on the Old Testament tradition, including the books of Maccabees; but for the last part he began to write on the basis of trustworthy historical sources of his own and thereby himself became a historical source. From about the 1st century B.C. onwards Josephus's historical information becomes increasingly detailed and complete, so that he becomes our main source for the history of Israel up to the year A.D. 73[2].

For this later period too we have in addition numerous isolated pieces of information referring directly or indirectly to the history of Israel, mainly deriving from the Graeco-Roman world. They are found, above all, in works concerning the history of the Hellenistic States and the Roman Empire, in which the history of Israel was now most intimately involved. Unfortunately these sources are rather scanty.

The study of historical sources cannot and must not be confined to the collecting and arranging of the relevant information. In certain circumstances the task of interpreting the relative usefulness and significance of the sources is even more important. This applies particularly to the history of Israel, and especially to its earlier stages, for which official records are few, and even those that do exist only represent a limited selection of which the underlying principle has to be discerned before they can be utilised. For the greater part, however, the Old Testament contains popular historical traditions especially concerning the early history of Israel, which were transmitted by word of mouth to begin with and not written down until later. They are usually the only information

---

[1] Edition of the text: *Flavii Josephi opera recogn.* B. Niese, I-VI (1888–1895).

[2] On the insurrection of A.D. 66–73 cf. Josephus, ἱστορία Ἰουδαϊκοῦ πολέμου πρὸς Ῥωμαίους, with a historical introduction that starts at the time of the Maccabeans.

which we have regarding certain events and processes so that there is no chance of checking their accuracy. In such cases it is absolutely necessary to investigate the source of these records, to ask what occasioned them, why they were made and made in this form, what they are intended to connote and what they are capable of signifying historically. This question must be applied to each single tradition. Even the purpose and nature of the beginnings of real historiography, which go back to a fairly early period in the age of David and Solomon and the productions of which have come down to us, in so far as they were included in his great compilation by the deuteronomist, must be investigated before their value can be assessed objectively. For it would certainly be wrong to regard as authoritative only the traditional material which happens to have been preserved with its particular contents and interests, and not to raise other relevant historical questions and pose other problems unrelated to this material. The available traditions may indeed help us to answer such questions even though they are not their real interest and concern; or they may by their very nature and limitations indicate that these questions are unanswerable. It may then be proper to draw cautious inferences from the facts which are recorded.

The differences of opinion which still persist, especially regarding the beginnings and earliest periods of Israel's history, are based very largely on uncertainties involved in the utilisation of the popular traditions of the Old Testament. This is not surprising, however, since the examination of the origins, motives and development of this tradition has not yet been undertaken at all systematically, much less has it led to positive results. There is still much to be done in this field. It is not enough, in considering the popular nature of this tradition, to dispute the historical credibility of certain passages according to our own discretion and to stick to the rest as the 'historical nucleus' and incorporate it in the history of Israel or, alternatively, to assess the historical credibility on the basis of the approximate age of the various traditions. What is important is rather to grasp as precisely as possible the historical assumptions behind these traditions in each individual case from the material of the tradition itself, and then to assess as objectively as possible what they can contribute to our knowledge of the outward course of the history of Israel, and what they cannot contribute. The same applies, however, to the literary historical narratives and to the later more comprehensive historical works, and the traditional materials incorporated in them. Only when we have grasped the

circumstances under which they arose and what they are driving
at, can we answer the vital question as to how they arrived at their
particular selection from the wealth of events and why they
presented it in the particular way they did. Only when we have
answered that can we discern the subjects on which they can be
expected to supply information and the weight which may be
attached to what they say and to what they suppress. It must be
clear from the outset that it is absolutely necessary to ask these
questions and to answer them as far as possible[1], but also that the
answers cannot be given with mathematical clarity and certainty,
since many unknown factors are involved and the answers must be
arrived at by taking all the circumstances into account and
reaching a synthesis as intelligently as possible. An exposition of
history based on this kind of approach may be called 'subjective',
even though it is committed to a conscientious interpretation of the
sources. In this sense, however, every exposition of history is
inevitably 'subjective' even if it is imagined to be 'objective',
since the fact is that the available traditions shed a purely accidental light on the course of events as a whole and can only be
evaluated within the framework of a specific approach to the
material. But, by doing justice to all the available information, such
a 'subjective' approach will be convincing and therefore justified.

Historical synthesis is indispensable even in the interpretation
and utilisation of archaeological findings, that is, the entirely
visible, concrete, verifiable remains of past history. In this case too
it is a matter of constantly fitting the isolated details into historical
contexts which have first to be reconstructed. Admittedly, the
sober consideration of all the probabilities and improbabilities is
a specially urgent necessity in this field. One has to be very clear
what the results of archaeological work can prove and what they
cannot prove. For more than a century now the excavators' spades
have brought to light from the soil of the Near East the material
which has made possible a mass of surprisingly many-sided and
accurate information on the great and rich world of the ancient
Orient and its stirring history. When one asks, however, what this
modern knowledge is primarily based on, the answer must inevitably be the innumerable written documents which have come to
light as a direct or indirect result of the excavations. What knowledge of any real accuracy and historical substance of the ancient

---

[1] Anyone who does not ask these questions misjudges the situation and inevitably
gives tacit answers; but these answers will not be considered and well founded, and
will therefore not withstand closer examination.

Orient should we possess if we had all the material remains except-
ing the literary relics in the widest sense of the word? Inasmuch as
even the latter have in the main become available as the result of
archaeological work this has acquired a position of absolutely
prime importance for historical knowledge, including knowledge
of the history of Israel. It is true that in the narrower sphere of
Israel itself, in Syria-Palestine, discoveries of written records are
rare surprises. And that is no mere accident. In contrast to the
great river valleys of lower Mesopotamia and of Egypt, the
hilly and heterogeneous land of Syria-Palestine did not develop great political organisations and there was therefore little
occasion for inscribed stone memorials or large buildings with
inscriptions. But whilst it was possible for writings of an everyday
character to survive in Mesopotamia in the form of clay tablets inscribed with wedge-shaped characters and also on inscribed sheets
of papyrus in the completely dry climate of Egypt, it was not possible
in Syria-Palestine where only the clay tablets of the Late Bronze
Age, inscribed with cuneiform characters, were able to survive for
centuries, whereas the papyrus perished entirely owing to the
winter rain and even the writing on potsherds only survived under
unusually favourable conditions. For the most part, therefore, the
written documents of the Iron Age failed to survive at all.

As far as the Israelite period is concerned, Syrian-Palestinian
archaeology is therefore almost wholly silent; and it is clear that
under these circumstances the historical interpretation of archaeological discoveries is particularly difficult. The understandable
enthusiasm with which, to begin with, unusually intensive excavations were carried out in Palestine, from purely Biblical motives,
with the aim of finding positive and indisputable traces of Israelite
history, has in many cases led to the drawing of over-hasty parallels
between the discoveries and known events of history, which have
turned out to be untenable; and although Syrian-Palestinian
archaeology has long since developed from an auxiliary discipline
of Biblical studies into an independent science with methods of its
own and aims evolving from its own work[1], it has still not entirely
overcome the improper search for direct Biblical connections. To

[1] Their results have been expertly and thoroughly collated with a wealth of illustra-
tions, in C. Watzinger, *Denkmäler Palästinas. Eine Einführung in die Archäologie
des Heiligen Landes*, I/II (1933–1935), and more briefly but still very reliably in
P. Thomsen, *Palästina und seine Kultur in fünf Jahrtausenden nach den neuesten
Ausgrabungen und Forschungen dargestellt*, 3rd ed. (AO, Vol. 30) and in W. F.
Albright, *The Archaeology of Palestine* (1951). W. F. Albright, *From the Stone Age to
Christianity* (2nd ed. 1946), offers a comprehensive evaluation of the results of the
archaeological work, especially for the inner continuity and progress of Israelite history.

look for its significance in the wrong direction is to make unfair demands on Palestinian archaeology and to overlook the really positive contribution it can make to our historical knowledge. In general, it must not be expected to yield positive evidence concerning particular historical events and processes, except when it leads to the fortunate discovery of written documents. But it can certainly shed a far-reaching light on the presuppositions and conditions of life and the changes they underwent in the course of time, and it can thereby reveal the background against which the historical personalities acted and the actual historical events took place; and in so far as these phenomena and movements are always closely related to that background, it makes a substantial contribution to our insight into the historical process. Thus an account of the history of Israel which does not refer constantly to the results of Syrian-Palestinian archaeology, is indefensible now that this source of information has become accessible. It has had the greatest possible and most enduring influence on our total conception of the history of Israel, by revealing through innumerable details the world in which this history ran its course and it has thereby enabled us to achieve a fresh and vivid understanding of the reality behind the historical events which have been transmitted by the literary tradition. It is true that in the nature of things it is only rarely that archaeological evidence is forthcoming to prove that a particular event actually took place and that it happened as described in the written records. The fact that an event can be shown to have been possible is no proof that it actually occurred, and the archaeological illumination of the general situation in any particular period does not in any way enable us to dispense with the study of the nature of the traditions enshrined in the records which have been handed down. On the other hand, however, information attested by the tradition can usually be understood more precisely and concretely, and therefore more positively and comprehensively, and appreciated and visualised more vividly in the setting of a particular period when illuminated by the material remains, than would be the case without them. At the same time, a picture which has only been drawn with single strokes in the literary records can often be supplemented and rounded off by the archaeological discoveries. Thus the history of Israel has gained substantially in colour and plasticity as a result of Syrian-Palestinian archaeology.

Everything we have said so far concerns the outward course of the history of Israel and the question of the available sources.

Everything that can make any contribution, direct, or indirect, is to be welcomed wholeheartedly. But the fundamental meaning of the history of Israel cannot be inferred from the innumerable sporadic assertions that occur in the sources or from the course of the actual history itself; *the* source of information on this subject is simply the witness of the Old Testament which explains that the history of Israel which is, like all human history, mysterious and ambiguous when judged merely from the outside, may be given a unified meaning by declaring outright that God, the Lord of the whole world, here used a people as his instrument so that in it 'shall all families of the earth be blessed' (Gen. xii, 3). That this testimony exists, is in the first place a historical fact, which is itself part of the history of Israel; and it would be unscientific to disregard this truly singular fact. This self-testimony makes the history of Israel not merely unique, as every national history on earth is unique and un-repeatable, but utterly unique in character among the histories of the nations. That this self-testimony is valid can no longer be proved. The outward history of Israel can be described without any deeper questionings and presented as a coherent whole, even if this self-testimony is ignored; and the questions as to the basis and meaning of many phenomena can be left alone as un-answerable: world history is, after all, full of such unanswer-able questions. But to ignore this question as to the deeper meaning of Israel's history is to leave out of account a certain fact —the fact that the main traditional source of information in the history of Israel, beside which all other sources are purely supple-mentary, is indissolubly bound up with this testimony. The Old Testament relates the history of Israel in such detail simply for the sake of this testimony. This fact must be taken seriously. The Old Testament is not merely a treasury of traditional historical information but, on a higher plane, *the* real source for the history of Israel besides which all other sources must be regarded as secondary, in so far as it not only gives a coherent account of the external course of this history over a fairly long period, but also utters the decisive word towards an understanding of this history[1].

[1] From the wealth of previous books on the subject we propose to mention here only those which still need to be taken directly into account and have more than a merely historical interest, which means that it is not necessary to include anything published before the opening up of the ancient Orient and its utilisation for the history of Israel. In the first place reference must be made to the work by R. Kittel which first appeared in 1888–1892 as *Geschichte der Hebräer* and from the 2nd edition onwards (Vol. I, 1912, Vol. II, 1909) as *Geschichte des Volkes Israel* made definite use of the new discoveries and knowledge of the ancient Orient. In the final revised edition (I⁵, ⁶, 1923; II⁶, 1925) it can still be considered a standard work. The first two volumes, which

dealt with the history up to 587 B.C., were followed much later by a third volume in two parts (1927–1929) which extends to the end of the Persian period. Admittedly, no one would now begin the history of Israel with a description of the whole primeval and early period of Palestine (against II[6], p. xi), since nowadays a history of Palestine is already a problem on its own and different from a history of Israel, and the cultural history of Palestine can only be treated, at any rate in its wider context, with that of Syria; but the incorporation of Israel in the greater entity of the world around it, which Kittel clearly discerned as his task, will always be a necessity for any historian of Israel. A more concise work is E. Sellin's *Geschichte des israelitisch-jüdischen Volkes*, I (1924), II (1932) which—with all kinds of original and not always tenable theses—extends to the period of Alexander the Great, since the third volume, which was to have brought the history of Israel to its appropriate conclusion in the first two centuries A.D., was never written. On the basis of an intimate knowledge of its setting, the history of Israel to the period of Ezra and Nehemiah has been written in an independent and stimulating way by E. Auerbach under the title *Wüste und Gelobtes Land*, I (1932), II (1936), in which the author brings out the influence of the neighbouring desert on the course of Palestinian and therefore Israelite history. There are other more detailed expositions of the subject by T. H. Robinson and W. O. E. Oesterley, *A History of Israel*, I/II (1932) and A. Lods, *Israël des origines au milieu du VIIIᵉ siècle* (1930) E.T. *Israel* (1932), and *Les Prophètes et le début du judaïsme* (1935) E.T. *The Prophets and the Rise of Judaism* (1937). For the final period of the history of Israel there is now the comprehensive work of F.-M. Abel, *Histoire de la Palestine depuis la conquête d'Alexandre jusqu'à l'invasion arabe*, I/II (1952); for the last phase of the history of Israel the very detailed treatment of E. Schürer, *Geschichte des jüdischen Volkes im Zeitalter Jesu Christi*, I (3, 4 1901), II (4 1907), III (4 1909) is still of basic importance: it starts with the Maccabean period and extends to A.D. 135. A. Schlatter, *Geschichte Israels von Alexander dem Grossen bis Hadrian* (3 1925) provides an easily understood account, based on penetrating independent study of the sources, of the concluding section of the history of Israel with special regard to religious and intellectual life. Among the smaller textbooks we may note H. Guthe, *Geschichte des Volkes Israel* (3 1914), extending to A.D. 135, still useful, though in many respects out of date, and A. Jirku, *Geschichte des Volkes Israel* (1931) which only goes as far as 587 B.C. W. F. Albright, *The Biblical Period*, deals with the history of Israel précis-fashion, including the Persian period, and the subsequent period is dealt with similarly by E. Bickerman in *The Historical Foundations of Postbiblical Judaism* (both of these in the symposium L. Finkelstein, *The Jews; their History, Culture and Religion* [1949]). A. Alt, *Kleine Schriften zur Geschichte des Volkes Israel*, I/II (1953) contains numerous separate studies of basic importance on problems of the history of Israel.

PART ONE

ISRAEL AS THE CONFEDERATION OF
THE TWELVE TRIBES

CHAPTER I

THE ORIGINS OF THE TRIBES OF ISRAEL

5. *The Homes of the Tribes in Palestine*

'ISRAEL', which, according to Old Testament tradition, was an association of twelve separate tribes, cannot really be grasped as a historical entity until it becomes a reality living on the soil of Palestine. Naturally, the Old Testament tradition is unquestionably right in regarding the tribes not as indigenous to Palestine but as having entered and gained a footing there from the wilderness and steppe at a definite point in time. Even if the event had not been recorded in so many words, it would be possible to infer that it had taken place from the location of the areas occupied by the tribes in Palestine and from their mode of living and dwelling there. It goes without saying that the tribes had a history of their own before they entered Palestine and in the Old Testament certain tribal traditions from that early period have been preserved which are undoubtedly genuine. We shall deal with them later on in greater detail. On the other hand, these traditions were first given their definitive form within an Israel that was already united in Palestine and they were conditioned by its point of view. Together with the historical events on which they are based they made a contribution of basic importance to the self-consciousness and faith of Israel when it was living in Palestine, but, at the same time, in their existing form they are based on presuppositions which did not exist until the tribes had already settled on Palestinian soil. Above all, as will be seen in a moment, the fusion of the tribes into the entity 'Israel' only became a final and enduring reality in Palestine; and the individual tribes only became consolidated into permanent historical entities in the process of their occupation of the land. The traditions are an essential and decisive part of the heritage of the Israel that we know in Palestine and it is in this context that we must regard them as a historical fact of fundamental significance, having its roots in the pre-history of Israel. On the other hand, the history of Israel, in the strict sense of the history of a more or less definable entity, only begins on the soil of Palestine.

To define this entity with precision it is necessary first of all to

53

establish the actual list of tribes reckoned as Israel and the areas
which they inhabited. This can be done by using all the various
data which are scattered about in the fragments of narrative tradition, as preserved, above all, within the framework of the great
collective work of the deuteronomist and to some extent also, in
that compilation of traditions, the Pentateuch, which evolved on
Palestinian soil. The most important source of all is provided by
a few traditions which deal specifically with individual tribes. A
comprehensive description of the tribal geography was later inserted in the deuteronomistic writings (Jos. xiii-xix, xxi) incorporating an old list of the borders of the tribal areas, which probably
derives from the period before political organisation took shape
and which states the various dwelling-places of the individual
tribes in the form of an enumeration of the permanent boundary
marks. It is true that it does not simply reproduce the tribal
territories at a particular historical date but describes the areas
to which the individual tribes laid claim, in accordance with
the theory that the *whole* land of Palestine was to belong to the
united tribes of Israel. Obviously, however, the territories actually
inhabited by the tribes form the basis of the list[1]; to eliminate the
purely theoretical elements we are not reduced to mere surmise
and supposition, for in Judges i, 21, 27-35 we have a list the basis of
which also derives from the pre-monarchical era and which, at least
as far as the tribes of central and northern Palestine are concerned,
briefly states which Canaanite city-state territories they were in
fact unable to occupy, although here too the supposition is that
they were really entitled to them[2]. In addition, there are one or two
further traditions which, whilst they do not deal with the geography
of the tribes, do contain some information about the continued
existence and make-up of the tribes of Israel. In Num. xxvi, 4bβ-51
we have a list of the families belonging to the tribes which is presumably fairly old, although it is impossible to give it a precise
date[3]; and in Gen. xlix, 1b-27/28 and Deut. xxxiii, 6-25 we find

---

[1] Cf. above all A. Alt, Das System der Stammesgrenzen im Buche Josua, Sellin-
Festschrift [1927], pp. 13-24=*Kleine Schriften zur Geschichte des Volkes Israel*, I
[1953], pp. 193-202, and also M. Noth, ZDPV, 58 (1935), pp. 185 ff.

[2] It is found in a conglomeration of supplements to the deuteronomistic work and it
is uncertain how it got there. In its present form it presupposes the later incorporation
of these city-state territories in the Kingdom of David and Solomon.

[3] This list was subsequently used to compile a later and apocryphal list of the numerical strengths of the single Israelite tribes as applicable at the time of the Exodus from
Egypt; and so it was assumed that Moses undertook a census of the people, and the
whole episode was inserted as an afterthought into the Pentateuch narrative which had
already been compiled; cf. M. Noth, *Das System der zwölf Stämme Israels* (1930),
pp. 122 ff.

collections of brief aphorisms about the individual tribes which were later inserted in the Pentateuch narrative in the form of 'The Blessing of Jacob' and 'The Blessing of Moses'; such sayings had probably been in circulation among the tribes for a long time, some expressing praise, others chaffing or mocking. They were compiled unsystematically and derive from various, no longer precisely definable, periods. The description of the behaviour of the various tribes of central and northern Palestine contained in the Song of Deborah (Judges v, 2-30) is based possibly not so much on the single event here commemorated as on the way the tribes habitually acted.

The tribes of Israel fall into a number of geographically correlated groups. As far as one can see, the tribe of *Judah* always played the leading part among the tribes of southern Palestine. It inhabited the southern part of the mountains west of Jordan, south of Jerusalem, and its area extended southwards almost as far as the city of Hebron. Bethlehem, at the Amarna period, 'a city of the land of Jerusalem'[1], was its centre. It is now impossible to say how this city, which was probably only temporarily subject to the rule of Jerusalem and had itself been a minor centre of government, came into the possession of the tribe of Judah. To the north the territory of Judah was bordered by the city-state of Jerusalem and the territories of the other city-states in its vicinity; to the east the 'wilderness of Judah', sloping down to the Dead Sea, formed a natural boundary. The few oasis settlements on the west bank of the Dead Sea may also have been inhabited by Judaeans. As far as these borders are concerned, the descriptions contained in Jos. xv, 1-12 correspond to the facts, but, for reasons which we shall discuss later, southwards and westwards they greatly extended the frontiers of Judah. In fact the mountains south of Judah were inhabited by other tribes, which will be mentioned directly, and even the city of Hebron belonged to one of them and not to the tribe of Judah. In the west, however, the southern part of the Palestinian coastal plain was in the hands of the initially powerful Philistines, who had subjugated the old Canaanite city-states formerly situated there; and only in the hill country between the mountains proper and the plain, in which there were comparatively few city-states, was there room for new settlements. This was the only direction in which the powerful tribe of Judah could expand; and in time Judaean clans did in fact advance into this hill country and apparently entered into normally peaceful relationships with the

[1] Cf. p. 32 above.

Canaanites already residing in some of the cities there[1]. The name Judah (יהודה) is not related to any well-known type of Semitic personal name and can hardly have been a personal name originally: in any case it cannot be explained philologically as a compound of the name for God (יהוה). On the other hand, we have evidence of a number of similarly constructed place-names[2] and the probability is that it was originally used in the phrase 'mountains of Judah' (הר יהודה) to describe part of a mountainous district south of Jerusalem[3] and in the phrase 'wilderness of Judah' (מדבר יהודה) to describe the area sloping down to the Dead Sea, to the east of the mountains[4]. It is probable that the clans which settled in this area called themselves later the 'people of Judah', 'Judaeans' (בני יהודה), and thus became the 'tribe of Judah'.

From various scattered references in the Old Testament we know that a few other tribes or clans resided south of these Judaeans in the most southerly part of the mountains. Hebron (in the area of the modern *el-khalīl*) which was probably already a Canaanite city, was in possession of the *Calebites* who belonged to the kindred of the Kenizzites[5], other parts of which were represented among the Edomites[6]. The traditions behind Num. xiii, xiv and Deut. i, 22-45 and Jos. xiv, 6aβb-15 are an attempt to explain how it came about that Hebron, a city of blessing and importance, was assigned to Caleb, the *heros eponymus* of the Calebites; they therefore presuppose the possession of Hebron by the Calebites. How far the area of the Calebites extended it is no longer possible to say with any certainty. According to 1 Sam. xxv, 1-3 a Calebite was living in Maon, which was about 10 miles south of Hebron (the modern *tell maʿīn*), and, according to 1 Sam. xxx, 14 the tribe of Caleb had a share in the Negeb, the somewhat indeterminate region of steppe south of the mountains west of the Jordan. The area occupied by the Calebites appears to have extended southwards from Hebron.

[1] This may be seen, above all, from Gen. xxxviii where incidents from tribal history appear with other narrative elements in a complex section now not analysable with any certainty (cf. M. Noth, *Überlieferungsgeschichte des Pentateuch*, pp. 162 f.) and also from the geographical list of the settlements which is contained in 1 Chron. ii, 4 (cf. M. Noth, ZDPV, 55 [1932], pp. 97-124). On the incident itself cf. M. Noth, PJB, 30 (1934), pp. 31-47.

[2] From the old Testament we know the city names ינבהה and יראלה; on the other hand, the place name יהוד (Jos. xix, 45) is difficult to separate etymologically from the name יהודה.

[3] Cf. Jos. xi, 21 and especially Jos. xx, 7; xxi, 11, where Hebron, which was not inhabited by Judaeans at all, is described as situated on the הר יהודה; cf. further 2 Chron. xxvii, 4. [4] Judges i, 16; Psalm lxiii, 1.

[5] In Num. xxxii, 12; Jos. xiv, 6, 14 Caleb is called a 'Kenizzite'; cf. also Jos. xv, 17; Judges i, 13; iii, 9. [6] Cf. Gen. xxxvi, 11, 42.

The *Othnielites* were another Kenizzite tribe: according to Jos. xv, 15-19 = Judges i, 11-15 they owned the city of Debir, which is said formerly to have been called Kiriath-Sepher. Unfortunately its situation is not known for certain[1]. But in all probability it lay south-west of Hebron, presumably on the heights of the mountains west of Jordan. We have no information at all as to how far the land of the Othnielites extended in this area.

The most southerly part of the mountains was also inhabited by the *Kenites* whose *heros eponymus* Cain appears in Gen. iv, 1-16. If it is correct that in Jos. xv, 56-57, the words זנוח הקין belong together[2] and are to be translated by 'Zanoah of the Kenites', then the Kenites lived south-east of Hebron; for in Jos. xv, 55-57 this Zanoah is mentioned along with a number of other places in this district. In any case we may take it that the Kenites lived somewhere in the southern part of the mountains west of Jordan, since in 1 Sam. xxx, 29 'the cities of the Kenites' are referred to in connection with other well-known places in the southern part of the mountains. They, too, had a share in the Negeb; in 1 Sam. xxvii, 10 there is a reference to the 'Negeb of the Kenites'. The Kenites do not appear to have become completely domiciled until relatively late and possibly only a part of the tribe settled permanently. In Judges iv, 11, 17; v, 24 we hear of a Kenite nomad pitching his tent somewhere or other in Galilee. It is true that, according to Judges iv, 11, he had 'separated himself from the (other) Kenites', but probably there was quite a number of such 'separated' Kenites. On the other hand, according to 1 Sam. xv, 6, in Saul's time the Kenites still regarded themselves as belonging to the nomadic kindred of the Amalekites. Perhaps, therefore, only a section of the Kenites established themselves in a small area south-east of Hebron near the border[3] between the cultivated land and the steppe, whilst other sections maintained their nomadic way of life in the steppe and wilderness and in isolated cases even in the heart of the cultivated land[4].

Finally, we know very little about the *Jerahmeelites* who must also be mentioned in this connection. In 1 Sam. xxx, 29 'the cities of the Jerahmeelites' are mentioned beside 'the cities of the Kenites'

---

[1] Cf. above (p. 33, note 1).   [2] Thus, according to the Septuagint.

[3] The fairly late information contained in 1 Sam. xv, 6 might originate in the fact of the juxtaposition of nomadic *and* established Kenites. According to Judges i, 16 (text. em.) it was especially the Kenite clan of בני הבב that settled in Palestine.

[4] The name of the tribe might indicate that it was an association of desert smiths (cf. Arabic *ḳain* = 'smith'); but the Kenites who had settled were certainly farmers like the other inhabitants.

and in 1 Sam. xxvii, 10 the 'Negeb of the Jerahmeelites' is referred
to alongside the 'Negeb of the Kenites'. In a later list Jerahmeel
appears as the brother of Caleb (1 Chron. ii, 9, 42). Although it is
impossible to determine their territory very accurately we must also
place the Jerahmeelites in the most southerly part of the mountains[1].

The tribe of *Simeon* evidently dwelt entirely in the far south;
we know little about it, for in the list of the tribal boundaries in
Jos. xiii ff. it is not mentioned at all, and in the historical tradition
of the Old Testament it plays no part whatsoever. Only in the
fragmentary narratives of unknown origin dealing with the
occupation of land by Israelite tribes, contained in Judges i, 1 ff.,
which were subsequently taken into the deuteronomistic compilation, does the tribe appear (Judges i, 3) alongside Judah,
and in Judges i, 17 we are informed, in the only concrete statement
we have about it at all, that the tribe took possession of the city
of Hormah, formerly called Zephath (the modern *tell el-mushāsh*
east of *bīr es-seba'* = Beersheba); and the fact that the Simeonites
resided in this southerly frontier area caused a late redactor to
assign the most southerly district of Judah (Jos. xv, 21-32) at any
rate in part to the tribe of Simeon (Jos. xix, 2-8). In the system of
tribal frontiers Simeon's area was simply made a part of the larger
unit of Judah (cf. also Jos. xix, 1, 9); and in the narrative in
Judges i, 1 ff. Simeon also appears entirely in the shadow of Judah.
It seems, therefore, that the tribe of Simeon, living as it did entirely
on the periphery of the Israelite territories, was in no position to
play an independent role in the historical period known to us. Its
name was almost certainly originally a personal name (cf. Ezra x,
31); it was therefore named after one of its ancestors.

The most important tribes historically were those of Central
Palestine. First among them was the '*house of Joseph*'. This term,
which has a very original and ancient ring about it[2], gives special
prominence to the significance of 'Joseph' within the totality of
the tribes of Israel and appears to indicate that in reality more than
a single tribe was concerned. It has its counterpart in the expression,
'the house of Judah', and the latter is used precisely when not

---

[1] Of the names of these tribes Othniel and especially Jerahmeel are evidently personal names, that is, names of real or fictitious ancestors of these tribes. On the name
of the Kenites cf. the previous note. There is still some doubt about the name Caleb,
which apparently means 'dog' (in an archaic form of the word) and may be a personal
name with this meaning; on the other hand, animal names might also be originally
tribal names, if not on the basis of an old system of totemism, at any rate in connection
with certain tribal tokens or the like.

[2] It occurs in fairly old contexts in Jos. xvii, 17; Judges i, 23, 35; 2 Sam. xix, 21;
1 Kings xi, 28 and also in Jos. xviii, 5; Amos v, 6; Ob. 18; Zech. x, 6.

merely the actual tribe of Judah but the whole group of south
Palestinian tribes is concerned, which were united under the name
of 'Judah' and then combined in a kingdom of their own called
'Judah'[1]. In fact the 'house of Joseph' was a particularly large
association of clans holding the whole of the central part of the
mountains west of Jordan and thereby possessing a more extensive
area than any of the other tribes. If this part of the mountains,
particularly in the northern half, was relatively intensely wooded,
so that clearings had to be made before it was available for settlement[2], this was hardly less true of the mountainous areas in the
south and north of the country where more numerous tribes lived
side by side. According to the description of the frontier in Jos.
xvi, 1-3, to the south the 'house of Joseph' occupied the area west
of Jordan as far as the latitude of the city of Bethel[3] (the modern
bētīn) and including this city; in the north—an exact description
of the northern border of the tribe of Joseph is not given in the
book of Joshua—its area extended as far as the southern edge
of the great plain of Jezreel, which interrupts the course of the
mountains west of Jordan. To the east, the slopes leading to the
Jordan Valley were probably very sparsely inhabited and in the
valley itself there were no settlements west of the Jordan worth
mentioning at all in this period. The coastal plain in the west, however, was and remained in the hands of ancient city-states, as far
as this partly marshy area was capable of being inhabited at all
(cf. Judges i, 29).

The great association of the 'house of Joseph' (obviously originally a personal name) was in fact divided in Palestine itself into
two tribes, Manasseh and Ephraim[4], of which *Ephraim* was the
greater and the more important. In Jos. xvi, 5-8 the territory of
Ephraim is specially marked off within the larger area occupied
by the house of Joseph. According to this description Ephraim
was the southerly neighbour of Manasseh and its territory extended northwards from Bethel in the south almost as far as the
city of Shechem (the modern *tell balāṭa* east of the city of *nāblus*)
which itself fell to the area occupied by Manasseh.

[1] Cf. above all 2 Sam. ii, 4, 7, 10, 11, also 1 Kings xii, 21, 23. The expression 'house
of Israel' was probably modelled on the expression 'house of Judah' as a result of the
juxtaposition of the kingdoms of Israel and Judah; thus 2 Sam. xii, 8; 1 Kings xii, 21
and elsewhere (not yet 2 Sam. ii, 10 and v, 3 cf. with ii, 4). 'Israel' was from the very
outset not a tribal name at all, but a comprehensive total description.
[2] Cf. Jos. xvii, 18.   [3] Cf. above, p. 32.
[4] It was originally the custom to name the two names in this order and it was only
later that the habit arose of putting Ephraim first because of its importance; cf. Gen.
xlviii, 1-20.

The name 'Ephraim' is obviously not a personal name, but the name of a place, as is already indicated by its ending, which often occurs in the names of places and countries. According to 2 Sam. xviii, 6 there was in the country east of Jordan a 'wood of Ephraim' which was probably named after a particular district: it certainly has nothing to do with the Ephraim west of Jordan. The latter presumably appears in its original connotation in the term 'Mount Ephraim' (הר אפרים) which often occurs in the Old Testament. This term usually denotes the whole of the great central part of the mountains west of Jordan—beyond the land of the tribe of Ephraim[1]. But it may be that this is a later extension of the original meaning, which may have been restricted to quite a small area. According to 2 Sam. xiii, 23 the sanctuary of Baal-hazor, which is usually placed, probably correctly, on the mountain summit now known as el-'aṣūr a bare 6 miles north-east of Bethel, was situated 'beside[2] Ephraim'; and here 'Ephraim' most probably denotes a village[3]. But again, it is questionable whether in this case 'Ephraim' as a place name was in fact original and not rather 'Mount Ephraim', that is, a closely confined mountainous district in which a village which grew up there was given the name of Ephraim[4]. However that may be, it at any rate seems to be certain that as a designation of a locality Ephraim originally had its real home in the extreme south-east part of what later became known, in a wider sense, as 'Mount Ephraim' and that it arose in the extreme south-east part of the area inhabited by the tribe of Ephraim. The tribal name of Ephraim would then appear to have come about by clans which settled in this area being called 'Ephraimites' (בני אפרים), just as the clans which settled on 'Mount Judah' acquired the name of 'Judaeans' (בני יהודה). Thereafter kindred clans further away to the west and north-west were probably included in the designation 'Ephraim', when a tribe was constituted in this area, and, with the name of Ephraim, that of 'Mount Ephraim' was also extended, until in the end it stretched far beyond the territory colonised by the tribe of Ephraim.

Quite early on, the vigorous tribe of Ephraim was no longer satis-

---

[1] This is clear above all in 1 Kings iv, 8; Jos. xx, 7; xxi, 21. Other old references to the expression 'Mount Ephraim' will be found in Jos. xvii, 15; Judges vii, 24; 1 Sam. i, 1.

[2] On the striking use of the preposition עם cf. Gen. xxxv, 4.

[3] This place Ephraim may have been situated on the ruined site of khirbet el merjame near sāmye; cf. W. F. Albright, JPOS, 3 (1923), pp. 36 ff. and AASOR, 4 (1924), pp. 127 ff. and also A. Alt, PJB, 24 (1928), pp. 35 ff.

[4] The change of meaning of this name may be compared with that of the name Gilead; on the latter cf. M. Noth, PJB, 37 (1941), pp. 59 ff.

fied with the territory west of the Jordan which could only offer limited scope for expansion, since in the mountains to the north and south other tribes of Israel were settled and, to the west, Canaanite city-state territories blocked the way to the coastal plain[1]. And so Ephraimite families went over the Jordan Valley into the central part of the country east of Jordan. Here, on both sides of the Jabbok (the modern *nahr ez-zerḳa*), was a well-wooded mountain country which had hardly been opened up at all. Admittedly it was not particularly inviting country, but it did offer scope to a land-seeking tribe not afraid of the hard labour of clearing the forest. Coming from their dwellings west of Jordan the Ephraimites reached the district south of the Jabbok which was the original home of Gilead, a name which still survives in the place-names of the district. The people that settled there called themselves 'Gilead-ites' (גלעדי) or 'people of Gilead' (אנשׁי גלעד)[2] and the 'Gilead' mentioned in the Song of Deborah (Judges v, 17) is a reference to them. That they were of Ephraimite descent we learn from Judges xii, 4 where it is stated that in the course of a violent and dangerous quarrel they were contemptuously called 'fugitives of Ephraim' by their fellow-tribesmen from the land west of Jordan. They initiated the settlement of the area in the centre of the land east of Jordan. Admittedly, their territory was not at all large and scarcely capable of further extension, since any expansion worth mentioning was prevented by the deep incision of the Jabbok Valley to the north and by the neighbouring Ammonites to the east and south-east.

The other tribe which established itself within the frame-work of the 'house of Joseph' as Ephraim's northern neighbour, seems to have had a rather complicated history. The Song of Deborah, one of the oldest passages in the Old Testament, mentions (Judges v, 14) *Machir* as well as Ephraim and the strangely tortuous formulation of Jos. xvii, 1 seems to suggest that the old system of tribal borders described in Jos. xiii-xix also assigned to Machir the remnant of Joseph's territory that remained after the territory of Ephraim had been subtracted[3]. But the tribe of Machir —or at any rate the main part of it—then migrated to the land east of Jordan, where it is usually located in Old Testament tradition; the people who remained in the land west of Jordan on the northern borders of Ephraim formed the tribe of *Manasseh*,

---

[1] Cf. Jos. xvii, 14-18.
[2] More details on this in M. Noth, PJB, 37 (1941), pp. 59 ff.
[3] Cf. also M. Noth, *Das Buch Josua* (² 1953).

which is clearly a personal name. Manasseh occupied the northern half of the central range of the west Jordan mountains from Shechem in the south. To the north its territory was still fairly intensely wooded and in the west, north and east it was encircled by the city-state territories in the coastal plain, in the plain of Jezreel and the Jordan Valley, which made expansion beyond the mountains impossible (cf. Judges i, 27-28). Machir, however, that is, the main constituent of the clans which to begin with had been Ephraim's northern neighbours, had meanwhile migrated into the opposite section of the land east of Jordan, into the mountain country north of the Jabbok, where they had become the northern neighbours of the east Jordan Ephraimites. From the first constituent of east Jordan colonial territory south of the Jabbok the name Gilead was now extended to the area north of the Jabbok and thus Machir became the 'father of Gilead', this being the almost stereotyped expression used in the old Testament (Jos. xvii, 1 and elsewhere). Numbers xxxii, 39-42 contains a few scanty notes about the process by which the land north of the Jabbok was occupied. This land was fairly extensive and was probably only sparsely populated in the more accessible areas. With advancing colonisation the name Gilead also travelled further. The occupation reached a limit only where the arable land passed over into desert in the east and where the existence of numerous Canaanite city-states in the north-east and north in the area around modern *irbid* (Arbela) made further expansion impossible. The greater importance of the west Jordan possessions compared with those east of Jordan was marked by the fact that 'Manasseh' now became the real tribal name and—without regard to the actual historical process—Machir was subordinated to Manasseh genealogically and made its son (Num. xxvi, 29 and elsewhere).

The southern neighbour of the house of Joseph and specifically of the tribe of Ephraim was *Benjamin*, a small tribe occupying a not very extensive area north-east of Jerusalem which still belonged to Canaan. Its borders are described very precisely in Jos. xviii, 11-20. According to this account, its lands included not only Jerusalem, which, according to Judges i, 21, Benjamin was unable to occupy, but also a group of Canaanite city-states north-west of Jerusalem which only subsequently entered into closer relationship with the tribe of Benjamin. The territory which the tribe of Benjamin actually inhabited was limited to part of the southern end of the Jordan Valley, west of the Jordan, around the oasis of Jericho and as far as the adjacent western section of the land rising to the

summit of the mountains where a few villages on the great road
north to south across the mountains between Bethel and Jerusalem
belonged to the Benjaminites. Most probably the name itself means
'he (who lives) in the south' and refers to the situation of the settlements in the land within the framework of the central Palestinian
group of tribes. If this is so, the tribe of Benjamin also acquired its
name as a direct result of its occupation of the land[1].

Finally, the tribe of *Gad* which lived in the land east of Jordan
and, alone among the tribes of Israel, probably made a permanent
settlement there from the very beginning, has to be reckoned
among the tribes of central Palestine. At any rate there is no
reason to suppose that Gad, like other parts of the house of Joseph,
only migrated later into the land east of Jordan from an original
home west of Jordan. A description of the borders of Gad appears to
be contained in the very complicated passage in Jos. xiii, 15 ff. where
this tribe seems to have been assigned a strip of the mountain east
of the Jordan from the Arnon (the modern *sel el-mōjib*) in the south
as far as the Jabbok in the north and, in addition, the whole of the
eastern half of the Jordan Valley. On the other hand, according to
an older and more concrete tradition, it had established itself on the
pasture land of the 'land of Jazer' (יעזר) (Num. xxxii, 1). Admittedly, it has so far only been possible to define the position of the
town of Jazer approximately; but this much is certain: the 'land of
Jazer' must have been somewhere in the east Jordan mountains
north-east of the northern end of the Dead Sea[2]. Gad therefore occupied only a small area, which was hemmed in on the east by the
possessions of the neighbouring Ammonites and also provided little
scope for expansion in the direction of the wooded mountain country
to the north; whilst in the south-east the cities on the tableland north
of the Arnon set a limit to peaceful expansion, so that the only outlet
was southwards along the outer edge of the mountains on the
eastern side of the Dead Sea, and the tribe of Gad did in fact
gradually expand in that direction[3].

In the Old Testament references to tribal territories the tribe
of *Reuben* is always mentioned in connection with Gad (Num.
xxxii, 1 ff.; Jos. xiii, 15 ff.); but the details indicate that these
references are not based on any clear-cut conception of a particular

---

[1] The tribe of *Banū-yamīna* which is known from the Mari-texts (cf. W. v. Soden,
WO, I, 3 [1948], is only connected with our Benjamin in name (it has the same meaning)
but not in fact.   [2] Details in M. Noth, ZAW, N.F. 19 (1944), pp. 30 ff.
[3] The name Gad is difficult to interpret; it may probably be regarded as originally
a personal name (cf. M. Noth, *Geschichte und Altes Testament = Alt-Festschrift*,
[1953], pp. 145 f.).

territory belonging to the tribe of Reuben but rather that the land
of Gad was always theoretically divided in various ways, half of it
being allotted to Reuben. The old inventory of the tribal borders
does not seem to have contained anything about Reuben but only to
have recognised the territory belonging to Gad in the land east of the
Jordan. It is difficult to believe, however, that there was not some concrete reason for the later attempts to find a place for Reuben alongside Gad in the tribal geography. Probably there were clans in the
vicinity of Gad which called themselves Reubenites, though we
know nothing for certain about their homes. Originally the tribe of
Reuben resided, not in the land east of the Jordan, but somewhere
or other west of the Jordan. The Song of Deborah still appears to
connect Reuben with residences west of the Jordan (Judges v,
15b-16)[1]; and in other places too there are at least traces of Reubenites formerly living west of the Jordan. According to Jos. xv, 6; xviii,
17 there was a place in the district on the lower edge of the mountains south of Jericho which was called 'stone of Bohan the son of
Reuben'. This stone had originally been called 'thumb-stone',
and the word 'thumb' had been mistaken for a personal name and
its bearer for a Reubenite, evidently because Reubenites had once
lived in the district in question—immediately opposite the territory
of the tribe of Gad on the other side of the Jordan Valley. The
formulation of this local name evidently took place at a time when
the tribe of Reuben was no longer known in the borderlands of
Judah and Benjamin, and all that survived was the memory of the
earlier presence there of parts of the tribe. West of this 'thumb-
stone' lay the plain of Achor (Jos. xv, 7) with the pile of stones to
which was linked the tradition of Joshua vii telling of Achan, of
the family of Carmi (Jos. vii, 1, 18), which is probably identical with
the Reubenite family of Carmi (Num. xxvi, 6). It is true that Achan
and the family of Carmi are expressly assigned to the tribe of Judah
in Jos. vii, 1, 18, but the only point that arises from that is that
Reubenites who resided in the vicinity of the tribe of Judah finally
joined the latter tribe. The fact that the name Hezron occurs
among the clans of Reuben in Num. xxvi, 6 and was, according
to Num. xxvi, 21, also the name of the subdivision of a Judaean
clan, can be explained in the same way. Consequently, as far as
we can tell from Old Testament tradition, the tribe of Reuben had
no real territory of its own. There are merely slight traces of an
earlier presence of Reubenites in the district of the Judaean-
Benjaminite border on the eastern slopes of the mountains west of

[1] There is no reference to the land east of the Jordan until the following verse 17.

the Jordan, and there is also the traditional view that Reuben lived with Gad exactly opposite in the land east of the Jordan. From this it may be inferred that the tribe of Reuben had once had its real territory somewhere in the land west of Jordan. All that tradition tells us for certain, however, is that disintegrated elements of the tribe, in so far as they were not simply absorbed into Judah, finally retreated, apparently mainly into the land east of the Jordan, to the very periphery of Israelite territory. Thus, the tribe of Reuben leads as shadowy an existence in the tribal geography as the tribe of Simeon which has been discussed above[1].

The north Palestinian tribes resided on the edge of the mountains which we call the mountains of Galilee, which rise northwards from the plain of Jezreel to the highest eminences of Palestine. The description of the borders contained in Jos. xix, 24-31 assigns an extensive territory to the tribe of *Asher*, including the northern part of the coastal plain and Carmel with its foreland. In fact, according to Judges i, 31, 32, the Asherites did not occupy the city territories in the plain, their actual possessions being limited to the western rim of the Lower Galilean mountains east of Acco and of the Canaanite towns situated in the plain around Acco. The little tribe of Asher, whose name could, but need not inevitably, be the name of a god[2], apparently had no necessity to expand eastwards and northwards into the almost empty lands in the interior of Lower and Upper Galilee; it was satisfied with the attractive hills and mountains above the plain of Acco. On the south-eastern edge of its territory on the western side of the great plain of *sahl el-battōf* which is set deep in the mountains of Lower Galilee, Asher came into contact with its Israelite neighbour.

This neighbour was the tribe of *Zebulun*, whose borders are described fairly exactly in Jos. xix, 10-16. According to this account, the tribe resided in the mountains on the south edge of Lower Galilee between the plain of Jezreel in the southern and *sahl el-battōf* (which we have just mentioned) in the north, in the vicinity of the later city of Nazareth, the modern *en-nāṣira*. Zebulun was also a small tribe, and its territory not very extensive. In the west it bordered on the coastal plain north of Carmel, into whose city-state territories Zebulun found no access (Judges i, 30); in the south was the great plain of Jezreel, the soil of which was, and remained firmly, in possession of the Canaanite city-states. Zebulun does not appear to have needed the large-scale extension of its

---

[1] The meaning of the name Reuben is obscure.
[2] It would then be the male counterpart of the name of the female deity אֲשֵׁרָה.

territory which could only have been effected by penetrating into the interior of Galilee. The name Zebulun cannot be explained for certain; it could originally have been a personal name[1].

In Deut. xxxiii, 18-19 Zebulun and *Issachar* are mentioned together, the main point being that they used to celebrate a sacrificial feast together 'on a mountain'. The mountain referred to must be Tabor, which towers up impressively like a dome in the north-eastern corner of the plain of Jezreel: for the sanctuary on Tabor was a border sanctuary between Zebulun and Issachar in the south-eastern corner of Zebulun and the north-western corner of Issachar. From the details of the territory of the tribe of Issachar in Jos. xix, 17-23 it may be gathered that Issachar occupied the southern spur of the Galilean mountains, which is bordered in the west by the plain of Jezreel, in the south by the broad valley of the *nahr jālūd* with the old Canaanite city of Beth-shan (the modern *tell el-ḥuṣn* near *bēsān*) and in the east by the Jordan Valley. We shall discuss later in greater detail the special conditions under which Issachar had been able to gain a footing here[2]. They explain the tribe's curious name, which arose after its occupation of the land. Issachar means 'hired labourer' and the name was evidently first given to it as a nickname, in connection with the satirical line about Issachar which has come down to us in Genesis xlix, 15 in the Blessing of Jacob, where Issachar's status is also referred to as that of a dependent labourer.

On Mount Tabor Zebulun and Issachar bordered on the tribe *Naphtali* whose territory, according to Jos. xix, 34, also reached as far as Mount Tabor and, according to Jos. xix, 32-39, lay along the eastern border of the Lower and Upper Galilean mountains. The fact that, in this description of the borders, the territory of Naphtali is made to extend fairly deep into the interior of Galilee and as far as the territory of Asher, is presumably merely due to the theory that the whole land was divided up among the tribes of Israel. The real centres of Naphtali will have been above the Sea of Tiberias and the adjacent northern part of the Jordan Valley. It is true that from that base Naphtali could, if necessary, have acquired further land to the west which was still in part wooded and uninhabited; but it is hardly to be supposed that the tribe made any extensive use of this possibility. The name Naphtali does not look much like a personal name and is altogether rather obscure; in this case too the point has at least to be considered whether it did not originally refer

---

[1] Cf. the personal name Zebul in Judges ix, 28 ff. as well as the Ugaritic *zbl*, which appears to be a particular honorary title.　　　　[2] Cf. pp. 78 f.

to a particular geographical region, in fact to the 'Mount Naphtali' (הד נפתלי) mentioned in Jos. xx, 7[1], though, according to the existing tradition, the mountain is supposed to have acquired its name from the tribe. In fact the mountain may have given its name to the clans that settled there, as happened in the case of Judah and Ephraim.

The tribe of *Dan* lived on the very periphery and in a rather isolated position, near the sources of the Jordan in the highest reach of the Jordan Valley. Its centre was the formerly Canaanite city of Laish (the modern *tell el-ḳāḍi*) mentioned in the Palestine list of Thothmes III. According to Judges xviii, 27, the tribe had acquired this city by military conquest and had given it the new name of Dan (Judges xviii, 29) after its own name. The tribal name could originally have been a personal name[2]. A part of the section referring to Dan in the old inventory of the borders is probably contained in Num. xxxiv, 7-11, where its borders, as those of the most northerly tribe, are introduced to establish the northern frontier of the whole territory of Israel, just as in Num. xxxiv, 3-5 the southern frontier of Judah described in Joshua xv, 2-4 serves to determine the southern frontier of the whole area. According to this, Dan had possessed not only the uppermost part of the Jordan Valley, but also part of the adjacent thickly wooded mountains to the east in the region now called *jōlān*; and this may in fact have been the case (cf. also Deut. xxxiii, 22), since the adjoining mountains westward were in the hands of the neighbouring tribe of Naphtali; in the north, however, the rather uninviting mountains of central Syria and, in the south, the marshes around the northernmost lake of the Jordan Valley were unsuitable for settlement, so that the opportunities for the tribe to expand lay in the east.

In this remote area Dan had found a home after a first attempt at occupation in quite another part of the country had failed. According to Judges i, 34-35, the Danites had first tried to gain a footing in the hill country between the mountains and the coastal

---

[1] According to this passage the place Kedesh (modern *kedes*) was specifically situated on the 'Mount Naphtali', which may therefore be sought north-west of the uppermost end of the Sea of Jordan, the lake that is now called *hule*. The Naphtalites will therefore have first gained a footing in this district. The same geographical connotation resides in the expression 'Kedesh-naphtali' (Judges iv, 6), in which 'Naphtali' may be the genitive of the region added to the place-name, as is certainly the case in the similarly compounded expression 'Jabesh-gilead' (1 Sam. xi, 1 and elsewhere) and probably in the expression 'Bethlehem-judah' (Judges xvii, 7 and elsewhere), in which 'Judah' also appears to have retained its original meaning as the name of a region.

[2] Cf. M. Noth, *Geschichte und Altes Testament = Alt-Festschrift* (1953), p. 146.

plain west of Jerusalem. But the earlier inhabitants[1] who ruled the
country from their towns had not allowed the tribe of Dan to
acquire the necessary land for settlement: an instructive example
of the fact that the Israelite tribes found no room in the parts of
the country which were already crowded with Canaanite cities and
were usually not in a position and probably did not even attempt
to make space for themselves by force of arms. So, according to
Judges xviii, the tribe of Dan withdrew again from this area and,
as the hitherto unoccupied land in the vicinity had meanwhile been
taken over by other Israelite tribes, it made a permanent home for
itself in the remote area in the far north, employing force—and
in this being an exception—to occupy a small Canaanite city.
Apparently it was thereby the last of the tribes of Israel to achieve
a permanent settlement for itself.

6. *The Occupation of the Land by the Tribes of Israel*

When one looks at the whole range of the Israelite settlements in
Palestine it is immediately obvious that the tribes of Israel entered
those parts of the country that had only been inhabited sparsely or
not at all in the Bronze Age[2]. They occupied the various parts of
the mountains west of the Jordan as well as the central section of
the highlands east of the Jordan whilst the plains on which nature
had bestowed its blessings remained in the hands of the older
Canaanite population which was concentrated in cities and alongside which the tribes now lived as a new element in the population.
This fact in itself shows very clearly that the Israelite occupation
did not ensue from a warlike encounter between the newcomers
and the previous owners of the land. In the parts of the country
occupied by the Israelites there were only a few scattered Canaanite settlements, though the tribes may have occupied some of these
by military force sooner or later. But such minor military conquests
did not involve any conflict with the main mass of the Canaanites,
who did not inhabit the region occupied by the tribes of Israel;
and where, in the mountains, there was a series of Canaanite cities

---

[1] In Judges i, 34, 35 they are called 'Amorites', the general name for the pre-Israelite
population. According to the stories of the Danite Samson which are set in the same
district (Judges xiii-xvi) the hostile neighbours were the Philistines, who had set up
their dominion over the 'Amorites' in the southern coastal plain.

[2] Cf., in addition to A. Alt, *Die Landnahme der Israeliten in Palästina* (1925),
especially pp. 31 ff., above all A. Alt, Erwägungen über die Landnahme der Israeliten
in Palästina, PJB, 35 [1939], pp. 8-63 = *Kleine Schriften zur Geschichte des Volkes
Israel*, I (1953), pp. 89-125 (especially pp. 121 ff.) and pp. 126-175.

in one neighbourhood, as in the vicinity of Jerusalem, no large-scale conflict occurred either: on the contrary, the tribes did not advance any further than the immediate vicinity of these city territories. The special case of the tribe of Dan, with its unsuccessful attempt to gain a footing in the hill country on the inner edge of the coastal plain, may be regarded as an example of the way the tribes were incapable of venturing, and in fact did not venture at all, to challenge the firmly established cities of the Canaanites with the dreaded chariots of iron of their rulers (cf. Jos. xvii, 16; Judges i, 19; iv, 3), to a large military conflict.

It is clear that, to begin with, the occupation of the land by the tribes took place fairly quietly and peacefully on the whole and without seriously disturbing the great mass of the previous inhabitants. We may think of it as having proceeded rather in the way in which even today semi-nomadic breeders of small cattle from the adjoining steppes and deserts pass over into a settled way of life in the cultivated countryside, the only difference being that at that time there was more uninhabited space available than there is today. Usually such semi-nomads make contact with agricultural land in the process of the so-called change of pasture: in the dry summer-time when their flocks of sheep and goats can no longer find enough fodder outside, they come by an explicit or tacit arrangement with the inhabitants into agricultural country where the fields have been harvested; and here their easily satisfied flocks find fodder enough. Unlike the camel nomads of the desert with their proud contempt for a settled way of life, these peaceful semi-nomads always hanker after a more settled life in the coveted agricultural countryside; and as soon as there is an opportunity, whether owing to gaps in the previous settlements or access to inhabitable but previously uninhabited districts, the day comes when they do not return to their winter pastures in the steppe and desert but settle down permanently in the agricultural countryside. The Israelites were land-hungry semi-nomads of that kind before their occupation of the land: they probably first set foot on the land in the process of changing pastures, and in the end they began to settle for good in the sparsely populated parts of the country and then extended their territory from their original domains as occasion offered, the whole process being carried through, to begin with, by peaceful means and without the use of force.

This means that the Israelitish occupation was a process that lasted for a good time, not merely in the sense that each individual tribe needed a certain time to occupy its own territory but also in the sense that the tribes did not all settle in the land at the same period. We know for certain that the tribe of Dan did not move into its final domains until after most or all the other tribes had already found their new homes. It may be that this was a unique case, since this tribe had first tried to gain a footing in an area that was particularly unfavourable because of the presence of Canaanite cities; and we have no information to indicate that other tribes attained the ultimate possession of their territory only after unsuccessful attempts to establish themselves. But various details concerning the distribution of the tribal areas in Palestine show that the total occupation by the tribes of Israel was a complicated process which must have passed through several stages and covered a fairly long period of time.

In this connection the situation of the tribe of Reuben, which was discussed on pp. 63 f., and which always appears at the head of the list in the traditional enumeration of the tribes, is specially noteworthy. In the old tradition no special area was assigned to this tribe. If there were Reubenite clans in the neighbourhood of the tribe of Gad, they had apparently only migrated later on to the land east of Jordan; in the opposite part of the land west of Jordan there were also a few traces of the former presence of Reubenites who had been absorbed to some extent in the association which made up the tribe of Judah. We have evidence therefore only of the remnants of the former tribe of Reuben, which must have dwelt somewhere in the central part of the land west of Jordan. But in the period of which we have more exact knowledge, this area, in so far as it was available to the Israelites at all and was not occupied by Canaanite city-state territories, was already in the hands of other tribes which were only able therefore to take possession, or at any rate, full possession, of their territories after the tribe of Reuben, for reasons unknown to us, had disappeared altogether, with the exception of a few insignificant remnants. It follows that Reuben must have been established before the other tribes completed their occupation.

This inference is confirmed by an evidently quite similar situation in the tribes of Simeon and Levi, which usually follow Reuben in the traditional list of the tribes. The old tradition does not assign any particular district to Simeon either; and there is only a brief record of the fact that Simeonite clans lived in the extreme south of the land and were counted as part of the greater whole of 'Judah'. Tradition has nothing to relate, however, of the areas occupied by the tribe of Levi and it is impossible to find any area where it could have dwelt in the same region as the other tribes[1]. But Simeon and Levi certainly once had their homes in Palestine since they are mentioned in the list of tribes; and the tradition of Gen. xxxiv originates in the fact that both tribes once lived in the vicinity of the formerly Canaanite city of Shechem in the central area west of Jordan. But it was there that the 'house of Joseph' resided later on, and, again, we have to conclude that the 'house of Joseph' was unable to occupy its new home until after Simeon and Levi had departed, and that it entered Palestine later than those two tribes. In the reference to Simeon and Levi in the Blessing of Jacob both tribes are cursed to be 'scattered in Israel' (Gen. xlix, 5-7) on the traditional basis of Gen. xxxiv, and Reuben also receives a curse (Gen. xlix, 3-4). This refers to the later situation of these tribes and also indicates that the situation was not the same from the beginning. This being 'scattered' was the precondition, however, of the entry of other tribes into their domiciles in Palestine.

This also demonstrates that the prehistory of the tribes of Israel and their occupation of the land were more involved than appears from the Old Testament tradition that was only evolved in a later age. This tradition proceeded from a situation in which the tribes were already living side by side in Palestine in an orderly way and had already accumulated some common historical experience. The assumption behind the tradition is that the events which led up to this situation were simultaneous and similar for all the tribes, in fact that Israel had been associated as a single unit in Palestine from the very beginning. Under the influence of a conception based on the development of large families and clans it thinks of the tribes and the whole of Israel as having arisen by propagation and ramification from the family of a common ancestor and having formed a unity based on blood relationship from time immemorial and being bound together by a common destiny. Thus the tribes were derived each from one ancestor who also gave his name to the tribe; and these ancestors appeared as brothers, as sons of a man called 'Israel' from whom the name of the whole derived[2]. It is quite true that in the building up of the tribes and also in their mutual connections the element of blood relationship did play an

---

[1] It is clear from the fact that it is mentioned in the list of the other tribes and also from Gen. xlix, 5-7 that the tribe of Levi was a 'secular' tribe like the other tribes. In what relation the later Levitical priesthood stood to it is a question on its own, which need not affect the above statement.

[2] The equating of the *heros eponymus* 'Israel' with the 'patriarch' Jacob occurs very early on in the Old Testament but is a secondary process in the historical tradition.

important part. But in addition to that there were usually particular historical circumstances which led to the amalgamation of certain more or less related clans into a tribe and to the association of a particular number of tribes into a tribal confederation.

That the Old Testament tradition took too simple a view of the events which led to the development of Israel as a totality is obvious from the fact, already mentioned, that the tribes of Israel did not all settle on the soil of Palestine at the same time but, judging from various statements in the tradition that has come down to us, their occupation of the land was divided into at least two distinct phases. The data are scanty and only incidental to the main stream of a tradition which was shaped by the conception of a common pre-history and a joint occupation of the land. We have to reckon with the possibility that the settlement of Israel in Palestine was an even more confused and complicated process, but owing to the lack of information, it is impossible to come to any firm conclusion one way or the other. But we know enough to infer that the individual tribes each had their own particular prehistory and that their mutual relationships were at best loose and fluid before they entered into a solid and lasting association one with another on the soil of Palestine under the collective name of Israel. Thinking again in terms of later conditions, the Old Testament tradition also simplified the facts by assuming that the individual tribes were firmly established as clear-cut entities from the very outset. Some of the Israelite tribes bear names that were originally place-names and derived from the areas in which the tribes in question settled[1]; in another case a tribe derived its name from the particular circum-stances in which it had acquired its land[2]. These tribes cannot have been given their names until their arrival on the soil of Palestine, which means that they were not finally constituted until their arrival there. The clans that were combined in these tribal units did not apparently bring a common tribal name with them which would have made the renaming which took place in Palestine unnecessary. It follows, therefore, that these tribes had not been self-contained units at all before their occupation of the land, but consisted of clans which did not form themselves into tribes until they began living together in Palestine. The same may be assumed to apply to the tribes from whose names nothing precise can be deduced and which perhaps adopted the name of their leading clan, which in its turn might have been called by the personal

[1] Thus Judah, Ephraim, Benjamin and probably Naphtali too; cf. pp. 56 f., 60 f., 63, 67.　　[2] This is true of Issachar; cf. pp. 76 f.

name of an ancestor[1]. The Old Testament tradition therefore not only goes beyond the facts by tracing back the names of the tribes beyond the period of the occupation, but also by assuming that the tribes had long existed as self-contained units. This too suggests that the process of the occupation must be reckoned to have lasted a long time, in the course of which the tribes were formed definitively, and that this process consisted of very many different and geographically widely separated movements of population.

It is true that the Old Testament records the conquest of the land of Palestine as the 'promised land' by the whole of the tribes of Israel, as a single, self-contained operation. The older strata of the Pentateuch narrative originally led up to such a presentation of the conquest, though it is impossible to reconstruct it in detail as only its beginnings are preserved in Num. xxxii, 1 ff., whereas its continuation was dropped in the final editing of the Pentateuch. But it is possible to infer from Num. xxxii, 1 ff., that, according to this presentation, the united tribes set out for their subsequent domiciles, presumably all at the same time, from the southern part of the land east of Jordan. This accords in substance with the account of the occupation of the land in the deuteronomistic narrative offered in Jos. i-xii on the basis of an old source which consisted of a series of separate narratives. According to this account, the combined tribes conquered the land west of the Jordan by force of arms and took possession of it after crossing the lower Jordan, that is, approaching it from the southern part of the land east of Jordan. But on closer analysis the old nucleus of Jos. i-xii proves that the stories related in those chapters did not deal with Israel as a whole at all but—apart from the specifically Ephraimite tradition in Jos. x, 1 ff. and the specifically Galilean tradition in Jos. xi, 1 ff.—exclusively with the tribe of Benjamin. Geographically the whole thing takes place within the small territory of the tribe of Benjamin; the special tradition of the neighbouring tribe of Ephraim links up with this quite well, whereas the special Galilean tradition stands completely on its own, quite unconnected geographically with what has gone before. But the Benjaminite tradition originally consisted of a series of aetiological narratives, which were collated on the asumption that it was from the east, across the lower Jordan, that the tribe of Benjamin entered into

[1] Manasseh may be considered an example of this—the name is undoubtedly a personal name. Manasseh was presumably a Machirite clan, which did not join in the migration into the land east of the Jordan, and gave its name to all the parts of Machir that remained behind in the land west of the Jordan, and finally included under this name even the East Jordanites who had migrated (cf. p. 61 f.).

its territory around Jericho and the adjoining western part of the mountains[1]. This assumption represents the tribe of Benjamin's own living tradition about its occupation of the land; and we have here a concrete example of the fact that an individual tribe possessed its own special tradition concerning the way it came into possession of its land[2]. But what is true of the tribe of Benjamin will also be true of the other tribes; and if the tribes each had their own occupation tradition in very early times, they will certainly each have moved into their subsequent territory in Palestine in their own special way. Almost all these special traditions of the tribes have been lost, however, because within the Old Testament tradition already, they were replaced by the conception of the joint conquest of Palestine by Israel as a whole, and only the Benjaminite narrative has been preserved because, for special reasons which we still have to discuss, it was specially suitable as a basis for the concrete version of the joint Israelite occupation of the land west of Jordan and was therefore developed and supplemented with this in mind; the Benjaminite foundation is still quite apparent, however.

We must therefore attempt to throw some light on the complicated process of the occupation by considering the situation of the various tribal territories and a few scattered particulars in the Old Testament. As far as the group of central Palestinian tribes is concerned we are on relatively safe ground. For Benjamin we have the hypothesis already mentioned of the sequence of aetiological narratives in the first half of the Book of Joshua; and this accords so well in content with the situation of the tribe's places of occupation that it is no doubt historically accurate. According to this account, the clans which formed the tribe of Benjamin made their way from the east or south-east through the southern part of the land east of the Jordan over the lower Jordan, established themselves in the territory belonging to the city of Jericho (the modern *erīḥa*)[3] and from there they climbed the west Jordan mountains up to the heights where the Canaanite cities north-west of Jerusalem put an end to their further advance to the west[4]. The 'house of Joseph'

[1] More details in M. Noth, *Das Buch Josua* ([2] 1953), pp. 20 ff.

[2] It is no longer possible to say to what extent special tribal traditions lurk behind the narrative fragments in Judges i, 1 ff. In quite a different context we have a special tribal tradition in the traditional basis of Num. xiii, xiv; cf. pp. 75 f.

[3] The question as to when Canaanite Jericho came to an end has not yet been completely elucidated archaeologically. Probably Benjamin did not find Jericho an established and fully inhabited city; cf. M. Noth, *op. cit.* p. 21.

[4] It is wrong to conclude from Gen. xxxv, 16-20 that Benjamin only subsequently branched off from the 'house of Joseph' in Palestine and constituted itself as an independent tribe alongside Joseph. The conversion of narrative details of the 'patriarch'-stories into tribal history (Gen. xxxv, 16-20 draws attention to Rachel's grave) is

came from the same direction; for it evidently occupied the area in which it subsequently settled, from the south-east corner. Those clans which formed themselves into the tribe of Ephraim first gained a footing on 'Mount Ephraim', from which the tribe derived its name, and this 'Mount Ephraim' is presumably to be sought slightly north of the Benjaminite area above the lower Jordan Valley[1]. Since the 'house of Joseph' appears in the Old Testament tradition as a coherent association of fair size, it is at least probable that not only the parts which joined to form the tribe of Ephraim but also the other parts of this association came from the same direction, and then occupied the whole of the great central part of the west Jordan mountains without a break.

The territory of Gad lay north-east of the Dead Sea along the route on which all these groups advanced through the southern land east of the Jordan; it may therefore be assumed that the Gadite clans carried out their occupation of the land as part of the same migration. They remained in a small area east of the Jordan Valley, either because they found homes there straight away with which they were so delighted that they were able to save themselves the journey through the Jordan Valley[2], or because they found the west Jordan territories which were accessible from the southern land east of the Jordan already occupied and had to be content with the modest space available east of the Jordan Valley.

It is no accident that the Benjaminite tradition contained in Jos. i-xii was later used as the basis of the description of the combined Israelite conquest of the land west of the Jordan, since, independently of that tradition, the older strata of the Pentateuch narrative made the united forces of Israel advance to their occupation of Palestinian soil through the southern land east of Jordan. In time, therefore, the specific and historically accurate memories of the occupation of the land by the important central Palestinian tribes were imposed on all the tribes of Israel. When the conception of a common history of Israel existing even before the occupation of the land was developed in the light of later conditions, it was the specifically central Palestinian traditions which determined the picture of the total occupation of the land by Israel as a whole.

Before the tribes we have mentioned established themselves in

inadmissible. Benjamin originated in the first place on the soil of Palestine no more and no less than the other tribes; and we have a specific tradition concerning the manner of Benjamin's occupation of the land.

[1] Cf. p. 60 f.   [2] The matter is described thus in Num. xxxii, 1 ff.

the central part of Palestine, the tribes of Reuben, Simeon and Levi had (as we have discussed on p. 69 f.) settled somewhere in the central territory west of Jordan, and had then, for reasons which are uncertain[1], migrated and dispersed and thereby made room for the tribes that came later. As we no longer know exactly where they settled to begin with, it is also impossible to describe the exact course of their occupation of the land. It is possible that they had entered the land by roughly the same route as the later tribes of central Palestine. In that case their starting-point will also have been somewhere in the steppes and deserts on the border of the southern land east of Jordan.

Matters were different with the south Palestinian tribes. For them we have, to begin with, a Calebite story which indicates that the tribe of Caleb entered its territory in Palestine from the south, that is, from the region of the so-called Negeb. For the tradition on which the story contained in Num. xiii, xiv is based, and which sets out to explain how it came about that Caleb attained possession of the important city of Hebron, undoubtedly originally amounted to the fact that Caleb was assigned the city of Hebron along with its fertile surroundings as a reward for its courageous behaviour, without having first to join in the great detour through the southern land east of the Jordan as is suggested by the later insertion of the tradition into the larger narrative complex of the Pentateuch. But the real starting-point of this narrative was the Negeb; it was from there that the thrust to the mountains in the north had been made which brought Caleb into possession of Hebron. The situation of the Calebite territory suggests that it is highly probable that this account of the journey of Caleb is historically accurate. By and large the most obvious assumption is that the tribes that had settled in the southernmost part of the west Jordan mountains had come from the adjoining semi-nomadic area to the south. In the case of Caleb there is the additional connection with a tribal association which was also represented among the Edomites[2]. The home of this tribal association of the Kenizzites can only have been in the Negeb, whence individual components had reached Edom over the *wādi el-ʿaraba* and others had come into the West Jordan mountains. The same applies to Othniel, whose relationship with Caleb and whose one-time membership of the tribal confederation we have just mentioned also suggest that it originally came from the Negeb. The Kenites had also apparently come from the south,

---

[1] According to Gen. xxxiv, military conflicts with the Canaanite city of Shechem appear to have been the cause for Simeon and Levi.   [2] Cf. p. 56.

so far as they settled at all in the vicinity of Caleb and Othniel; since, according to 1 Sam. xv, 6, they had once belonged to the same tribal confederation as the Amalekites, whose territory was somewhere in the northern part of the Sinai Peninsula.

How much one has to reckon on unusual and unexpected tribal migrations is shown by the case of the tribe of Simeon which, although it resided in the extreme south in the region of Beersheba and therefore actually in the Negeb itself, had not come from this semi-nomadic area, at any rate not directly, but had migrated from the very heart of Palestine, and, after it had become unable to maintain itself any longer in its original Palestinian settlements, had found a place on the extreme border of Israelite territory, like the tribe of Dan in the extreme north. It is permissible to assume that the southern part of the mountains west of Jordan was already occupied when the remnants of Simeon had to seek for new homes, so that it was only in the Negeb that they found a district in some degree suitable for permanent settlement.

It is also very difficult to establish anything for certain about how the tribe of Judah came into occupation of the land. From the south the cities of Hebron, and possibly Debir too, obstructed the access to its territory, and city-states in the region of Jerusalem also made access difficult from the north. The tribe of Judah established itself between these two regions. The situation of its territory suggests that it may either have moved in from the Negeb from a southerly direction or from the most southerly end of the Jordan Valley, and therefore, ultimately, from the east. The fact that, in the traditional enumeration of the twelve tribes of Israel, Judah appears in the leading group with Reuben, Simeon and Levi, suggests that it gained a footing in Palestine in the opening phase of the occupation; and as this oldest group of tribes appears to have settled predominantly in the central land west of the Jordan, we are probably entitled to assume that they came in over the lower Jordan from an easterly direction, and this may well have been true of Judah too. There is, however, a complete lack of concrete evidence to make even a moderately firm decision possible.

The course of events is least certain of all in the case of the Galilean tribes and the traditions that have come down to us about them are far and away the scantiest of all. It is highly probable that the ways by which the individual tribes in this group came into possession of their land in Palestine varied considerably. The only case about which we have more detailed information shows how complicated the prehistory of the occupation could be. We refer to the tribe of Dan, which ultimately found a place for itself in the far north near the sources of the Jordan after a vain attempt to gain a footing in quite a different place in Palestine. The situation was, again, quite different in the case of the tribes of Zebulun and Issachar. After the organisation of the traditional twelve-tribe system, which we have still to discuss, these two tribes formed a special group on their own, with Reuben, Simeon, Levi and Judah, that is, with the tribes that had settled in the central land west of the Jordan in a very early stage of the occupation, and it is therefore probable that they had entered the land about the same time and in a similar fashion, and had been in more or less close touch with them. Of the Galilean tribes, their homes were nearest to the central part of the west Jordan mountains, only separated from it by the plain of Jezreel or the valley plain of *nahr jālūd* with its city-state territories. It cannot be proved with any certainty, and need not necessarily be assumed, that the tribe itself had once resided there with those other tribes and had only subsequently been forced, for reasons unknown to us, to migrate from there to near-by southern Galilee[1]. But it may be considered probable that they had moved into their later dwelling-places from a southerly or south-easterly direction. The tribe of Naphtali, on the other hand, must have come through the northern land east of the Jordan from an easterly direction, particularly if it may be assumed to have first gained a footing on the 'Naphtali' mountains in the region of Kedesh. It is almost impossible to say anything for sure as to how the tribe of Asher reached its territory.

In the Old Testament we have one or two striking statements from which we are able to gather something about the special conditions in which various of the Galilean tribes came into possession of their land in Palestine. In Jacob's blessing the tribe of Issachar is criticised and mocked because—as 'a strong ass couching down between two burdens'—it 'bowed its shoulder to bear' and 'became a servant unto tribute' for the sake of peace and quiet and a pleasant land (Gen. xlix, 14-15), and the name Issachar (hired labourer) is undoubtedly due to the same cause. If this statement was true, Issachar had acquired its territorial possessions at the price of its independence. What actually happened may be inferred from a few statements in the Amarna tablets, according to which the Canaanite city of Shunem (the modern *sōlem*) which was

---

[1] Since we do not know what special circumstances prevailed in this particular case, it is impossible to draw any positive conclusion regarding the earlier dwelling-places of Issachar from the fact that, according to Judges x, 1, 2, the Issacharite Tola lived and was buried in 'Shamir in Mount Ephraim' (exact position unknown).

situated in the later Issacharite territory, was destroyed in the Amarna period and its soil had to be cultivated ('tilled') by forced labour on behalf of, and in the interests of, the then Egyptian sovereign and under the supervision and at the suggestion of the Canaanite city governors[1]. The land-seeking clans apparently offered their services and were settled on the territory of the former city of Shunem and formed themselves into the tribe of 'Issachar' and from Shunem they finally occupied the adjoining mountain country to the east. Several other striking statements in the Old Testament about Israelite tribes can probably best be understood in the light of this fairly concrete situation In the same Blessing of Jacob it is said of Zebulun that it 'shall dwell at the haven of the sea' and 'shall be for an haven of ships'[2] (Gen. xlix, 13). Now the dwelling-places of this tribe that are known to us did not lie on the coast at all or even anywhere near it; and there is no reason to assume that Zebulun had lived by the sea at some previous time, since all the inhabitable places on the coast had been occupied long before the tribes of Israel appeared. It is more likely that this reference to Zebulun, which was probably intended as a criticism, means that the Zebulunites had to perform certain compulsory tasks, above all in the harbours of the northern coastal plain. And it is not difficult to surmise that the acceptance of this permanent obligation was the price the clans which made up Zebulun had to pay in return for permission from the neighbouring Canaanite cities to settle in the lower Galilean mountains in the hinterland of the coastal plain. This supposition is confirmed by the fact that in Judges v, 17b Asher is also said to have 'continued on the sea shore', although in fact Asher no more lived on the coast than its neighbour Zebulun, but in the mountainous hinterland of the northern coastal plain. The remark may therefore be assumed to mean the same as the reference to Zebulun. Owing to their dependence on the neighbouring Canaanite cities much of the latter's wealth flowed into these tribes on the edge of the northern coastal plain and the plain of Jezreel. There are allusions to the good life in Asher in the Blessing of Jacob and in that of Moses too (Gen. xlix, 20; Deut. xxxiii, 24); and in Deut. xxxiii, 19 Zebulun and Issachar are even said to 'suck of the abundance of the seas', which can only mean that they too gained indirectly from the

[1] The references and their precise explanation will be found in A. Alt, PJB, 20 (1924), pp. 34 ff.
[2] In the passage about the 'ships' the text is not quite in order and impossible to reconstruct with certainty. The final remark, that Zebulun's border 'shall be unto Sidon', appears to be a postscript.

commercial profits of the Canaanites. In Lower Galilee, therefore, the situation of the tribes was determined in a special way by the direct vicinity of the plains with their cities, and here the occupation of the land seems to have taken place under special conditions.

It is very curious that in Judges v, 17a the tribe of Dan is also said to have 'remained in ships' although its dwelling-place lay far away from the sea by the sources of the Jordan, a fact which is obviously taken for granted in the Song of Deborah, and in Judges xviii, 28 the city of Laish is explicitly stated to have been 'far from Sidon'. But perhaps the latter remark is significant in so far as it does establish some connection between the territory of Dan and the city of Sidon (cf. also Judges xviii, 7) and the Mediterranean coast; and it looks as if at the time Sidon had sovereign rights in the uppermost reaches of the valley of the Jordan. The reference to Dan in Judges v, 17a can therefore probably be taken to mean that this tribe also had to buy its settlement by accepting a certain amount of compulsory labour service in South Phoenician seaports. Of all the Galilean tribes Naphtali is the only one which we do not find mentioned in this connection and that is probably no accident, since Naphtali occupied the territory in the mountains west of the Lake Huleh (*bahret el-ḥūleh*) and the Sea of Tiberias which was least favoured by nature. The Naphtalite clans probably contented themselves with these modest dwelling-places and thereby preserved their independence.

Since the occupation of the land by the Israelite tribes was therefore a process which covered a long period of time and consisted of various, geographically distinct movements, it is impossible to assign an exact date to the occupation as a whole. All one can do is to give an approximate *terminus a quo* and a *terminus ad quem*. Later on, the Old Testament tradition greatly simplified the process and concentrated it all into a single brief episode, so that as a source of direct information about the temporal duration and sequence of these movements it is quite unreliable; and we neither have nor can expect to have any historical information about these matters outside the Old Testament since, on the whole, the occupation took place more or less unobtrusively, away from the main scenes of the earlier history of Palestine, with no particularly striking events which might be expected to have attracted the attention of the ancient Oriental powers of the time and occasioned some kind of written record. The Amarna period may be considered the *terminus a quo*, but not because otherwise the process of the occupation of the land would be bound to have been mentioned in the political correspondence of the Amarna tablets[1]; the city-states of Palestine, from whose domains the Amarna tablets derive, in so far as they are concerned with Palestine at all, were hardly affected to any degree by the Israelite occupation to begin with. But there are two points which suggest that in the Amarna period the Israelite tribes had not yet settled in the land. At that time Bethlehem was still 'a city of the land of Jerusalem'[2] and only later became the centre of the tribe of Judah as it was being constituted; and only at that period did the destruction of the city of Shunem produce that gap in the Canaanite system of city-states in the vicinity of the Jezreel plain which was later occupied by the tribe of Issachar[3]. Judah and probably Issachar as well were part of the older group of Israelite tribes which were the first to settle in the land. On the other hand, in the case of Issachar, the actual sequence of events suggests that this tribe moved into its territory not long after the end of the Amarna period. We must therefore place the beginnings of the Israelite occupation in the second half of the 14th century B.C. The final conclusion of the process will probably have taken place at least a hundred years before the accession of Saul. It is true that we have no reliable information at all regarding the temporal duration and sequence of the events recorded as having occurred on the soil of Palestine before the formation of the Kingdom of Israel. But the list of the 'Judges of Israel' in Judges x, 1-5; xii, 7-15[4], which belongs to this period, alone embraces sixty-eight years and it is not certain that the series is complete at either end. Judging from this, the occupation had ended at the latest *circa* 1100 B.C.

These dates, especially the last, merely represent the extreme possibilities and they must not be assumed to mean that the occupation took two hundred years all told. That is unlikely. But the tradition being what it is, all we can do is cautiously to mark out the extreme limits of probability. Presumably the occupation took place within a considerably shorter period of time, in the course of a few decades; and the conditions prevailing in the tribe of Issachar, which we have already discussed, suggest that the process took place more in the first than the second half of the period, that is, approximately the 13th century B.C. But it must be remembered that this more precise dating is nothing more than a likely supposition.

[1] The Ḫabiru-Hebrews of the Amarna tablets are not to be identified with the Israelites. Cf. above, p. 33 f.
[2] Cf. above, p. 32.   [3] Cf. above, pp. 78 f.
[4] More details on this traditional element will be found below at pp. 101 f.

In recent times attempts have been made to date the process or its individual elements more exactly on the basis of archaeological data. It is now possible to assign related strata of settlements on ancient sites which have been excavated, to a period of only a few decades, even without the aid of epigraphic discoveries, simply on the basis of the evidence of the material remains. The idea inevitably suggests itself of relating the destruction of Palestinian cities, for which there is clear evidence within the period in question, to the appearance of the Israelites in Palestine and dating that appearance accordingly[1]. But so far there has been no absolutely certain evidence of this kind, and such evidence is in fact hardly likely to be found. For the Israelite tribes did not acquire their territories by warlike conquest and the destruction of Canaanite cities[2], but usually settled in hitherto unoccupied parts of the country. These destructions were more probably due to the continual conflicts of the city governments among themselves, which are known to have occurred in the Amarna period, and, *circa* 1200 B.C., to the warlike emergence of the 'Sea Peoples' in the regions of the city-states of Palestine. The Israelites established themselves chiefly in settlements newly founded by themselves. If the beginnings of these settlements could be dated with archaeological accuracy, that would help to ascertain the date of the occupation. But that is scarcely possible. It is true that these new foundations at the beginning of the Iron Age had an enclosure erected with stones instead of the strong city walls of the Bronze Age Canaanite cities which have maintained the successive strata of the settlements intact for thousands of years. The old sites which date only from the Iron Age have usually disintegrated and their remains have been scattered in the course of time and have disappeared: all that has survived on the old sites are miscellaneous relics, usually without any ascertainable stratification. It must also be remembered that the civilisation of the Early Iron Age was very much more poverty-stricken and less sharply defined in stages than that of the preceding Bronze Age, and this fact makes it impossible to date the, for the most part scanty, remains at all accurately. It follows that the beginning of the Israelite settlement cannot be dated any more exactly and definitely from an archaeological point of view than from the evidence of the literary tradition. Hence the matter must

---

1 W. F. Albright has repeatedly attempted this in numerous articles.

2 The conquest narratives in the first half of the Book of Joshua (cf. especially Jos. vi; viii; x, 28 ff.; xi, 10 ff.) originate in aetiological traditions which proceeded from the later devastated condition of the sites in question (cf. M. Noth, *Das Buch Josua*, [2 1953]).

be left at a cautious defining of the period of the Israelite occupation.

This occupation of the land was, however, part of a wider historical movement. At the same period land-seeking elements appeared everywhere on the borders of Syria and Palestine and, even beyond, in Mesopotamia between the upper reaches of the Euphrates and the Tigris and in the middle of the Euphrates. They settled in large numbers especially in the Syrian interior and in the adjacent area on both sides of the upper Euphrates, and then established more or less permanent and, according to local conditions, more or less comprehensive political organisations. In the immediate vicinity of the Israelite tribes, numerous clans settled, as part of the same movement, in the southern part of the land east of the Jordan, which had hardly been inhabited at all for centuries, southwards towards the Gulf of *el-'akaba*, and here they formed themselves into the peoples of the Ammonites, Moabites and Edomites[1] and apparently very early founded kingdoms. In Syria and Mesopotamia these elements were known by the collective name of Aramaeans, a term which occasionally occurs among the neighbouring Assyrians in Middle Assyrian royal inscriptions and then is also frequently mentioned in the Old Testament[2]. This great movement, of which the settlement of the Israelite tribes was part and which consisted of many different elements, took place during the transition from the Bronze to the Iron Age, proceeding from the Syrian-Arabian desert into the bordering agricultural lands. It is therefore natural to call the movement the 'Aramaean migration' and it is perfectly in order to do so provided one remembers that it was not in fact a uniform and deliberately planned process. In the Old Testament itself the ancestor of Israel is described as an 'Aramaean' in a solemn, cultic profession of faith (Deut. xxvi, 5); and the Israelites once spoke an ancient Aramaic dialect before in Palestine they adopted the Canaanite language native there, literally 'the language of Canaan' (Isa. xix, 18), which was admittedly closely akin to their own ancient Aramaic. The Hebrew of the Old Testament still shows traces of the mixture of various dialects.

To take this view involves the rejection of a theory which is very old and has been revived in various forms and on different grounds right up to the most recent times: the theory that the prehistory of

[1] Further details on these peoples in WAT, pp. 68 ff.
[2] On the prehistory of the name Aramaean cf. A. Dupont-Sommer, Supplements to VT, I (1953), pp. 40 ff.

the Israelite tribes was bound up with the Hyksos movement[1].
Since it has been established that the Israelites cannot be simply
identified with the conquering ruling class of the Hyksos, it has
been thought that they came with the Hyksos migration, namely
from Mesopotamia, whence the Hyksos appear to have come and
where, according to an Old Testament tradition, the forefathers of
Israel had lived[2]. The numerous texts from the 15th century B.C.
in which there are references to legal and social institutions such as
are familiar from the Old Testament stories of the 'Patriarchs'[3],
which have been found in the ancient city of Nuzu east of the
Tigris (near the modern *kerkūk*), appear to support this theory. At
that time Nuzu was a Hurrian city and still had connections with
the Hurrian elements of the former Hyksos movement, and so the
Israelites would have become familiar with these Hurrian institutions through their connection with the Hyksos, and so introduced
them into Palestine. But the arguments on which these suppositions
are based are unsound. These institutions, if there is a real link
of the kind supposed, could have been introduced into Syria-
Palestine by the Hykos themselves and could have become known
to the Israelites when they entered Palestine. But the tracing of
Israel's ancestors to Mesopotamia is based on the accurate tradition
of the Aramaean relationship[4], which was then specifically applied
later on to the main Aramaean centre on both sides of the upper
Euphrates. Against linking the Israelite occupation and the 'Aramaean migration' with the Hyksos movement there is the fact that,
to the best of our knowledge, the occupation took place much later
than the appearance of the Hyksos and that the Aramaeans did not
emerge as a migrant stratum until long after the period of the
Hyksos; but above all, there is the fact that the Israelite occupation
took place in the very regions of Palestine which played no part at
all in the Hyksos period and were not directly affected by the Hyksos
rule at all, and it proceeded from directions which had nothing in
common with the direction of the Hyksos movement. The Hyksos
rule in Palestine extended to the city-state regions of the land; but
it is clear that originally the Israelite tribes had no connection of
any kind with that system of government, but only established a
connection sooner or later according to local conditions.

[1] Thus first of all Josephus, *Contra Apionem*, I, 14, § 75 ff. In modern times the
opinion has been shared particularly by Egyptologists.

[2] Cf. especially Gen. xxiv, 10 ff.; xxvii, 43 ff.; also Gen. xi, 10-32; xii, 5.

[3] Cf. most recently C. H. Gordon, BASOR, 66 (1937), pp. 25 ff.; M. Burrows, JAOS,
57 (1937), pp. 259 ff.; R. de Vaux, RB, 56 (1949), pp. 22 ff.

[4] In its original form the tradition exists in the story of the relationship between
Jacob and 'the Aramaean Laban' (cf. especially Gen. xxxi, 19 ff.).

CHAPTER II

THE CONFEDERATION OF THE
TRIBES OF ISRAEL

7. *The Twelve-tribe System*

THE tradition that has come down to us refers to the Israelite tribes only as members of a larger whole. References to the dwelling-places, characteristics, particular destinies of individual tribes are also based almost entirely on the assumption that they are members of a larger whole. This assumption is expressed in the well-defined tradition of the 'twelve tribes' which made up 'Israel'. This traditional element of the twelve-tribe system has come down to us in two forms which differ only on one point. In one form the tribe of Levi is included and Joseph appears as *one* tribe, whereas in the other form Levi is left out and Joseph's place is taken by Manasseh and Ephraim, the subdivisions of Joseph, which appear as independent tribes. The first form is found above all in the story of the birth of the ancestors of the tribes as sons of Jacob, in Gen. xxix, 31–xxx, 24 and also within the setting of Jacob's Blessing in Gen. xlix, 1b-27, whilst the second form is found above all in the great list in Num. xxvi, 4bβ-51[1]. Since Levi had completely disappeared as a 'secular tribe' in the historical period of which we have more detailed knowledge, the form in which it is included must be considered the older of the two. Both forms share a quite definite grouping of the tribes which is expressed in Gen. xxix, 31 ff. in the derivation of their ancestors from different mothers and in Gen. xlix and Num. xxvi in the sequence in which they are enumerated. The older form begins with a group of six tribes which, following Gen. xxix, 31 ff., are usually called 'Leah tribes'. The tribes of Reuben, Simeon, Levi, Judah, Zebulun and Issachar[2]

---

[1] Further references and all details will be found in M. Noth, *Das System der zwölf Stämme Israels* (1930).

[2] The sequence Zebulun-Issachar appears in Gen. xlix and perhaps also in the oldest narrative stratum of Gen. xxix. 31 ff. whilst in the form of Gen. xxix. 31 ff that has come down to us and in Num. xxvi Zebulun follows Issachar.

are listed in a more or less established order. In the later form Gad takes the place of Levi, so that this form also opens with a group of six tribes. The 'Rachel tribes' form a further group, consisting of Joseph and Benjamin in the older and Manasseh, Ephraim, Benjamin in the later form. The rest of the tribes appear in a third group, which is the least fixed in form. According to Gen. xlix Dan, Gad, Asher, Naphtali[1] belong to this group whilst in the later form represented by Num. xxvi Dan, Asher, Naphtali appear in this group.

To assess this traditional element of the twelve-tribe system objectively it must be remembered, on the one hand, that it obviously does not represent simply the organisation of Israel as given or naturally developed at a particular time, or, in view of the two forms, at particular times. It in no way corresponds to the actual situation in the period of which we have more exact historical knowledge. It begins the sequence of tribes with the more or less forgotten tribes of Reuben, Simeon and Levi, and, on the other hand, the southern neighbours of Judah are missing, among which at any rate Caleb, with its possession of the city of Hebron, must have been at least as important as any of the Galilean tribes, all of which are listed as independent members, whilst the southern tribes—apart from the wholly peripheral Simeon—are to be regarded as included in Judah. But the system does not simply reproduce the situation of an earlier, historically uncertain period in which Reuben, Simeon and Levi were still playing their original roles and would therefore merit pride of place in the system, whilst the southern tribes had perhaps not yet settled in the land at all. This assumption is out of the question since the dispersion of Reuben, Simeon and Levi was the precondition of the occupation of the land by the 'Rachel tribes', which nevertheless do appear in the system. But one cannot ascribe the origin of the system to the period before the occupation since, on the whole, the tribes themselves did not become established entities until the occupation. It is therefore impossible to conceive of any period in which the actual situation of Israel corresponded exactly to the traditional system in either of its forms.

We must not, however, conclude from this that the system arose as a purely theoretical construction at a time when the tribes themselves were no longer playing any essential part historically and an

---

[1] This is the sequence in Gen. xlix. In Gen. xxix, 31 ff. these tribes are again grouped differently; but probably this was due merely to the shaping of the narrative and is of no historical importance.

arbitrarily constructed picture of ancient Israel as divided into twelve parts was no longer hindered by historical reality. For, apart from the question whether such a period ever existed, the system undoubtedly links up with the actual existence, if not of all, yet of most of the tribes which are enumerated in it, and in such a way that the details cannot be explained in purely theoretical terms. It is impossible to explain either the choice of these particular twelve names or the fact that the system has come down to us in two different forms, though they actually differ only on one point, nor is it possible to explain the established order of the names beginning with Reuben and Simeon, or the particular form of grouping, in which tribes living separately from one another appear together in the first and third of the above-mentioned groups, if the whole system is attributed to a more or less arbitrary compilation. Obviously definite, quite concrete historical presuppositions are involved and if, according to what has been said above, the system cannot be derived simply from the historical situation in particular periods, nevertheless it probably originated in a complicated historical process.

Admittedly, the system is so bound up with the very suspicious element of the apparently artificial number twelve, that that element must obviously be regarded as a quite essential constituent of the system, as is indicated above all by the fact that the number twelve was strictly adhered to in the transition from the earlier to the later form. This number twelve proves to be a historic factor shedding light on the origin and significance of the tribal system as a whole, for lists of twelve tribes—occasionally of six tribes too—also arose outside Israel and have come down to us. H. Ewald[1] was the first to point out that the Old Testament itself provides the nearest examples, since it contains in Gen. xxii, 20-24 a list of twelve Aramaean tribes, in Gen. xxv, 13-16 a list of twelve Ishmaelite tribes, and in Gen. xxxvi, 10-14 one of twelve Edomite tribes, whilst in Gen. xxxvi, 20-28 there is a list of six Horite tribes. The Israelite system of twelve tribes does not therefore by any means represent an isolated phenomenon and, for that reason, it cannot be attributed historically either to the chance circumstance of the co-existence of twelve brothers as ancestors of the tribes, or to a secondarily constructed picture of the schematic dividing up of a larger whole; on the contrary the number is the result of certain established principles such as were customary in tribal societies which were still lacking settled political institutions. This is certainly

[1] H. Ewald, *Geschichte des Volkes Israel*, I, 3rd ed. (1864), pp. 528 ff.

true of all the examples known to us from the Old Testament. Admittedly these bare lists still say very little about the purpose of these organisations. The fact that similar associations of twelve tribes existed in ancient Greece and Italy is more helpful; and of these there are various traditional accounts which indicate that a cult observed in common formed the centre and that the members of these associations used to meet for particular festivals at the central shrine, in fact that certain cults were entirely sustained and administered[1] by such associations of twelve or six tribes. There seem therefore to have been quite practical reasons for the fixed and constantly maintained number twelve (or six), inasmuch as the members of these associations had to assume responsibility for the upkeep of the common shrine and its worship in a monthly or bi-monthly rota. In Greece such a sacred society was called an amphictyony, a 'community of those who dwell around' (around a particular shrine); and this expression may serve as an appropriate technical term for this kind of association.

We are thus concerned with a sacral association of the Israelite tribes, an 'ancient Israelite amphictyony'. The number twelve was part of the institution which had to be maintained even when changes took place in the system: it proves therefore to have been neither the mere result of the natural ramification of a human group nor the invention of a later period, but rather an essential element in the historical organisation of such a tribal confederation. The fact that the twelve-tribe system was part of a historically evolved and historically changing institution suffices to explain the traces of a complicated origin and development which are present in the system itself. The traditional precedence of the tribes of Reuben, Simeon (and Levi) can only have originated in a situation in which these tribes played an important part. That can only have been the case in a period in which the later central Palestinian tribes had not yet occupied their subsequent dwelling-places. These latter tribes belong to a different sub-group from the former. Reuben, Simeon (and Levi) lead the special group of the 'Leah tribes'; and the strictly maintained number six is a striking feature of this group. When, owing to the omission of Levi[2], a gap arose in this group, the total

---

[1] Details and references in M. Noth, *op. cit.* pp. 47 ff.

[2] It is impossible to ascertain the reasons for this omission, particularly as Reuben and Simeon, which had probably lost their old position as much as Levi, continued to be counted, fictitiously, as tribes. Probably the elimination of Levi from the system is connected with the fact that, as is stated explicitly in the Old Testament tradition, people thought of the secular tribe of 'Levi' as having survived in the institution of the 'Levitical priesthood'. Whether in fact there is a historical connection between the two or merely an identity of name is another question.

number of twelve tribes was maintained not merely by dividing Joseph into Manasseh and Ephraim in the 'Rachel group' but also by transferring Gad[1] to the position of Levi in the order of the list (cf. Num. xxvi) and thus the numerical continuity of the group of six tribes was preserved. The only reason for that must be that the number six of the first group was as vital a part of the institution as the number twelve was of the whole, that the group of six tribes had special functions within the life of the whole, which required its preservation in the greater whole. If one remembers, finally, that outside Israel six-tribe associations can be proved to have existed alongside numerous twelve-tribe associations, one must conclude that the 'Leah tribes', Reuben, Simeon, Levi, Judah, Zebulun and Issachar, had once formed a six-tribe association at a time when the first named of these tribes were still in full possession of their original position and Joseph and Benjamin had not yet completed their occupation, and that this six-tribe association was the fore-runner and basis of the later twelve-tribe association. As far as we know, those six tribes were among the Israelite tribes which had settled in Palestine in a relatively early stage of the occupation. When after a violent upheaval of the hitherto existing conditions, of which we have only the most tenuous information, and which affected the tribes of Reuben, Simeon and Levi above all, and created a vacuum in the central part of the mountains west of the Jordan, new clans moved into the land and formed themselves into new tribes, the old six-tribe association was extended into a twelve-tribe association but in such a way that the old six tribes, even though they now existed only in scattered remnants, not only continued to be reckoned as full partners but were given first place in the enumeration of the members of the system and were even preserved as a self-contained group within the whole, probably in consideration of the special rights and duties in the life of the enlarged association which still devolved upon them by reason of seniority.

Joseph and Benjamin were the chief newcomers. Whilst Benjamin was constituted with a probably small number of clans as an independent tribe within a narrowly confined area and was always counted as an independent member in the system, the 'house of Joseph' represented an apparently very comprehensive association of clans, which soon divided into two tribes when the occupation of the land began. The term 'house of Joseph' does not suggest

[1] It is impossible to know why Gad was incorporated secondarily in the group of six tribes.

a real tribal name, whereas Machir (Manasseh) and Ephraim, when they became established in Palestine, appear to have formed themselves, like the other tribes, into fixed and self-contained tribes on the basis of dwelling together within a particular area. The question remains, where the name '(house of) Joseph' came from. As it is not likely that two tribes subsequently joined together under a common name in Palestine, it must be assumed that the name '(house of) Joseph' derives from the period before the occupation as a description of a fairly large association of clans which finally settled in the central land west of the Jordan. They were received into the twelve-tribe system first of all as a single member under the old common name, because there was only one place vacant for them within the framework of the established twelve, if the four tribes on the border—three Galilean and one east Jordan tribe—were to be incorporated simultaneously in the twelve-tribe association. We know nothing further at all about the prehistory of these four tribes, the time of their occupation of the land and the circumstances of their entry into the twelve-fold amphictyony.

Once the twelve-tribe association had been constituted on the model of the six-tribe association, the only change it underwent was caused by the withdrawal of Levi, which offered an opportunity for the tribes of Machir (Manasseh) and Ephraim to be incorporated into the system as separate units in place of the old entity of the 'house of Joseph'. Apart from that, no further change was made in the firmly established system, even when the composition of the tribes underwent various changes in the course of the historical development. This complicated evolution of the twelve-tribe system also explains why none of the forms that have come down to us reproduces the state of affairs prevailing at a particular time, since to some extent earlier organisations, to which the later elements were added, were always preserved within it. But all this merely shows that the system itself is a historical phenomenon related to a historical institution.

All these are conclusions based on the presence of traditions concerning the twelve-tribe system, compared with other similar traditions from outside Israel. The question is how far it is permissible to use this comparative material to complete the picture of the Israelite twelve-tribe system. The Greek amphictyonies, of which we have fairly extensive knowledge[1], offer the best example of a similar institution outside Israel. But one must be careful how one uses this

[1] Cf. G. Busolt, *Griechische Staatskunde* (Handb. d. Klas. Altertumswiss. IV, I, 1), II ([3] 1926), revised by H. Swoboda, pp. 1280 ff.

material, since it derives from a relatively remote area, from a comparable, but different, historical setting; nevertheless if statements in the Old Testament tradition correspond to it and find in this context an illuminating explanation, we should not disregard it.

Wherever we have any exact information at all about them, the essential feature of the institutions of these tribal associations was always the central shrine. We may certainly reckon with this in the case of the Israelite association. In all probability the divine throne of the sacred Ark[1] formed the centre of worship; the role which this chest played later on in the struggles with the Philistines, and under David and Solomon, makes it extremely likely that it had long held a position of central importance in the life of the tribes of Israel. We have no reliable information about its origin. Presumably it had originally been a travelling shrine of wandering clans[2]. Who brought it into Palestine and why it became the main sacred object of the Israelite tribal association is completely unknown, since all traces of ancient traditions concerning it have vanished. The question whether it played the central role from the very beginning even in the older association of the six tribes or was only later set up in the central place of worship as a particularly venerable sacred object, cannot be answered. But in this context the fact of primary importance is that, as far as can be inferred from the later history, it was the common cult object which united the association of the twelve tribes of Israel.

Among the established tribes in Palestine the Ark was no longer a real travelling shrine but, though it had as yet no permanent resting place[3], it was set up in one place for a more or less prolonged period and this place then formed the central place of worship, the geographical centre of the ancient Israelite amphictyony. It appears that, according to several traditions preserved in the Old Testament, the undoubtedly very ancient tree shrine east of the city of Shechem in the middle of the mountains west of the Jordan (the modern *tell balāṭa*) was the centre of worship of the tribes of Israel; and that seems to have been the earliest state of affairs which it is still possible to discern. It seems reasonable to assume that the old six-tribe association of the 'Leah tribes' which seem to have resided mainly in the central part of the mountains west of the Jordan,

---

[1] Num. x, 35 f. and Jer. iii, 16 f. suggest that it was highly probable that the Ark was originally conceived as the empty throne of the invisible deity.

[2] Cf. especially the obviously old 'sayings of the Ark' in Num. x, 35 f. Their incorporation in the present context and also the remark about the Ark in Num. xiv, 44 probably point to the truth, as does the late description in Exod. xxv, 10 ff.; xxxvii, 1 ff. which refers to the Ark as a portable sanctuary.

[3] With reference to this, it is stated in 2 Sam. vii, 6 that the Ark had 'moved around' until the time of David.

already had its religious centre here and that the twelve-tribe association was in this case linking up with an older tradition. But that
is merely a possibility. So far as the twelve-tribe association is
concerned, however, we have, to begin with, the story of the 'diet
of Shechem' in Jos. xxiv, a special section which now exists in a
deuteronomistic revised version as a later addition to the deuteronomistic history. According to this, Joshua gathered all the tribes
of Israel to Shechem, to the holy place 'before God' and summoned them to decide whether they desired to serve Yahweh or
other gods, and after they had decided for Yahweh he made a
covenant between God and people and 'set them a statute and an
ordinance in Shechem' and in witness thereof 'took a great stone
and set it up there under the oak that was in the sanctuary of
Yahweh'. This tradition, or at any rate its transmission and
preservation, certainly refers to a regular observance which took
place before the sacred stone in the oak shrine at Shechem and
which evidently included a public profession of faith in Yahweh,
an act of covenant-making and a proclamation of the statutes of the
law. And the statement in the secondary deuteronomistic passages
Deut. xi, 29 ff.; xxvii, 1-26; Jos. viii, 30-35[1] according to which,
immediately after their occupation of the land, the tribes of Israel
set stones and an altar near Shechem and inscribed the 'Law (of
Moses)' on the stones and spoke solemn blessings and cursings,
must originate in the same ceremony. In these latter, fairly late
passages, the traditional material may have been subsequently
elaborated and reshaped; but that it refers to the same thing as
Jos. xxiv is clear enough. According to this then, a ceremony was
performed at the sanctuary, probably at regular intervals, until comparatively late, and this referred to a relationship to their God which
was significant for the whole of the tribes of Israel. In addition,
Yahweh appears to have been worshipped as the 'God of Israel' at
this very shrine near Shechem (Gen. xxxiii, 20; Jos. viii, 30; xxiv,
2, 23)[2]. All of which suggests that this shrine was once of central
importance for the whole of the Israelite tribal association; and as
religious observances have a habit of preserving with great per-
sistence not only their actual form but also their association with a
particular place, there is everything to be said for assuming that,
even after the centre of worship of the tribal association had been
transferred to other shrines, the old ceremony still continued to be

---

[1] These items are not identical in form or content, but obviously all proceed from the
same situation.
[2] Cf. C. Steuernagel, *Wellhausen-Festschrift* (BZAW, 27 [1914]), pp. 329 ff.

observed near Shechem. This is taken for granted anyway in the passages of Old Testament tradition we have mentioned[1].

It follows that the shrine near Shechem was probably once the amphictyonic centre of the Israelite association of tribes; and that appears to be the earliest state of affairs it is possible to discern with any certainty. According to what was said above, the Ark of Yahweh must have been set up on that spot at that time. Admittedly, there is no evidence that it was, but that is not surprising, since in the period of which we have direct historical records, the central shrine of the tribes, and therefore the Ark, had already been shifted from Shechem, and on the old spot only certain traditional ceremonies which derived from the one-time importance of the shrine near Shechem had been preserved because of the usual conservatism inherent in religious observances.

It is much more difficult to answer the question whether it is possible to extract anything further of historical value from the old tradition in Jos. xxiv. Even though the transmission of this story is based on the regular repetition of the ceremonies described therein, nevertheless it recounts a unique event as the justification for these repeated observances; and its uniqueness is obvious above all from the part which the person of Joshua plays in it. The question is whether the person of Joshua is part of the basic substance of this traditional material. Now the Ephraimite Joshua[2]—apart from his doubtless secondary appearance in a few passages in the Pentateuch—did not originally appear in the originally Benjaminite aetiological narratives of the occupation of the land in Jos. ii-ix, and is no more firmly rooted in the probably equally Benjaminite narrative of the battle in Jos. x, 1 ff. than in the Galilean narrative of Jos. xi, 1 ff. The possibility must nevertheless be taken into account that, historically, Joshua derives from the context of Jos. xxiv. That raises the question whether Joshua did not in fact play a part in the history of the twelve-tribe association. On the basis of Jos. xxiv, one can at least ask whether he was not the man who first gave the twelve-tribe association in Shechem its 'statute and ordinance' and therefore occupied a leading position in the establishment of this amphictyony. If this was the case, it would not be difficult to imagine that, as the founder of the statutes of the

---

[1] In them there is no mention of the Ark, apart from Jos. viii, 30 ff., which is probably the latest passage, which mentions the Ark only because of the part it plays in Jos. iii, iv, vi. These traditional fragments no longer recognise the sanctuary near Shechem as the central sanctuary, but merely as the place where customs are observed which had been maintained at the former site of the central sanctuary.

[2] Joshua's burial place was shown in an Ephraimite place (Jos. xxiv, 30).

twelve-tribe association on Palestinian soil, he became the leader of the joint enterprise, once the idea of the unique event of an occupation of the land by Israel as a single unit had been formed. This supposition, based on Jos. xxiv, concerning the historical starting-point of the tradition concerning Joshua cannot, however, now be established with certainty from the sources available to us and it is therefore simply a possibility.

For reasons unknown to us the amphictyonic central shrine near Shechem was in time abandoned and shifted elsewhere. As it was only possible for it to play its role[1] by a friendly agreement with the city-state of Shechem on whose territory it was situated, perhaps a conflict with the Shechemites induced the tribes of Israel to shift it[2]. But possibly at this early period an occasional change of the central place of worship was provided for because the Ark was formerly a travelling shrine which it was not intended should become the object of a local cult after the manner of the Canaanites. At any rate the South Ephraimite shrine of Bethel (the modern *burj bētīn* near *bētīn*) seems for a time to have taken over the role of the central shrine. This is suggested by the statement in Judges xx, 26 f. (cf. xx, 18; xxi, 2) according to which, at the time of the story contained in Judges xix f., the Ark stood in Bethel. As the Ark is not connected with Bethel anywhere else and it is not quite clear how such an assumption could have come about of its own accord[3], it may be taken for granted that the information is historically accurate. Its accuracy is also confirmed by the striking performance of a pilgrimage from Shechem to Bethel, on which the story contained in Gen. xxxv, 1-7 is presumably founded[4]. According to this, certain preparatory actions were carried out in Shechem and then after the pilgrimage the real religious ceremonies were performed in Bethel. It looks as if a ceremony that had originally been self-contained was split up and only certain remnants were preserved at the original place of worship and that the main ceremony was transferred to another place. If one notes, moreover, that the 'putting away of the strange gods' which, according to Gen. xxxv,

[1] The city-state of Shechem had probably entered into friendly relationships with the tribe of Manasseh very early on and had actually been drawn into the association of this tribe; cf. below, p. 145.

[2] We hear of such a conflict in Judges ix (cf. below, pp. 152 f.). But another event of a similar nature which has not come down to us might equally well have been the reason for this transference of the central sanctuary.

[3] The meeting-place of the tribes in this story was Mizpah (Judges xx, 1 ff.), and the only part that Bethel plays in it is as the site of the Ark.

[4] Cf. A. Alt, *In piam memoriam Alexander von Bulmerincq* (1938), pp. 218 ff. = *Kleine Schriften zur Geschichte des Volkes Israel*, I (1953), pp. 79 ff.

2, 4, was carried out in an actual ceremony at the shrine near Shechem, is textually unmistakably related to Jos. xxiv, 14, 23, this
pilgrimage from Shechem to Bethel was in fact occasioned by the
transference of the amphictyonic central shrine from the one place
to the other.

Then, sooner or later, Bethel itself was abandoned. For a time,
the Ark appears to have found a home in the shrine of Gilgal in
the urban region of Jericho which was occupied by Benjaminites.
The part which the Ark plays in the basic material of the narrative
in Jos. iii, iv concerning the Israelites' crossing of the Jordan on their
entry into the land, which undoubtedly originated in Gilgal, can
hardly be taken to mean anything but that the Ark was one of the
local appurtenances of Gilgal[1]. If, all the same, the Ark had no fixed
abode before David, we may not be far wrong in assuming that the
shrine of Gilgal also provided it with a home for a time. But we
know nothing for certain. In Gilgal, too, and wherever else it may
have stood, it did not remain permanently. At any rate, we find it
finally in Shiloh (the modern *khirbet sēlūn*) in the midst of Ephraimite territory. Here the Ark even possessed a temple (1 Sam.
iii, 3; cf. also Jer. vii, 14; xxvi, 9) which was probably not the case
in Shechem and certainly not in Bethel and Gilgal. It is impossible
to say why Shiloh was chosen. The terebinth near Shechem had
been a centrally situated shrine which, seeing that it belonged to
one of the few old Canaanite city-states in the mountains and in a
region inhabited by the tribes, was undoubtedly of a venerable age
when the Israelites appeared in the land. The same applies to
Bethel; this shrine belonged to the city which had existed since the
Middle Bronze Age[2]. It had originally borne the name of Luz
and was then called Bethel, after the shrine (the modern *bētīn*),
and had probably been, with Shechem, one of the most important
ancient shrines in the central part of the mountains west of the
Jordan, so that after Shechem had been abandoned, the idea of
transferring the amphictyonic centre there inevitably suggested
itself. Gilgal too was undoubtedly an ancient and probably much
frequented shrine on the territory of the former city-state of Jericho.
Shiloh, on the other hand, was a place of no particular importance
in Mount Ephraim which was colonised by the Ephraimites[3] and
then only acquired temporary importance because the Ark was set

[1] H.-J. Kraus, *Vetus Testamentum*, I (1951), pp. 184 f. has rightly drawn attention
to this.

[2] This has been shown by the excavations on the site itself; cf. the preliminary reports
by W. F. Albright, BASOR, 55 (1934), pp. 23 ff., 56 (1934), pp. 2 ff.

[3] Danish excavations have revealed ancient Shiloh.

up in its shrine. We know too little about the events of that early period to be able to decide why the Ark was brought to Shiloh. It remained there until it finally fell into the hands of the Philistines who probably destroyed the city and shrine of Shiloh as well. In connection with the emergence of the monarchy the question of the central place of worship was considered completely afresh.

Israel was constituted as a historical entity in the form of an amphictyonic twelve-tribe association; this fact was of basic significance for the whole subsequent course of its history. Israel, at any rate, always thought of itself as a community of twelve tribes, and upheld the conception in spite of all later attacks on its external form. To the very end of Israel's history it never became a pure fiction, since there were always descendants of the old tribes to sustain the tradition. On the other hand, however, Israel's organisation into twelve tribes later tended to become part of a purely theoretical tradition, with no correspondence to the actual facts. To some extent this was the case from the very beginning, since even in the older twelve-tribe system members of the preceding six-tribe system were included though only scattered remnants of them survived. Probably the same thing happened later on with other tribes. Nevertheless, the system, of which the fixed number of twelve was part, continued to be maintained; and the system held together the surviving remnants of tribes under the traditional names.

Israel entered history in an outward form that was in no way unusual. The fact that similar amphictyonic twelve-tribe associations existed in the vicinity of Israel and beyond, in the ancient Mediterranean world, has enabled us properly to understand the Israelite twelve-tribe system. Israel formed itself into a twelve-tribe association in the course of a great movement towards the occupation of territory, a movement which, extending far beyond Israel itself, in the form of an Aramaean migration, led many other elements from the wilderness into the agricultural land of Syria and Palestine (and of Mesopotamia) and within this great movement there is evidence of other twelve-tribe associations besides that of Israel. Israel not only entered into a world with whose history its own was bound up in a great variety of ways from now on, but became what it was in association with larger historical movements. The special nature of Israel cannot therefore be sought merely in the processes and formations we have discussed.

Here belongs too the gathering round a central shrine, an essential feature of the life of all these twelve-tribe associations. In Israel the central shrine no more excluded the use of other shrines than it did in other tribal associations; at these other shrines local communities and the clans which comprised them practised their local cults; and further, it was perhaps here that the individual tribes met on their own account and traditional bands of pilgrims came together. But for Israel as a whole only the worship at the central shrine was official, and it was here alone that the basic community of Israel was expressed in worship. The central shrine became a place of worship of particular significance for Israel; and the trend towards an even more far-reaching centralisation of religious observances, which was to play such an important part later on, existed in Israel from the very beginning. There was, however, nothing exceptional or peculiar about Israel's position in this matter: it simply followed a development shared by all twelve-tribe associations. The special feature about Israel's position was merely that the old pattern was preserved more widely than elsewhere even when historical conditions changed.

8. *The Institutions of the Confederation of the Twelve Tribes*

The Old Testament tradition provides us with almost no direct information about the life and functions of the Israelite twelve-tribe association, and it is only possible to a limited degree to draw indirect conclusions from various scattered data. But this is not surprising since it is not usual to record and transmit much about institutions which function in an orderly way and are therefore not particularly noteworthy. Usually they are not mentioned in documents until the stage of official record-making has begun and that stage was not reached in Israel until the rise of the monarchy. It is precisely because the constitution of the amphictyonic twelve-tribe association was so essential for Israel that it remained a continuous and therefore self-evident institution until the kingdom was formed, that the Old Testament has so little to report about it.

The common worship at the central shrine 'before Yahweh', that is, before the Ark as the place of God's presence (cf. Judges xx, 26 f.), was its primary feature, as the visible expression of Israel's communal life. But we have no details about this worship. It may be assumed that it included regular offering of sacrifices at particular times, made in the name of the whole of Israel, and the holding of pilgrim festivals probably at least once a year. The old ordinance that 'three times in the year all thy males shall see the face of Yahweh' (Exod. xxiii, 17; xxxiv, 23) can only refer to the local shrines throughout the country and to the three agricultural festivals which were celebrated at these shrines, as it would have been impracticable to carry it out at the central shrine. When, on the other hand, we hear in 1 Sam. i, 3 ff. that Elkanah, the father of Samuel, went with his family to Shiloh 'year by year' (verse 7) 'to worship and to sacrifice there in the house of Yahweh' it may have been an annual amphictyonic festival at which all the tribes had to be represented officially, but to which many other Israelites came as well, especially if the central shrine was as accessible for them as it was for the Ephraimite Elkanah.

On the occasion of these festivals the tribes no doubt met to consult on questions of common interest, through their official representatives. It appears that these deputies were called נשׂיא and that this term may be taken to mean 'speaker', following the Hebrew expression נשׂא קול etc.[1] At any rate there are lists of twelve נשׂיאים in Num. i, 5-16; xiii, 4-15; xxxiv, 17-28, one belonging to each of the twelve tribes; and in Gen. xxv, 16 there is a reference to twelve נשׂיאים who evidently belonged to the Ishmaelite twelve-tribe system. As officials within the framework of a sacral institution these נשׂיאים were under the special protection of divine law, as is obvious from Exod. xxii, 28 where the cursing of a נשׂיא is forbidden, in direct connection with the injunction not to curse God himself. But we are not given any details about the office and tasks of the נשׂיא.

Emphasis was perhaps not laid on the cultic actions in the narrower sense in the Israelite twelve-tribe association. It is true that the institution of a permanent priesthood may have existed at the central shrine. In the temple of Shiloh, Eli and his sons officiated as priests before the Ark (1 Sam. i-iii) and when the Ark was marched out into the war against the Philistines it was accompanied by the sons of Eli (1 Sam. iv, 4, 11)[2]. To judge from this, the office of priesthood before the Ark appears to have been hereditary. But we do not even know whether the priesthood at the amphictyonic central shrine was appointed by the tribes as a whole or whether it was the old local priesthood of Shiloh which undertook the care of the Ark when the central shrine was transferred to Shiloh, as previously the local priests of Shechem and Bethel and Gilgal will have done, or whether the נשׂיאים of the tribes may not have per-

[1] Further references and details in M. Noth, *op. cit.* pp. 151 ff.
[2] It is not expressly stated that the sons of Eli carried the Ark itself; only the presence of priests at the Ark was necessary; the actual carrying was probably performed by subordinate cult-officials.

formed the necessary priestly functions at the great amphictyonic festivals. All that is quite uncertain and the scanty and scattered data of the Old Testament tradition leave various possibilities open. It is noteworthy that, at any rate in the case of Shechem, Bethel and Gilgal the amphictyonic central act of worship took place at ancient Canaanite shrines, even though Shechem, Bethel and Gilgal were in close touch with the tribes of Manasseh, Ephraim and Benjamin. Along with the holy places, no doubt much of the native Canaanite cultic traditions and practices also passed into the religious life of Israel. And that applies not only to the numerous local shrines throughout the country but also to the official worship of the whole society, which took place before the ancient sacred terebinth of Shechem (cf. Gen. xii, 6), before the equally venerable upright stone, the 'Massebah' of Bethel (cf. Gen. xxviii, 18, 22) and similar places. But all this merely accords with the fact that in Israel, in the sphere of public worship, the traditions of the new country were adopted to a very wide extent after the occupation: sacrifices were made in the manner native to the country[1], the agricultural festivals that were indigenous in Palestine were celebrated, the places that had been holy from time immemorial were venerated. This did not involve a change-over to Palestinian cults, with their gods; but, in addition to all kinds of customs which Israel had brought with it from the wilderness, Israel did in fact widely adopt in its worship the framework which it found in Palestine and the customary forms: it was only particular customs belonging to such cults as that of the Mother Goddess and the young vegetation god that were rejected as foreign and idolatrous. It follows that Israel's religious organisation was not in fact an expression of its own intrinsic character at all. It was entirely taken for granted that this sphere was part and parcel of its life and as a twelve-tribe association Israel, like other analogous associations, had its religious centre with pilgrim festivals and sacrifices. But religious observances apparently were not regarded as of prime importance in Israel and it is scarcely an accident that, compared with other documents of religious history deriving from the world surrounding Israel[2], the Old Testament shows surprisingly little interest in purely cultic procedures and problems.

[1] The thesis expressed in the title of the book by R. Dussaud, *Les Origines cananéennes du sacrifice israélite* (1921), has been entirely confirmed by the texts of Ugarit which were found later, with whose devotional terminology that of the Old Testament shows various points of contact.

[2] The texts of Ugarit, with their devotional-mythological contents, must now be compared.

The scanty information which we have in the Old Testament about the religious ceremonies performed at the amphictyonic central shrine lays more stress on other things than the specifically cultic actions. In Jos. xxiv there is no mention at all of sacrifices, but rather of a profession of faith in Yahweh and of the making of a covenant (though nothing is said about its outward form), and of the establishment of a 'statute and an ordinance' which were written 'in the book of the law of God', and, finally, there is mention of the setting up of a great stone under the oak tree that was in the sanctuary of Yahweh. And the late, only secondarily deuteronomistic passages in Deut. xi, 29 f.; xxvii, 1 ff.; Jos. viii, 30 ff.; are similar; in these passages it is true that we read of the setting up of an altar and the offering of sacrifices (Deut. xxvii, 5-7; Jos. viii, 30-31), but above all of the writing of the 'words of the law' on great stones set up there (Deut. xxvii, 2-4, 8); Jos. viii, 32) and of a reading of the 'words of the law' (Jos. viii, 34-35, cf. Deut. xxvii, 9 f.) and of a solemn pronouncement of blessings and curses which is no doubt connected with the 'words of the law' (Deut. xi, 29-30; xxvii, 11-13; cf. Jos. viii, 33 and also Deut. xxvii, 14-26). Admittedly, the deuteronomistic passages seem to combine various conceptions in a far from uniform and somewhat obscure manner, and to contain a late and hardly authentic element in the reference to the writing of the words of the law on great stones. They cannot therefore be used as primary sources of information about the ceremonies at the central shrine, of which they clearly evince no direct knowledge; but they do seem to contain a fragmented reflection of these observances and one that is evidently in accord with Jos. xxiv, which states that the 'statute and ordinance', the 'words of the law' played a vital part in the tribal gatherings at the central shrine. They included blessings and curses for the observance and infringement of the statutes of the law, and the foundation of the validity of these statutes was the covenant between God and people which, according to Jos. xxiv, 25, was regularly renewed at the central shrine. We can obtain from all this an approximate picture of what Israel considered essential in the celebrations held at the solemn gatherings of the tribes, but we must be careful not to attempt to reconstruct the whole situation from the scanty and purely indirect information in the Old Testament. The passage in Deut. xxxi, 10-13 offers no more concrete evidence: it should probably be utilised in this connection, however, although it does not mention the location of the central shrine and is presumably already intended to refer to the Temple at Jerusalem. It is one of the secondary passages of the deuteronomistic history and contains the instruction that every seven years at the autumn festival, when 'all Israel comes together to see the face of Yahweh its God', the law shall be read publicly for the instruction of all Israel. This refers more precisely to the later deuteronomic law, but seems to connect the instruction concerning the reading of the law at the end of every seven years with an old custom which had been observed, possibly from the very beginning, at the central Israelite shrine. If this be so, apart from the ceremonies which presumably took place once a year, a particularly solemn celebration took place every seven years at the central shrine in which the reading of the law played a leading part.

From the very beginning, then, Israel's speciality did not consist in a particular and unique form of worship at the central shrine but in the fact that it was subject to a divine law which was recited at the tribal gatherings at regular intervals and to which Israel committed itself in constantly renewed acts of affirmation. This is consonant with the fact that the only office for all Israel explicitly mentioned in the oldest Old Testament tradition was not a priestly but a judicial one. In Judges x, 1-5; xii, 7-15 we have a list of so-called 'minor judges'. They are so described to distinguish them from the 'major judges' about whom detailed records exist in the 'Book of Judges' but who, from all accounts, were not judges at all but charismatic leaders of tribes in various warlike conflicts and were only incorporated in the list of 'judges' by the author of the deuteronomistic chronicle because one of them, Jephthah, was also represented in the list of the 'minor judges'[1]. The older tradition knew only the 'minor judges' as the judges of Israel, and to them alone does the title 'judge' properly apply, in accordance with the traditional material. In the above-mentioned list they appear as the bearers of an office which was administered by *one* man; and the list mentioned six such judges, who filled the office of judge in an uninterrupted sequence. In each case only the name, descent and native place is briefly mentioned, then the duration of the tenure of office is recorded and finally the place of burial briefly stated; in some cases brief anecdotal remarks are also included within this framework[2]. Apart from these data, this traditional material appears to be based on official records. This applies especially to the references to the years during which they 'judged'

[1] On this literary process cf. M. Noth, *Überlieferungsgeschichtliche Studien*, I (1943), pp. 47 ff.
[2] Details in M. Noth, *Festschrift Alfred Bertholet* (1950), pp. 404 ff.

Israel. It deserves to be noted that we have here the only exact and obviously authentic chronological information (not merely in round figures) which the Old Testament contains for the period before the founding of the Kingdom. The fact that this information was recorded officially and transmitted to posterity can probably only be explained by the fact that in the earliest period of Israel's history dates were based on the period of the judges' years of office. If that is so, it follows that this was the central office in the Israelites' twelve-tribe association and that the law played a decisive role in this association[1].

Apart from the scanty details contained in the list, however, we have no further information about the position and functions of the judicial office. Were the judges who came from quite different tribes in an apparently irregular succession, elected from time to time by the tribes? Was the election made by the official representatives of the tribes, the נשיאים, on the occasion of one of the great federal gatherings at the central shrine? Or was the choice left to a divine decision which was obtained by drawing lots at the central shrine?[2] Various possibilities are conceivable, but we have no precise evidence on which to come to a decision. We can also only surmise what the rights and duties of the office were. It is hardly likely that it included the administration of justice, for that lay in the hands of the elders of the clans (זקנים), whose custom it was to administer justice 'in the gate', *i.e.* in the passage-way of the city-gate and on the square in front of it, as the centre of the whole of public life, according to the traditional and, to begin with, purely oral statutes of the 'civil law' later fixed in written form; or it lay in the hands of the priests at the country shrines, before whose sacral court certain cases were brought or who in cases where it was impossible to establish the facts were asked to secure a 'judgement of God'[3]. The 'judge of Israel' could be applied to at the most as a court of appeal, but it is doubtful whether an appeal against any sentence, once it had been passed, was considered admissible at all. It is far more likely that the central judicial office of Israel was related to the law that was valid in the whole of Israel,

---

[1] If the cult had been all-important, dates could have been based on the years of the (high) priests of the central sanctuary, in so far as such existed.

[2] This might be compared with the story of the drawing of lots to make Saul king in 1 Sam. x, 19b-21, though it is of late date (cf. also Jos. vii, 16-18); but at any rate it proves that the method was known in Israel.

[3] More details on this will be found in A. Bertholet, *Kulturgeschichte Israels* (1919), pp. 194 ff. and in L. Kohler, *Die hebräische Rechtsgemeinde* (*Der hebräische Mensch* [1953], pp. 143 ff. E.T. *Hebrew Man* (1956), pp. 149 ff.).

the divine law to which Israel was subject and which had to be regularly proclaimed anew, and that the 'judge' of Israel was the one who had to know and interpret it and give information about it, who had to see that it was observed and perhaps had himself to proclaim it in public, and whose duty it was to apply it to new situations and thereby assume responsibility for its development and constantly instruct the tribes about the meaning and application of its individual clauses. From the little we know about the earlier period of Israel's history it is probably permissible to infer so much, and the existence of this office of judge testifies to the basic importance which was attached to the divine law in Israel[1].

The question suggests itself as to whether the numerous and comprehensive collections of legal ordinances which we have in the Old Testament have not preserved the formulation of the oldest divine law of Israel. For even if it was handed down by word of mouth to begin with, in time it was probably set down in writing, and one would certainly expect it to have been incorporated in the Old Testament tradition. But we have no real chance of determining whether this in fact occurred, particularly as nothing is known for certain about its contents in any case. It is true that other tribal associations, like the Greek amphictyonies, had their 'amphictyonic law' which was binding on all their members; but on this point historical parallels are not very helpful, since it is highly probable that the divine law of Israel was something special and unique. The oldest traces of genuinely Israelite legal ordinances in the Old Testament may well be the original federal law of Israel[2] and the later books of the law as far as and including

[1] Historical parallels are not required to confirm these conclusions drawn from Old Testament statements; but they are not unwelcome when they can be quoted, even if they are so far distant in time and place that no historical connection can be assumed to exist. A. Klostermann in *Der Pentateuch*, N.F. (1907), pp. 348 ff. has performed a useful service in studying closely the office of Icelandic 'law speaker' and using it to explain the institution of the 'minor judges' (*op. cit.* pp. 419 ff.) and the derivation of the form of the deuteronomic law from the interpretative recitation of the law. In spite of the detailed criticism of A. F. Puukko, in *Das Deuteronomium* (BWAT, 5 [1910]), pp. 175 ff., of the inferences drawn by Klostermann regarding Deuteronomy, the latter's comparison of the Israelite institution with the Icelandic 'law speaker' has proved more and more to be relevant; cf., besides the agreement with reservations of M. Weber, *Gesammelte Aufsätze zur Religionssoziologie*, III (1923), p. 93, above all A. Alt, *Die Ursprünge des israelitischen Rechts* (1934), pp. 31 ff. = *Kleine Schriften zur Geschichte des Volkes Israel*, I (1953), pp. 300 ff. on the judges of Israel and G. v. Rad, *Deuteronomium-Studien* (1947), pp. 7 ff. E.T. *Studies in Deuteronomy* (1953), pp. 11 ff. on the connection between Deuteronomy and the recitation of the law.

[2] Of the statutes which were formulated 'apodictically' or 'casuistically' (on this distinction cf. A. Alt, *op. cit.* pp. 12 ff. and pp. 285 ff.) only the former are to be considered genuinely Israelite; they usually formulate prohibitions with the words 'thou shalt not . . .'.

the so-called Holiness Code in Lev. xvii-xxvi, and the deuteronomic law in Deut. xii-xxvi, may well be seen as further developments of the earliest statements. These earliest statements are to be
found within the so-called Book of the Covenant in Exod. xxi-xxiii;
and so the genuinely Israelite part of the Book of the Covenant,
the religious and moral prohibitions in Exod. xxii, 17 ff.[1] have
most right to be considered elements of the original divine law of
Israel[2]. Their content cannot be summarised in a sentence; but it
was their concern, as it was that of the Old Testament ordinances
in general, to preserve Israel's relationship with God intact and to
prevent its possible disturbance in all departments of life by the
prohibition of unlawful acts[3]. Israel was subject to a divine law
which required to be proved and tested in all the situations of
life and presupposed a strictly regulated relationship of Israel to
its God. This divine law was proclaimed and interpreted to the
tribes again and again at their assemblies and the central office of
the 'judge of Israel' carefully guarded it. The enforcement of this
divine law separated Israel from other peoples and the precondition of the divine law was the unique quality which determined
the existence and nature of Israel[4].

The tribal association was not merely committed to this divine
law but it was also bound to punish violations and could if necessary be summoned to enforce such punishment against any of its
members, just as in other tribal associations, such as the Greek
amphictyonies, refractory members could be brought to heel by
force. The punishment of transgressors took place in Israel in
order 'to put aside the evil (or the evil one) from the midst of
Israel' (so the deuteronomic formula in Deut. xiii, 6 and other
places.) In order to cancel the transgression of the divine law the
transgressor was 'rooted out of his people'—usually being stoned
by the whole people—as though he had never belonged to this
people. We hear of the violent punishment of a transgressor of the
divine law in the only Old Testament tradition which shows the

[1] For the literary analysis of the book of the Covenant and the analysis of its content,
and on the above description cf. A. Jepsen, *Untersuchungen zum Bundesbuch* (1927).
[2] The statement must be formulated carefully since a self-contained corpus of legal
statutes does not in fact exist in Exod. xxii, 17 ff.
[3] More details on this in M. Noth, *Die Gesetze im Pentateuch* (Schriften der Königsberger Gelehrten Gesellschaft, geisteswiss. Klasse, XVIII, 2 [1940]), pp. 40 ff.).
[4] The view of J. Wellhausen and his school that 'the law' was a late, post-prophetic
phenomenon in Israel, is only correct to the extent that the legal sections contained in
the Old Testament, which are very disparate, are on the whole fairly late. But as the
formulation of the divine law, the 'law' had its roots and its beginnings in the very
earliest constitution of the Israelite association of the twelve tribes.

sacral tribal association as such in the period before the formation of the Kingdom, because it was evidently quite an unusual case which seemed worth recording for the benefit of posterity. According to the story contained in Judges xix, xx which is certainly based on an old tradition and only appears to have undergone slight literary elaboration, there took place in the period in which 'there was no king in Israel' (xix, 1) in the Benjaminite city of Gibeah (the modern *tell el-fūl*) a sexual offence against the wife of a Levite who had claimed hospitality in the city for a night. This meant that a נבלה בישראל had occurred (Judges xx, 10; cf. xix, 23)—a 'folly wrought in Israel'—this technical term apparently signified a violation of the divine law then in force in the tribal society, which was especially strict in sexual matters, in intentional contrast to Canaanite ways; and as the inhabitants of Gibeah had taken part in the crime *en masse*, the Levite whose wife had been raped to death summoned the tribal association by dividing his wife into twelve pieces and sending one piece to each of the twelve tribes[1] accompanied by the formula that was probably specially provided for a case of this kind: 'Consider it, take advice, and speak your minds' (Judges xix, 30 LXX). The association of tribes came together at this extraordinary assembly in Mizpah (probably the modern *tell en-naṣbeh*), almost certainly because Mizpah was nearest to the scene of the crime, and decided to punish the deed as נבלה בישראל. But as the tribe of Benjamin, to which the city of Gibeah belonged, refused to hand over the guilty fellow-tribesmen of Gibeah (Judges xx, 13) and thereby declared its solidarity with the criminals, the other tribes waged a federal war against the tribe of Benjamin which ended in a defeat for the Benjaminites. Apparently that was considered the end of the matter: the crime had been dealt with.

The case shows the importance and seriousness that were attached to the observance of the statutes of the divine law in the twelve-tribe association. In the regular proclamation of these statutes, in the care that was taken to see that they were carried out, and in the punishment, if necessary by force of arms, of the transgressor, the life of the twelve-tribe association was apparently primarily expressed—apart from the common acts of worship at the central shrine. It does not appear from the tradition that has come down to us that the twelve-tribe association was a political and military institution concerned with external affairs except in

[1] On the prehistory of this method of calling to arms cf. W. Wallis, ZAW, 64 (1952), pp. 57 ff.

so far as a federation of twelve tribes inevitably implied a power complex, even though the aggressive development of power was not one of its intrinsic tasks. In practice, at any rate, the waging of war against hostile neighbours was usually left to the individual tribes or, in certain cases, to a voluntary amalgamation of several tribes. Thus the individual tribes had in fact usually to depend on themselves for the maintenance and extension of their newly acquired possessions in the land, and they waged the necessary struggles for themselves, on their own. They had their own political and military organisation specially designed for the purpose.

We know very little about the organisation of the individual tribes, but we must certainly assume that it was not substantially different in Israel from what it was in the other groups which settled in Syria and Palestine in the process of the Aramaean migration, and that it was substantially the same in all the tribes of Israel. The most important points about the inner structure of the tribes may be gathered from Jos. vii, 16-18[1], according to which the tribes were made up of clans (משפחות[2]). The tribes—in the Old Testament the 'tribe' is called שבט or מטה, *i.e.* 'branch', 'staff', 'stick', following the same idea as the German 'Stamm'— contrary to the traditional idea, were formed only when they reached Palestine as part of the historical process of the occupation of the land and consisted of the clans which settled in a particular limited area and were not simply held together by bonds of kinship. But the clans may well have represented older associations which had existed before the occupation and which then stayed together in local communities in Palestine and preserved their old fellowship, for example, in certain definite acts of worship in which the clan as such took part[3]. Unfortunately it is no longer possible to ascertain the original meaning of the word משפחה, but it is likely that basically the clan represented a union of blood-related groups and that it was the biggest unit still held together by ties of blood relationship[4]. The clans for their part consisted of a series of large families (בית or בית אב), *i.e.* the descendants of common ancestors

[1] This might be compared with 1 Sam. x, 20 f. where, however, one link in the chain is missing.

[2] Cf. also the long list in Num. xxvi, 4bβ-51, in which are enumerated by name the משפחות as the subdivisions of all the Israelite tribes.

[3] Thus 1 Sam. xx, 29 presupposes that a clan like the Judaean clan to which David belonged was in the habit of observing its 'family sacrifice' (זבח משפחה) in its own place —in this case, it was Bethlehem—on which occasion the other scattered members of the clan also came together.

[4] Such a clan would correspond roughly to a Greek *phratry* or Roman *gens*.

over about three or four generations who expressed their kinship not only in special acts of worship like the clans, but were probably held together by a common economy as well. The clarification of these relationships is made more difficult because in the Old Testament the terms are not always used precisely and consistently, and because the actual situation, especially the subdivisions of the clans, was very often even more complicated owing to all kinds of secondary ramifications and amalgamations of which we have no information at all. On the whole, however, the picture which emerges from Jos. vii, 16-18 is probably a fairly accurate reflection of the normal state of affairs.

The organisation of the tribal militia which the tribes employed when they went to war corresponded to the structure of the tribes. The tribes waged their wars by calling out their able-bodied, free men, who provided their own weapons. The tribes had no real professional soldiery such as was represented by the ruling class in the Canaanite cities with their war-chariots. There were individual 'dedicated warriors', Nazirites, who like Samson, the embodiment of the original form of Naziritism, submitted voluntarily to the law of sacred chastity by not cutting their hair and abstaining from wine, that enervating product of the agricultural land, and were then able to accomplish mighty deeds of warlike strength; and leaders in battle driven by the spirit of God, like the majority of the so-called 'great judges' of the Book of Judges. These were a well-known phenomenon, but they were not professional warriors who practised the art of war for its own sake, but charismatics, empowered for unusual achievements in time of war. Israel's military strength, however, was based on the tribal militias which marched to war on foot—without the aristocratic weapon of the horse-drawn war-chariot. The formation of the militia of a tribe corresponded to its subdivisions. The men of a clan liable to serve in the militia formed a unit of their own in war and this was called a 'thousand'. The word 'thousand' (אֶלֶף) is occasionally used simply as a term for 'clan', where the 'thousands' of a tribe are mentioned in contexts where there is no reference to the militia (1 Sam. xxiii, 23; Mic. v, 1; also Judges vi, 15). When it appears in some late passages of the Old Testament as an alternative for 'tribe', this is a secondary and improper use of the term. Naturally the clans differed greatly in strength; and 'thousand' is a traditional term, in which the number is in itself of no significance. Nevertheless, the use of the word 'thousand' for the military unit of a clan gives us at least an approximate idea of the number of men fit to bear arms within a clan. If 'fifties' occasionally appear as well as 'thousands' (1 Sam. viii, 12; cf. also 2 Kings i, 9 ff.)[1], possibly these were the units formed by the large families within the militia and they may indicate the approximate war strength of a large family[2].

The social order in Israel was patriarchal. No definite evidence survives of an older matriarchal order in Israel[3]. The large family was subject to the *patria potestas* of the grandfather as the head, together with the grown-up and married sons. But the larger units were led by councils of elders which administered justice, represented their association in negotiations and made other decisions. Here leadership was entirely by committee. Unfortunately we have no precise information about the structure of these councils. The heads of the constituent large families, or at least of the most important and respected of these, probably acted as elders (וקנים) of the clans. Since the clans lived together in local units in Palestine, the elders of a place (1 Sam. xi, 3; xvi, 4; 1 Kings xxi, 8; Deut. xix, 12 etc.) may be taken to have been the elders of the clans in question. But the institution of the elders of the clan certainly goes back to the period before the occupation when the clans were still nomadic units, and it was brought into Palestine with them; for such institutions are usually ancient and tend to be stubbornly preserved. The office of elder probably had its roots and real home in the clan. When the tribes established themselves as fixed entities in Palestine, councils of elders were also formed for them; in the Old Testament we occasionally hear of the 'elders of the tribes' (Deut. xxxi, 28) as well as the elders of certain individual tribes (1 Sam. xxx, 26; 2 Sam. xix, 12; Ezek. viii, 1; also Judges xi, 5), who led and represented the tribes. The institution was obviously transferred from the clans to the tribes. Unfortunately we are told nothing at all about the structure of the councils of the elders of the tribes. Perhaps they merely consisted of all the elders of the constituent clans. The Old Testament also makes repeated reference to the elders of Israel. But Israel as a

---

[1] According to a not improbable supposition of E. Meyer, in *Die Israeliten und ihre Nachbarstämme* (1906), p. 501, the word חמשים (Exod. xiii, 18; Jos. i, 14; iv, 12; Judges vii, 11) really meant 'arranged in fifties', that is, organised on a war footing, because the basic unit of the levies was the group of fifty; a different view is given by L. Koehler, *Lexicon s.v.*

[2] 'Hundreds' occur in the Old Testament above all in mercenary contingents (that is, not in levies) (1 Sam. xxix, 2; 2 Sam. xviii, 1, 4; 2 Kings xi, 4, 19) and also in summary and not very reliable lists as for example Exod. xviii, 21. 'Hundreds' apparently played no part in the Israelite levy, probably because there was no corresponding element in the organisation of the tribes.

[3] But cf. A. Bertholet, *Kulturgeschichte Israels* (1919), pp. 83 ff.

whole was not a political organisation but rather a sacral amphictyonic association, whose members were represented by their
נשׂיאים at the federal assemblies; and it is not very likely that there
existed a council of elders for the whole of Israel. The 'elders of
Israel' were either the elders of many or all the single tribes, as in
2 Sam. iii, 17; v, 3; xvii, 4, 15; 1 Kings viii, 1 who met together,
or a secondary fiction which imagined Israel as a total unit organised on the analogy of the clans and tribes.

CHAPTER III

THE TRADITIONS OF THE SACRAL CONFEDERATION OF THE TWELVE TRIBES

9. *The Deliverance from Egypt*

OUTWARDLY Israel took the form of an amphictyonic association of twelve tribes similar to the associations that existed elsewhere in similar historical circumstances. In this sacral association it was subject to a divine law, the constant proclamation and observance of which was one of the most important, if not the most important, task of the society and its organs and institutions. This divine law was not unlike the amphictyonic law which prevailed in similar associations. But in content it was substantially more than a mere amphictyonic law. For it was clearly not concerned with the obligations of the individual members of the confederation towards the central sanctuary or the relations of the members of the confederation to one another and to foreign powers. It was concerned rather with Israel's relationship to its God and was intended to safeguard the inviolability of this relationship in every respect. In the law this relationship appears as a specific and unique commitment for Israel which is not derived merely from the simple process of gathering round a common central shrine. In Israel the situation was not, as appears to have been the case in the Greek and Italic associations which are somewhat more exactly known to us, that a number of tribes were united around what was probably a very ancient rite connected with a particular age-old holy place, and were kept together by the common observance of this rite. It is true that—at any rate to begin with—the local centre of the Israelite amphictyony was always an ancient Canaanite shrine. But it was not the old Canaanite cult in use at this shrine that had brought and kept the tribes together; what happened was that Israel's own form of worship, with the shrine of the Ark, found a home for itself in an ancient Canaanite place of worship[1] but was not so

---

[1] According to the ancient world it was impossible to declare or make any place at all a place of worship; it had to be hallowed by some event or other or be traditionally holy. Thus the central place of Israelite worship could only be established in some place that was already holy, *i.e.* in some Canaanite place.

bound up with this place that it could not be shifted, if the occasion arose, to another place. This raises the question of the form of worship observed by the Israelite tribes and their special relationship to God.

The question is answered by certain traditions which were current among the Israelite tribes. They have come down to us in the great compilation of the Pentateuch, which, admittedly, only attained its ultimate form at a later date as the consummation of a long and complicated series of literary processes, though it has its source in an ancient stock of oral traditions which was developed quite early on and is rooted in a number of themes which had evidently been current among the Israelite tribes from the earliest times in connection with certain religious observances[1]. These themes are concerned with historical events which took place in the period before the occupation of the land, and concern certain encounters with the God whom the Israelites served in their worship and above all in their central rites, and to whose statutes they were subject: statutes intended to maintain the integrity of their relationship to this God. As far as we can trace them back any further at all, the traditions in question proceed from the existence of 'Israel' as an independent entity, in other words, from a fact which had no definitive existence until after the occupation of Palestine. The traditions exist, therefore, only in the form in which they were cherished among the tribes which had settled in Palestine. They can only be understood historically as the traditions of the tribes united in Palestine concerning the crucial foundations of their faith. As such they were of fundamental importance. But we have also to try to fit the historical information which they contain into historical contexts, even if by so doing we are ultimately bound to go back to the sphere of the historically inexplicable (cf. p. 3).

One of the original articles of Israel's faith was that it had once been 'brought out of Egypt' by its God Yahweh (cf. Num. xxiii, 22-xxiv, 8; 2 Sam. vii, 23; 1 Sam. iv, 8; Judges vi, 13; and also Exod. xx, 2 and elsewhere); and the time when the Israelites were 'brought out of Egypt' by their God appears as the beginning of their relationship to God (2 Sam. vii, 6 and elsewhere). At the offering of the first fruits of the field in the sanctuary it was the custom to recite a religious formula the main theme of which was the 'bringing forth out of Egypt' (Deut. xxvi, 5-9). References to

[1] On this point and what follows more details will be found in G. v. Rad, *Das formgeschichtliche Problem des Hexateuchs* (1938) and in M. Noth, *Überlieferungsgeschichte des Pentateuch* (1948).

this 'bringing forth out of Egypt' appear in all kinds of places in the Old Testament tradition, sometimes in formal phrases, sometimes in more or less elaborate statements, and it forms a leading theme in the Pentateuch (Exod. i-xv). From all the more detailed references and especially from the relevant section in the Pentateuch it appears that 'bringing forth out of Egypt' connoted not merely the point of departure of the migration of the Israelite tribes but a mighty deed of the God of Israel. Israel had been enslaved in Egypt and was to be held there, but its God had wonderfully delivered it from bondage and saved it from the power of the Egyptians. There is no doubt that the concrete statement in this confession is based on a definite historical occurrence and it is not difficult to discern the circumstances in which it took place.

It was not unusual for Egypt to see all kinds of elements from the neighbouring Asiatic lands and primarily the Sinaitic desert appearing on the eastern border of the Delta. They came to Egypt in the first place owing to the lack of food caused by a deficiency of rain and they desired to be admitted, and were admitted, to the blessed land of the Nile which did not depend on rainfall. In the Papyrus Anastasi VI from the period of the Pharaoh Seti II (*circa* 1205 B.C.) there is a report to his superior by an Egyptian frontier official from the eastern frontier of the Delta, in which it is stated, among other things, that on the frontier the transit of Bedouin tribes[1] from Edom through the fortress of Merneptah in *ṭkw*[1] to the marshes of pr-ꜣtm[2] of Merneptah in *ṭkw* had been stopped (?) 'in order to keep them and their flocks alive in the possession of the king . . .'[3]. This statement in the official's report obviously did not refer to anything out of the way for Egypt. Such things often happened, no doubt; and the frontier official reported them to his superior as it was his duty to report on all important as well as unimportant incidents on the frontier. The 'Bedouin tribes of Edom' were probably groups of breeders of small cattle with their flocks— no doubt quite small flocks—from the steppe beyond the Sinaitic desert[4], like the Israelite tribes before their occupation of Palestine;

---

[1] The name of this Egyptian city appears in the Old Testament in the Hebraized form Succoth (probably the modern *tell el-maskhūṭa* in the Eastern part of the *wādi ṭumēlāt*).

[2] This is the Pithom which we know from the Old Testament (the modern *tell er-reṭāble*, about 6 m. west of the *tell el-maskhūṭa* in the *wādi ṭumēlāt*).

[3] Translation of the text in AOT², p. 97; TGI, pp. 34 f. Cf. ANET, p. 259.

[4] Even if the reference in this text really is to the name 'Edom' which we know from the Old Testament, we can say nothing for certain about the origin of these Bedouin tribes, since we have no details about the specific meaning and connotation of the name Edom in the 13th century B.C.

lack of food had persuaded them to try to 'preserve their life' in Egypt. They were admitted to Egyptian State territory in the *wādi ṭumēlāt*, which extends from the most easterly arm of the Nile eastwards to the modern 'Crocodile lake' (*birket et-timsāḥ*) roughly in the middle of the Suez Canal, and represents a tract of cultivable land on the eastern border of the Egyptian Nile delta immediately adjacent to the Sinaitic desert. This *wādi ṭumēlāt* or a part of it seems to have had a name in ancient times which appears in the Old Testament in the form of 'Goshen'; and, according to Exod. viii, 18; ix, 26 it was in the 'land of Goshen' that the Israelites had resided in Egypt. The reference in the frontier official's report recalls, therefore, in almost every respect, what the Old Testament tradition says about the reasons for and the circumstances surrounding the Israelites' sojourn in Egypt; and the date of the incident mentioned in the report cannot be very far from what is reported in the Old Testament. I am not suggesting that the two incidents are identical, but rather that the frontier official's report shows that the Old Testament tradition refers to the kind of incident that was often taking place, and illustrates the sort of motive which led the Israelites into Egypt.

These Israelites lived in Egypt in circumstances of which we have no details, as people with inferior rights who were usually called 'Hebrews'[1]; and the fact that the Old Testament often uses the word 'Hebrews' when referring to the Israelites in Egypt (Exod. i, 19; ii, 7, 11, 13; v, 3 and elsewhere) is entirely in accordance with the actual situation. The Egyptians were quite familiar with this foreign term which they transliterated as *'pr*. These *'pr* undertook or were compelled to undertake all kinds of service, and in Egypt all service was directly or indirectly for the state. This is mentioned in various Egyptian texts. Under Rameses II *'pr*-people appear who 'haul stones for the great fortress of the city of Raamses, the beloved of Amon' and 'haul stones for the god Re, the Re of Rameses, the beloved of Amon, in the southern quarter of Memphis' —they were used as labourers in the building of cities and temples. Under Rameses III we hear of *'pr*-people who had settled in the lower Egyptian city of Heliopolis; and under Rameses IV we come across *'pr*-people among the workers in the quarries of *wādi ḥammāmāt* east of the Pharaonic city of Thebes[2]. Again, this is

---

[1] Cf. above, pp. 33 f.

[2] Cf. M. Chabas, *Mélanges égyptologiques*, I (1862), pp. 42 ff. German translation of the texts in H. J. Heyes, *Bibel und Ägypten*, I (1904), pp. 146 ff. and in A. Jirku, *Die Wanderungen der Hebräer im 3. und 2. Jahrtausend v. Chr.* (1924), pp. 24 f., TGI, pp. 30 f.

entirely in accordance with the tradition of the compulsory labour to which the Israelites were subjected in Egypt and, in particular, with the strikingly concrete information in Exod. i, 11 that the Israelites were used in the building of the cities of Pithom and Raamses in the eastern delta[1]. The point is not that the Egyptian texts refer specifically to the Israelites as 'Hebrews' but they do show that 'Hebrews' performing compulsory labour in Egypt were nothing unusual, and they therefore confirm in a most striking way the information about the fate of the Israelites in Egypt contained in the Old Testament.

Admittedly, all this merely forms the concrete background to what is the essential content of the acknowledgement of the 'bringing forth out of Egypt'. According to this, the Israelites left Egypt ultimately, and this involved them in conflict with the Egyptian power, from which the mighty hand of their God delivered them. Historically it is impossible to say much for certain about the circumstances surrounding this migration from Egypt. That the Israelites, who had probably gone to Egypt in the first place only under the pressure of dire distress and had been forced to submit to compulsory labour amid conditions of slavery, finally longed to recover their old freedom is understandable[2]. That the Egyptians—in a period of assiduous building activity, as under Rameses II, whose interests were concentrated on the eastern Delta—did not want to lose this labour force, is also understandable. The Israelites therefore tried to escape against the will of the Egyptians. In the Old Testament the story of the killing of the Egyptian first-born, and then further the story of the Egyptian plagues and of the long, futile negotiations with the Egyptians concerning the release of the Israelites, which only bore fruit at the very end, were developed in conjunction with the historical explanation of the old traditional custom of the sacrifice of the Passover observed by the nomadic shepherds[3]. In Exod. xiv, 5a, however, a remnant of an earlier account has

---

[1] On the situation of Pithom cf. above, p. 112, note 2. The city of (Per-)Rameses = 'house of Rameses' completed by Rameses II was probably on the site of, and around, the ancient city of Zoan (the modern ṣān el-ḥagar) about 30 m. north of Pithom, near the old mouth of one of the eastern arms of the Nile.

[2] This longing is particularly easy to understand if the immigration to Egypt had taken place not very long before and the memory of it was still alive. The computing of the sojourn in Egypt at 430 years in Exod. xii, 40 f. P (cf. the round figure of 400 years in the note added in Gen. xv, 13b) is no doubt much too high. It is countered by the older reference to four generations in Gen. xv, 16 E which is more likely to be correct, though even that figure may be too high. We have nothing to work on for a more exact computation.

[3] More details on this will be found in M. Noth, *Überlieferungsgeschichte des Pentateuch* (1948), pp. 70 ff.

apparently been preserved, according to which the Israelites had 'fled' from Egypt without the knowledge of the Egyptians; and this account is more likely to be in accordance with the facts. It is true that it is no longer possible to discover any historical details regarding the circumstances of, and opportunities for, this flight. But there that great event took place which was always thought of first when Israel remembered the 'bringing forth out of Egypt' in its confession of faith. By the side of a sea which blocked their way in one direction and appeared to make escape impossible, the escaping Israelites were attacked by a detachment of Egyptian chariots[1]. This incident certainly occurred on the eastern border of the delta where the Israelites were bound to attempt to leave the sphere of direct Egyptian suzerainty. It is impossible to ascertain the locality of the incident more precisely and it would still be impossible even if we had exact information regarding the extent of the arms of the sea and the lakes in the modern Suez Canal area at the time in question. There is no reliable information about this in the Old Testament. It is true that in Exod. xiv, 2 there are some very precise references, and these are sufficiently clear to enable us to say with fair assurance that they concern the district of what was called the Sirbonian Sea in Hellenistic and Roman times, *i.e.* the modern *sebkhat berdawīl*, the great lagoon which is about a day's journey east of the north-east corner of the delta[2], and it is quite possible that these references are accurate. But they are only contained in the late Priestly Code and probably represent a later effort to set the great, decisive event in a particular place in keeping with the traditional setting of the historical events. It is true that it is far and away the oldest such attempt known to us, but it was separated from the event itself by more than 500 years and was probably not based on an unbroken tradition, since the earlier strata of the Pentateuch narrative do not seem to be aware of any such precisely defined place—at any rate, nothing of the kind has come down to us—but merely refer rather vaguely to a place 'on the sea'[3]. Inevitably, this 'sea' that exerted a decisive influence on

---

[1] That the Pharaoh himself was present is not even to be inferred with any certainty from the phrasing of Exod. xiv, 6 f. J (cf. verse 9aα) and Exod. xiv, 8 P (cf. verse 9aβ P), and is historically out of the question in any case, since if he had been present we should hear about it in Egyptian sources for the well-known history of the Pharaohs of the New Kingdom, whereas the disaster that befell a group of Egyptian chariots was not so important for Egypt that we should expect to find an Egyptian record of it.

[2] For the details see M. Noth, Der Schauplatz des Meerwunders, *Festschrift Otto Eissfeldt* [1947], pp. 181 ff..

[3] Outside the Pentateuch narrative (and in some passages in the Pentateuch, probably only secondary) this sea is specifically called the 'Reed Sea' (provided יַם־סוּף really

the course of events, must have lain in the vicinity of the modern Suez Canal, whether one follows Exod. xiv, 2 in referring to the lagoon of the *sebkhat berdawīl* or one of the lakes on the isthmus of Suez[1] which are now crossed by the Suez Canal, or prefers to follow the example of the early Christian pilgrims in thinking of the northern end of the gulf of Suez near the modern city of Suez (*es-suwēs*).

Our lack of knowledge about the localisation of the events which took place is in part responsible for the mystery and obscurity in which they remain for us. According to what is probably the earliest reference to the incident, contained in the short Hymn in Exod. xv, 21b, the essential feature was that Yahweh 'threw' the Egyptian chariots 'into the sea' with 'horse and rider'. The detachment of Egyptian chariots sank in the water owing to some unexpected disaster and the escaping Israelites were thereby suddenly liberated from supreme and apparently inescapable danger. They were convinced that God had thereby openly intervened to help them in a mighty act and had set the seal on their escape from Egypt. Although they acknowledged that this divine miracle was fundamentally inexplicable and passed it on to posterity as such, attempts were naturally made later on to reconstruct the incident in greater detail—going beyond the description given in Exod. xv, 21b by imagining that a wonderful way of escape had been opened up for them through the 'sea' that barred their way and which engulfed the Egyptians when they went the same way. These attempts to reconstruct the incident probably include the simple account in Exod. xiv which makes Yahweh 'cause the sea'—this could have been quite a shallow lake—'to go back by a strong east wind' (verse 21a), so that the Israelites were able to move on, whilst the Egyptians who had pursued them were driven into a state of utter panic by some mysterious divine action (verse 24b), and fled blindly into the sea that had returned meanwhile to its old place (verse 27aβ). The phenomenon of the pillar of fire and cloud, which,

means that) (Jos. ii, 10; iv, 23 and elsewhere). If, as is the case in all the passages in the Old Testament which it is possible to interpret with certainty, this should refer to the gulf of *el-'aḳaba*, then we should have here a localisation deviating strikingly from Exod. xiv, 2, which would show that an ancient and authentic local tradition about the miracle at the sea did not exist: it could not be historically accurate anyway, but could only be based on a secondary association of the story of the deliverance out of Egypt with the story of the occupation of the land from the southern land east of the Jordan. It is, admittedly, not absolutely impossible that in this context the 'Reed Sea' connoted the Gulf of *es-suwēs* or some other sheet of water on the eastern edge of the Nile delta.

[1] It is possible that in the 2nd millennium B.C. the Gulf of *es-suwēs* still had a shallow connection by water with the Bitter Lakes and even with the *timsāḥ*- lake, whilst further to the north the *ballāḥ*-lake was connected by water with the Mediterranean, so that there was only a relatively narrow isthmus between the *timsāḥ*-lake and the *ballāḥ*-lake.

to begin with, came as a protection between the Israelites and the Egyptians (verses 19b, 20) and through which Yahweh 'looked unto the host of the Egyptians' (verse 24) to frighten and trouble them, already includes a secondary element from a completely different context, namely, the Sinai tradition. Later on the incident was conceived even more impressively as is clear above all from the account of the Priestly Code in Exod. xiv, according to which a way was made for the Israelites through the sea, which rose up as a 'wall' on both sides (verse 22), and closed in again over the pursuing Egyptians. All these are different ways of reconstructing the miracle of the deliverance, later rationalisations of the incident which are, admittedly, in the first place, simply an attempt to testify each in its own way to the great divine act of the 'bringing forth out of Egypt'. And in the last resort that was all that really mattered, even if there was no authentic tradition about the actual course of events. There can be no doubt, however, that this was a real event; we can discern to some extent the conditions and circumstances which led to it and can fit it into a historical situation of which we have quite reasonable knowledge. The incident itself, which the Israelites experienced as an unexpected and mighty act of deliverance of their God, remains veiled from our sight.

One of the historical questions which the incident raises concerns the people who were involved in it. Hitherto they have been described as 'Israelites' in accordance with the tradition which was transmitted in the confederacy of the twelve tribes. But the 'Israel' of the twelve tribes only evolved on the soil of Palestine and even the name 'Israel' is not certainly attested before the entry into Palestine[1]. The traditions concerning prehistoric events were shaped from the point of view of the situation as it was in Palestine and these traditions referred to 'Israel' as if 'Israel' had already existed for a long time. Historically speaking, the 'bringing forth out of Egypt' cannot have referred to the later Israel whose ancestors had not all shared a common pre-history. The departure from Egypt and the deliverance which took place 'by the sea' do not suggest a great number of complete tribes but a numerically fairly small group which was in a position, because of its size, to 'flee' from Egypt. It is usual to think, therefore, of individual components of what later became Israel, which had been in Egypt and may be considered the real transmitters of the tradition of the 'bringing forth out of Egypt'. The question is then asked, What group of tribes was actually involved? and the choice easily falls on the

[1] Cf. above, p. 3.

'Rachel' group. But the reasons for this are not very sound. It is true that these important central Palestinian tribes were eventually able to force the whole of Israel to acknowledge their special traditions, but this is only one of a number of different possibilities, and not absolute proof. The fact that Joseph and his brother Benjamin play such a large part in the account of the migration to Egypt is due not to historical reasons but to the way the tradition was passed on. For the so-called 'story of Joseph' is not based on a foundation of tribal history at all, at least not in the sense of portraying the special destiny of a single tribe or group of tribes, personified in the figure of the ancestor. It is a fairly late narrative element within the whole corpus of the Pentateuch tradition and conceived from the very outset from the point of view of Israel as a whole. It is not a story of Joseph but a story of 'Joseph and his brethren', and Joseph plays a special part in it, with Benjamin only because it was moulded among the tribes of central Palestine, incorporating to some extent the motif of the youngest son who is favoured by the father and therefore hated by his older brothers, since, according to the personification of the twelve-tribe system in the narratives of Gen. xxix, 31–xxx, 24, Joseph and Benjamin were the youngest sons of Jacob. It is impossible to draw any historical inferences from the story of 'Joseph and his brethren'. Finally, the fact that in the Pentateuch the context leads from the deliverance out of Egypt to the occupation of the land from the southern land east of the Jordan and therefore to the manner in which the central Palestinian tribes occupied the land cannot be cited as evidence that events in Egypt specifically affected the 'Rachel' tribes. Like the interrelationship between the various themes in the Pentateuch, this connection between various events is secondary and there is a striking gap between the information about events in and around Egypt and the statements about the appearance of the Israelites in the southern land east of the Jordan, which shows that there is no simple continuity in the narrative. The reason is that the elaboration, for the purposes of the narrative, of the confession of faith in the divine bestowal of the land of Palestine, which led on from the development of the motif of the 'bringing forth out of Egypt', took place in the end among the central Palestinian tribes, and was based on their particular memories of the occupation of the land. This happened in such a way that these particular memories of the occupation were already regarded as descriptive of all Israel when they were joined to the stories concerning the sojourn in Egypt. The basis of the central Palestinian tradition is therefore only the theme of the occupation of the land, not that of the sojourn in Egypt as well, much less a combination of these two themes.

In any case, however, it is wrong to ask which of the Israelite tribes were in Egypt since the tribes were only formed into permanent units when they arrived in Palestine. In some cases it can be proved, and it is probable in the others also, that they were first given their names there too. The later tribes did not exist at all in Egypt. This makes the question as to who actually was in Egypt even more difficult to answer; we can only say that they were elements which became part of the tribes which were formed when the land was occupied. They were probably not absorbed by a single tribe, or even a single group of tribes, but by the whole range of the Israelite tribes[1]. It may be surmised that those who migrated to Egypt had previously had a connection with the nomadic shepherds who sojourned on the borders of Palestine, who had perhaps already been in touch with this land in the process of changing pastures, and who, in the course of time, formed the tribes of Israel. After the deliverance out of Egypt, these migrants may well have returned to this sphere again. We have no knowledge whatsoever as to how this came about, since the route taken by the Israelites on their departure from Egypt, which is presupposed rather than actually laid down in the Pentateuch, was based on the later combination of the various themes of the narrative and not on an original tradition. After crossing the desert of Sinai, the elements which came from Egypt at any rate reached the territory of the clans who were living in the vicinity of Palestine and who coveted this land. They were probably related to these clans and brought them the news of the divine miracle 'by the sea', which moved them so deeply that they passed the story on everywhere and transmitted it to their descendants as though it had happened to them all. In this way the confession of faith in the God who had manifested himself so gloriously by delivering them from the hand of the Egyptians became the common property of the whole of Israel and one of the foundations of the faith which was vital in the institution of the sacral confederation of the twelve tribes under the protection of the binding law of God.

Any attempt to fix the sojourn in Egypt chronologically can

---

[1] Presumably only one of the different, chronologically separate phases of the Israelite occupation is involved. To judge from the estimate of the time when the sojourn in Egypt took place, which we are about to discuss, it is probable that the old 'Leah'-tribes were already in Palestine (cf. above, p. 80) when these events occurred in and around Egypt, and that the migrants who returned from Egypt were therefore absorbed by other groups of tribes.

only be made on the basis of statements in the Old Testament. As far as Egypt is concerned the process of the arrival and departure of Asiatic neighbours was too frequent and repeated an occurrence, and even the disaster that befell a detachment of chariots on the eastern border of the delta too insignificant an incident for us to expect any information on the subject from Egyptian sources, which might establish the exact date of the event that had such a profound effect on Israel. As far as Palestine is concerned, the occupation of the land by nomadic shepherds in the course of the Aramaean migration was too long a process and too remote from the scenes of the previous history of the country for us to expect to find any information on its individual stages in Palestinian sources outside the Old Testament. Now the Old Testament does not contain any early, reliable information about the duration of the sojourn in Egypt, which was in fact probably quite short[1], but it does contain a strikingly concrete item of information about the compulsory labour to which the Israelites were subjected in Egypt which it is possible to fix chronologically. According to Exod. i, 11, the Israelites were employed in the building of the cities of Pithom and Raamses in the eastern delta[2]. This takes us to the period of the Pharaoh Rameses II (1290–1223 B.C.). According to the evidence of discoveries made on the *tell el-maskhūta*, Rameses II began with the building of granaries in Pithom, and, above all, this Pharaoh is known to have developed the city of (Per-)Rameses as a delta residence and named it after himself. The reference to the two city names in Exod. i, 11 does not at all look like a secondary elaboration and it fits in so well with all we know from other sources about the sojourn in Egypt that it must be considered a reliable tradition. If this is so, the information has more weight than any dubious supposition regarding the historical circumstances and the date of the sojourn in Egypt[3]. Rameses II must therefore be regarded as the so-called 'Pharaoh of the oppression'. In view of this Pharaoh's long reign it is impossible to be very precise about the actual dates; one can hardly say more than that the sojourn in Egypt and the departure from that country took place during the 13th century. This does not fit in at all badly with the course of events in Palestine; at that time the occupation of the land was

---

[1] Cf. above, p. 114, note 2.

[2] On the localisation of the two cities cf. above, p. 112, note 2, and p. 114, note 1.

[3] This is also true of the late chronological constructions in the Old Testament itself, such as the chronological framework of the deuteronomistic history, to which the chronological reference in 1 Kings vi, 1 belongs (on how this came about cf. M. Noth, *Überlieferungsgeschichtliche Studien*, I [1943], pp. 18 ff.).

probably being carried out by the younger strata of the Israelite tribes, who were joined by the elements coming out of Egypt.

10. *The Patriarchs*

One of the traditions that survived among the confederacy of the twelve tribes of Israel was that of the so-called Patriarchs. As in the similar case of the tradition regarding the deliverance out of Egypt, the background of the tradition was a historical manifestation from Israel's earliest history; but it acquired historical significance as part of the faith of Israel. The fundamental constituent of this tradition, as it appears in the Pentateuch as a whole, evidently lies in the divine promises regarding the possession of the land of Palestine and regarding their descendants, promises that were bestowed on these patriarchs in repeated divine revelations in various holy places in the land, and which were ultimately fulfilled in the occupation of the land by the Israelite tribes, who constituted a numerous people. The occupation of the land was thus proved to be a work achieved under divine guidance which had long been envisaged and prepared. The tradition of the patriarchs was conceived and developed from this point of view in the Israelite confederation of the twelve tribes. But it was connected with certain human figures which it refers to by name and of whose life it has all kinds of concrete details to record; and so the question arises as to what extent and in what respect the tradition was based on historical reality.

Evidently numerous local Palestinian traditions became attached to the personalities of the patriarchs which were not originally associated with them at all and which must be ignored if the question as to the nature of the patriarchs is to be answered; since it was only after the patriarchs had taken their place in the tradition that they attracted local traditions[1]. They occupied this place as the recipients of divine promises—this was originally the specific nature of the whole phenomenon and the fundamental significance of the whole complex of tradition—and as the founders of the cult at the places hallowed by the divine promises and the encounter

---

[1] Among these local traditions acquired secondarily will have to be reckoned, in the case of Abraham, the whole story of Sodom (Gen. xviii, xix), the aetiology of the substitution of the sacrifice of a son by that of a ram in the mountain sanctuary in 'the land of Moriah' (Gen. xxii, 1-19); in the case of both Abraham and Isaac, the stories of wells from the Negeb (Gen. xxi, 25 f., 30; xxvi, 14 ff.); in the case of Jacob, the stories of Jacob and Esau which are native to the land of Gilead including the aetiology of the Israelite-Aramaean frontier on 'mount Gilead' (Gen. xxxi), the explanation of the name Mahanaim (Gen. xxxii, 1, 2 and 4 ff.), the story of the night-spirit at the Jabbok ford near Peniel (Gen. xxxii, 23-32) and similar stories.

with God that these promises implied. These places were places of worship which continued to enjoy the high regard of the Israelite tribes for a long time: they included the tree sanctuary east of Shechem (Gen. xii, 6; xxxv, 2, 4); the holy place of Bethel (Gen. xii, 8; xiii, 3; xxviii, 11-22; xxxv, 1, 3, 5, 7); the sanctuary of Beer-sheba (Gen. xxi, 22 ff.; xxvi, 23 ff.; xlvi, 1-4); the sacred terebinth of Mamre near Hebron (Gen. xiii, 18; xviii, 1 ff.). All the basic elements of the characteristic type of patriarchal narrative are to be found in summary form in the first passage of this kind in the Old Testament. This is the statement regarding the appearance of Abraham at the 'oracle-giving terebinth' near Shechem which is given in Gen. xii, 6 f.: God 'appears' to Abraham, promises 'this land' to his descendants, and Abraham immediately builds an altar on the site for 'Yahweh who appeared unto him'. The only point that needs to be added is that these 'descendants' (the 'seed' of Abraham) used to sacrifice on the altar on this hallowed spot 'to the God of their father Abraham'. It follows that information about the patriarchs survived and was handed down in connection with the sacred objects established by them (altars or massebahs)[1] at the holy places in question, and that their names lived on in association with the deity ('God of Abraham' etc.), named after them and worshipped by their descendants.

We have here a particular type of phenomenon of religious history, which may be compared with similar phenomena of which there exists illuminating evidence on the borders of Palestine, though only from the Hellenistic-Roman period: the worship of θεοὶ πατρῷοι, i.e. ancestral gods who were invoked by the descendants because they had once appeared to their forefathers and been of assistance to them; this comparative material throws light on the basic element in the tradition of the patriarchs[2]. If, therefore, the figures of the patriarchs lived on among the Israelite tribes as the recipients of divine manifestations and the founders of cults which continued to be practised by their descendants and with which their names remained associated, they were clearly

[1] Massebahs, upright stones, were among the usual contents of Canaanite shrines, originally intended as abodes of the local deity, and later interpreted as memorial stones.
[2] We owe the recognition of this important fact to A. Alt, *Der Gott der Väter* (1919). The comparative material which Alt presents *in extenso* is to be found in Greek and Nabataean inscriptions, especially from the northern area east of the Jordan. Earlier interpretations of the figures of the patriarchs, both as personifications of tribes for which there is no real evidence, and the even less tenable mythological interpretation of them as originally deities, and the quite arbitrary interpretation of them as fairy-tale figures, have thereby been exploded once and for all, so that there is now no need to discuss these interpretations.

men who had once lived as historical persons.

One of the special and evidently original elements in the Old Testament tradition of the patriarchs was the promise of descendants and the promise of the land of Palestine; the esteem in which the patriarchs were held as the recipients of this promise remained great precisely because this promise had ultimately been fulfilled. But the promise itself was bound up with the situation in which the clans which subsequently combined into 'Israel' sojourned on the borders of Palestine and were still merely at the stage of coveting the land and had at most made contact with Palestine through the summer pastures. The way of life of the patriarchs is described as essentially that of nomadic shepherds who have not yet really settled down, who live in tents and who are concerned above all with pastures and watering-places for their herds of small cattle. If that description is correct, the patriarchs as historical personalities did not really belong to Palestine at all but only to its vicinity. The question is whether the divine manifestations which were vouchsafed to them occurred at sanctuaries in Palestine itself— when the change of pasture brought them into Palestine in the summer months, for example—or whether they did not usually take place somewhere outside Palestine in the steppe. It may be presumed that it was their descendants who first established the worship of the 'god of the fathers' in Palestine after they had settled there and had seen the fulfilment of the promises made to their forefathers, and that they continued to practise this worship at the holy places in Palestine, and that it was only then that the tradition of the patriarchs assumed the form in which the patriarchs had all their encounters with the deity at these same holy places. If that is so, then we have no evidence, beyond what has been said already, for making any definite historical assertions about the time and place, presuppositions and circumstances of the lives of the patriarchs as human beings. Even the original tradition of the patriarchs was not, however, much concerned with their human personalities, but rather with the divine promises that had been made to them.

Nevertheless it might be possible to find in the relatively familiar history of the ancient Orient in the 2nd millennium B.C. a situation in which the patriarchs might have appeared in the vicinity of Palestine as, in accordance with Old Testament tradition, the first heralds of the later Israel[1]. The Old Testament tradition itself

---

[1] Cf. the penetrating and thorough researches of R. de Vaux, Les Patriarches hébreux et les découvertes modernes, RB, 53 [1946], pp. 321-348; 55 [1948], pp. 321-347; [1949], pp. 5-36.

suggests this possibility, since, in the story recorded in Gen. xiv, it shows Abraham acting within a comparatively broad context of ancient oriental history. But the story contained in Gen. xiv is in every respect so isolated within the whole tradition of the patriarchs that the question is whether it can be included among the authentic basic material of this tradition at all. In addition, the historical elucidation of Gen. xiv has attained no clear results in spite of much effort. It is true that kings of the ancient Orient appear in Gen. xiv with such concrete names and descriptions that they must be presumed to represent historical personalities; but it is so difficult to place the total content of the story in a definite historical period that one cannot help thinking that historical figures of the ancient oriental world were only later brought into a secondary historical relationship with one another. The relatively late chronological references in the Old Testament must be considered equally unreliable as evidence for fixing the period of the patriarchs and so for some kind of historical arrangement of them. On the other hand, there is a possible connection between the patriarchs and the elements which appeared in the 19th-18th centuries B.C. in Mesopotamia and in Syria-Palestine (see above, p. 24), the names of which have come down to us through the Egyptian execration texts (cf. above, p. 18). Since these names are strikingly similar in form to earlier Israelite personal names, it is not unlikely that there was at any rate a distant relationship between these immigrants of the 19th-18th centuries and those who carried through the later 'Aramaean migration' (cf. above, p. 83)[1]. Now, if the Old Testament makes the patriarchs appear as the precursors of the clans which later combined to form 'Israel', it may be feasible to see their history within the framework of the migratory movement of the 19th-18th centuries, the more so as the forms of two of the three patriarchal names known to us, Isaac and Jacob, are typical of this stratum of immigrants. Against this assumption, however, there is the fact of the great distance of time, whilst the Old Testament brings the patriarchs very close to the historical events which had a fundamental effect on the life of what was later to become Israel. And it is unlikely that the tradition of the patriarchs could have entered the evolving tradition of the Pentateuch after an interval of more than 500 years. It is more likely that the historical figures of the patriarchs, however intangible, already belonged to the 'Aramaean migration'.

It may be assumed that numerous such 'patriarchs' were known

[1] Cf. M. Noth, *Geschichte und Altes Testament = Alt-Festschrift* (1953), pp. 127 ff.

among the Israelite tribes. The fact that Abraham, Isaac and Jacob were particularly remembered was due to the peculiar evolution of the Pentateuch tradition. At an early stage this tradition was developed, to begin with, among the tribes of Central Palestine; and just as the theme of the occupation of the land was developed from their particular point of view, so the theme of the patriarchs was evolved from the point of view of the promise that was ultimately fulfilled in the occupation of the land by the Israelite tribes. But in the 'house of Joseph' Jacob figured as the original recipient of the promise; according to the tradition, the figure of Jacob was associated with the sanctuaries of Shechem and Bethel, and further, there were particularly associated with him stories which were native to the Josephite settlement east of the Jordan. In the course of the development of the Pentateuch tradition the figure of Jacob was, to begin with, the sole representative of the patriarchs[1] and, in spite of his originally belonging specifically to the 'house of Joseph', as a result of his association with the tradition of the occupation of the land, he acquired a significance for, and was acknowledged by, Israel as a whole. As part of the make-up of a 'patriarch' in the sense we have described was the role of the ancestor who had received divine promises for his descendants, Jacob logically became the tribal ancestor of the whole of Israel and the eponyms of the twelve tribes became his sons. Thus Jacob, who was well known among the clans of the 'house of Joseph' in their particular area of the land and whose name was handed down as name of ancestor by these clans in connection with the worship of the 'God of Jacob' and whose memory survived at some of the sanctuaries in Palestine, finally assumed the central role of ancestor of the whole of Israel and in this role he became a figure of historic importance for the confederation of the twelve tribes. The same kind of thing applies to Isaac and Abraham, who were added later on when the Pentateuch tradition was further developed among the southern tribes. They belong to the same type and only differ from Jacob in that stories about them circulated among the inhabitants of the Negeb. Their historical setting has therefore to be sought among the nomadic shepherds on the southern border of Palestine. It was here that the 'God of Isaac' and the 'God of Abraham' were worshipped on the basis of the divine

---

[1] The confessional formula in Deut. xxvi, 5-9 only mentions Jacob as patriarch (without referring to his name) and, with reference to his person, begins the summary enumeration of the basic events in Israel's early history up to and including the occupation of the land.

manifestations which had occurred, and the names of Isaac and Abraham were preserved in association with these cults. When their worshippers settled down, all kinds of Palestinian traditions were connected with their names. Among the southern tribes they therefore became ancestors of Israel. When the Pentateuch tradition, which was first evolved in Central Palestine, was further developed by the southern tribes, they were given genealogical precedence over Jacob. Because their only real home was among the southern tribes, however, they apparently never acquired such universal significance among the Israelite tribes as the central Palestinian, Josephite figure of Jacob. Outside the Pentateuch at least the names of Isaac and Abraham appear incomparably less frequently in the Old Testament than that of Jacob, which appears either as the name of the patriarch or as a poetic term for Israel in the most varied contexts as something obviously quite familiar.

The fact that the patriarchs and the narratives concerning them were originally limited to particular clans or tribes also suggests another probability that it is impossible to prove only because we do not know whether, owing to the peculiar development of the Pentateuch tradition, knowledge of 'patriarchs' who were known among other Israelite tribes may have been lost. To judge from the stories of the patriarchs which have come down to us, it might be supposed that the patriarchs and so the worship of a $\theta\epsilon\grave{o}s$ $\pi\alpha\tau\rho\hat{\omega}os$ were the special concern of the later stratum of Israelite tribes and not of the earlier group of 'Leah' tribes. Jacob belonged to the 'house of Joseph' and Isaac and Abraham played a part in the tribes of the South Judaean mountains and the Negeb. It is above all a striking fact that none of the patriarchs had any association with the 'Leah' tribe of Judah which was of such great historical importance; even the terebinth shrine at Mamre near Hebron which was the scene of a relatively late complex of stories concerning Abraham, was not Judaean but Calebite, and the original tradition of Abraham, which, like that of Isaac, was native to the Negeb, did not extend further to the north at all[1]. The whole tradition of the patriarchs was therefore, like the tradition concerning the exodus from Egypt, presumably a later contribution to the stock of Israelite traditions, though it should be borne in mind that specifically Judaean traditions appear to be almost completely lack-

[1] For this reason alone the idea which first appears in the chronistic history (2 Chron. iii, 1), that the 'mount Moriah' of Gen. xxii, 2 is identical with the Mountain of the Temple in Jerusalem and not situated much further to the south, is quite improbable.

ing in the Pentateuch, and the actual tribe of Judah evidently did not take part in the formation and development of the Pentateuch narrative[1].

However that may be, the tradition of the patriarchs as such became part of the tradition of Israel as whole, at least in the figure of Jacob, and through its connection with the tradition of the exodus from Egypt and the occupation of the land, it acquired a significance as an article of faith among the Israelite confederation of the twelve tribes which far exceeded the original significance of the cults inaugurated by the patriarchs as recipients of the promises. The promises made to the patriarchs had, it was inevitably thought, been fulfilled in the occupation of the land by the clans which considered themselves the descendants of the patriarchs. Through the association of the patriarchs with the other traditions, however, the promises not only acquired a significance for Israel as a whole, but they also became the elements of an act of divine guidance in which the goal of the occupation of the land by a numerous people was not attained simply and suddenly, but by the roundabout way of the sojourn in Egypt and the miraculous deliverance from the hand of the Egyptians. Thus the entry of the tradition of the patriarchs into the faith of the Israelite confederation of the twelve tribes made a substantial contribution to the development of the theological explanation of the divine action which had led Israel to its present position in history, a people of God in the land which its God had given to it[2].

11. *The Covenant of Sinai*

The tradition of Sinai was included in the Pentateuch material at a relatively late date, though before the earliest literary form of the Pentateuch tradition known to us and therefore probably still in the period when the tribes were living on their own, before the beginning of the formation of the Kingdom. It deals with the revelation of God which was bestowed on the Israelites on the holy mountain in the wilderness, which was followed by the binding of the participants to the God who made himself known to them, and their subjection to the will of God declared to them. To the basic material of this Sinai tradition, later to be elaborated, however, belonged the story of the manifestation of God on the mountain amid

[1] The Galilean tribes did not contribute anything to the Pentateuch tradition either.
[2] Cf. G. v. Rad, Verheissenes Land und Jahwes Land im Hexateuch, ZDPV, 66 [1943], pp. 191-204.

mighty and terrifying natural phenomena which the people witnessed in awe at the foot of the mountain (Exod. xix in various later literary forms), and of the establishment of a permanent relationship between God and the people in the form of a covenant similar to the agreements concluded between human partners (Exod. xxiv, 1-11; xxxiv, 1-28, in several variant forms). This making of a covenant signified the submission of the people to the rule of the God who had appeared to them[1] and the acknowledgment of the claim of this God to their exclusive worship even if the oldest tradition did not know anything about a divine law formulated in definite ordinances. At any rate the binding of the people to its God, who might now be described simply as 'the God of Israel', formed the real substance of the covenant-making in the Sinai tradition. Of the various laws which were later gradually added to the story of Sinai as precise indications of the obligations of the covenant, none can be traced back with any certainty to the original content of the tradition and most of them do not even go back to its earliest literary version.

There is no doubt that the Sinai tradition, the basic substance of which is quite unique and unrelated to any other phenomenon in the history of religion, derived from an actual event. It must be admitted that the event is wrapped in mystery, and we are even in the dark about its historical background and context. This is mainly owing to the fact that, to begin with, the Sinai tradition was an independent entity on its own, whose setting was a festival for the making or renewing of the covenant which was regularly observed by the Israelite tribes[2], and that it was only later that it was included among the themes of the Pentateuch as part of a larger narrative complex.

It is not even possible to say anything for certain about where the incident took place on which the tradition is based. The Pentateuch narrative and certain passages outside the Pentateuch refer to the mountain where God revealed himself as 'Sinai', whereas in the deuteronomic-deuteronomistic literature and in some passages which derive from this source the name 'Horeb' appears. The juxtaposition of these two names and their interrelationship is a complete mystery; and only one point is clear, namely that the name 'Sinai' is the older of the two in the tradition that has come

[1] J. Begrich, ZAW, N.F. 19 (1944), pp. 1 ff. has tried to show that the Old Testament word for 'Covenant' connotes not so much a double-sided agreement between equal partners as a more or less one-sided enactment.

[2] More details on this will be found in G. v. Rad, *Das formgeschichtliche Problem des Hexateuchs* (1938), pp. 11 ff.

down to us[1]. We therefore usually give preference to this name. Whereabouts, then, is this 'Sinai'? Until the Byzantine period there is no evidence for the view that it is to be found in the mountainous southern part of the Sinaitic peninsula which is traditionally named after it, between the gulfs of *es-suwēs* and *el-'aḳaba*; whether we think specifically of the *jebel mūsa* = 'mountain of Moses' (7467 ft.) favoured by modern local tradition on account of its name or the *jebel ḳāterīn* = 'mount Catherine' (8664 ft.) with the Monastery of St. Catherine as the vehicle of the Byzantine-Christian tradition, or, finally—for reasons to be mentioned in a moment—of the *jebel serbāl* (6830 ft.) which lies somewhat further to the west. The Byzantine tradition certainly links up with the fact that its 'Sinai' was already traditionally sacred in that period, and the very numerous Nabataean rock inscriptions which have been discovered, especially at the entrances to the massif of the *jebel serbāl* and which derive from Nabataean pilgrims, some of whom came long distances, prove that in the 2nd and 3rd centuries A.D. after the fall of the Nabataean state and after the abolition of the famous sanctuaries in the Nabataean capital of Petra, a mountain shrine in the southern part of the traditional Sinaitic peninsula had attracted Nabataean pilgrims[2]. This certainly presupposes that a pilgrims' shrine had already existed in the district for a long time, and since the sacredness of a place is usually preserved with great tenacity in spite of changes in cult and religion, and is more or less undisturbed by the comings and goings of different human groups and peoples, it may be assumed with great probability that in the district in question there had been a sacred mountain from time immemorial which may well have been the 'Sinai' of the ancient Israelite tradition.

It must be remembered, however, that the positive arguments in favour of this supposition are very weak. There is evidence only from the 6th century onwards of a tradition that the ancient holy mountain which definitely existed in the southern part of the 'Sinaitic' peninsula, was identical with the 'Sinai' of the Old Testament. This means that, measured against the antiquity of the events which took place on 'Sinai', the tradition is very late, and may well be purely secondary. It cannot be argued that there is a tradition of a route for the Israelite wanderings in the wilderness preserved in the Pentateuch narrative which would suggest

[1] The occurrence of the name 'Horeb' in some passages in the Pentateuch narrative is probably entirely secondary; cf. M. Noth, *Überlieferungsgeschichtliche Studien*, I (1943), p. 29.
[2] Cf. the treatment and utilisation of these inscriptions by B. Moritz in *Der Sinaikult in heidnischer Zeit* (Abh. d. Goett. Ges. d. Wiss., N.F. 16, 2), 1916.

placing 'Sinai' in the so-called Sinaitic peninsula. In the first place, it is almost impossible to localise any of the place-names which appear in this connection with any degree of certainty. And then it is very doubtful whether the references to places in the various strata of the Pentateuch narrative are intended to suggest any particular route; even if that were the case, it would not be a primary source, since the Sinai theme was only included in the Pentateuch narrative at a relatively late date and connecting links, such as points on the route to and from Sinai, were only drawn in secondarily. General considerations are useless, however, in any attempt to locate Sinai, since we have no knowledge of the historical and geographical context to which the originally separate Sinai tradition belongs. Presumably pilgrimages were made to the holy place Sinai and such pilgrimages may draw their participants a long way from areas in which they live or move about, particularly if these are areas which have no firmly settled population. The celebrated Sinai inscriptions from the district of the turquoise mines of *serābīṭ el-khādem* in the northern part of the mountains of the Sinai peninsula, to which the Egyptians had laid claim from the earliest times, were discovered by Flinders Petrie in 1905[1], but they must be completely excluded from the 'Sinai' problem, though they have occasionally been called in as evidence. It is true that the inscriptions are written in a Canaanite alphabet and have become famous as the oldest known evidence of this type of script; they are, moreover, obviously written in a Canaanite dialect, but have nothing at all to do with the Israelites. They derive from the 15th century B.C., that is, from a period when it is hardly possible that the Israelites were making pilgrimages to Sinai, and they are to be traced to Canaanite mine-workers in the service of the Egyptians[2].

It is, admittedly, impossible to deny that Sinai may have been situated in the southern part of the traditional Sinaitic peninsula but it cannot be proved, and it is quite possible that it lay elsewhere. In recent times it has often been suggested[3] that it may have lain

[1] Cf. F. Petrie, *Researches in Sinai* (1906). In the meantime further expeditions have examined these inscriptions more closely and discovered new ones.

[2] On the dating, reading and interpretation of these inscriptions cf. recently W. F. Albright, BASOR, 110 (1948), pp. 6 ff.

[3] The thesis that Sinai was located in the northern part of the Sinaitic peninsula (propounded among others by R. Kittel, *Geschichte des Volkes Israel*, I [eds. 5/6 1923], p. 346; A. Jirku, *Geschichte des Volkes Israel* [1931], p. 72) in the vicinity of the springs of Kadesh-barnea ('ēn ḳadēs) may be passed over since there is no evidence for its validity. The assumption that the Israelite tribes spent a long time in this area has no basis in the primary tradition of the Pentateuch (the statement in Deut. i, 46 is based on a secondary historical reconstruction) and the requirement that Sinai should be easily accessible overlooks the complications of events in Israel's early history.

in north-western Arabia east or south-east of the gulf of *el-ʿaḳaba*.
One of the arguments used in support of this theory must be
rejected straight away. It is suggested that Sinai must have lain in
the district occupied by the Midianites, and that, according to the
available information, the Midianites inhabited the eastern side of
the gulf of *el-ʿaḳaba*, even though as nomads they often strayed far
from their proper area. But there is no reference at all to the Midianites in the basic material of the Sinai tradition; it is only in later
connecting narratives such as Exod. iii, 1 ff., Num. x, 29 ff. that
they appear in connection with Sinai owing to a secondary and
questionable identification of Sinai with the 'mountain of God'
mentioned in Exod. xviii (where a meeting took place between
Midianites and Israelites). Another argument, however, deserves
serious consideration. A few details in the description of the circumstances that attended the great revelation of God in Exod. xix
suggest that Sinai was an active volcano, especially the statement
that the whole of Sinai 'was altogether on a smoke, because Yahweh descended upon it in fire; and the smoke thereof ascended
as the smoke of a furnace, and the whole mount quaked greatly'
(verse 18). There is also the strange phenomenon of the 'pillar of
cloud' and 'pillar of fire' which led them on their way (Exod.
xiii, 21 f.) and which can hardly have originated except in the
Sinai tradition. The significance of these very concrete details is
not reduced by the fact that a variant in Exod. xix appears to refer
only to 'thunders and lightnings and a thick cloud upon the mount'
(verse 16). Now no active volcanoes have existed in the traditional
Sinaitic peninsula in historical times but only on the other side of
the gulf of *el-ʿaḳaba* in north-western Arabia in the area of the
caravan route south-east of *tebūk* which leads to southern Arabia,
about 125 miles south-east of *el-ʿaḳaba*. The considerable distance
of this area from Palestine and its borders is not of decisive importance, since it is hardly likely in any case that Sinai was situated
on the route of the migrant Israelites, and was not rather the
goal of a pilgrimage for which even great distances were no real
obstacle. On the other hand, it is just possible that among the tribes
wandering about in southern and eastern Palestine volcanic manifestations which were well known in north-western Arabia were
traditionally thought of as phenomena accompanying theo-
phanies, and that they were mentioned even when the theophany
occurred in a place with no volcanoes. In favour of locating Sinai
in north-western Arabia there is, finally, the point that Num.
xxxiii, 1-49 appears to contain the list of halting-places on a journey

to Sinai and that this route leads from Palestine via el-'akaba not, apparently, to the traditional Sinaitic peninsula but, presumably, to north-western Arabia[1]. To sum up, there are sound reasons for assuming that Sinai lay in the volcanic area of north-western Arabia, but these reasons are not unambiguous or adequate enough to prove the correctness of this assumption.

A few passages in the Old Testament outside the Pentateuch refer to Sinai in striking connection with the name Seir, which was applied pre-eminently to the mountainous country on the eastern side of the wādi el-'araba between the Dead Sea and the gulf of el-'akaba. They refer to the coming of Yahweh from Sinai. This is quite clearly the case in Deut. xxxiii, 2 where 'Yahweh came from Sinai' is paralleled by his 'dawning from Seir upon them'; and in Judges v, 4 too the 'going out of Seir' and 'marching out of the field of Edom' obviously refer to the God coming from Sinai, whether the explicit reference to the name Sinai in the following verse is original or not. On the other hand, in Deut. xxxiii, 2 with Seir there is also a reference to 'Mount Paran'[2], which is almost certainly identical with the modern jebel fārān on the western side of the wādi el-'araba[3]. It seems that these references to place-names are only very approximate, and it is therefore sometimes also assumed that the direction from which Yahweh was expected to come from Sinai was indicated very vaguely from the point of view of Palestine. But the wording in Judges v, 4 suggests that the district of Seir really was the starting-point from which Yahweh came; and since any other certain localisation of Sinai is impossible, the two passages referred to would certainly suggest that the district of Seir should also be borne in mind, though it is impossible exactly to define the scope of the term Seir and so this does not provide a very accurate indication of locality even if a precise factual indication is indeed present at all.

The historical circumstances in which the pilgrimage to Sinai and the divine revelation on Sinai took place are just as doubtful as the place where the revelation occurred. The Pentateuch tradition refers simply to 'Israel' having been at Sinai. But the same thing applies here as in the case of the departure from Egypt and the deliverance 'by the sea'. Since the 'Israel' of the twelve tribes was not formed until the settlement on Palestinian soil and the in-

---

[1] More details in M. Noth, Der Wallfahrtsweg zum Sinai, pJB, 36 [1940], pp. 5 ff.
[2] The naming of Meribath-Kadesh in Deut. xxxiii, 2 which has been obtained by textual conjecture is very uncertain; cf. F. M. Cross and D. N. Freedman, JBL, 67 (1948), p. 193.
[3] 'Mount Paran' appears in a similar context in Hab. iii, 3.

dividual tribes did not become fixed entities until then, the 'Israel' which was present on Sinai cannot have been the 'Israel' of the later period or even a particular group of its tribes. All that can be said is that the divine revelation on Sinai was imparted to clans which later became incorporated in the tribes of Israel, though it is still impossible to say anything definite about their number and structure. What they experienced affected the whole of the later tribes of Israel so powerfully that what took place on Sinai became a substantial and fundamental element in that common Israelite tradition which henceforth inspired Israel as a corporate unit. It is therefore probable that those who participated in the incident that took place on Sinai were not merely incorporated into one of the subsequent tribes of Israel but were rather spread more broadly in the tribes.

There remains the problem of the historical connection between the encounter on Sinai and the departure from Egypt. In the Pentateuch narrative the two events follow on from one another smoothly and fairly directly, in fact the pillars of cloud and fire are made to appear to the Israelites departing from Egypt before the deliverance 'by the sea' (Exod. xiii, 21 f.). But the Sinai theme was not added to the others until much later, and the story of the departure and entry had been presented in short didactic summaries long before any mention was made of Sinai[1]. Meanwhile, the Sinai theme was transmitted independently within the framework of the festival of the making or renewal of the Covenant. In the oldest tradition there was evidently no connection between the two events, and it was only as the Pentateuch narrative developed that all the existing traditions concerning the prehistory of Israel were brought together and referred to 'Israel' as a whole and the story of Sinai was incorporated in a quite natural manner in the story of the departure from Egypt and the occupation of the land. If there was therefore no original traditional connection, it is just as unlikely that there was any historical connection. If, moreover, Israel did not yet exist at all as a unified and fixed entity in this early period, it is quite unlikely that the same elements of what later became 'Israel' took part in the events in and around Egypt and also in the encounter on Sinai. But if they were two different groups, the incident that took place on Sinai becomes an even more completely isolated historical event, about the reality of which there can be no doubt, the historical framework of which is, however,

---

[1] Cf. the discussion of the 'minor historical Credo' and its free variations in the cultic poetry in v. Rad, *op. cit.* pp. 3 ff.

completely beyond our ken. The one and only connection with historical facts known to us is that ancestors of what was later to become 'Israel' took part in it.

This also means that it is impossible to assign a date to it and even impossible to fit it into any sequence of historical events or, above all, to define its relationship in time to the departure from Egypt. All one can do is to draw attention to the following circumstance. The deliverance from Egypt which took place 'by the sea' was so much to the fore in the Israelite tradition, as far as it is known to us, as the precondition of the occupation of the land, that one gets the impression that, as the divine action on which the very existence of Israel was based, it was a more lively and immediate memory than the divine appearance on Sinai, which was only transmitted within the framework of a regular religious observance. In view of this, the encounter on Sinai may be assigned to a comparatively early date and those who took part in it may be regarded as members of a fairly ancient stratum of what later became Israel, whilst the participants in the events which took place in and around Egypt belonged to later generations.

It is even more difficult to establish the content and nature of the event which took place on Sinai than it is to discern the outward circumstances and context. The only historical evidence available to us is the religious rite which bore repeated witness to the fact that God had appeared to the clans that came on pilgrimage to Sinai. The actual incident extends into the realm of the historically inexplicable in the sense outlined above on page 3. But this mysterious event and all that followed from it, the binding of the people to the God who had appeared and their submission to his exclusive ('jealous') claim and will, took place in historically conditioned forms. If a pilgrimage to Sinai was the outward occasion, Sinai must already have been a sacred mountain to which pilgrimages were made, and also a place at which a deity was revered. In fact this older cult of Sinai appears at least in one respect to have had a permanent influence on the faith of Israel. Everything suggests that the divine name of Yahweh derives from the pre-Israelite cult of Sinai as the name of the deity who was worshipped on Sinai. This is suggested by the Pentateuch itself since the name Yahweh is imparted to Moses on his first visit to the subsequent site of the divine revelation (Exod. iii, 14 E.), though the narrative in which this occurs is admittedly comparatively late. Another point in support of this argument is the view, occasionally put forward in the Old Testament, that Sinai was the dwelling-place of Yahweh and that from time to time He comes from Sinai (Judges v, 4 f.; Deut. xxxiii, 2 and also Hab. iii, 1) and that to find Him one must travel to the sacred mount of God in the desert (1 Kings xix, 8 ff)[1]. Indeed, if the supposition is correct that the curious expression זה סיני in Judges v, 5 is to be translated as 'the one from Sinai'[2], then, whether or not the words in the passage are part of the original text, Yahweh was here being called 'the (God) of Sinai' in a stereotyped phrase. If this is a correct interpretation, we may imagine that the decisive revelation of God took place on this site in the name of this same Yahweh in the course of a pilgrimage to the holy mount of the Yahweh of Sinai amidst awe-inspiring, possibly volcanic, natural manifestations.

It has been generally assumed that Moses' historical work had its real centre on Sinai; whatever judgement may be passed on the content of the Moses tradition, that he was the leader of the people on Sinai, the interpreter of what took place there and the organiser of the people of God on the basis of more or less firmly defined formulations of the divine will, seems to be more or less established. This view of Moses has its ultimate source in the deuteronomic-deuteronomistic literature of the Old Testament in which Moses' role as mediator at the giving of the law on the holy mount is regarded as the decisive element in his work; and this is connected with the fact that it considered the theophany on the mountain and the legislation enacted there as the most important of the traditional events of Israel's pre-history. These events were singled out for special treatment[3]. This led to Moses being thought of primarily as the law-giver; and in the later literature of the Old Testament the name Moses appears above all in connection with the 'Law (book) of Moses'. The deuteronomic-deuteronomistic literature naturally refers back to the role which Moses played in the Pentateuch narrative; but in the latter the appearance of Moses on Sinai is merely one link in a long chain and Moses on Sinai is no more and no less the messenger of God and the spokesman of the people than in other events which took place between the departure from

---

[1] The name 'Horeb' in 1 Kings xix, 8 is probably a (deuteronomistic) addition; according to what follows, the 'mount of God' at any rate means the place which is called Sinai in the Pentateuch narrative. On the possibility that, even apart from Elijah, pilgrimages continued to take place for a long time to the holy mountain from Palestine, cf. M. Noth, PJB, 36 (1940), pp. 7 f.

[2] Thus W. F. Albright, JBL, 54 (1935), p. 204.

[3] The deuteronomic law, formulated as a speech by Moses, was naturally specially interested in this. Following the same line, the deuteronomistic history begins in Deut. i, 1 ff. with the sojourn of 'Israel' in Horeb. In the same way too the Priestly strand of the Pentateuch narrative concentrates its whole interest on the legislation on Sinai.

Egypt and the entry into the Promised Land. For from his first appearance among the Israelites who were performing compulsory labour in Egypt, right up to his death shortly before the entry into the Promised Land, Moses is, from the point of view of the Pentateuch, the head of the wandering people, and, though often attacked, he is always confirmed anew by God.

It is this view of Moses, however, as offered by the oldest surviving tradition, which raises the historical problem of his personality. Since the Pentateuch narrative was compiled step by step from a series of originally independent themes, the regular appearance of Moses in most of these themes cannot be original but must be the result of later assimilation; and the inevitable question is to which theme or tradition Moses was originally attached and where we must look for his position in history. The question is extraordinarily difficult to answer[1]. It is highly likely, however, that it is possible to establish, negatively, that, according to the earliest tradition available to us, he was not especially firmly rooted in the Sinai theme, since nothing is said about him in that tradition apart from his general role as a leader. His personality appears in very much more concrete and specific circumstances in other places in the Pentateuch narrative[2]. This suggests that Moses had no historical connection with the event which took place on Sinai. Historically, it is therefore hardly justifiable to describe him as the organiser and law-giver of Israel[3]. The fact that it is impossible to name any specific human person who played an active or interpretative part on that occasion makes the Sinai event even more mysterious.

Nevertheless, the core of the Sinai tradition was a historical occurrence, however little it may be historically grasped in detail. The same thing applies here as in the case of the deliverance 'by the sea'. We can analyse into their individual elements the tradi-

---

[1] Cf. the discussions in M. Noth, *Überlieferungsgeschichte des Pentateuch* (1948), p. 172 ff.

[2] In view of his obviously Egyptian name one might look for his original role within the framework of the deliverance from Egypt, possibly as the messenger of God who announces the imminent action of God (cf. Exod. iii, 16-17aα). But perhaps the most concrete fact of all is the tradition of the tomb of Moses which was situated in a very definite spot. According to this, Moses would belong historically to the phase of the preparations for the occupation of the land by the tribes of central Palestine. More details about his specific role and significance will have been lost in the process of expanding his personality into one of relevance to Israel as a whole, so that it is impossible to say anything definite about it.

[3] To describe him as the 'founder of a religion', or even to speak of a 'Mosaic religion', is quite misleading and incompatible with the Moses tradition as it was developed later on.

tions by which the sacral confederation of the twelve tribes lived, and analyse the historical content of these elements, but we must state quite definitely in conclusion that these traditions have come down to us only as parts of a larger whole, that they are all related to the greater entity of 'Israel' and concerned with Yahweh as the 'God of Israel'. Within this larger whole the God who appeared on Sinai is, needless to say, the same as the God who showed his power in the deliverance 'by the sea'. And the basic elements of this larger whole existed at a very early date. It is true that the growth of the Pentateuch was a long process even in the stage of purely oral transmission which had probably already been very largely concluded before the beginning of the formation of the kingdom, and the beginnings of which go back to the earliest period immediately following the occupation of the land by the tribes. But these beginnings already presuppose the existence of 'Israel' as a unit and the unity of the traditions based on the faith in the 'God of Israel'. The gradually evolving narrative of the Pentateuch thus becomes important as a source of evidence for Israel's unity and consciousness of unity immediately after the occupation of the land, and the gradually developing tradition of the Pentateuch, the religious content of which is quite without parallel, becomes a clear token of the particularity and qualitative uniqueness of Israel's position among the nations. At the same time, how the unit of 'Israel' came into being in the first place remains a problem.

If the twelve tribes of Israel first met on the soil of Palestine, if it was various sections of this 'Israel' that had witnessed the deliverance from Egypt and the meeting with God on Sinai and the occupation of the land from the southern land east of the Jordan: if these events were unrelated in time or content[1] then the question is, how did it happen that 'Israel' felt itself so much a unified whole so soon after the occupation of the land that a framework of traditions came into being which was concerned with the common prehistory of 'Israel'? Clear though the facts themselves are, it is impossible to answer this question with any certainty, since the tradition does not take this process into account and does not say anything about it. Only conjectures are possible, but they must be made, since the question requires at least a feasible answer. And

---

[1] There have been many modern attempts to establish some sort of connection between these happenings, without following the sequence of events transmitted in the Old Testament. In view of the nature of the tradition these attempts must inevitably remain questionable. From the most recent period we may mention Th. J. Meek, *Hebrew Origins* (² 1950); H. H. Rowley, *From Joseph to Joshua* (The Schweich Lectures, 1948 [1950]).

this answer must be based on the supposition that the unity of 'Israel' and its faith did not suddenly appear one fine day but gradually grew up in Palestine from a nucleus. If it were true that the content of the Sinai tradition referred to an event of the fairly remote past, those who took part in the encounter with God on Sinai would have to be included among the earliest of those who later became 'Israel'[1], and, in the course of time, further groups will have joined with them and become associated with their extraordinary and momentous traditions. Among these people the encounter on Sinai would have meant that subjection to the will of God as formulated in a divine law was decisive, and the significance of the divine law and a central judicature would both have their roots therein. When other elements in Palestine were added, which had taken part in the deliverance 'by the sea', the conviction would have at once impressed itself on their minds that the mighty God to whom they owed the deliverance out of Egypt could have been no other than the God who appeared on Sinai. And when Israel formed itself into the sacral confederation of the twelve tribes with the confession of faith in Yahweh as the God of Israel, the various traditions would have coalesced into the image of a coherent prehistory shared by the whole of 'Israel', though in such a way as to make the liberation from Egypt, combined with the promise to the Patriarchs, the main point of interest, as evidence of the mighty deeds of the God of Israel, whilst the ancient Sinai tradition remained on its own in the background to begin with. In the end, however, it was to be incorporated in the total corpus of the traditions. The Sinai tradition would have contributed the name of Yahweh to the corpus of these traditions from the very beginning. It is clear that all this is a hypothesis which it is impossible to prove: it is merely an attempt to provide an answer to an inevitable question.

But what did its special position among the nations, based, according to its tradition, on a peculiar relationship to God, mean for 'Israel'? The earliest tradition says nothing on this point. But one of the earliest theological formulations of the old tradition, the Yahwistic narrative, conceives the history of Israel as part of a universal divine purpose for the blessing of humanity (Gen. xii, 1-3). One can at least wonder whether the Yahwist was not expressing something that even before him and, perhaps even from the very first, was present in the faith of Israel.

---

[1] Anyone who is interested in hypotheses may think of elements which were absorbed by the older group of the so-called 'Leah'-tribes.

PART TWO

THE LIFE OF ANCIENT ISRAEL IN THE PALESTINIAN-SYRIAN WORLD

CHAPTER I

THE CONSOLIDATION OF THE TRIBES IN PALESTINE

12. *Their Relationships with the Earlier Inhabitants of the Land*

THE country in which the Israelite tribes settled was an inhabited land. In the Old Testament the people that had lived in the land in pre-Israelite times are usually called 'Canaanites' without regard to their ethnic differences, and we shall also use the term in that sense[1]. The Canaanite population was concentrated in the numerous fortified cities which were, admittedly, not distributed evenly throughout the country but were most frequent in the plains favoured by nature, whilst there were only occasional cities in the more sterile and mountainous parts of the land. These cities, which were fortresses enclosed by a wall, with houses closely crammed together, with adjoining territory providing the necessary agricultural land, had already passed through their prime in the Bronze Age but they were still the heirs of a rich urban civilisation. The irregular distribution of these cities allowed the Israelites to gain a footing in the parts of the country which were inhabited only sparsely or not at all, areas which were still very largely wooded and still in need of clearing to be suitable for human settlement, without having to turn out the older Canaanite inhabitants from their properties; and on the whole they did not expel them. The Canaanites remained in the land and, generally speaking, were able to continue unimpeded with their own way of life and with their possessions undiminished. But in the places of which they took possession the Israelite tribes frequently established new settlements, which they also called 'cities', and which were, like the Canaanite cities, enclosed by a wall in a situation as fortified as possible or at least not

[1] In addition to the description 'Canaanite' the terms 'Amorite' and 'Hittite' occur in the Old Testament with the same meaning. This use of the term 'Canaanite' does not throw any light on the etymology of the name Canaan which has not yet been completely explained (cf. above, p. 22, note 3) and its original reference to the area of the Phoenician coast, nor on the use of the term 'Canaanite' to describe a group of Semitic dialects native to Syria and Palestine which has become a convention in modern philology.

easily accessible, with densely packed dwellings in a confined space. Usually, however, they did not have such strong and carefully built walls as the Bronze Age cities. Their walls were much less resistant to the destructive influences of time, and the archaeological traces of the Israelites' Iron Age settlements have been obliterated more thoroughly and intensely than those of the earlier Bronze Age cities of the Canaanites.

With the settlement in Palestine, the change over to agriculture as their main activity and the concentration of the population in 'cities' or places like cities, the Israelites' way of life approached that of the indigenous Canaanite population, which lived mainly in special parts of the country but was also represented here and there in the mountains occupied by the Israelites, and they entered into neighbourly relations with them in many places. This led in time to the development of a particular kind of relationship between the two parties. We have only sporadic and more or less fortuitous information about this, but what we have shows that their mutual relations varied enormously according to time and place.

On the whole, the Israelite tribes, who had come from quite different circumstances, regarded the Canaanite way of life as alien and it remained alien so long as the independent character of the Canaanites survived in the land. This is true at any rate of the period preceding the formation of the kingdom in Israel and true also of the Israelite circles which deliberately maintained their old authentic traditions. In spite of their settlement in Palestine, the genuine urban culture, whose rich diversity was maintained even in the Iron Age, continued to be alien to the Israelites, who were used to simplicity and straightforwardness; what the essentially agricultural and cattle-rearing Israelites considered 'Canaanite', above all, was the interest in industry, commerce and profit-making which was rooted in their urban civilisation. At a later date the merchant and trader could be described simply as a 'Canaanite' (Isa. xxiii, 8; Zeph. i, 11; Zech. xiv, 21; Prov. xxxi, 24; Job xl, 30 (=xli, 6 in the English Bible), and this activity was thereby characterised as something alien to Israel's own character; in Hos. xii, 8 (= 7 in the English Bible) there is a specific reference to the deceitful conduct of such 'Canaanites'[1]. The Israelites, whose tribal organisation was based on the equal rights of all the free members of the tribe, regarded the social stratification in the

---

[1] When Israelites take part in this behaviour, they turn themselves into 'Canaanites', which is probably the meaning of this difficult sentence in Hosea.

Canaanite cities as alien to their own social outlook: here there was a ruling, property-owning aristocracy on the one hand, with a feudal lord at the summit, who called himself a king or was at any rate usually called by that title in the Old Testament, and, on the other hand, a subject population devoted primarily to agricultural work. The military technique of chariot fighting as practised by the ruling classes of the cities was alien to the Israelites, and was also an object of terror to them. To begin with, the tribes which were accustomed to take the field with a militia of fighting men bearing their own weapons, felt thoroughly inferior to these contingents of iron chariots[1] and as a result they did not, generally speaking, dare to undertake any warlike attacks on Canaanite cities (Jos. xvii, 16, 18; Judges i, 19; iv, 3, 13) where the mode of fighting not only filled them with feelings of inferiority but inspired them with awe. Above all, however, it was the life and faith of the Canaanites that was alien to the Israelite tribes. They seemed to them to be morally inferior and degenerate, lustful and unprincipled. In the original form of Gen. ix, 20-27 'Canaan', the youngest son of Noah, the representative of the Canaanites, is described as shameless and perverse. The intention behind the story told in Gen. xxvi, 7-11[2] is to point out that anyone who comes into the region of a Canaanite city must reckon with the possibility of his wife falling victim to the inhabitants' covetousness and himself, as the woman's husband, running the danger of being treacherously murdered. A girl who appears unprotected in the vicinity of a Canaanite city may easily be raped by one of the inhabitants, possibly even the son of the city king himself (cf. Gen. xxxiv, 1 f.). For the Israelite tribes, who were used to the strict discipline of a patriarchal society, all this moral laxity was contemptible and shocking. It was no doubt bound up to some extent with the special character of the Canaanite cult to which the Israelites, with their devotion to the demands of a stern deity, were particularly antagonistic. The cults which flourished among the Canaanites were the immemorial rites of the great fertility-bestowing mother-deity, generally called Astarte in Canaan, and of a youthful deity who represented the annual blossoming and dying of vegetation. These cults included the celebration of a 'holy marriage' (ἱερὸς γάμος) at a holy place with

---

[1] These contingents of chariots (רכב is used as a collective noun) consisted of war chariots, which were naturally not made entirely of iron but only provided with iron fittings. The chariots were made of wood and when the Israelites captured them they burnt them (Jos. xi, 6, 9 [the single chariot is called מרכבה]; cf. Ps. xlvi, 10 [=9 in the English Bible]).

[2] The transfer of this scene to Egypt in Gen. xii, 10-20 is a secondary tradition.

female representatives of the deity and 'sacred' prostitution and the cultic sacrifice of female chastity. There was also the cult of the multiform Baal, the fairly ancient Baal of heaven, and the numerous local Baals which were also givers of life and fertility and held sway in the sphere of sensual life. The Israelites were bound to reject all this, especially the worship of female deities.

On the other hand, however, they had inevitably to establish certain relations with this Canaanite world. The change over to a settled and predominantly agricultural way of life based on the land involved an adaptation to the new conditions, a readjustment to the customs current among the previous inhabitants, since ideas and attitudes are intimately bound up with a people's whole way of life. I do not mean that considerable elements among the Israelites succumbed to the danger of wholesale Canaanisation and simply became Canaanites even in the sphere of worship, and so were absorbed into the Canaanite population; naturally we have no information on this point but we must assume that a certain amount of assimilation occurred. The degree of assimilation will hardly have been on a large scale, however, and is therefore of no great historical significance. On the other hand, even the broad masses of the Israelites who remained fully aware of the differences separating them from the Canaanites, inevitably adopted something of the Canaanite character and way of life. This also applies to the religious sphere which was necessarily closely connected with the whole way of life. The very fact that the Israelite tribes conducted their worship largely at the age-old shrines of the land led to the adoption of the native cult-traditions. This is true of the central amphictyonic rite (cf. above, p. 91 ff., 97 ff.) and even more of the numerous local rites observed by the tribes or clans that had now become local communities. The point is not that foreign gods were worshipped in these places, but the forms that were traditional in the land had a decisive influence on the Israelites' rites. Thus, the great agricultural religious festivals (cf. above, p. 97), which were closely connected with the seasons of the year in Palestine were taken over, and the whole system of sacrifice in general followed the ancient traditions of the country. Even though the specifically Canaanite rites of which we have spoken were excluded as essentially foreign, a far-reaching process of Canaanisation took place in the field of worship. The Israelite faith entered quite concretely into the world in which the Israelites were now living. In daily life and work a strong approximation resulted quite automatically from the fairly similar outward conditions under which both peoples were now living; and as long as they were new-comers the Israelites no doubt learnt and adopted a good deal from the Canaanite inhabitants.

It is therefore not surprising that in spite of all their feeling of alienation the Israelites' relations with their Canaanite neighbours were by no means entirely hostile. Sporadic information throws some light on the multiplicity of the various relationships which developed between Israelites and Canaanites in the course of time. The information available is nothing like sufficient to enable us to survey the whole field, but it does show what a variety of developments was possible. So far as relationships were established at all, by reason of neighbourhood or communications, a peaceful *modus vivendi* was often found possible. One way was for one of the parties to enter more or less voluntarily into some form of dependence on the other. In the period of the occupation of the land the tribes of Issachar, Zebulun and Asher, which settled on the borders of the plain of Jezreel and the plain of Acco, apparently entered into a feudal relationship with the city governments in the plains, and probably received a share of the profits accruing from their rich estates in return for their services. They did not have to surrender their identity as members of the Israelite confederation, and did not remain in this state of dependence permanently, but to begin with they did, nevertheless, enter into this one-sided relationship. The fact that the ancient city of Shechem, which lies in a rather isolated position in the mountains of Central Palestine, was admitted into the society of the tribe of Manasseh with the status of a Manassite clan, forms a counterpart to this example. In the great list of clans in Num. xxvi which is arranged according to tribes, Shechem appears among the Manassite clans (verse 31b) and hence within the organisation of the tribe of Manasseh as a minor member of the Israelite confederation of the twelve tribes, and probably also as a participant in its divine worship, without abandoning the political and social structure of the old political order (see below, p. 152 f. on Judges ix). We have no idea how this came about, and can only presume that the fact that Israelite clans had taken part in the worship at the shrine of Shechem from a fairly early period (cf. Jacob's association with this shrine), played a part, and that for a time Israel's central amphictyonic rite was performed there. Anyway, this attachment of Shechem to Manasseh must have taken place very early on, since it is taken for granted not only in the list in Num. xxvi which goes back to the pre-monarchical period, but also in the story contained in Judges ix. In a similar way, the four Canaanite cities mentioned in Jos. ix, 17, which were situated in the mountains north-west of Jerusalem, appear as belonging to the tribe of Benjamin. The cities in question are Gibeon (not yet identified for certain), Chephirah (the modern *khirbet kefîre*), Beeroth (not yet identified precisely) and Kiriath-Jearim (*dēr el-azhar* near *el-ḳerye*). Their territories appear in the description of the frontiers for Benjamin (Jos. xviii, 11-20) which derives from the pre-monarchical period, as part of Benjamin's tribal area[1]. On the other hand, however, their names do not appear in the list in Num. xxvi, so that we have perhaps to assume that they were not received into the tribal unit of Benjamin until after this list had been compiled. Again, we know nothing as to how the annexation took place; in Jos. ix we have an aetiological narrative which takes for granted the fact that the four cities belong to Benjamin, and which undertakes to explain it. It amalgamates it, however, with the quite different fact that Gibeonites had to serve as 'hewers of wood and drawers of water' at the shrine of Gilgal near Jericho.

The facts mentioned so far indicate that in the parts of the land which were crowded with Canaanite cities, above all in the plains, the Canaanites had the upper hand to begin with, whereas in the mountains the Israelite tribes prevailed over the more scattered cities, without necessarily having recourse to arms. But in such a distinctly intermediary area as the hill country between the southern Palestinian mountains and the southern part of the maritime plain, what was apparently a fundamentally peaceful process of mutual assimilation ensued. It was here that the vigorous tribe of Judah was seeking to expand, and it found a chance to do so in this direction from its settlements in the mountains: the result was co-existence between Judaeans and Canaanites, with connubium and other friendly relationships. The position of the Canaanite cities in this area does not seem to have been affected and the Judaeans only settled in intervening smaller settlements which they found when they arrived or which they established for themselves. This is clear from Gen. xxxviii. Admittedly, it is impossible in this passage to separate the element of tribal history, which is undoubtedly present, from the purely narrative element.

---

[1] This description of the frontier must be considered with some reserve, since the system of describing the frontiers in the book of Joshua does not merely refer to the actual dwelling-places of the tribes in Palestine (cf. above, p. 53). Moreover, the later editor of the system included Kiriath-Jearim in Judah. But in connection with Jos. ix, 17 historical significance must obviously be attributed to the incorporation of the four city territories in the tribal area of Benjamin.

Certainly the whole passage cannot be derived from tribal history. But the story of the birth of Shelah, who, according to Num. xxvi, 20, was the *heros eponymus* of a Jewish clan, is certainly a personification of a chapter of tribal history. According to Gen. xxxviii, 5, Shelah was born in Chezib (=Achzib, Jos. xv, 44). This was a small place in the hill country which is probably identical with the modern *tell el-bēḏa*[1]. According to Gen. xxxviii his father was Judah the tribal ancestor, whereas his mother was a Canaanite. His descendants, the Shelanites, who are reckoned to Judah, certainly settled in the region of Chezib[2].

It is true that the contacts between Israelites and Canaanites, so far as they occurred at all, were not entirely of a peaceful nature. Warlike encounters between them evidently occurred at a very early stage. The information we have is only sporadic and fortuitous but it gives us some idea of what may have happened, without allowing us to survey the encounters as a whole. Not surprisingly, we learn from Israelite sources only about the conflicts which ended in victory for the Israelites. No doubt the contrary also occurred. The fact that the Canaanite city rulers were able for the most part to maintain their properties is in general to be attributed to the fact that the tribes did not dare to attack them, but in isolated cases it may have been due to the fact that the cities were able to defend themselves against the encroachments of the Israelites by force of arms. Occasionally, the cities themselves probably attacked their unwanted and troublesome new neighbours, and they may have been successful in wresting this or that piece of their territory from them again. But more significant incidents of this kind are hardly likely to have occurred. The Israelite tribes were also capable of warding off such attacks. We have an example in Jos. x, 1-15 in the story of the Battle of Gibeon. The core of the tradition is apparently that the 'kings of the Amorites that dwell in the mountains'[3] (verse 6) undertook an attack on the neighbouring Israelites—to judge from the site of the battle, the tribes in question may have been Benjamin and Ephraim—but were thoroughly routed[4]. Such

[1] This identification has been suggested by K. Elliger, ZDPV, 57 (1934), pp. 123 f.

[2] 1 Chron. ii and iv also contain a series of references which appear to indicate that the Judaeans settled between the cities of the hill country; cf. M. Noth, ZDPV, 55 (1932), pp. 97 ff.

[3] The name 'Amorites' is used here in the same general sense as the name 'Canaanite'. The cities of these 'Amorite kings' were probably situated somewhere in the vicinity of Gibeon.

[4] The present connection between Jos. ix and Jos. x can hardly be an original element in the tradition. It might be asked whether the annexation by the tribe of Benjamin of the four cities mentioned in Jos. ix, 17 was not rather a result of the Battle of Gibeon

incidents may occasionally have taken place at other times and places. There may have been plenty of such incidents, but it should be remembered that, on the whole, they were very limited in extent and significance.

Above all, however, the Israelite tribes succeeded more than once in conquering individual Canaanite cities by force of arms and obtaining possession of their settlement and territory. According to the information available, the cities in question were in more or less isolated spots away from the great city-state territories. In Judges i, 10-15 = Jos. xv, 14-19 (cf. Jos. xiv, 12) there is a reference to the fact that the Calebites[1] had conquered the city of Hebron and the Othnielites, to whom they were related, had conquered the neighbouring city of Debir. They were, at any rate, subsequently in possession of these cities and the tradition which derives from this fact may be accurate in its reference to a conquest by force of arms. According to the note in Num. xiii, 22b, Hebron was formerly a Canaanite city; and the same may be true of Debir, though there is no positive archaeological[2] or literary[3] evidence on this point. Farther to the north, according to Judges i, 22-26, the 'house of Joseph' conquered the city of Bethel which was situated right on the southern border of its settlement. Archaeological evidence shows that Bethel (the modern *bētīn*) was already a city in the Middle and Late Bronze Age. According to Judges i, 23b (cf. Gen. xxviii, 19b and elsewhere) this city had previously been called Luz, whilst the name Bethel probably belonged originally merely to the shrine that lies to the east of it (on the site of the modern *burj bētīn*), where Israelite clans had probably taken part in the worship from very early times: the name was probably only subsequently transferred to the city. It may be that the change of

and therefore at any rate indirectly a consequence of a warlike encounter: in other words, not simply an act of peaceful agreement, as was assumed above on p. 146. On the analysis of the historical tradition of Jos. x cf. M. Noth, PJB, 33 (1937), pp. 22 ff.

[1] In Judges i, 10 the name 'Judah' may be assumed to have been originally 'Caleb' (as in Jos. xv, 14).

[2] The locating of Debir at *tell bēt mirsim* (about 18 m. north-north-east of Beersheba), which is advocated above all by the eminently successful excavator of *tell bēt mirsim*, W. F. Albright (cf. AASOR, 12 [1932]; 13 [1933]; 17 [1938]; 21/22 [1943]), is very questionable. To judge from the references in the Old Testament, one would prefer to look for it nearer to Hebron in the mountains.

[3] The assumption that Debir is called by its older name of Kiriath-Sepher (Jos. xv, 15 f.; Judges i, 11 f.) in the form of *bt-ṭpr* in the Egyptian *Pap. Anastasi*, I, 22, 5 from the period of the Ramessides (about the 13th century B.C.) must be abandoned; *bt-ṭpr* was probably somewhere quite different. An older name, Kiriath-Arba, has also come down to us for Hebron (Jos. xiv, 15; xv, 13; Judges i, 10 and elsewhere). Were these two cities renamed after the above-mentioned conquest and resettlement? Cf. above, p. 33, note 1.

name was connected with the occupation by the 'house of Joseph'. In the land east of Jordan the tribe of Gad succeeded in conquering the city of Heshbon (the modern *ḥesbān*), which was directly adjacent to its territory, and ruled by the city king Sihon, as the old song of victory in Num. xxi, 27-30 informs us, to which the framework of a story was added in Num. xxi, 21-31. In the remote uppermost part of the Jordan Valley the city of Hazor (the modern *tell waḳḳas*), of whose existence in the Middle and Late Bronze Age there is documentary evidence in Egyptian sources and the Amarna tablets, was conquered and destroyed by Israelites, and probably by the neighbouring tribe of Naphtali, and its territory annexed. This event forms the basis of the story contained in Jos. xi, 1-15. In the late Canaanite period the city of Laish (the modern *tell el-ḳādi*) which was situated near the sources of the Jordan—a fact which is confirmed by Egyptian sources—was, according to Judges xviii, 27 f. captured and settled in by the tribe of Dan in their search for land, and they called the city by their own name of Dan. It is true that the tribe of Dan thereby entered into some kind of dependence on the Phoenician coastal cities which apparently ruled over Laish and its territory[1].

In the Old Testament tradition all these conquests are directly related to the occupation of the land[2]. It should be remembered, however, that the occupation was a long process which certainly did not begin with the conquest of cities. On the contrary, the attacks on isolated Canaanite cities probably did not take place until the Israelite tribes had established themselves in their vicinity, in uninhabited or only sparsely inhabited areas and had thus gained a footing for themselves in Palestine. The occupation of Canaanite cities which were situated for the most part on the borders of Israelite territory, may be thought of at most as the very last stage in the process of occupation, if it is not in fact even better to think of it as a development and rounding off of the process of occupation, and a coming to terms with the earlier inhabitants after the real occupation was over[3].

[1] Cf. the striking reference to Sidon in connection with Laish in Judges xviii, 7, 28 and see above, pp. 79 f.

[2] The well-known stories of the conquest of the cities of Jericho (Jos. vi) and Ai (Jos. viii) have not been taken into consideration. They are in fact aetiological legends based on the fact that these cities were in ruins. But the destruction of these cities—as is certain in the case of Ai (the modern *et-tell* near *dēr dubwān*), and probable in that of Jericho (the modern *tell es-sulṭān* near *eriḥa*)—had taken place before the Israelites' occupation, so that the latter were able simply to take possession of the ruins and the surrounding areas.

[3] Cf. especially A Alt, PJB, 35 (1939), pp. 14 ff. = *Kleine Schriften zur Geschichte des Volkes Israel*, I (1953), pp. 131 ff.

We only hear once of a war of any importance waged by Israelite tribes against Canaanite cities within the city-state system proper, that is, in one of the plains; this is no accident, since such events were obviously quite exceptional. The prose narrative of Judges iv and the ancient song of victory in Judges v are concerned with the famous victory which Israelite tribes obtained over the chariot armies of king Sisera in the plain of Jezreel 'in Taanach by the waters of Megiddo' (Judges v, 19). We know little about the background of this victory[1]. Sisera was king in Harosheth (*tell 'amr* near *el-ḥāriṭīye*) at the north-western end of the plain of Jezreel. His name is possibly Illyrian[2] and, if so, he may have been a member of the ruling class of the 'Sea Peoples' (see above, p. 37 f.). It may be that he exercised a kind of sovereignty over the cities in the plain of Jezreel which were occupied partly by 'Canaanites' and partly by 'Sea Peoples', and perhaps in the plain of Acco too. According to the Old Testament tradition the conflict was started by the neighbouring tribes of Naphtali and Zebulun (Judges iv, 6, 10)[3]. There is no mention of the cause of the conflict and one can merely presume that the reaction was provoked by the fact that the Galilean tribes on the borders of the plains were in a state of dependence on the cities in these plains (cf. above, p. 78 f.) But the lead was taken by the tribe of Naphtali which was in no such condition of dependence. Barak, a man of Naphtali from Kedesh in Naphtali (the modern *ḳedes*) became the leader, inspired by a 'prophetess' called Deborah (Judges iv, 4). This is the first known example of charismatic leadership among the Israelite tribes. In the name of the God of Israel, a man is summoned to a particular undertaking by a messenger ('prophet'), and though he has no official status of any kind, he embarks on this task and finds followers, as one called by God; and the war which is waged is a 'holy war'[4]. Barak's call was answered by his own tribe of Naphtali and the neighbouring tribe of Zebulun. From Kedesh where his followers were assembled, they proceeded to the holy mountain of Tabor in the north-eastern corner of the plain of Jezreel, and from there they sallied forth against the chariots of Sisera which had gathered meanwhile in the plain of Jezreel. They achieved a complete victory over this dreaded

[1] For conjectures on this point see A. Alt, ZAW, N.F. 19 (1944), pp. 72 ff.
[2] Thus A. Alt, ZAW, N.F. 19 (1944), p. 78, note 3.
[3] In the Song of Victory in Judges v there is a secondary extension of the circle of participants.
[4] Cf. G. v. Rad, *Deuteronomium-Studien* (1947). pp. 31 ff. (E.T. pp. 45 ff.) and especially G. v. Rad, *Der heilige Krieg im alten Israel.*

enemy, and this the Israelites could attribute only to the mighty aid of their God, in whose name Barak had entered the fight. Sisera himself was forced to flee on foot after the power of his chariots had been broken, and he was slain in the tent of a Kenite sojourning in the vicinity where he had sought refuge. The victors pursued and destroyed the enemy forces.

There is no reference to the results which followed from this event. It is not said, and it is therefore unlikely, that the Israelites proceeded to conquer and take possession of the cities in the plains either as a whole or one by one. The way they were later incorporated in the kingdom of Israel (cf. below, p. 163 f.) definitely indicates that they continued to exist as Canaanite cities. It may be assumed, however, that, though there is nothing to this effect in the tradition, the dependence of the Israelite tribes on the Canaanite cities now came to an end, if indeed it had lasted as long as this, and that at any rate these tribes henceforth enjoyed complete freedom just like the other tribes. But the most important result of the victory from the point of view of the Israelite tribes was undoubtedly the experience which they gained of being, with the help of their God, a match for and even superior to the might of the Canaanite chariots. This meant the disappearance of their feeling of insecurity and fear of the military technique and power of the earlier inhabitants of the land; and so it became possible for the tribes to attain a position of superiority over the Canaanite city state-system. At the same time, this victory proved that the God who, according to the traditions of the sacral confederation of the twelve tribes had intervened with his mighty aid in their early history and had led the tribes into the Promised Land, was still a living force in the present, and helping the tribes to maintain themselves in the Promised Land against its previous inhabitants. All this was of fundamental importance beyond the immediate circle of the tribes that had taken a direct part in the fight. This is also shown by the song of victory in Judges v, the so-called Song of Deborah, which is one of the oldest passages in the Old Testament. It links up with the prehistoric traditions by speaking at the beginning of the coming of Yahweh from Sinai and celebrates the great occurrence as an event of concern to all the Israelite tribes, except that the remote and somewhat isolated tribes in the south are not taken into account.

We have no evidence at all on which to assign a date to the victory over Sisera[1], even very roughly, but we shall not be far

[1] As this victory does not appear to have had any direct and tangible effects on Canaanite cities, it is impossible to date it archaeologically—for example from the

wrong if we assume that it presupposes the lapse of a certain time during which the tribes were settling down and securing and developing their territories. It may be assumed that this victory marked the end of the process of consolidation on the soil of Palestine and gave final definition to the Israelites' position in relation to the previous inhabitants. Admittedly, this relationship was full of latent tensions owing to the differences between the character of the two peoples, and even when the relationship was firmly regulated these tensions were bound to lead to greater or smaller conflicts.

We hear of such a conflict in the story of Abimelech, the 'son of Jerubbaal'[1] (Judges ix). This was an occurrence of a particular kind which arose out of the special relationship between the city of Shechem and the tribe of Manasseh, but it is of general significance inasmuch as it indicates how the differences between the political and social structure of the Israelites and Canaanites easily led to tension and conflict, even when a definite agreement between the two parties was in existence. The same cause will have led to friction in other places too, even though the tradition does not mention it[2]. According to Judges ix the background of Abimelech's undertaking was the incorporation of the old Canaanite city of Shechem in the unit of the tribes of Manasseh (cf. above, p. 145). This incorporation evidently involved Israelite-Canaanite intermarriage in this area. At this time the clan of Jerubbaal, which was living in the city of Ophrah, had the lead in Manasseh, and this predominance extended to the city-state of Shechem. An ambitious member of the clan, Abimelech, whose mother was a Shechemite, was able to exploit the dislike of the old Shechemite ruling aristocracy[3] for the rule of the clan of Manasseh, and with their aid he succeeded in killing off most of the other male members of the clan of Jerubbaal. He thereupon had himself made king of Shechem by the aristocracy of the city: he was himself a Shechemite, at least on

historical vicissitudes of the city of Megiddo (the modern *tell el-mutesellim*) which can be reconstructed from archaeological evidence; cf. especially A. Alt, ZAW, N.F. 19 (1944), pp. 67-85.

[1] The equation Jerubbaal = Gideon (Judges vii, 1; viii, 35; cf. vi, 25-32) is certainly secondary, though possibly fairly old; it is probably based on the fact that Gideon's home was also in Ophrah. But we probably owe to it the preservation of the story of Abimelech as an appendix to the stories of Gideon.

[2] The relationship of the tribe of Benjamin with the four Canaanite cities which were annexed to it (cf. above, p. 146) does not seem to have continued without difficulties. At least, we hear that the Benjaminite Saul as king later intervened with force in some of these cities; cf. 2 Sam. xxi, 1 ff. (Gibeon) and 2 Sam. iv, 2, 3 (Beeroth).

[3] At that time Shechem was governed not by a city king but aristocratically—there is evidence to prove that Canaanite cities were occasionally governed in that way even in the Amarna period.

his mother's side. But he did not want to be merely a minor Canaanite city-king in the old Canaanite style: probably with some pressure and force he extended his rule to the Manassite and Ephraimite clans living in the mountains around Shechem[1]. His dominion thereby became a hybrid and inorganic structure and it was this that ruined him after a fairly short time. As he refused to be merely the city king of Shechem, but wanted to rule as far as possible over Israelite tribes as well, Abimelech moved his residence in due course from Shechem to Arumah (the modern el-'orme, about 6 miles south-east of Shechem in Ephraimite territory), and installed an official (פָּקִיד) as his deputy in the city-state. The Shechemites, who had helped him to become king, took offence and charged him with disloyalty. They gathered in force to rebel against Abimelech. Thereupon Abimelech attacked the city—evidently with the mercenaries he had levied with the Shechemites' money to exterminate the clan of Jerubbaal and to establish his rule—and conquered and destroyed it. But he had thereby destroyed the basis of his own kingship and this soon led to his destruction. He apparently still tried to extend his rule in one direction and another by conquests in Manassite-Ephraimite territory. At least we find him finally occupied with an attack on the city of Thebez (the modern ṭūbāṣ, about 9 miles north-east of Shechem). In this attack he lost his life. His kingship, which was entirely his own personal achievement, thus came to a rapid end.

The emergence of Abimelech was merely an episode. It apparently had no historical consequences[2]. One can hardly call this adventure of Abimelech a prelude to the subsequent formation of a kingdom in Israel. After his death the relationship between Shechem and Manasseh will have reverted to the old arrangement. But the story of Abimelech is remarkable as evidence of the tensions existing between the Israelite and Canaanite systems, which he tried to turn to his own advantage, but which finally destroyed him. It is also worthy of note that, in the tradition that has come down to us, Abimelech was the first Israelite—though on his mother's side he was an Israelite-Canaanite half-caste—to call himself a 'king'.

[1] Already in the Amarna period the city king Labaya of Shechem had extended his rule far over the mountains of Central Palestine (cf. A. Alt, *Die Landnahme der Israeliten in Palästina* [1925], pp. 18 ff. = *Kleine Schriften zur Geschichte des Volkes Israel*, I [1953], pp. 108 ff.). At this time, however, this area will hardly have been already occupied by Israelite tribes. Labaya therefore found a different situation from the one which existed at the time of Abimelech.

[2] It is at least possible, but by no means certain, that the transfer of the amphictyonic central sanctuary from Shechem to Bethel was connected with the disturbances of the Abimelech period (cf. above, pp. 94 f.).

13. *The Israelites' Struggles with their Neighbours*

On the eastern side the Israelite confederation of tribes had a series of neighbours who had come into Palestine from the desert and steppe, and settled there about the same time as the Israelite tribes, and in a similar way, as part of the same movement. They had settled in the, to some extent, favourable and fertile areas on the eastern border of Palestine, and had formed themselves into separate nations in the course of time, especially in the southern part of the land east of Jordan. They had here organised themselves into states at a comparatively early date. We know almost nothing about the gradual process of their occupation of the land and their consolidation in it, as there are no records. All that can be established archaeologically is that the southern part of the land east of Jordan, northwards as far as the region of the Jabbok, had hardly been settled permanently in the Middle and Late Bronze Age, and only began to be occupied with permanent settlements in the course of the 13th century[1]. To begin with there was no occasion for warlike conflicts with the peoples here coming into being, closely related to the Israelite tribes in character and each having its own area. But the striving to extend their own territory, which is always characteristic of vigorous peoples, did occasionally lead to conflicts, and according to the traditions that have come down to us the initiative appears to have been taken by the eastern neighbours, whose living space was confined by the desert on the east, and who naturally tried to attack westwards from time to time. The Israelite tribes were therefore forced to defend their territory against these attacks.

In the southernmost land east of Jordan, south of the *wādi el-ḥesa*, which flows into the southern end of the Dead Sea, the Edomites had settled in the mountains east of the great cleft of the *wādi el-ʿaraba*. They had formed a state early on with kings, possibly elected (cf. Gen. xxxvi, 31-39). Edom was situated in a remote spot with no direct frontier with the Israelites, so that there was no occasion for hostilities.

North of the *wādi el-ḥesa*, on the eastern side of the Dead Sea, was the region of the Moabites. Their land extended northwards as far as the Arnon (the modern *sēl el-mōjib*); but throughout their history they aspired to acquire the fertile plain north of the Arnon, and at various times they did in fact possess various parts of this plain. Their only chance of extending their possessions was in

[1] Cf. N. Glueck, AASOR, 14 (1934) and 15 (1935).

a northerly direction beyond the Arnon; in this area they came into contact with the Israelite tribes. To begin with, the table-land north of the Arnon appears to have been occupied in the course of the 13th century B.C. with all kinds of minor urban domains such as Heshbon, which the neighbouring Gadites were able to conquer in the end. It is impossible to say for certain who had founded these cities, of which there were a few also south of the Arnon[1], or who lived and ruled in them[2]. South of the Arnon they were absorbed at an early date by the Moabite state as it came into being, whilst north of the Arnon between Moab and Israel they were possibly able to maintain their independence somewhat longer. The Moabites formed a state of their own at a relatively early period and, like the Edomites, they had kings long before even the idea of a monarchy arose in Israel. It is true that we know nothing at all about how the state was developed in Moab, and it may be doubted whether a monarchy ruling over the whole country existed here from the very beginning. One has the impression that the Moabite kings whom we meet in the earliest period in the Old Testament were minor kings of whom there may, to begin with, have been several ruling simultaneously in Moab.

The earliest state of affairs which it is possible to discern is that the Moabites had advanced fairly far to the north of the Arnon —at least along the mountains which accompany the eastern border of the Dead Sea, assuming that the cities farther to the east, in the centre of the table-land, were still independent at that time[3]. Between Heshbon (*hesbān*), and the northern end of the Dead Sea, there lay the mountain summit of Peor with the once-famous shrine Baal-Peor, in a promising spot on a terrace of the mountains east of Jordan, which rise up from the Jordan Valley on the site of the modern *khirbet esh-shēkh jāyil*; Israelites—primarily members of the neighbouring tribe of Gad—and Moabites met at this shrine. It was apparently a frontier shrine, and at the time Moabites were living in the immediate vicinity. This situation is the background of the short narrative in Num. xxv, 1-5 and above all of the stories of Balaam in Num. xxii-xxiv[4]. The latter also show that the

[1] According to the archaeological evidence an example of this is the ancient site of *el-bālū'a*.

[2] Cf. A. Alt, PJB, 36 (1940), pp. 29 ff., which deals particularly with the stele of *el-bālū'a*, which, curiously enough, bears an inscription in Cretan linear B.

[3] More details on the following will be found in M. Noth, ZAW, N.F. 19 (1944), pp. 17 ff.

[4] It is true that in the traditional context the stories of Balaam are transferred to the period of the occupation of the land, but originally they presupposed that the Israelites had already consolidated their territorial possessions.

neighbourly relationships were not always friendly. It is true that there is no mention of warlike altercations with Balak, the 'king of the Moabites' in the stories of Balaam, and in the end the *status quo ante* between Israel and Moab remains unchanged, but they do presuppose that the two parties were enemies in spite of their joint participation in the cult of Baal-Peor.

In this early period, however, the possessions of the Moabites even extended as far as the Jordan Valley west of Beth-Peor. Here lay the ערבות מואב on the east side of the Jordan opposite the ערבות ירחו on the other side; these refer to the parts in the Jordan Valley (הערבה) which belonged to Moab, or to the city-state of Jericho. Now the term ערבות מואב only occurs in the latest literary stratum of the Pentateuch narrative; but it must have originated in a much earlier period, and only the early period dealt with here is feasible. The most southerly part of the Jordan Valley on the northern border of the Dead Sea, on the east side of the Jordan, had there-fore at one time been the possession of the Moabites, at the very time when they were neighbours of the Gadites at the shrine of Baal-Peor. This extension of Moabite territory right down into the Valley of the Jordan is presupposed in the story of Ehud in Judges iii, 12-30. According to this, the Moabites had even attacked at one time beyond the Jordan and occupied the territory of the former city-state of Jericho, and forced its Benjaminite owners to pay tribute to them, until in the end the Benjaminite Ehud succeeded in killing Eglon the 'king of Moab'[1] when paying the tribute and, exploiting the confusion this caused among the Moab-ites, he destroyed the Moabite garrison on the west side of the Jordan, with Benjaminites and Ephraimites whom he swiftly sum-moned to his aid. The aim of warding off the attacks of the Moabites on the land west of the Jordan was thereby achieved, and the situation restored, which was evidently considered normal at the time, namely that the lowest part of the course of the Jordan was the Israelite-Moabite frontier; the possibility of crossing over to the eastern side of the Jordan is not envisaged at all in the story of Ehud.

Nevertheless this still implies a quite extraordinarily wide exten-sion of Moabite territory in a north-westerly direction. But this situation did not last very long. At least, at the beginning of the Israelite monarchy, we already find not only a great part of the plain north of the Arnon under the rule of the Israelite state, but it

---

[1] Unfortunately it is not clear from the story of Ehud where the murder of Eglon took place (whether it was west or east of the Jordan).

was evidently already inhabited by Israelites to some extent. This can hardly have happened all at once and will not have been possible without warlike struggles and, possibly, numerous minor battles. We are in the dark about all this, since the tradition regarding the pre-monarchical period of the Israelites' life in Palestine mainly records such events as are linked with particular leaders. It was, at any rate, the tribe of Gad, which was able to extend its territory at the expense of the Moabites. Perhaps the successful conquest of the neighbouring city-state of Heshbon had so strengthened the position of this tribe that it was now able to prevail over the Moabites. For Moab was a small people and the Moabite state a small state, which was unable to develop any great power and only achieved successes against Israel when, for some reason or other, the situation was particularly in its favour. To begin with, the Moabites had been able to strike out a fair way northwards beyond the Arnon when the Israelite settlement in the land east of the Jordan had still been very weak, and the tribe of Gad had been limited to a small and far from favourable area consisting for the most part of pasture land (cf. Num. xxxii, 1). But later on Gad had advanced, at any rate on the western border of the table-land, right up to the Arnon, as king Mesha of Moab remarks in his inscription (line 10) in the middle of the 9th century B.C., that 'the men of Gad' had 'lived in the land of Ataroth (the modern *ʿaṭṭārūs* about 8 miles north of the Arnon) from time immemorial; and the city of Dibon (the modern *dībān*, 3 miles north of the Arnon) is described as '*Dibon-gad*' in Num. xxxiii, 45 f., and was therefore not only incorporated in Israelite state territory later on but also inhabited by Israelites (Gadites). This advance made by the tribe of Gad certainly took place in the period before the formation of the kingdom. We do not know how far Gad was able in the course of its expansion to seize other cities further to the east on the table-land.

The Ammonites resided north-east of Moab in the region of the upper course of the Jabbok. Their centre was the city of Rabbah (also called רַבַּת בְּנֵי-עַמּוֹן after them) on the site now occupied by the capital of Jordan, *ʿammān*, in whose name the old name of the Ammonites survives. They too had a monarchy and formed a small state very early on, at any rate long before the Israelites. The association which they had with their northern neighbours the Aramaeans, which occasionally came into prominence later on, suggests that they were closely related to them. To begin with, they had no relations with Israel, since they lived away from Israelite territories. It was only when the ancient land of Gilead, south of the

Jabbok, was colonised by Ephraimites from the west Jordan mountains of Ephraim that contacts resulted, the more so since the Ammonites had a tendency to expand to the north-west. Here lay the small fertile plain that is now called *el-buḳe'a*, north of the modern cross-roads at *eṣ-ṣuwēliḥ*; and the Ammonites settled in this plain particularly as they had not much scope for expanding in other directions. They thereby became direct neighbours of the Ephraimite settlers in the land of Gilead; and they were bound to come into conflict with them if they wished to advance still farther to the north-west. That they did in fact once attack the land of Gilead we learn from the story of Jephthah in Judges x, 6-xii, 6[1]. According to this they one day occupied the place named Gilead (the modern *khirbet jel'ad*), which was a settlement on 'mount Gilead', from which the whole district had taken its name; and this occupation was no doubt achieved by force of arms (Judges x, 17a). To ward off this attack the Gileadites first of all looked for a leader, and as they could not find one in their own ranks they thought of one Jephthah, a son of a Gileadite of inferior status, who had been excluded from the family inheritance, and who went about in the 'land of Tob'[2] at the head of a band of adventurers and had meanwhile proved his worth in warlike deeds. Jephthah gathered together the militia of the Gileadites in Gileadite Mizpah (probably somewhere in the modern *rēshūni*, a few miles north-west of Gilead), at whose shrine 'the spirit of Yahweh came upon Jephthah' (Judges xi, 29) so that he now marched forth as a charismatic leader at the head of the Gileadites against the Ammonites, conquered them and drove them out of Gilead again[3]. He thus secured the land of Gilead for its Ephraimite inhabitants, for we hear nothing of any further effort by the Ammonites to seize the land of Gilead[4]. Admittedly, the Ammonites remained undisturbed in their territory (no doubt including the *buḳe'a*). It had been a purely defensive victory. But Jephthah later occupied the office of 'judge of Israel' for six years until his death (Judges xii, 7).

North of Ammon, in Israel's early period, the Aramaeans were

---

[1] The passage in Judges xi, 15-26 in which Moab appears quite inappropriately as an enemy is a secondary interpolation. Judges xi, 30-31, 34-40 and Judges xii, 1-6 contain separate stories.

[2] Unfortunately it is impossible to identify the situation of this 'land of Tob', which may be compared with 2 Sam. x, 6, 8. It was probably one of the districts east of Jordan which was still but sparsely inhabited at that time, most likely north of the Jabbok.

[3] Unfortunately it is impossible to identify the places mentioned in Judges xi, 33 which define the scene of the battle.

[4] Later on the Ammonites undertook another attack, under different conditions, on the Israelite possessions east of Jordan (cf. pp. 167 f.).

on the point of gaining a footing on the soil of Palestine and constituting themselves in what were apparently, to begin with, not very firm political units[1]. A group of Aramaeans settled for a time south of the Jabbok immediately to the east of the land of Gilead; and it was here that the first historical encounter between Israelites and Aramaeans that is known to us took place, and this was of a peaceful nature. By agreement between the two parties a stone was set up on 'mount Gilead' to mark the frontier which they bound themselves not to transgress with evil intent (Gen. xxxi, 44-54). In the popular story of this agreement Jacob represents the Israelites, that is to say in fact the Gilead Ephraimites, and Laban the Aramaeans who were their eastern neighbours. It was apparently only a temporary state of affairs, since it is unlikely that the probably small group of Aramaeans had gained a very firm footing at this place. At any rate we do not hear any more of Aramaeans south of the Jabbok. Probably the Ammonites moved forward to this place.

For the rest, in the early period the Israelite tribes had no contacts with the Aramaeans, who were later to intervene so persistently for a time in Israelite history. It was only the gradual occupation of the land north of the Jabbok, the modern region of *'ajlūn*, by Manassites who came from the land west of Jordan which brought Israel into direct touch with the Aramaeans who had settled north-east and north of the *'ajlūn*. But this did not take place until later. For the time being the territory of the Canaanite city-states of the northern land east of Jordan began on the borders of the *'ajlūn*. In contrast to the southern land east of Jordan, the city-state system had survived here even in the Middle and Late Bronze Age and right into the Iron Age. On both sides of the Yarmuk, in the land of Bashan, there were numerous urban centres on the fertile table-land west of the steeply rising basalt mountain of *jebel ed-drūz*. The Old Testament tradition tells of a king Og of Bashan, who resided in Ashtaroth (the modern *tell 'ashtara*) and Edrei (the modern *der'a* on the southern border of the Yarmuk Valley)[2], and had ruled over the many cities in Bashan (Deut. iii, 1-7; cf. Num. xxi, 33-35; Jos. xiii, 12, 30 f.). This story is, admittedly, only found in deuteronomistic and secondary deuteronomistic passages; but there is no doubt that the deuteronomistic historian included it as an already existing tradition. It implies quite correctly that Bashan was an area with old-established cities.

---

[1] Details in M. Noth, BBLAK, 68 (1946-1951), pp. 19 ff.
[2] Originally Ashtaroth alone was regarded as the seat of Og (cf. Jos. ix, 10), and Edrei, the site of the battle, was only added later.

This was of interest to Israel when the Manassites in the land north
of the Jabbok extended their settlement into the neighbourhood of
this region of city-states. The figure of king Og is, however, far
from clearly defined historically. That one of the city kings seized
the dominion over the whole area of city-states is very curious and
conceivable at most only as a passing episode of which the Israelites
might have received word. But the fact that this king Og is included among the 'Rephaim', that awe-inspiring population of
giants from primeval times who were associated in the northern
land east of Jordan with the very numerous ancient megaliths[1],
shows that at best we have here a historical phenomenon only in
rather vague outline, which has been elaborated with details
which are historically out of place. The Israelites encountered
king Og of Bashan merely in stories emanating from the city-state
territory of Bashan but not directly as a historical figure; and so
the victory of the Israelites over Og at Edrei can scarcely be called
a historical event, but merely an indirect expression of the fact
that Israel claimed possession of the city-state territory in the
Northern land east of Jordan without ever really having possessed
it. It is highly probable that no warlike conflicts with the city-states
took place at all in the early period, but that a state of peaceful co-
existence developed such as was customary in the other parts of
Palestine; all the more so since the Manassite settlement of the
'ajlūn was hardly very dense and there was therefore no pressing
necessity to extend this territory, just as the cities in the land of
Bashan can hardly have had any reason to encroach from their fertile
table-land onto the wooded mountain country north of the Jabbok.

On the eastern side, where the neighbours lived against which
Israel had to assert itself in its early period, Palestine was open to
invasions from the desert, aimed not at a gradual occupation of
Palestinian soil but merely at plundering its produce. The danger of
such invasions had existed ever since the domestication of the camel
in the desert had been developed to such an extent that it became
possible for fairly large groups not merely to live in the desert in
comparative independence of watering-places, but also to traverse
fairly large tracts without water, and to move quickly over great
distances. In earlier times the camel had not been entirely unknown
in the ancient Orient, but according to our literary and archaeological sources, it did not play any part worth mentioning until the

---

[1] The fact that, according to Deut. iii, 11, king Og's 'bedstead of iron', probably a
basalt dolmen, was shown in Ammonite Rabbah, makes the lack of uniformity in the
tradition especially clear.

Late Bronze Age. It was only after the occupation of the land by the Israelites that the camel was sufficiently domesticated for that special kind of bedouin existence to develop, of which we first gain more precise information in the early Arab period[1]. Very soon, however, the new opportunities arising from the use of the camel made their influence felt in Palestine, which was so near to the desert. This new departure forms the background to the stories of Gideon in Judges vi-viii which tell of the invasions of the land west of the Jordan by the Midianites coming from the east[2]. The Midianites evidently constituted a large and fairly widespread association of tribes in the desert east and south of Palestine[3]. At a certain period they began to make a deep inroad into Palestine with their camels; in fact they threatened the country right up to the coast[4], and this always just after sowing had been completed and the seed was coming up. They let their camels graze off the young crop and took what they needed of the produce of the land and the cattle of the inhabitants—anything they had not already destroyed during their invasions. The most threatened areas were naturally such fertile plains as the plain of Jezreel (Judges vi, 33); but the Israelite possessions in the hill country were not spared. The appearance of the Midianites, which for a time apparently occurred every year, spread extreme panic in the country where the appearance of these swift-moving camel nomads was obviously a complete novelty and a sinister phenomenon. The terror they aroused can still be felt in the story of Gideon, where it refers to the 'camels without number' of the Midianites (Judges vi, 5; vii, 12) and how because of their coming men would take refuge in every conceivable hiding place in the mountains, in caves and on the mountain-tops (Judges vi, 2).

It was the great achievement of Gideon, a Manassite of the clan

---

[1] Cf. W. F. Albright, *From the Stone Age to Christianity* (²1946), pp. 120 f.; *Archaeology and the Religion of Israel* (²1946), pp. 96 ff. Albright assumes, and, to the best of our knowledge, rightly, that the real domestication of the camel took place *circa* 1100 B.C.

[2] In Judges vi, 3, 33, vii, 12 the Amalekites and the 'children of the east', *i.e.* the inhabitants of the eastern desert in general, are mentioned along with the Midianites.

[3] According to Num. xxii, 4, 7 the Midianites participated in the worship of Baal-Peor (cf. above, p. 155), which is not surprising as they resided in the vicinity of the southern land east of Jordan. On the other hand, we also find them in the southern desert; for it was no doubt here that the story of Israel's encounter with the Midianites at the 'mount of God' was enacted (Exod. xviii, 1 ff.). If they were a great tribal unit, this wide distribution is not surprising. The place *madyan* which lies on the eastern side of the gulf of *el-'aḳaba* provides evidence, dating from Roman times, that they lived there (the evidence is given, for example, in R. Kittel, *Geschichte des Volkes Israel*. I, 5, 6 [1923], p. 347, note 1); they may have originated in this remote district.

[4] In Judges vi, 4 Gaza is mentioned in this context.

of the Abiezrites which dwelt in Ophrah, that he dared to meet the danger. The tribe of Manasseh, settled next to the plain of Jezreel on the south, certainly suffered from these attacks on the plain. At the head of a small band of brave comrades of the tribe (cf. the episode described in Judges vii, 2-7) Gideon invaded the camp of the host of the Midianites, who were resting for the night beside the well of Harod (the modern *'ēn jālūd*) at the north-western foot of Mount Gilboa (the modern *jebel fuḳū'ā*), that is, at the south-western end of the plain of Jezreel, after an evidently successful bout of plundering in the plain. This well-prepared and completely unforeseen attack terrified the Midianites so much that they made for the open country on their camels and fled to the Jordan through the plain of the *nahr jālūd* and across the Jordan farther eastwards[1]. Gideon's victory over the Midianites appears to have put an end to the nuisance which they had been causing, or at any rate to have roused the inhabitants' determination to defend themselves, so that we hear no more about attacks by the Midianites. The terror which they had spread makes it easy to see why Gideon's victory, which broke the spell, was remembered for so long. When, in Isa. ix, 3 (4 in the English Bible) the 'day of Midian', that is, the day of the victory over the Midianites, is quoted as an example of an especially brilliant victory, the reference is no doubt to the surprising success of Gideon the Manassite.

In the early period the existence of Israel in Palestine was not really fundamentally threatened from the east, either by the small neighbouring peoples on the eastern border or by the nomads who made occasional incursions. Nor were they threatened by the older Canaanite population, which no longer had any great military force at its disposal. The threat came from the elements which set foot in the land from the west about the same time as the Israelite tribes: from the Philistines and the 'Sea People' elements related to them, who had established themselves as a ruling class in a series of ancient Bronze Age cities in the maritime plain. They represented the strongest force in the country and were developing great military resources, to begin with, mostly in the area of the Canaanite city-state territories. At the outset there was no large-scale military conflict with the Israelite tribes if one overlooks the fact that Sisera may have been a member of the 'Sea People' ruling class.

[1] It is impossible to reconstruct the details of the event. The main narrative in Judges vii, 1–viii, 3 closes with aetiological elements concerned with place-names (vii, 25); and Judges viii, 4-21 contains the end of a parallel story, which deviates in a number of points from the main narrative. It is impossible to be certain about the relationship of the two stories to each other and to the historical events.

But in any case Sisera stood at the head of a group of old Canaanite city-states in the plain of Jezreel and possibly the plain of Acco as well, against which Barak won his famous victory (cf. above, p. 150 f.). Of the Philistines, in the narrower sense of the term, who ruled in their five city-states in the southern part of the maritime plain of Palestine, we hear in the stories about Samson in Judges xiii-xvi. The tribe of Dan, to which Samson is assigned, and which tried to gain a footing in the hill country in the neighbourhood of the modern ṣarʿa, lived under the pressure of the adjacent Philistines; and all that is related of Samson is that he played all kinds of tricks on the Philistines until he finally succumbed to their superior might. But the tribe of Dan then had to withdraw from the hill country[1] and left behind at most only a few remnants in the district of ṣarʿa. For the rest, they tried to find a new territory in the far north of the country by the sources of the Jordan.

The Philistines were able—possibly in association with the other 'Sea People' elements farther to the north—to set about subjugating the whole country, at any rate west of Jordan. And they began the attempt quite soon. A decisive struggle with them for supremacy was in store for the Israelite tribes; and the conflict led Israel on to the path of political power which it had not trodden before. It is very characteristic that the struggle for consolidation in the land which took place with the earlier inhabitants and neighbouring peoples after the Israelites had occupied the land was not regarded as a concern affecting Israel as a whole. The individual tribes had to guard their possessions for themselves and, where necessary or desirable, to try to extend their settlement on their own. In certain cases neighbouring tribes may occasionally have combined to protect their common interests. But in this early period we hear nothing at all of joint undertakings by the whole association of the twelve tribes for the protection or extension of their property and life, and evidently nothing of the kind in fact occurred. It was only the late deuteronomistic conception of an 'age of the judges' which magnified the occasional charismatic leaders of individual tribes and groups of tribes into personalities of importance to Israel as a whole, whereas we know from the traditions that survive that their role was strictly limited. They acquired this exaggerated importance by being combined with the quite different office of 'judge of Israel' (cf. above, p. 101 f.) which, though it did refer to Israel as a whole, was only entrusted with internal functions.

[1] According to Judges i, 34 f. the Danites had to yield to the pressure of the 'Amorites'. That may be true; but no doubt the Philistines stood in the background.

CHAPTER II

THE TRANSITION TO THE DEVELOPMENT
OF POLITICAL POWER

14. *The Episode of the Monarchy of Saul*

F R O M time immemorial the Canaanite cities in Syria-Palestine had normally had city kings with a feudal ruling class. The Philistines —and probably the other 'Sea People' groups in the land as well— had their 'princes'[1], who also resided in the urban centres with a heavily armed retinue of warriors[2], and, in addition, a following of mercenary leaders who were invested with a piece of land and had to perform military service with the mercenaries they collected together[3]. They therefore represented an intensely concentrated military force. The neighbouring peoples in the southern land east of Jordan, who had settled about the same time as the Israelite tribes, had apparently succeeded in developing simple political organisations, each with its own monarchy, soon after their occupation of the land; and even the groups of Aramaeans on the borders of the northern land east of Jordan, who only gradually became consolidated in Palestine, soon reached the point of establishing political organisations which were, to begin with, however, very unstable, with kings at their head[4].

It was only in the sacral association of the tribes of Israel that a concentration of political power and the formation of a state were not achieved until long after they had occupied the land and settled down. The individual tribes were left to look after their own stability and security. It is clear that there were certain impediments which hindered further political developments. An anecdote in Judges viii, 22-23 records that after his brilliant victory over the Midianites Gideon was asked by the Israelites to accept the hereditary office of 'ruler' in Israel; he replied as follows to this

---

[1] The Old Testament calls them specifically סְרָנִים, a term which has been connected with the word τύραννος, which is non-Greek in origin.
[2] Cf. as an example the description of Goliath in I Sam. xvii, 4 ff.
[3] David was in this position for a time; cf. I Sam. xxvii, 2 ff.; xxix, I ff.
[4] More details in M. Noth, BBLAK. 68 (1946–1951), pp. 25 ff.

request: 'I will not rule over you, neither shall my son rule over you: Yahweh shall rule over you'. This brief story may have been drafted long after kings had appeared in Israel, and may therefore have been aimed indirectly against the already existing institution of monarchy, but it fairly certainly reflects an attitude that was current among the tribes of Israel before the rise of the monarchy, since only this kind of outlook can explain the historical fact that the idea of monarchy became effective so late and went so much against the grain in Israel. The argument for rejecting the idea of hereditary monarchy which is given in this little anecdote probably reflects the attitude to the institution that was prevalent among the tribes, who were, after all, familiar with a great variety of forms of monarchy in the world around them. The exclusive committal of the sacral association of the Israelite tribes to its God and to his will here had its effect on their history, and the particularity of Israel thus appears as a historical fact.

The fact that a monarchy was finally established in Israel[1], thereby turning Israel from the line to which it had kept so strictly hitherto to the road to political power in relation to the surrounding peoples, was a result of the development of the historical situation in Palestine, which very seriously threatened not only the individual tribal units but the continuity and existence of Israel as a whole. The historical background to Saul's elevation to the monarchy was the growing power of the Philistines, who were attempting to gain absolute control over the whole country.

In an old story about the fate of the Sacred Ark, deriving roughly from the time of David, which is contained in 1 Sam. iv, 1b-vii, 1 and 2 Sam. vi, 1-16a, 17-19[2] we learn of one of the first large-scale military clashes between the Israelites and Philistines. This took place *circa* 1000 B.C.[3]. The Philistines gathered their forces in Aphek (probably the modern *tell el-mukhmar* near *rās el-'en*[4]) on the upper course of the river which is now called *nahr el-'auja* that flows into the Mediterranean north of *yāfa*. Aphek lay right up on the northern border of their territory. It was a favourable point of departure for an attack on the mountains of Central Palestine, which rise close by on the east of Aphek, where the central Israelite

---

[1] Cf. on the following, above all, A. Alt, *Die Staatenbildung der Israeliten in Palästina. Verfassungsgeschichtliche Studien* (Reformationsprogramm der Universität Leipzig, 1930) = *Kleine Schriften zur Geschichte des Volkes Israel*, II (1953), pp. 1 ff.

[2] On the extent and nature of this 'story of the Ark' cf. L. Rost, *Die Überlieferung von der Thronnachfolge Davids* (BWANT, III, 6 [1926]), pp. 4 ff.

[3] Only very rough dates are possible even for this period; cf. below, p. 225.

[4] Cf. M. Noth, *Das Buch Josua* (² 1953), p. 72.

tribes had established themselves. Such an attack was evidently their intention, since it was certainly the Philistines who took the initiative. With the other 'Sea People' groups in the land, they had substantially achieved predominance in the maritime plain which was occupied by Canaanite city-states, and were bound, if they intended to extend this supremacy over the whole country, above all to subjugate the Israelite tribes. In view of the imminent danger the Israelites gathered at a place called Ebenezer, which is on the edge of the mountains opposite Aphek and roughly on the site of the modern *mejdel jāba*. It is impossible to say for certain who actually took part on the Israelite side. The main participants were probably the militia of the tribe of Ephraim which was most immediately threatened from Aphek. But some of the neighbouring tribes of the central Palestinian mountains will also have been involved in some measure, and, in view of the enormous danger, reinforcements from other tribes may also have been present. In an initial encounter the Philistines were victorious. Thereupon the amphictyonic shrine of the Ark was fetched from Shiloh to guarantee the presence of their God among the hard-pressed Israelites in a second battle. The 'story of the Ark', which is especially concerned with fate of the sacred Ark, records only this fact. The transporting of the Ark to the camp could only mean that the whole association of Israelite tribes was being deployed against the Philistines. So far as we know from the tradition, it was the first time the whole tribal confederation had come forward in defence of Israel, the reason being that this was in fact the first time the existence of Israel as a whole in Palestine had really been threatened by the power of the Philistines. The fact that there were two battles in succession against the Philistines probably means that at first, as hitherto, those parts of Israel primarily affected had resisted the Philistines' attack, and, when this defensive effort had completely failed, the whole confederation of the tribes had been summoned, together with its central sacred object. But in the second battle too, the Israelites were utterly defeated by the overwhelming might of the Philistines, so thoroughly indeed that the Israelite armies were completely disintegrated and the sacred Ark captured by the victors (1 Sam. iv, 10, 11).

The results of this defeat were extraordinary. When, four centuries later, the prophet Jeremiah said that the temple in Shiloh which had housed the Ark had once been destroyed and that even in his time it was still possible to see the ruins of this temple (Jer. vii, 12, 14; xxvi, 6, 9), in all probability this destruction had been

carried out by the Philistines after their victory at Ebenezer, which
gave them free access to Shiloh (*sēlūn*)[1]. After the Ark itself had
fallen into their hands they also destroyed the temple which had
housed it, thus destroying the central shrine which had held the
Israelite tribes together. In addition, they subjugated the Israelite
tribes themselves. They installed garrisons in Israelite territories.
We hear of one such 'governor' or 'garrison' (נְצִיב) in Benjaminite
Gibeah (the modern *tell el-fūl*, 4 miles north of Jerusalem) in 1
Sam. x, 5; xiii, 3. We are not told where else they had such garrisons. They will, at any rate, have occupied the central mountains
west of Jordan in this way. Israel was also disarmed. The Philistines attempted to prevent the manufacture of new weapons by
forbidding the Israelites to work in metal, so that they were forced
to go to the Philistines for the tools they needed for agricultural
and other peaceful uses (1 Sam. xiii, 19-22). Naturally, they were
able to enforce these prohibitions only so far as their occupation
extended, and the emergence of Saul suggests that their authority
was not so effective in the more remote provinces. *De jure*, however, the Israelite tribal confederation was subject to Philistine
rule, and to all intents and purposes the Philistines had attained
their object of dominating at any rate the land west of Jordan.

It is not surprising that Israel's situation encouraged other of her
neighbours to expand their territory at her expense and to satisfy
some of their old desires. The Ammonites now renewed the attempt
which had been wrecked by Jephthah's victory. They apparently
occupied the old land of Gilead south of the Jabbok, and encroached on the land north of the Jabbok. At any rate, we find
them occupied at this time with an attack on the city of Jabesh[2],
probably a Manassite foundation in the colonial land of the modern
'ajlūn, situated in the area of the *wādi yābis*, in the name of which
the old name of the city survives[3]. In 1 Sam. xi, 1 ff. we read how
the people of Jabesh, being too weak to resist by themselves,
declared themselves ready to come to terms with Nahash, the king

[1] The archaeological discoveries also show that Shiloh was destroyed about this time.
[2] In the fuller name 'Jabesh (in) Gilead', which is mostly used, the extension of the
name Gilead to the land north of the Jabbok is already presupposed. Cf. M. Noth,
PJB, 37 (1941), pp. 72 ff.
[3] According to Eusebius (*Onomastikon*, 110, 12 f. in E. Klostermann's edition),
Jabesh lay on the later Roman road from Pella to Gerasa, that is, on the upper course
of the *wādi yābis* in the mountains, and, according to archaeological discoveries (cf. N.
Glueck, AASOR, 25-28 [1951], pp. 211 ff.) on the site of the present ruins *tell el-maḳlūb*
on the northern side of the valley. N. Glueck (*op. cit.* pp. 268 ff.) and, following him,
the *Westminster Historical Atlas to the Bible* (1945), place Jabesh at the lower end of
the *wādi yābis* in the Jordan Valley and, in particular, on the *tell abu kharaz*, but this
argument fails to weigh against the very precise reference made by Eusebius.

of the Ammonites, but were scornfully rejected. They asked for seven days' respite to seek for help among the Israelite tribes, and this respite was apparently accorded to them in the certain expectation that they would never find the help they were seeking. Whether or not one regards the incident as likely, it does at least describe the situation in the land east of Jordan very strikingly; on the one side the aggressive activity and certainty of victory of the small people of the Ammonites and on the other the helplessness of the Ephraimite-Manassite settlers east of the Jordan who no longer had any support to fall back on in their motherland west of the Jordan, evidently because the power of the Israelite tribes had been completely paralysed by the Philistines. At the same time, it is clear that the arm of the Philistines did not fully extend as far as the land east of Jordan, so that it was possible for things to happen there which were beyond their control.

This situation forms the background to Saul's elevation to the monarchy. Saul, the son of Kish, was a Benjaminite from the Benjaminite village of Gibeah (the modern *tell el-fūl*)[1]. He evidently belonged to the stratum of the permanently established free members of the tribe, who lived very largely on agriculture. The main stages in the process by which he became king have no doubt been correctly recorded in 1 Sam. xi, but the details of the process will not bear closer historical scrutiny. According to 1 Sam. xi, Saul's first public appearance took place when the 'spirit of God' came upon him and he began to act spontaneously (verse 6). This happened when Saul heard of the hard-pressed Jabeshites' search for help, to which the Israelite response had otherwise been merely one of despair and lamentation. This recalls the emergence of those charismatic leaders of tribes and groups of tribes which, summoned in the name of God or constrained by the spirit of God, had fought for the rights of the Israelites in the land and had prevailed (cf. above pp. 150 f.). In fact Saul's first undertaking belonged very nearly to this category. If the actions of the charismatic leaders had often been preceded by a call, tradition records a corresponding call in the case of Saul. In a popular story (1 Sam. ix, 1–x, 16) which was placed before Sam. xi in the older Saul tradition, without being closely connected with it, there is a reference to Saul's meeting with Samuel, the 'man of God' or 'seer' at an unnamed spot in the general vicinity of Gibeah, at which Samuel anointed

---

[1] In 1922, and again for a short time in 1933, W. F. Albright made successful excavations on the *tell el-fūl*; cf. W. F. Albright, in AASOR, 4 (1924), and BASOR, 52 (1933), pp. 6-12.

Saul in the name of Yahweh to be *nāgīd*, that is, the ruler appointed
by God (x, 1). This story is obviously very anecdotal, and even
on the main point, the anointing to the office of *nāgīd*, the later
kingship of Saul may have been casting its shadow ahead, since
this rite goes far beyond the appointment of the charismatic leader,
as it had always been enacted hitherto, inasmuch as the anointing
implied the conferment of an office and the title of *nāgīd* appears
to have denoted the man destined for a future office[1]. According to
1 Sam. xi, however, it must at least be doubted whether there was
any thought of a future monarchy when this calling of Saul took
place, or whether it was not evoked rather by the immediate emergency: this is all the more likely to have been the case since there
was no tradition behind the idea of monarchy in Israel and it was
bound to encounter serious misgivings (cf. above pp. 164 f.). But
if this is so, the story recounted in 1 Sam. ix, 1–x, 16 is correct in
so far as Samuel inspired Saul to make his first public appearance
in the name of the God of Israel.

When the distress of the people east of Jordan, and especially
the people of Jabesh, came to his knowledge, Saul acted with
spontaneous enthusiasm as the one called to be their leader. He
summoned the armies of the whole confederation of the twelve
tribes in a way that was probably customary at the time[2], and he
assembled his followers in Bezek (the modern *khirbet ibzīḳ*) on the
road down from Shechem to Beth-shan roughly opposite Jabesh,
at a spot from which it was possible to reach the Jordan Valley
directly and then advance further over into the *'ajlūn*. The em-
ployment of the whole tribal association to defend their existence
against danger from outside, accorded with the need of the moment.
Hitherto this had not been the custom, but if the supposition suggested on p. 166 is correct, there had been a precedent in the
decisive, albeit disastrous, battle against the Philistines at Ebenezer.
It is stated explicitly in 1 Sam. xi, 7 that the tribes followed Saul's
call in 'the dread of Yahweh'. The question may be asked how far
this was actually possible under the rule of the Philistines and in
the state of disarmament imposed by them. It may be that there
was no garrison, and therefore no real enforcement of Philistine

---

[1] It may be asked, however, whether the title *nāgīd*, which only occurs in the Old
Testament as a term for the king designate, did not formerly have the more general
meaning of the man called by God to undertake a military action.

[2] On the dividing up of the oxen mentioned in 1 Sam. xi, 7, cf. Judges xix, 29 which
may refer to a variation of the usual custom arising from a special case. The method of
the summons to arms described in 1 Sam. xi, 7, with conjuration expressed in an oath,
makes an impression of great originality (cf. above, p. 105, note 2).

sovereignty on the eastern border of the mountains west of Jordan and in the land east of Jordan where the event took place, and that disarmament had not actually been carried out there. It may also be that the Philistines were not interested in military conflicts of the other Palestinian peoples among themselves or were perhaps not reluctant to see them take place, since even an increase in the power of the Ammonites could hardly be welcome to them. At any rate, in spite of the pressure of the Philistines, Saul found sufficient armed followers to risk the attack on the Ammonites and the deliverance of the hard-pressed city of Jabesh.

He achieved a brilliant success. Jabesh was relieved and the danger from the Ammonites in the land east of Jordan apparently eliminated. Apart from this immediate result, the victory had a great psychological effect on the hard-pressed Israelites. It was an encouragement to the Israelite tribes; and it is not surprising that they now began to come to themselves again and to act with resolution. What happened now had far-reaching consequences. There is a brief report in 1 Sam. xi[1], according to which, after the Ammonite war, Samuel summoned the Israelite tribes to the ancient shrine of Gilgal near Jericho (its exact location is still unknown). As 'man of God', which would in itself command respect, and now for the first time really as the spokesman of God who had called and inspired Saul to his act of liberation, an authority in Israel, even though bearing no office, Samuel may in fact have played an active part in the events that now took place. He chose the shrine of Gilgal for the assembly of the tribes, because after the disappearance of the former shrine which was brought about by the loss of the Ark and the destruction of the temple of Shiloh, it was a suitable place for several reasons. It was an ancient and famous shrine on the Benjaminite-Ephraimite frontier, no doubt much frequented by the tribes of Central Palestine, and had possibly already played the part of the central Israelite shrine for a time (cf. above, p. 95); its situation was relatively central for all the Israelite tribes, and yet at the same time probably outside the area directly controlled by the Philistines. Whereas the Philistines certainly kept the site of the previous federal shrine at Shiloh under constant supervision and occupied the central Palestinian mountains, the Jordan Valley, with the shrine of Gilgal, was presumably, like the land east of Jordan, not occupied by a permanent Philistine gar-

---

[1] In addition to 1 Sam. xi we have, in the fragment of narrative in 1 Sam. x, 21bβ-27a, an old reference to Saul's election to the monarchy (cf. O. Eissfeldt, *Die Komposition der Samuelisbücher* [1931], pp. 7 f.). But the part played here by Saul's physical height is obviously anecdotal and this is certainly not a historical record.

rison, and what took place there was not directly or immediately known to the Philistines.

Here in Gilgal 'the whole people' 'made Saul king before Yahweh', *i.e.*, in the sanctuary there (1 Sam. xi, 15). Though it took place in the sanctuary and in an atmosphere of religious consecration, the ceremony was not really a sacral rite like the appointment of a charismatic leader, but rather a political act. Israel was acting as a 'people', no longer as a sacral confederation of tribes. It was embarking, though to begin with in quite a modest way, on the road to political power and thereby making a decision which was to have a quite fundamental determining influence on the further course of its history. It is clear that the historical situation in which Israel found itself at this time, which involved a threat to its whole existence from the Philistines, was the direct reason for this new departure. If Samuel did actually take the initiative, he will have done so in view of this situation, and will have received the consent of the tribes also in view of the immediate situation. It is clear that the new king, who had proved his worth in the victory over the Ammonites which had just been won, was expected to deliver Israel from this threat to its whole existence and to wage a successful war against the Philistines. A first step in the direction of employing the whole tribal confederation as a single force had already been taken, inasmuch as the levies of the whole of Israel had been raised probably both in the decisive and disastrous battle against the Philistines and in the victorious struggle against the Ammonites, in contrast to earlier conflicts with the previous inhabitants of the land and the neighbouring peoples. One swift campaign did not suffice, however, against the Philistines, as it had done against the much less formidable Ammonites. Against the Philistines a permanent and stable military command seemed to be necessary and the new king was no doubt intended to act primarily as leader of the levies of Israel, and it was in such a capacity that he did in fact come forward. The Israelites easily found a model for the new institution of the monarchy in their own historical environment. It is true that, apart from the name, their monarchy had hardly anything in common with the Canaanite city monarchy and its knightly charioteers. The Philistine system of government, which had proved so successful a factor in the struggle against the Israelites, could hardly be imitated over night, based as it was on a professional army and a system of mercenaries. But the kindred neighbouring peoples in the east had a national monarchy, of whose character and functions we have no detailed information, but which took the lead in warfare with external enemies, and so had proved its worth in warfare. This was the chief model for the new institution in Israel, all the more so since the social structure among these peoples was presumably similar to that prevailing in Israel.

But the very fact that the monarchy in Israel was based on a model that had proved its worth in other peoples inevitably made it a problem for Israel. Was it right for Israel to try to be a nation like other nations and to install a king on the model of foreign monarchies and, in spite of its distress, to embark on the road to political power? Modest though the first steps which it took in this direction were, it was a fundamentally new departure for Israel. The older stories of the election of Saul to the throne obviously refer to the event with unfeigned satisfaction; they see in it a work of the God of Israel[1] and they show an obvious delight in the personality and the first actions of the new king. Those who scornfully expressed their doubts concerning the value of the new institution and its representative are dismissed as 'good for nothing' (1 Sam. x, 27a). This clearly suggests that the appointment did not proceed without opposition; and the question must be considered whether this opposition was really so frivolous as it was made out to be. Fundamental doubts about the value of Saul's monarchy are, it is true, found only much later in the deuteronomistic history[2], where the whole proceeding is introduced by the people's demand for a king 'like all the nations' (1 Sam. viii, 5) and this demand is interpreted to mean that the kingship of God over Israel, which really ought to continue, was being rejected by the people. But it is likely that in this an attitude to monarchy as such was being expressed which was certainly later confirmed time and again by the experiences which the people had of the institution[3], but which had, however, existed from the very beginning and had made itself felt

---

[1] In 1 Sam. ix, 1 ff. Yahweh's initiative is put into effect by Samuel, and, with reference to 1 Sam. xi, the affair is so described as if Saul was being called to be the future king from the very outset (cf. also 1 Sam. x, 16: 'the matter of the kingdom', so that by electing Saul to be king the people was ultimately merely fulfilling the divine will). The fragment of narrative in 1 Sam. x, 21bβ-27a also says that Saul, whose height had proved him to be the king, had been 'chosen' by Yahweh.

[2] The deuteronomistic historian supplemented the old tradition of Saul in accordance with his own ideas, by adding 1 Sam. vii, 2b-17; viii, 1-22; x, 17, 27a; xii, 1-25. Admittedly he made it easy for himself to reject the institution of the monarchy by making Samuel win the decisive victory over the Philistines (1 Sam. vii, 10b-11), thereby fundamentally misrepresenting the real historical background to the emergence of the monarchy.

[3] In the formulation of the 'law of the king' in 1 Sam. viii, 11-18 the later development of the monarchy played an essential part.

even before the rise of the monarchy (cf. above, p. 164 f.). It must be admitted that this attitude was well justified. It is true that the organisation of the sacral confederation of the twelve tribes had its counterparts in the surrounding world, but the monarchy and the consequent development of political power was a secular, 'heathen' affair to a much more marked degree than that earlier institution which left to the individual tribes and groups of tribes the relatively simpler consolidation of their life in relation to the outside world.

For the time being, however, the emergency was so great that there was hardly time for detailed discussion, and the hope placed in the new king, who had proved his worth so brilliantly in the battle against the Ammonites, was so great that all doubts about him faded into the background. The situation impelled Saul to take up the struggle against the Philistines and he apparently embarked on the task without delay. In 1 Sam. xiii, 2 to xiv, 46 there is an ancient narrative about Saul's successful attack on the Philistine garrisons. It is true that the story concentrates mainly on the person of Saul and, above all, on that of his son Jonathan, and less on the conflict with the Philistines, and great emphasis is therefore laid on anecdotal details, but it does reveal the historical background of the conflict fairly clearly. According to this account, Saul immediately made the necessary preparations in Gilgal by forming a body of picked troops from the crowd assembled there and sharing the command with his eldest son Jonathan (cf. 1 Sam. xiv, 49), who appears in the tradition as a particularly attractive figure. The first step then was that Jonathan undertook with his followers an apparently surprise attack on the Philistine garrison in Gibeah, which led to its destruction (1 Sam. xiii, 3[1]). Apparently Saul's appointment as king and the military preparations had taken place so swiftly that the Philistines were quite unprepared for the attack. But this was only the opening of the struggle. The Philistines quickly assembled their available forces, that is, the garrisons occupying the mountains west of Jordan and in the area that was especially threatened; they moved into camp near Michmash (the modern *mukhmās*) about 5 miles north-east of Gibeah and reconnoitred the surroundings from there (1 Sam. xiii, 16-18). Saul, however, who had moved with his followers into

---

[1] In 1 Sam. xiii, 3 the name 'Geba' which is now given there is usually corrected into 'Gibeah' on the basis of the preceding verse. This is not absolutely certain. The similarity between the two names and the fact that they can be easily confused makes it impossible to come to a definite decision, particularly as the two places are fairly close to each other.

the same district of Michmash, encamped with his son Jonathan near Geba (*jeba'*) which lay opposite Michmash to the south-west and was separated from it by the deep incision of the *wādi eṣ-ṣuwēnīṭ*. But once again a surprise attack on the Philistines was successful, and here again Jonathan is credited with the initiative. This second success gave new courage to the Israelite tribes, who had been terrified by the overwhelming power of the Philistines at the first outbreak of hostilities (cf. 1 Sam. xiii, 6); and they evidently drove the Philistine garrisons out of the whole district, where they would hardly have been very strong in numbers.

To understand what happened and the results that ensued, it must be remembered that this initial success of Saul was not a victory over the assembled military might or even a considerable levy of the Philistines: the Philistine garrisons had merely been expelled from Israelite territory by surprise tactics. Nevertheless, this meant a good deal in the situation prevailing at the time, and the Israelite tribes' decision to make Saul king after he had proved his worth so brilliantly in the victory over the Ammonites, and entrust him with the battle against the Philistines, seemed to have been rapidly justified by the course of events. The Israelite tribes were able to breathe again. Admittedly, a decisive battle against the Philistines was bound to be imminent, since neither Saul nor the Israelite tribes could have any doubt that the Philistines would very soon set out with their united forces to recover their lost position, and that the real decision would then be made. To begin with, the conflict was limited to minor encounters on the frontier, of which we learn from a few general observations[1] and from various anecdotes[2]. They had no great influence on the course of events. But Saul had to endeavour to prepare for the impending conflict.

We hear practically nothing about a development in the organisation of the monarchy under Saul, and probably little of any significance occurred in this respect. He did attend to Israel's armed forces to some extent. According to 1 Sam. xiv, 52 he gathered together a standing army, probably small in numbers, for the war against the Philistines, and for this purpose drew to himself men who appeared to be particularly valiant. His immediate personal entourage remained confined to a few men who had an important part to play in his conduct of the war. In 1 Sam. xx, 25 there is a reference to the circle that used to gather round him daily at meal

---

[1] 1 Sam. xiv, 52a; xviii, 17b, 21 a, 25, 27a.
[2] Cf. 1 Sam. xvii, 1 ff.; xviii, 6 f.; xxiii, 1 ff.

times; it included, in addition to his son Jonathan, who had already proved his worth in the opening battles against the Philistines, his cousin Abner whom he had made 'captain of his host', that is, leader of the levies of the Israelite tribes (cf. 1 Sam. xiv, 50, 51) and, in addition, David, whom Saul had appointed his personal armour-bearer (cf. 1 Sam. xvi, 14-23). He resided in his native Benjaminite Gibeah (*tell el-fūl*); and there he had built for himself a modest citadel, the foundations of which have been uncovered by excavations on the site[1].

According to 1 Sam. xv, 1 ff. Saul also won a victory over the Amalekites, that body of nomadic tribes in the southern desert with whom the southern tribes of Israel lived in a state of more or less constant enmity (cf. Exod. xvii, 16). The account of this victory appears in a special tradition which has no clearly discernible literary or material connection with the other stories about Saul. Presumably, the Amalekites in the south had, like the Ammonites in the east, taken advantage of the weak state into which the Israelites had been brought by the Philistines, to extend their own territory; and after successfully warding off the Ammonites and achieving an initial success against the Philistines, Saul probably restored Israel's position in regard to the Amalekites.

More important, however, and of greater consequence, was the fact that after Saul had been made king it very soon appeared that, in spite of the brilliant initial successes, the institution of the monarchy was bound to come up against internal difficulties within the sacral association of the Israelite tribes, because, though temporary charismatic leadership was compatible with the traditions of a tribal association subject to a divine law, a 'secular' monarchy was not: and, on the other hand, it was impossible to base the institution of monarchy on the sacral association of the tribes. So the combination of leadership and monarchy in the person of Saul was not a reliable foundation for a permanent institution. These internal difficulties came to the surface in the quarrel between Samuel and Saul which is explained in two different ways in 1 Sam. xiii, 7b-15a and 1 Sam. xv, 1-35. It is therefore impossible to establish the cause of the quarrel with any certainty, but in any case—both passages are in agreement here and it is consonant with the whole nature of the matter—it stemmed from the fact that the relationship between the king's sacral and secular functions was ill-defined and the secular requirements of the monarchy conflicted

[1] Cf. W. F. Albright, BASOR, 52 (1933), pp. 7 ff.

with the ancient sacral traditions. Samuel, who had apparently played an active part in Saul's election to the monarchy, rejected the consequences which flowed inevitably from the establishment of the monarchy, and made himself the spokesman of the old traditions, to which no doubt large sections of the Israelite tribes felt themselves committed. In fact, when Saul now pursued, as he was bound to do, his own way as king, Samuel retracted the call which he had previously issued to Saul and declared that Saul had been 'rejected' by God (1 Sam. xv, 23, cf. xiii, 14). The kingship of Saul, which was not yet firmly established on its own feet, but was linked to the calling of the charismatic leader, thereby lost its support and no doubt much of its authority among the tribes. Saul himself became uncertain of himself and suspicious. 'The Spirit of Yahweh departed from Saul, and an evil spirit from Yahweh troubled him' (1 Sam. xvi, 14). David, his young armour-bearer, became the special object of his suspicions. David's radiant personality had won the ready sympathies of the Israelites (cf. 1 Sam. xviii, 7) whilst Saul's reputation dwindled rapidly after his initial successes. The external emergency which had occasioned his elevation to the kingship turned out to be an insufficient basis for the establishment of a monarchy over the Israelite tribal confederation; and as soon as the external pressure had abated—albeit only temporarily—the problematical character of the institution emerged.

It is true that this internal conflict did not have time to come to a head since the external enemy, the Philistines, brought Saul's kingship to a violent end. The elimination of their garrisons inevitably stirred the Philistines into action. To begin with they had merely allowed themselves to be surprised, but in view of their military superiority they had every prospect of regaining the position they had lost. For in spite of the fact that Israel's armies were now united under a royal command it had not really added to its power since the defeat at Ebenezer and it was also labouring under internal difficulties. The Philistines will scarcely have allowed much time to elapse before making their decisive counter-thrust. In the editorial note in 1 Sam. xiii, 1 which is probably only deuteronomistic, Saul is said to have reigned for two years over Israel; but the statement is incontestable on textual grounds[1] and probably historically too, so that it must be assumed that the

[1] The usual alteration of the text ('twenty years') is based not on textual but historical considerations. But the deuteronomist doubtless wrote 'two years', since only this figure fits into his chronological system; cf. M. Noth, *Überlieferungsgeschichtliche Studien*, I (1943), pp. 18 ff.

deuteronomist was incorporating part of a sound tradition[1]. This statement implies that, after Saul's successful surprise attack, the Philistines prepared for their counter-attack in the following year; and even if the traditional record did not state this explicitly we should be bound to assume it as a probability. The Philistines can hardly have wanted to give Saul time to consolidate his monarchy before engaging in battle with him. As it was the custom to embark on large-scale campaigns in the spring after the end of the winter rains (cf. 2 Sam. xi, 1), the Philistines no doubt chose the spring of the year following Saul's appointment as king as a suitable moment for their counter-attack.

We learn what ensued in considerable detail from the traditional account of David's rise which is contained in 1 Sam. xvi, 14 ff Once again the Philistine rulers gathered together their armies in Aphek (1 Sam. xxix, 1)[2]. This time, however, they did not attack the central Palestinian mountains from there directly but advanced northwards through the maritime plain and then—no doubt by the usual route or through the modern *bilād er-rūḥa*—into the plain of Jezreel to the city of Jezreel (the modern *zer'īn*), cf. 1 Sam. xxix, 11b. This presupposes that they joined up with the other 'Sea People' elements in various cities in the northern coastal plains and the plain of Jezreel. In this way they attacked Saul at a particularly vulnerable point in his domain, where the geographically relatively ill-defined area of Israelite settlement was hemmed in particularly closely by Canaanite city territories so that the Galilean tribes were connected with the tribes in central and southern Palestine merely by a narrow bridge of Israelite territory. They thereby prevented Saul from bringing all his forces together, and in fact, according to 1 Sam. xxxi, 7 'the men of Israel that were on the other side of the valley and they that were on the other side of Jordan'[3], that is, the tribes in the Galilean hills and the land east of Jordan, did not take part in the battle against the Philistines. Saul set out against the Philistines with the armies of the central and south Palestinian tribes 'by a fountain which is in Jezreel' (1 Sam. xxix, 1), probably by the source of the Harod

[1] It is difficult to believe that the deuteronomist invented this figure for the sake of his chronological system, since he could have built this up in another way to suit his scheme. The reference to the king's age on his accession which is provided for in the deuteronomistic scheme of the introduction of reigns has been omitted in 1 Sam. xiii, 1, probably because the deuteronomist had no evidence.

[2] Cf. above, p. 165.

[3] The usual alteration of the text in this passage is not justified on textual or material grounds; there were no Israelites in the 'cities of the plain' and there were no 'cities of the Jordan' at all.

(the modern *'ēn jālūd*), south-east of the city of Jezreel at the foot
of Mount Gilboa where Gideon undertook his famous attack on the
Midianite camp. The situation was hopeless from the very outset,
and Saul gave up his cause for lost even before the battle had begun.
A special tradition contained in 1 Sam. xxviii, 3-25 relates how
before the battle he went in his despair in disguise to a necromancer
in near-by Endor (the modern *khirbet eṣ-ṣafṣāfe* near *endūr*) to
enquire of Samuel's ghost about his fate, and how, through the
woman's arts, he was merely given the answer that his monarchy
and his life were lost.

In fact, according to 1 Sam. xxxi, the Philistines' attack sufficed
to break up Saul's armies straight away. They scattered and took
their flight over Mount Gilboa, pursued by the victorious Philistines. In the course of the pursuit Saul's sons lost their lives, together with a great part of the Israelite armies. Saul committed
suicide so as not to fall alive into the hands of the Philistines. The
Philistines' victory was complete and Israel's situation more
desperate than after the second battle of Ebenezer. The Philistines
occupied the territory of the Israelite tribes all over again, including this time Galilee and the land east of Jordan (1 Sam. xxxi, 7).
They took cruel vengeance on Saul and his sons when they found
their corpses on Mount Gilboa. They cut off Saul's head and
carried it through their cities with his armour as a trophy of
victory. They fastened his body and those of his sons to the wall
of Beth-shan (the modern *tell el-ḥuṣn* near *bēsān*), which lay not
very far from the battlefield in the lower part of the broad valley
of the *nahr jālūd* and was at that time still the seat of a government of 'Sea Peoples' related to the Philistines[1]. Thus Saul and
his sons would have been denied the last offices of burial if people
from Jabesh, which lay across the Jordan not far from Beth-shan,
who owed to Saul their deliverance from the Ammonites, had not
fetched their bodies secretly by night from the wall of Beth-shan
and buried them in Jabesh. The Philistines had now attained their
goal and the question of sovereignty in Palestine appeared to have
been settled in their favour once and for all. The final outcome of
Saul's short reign was as hopeless for Israel as it could possibly be.

[1] Cf. A. Alt, Zur Geschichte von Beth-Sean 1500–1000 B.C., PJB, 22 [1926],
pp. 108-120.

15. *David's Empire*

The situation in which Israel found itself after the death of Saul forms the background to the amazing rise of David. With the coming of David, following the monarchy of Saul, which was a mere episode, Israel's progress to political power entered a completely new and decisive phase. Unlike Saul, David set out on the road to political power quite deliberately and consistently from the very beginning. That is why in the Old Testament a new kind of historical tradition begins with David. The tradition of David must be regarded as, for the most part, a historical record, a work of 'scholarship', whereas for the earlier historical period up to and including Saul we have mainly popular stories and also traditions concerning pre-historical times, based on religious confessions. The development of political power and the active participation in historical events was the precondition for the beginning of historical writing. For the history of David we have at our disposal source material which allows us to discern the historical processes and, above all, their mutual relationships more clearly than was possible from the earlier popular stories. This also applies to David's rise to power, for which we have a connected narrative which deals with precisely this historical theme and traces David's progress from his beginnings up to the establishment of the Judaean-Israelite state with obvious expert knowledge and a sure grasp of the underlying circumstances[1].

David[2] was a Judaean from Bethlehem (the modern *bēt laḥm*, 5 miles south of Jerusalem), the capital of the tribe of Judah. In the person of David the tribe of Judah, the most important of the southern Palestinian tribes, emerges for the first time as a factor of historical importance. David's career began when he first attracted attention as a capable and talented young man who was drawn into Saul's immediate entourage as his armour-bearer

---

[1] 1 Sam. xvi, 14–2 Sam. v, 25. This work was subsequently extended, particularly in its first part, by some secondary additions, but it is still possible to reconstruct its original form with fair certainty.

[2] The name David has become a problem because in the Mari-texts a word *dawidūm* often occurs with the meaning 'commander', 'troop leader' (cf. W. v. Soden, WO, I, 3 [1948], p. 197), which can hardly be separated from the name David. If it is the same, it hardly looks as though 'David' was originally a personal name at all. Perhaps David first gave himself or was given this name during the period he was a leader of mercenaries (see below) and the title may have become a pseudo-personal name for him and taken the place of another personal name, unknown to us, which was his original name.

(1 Sam. xvi, 21)[1]. He was not, however, for long a member of Saul's entourage. Having quickly acquired popularity on account of his particularly attractive personality, he became the special object of Saul's suspicions and preferred to escape from the king's growing animosity towards him. He fled to his homeland, but did not remain in Bethlehem: he retired to the southernmost part of the mountains west of Jordan and gathered together a band of adventurers, with whom he supported himself by all kinds of plundering expeditions (for an example see 1 Sam. xxv, 2-43), and he was now pursued all the more by the hostility of Saul, who failed, however, to catch him. This period in his life had a decisive influence on his further development, for it turned him into a *condottiere*, a professional warrior, for whom warfare—at first only on a small scale—became his whole life. At the same time, evidently in order to profit therefrom later on, he established good relationships with the tribes that had settled south of Judah. According to 1 Sam. xxv, 43 he married one Ahinoam from Jezreel, which was probably a Kenite place[2] (south-east of Hebron, though we do not know precisely where) and, according to 1 Sam. xxv, 42, one Abigail, the wife of the rich Nabal from Maon (the modern *tell ma'īn* about 10 miles south of Hebron) whose death had been caused at a lavish sheep-shearing feast by fear of a sudden hostile visit from David and his men. This Nabal was probably also a Kenite[3].

For David and the band of men gathered around him the Philistine military system which employed mercenaries[4] as well as heavily armed hand-to-hand fighters, offered the best opportunities. One day, therefore, David offered the service of himself and his men to the Philistine ruler Achish of Gath (1 Sam. xxvii, 2 f.). Achish gave him Ziklag with the adjoining territory, in return for which he had to render military service when required. The whereabouts of Ziklag is no more certain than that of Gath; it was probably on the inner edge of the southernmost part of the maritime plain. It was certainly a risky move for David to go over to the Philistines, with whom an imminent life-and-death struggle awaited the Israelites. It is true that mercenary leaders are not usually very particular about whose service they enter provided they are well paid, and in any case this was David's simplest and surest way of escaping from

---

[1] The well-known story of Goliath contained in 1 Sam. xvii is secondary, both textually and materially, compared with the narrative in 1 Sam. xvi, 14-23.

[2] Cf. M. Noth, *Das Buch Josua* ([2] 1953) on Jos. xv, 55-57a.

[3] Maon was situated in the same later Judaean district as Jezreel; cf. Jos. xv, 55 f.

[4] Apart from David himself we have another example of this phenomenon in the 'Gittite' Ittai with his 600 men (2 Sam. xv, 18 ff.).

Saul's ambushes. But to the Israelite tribes the move was bound to seem a betrayal of their cause, even though David himself regarded it from the outset as in no way a transference of allegiance to the Philistines, but merely as a means to an end in his own career. In his choice of means he evidently had few inhibitions. He was playing a double game. From Ziklag he continued to develop his contacts with the south-Judaean tribes. With his men he undertook all kinds of plundering expeditions in the surrounding country and made presents of the spoil to the elders of various places in the area occupied by these southern tribes (1 Sam. xxx, 26-31). There was no need for his liege lord Achish to know this: he was kept in the belief that David had broken with Saul and the Israelite tribes once and for all. Admittedly the Philistines did not trust him absolutely. The other Philistine rulers insisted, against the wishes of his liege lord Achish, that David and his men should be excluded from taking part in the decisive battle against Saul (1 Sam. xxix, 2-11a), although he was naturally under an obligation to serve in such a great enterprise: they were afraid he might betray them. David was spared, therefore, from having to take an active part on the Philistine side in the struggle against Saul and the Israelite tribes.

The news of the disaster which had befallen Saul, that reached David in Ziklag, was evidently no surprise to him and could not, in view of the situation, be a surprise for such a shrewd man anyway. In fact it appears that he had evidently already considered and prepared for what he would do if the event which he expected actually occurred. He now acted very methodically and skilfully, making first of all for the one goal that was within his immediate reach, thereby making a move forwards which he certainly did not regard as the final stage in his progress. He was skilled in the great art of waiting until things came within his grasp, and this was the way he created the great empire which represents the climax in the development of political power in the history of Israel. In 2 Sam. ii, 1-3 we read that after Saul's terrible end David moved up to Hebron with all his followers and entourage and settled there. Calebite Hebron formed not merely the natural centre of the south Palestinian mountains but also possessed in its immediate vicinity the famous tree sanctuary of Mamre (the modern *haram rāmet el-khalīl*) which was probably at the same time the religious centre for all the south Palestinian tribes which appear to have been united around this centre in a confederation of six tribes forming a separate group within and alongside the great Israelite confederation of the twelve tribes. These six tribes (Judah, Caleb, Othniel, Cain, Jerahmeel, Simeon) led a life of their own, which, though it did not isolate them from the larger whole, did give them a special position. This fact now became historically important because David turned it to account. David was himself a Judaean; through his first marriages he was related to the Kenites; from Ziklag he had deliberately cultivated relations with the southern tribes. These relationships now inevitably bore fruit.

'The men of Judah came, and there [in Hebron or Mamre] they anointed David king over the house of Judah' (2 Sam. ii, 4a). The term 'house of Judah' is used here in contrast to the simple term 'Judah' evidently to signify the whole confederation of the six southern tribes. Who induced the six tribes to take this momentous step? The institution of monarchy, until recently quite foreign to Israel, had led to a fearful catastrophe soon after its emergence in the person of king Saul. It is hardly likely that, in these circumstances, the idea of a king in Israel can have taken such firm roots in Israel that, following the death of Saul, the election of a new king was bound to appear a matter of course and merely a question of choosing the right man. We are not given any details regarding the process by which David was elected king over the 'house of Judah' but we shall not be far wrong if we assume that David himself played a part in persuading the southern tribes to make this move. His personal influence was no doubt great. As Saul's armour-bearer he had already rapidly made himself universally popular. Moreover, for the southern tribes he was a man from their own circle, and, after his separation from Saul, David had proved himself emphatically a man of the southern tribes. If the institution of monarchy had been brought into rapid disrepute by Saul, the Benjaminite Saul was himself to blame for his own failure: David, the Judaean, would certainly make a better job of it. The long-standing special position of the southern tribes over against the larger whole, no doubt played a fundamental part, and David will have exploited this situation in his own interest. Since under David's monarchy the southern tribes constituted a state on their own, 'the house of Judah', they not only thereby underlined and intensified their special character but brought about a political division within the totality of the Israelite tribes which continued in a more or less pronounced form throughout the history of Israel and had the most unfortunate effects on its outward course.

The 'anointing' of the king was a rite of consecration enacted at a shrine; and in this case it probably took place at the religious centre of Mamre. This ceremony followed the election of David to the monarchy by the 'men of Judah'[1], and the election appears to have taken place without any religious foundation such as the designation by a prophet. It was a purely political act. That is typical of David's rise to power. His own personality and connections and his military entourage were the basis of his accession to the power represented by the kingship over the house of Judah. But how could the Philistines allow all this to happen after their great victory over Israel? There can be no doubt that David still remained their vassal and that, as tenant of Ziklag, he was still obliged to render military service with his band of mercenaries. Evidently, the Philistines had no objection to the 'men of Judah' electing this vassal of theirs as king. Whether or not the Philistines trusted David, at any rate they may have thought it a gain for themselves that the establishment of a separate Judaean monarchy involved a splitting up and therefore a weakening of Israel. It eliminated the confederation of the twelve tribes as a political and military unit since the southern tribes had acted regardless of the continuance of this association. For the time being, therefore, the Philistines gave at any rate their tacit consent to the course of events.

They maintained the same attitude to events which took place among the other tribes, since these events also appeared to involve the permanent division of Israel into two parts. Saul's captain, Abner, had survived the disaster on Mount Gilboa and he now assumed the leadership. He took Eshbaal, Saul's sole surviving son[2] across into the land east of Jordan, as far away as possible from the Philistines, to Mahanaim (the modern *tell ḥedjaj*) the capital of the Ephraimite territory in the land of Gilead south of the Jabbok and made him king there. This was a purely arbitrary action (2 Sam. ii, 8-9). Eshbaal's kingship was entirely without religious foundation. But the defeated and bewildered Israelite tribes apparently agreed to his appointment. They knew from the other monarchies in the world around them that monarchy was hereditary and, apart from Saul's sole surviving son, no other suitable candidate was available. Although it had been anything but a success under Saul, monarchy was the only institution to hand. Since the southern tribes had gone their own way with David, Eshbaal's sovereignty covered the somewhat ill-defined

[1] 2 Sam. ii, 4a contains an abbreviated statement. The 'men of Judah' could only proclaim David king, whilst the anointing was no doubt performed by a priest.

[2] The name Eshbaal is only preserved unchanged in 1 Chron. viii, 33; ix, 39, whilst in 2 Sam. it is distorted into the form Ishbosheth, because it contains the name of the God Baal which later became taboo.

territory of the tribes in the mountains, both east of Jordan and in Galilee and Samaria, as is recorded fairly precisely in 2 Sam. ii, 9. Like Saul, Eshbaal called himself 'king of Israel' and claimed to rule over all the Israelite tribes. But as the southern tribes had separated themselves from the rest, the political concept of 'Israel' under Eshbaal in fact only covered the major part of the tribes excluding the southern tribes, and from this time this limitation of the name 'Israel' continued in force within the political sphere, with 'Judah' and 'Israel' confronting one another as separate entities. The name 'Israel' now had two different meanings: as a term covering the whole of the tribes of Israel which represented and continued to represent the traditions of the basic deeds of God in their prehistory, 'Israel' was still used in the language of faith, but 'Israel' also signified a particular political structure which included only a section of the Israelite tribes and soon absorbed non-Israelite elements.

'Israel' and 'Judah' under Eshbaal and David were soon involved in military conflicts in the frontier region, which were presumably caused by the fact that Eshbaal, or rather, Abner, whose importance and influence continued to be greater than that of the king, undertook the almost hopeless task of subjugating the southern tribes by force. Naturally, David was not only a match for his opponents but was stronger than they. But these battles were only of minor importance and had no special consequences, apart from the fact that in their course Abner slew a brother of Joab, a member of David's immediate personal entourage, who was to play a part as the captain of his armies and hence, from now on, was consumed with a passion for revenge against Abner which he put into effect soon afterwards (2 Sam. ii, 12–iii, 1). This happened in the following way.

Eshbaal was unwise enough to fall out with Abner, because Abner had taken one of Saul's concubines. The unscrupulous Abner at once betrayed Eshbaal and got in touch with David through messengers, with the object of presenting him with the tribes under Eshbaal's rule (2 Sam. iii, 6 ff.). David was prepared to receive Abner with a view to further negotiations on the one condition that he brought him Saul's daughter Michal to be his wife[1]. This episode is typical of David's aims and methods. Abner

---

[1] The later tradition made Michal become David's wife during Saul's lifetime, in the context of David's victory over Goliath (1 Sam. xviii, 27). This is historically incorrect and the reference to this tradition in 2 Sam. iii, 14 is shown by the context to be secondary. In 2 Sam. iii, 15 the context requires 'Abner' (instead of 'Ishbosheth') as the subject of the sentences.

naturally took into account the fact that David regarded his kingship over Judah only as a beginning and aspired to rule over
all the Israelite tribes, and Abner was obviously right. David's
intended marriage with Michal was also designed to promote
this end, since one day, when all of Saul's sons had gone, Saul's
inheritance[1] and the succession to his throne[2] might fall to him
even if Abner's plan failed. Moreover, Abner reckoned that the
non-Judaean tribes would thus also be easily won over to the idea
of making David their king; here too he was right. From the time
when he had been Saul's armour-bearer David had not been
unknown to them and had enjoyed great popularity. Since he had
been king of Judah he had lost no opportunity of establishing
unofficial relationships with them[3]. Nevertheless, David was wary
about Abner's proposal. He knew him personally, as they had both
been members of Saul's entourage. For Abner the condition that
he should bring Michal with him meant the clear and final consummation of his break with Eshbaal and the transfer of his
allegiance to David. Abner fulfilled the condition, negotiated with
David in Hebron and came to terms with him. But the plan was not
carried out, since, on his journey back, Abner was murdered by
Joab at the gate of Hebron on the pretext of vengeance for the
murder of his brother, but in fact owing to jealousy and the
fear that Abner's connection with David might endanger his own
position.

David rejected the not entirely unwarranted suspicion that he
had engineered the murder of Abner, who was a power in Israel; he
arranged for Abner to be buried in Hebron with full honours in
his own presence. It is indeed improbable that he wanted this
murder, as it could easily have lost him the sympathy of many
people who were important for the next period in his career, and
in 2 Sam. iii, 37 the chronicler is able to state with satisfaction that
'all the people [probably in Hebron] and all Israel understood that
day that it was not of the king to slay Abner the son of Ner'. It was
not long before the Israelite tribes' confidence in David, and affection
for him, led him to the goal which he desired. One day the weak

---

[1] The age and application of the Israelite laws concerning the daughters' right of
succession, where there were no sons, are doubtful, however; cf. the late passage in
Numbers xxvii, 1-11.

[2] Naturally, there was not yet any definite right of succession to the throne. But, as in
the case of Eshbaal, it was easy enough to fall back on a member of the family of the
previous king in the search for a successor.

[3] As an example the writer in 2 Sam. ii, 4b-7 tells of a message which David sent to
the people of Jabesh, after he had learnt that they had buried Saul and his sons. His
sole intention in sending this message must have been to make them think well of him.

Eshbaal, who now lacked the strong hand of Abner, was murdered in Mahanaim during his midday sleep by two professional soldiers ('captains of bands') from the originally Canaanite city of Beeroth which had been absorbed by the tribe of Benjamin. The inhabitants had probably been forced to leave the city in a conflict with Saul and now took their revenge on the son of Saul (2 Sam. iv, 1 ff.). Eshbaal was not a king for long. The note in 2 Sam. ii, 10 gives him a reign of two years, *i.e.* a period from his election until an unknown day in the following year. This statement cannot be refuted on textual or material grounds. It is unlikely anyway that this weak monarchy could have survived for long without proper foundations. That Eshbaal was murdered probably suited David quite well. But that the two murderers soon appeared before him in Hebron with Eshbaal's head, in order to receive his praise and reward, could only embarrass him. If the murder of Abner had already aroused suspicions, it now seemed obvious that David was trying to make his way by murder generally. David had both the men killed at once and Eshbaal's head buried in Abner's tomb in Hebron. Again it is in fact unlikely that David tried to accelerate the almost inevitable course of events by instigating a murder instead of calmly and shrewdly awaiting the end of Eshbaal's reign as king; and once again the Israelites appear to have believed him when he claimed that he had had no share in the murder of Eshbaal.

There now remained practically only one path for the tribes of Israel to take. They had to hold fast to the institution of monarchy whether they liked it or not. After the southern tribes had founded their monarchy, the old confederation of tribes could not be developed into a political organisation such as appeared to be necessary in the present emergency. Among their own people they evidently found no man whom they could have made king. Of Saul's male descendants the sole survivor was now a lame son of Jonathan (cf. 2 Sam. ix, 1-3) who was out of the question. Meanwhile, however, David had become Saul's son-in-law through his marriage with Michal; he had also fostered and established other connections with them and had proved his worth as king of Judah. The elders of the tribes of the state of Israel therefore came to David in Hebron and offered him the kingship over Israel too. David made a 'covenant' with them and they anointed him 'king over Israel' (2 Sam. v, 1-3). This again was a political move. It is true that the contract was concluded 'before Yahweh', that is, in the sanctuary; but that merely means that this agreement was placed under divine protection, as in the case of other human agreements. The anointing was a sacral act following his election to the kingship but did not in itself constitute the election to the kingship. It is true that in 2 Sam. v, 2b there is an explicit reference to the fact that Yahweh had said to David: 'thou shalt be a captain (*nāgīd*) over Israel' (cf. above, p. 169). We are not told what this statement refers to. If the voice of a prophet unknown to us had uttered these words, it hardly meant more than that the elders of the tribes were confirmed in the move which the situation demanded in any case; and the agreement concluded in Hebron was still the important thing.

David was now 'king of Judah and Israel'. Two different acts at different times had made him first king over Judah and then king over Israel (in the narrower political sense of the term). Both kingships had their own legal basis and it was no longer possible to amalgamate them in a unified political structure. At any rate, David considered it right to keep to the foundations which had developed historically. The only factor uniting the two political structures was the person of the king himself: the link between them was a 'personal union'. Even after David had been elected king over Israel the juxtaposition of 'Israel' and 'Judah' continued; and the division of the Israelite tribes into two different states went on unaltered. Neither of the two states was a 'national state', in the way that Saul's kingship over the whole confederation of Israel had been a kind of 'national monarchy'; and the functions of the tribal confederation could not be continued by either of the states. Both states had been brought into existence by the special conditions which followed Saul's disastrous end.

The union of the two states in the control of one man could no longer be a matter of indifference to the Philistines. Until then they had presumably regarded David and Eshbaal as vassals under Philistine sovereignty. We are not told how far this vassal relationship worked in practice The co-existence of the two states may have suited them very well, and they do not appear to have interfered in the internal affairs of Israel so long as their sovereign rights were not affected. But the amalgamation of Judah and Israel in the person of their vassal David was bound to appear to them as a power which threatened them and so induced them to intervene. In fact we read in 2 Sam. v, 17 that when they heard that David had been anointed king over Israel, all the Philistines immediately[1] 'came

[1] In 2 Sam. v the story of David's conquest of Jerusalem takes precedence, though it took place a good time after David had united the two kingdoms (cf. below, pp. 189 ff.).

up to seek David'. They occupied the valley of Rephaim (verse 18) immediately west of the city-state of Jerusalem (the modern *el bak'a*). There were good reasons for this. The territory of Jerusalem separated the areas occupied by the states of Judah and Israel from one another. By attacking at this point they had hopes of preventing David from entering on his reign over Israel or at least making it impossible to assemble the armies of the two kingdoms. For David everything was now at stake. He could only maintain the position he had achieved if he succeeded in warding off the Philistines and destroying their supremacy; for their part the Philistines could only hold their supremacy if they were able to remove David from his kingship over Judah and Israel. The question as to who was to be supreme in Palestine had to be decided now. The decision went in David's favour. David set forth against the Philistines[1] with his band of professional soldiers[2] and probably made a surprise attack near the shrine of Baal-Perazim on Mount Perazim[3]. It is impossible to identify this place exactly. It was probably on the southern border of the plain of Rephaim. David certainly came from the south, from Hebron, and will have approached the plain of Rephaim on minor roads, and therefore unnoticed[4]. He succeeded in vanquishing the Philistines completely. He beat them by using their own methods. He had been a mercenary leader under the Philistines and knew their style of warfare. He

Historically the conflict with the Philistines no doubt preceded the conquest of Jerusalem. 2 Sam. v, 17 refers back quite correctly to 2 Sam. v, 1-3; and the only question is whether the writer of the story of David's rise to power put the story of the conquest of Jerusalem first, because he regarded it as particulary important, and then reported at a later stage on the victories over the Philistines in 2 Sam. v, 17-25, though with an explicit link with verses 1-3 (2 Sam. v, 4-5, 11-16 are secondary in this context from a literary point of view), or whether it was only a later writer who introduced the anticipatory passage about Jerusalem, so that the original order—corresponding to the historical sequence of events—was 2 Sam. v, 1-3, 17-25, 6-10 (with verse 10 as the emphatic conclusion).

[1] According to verse 17 David 'went down to the stronghold' and, according to verse 9, this can only mean the 'stronghold of Jerusalem. This can hardly be the original wording but a secondary reference to the Jerusalem story which now precedes. 1 Chron. xiv, 8 offers instead the general statement: 'he went out against them'. That too can hardly be the original text. Probably the traditional text was no longer intact at this point and was 'improved' in various ways, so that it is now impossible to reconstruct the original text.

[2] In verse 21 there is a specific reference, quite rightly, to 'David and his men'.

[3] In Isaiah xxviii, 21 there is mention of Mount Perazim, which was no doubt well known to the Jerusalemites and which lay in their neighbourhood, in an allusion probably to the victory that David had won there, at which Yahweh had intervened with great power. In 2 Sam. v, 20 the name 'Perazim' is given a secondary explanation quite artificially from David's victory over his enemies.

[4] Cf. A. Alt, PJB (1927), pp. 15 f., where it is suggested that the sanctuary of Baal-Perazim is identical with the modern sanctuary of *sitt el-bedrīye* on the rounded hill-top of *esh-sherāfāt*.

confronted them, not, like Saul, with the large, but unwieldy, militia of the tribes, but with a band of mercenaries which he may have strengthened and developed meanwhile as king of Judah and which had a professional understanding of the art of war. He beat the Philistines with the aid of this nimble instrument and with his own inimitable skill. In view of the all-important nature of the conflict, however, the Philistines made another attempt. The first time, underestimating the strength and military skill of the enemy, who was their own vassal, they had presumably not raised their full strength. The only point in making this second attempt, presumably quite soon after the first defeat, was to enter the fray with all the military forces at their disposal. They appeared once more on the plain of Rephaim. And David beat them again, this time at a place described as 'over against the mulberry trees' (2 Sam. v, 23). This place, probably well known to the near-by inhabitants of Jerusalem, is naturally impossible to identify. Perhaps this time David came upon the Philistines with his troops from the side of the state of Israel, from the north—no doubt as suddenly as before. Anyway, according to 2 Sam. v, 25, the pursuit of the utterly defeated Philistines took place north of the plain of Rephaim 'from Gibeon[1] until thou come to Gezer' (*tell jezer* in the maritime plain south of Lydda). Pursuing them right up to the borders of their own territory, David completed his victory over his most powerful and most important enemies.

The Philistines made no further attempt. They were forced to surrender their supremacy in the land. The period of their predominance had come to a rapid end. Henceforth they were limited to their old possessions in the southern part of the maritime plain and formed one of the small neighbouring states which gave trouble to Judah and Israel as occasion offered but were no longer able to make any decisive historical interventions. David's decisive victories over the Philistines were the fundamental and the most lasting successes of a life that was rich in success. They gave him freedom to develop and elaborate his political system along his own lines.

No doubt one of his first measures was to give the kingdom a centre. He still resided in Hebron ,which, though it formed a natural centre for the kingdom of Judah, was not in the long run a suitable place from which to govern the greater kingdom of Israel as well. Hebron was not only too far from the centre to be a suitable

---

[1] Instead of the 'Geba' which is given in the text, one should read 'Gibeon', in accordance with 1 Chron. xiv, 16.

capital for the dual monarchy, but in Hebron David was and remained primarily king of Judah, and the tribes in Israel did not want to be ruled by the king of Judah but by the David they had themselves elected king of Israel. He could not, however, make an Israelite city such as Shechem his residence, natural centre of the land though it was, out of consideration for the Judaeans who had been the first to make him king and would hardly have forgiven him if he had moved to the kingdom of Israel. In view of the jealousy and bad feeling between the two kingdoms of Judah and Israel which he had to take into account and which was to lead to open conflict even during his reign, with the sure instinct of the wise statesman he chose a city on neutral soil between the territories of the two kingdoms. This was Jerusalem, which had not yet been conquered by the Israelite tribes and was still occupied by a group of earlier inhabitants of the country, the Jebusites. The territory of the kingdom of Judah began south of Jerusalem and that of the kingdom of Israel north of Jerusalem[1]. It was an ancient city, the first literary reference to which appears in the Egyptian 'execration texts' at the beginning of the second millennium B.C.[2]. The Amarna tablets show that it was the seat of the city ruler Abdiheba[3]. In the Amarna period it had played a certain part as a ruler's residence in the mountainous area where there were few cities; but up to now it had not been one of the really important cities of the land. It lay on a hill within the hollow of a valley[4] in a strong position, but not one commanding a large area, at a height of about 2500 ft. on the rather inaccessible southern part of the hills west of Jordan. It was near the main north to south road over the hills, which followed the watershed, but lacked good communications with the east and west. It was in no sense the obvious centre of the land and the natural features of its position did not mark it out as the capital. What it became under David, and what it has meant in history right up to our own day, it owes not to nature but to the will and the insight of a man who, disregarding the natural conditions, made a decision that was right in a particular historical situation.

David took his time over this step too. According to 2 Sam. ii, 11,

[1] Cf. above all A. Alt, 'Jerusalems Aufstieg', ZDMG, N.F. 4 (1925), pp. 1-19.
[2] In K. Sethe (cf. above, p. 18, note 3) e 27/28 f. 18.
[3] The Amarna letters Nos. 285-290 derive from this Abdiheba (Knudtzon).
[4] Pre-Davidic and Davidic Jerusalem lay on the so-called 'south-east hill' above the Gihon fountain and outside the residential area of the modern city; cf. *Westminster Historical Atlas to the Bible* (1945), Pl. xvii. The comprehensive work by J. Simons, *Jerusalem in the Old Testament. Researches and Theories* (1952), should now be consulted on all questions regarding the ancient topography of Jerusalem.

v, 5a he resided in Hebron for seven and a half years, of which only two coincided with the simultaneous reigns of Eshbaal and David For a time, therefore, he ruled over both kingdoms from Hebron. Then he conquered Jebusite Jerusalem with his mercenaries (2 Sam. v, 6-9)[1] and made it his residence as 'the city of David'. It was not attached to either the kingdom of Judah or the kingdom of Israel but remained a city-state and David now became the city ruler of Jerusalem as legal successor to the previous Jebusite city ruler. The city was not inhabited by either Judaeans or Israelites, but continued to be occupied by its previous inhabitants and only received the king and his entourage, his household and his mercenaries. All these made up a considerable body of people, however, corresponding to the size of the political organisation that was now ruled from here.

David then moved into his new capital the ancient tribal relic of the Ark, which had apparently not been taken much notice of for some time, or perhaps, since the Philistines had captured it, had been carefully shunned in the old Canaanite city of Kiriath-Jearim which was annexed to the tribe of Benjamin. By bringing it to his capital David restored it to a place of honour (2 Sam. vi, 1-15; 17-19). He wanted to give this city the dignity pertaining to this central relic of the confederation of the twelve tribes and thus boldly linked to it the ancient sacral tradition which bound the tribes together, and thereby made use of it for his own ends. In fact the position in world history which Jerusalem has occupied ever since is due to this very act. David presumably set up the Ark in the city shrine, which was probably on the rounded hill-top dominating the city on the north where Solomon later erected his buildings. The ancient Israelite shrine now stood in a Canaanite place of worship in a Canaanite city which, though it was now David's royal city, had hitherto known no Israelite traditions of any kind. The priests who served it were royal officials (2 Sam. viii, 17a, 18b; xx, 25b, 26). Admittedly, the Ark had stood in former times in one or an other of the old local sanctuaries and the Israelite tribes now revered the sanctuary of Jerusalem as their own religious centre. 'Mount Zion'—this was the name of the hill-top on which Jerusalem's place of worship stood—became a concept in Israel's religious vocabulary.

The territories of the kingdoms of Judah and Israel were not very clearly defined owing to the contiguity of Israelites and Canaanites.

---

[1] In 2 Sam. v, 6 the writer refers correctly again to the 'king and his men', whereas 1 Chron. xi, 4 tendentiously substitutes, 'David and all Israel'.

This was true in particular of the kingdom of Israel. By incorporating the hitherto independent Canaanite city-states David gave the kingdoms of Judah and Israel the territorial unity which they had been lacking. We have no direct information about this, but it is possible to infer it indirectly. In 2 Sam. xxiv, 5-7 there is a description of the territorial frontiers of Israel and Judah. It is true that, according to the text, it describes the route which David's officers took for the purpose of the census of the people which was evidently conducted with a view to a reassembly of the levies. But in fact a description of the frontiers is offered for this route. It begins in the southern land east of Jordan on the Arnon (*sēl el-mōjib*) with the city of Aroer (the modern *khirbet 'arā'ir*) and therefore includes the whole plateau north of the Arnon with its cities in the east roughly as far as the line Aroer-Dibon (*dībān*)—Medeba (*mādeba*) in David's domains, then lists the 'land of the Hittites' between the land of Gad[1] and the Ephraimite-Manassite territory of the land of Gilead on the one hand, and the city of Dan by the sources of the Jordan on the other. 'The land of the Hittites'[2] can only mean an ancient city-state territory and, according to the context, a strip of city-state territories north-east and north of the *'ajlūn* must be meant, which David had also subjugated. Then there follow from the 'stronghold of Tyre'[3] onwards—this probably means the mainland base of the island city of Tyre (probably the modern *tell reshēdīye*)—evidently in a southerly direction 'the cities of the Hivites and of the Canaanites', that is, the city-states of the maritime plains north and south of the Carmel salient as far as an unnamed southern frontier which must be located roughly on the *nahr el-'auja*, beyond which in the maritime plain began the territory of the Philistine cities, which, though stripped of their power, had remained independent states. The statements contained in Judges i, 27-35, according to which the Canaanite cities which were not conquered by the tribes to begin with were later, 'when Israel was strong,' rendered politically dependent, though not occupied, must be taken as referring to this measure of David's. From this passage we learn in particular that the great cities in the plain of Jezreel were subjugated as well, which one would anyway have

---

[1] The name Jazer describes the province of Gad (cf. Numbers xxxii, 1), whereas the curious יהם (with the article that precedes it), is obviously erroneous. One would expect a verbal form in its place.

[2] Verse 6 should be read thus, following one part of the Septuagint tradition instead of the obviously distorted text. It is impossible to reconstruct the following word with any certainty.

[3] 'Sidon' in verse 6 is possibly intended to mean 'Phoenicia' quite generally. This is admittedly difficult to decide, since the preceding words are again distorted.

assumed to be the case in the nature of things. If, in accordance with the enumeration of the provinces of the kingdom of Israel in Solomon's time which is given in 1 Kings iv, 7-19, Israelite tribal territories and Canaanite city territories together constituted the territory of the kingdom of Israel, the subjugation of the Canaanite cities which this presupposes can hardly be ascribed to Solomon, of whom there is otherwise no record that he extended the area of his kingdoms, but must have been the work of David.

This means that the Israelites had achieved a final victory over the old Canaanite population and the kingdoms of Israel and Judah had received a generous accession of territory, to round off their domains. The process was most advantageous to the kingdom of Israel, in which the settlements of the tribes or groups of tribes were far from self-contained and much divided by city territories. At the same time, whilst the kingdom of Israel was greatly expanded, for the kingdom of Judah it presumably merely involved the lesser acquisition of city-state territories in the adjacent hill country to the west. It is true that this accession of power and territory also meant the loss of national compactness, especially for the kingdom of Israel and to a lesser degree for the kingdom of Judah as well. The Canaanite system was now incorporated in the kingdoms of Israel and Judah. For the inhabitants of the cities, whose ways were so foreign to the Israelite tribes, evidently remained substantially untouched by these annexations, and the political and social structure of their lives probably remained fundamentally the same. The place of the city kings was merely taken by the king of Israel or Judah; and where the cities had been governed aristocratically, the ruling class now had to acknowledge the sovereignty of this king as their overlord. Their submission was enforced, on the whole, by the superiority of David's power which had been revealed so clearly in his victory over the Philistines. Anyway, we do not hear that warlike undertakings were required to secure their submission. In both kingdoms the Israelite tribes were the uppermost and decisive element; but the Canaanite inhabitants were now a more-or-less important factor as well.

On the basis of his authority as king of Judah and Israel, David also subjugated his neighbours. He thereby created a great empire extending far beyond the confines of the Israelite tribes, and well rounded-off on all sides, including a greater part of Palestine and Syria. Large-scale political organisations had occasionally existed on Palestinian-Syrian soil, especially in the period when Palestine and Syria had been under Egyptian rule[1]. The Egyptian model also played an apparently not insignificant part in the internal organisation of David's empire. In 2 Sam. viii, 1-14, there is an annalistic compilation of David's exploits to extend his power, presumably in chronological order; and in 2 Sam. x, 1–xi, 1, and xii, 26-31, there is a more detailed account of his conflicts with the Ammonites and Aramaeans. The list in 2 Sam. viii begins appropriately enough with the Philistines (verse 1); the note in this verse that David 'smote the Philistines and subdued them' refers presumably to David's victories over the Philistines which are recorded in 2 Sam. v, 17-25, which, whilst they did not make the Philistines permanently dependent on David politically, forced them to acknowledge his superiority and sovereignty over the major part of the land[2]. In their small province, however, they remained the only power which David did not subjugate sooner or later. In 2 Sam. viii, 2, there follows the note about the subjugation of Moab, whose territory at that time only began south of the Arnon, since David had extended the state of Israel as far as the Arnon. No mention is made of any special reason for the war with Moab. David defeated Moab and after the victory he had two-thirds of the Moabite army slaughtered. It may possibly be inferred from this cruel treatment that Moab had wantonly seized on some frivolous excuse to go to war with David. David turned Moab into a vassal state and forced it to pay tribute to him; evidently the monarchy in Moab continued, but was compelled to acknowledge David's suzerainty.

After this, David's wars with the Aramaeans are reported in 2 Sam. viii, 3-8. According to 2 Sam. x-xii they were caused by the rashness of the Ammonites. Completely disregarding the new situation in Israel, the Ammonites, who were probably still planning to expand at the expense of the Israelites east of Jordan, in spite of their having been conquered by Saul, treated a deputation from David, which was making a courtesy visit on the occasion of a change of Ammonite sovereign, with such contempt that a war with David became inevitable. Because of their own insignificant resources the Ammonites tried to secure the help of their neighbours and relations, the Aramaeans. The latter had meanwhile established a few minor states. North of the Ammon the nearest neighbour east

[1] Cf. A. Alt, 'Das Grossreich Davids', ThLZ, 75 (1950), columns 213-220.
[2] The expression מחג האמה, in verse 1b, which must certainly not be 'improved' in accordance with 1 Chron. xviii, 1, is unfortunately quite obscure. The explanation given by O. Eissfeldt in ZDPV, 66 (1943), pp. 117 f., is not really satisfactory. It is not certain that the text is in order

of the *'ajlūn* on the farthest border of Palestine was the Aramaean State of Beth-Rehob (the modern *riḥāb*). The 'men of Tob' are to be sought not far from here, probably an Aramaean group with no very firm political organisation. Their help was also enlisted by the Ammonites. There was, in addition, the monarchy of Maacah, presumably an Aramaean domain too, which was probably situated at the southern foot of Mount Hermon. The Ammonites succeeded above all, however, in obtaining the assistance of king Hadadezer of Zobah. He ruled over the Aramaean tribes on the eastern side of the Anti-Lebanon, which were probably not yet fully established; he also governed the Aramaean tribes in the steppe as far as the Euphrates. All these Aramaeans came with a great body of men to relieve the Ammonite capital Rabbah (the modern *'ammān*), which David had meanwhile ordered to be attacked by the Judaean-Israelite militia under Joab. Joab succeeded in defeating these Aramaeans so completely that they refused to give any further aid to the Ammonites, and most of them also desisted from any further conflicts with David. Only Hadadezer himself made another personal effort, with freshly assembled forces, which now included the Aramaeans from Damascus, who had evidently established an Aramaean domain in this famous old oasis city and probably ruled over some of the city-state territories to the south of Damascus as well. Once again, however, David, who appears to have been present in person this time, succeeded in obtaining a decisive victory near a place called Helam, which must have been somewhere in the northernmost land east of Jordan. As a result of this victory the Ammonites' cause was lost. In the following year David gave orders to Joab to lay waste the Ammonites' land and besiege their capital Rabbah. Finally David himself hastened to be present at the capture of the city's citadel. He punished the Ammonites severely and not without good cause. He had the inhabitants of the Ammonite cities led away as slaves. He put the Ammonite crown on his own head, however; in other words he did away with the native monarchy and made himself king of Ammon. The kingship over Ammon was added to the kingships over Judah and Israel and over the city-state of Jerusalem. But on Aramaean territory the city-state area of the northern land east of Jordan was organised as far as Damascus as a province of the empire of David, under governors residing in Damascus, appointed by David, and under the obligation of regular payment of tribute. The minor Aramaean domains on the borders of the northern land east of Jordan may have been annexed to this province in one form or another. In this way David extended his rule far to the north-east. As the ruler of widely scattered and far from firmly established Aramaean tribes, Hadadezer of Zobah could hardly be permanently subjugated to David's rule. After his defeat he was forced to make a single payment of golden shields or quivers[1] which David took to Jerusalem as trophies, and he was thereby forced to make at least formal acknowledgement of David's supremacy. He was obliged to deliver supplies of bronze, but they were probably not intended to be kept up permanently. These may have come from the *beḳaʿ* between Lebanon and Anti-Lebanon over which Hadadezer had extended his rule[2], and where the presence of mineral deposits had been exploited even in ancient days. David's influence extended, therefore, indirectly at any rate, into the depths of central Syria, and it is not surprising that the king of Hamath on the Orontes in northern Syria (the modern *ḥama*) tried to establish good relations with him, now that he had become so powerful, by sending him a deputation with lavish presents: the fame of his victories had reached as far as Hamath (2 Sam. viii, 9 f.)[3].

Finally David's victory over Edom is recorded in 2 Sam. viii, 13 f. In this case, too, we do not know what caused a military conflict and what was the reason for the cruel treatment meted out to the Edomites which is reported in another context in 1 Kings xi, 15-17. According to the latter account, David defeated Edom—in the 'valley of salt' as it is called in 2 Sam. viii, 13[4]—and Joab ravaged for six months in Edom 'to cut off every male in Edom'. The royal house was also eliminated and only the little prince Hadad managed to escape to Egypt through the Sinaitic desert with some faithful servants. David also organised Edom as a province under its own governors; and this province, remote though it was, was important because it made access possible to the gulf of *el-ʿaḳaba* and hence to the Red Sea and because it included the numerous mineral deposits on the borders of the *wādi el-ʿaraba* which had already been exploited: the possibilities which this opened up were exploited later on under Solomon.

[1] It is impossible to establish the meaning of the word שלטי.

[2] In 2 Sam. viii, 8, the two cities of Tebah (the form in the original text) and Berothai are mentioned as the sites of mineral deposits. Unfortunately it is impossible to localise them exactly, as we have no certain evidence.

[3] The excavations at *ḥaṃa* (cf. H. Ingholt, *Rapport préliminaire sur sept campagnes de fouilles à Hama en Syrie* [1932–1938], 1940) have shown that Hamath was resettled *circa* 1200 B.C. as a seat of government by a population which used the 'Hittite hieroglyphs' as their script (cf. WAT, p. 166 and illust. 8c). The king who was a contemporary of David belonged to this people.

[4] This 'valley of salt' was probably east of the *wādi el-ʿaraba* (cf. also 2 Kings xiv, 7) and probably not in the modern *wādi el-milḥ* ('valley of salt') east of Beersheba.

In conclusion, David maintained peaceful and friendly relationships with king Hiram of Tyre and all the Phoenician coastal cities
for which Tyre appears to have been the main centre at the time[1].
Through him David obtained, no doubt in return for services
rendered, the coveted and precious cedar wood from the Lebanon
as well as expert craftsmen for the royal buildings in Jerusalem
(2 Sam. v, 11)[2].

After all his victories David was king of Jerusalem, king of the
states of Judah and Israel, whose extent had been substantially enlarged by the annexation of Canaanite city-states, king of Ammon,
ruler of the provinces of Aram (Damascus) and Edom, which were
administered by governors, and sovereign over the vassal monarchy
of Moab and possibly also nominally sovereign over Hadadezer
of Zobah. The whole realm had become an extremely complicated
political structure and had grown far beyond the confines of a
purely Israelite state. It had become a Palestinian-Syrian empire
united in the person of the king and embracing numerous different
peoples. David's political organisation was the first great independent power structure on Palestinian-Syrian soil of which we have
knowledge[3], embracing directly or indirectly most of Palestine and
Syria: a tremendous phenomenon from the point of view of world
history and basically the achievement of one intelligent and un-
commonly successful man. The general historical situation in the
Orient had been in his favour. In Egypt and Mesopotamia there
was at the time no greater power which might have encroached on
Palestine and Syria and enforced a claim to rule over it. The Egypt
of the 21st Dynasty was weak, disunited and restricted by the theo-
cratic rule of the priests of Thebes[4]. In Mesopotamia Babylon had
long since lost its importance as a political power as a result of the
foreign rule of the mountain people, the Cassites, which had now
lasted for centuries. After the golden age of the Middle-Assyrian
empire, Assyria, the rising power of the time, had declined again
around the turn of the millennium. In Asia Minor there had been
no power of any significance since the fall of the mighty empire
of the Hittites. It was therefore possible for new forces to develop
in Syria-Palestine without interference from outside, and so

[1] Cf. W. F. Albright, Studies in the History of Culture (1942), pp. 33 f.
[2] The note in 2 Sam. v, 11, was probably originally part of the context of 2 Sam. viii,
1-14, and was only transferred to its present position because of its reference to Jerusalem.
[3] Perhaps the Hyksos had at one time formed a great Palestinian-Syrian state,
before they conquered Egypt and transferred their seat of government there.
[4] Cf. Ed. Meyer, Gottesstaat, Militärherrschaft und Ständewesen in Ägypten. Zur
Geschichte der 21. und 22. Dynastie (Sit. Ber. d. Preuss. Akad. d. Wiss., phil.-hist. Kl.
XXVIII), 1928.

David's empire had developed in the southern part of Syria-Palestine.

Within a short time the situation had changed completely for the Israelite tribes. It was not long since that they had had to be content to maintain themselves against the previous inhabitants of the country; even more recently they had had to submit to the supremacy of the Philistines. Now, however, the king they had chosen ruled over an imposing empire and was widely esteemed and no doubt also widely feared. Their external security was assured and they were sharing in an impressive historic process which was enhancing their position and was bound to increase their self-awareness and self-confidence. For the first time in their history they were taking part in a great historical movement, not passively but creatively. Admittedly the participants were no longer merely the Israelite tribes, and it may be asked whether, despite their admiration for David's greatness and success, the tribes did not note with some anxiety that what was taking place went far beyond the bounds of the authentic history of Israel. The Israelite tribes formed the nucleus of David's empire only to a limited extent. They were divided between two separate political organisations and these organisations were no longer purely Israelite. David no longer waged his wars simply with the armies of the tribes. It is true, he still used the tribal militia or had it used, above all against the neighbouring peoples east of Jordan[1], and they even took the old tribal relic of the Ark with them[2], as though David was still waging a 'holy war'. David evidently took the Ark very seriously because it represented the confederation of the tribes. The military force which David preferred, however, was his band of mercenaries[3] who were by no means purely Israelite but, presumably, a very motley assortment[4], and in any case they belonged to him personally and not to the Israelite tribes. He had begun his climb to power as a leader of mercenaries and he had won with them such important successes as the decisive victory over the Philistines and the conquest of the city-state of Jerusalem. Later on he will have continued to use his mercenaries in important enterprises. The political structure that arose in this period was not so much an Israelite empire as David's empire. All the same, the tribes still regarded him as one of their

[1] Cf. 2 Sam. xi, 1 (Joab the captain of the host with 'all Israel' against Ammon); 1 Kings xi, 15 (Joab the captain of the host in Moab); 2 Sam. x, 17 (David with 'all Israel' against the Aramaeans).   [2] Cf. 2 Sam. xi, 11.

[3] Beside the captain of the host David had a special commander in charge of the mercenaries (2 Sam. viii, 18; xx, 23).

[4] Cf. already 'the thirty heroes of David' and K. Ellinger, PJB, 31 (1935), pp. 29-75.

own, and their central shrine was in David's royal city; and they had had at any rate a share in his ascent to power.

The existence of David's empire was so dependent on the strong personality of its founder that its survival beyond his death only seemed assured provided a successor of more or less equal stature could be found. David no doubt realised that too, and he must have realised equally well that owing to the complete lack of any traditional right of succession and the importance of his own personality for the establishment of his complicated empire, much depended on his personal decision regarding a successor. Strangely enough, David failed in this respect, mainly because he was apparently unable to make up his mind and delayed making the necessary decision far too long. The final period of his reign was therefore filled with all kinds of disturbances caused by various of his sons attempting to enforce their claim to succeed their father. A historical work that was probably written before the death of Solomon describes these troubles concerning the succession and also the ultimate solution of the problem with considerable exact knowledge [1]. That one of David's numerous sons would succeed him was practically certain. If Saul's sole surviving male descendant, a son of Jonathan named Merib-baal[2], who was a cripple, believed his great hour might still come when he would be offered the throne (2 Sam. xvi, 3) this merely showed how childish he was. After the terrible failure of Saul's monarchy there could hardly be many people among the Israelite tribes in favour of a continuation of this monarchy, even in Saul's own tribe of Benjamin, despite the fact that the monarchy of David the Judaean, who had taken Saul's place, still met with embittered hostility in this tribe (cf. 2 Sam. xvi, 8). The new state had so little in common with Saul's monarchy and was so much David's personal achievement that only members of David's family could be seriously considered fit to succeed him. Moreover, the 'prophet' Nathan, who evidently played a not unimportant part at David's court in Jerusalem had solemnly proclaimed in the name of his God that David's dynasty would endure beyond his death, saying that David's successful rise to power had proved that Yahweh had chosen him to be the king (2 Sam. vii, 8 ff.)[3].

[1] We have this historical work in 2 Sam. vii; ix, 1-xx, 22; 1 Kings i, ii; cf. L. Rost, *Die Überlieferung von der Thronnachfolge Davids* (BWANT, III, 6), 1926.

[2] The original form of the name is only contained in 1 Chron. viii, 34; ix, 40. In 2 Sam. iv, 4; ix, 6 ff. and elsewhere the name appears in the distorted form Mephibosheth.

[3] Probably the remark in 2 Sam. vii, 8, should be taken as meaning that Yahweh had called David to be *nāgīd* over Israel. We do not hear anything about such a call having

The practical question was therefore which of David's sons was to succeed him. If a dangerous state of chaos was to be avoided when he died, the question had to be settled during his lifetime. When David had asked for the hand of Saul's daughter Michal (cf. above, pp. 184f.) and had made her his wife, his idea had no doubt been that a son, possibly the eldest son of this marriage, who would have been a grandson of Saul, would become the favourite among his sons and might attract the sympathies of those who still supported the house of Saul. But as is stated explicitly in 2 Sam. vi, 23, the marriage of David and Michal remained childless. The obvious possibility that a son of this marriage might be elected to succeed his father was therefore ruled out. For the rest, according to the ancient Israelite law of succession, which assigned the main share of the inheritance to the father's first-born son without regard to the mother's position among the father's wives (cf. Deut. xxi, 17), the idea that David's eldest son should succeed him was quite natural; and, as far as we know, in the house of David the monarchy did in fact usually continue to pass to the king's eldest son. In the case of David himself, the founder of the monarchy and dynasty, the eldest son 'born in the purple', that is, the first son born after David's accession to the throne, might have had special priority. David's sons themselves apparently paid no particular attention to this latter aspect but regarded themselves as the presumptive successors to the throne in the sequence of their respective ages. In 2 Sam. iii, 2-5, there is a list of the five eldest sons of David, who, according to the editorial notes on this list, were born in Hebron, during the period of David's Judaean monarchy, but, as David had had at least two wives considerably earlier (cf. 1 Sam. xxv, 42-43) some of the sons were probably somewhat older. The list given in 2 Sam. iii, 2-5, is supplemented by the enumeration of the sons of David who were born in Jerusalem, which appears in 2 Sam. v, 13-16.

In 2 Sam. iii, 2, Amnon is described explicitly as David's first-born son, his mother being the Ahinoam from South Judaean Jezreel, by marrying whom David had strengthened his ties with the South Judaean tribes. Amnon was evidently regarded by himself and by others as the future king. The writer of the story of the succession to the throne also hints at this; obviously this is the sole reason why in 2 Sam. xiii, xiv, he tells the story of the murder of Amnon by Absalom in such detail as part of the story of the

played any part in David's rise to power (cf. above, p. 186). Possibly it was only established retrospectively that David must have been called by Yahweh to be *nāgīd*. 2 Sam. vi, 21, will have to be judged in the same way.

succession. Amnon was unwise enough to supply Absalom with a pretext for murdering him, by raping his half-sister Tamar. In fact, Absalom thereby removed the next man ahead of him as a claimant to the throne. According to 2 Sam. iii, 3, since David's second eldest son, who is mentioned here, disappears for some unknown reason, Absalom, as the third oldest son, was the next candidate after the death of Amnon. It is true that, to begin with, the murder of Amnon cost him his father's good-will. But with the help of Joab, the military commander, he finally obtained David's absolute forgiveness. David probably had a weak spot for his sons in general and for Absalom in particular. (2 Sam. xiii, 39; xiv, 1).

Even in David's own lifetime Absalom tried to seize the throne by force. This led to the so-called 'rebellion of Absalom', the course of which is described in great detail in 2 Sam. xv-xix. Absalom succeeded in gaining the sympathy and support of the Israelite tribes, especially in the kingdom of Judah, but in the kingdom of Israel too, apparently, so that in the end he was able to take the risk of having himself proclaimed king in the ancient and royal Judaean city of Hebron (2 Sam. xv, 10). This signified the deposition of David. We do not learn exactly what had in the meantime made David so unpopular in Israel that Absalom apparently had no difficulty in setting himself up as king. In time every regime loses sympathisers and acquires enemies; and it is easy to conceive that the Israelite tribes were more and more dissatisfied with the growth of David's dominion into an empire extending far beyond the territory of the Israelite tribes. At any rate, the defection of the tribes from David became so serious that in effect all that the ageing king had left was the personal loyalty of his own mercenaries. He therefore decided to escape to Mahanaim in the land east of Jord'an with his mercenaries, to avoid being surprised by Absalom and his followers in Jerusalem. Absalom was thus able to enter David's royal city and to take over the government of the city in due form. In the armed conflict that ensued, however, David's professional soldiers proved superior to the militia of the Israelite tribes that Absalom had assembled, though this was no doubt far stronger numerically. The decisive battle took place somewhere in the wooded hill country in the central land east of Jordan south of the Jabbok, in the 'wood of Ephraim' (2 Sam. xviii, 6). Absalom had led the militia there to attack David's position east of Jordan. He lost the battle and was killed as he was taking flight, despite David's explicit order to his soldiers that his life should be spared. There now remained nothing for the Israelite tribes in the kingdoms of Judah and Israel to do but to recall David as their king (2 Sam. xix, 10, 11). This led to a very remarkable sequel, which revealed the latent conflict between the kingdoms of Judah and Israel within David's political organisation and at the same time showed David making a definitely unwise move for the first time. David—while evidently still in Mahanaim—ordered the Judaean tribes to summon him to the throne of Judah as one of their own (2 Sam. xix, 12 ff.). Had he become so impatient that he could not wait for what was bound to come about in any case? When the Judaeans' representatives, following his summons, fetched the king from the Jordan and escorted him to the shrine of Gilgal near Jericho, the representatives of the tribes of the kingdom of Israel appeared and reproached David for not getting them to come and fetch him, since they represented the majority of the tribes. The result was that under the leadership of a Benjaminite called Sheba the watchword went out to the indignant tribes of the kingdom of Israel: 'We have no part in David neither have we inheritance in the son of Jesse: every man (go home) to his tents, O Israel!' (2 Sam. xx, 1). And the first thing David had to do after his return to Jerusalem was to call up his mercenaries and the Judaean militia to suppress the rebellion in the kingdom of Israel by force of arms. He soon succeeded in this (2 Sam. xx); but this quarrel between the kingdoms of Judah and Israel that erupted under David was a bad omen for the future.

In the end, therefore, David had regained his full supremacy. But the problem of the succession was still not solved. After the elimination of Absalom, Adonijah was now David's eldest son (2 Sam. iii, 4) and Adonijah proceeded to claim the throne (1 Kings i, 5). If Absalom had sought his followers among the broad masses of the Israelite tribes, Adonijah sought and found the support of a few influential men from David's entourage. He won over Joab the captain and Abiathar the priest from the royal sanctuary in Jerusalem (1 Kings i, 7). But this also meant—for this is the way things happen in the atmosphere of a royal court—that other equally influential men were ranged against Adonijah, including, no doubt not by accident, the mercenary leader Benaiah, who was Joab's rival, together with David's personal retinue, and Zadok, the other priest of the royal sanctuary, who were joined by Nathan, the court prophet (1 Kings i, 8). This opposition party succeeded in obtaining a decisive influence over king David who was now very old. They used one of the king's wives, the Bathsheba whom David, enchanted by her beauty, had once taken for himself adulterously, and whose husband Uriah he had had treacherously murdered (2 Sam. xi, 2 ff.). She had become David's wife and the mother of his son Solomon. At the time Nathan had remonstrated very earnestly with David on account of the crime he had committed against Uriah and Bathsheba (2 Sam. xii, 1 ff.). He now exploited the influence which Bathsheba among the king's wives still had. It is impossible to ascertain to what extent Bathsheba played an active part in what now followed and how far she was merely used by Nathan, who was clearly the leader of the party opposed to Adonijah; it is also impossible to establish how far what was said to David was the whole truth or merely a semblance of the truth. In any case, it was reported to him that Adonijah had made himself king on his own responsibility, whereas David had once promised to Bathsheba that her son Solomon should succeed him (1 Kings i, 11 ff.). The result which they hoped for was achieved, and David at last uttered his decision regarding the succession to his throne and appointed Solomon to reign in his stead, and had him anointed by Zadok the priest without delay, and then proclaimed him king in Jerusalem (1 Kings i, 28-40).

David's authoritative ruling had solved the problem of the succession at one blow. Adonijah at once abandoned his cause and Solomon was already king and co-regent with David. That the choice fell on Solomon can hardly have been due to his personal qualities, judging from all we hear about him. He was by no means the eldest of David's numerous sons, and he was not even the first of those 'born in the purple' (cf. 2 Sam. v, 14). What distinguished him from the others was that his mother Bathsheba was David's favourite wife, whether or not he had really promised her explicitly that her son Solomon should succeed him as king. In view of the priority which she enjoyed, some of the leading officials at court appear to have sided with Solomon, and, by playing a clever hand, finally to have obtained David's ruling that he should succeed him. If, despite the detailed and vivid account which is given within the framework of the tradition regarding the succession to the throne of David in 1 Kings i, the background and the actual course of events are not entirely clear, it is at any rate obvious that Solomon became David's successor, in opposition to Adonijah, as a result of an intrigue at court.

The successor whom David ultimately chose did not prove equal to his task: the history of his reign shows that. The only question is whether any of the others of David's surviving sons would have

been any more suitable. The task which confronted David's successor was extraordinarily difficult. The extremely complicated
empire which David had built up could only be held together and
consolidated by a successor who was to some extent the great king's
equal in wisdom and strength; and such a man was not easily to be
found.

16. *The Reign of Solomon*

It is noteworthy that the tradition concerning Solomon which has
been preserved within the framework of the great deuteronomistic
history is quite different in kind from the tradition regarding David
that has come down to us. It is true that the latter does not provide
a complete picture of David's reign, since it is made up, above all,
of the two great narratives concerning the rise of David up to his
accession to the kingdoms of Judah and Israel and Jerusalem, and
concerning the struggles about David's succession up to the accession of Solomon. On the development of David's empire all we
have is the brief annalistic record in 2 Sam. viii, 1-14, and a few
scattered details elsewhere. The great events of the time did,
however, clearly influence the two main narratives, and the nar-
rators continually attempted, within the framework of their own
particular themes, to show the significance of what had taken place.
They thus present a living and full-blooded picture of David. Concerning Solomon's reign, the traditional records merely cover a
mass of details; apparently no one was stimulated to compile a
connected historical account of his reign. For his section on Solomon (1 Kings iii-xi) the Deuteronomist was able to make use of
a 'Book of the Acts of Solomon' (1 Kings xi, 41) from which he
extracted the essential details. This book evidently represented a
compilation and elaboration of the material provided by the king's
official records and contained a wealth of sometimes very concrete
detail about a great variety of governmental measures taken in
Solomon's reign[1]. The Solomonic tradition also contains a number
of anecdotes about Solomon which evidently continued to circulate
for a long time. The subject of these anecdotes is Solomon's wealth
and wisdom. The royal household and buildings provided reason
enough for the idea that he was immensely wealthy; and the fact
that, rightly or wrongly, he was credited with the writing of proverbs (cf. 1 Kings v, 12-13) helped to add continually to his post-
humous fame as the pattern of the 'wise man'.

[1] For further details see M. Noth, *Überlieferungsgeschichtliche Studien*, I (1943),
pp. 66 f.

After the death of David, Solomon succeeded his father without difficulty or untoward incidents, once David had made up his mind and had him anointed king. He had, however, attained this goal as the candidate of a particular party at court and there had also been an opposition party in support of Adonijah who was, at the time, David's eldest son. At the very beginning of his reign Solomon eliminated the leaders of this opposition party, including Adonijah himself, in the most brutal fashion, as recorded in the story of the succession to David in 1 Kings ii, 13-44, 46a, which only then proceeds to state that 'the kingdom was established in the hand of Solomon' (1 Kings ii, 46b). David's mercenary leader Benaiah rendered very material services to Solomon in the removal of his enemies (1 Kings ii, 25, 34, 46a) and was rewarded by being made supreme commander of the army (1 Kings ii, 35a). It may be that Solomon had reason to establish his power against strong and influential enemies in this way, and that in so doing he was to some extent following his father's advice (cf. 1 Kings ii, 5 f., 8 f.). But it is probably more than a mere accident that we do not hear of David having paved his way to power by liquidating his personal enemies in this cruel way. David's superior power had raised him above such a necessity. Faced with the interplay of the opposing forces at the court in Jerusalem, which had meanwhile become large and influential, Solomon's personality was not apparently strong enough to absolve him from the necessity of having to watch jealously over the safety of his realm, at any rate to begin with.

Solomon had entered upon a great inheritance. The prestige which the great Davidic empire had enjoyed in the world of Palestine and Syria and even further afield in the ancient Orient continued in the main under Solomon, but he failed to add to his father's inheritance. There is nothing in the records concerning any military enterprise on the part of Solomon, and in fact he probably did not engage in war at all. At the outset the political structure bequeathed by David seemed firm and secure enough to make any further expansion of military power unnecessary. But in a situation of that kind a standstill usually means the beginning of a decline. And the decline of David's empire did in fact begin under Solomon. According to 1 Kings xi, 14-22, and xi, 25aβb, the news of David's death and of the death of his brutal and dreaded commander Joab, whom Solomon had had killed at the outset of his reign as one of his enemies, had caused the Edomite prince Hadad, who had once escaped to Egypt (cf. above, p. 196), to return to his Edomite homeland where he made himself king over Edom. This seems to have occurred fairly early in Solomon's reign. Admittedly there can be no question of Hadad having ruled over the whole of the former territory of Edom, since Solomon apparently had unrestricted access to the gulf of *el-'akaba* and the port of Ezion-geber which he had developed and used (1 Kings ix, 26), through the *wādi el-'araba*, that is to say, through a substantial part of the province of Edom. Hadad's rule can therefore only have extended to parts of the more inaccessible Edomite mountains east of the *wādi el-'araba*. The emergence of Hadad does show, however, that it was not long before Solomon no longer had complete control of the province of Edom; and Solomon apparently took no measures to regain complete possession of Edom. The fact that, according to 1 Kings xi, 23-25aa, an Aramaic adventurer named Rezon was able to seize the city of Damascus with a warlike band that he had collected, and made himself king there, was even worse. This, too, may not have involved the loss of the whole province of Aram during Solomon's reign. But the most important city in this province, the seat of the Davidic governors, had thereby fallen into foreign hands and, again, Solomon does not seem to have done anything to restore his threatened authority in the province of Aram. We are not told exactly when this happened but, to judge from the wording of 1 Kings xi, 25aa, it was probably early in Solomon's reign. The foundations were thus laid for the Aramaean kingdom of Damascus which was soon to develop with vigour and become, for a time, the strongest power in Syria-Palestine. For Solomon the inevitable result of losing Damascus was that the influence which David had exerted on the Aramaeans in the remoter parts of Syria came to an end. Otherwise, however, Solomon was able to preserve the complicated political structure established by David. He managed to suppress a serious rebellion in the kingdom of Israel. According to the scanty details in 1 Kings xi, 26-28, 40, which provide no really clear picture, the Ephraimite Jeroboam, who had been discovered by Solomon during the building operations in Jerusalem and entrusted with an office[1] in the house of Joseph, revolted against the king for reasons unknown to us. We do not know whom Jeroboam had behind him

---

[1] The word סֵבֶל which is used in 1 Kings xi, 28, to describe the sphere of this office is usually translated by 'compulsory labour', thus making Jeroboam an official within the Solomonic organisation of compulsory labour. But it should be noted that, although the word means something like 'bearing burdens', it is not the usual word for 'compulsory labour' (מַס, cf. under Solomon 1 Kings iv, 6; v, 27-28 [English Bible, v, 13, 14]; ix, 15, 21). Moreover, it is at least doubtful whether the 'house of Joseph' was used for compulsory labour (cf. below, pp. 210 f.). It is therefore still uncertain what the special task was with which Jeroboam was entrusted by Solomon.

nor how widespread the revolt was. In any case, the undertaking failed; but Solomon was not able to arrest Jeroboam, who managed to escape to Egypt and remain there. After Solomon's death he was to play an important role once more[1].

Whilst menacing incidents occurred in some of the outlying provinces, which Solomon evidently did not consider necessary to counter by force of arms, he devoted himself to the internal development of the kingdom and, above all, to a comprehensive scheme of building activity intended primarily to add lustre and distinction to the royal house. The most detailed accounts of Solomon's activities, which derive from the 'Book of the Acts of Solomon', deal with the royal buildings. Above all, Solomon extended the royal city of Jerusalem. David had been very largely satisfied with the old and narrow Jebusite Jerusalem on the so-called south-eastern hill above the spring of Gihon[2], and had merely had a new royal palace built in place of the Jebusite palace or may only have had the latter extended (2 Sam. v, 11). Solomon continued to 'repair the breaches' of the 'city of David his father' (1 Kings xi, 27). But the old 'city of David' no longer met his needs. Therefore, soon after his accession[3] he began to extend Jerusalem by adding an entirely new piece of land for his extensive palace buildings. The old Jerusalem, which was limited on the eastern side by the deep incision of the valley of the Kidron and on the west by the shallower valley we call the 'city valley', could only expand on the northern side where the hill on which the old city was sited reached a greater height. Therefore, Solomon erected his buildings north of the city of David, thereby giving Jerusalem extraordinary length from north to south compared with the very narrow breadth from east to west[4] caused by the two valleys already mentioned. The

[1] We do not know exactly when Jeroboam's revolt took place. Perhaps quite early in Solomon's reign, since the building activities in the city of David which first brought Jeroboam to the fore probably belong to the beginning of Solomon's reign; the only question is how long Jeroboam was one of Solomon's officials before he 'raised his hand against the king'.

[2] On the natural setting and architectural history of Jerusalem cf. H. Guthe, *Bibelatlas* (2 1926), No. 2a, I, and No. 3, II, and also K. Galling, ZDPV, 54 (1931), pp. 85 ff., Pl. 6, and J. Simons, *Jerusalem in the Old Testament* (1952), especially pp. 60 ff.

[3] According to 1 Kings vi, 1, 37, 'Yahweh's Temple', which formed part of the whole complex of the new buildings in Jerusalem, was begun in the fourth year of Solomon's reign.

[4] Contrary to earlier assumptions, the settlement of the so-called west hill on the farther side of the 'city valley' did not take place until very much later and not at all during the age of David and Solomon (cf. Galling, *loc. cit.*). No archaeological remains of pre-Hellenistic times have been found so far on this west hill (a point that is conceded by Simons, *op. cit.* pp. 251 f., in spite of the fact that on the whole his views are contrary to mine).

buildings of Solomon's royal palace, which were enclosed by a wall of their own, towered above the old Jebusite city and took up at least as much space. Solomon worked on this great scheme for a long time[1]. The royal temple was also built within this complex and it has become the most famous of Solomon's buildings: the Temple of Solomon. The Deuteronomist was already particularly interested in this building and therefore extracted from the 'Book of the Acts of Solomon' all the facts concerning the building of the Temple and the compiling of the inventory needed for this (I Kings vi, 1-38; vii, 13-51). The Temple was erected on the site which is now occupied by the Islamite shrine called the 'Dome of the Rock' (*kubbet es̱-s̱akhra*); and the 'Holy of Holies', the Adyton of this temple, towered above the highest elevation of the whole palace area. This highest point is the 'sacred rock' in the middle of the Dome of the Rock, still clearly visible today[2]. This rock had presumably been a sacred spot from time immemorial, the ancient 'high place' of pre-Israelite Jerusalem. Thus Solomon had so designed the whole lay-out of the palace area that the royal sanctuary of the Temple should stand on this ancient holy site. In any case, he could not have desecrated a traditional place of worship by covering it with palace buildings, but could only develop it as a holy place within the whole design. The building itself followed the local, that is, the Canaanite, traditions; for a temple is an urban sanctuary and the Israelite tribes adopted their urban culture from the Canaanites who had preceded them. Furthermore, Solomon used Phoenician craftsmen for his buildings (I Kings v, 32 [English Bible, v, 18]; vii, 13 ff.). It is also possible that the plan of the Temple as a long building with an Adyton, probably raised, at the rear end of the actual Temple, and an entrance hall in front, corresponded to the Syrian-Palestinian building style, which had itself been affected by Mesopotamian influence in the second millennium, but had perhaps incorporated various Egyptian elements as well, in keeping with the generally hybrid nature of Syrian-Palestinian culture[3]. As is

---

[1] There is a short report on the palace buildings as a whole in I Kings vii, 1-12. According to verse 1 they took altogether thirteen years. According to I Kings vi, 37-38, the sanctuary of the Temple which formed part of the whole complex, was begun in the fourth year and finished in the eleventh year of Solomon's reign.

[2] Cf. H. Schmidt, *Der heilige Fels in Jerusalem* (1933).

[3] Cf. K. Möhlenbrink, *Der Tempel Salomos* (BWANT, IV, 7 [1932]), who emphasises the connections with the Assyrian method of building temples, and C. Watzinger, *Denkmäler Palästinas*, I (1933), pp. 88 ff., who rightly lays stress on the connections with pre-Israelite Syria-Palestine, and, above all, A. Alt, 'Verbreitung und Herkunft des syrischen Tempeltypus', PJB, 35 (1939), pp. 83-99, especially pp. 96 f. = *Kleine Schriften zur Geschichte des Volkes Israel*, II (1953), pp. 100-115.

implied by the old votive utterance in 1 Kings viii, 12, 13, the Temple was conceived as the dwelling of the deity; in particular, the darkened Adyton was regarded as the place of the presence of God who 'said that he would dwell in the thick darkness' (1 Kings viii, 12). Solomon moved into this Adyton the ancient tribal relic of the Ark which David had brought to Jerusalem, as a throne for the invisible divine presence and set it up in place of the image or symbol of God which normally stood in the Adyton in the local type of temple. Thus the royal sanctuary within the complex of palace buildings, served by priests who were royal officials, became at the same time the central shrine of the Israelite tribes.

In addition, Solomon built in other cities, above all in formerly Canaanite cities which David had incorporated in the kingdoms of Judah and Israel and in which, as legal successor of the former city rulers, the king was the landowner. According to 1 Kings ix, 19, Solomon built cities for his chariots and teams of horses (for the chariotry), that is to say, he had special grounds laid out for this purpose in existing cities. The American excavations in Megiddo (the modern *tell el-mutesellim*) have thrown remarkable light on this activity, since they have revealed the remains of a great complex of stables for which Solomon was no doubt responsible[1]. To judge from this, Solomon built a great complex of stables around three sides of an inner courtyard which was capable of accommodating several hundred horses, in the north-eastern section of the ancient and important Canaanite city of Megiddo on the south-western border of the plain of Jezreel, which gradually declined at the end of the Late Bronze Age and was finally incorporated in the kingdom of Israel under David, losing its political freedom[2]. According to this clear evidence, the characteristic features are the rows of stone pillars on both sides of a rough-cast central corridor which separated the horse-boxes from one another. Hence other similar but less well-preserved and therefore less obvious buildings in various cities in Palestine may also have been stables erected by Solomon. In 1 Kings ix, 19, no names are given to the 'cities for his chariots and cities for his horses'; but in verse 15b and 17 there is a list of the cities which Solomon 'built', though the purpose of the building is not mentioned. Megiddo is included among these cities. It would seem, therefore, that at any rate some of the other

---

[1] Cf. P. L. O. Guy, *New Light from Armageddon* (Oriental Institute Communications, 9 [1931]), and C. Watzinger, *op. cit.* pp. 87 f., and especially figs. 80, 81.

[2] This discovery in Megiddo represents the most important surviving remains so far discovered of Solomon's copious building activities in the land.

cities mentioned may have been 'cities for his chariots and cities for his horses'[1]. It is clear that Solomon maintained a very considerable force of chariots which were distributed among various garrisons in the land, following the example of the ancient Oriental monarchs of his time. David had already maintained a standing army in his contingents of mercenaries, in addition to the tribal militias. But they still fought on foot[2]. He had not known what to do with the teams of horses (and chariots)[3] captured from the Aramaeans; apart from a small reserve, he had made this particularly valuable booty useless (2 Sam. viii, 4). Solomon, however, surpassed the simplicity which still marked the age of David. He waged no wars and never really used his chariots at all: they merely served to add to his royal lustre[4]. Apart from the 'cities of chariots and horses', I Kings ix, 19 also refers to 'store-cities' built by Solomon; this must mean that he had royal warehouses built in existing cities which were probably used to store the tribute in kind collected from the country for the court.

Solomon's building activities required an enormous labour force which the country had to raise at a time when all the basic operations still had to be done by hand. Solomon also greatly developed the institution of forced labour, that is, the compulsory use of subjects for the carrying out of work for their overlord. We have no details as to how the groups of forced labourers were selected or how long they were required to serve. Organised forced labour had already existed under David. In the latter part of his reign (2 Sam. xx, 23-26) the list of his senior officials included a 'chief of forced labour' (verse 24a), though it had not done so in his early period (cf. 2 Sam. viii, 16-18). David will also have employed forced labour on his royal buildings. The records do not contain much

[1] The city of Gezer is also mentioned in this context; and in fact the famous row of massebahs 'of Gezer' (cf. Gressmann, AOB², Nos. 411, 412) is probably nothing but part of the row of pillars of a Solomonic stable building. According to I Kings x, 26, Solomon also had chariots and horses in Jerusalem itself, *i.e.* inside his great palace grounds, which one would assume to have been the case anyway.

[2] At this time even the king did not yet go into battle in a chariot (cf., on the other hand, for a later period, I Kings xxii, 34, 35, 38) but, when he did not go on foot, rode on a donkey or a mule; it is true that we do not hear that David did this, but it is reported of Absalom who was made king (2 Sam. xviii, 9).

[3] It is surprising that the Aramaean king Hadadezer of Zobah went into battle in a chariot; he must have had under his command, probably in Syria and perhaps in the northern land east of the Jordan too, old city-states which had to provide him with contingents of chariots.

[4] When they were preparing to succeed to the throne, David's elder sons had already provided themselves with chariots in the 'modern' fashion (2 Sam. xv, 1; I Kings i, 5); but they too had only used the chariots as tokens of royal dignity. They did not intend to go into battle with them (cf. the last note but one).

about David's building activities (2 Sam. v, 11) and they will, in
fact, have been on a modest scale and perhaps confined to Jerusalem. This state of affairs was changed under Solomon. During
his reign Adoniram was still 'over the forced labour' as he had
been in David's reign (1 Kings iv, 6b) but his work was certainly
far more extensive. The tradition of Solomon includes two contra-
dictory statements about compulsion for forced labour. According
to 1 Kings v, 27 (English Bible, v, 13), the force was raised 'out of
all Israel', whereas in 1 Kings ix, 15a and 20-22, it is emphasised
that only the non-Israelite population of the old Canaanite city-
states, which were now incorporated in Judah and Israel, were
called on to supply forced labour. Of these city-states, which the
Israelite tribes had been unable to conquer in the period before
the formation of the monarchy, it is stated explicitly in Judges i,
27 ff., that later on, 'when Israel had become strong', *i.e.* when,
with the advent of the monarchy, she had proceeded to develop
her political power, they were compelled to perform forced labour
(למס verses 28, 30, 33, 35). Probably the reference in 1 Kings ix,
15a and 20-22, is substantially correct and the statement in
1 Kings v, 27 (English Bible, v, 13), employs too brief a formula
and is therefore inaccurate. Whilst perhaps the free men of the
Israelite tribes were legally liable for army service, they were not
liable for forced labour and it would have been a monstrous infringement of their legal rights on the king's part to have compelled them to do forced labour. In the Canaanite cities, on the
other hand, the king had at his disposal a slave population which
had already had to perform forced labour for the city rulers and
now had to do it for the king in Jerusalem[1].

Solomon also needed an enormous amount of material for his
buildings. The stone he required could be quarried in the mountains. But the lack of forests in the land made it necessary to
import the timber required. From earliest times one of the main
sources of timber in the ancient Orient had been the wooded
Lebanon on the northern borders of Palestine. Solomon therefore
concluded a treaty with king Hiram of Tyre (1 Kings v, 15-26
[English Bible, v, 1-12]), who had already sought the favour of the
mighty David and had already supplied him with timber for his
buildings. Hiram contracted to supply timber and to enlist expert
craftsmen, of whom there was a shortage in Solomon's predominantly rural kingdom, for the great and varied building under-

[1] The Israelite tribes' complaint about his reign after the death of Solomon (1 Kings
xii, 4) can therefore hardly refer to forced labour, but to such things as taxes, etc.

takings. In return, Solomon agreed to maintain a regular supply of wheat and olive oil to the commercial city-state of Tyre, which had little agricultural land[1]. To keep up these quite considerable supplies Solomon had to commandeer the produce of his subjects, especially of the agricultural Israelite tribes, for the sake of his building.

Solomon's buildings in Jerusalem were the setting for a brilliant and expensive royal household; for this, too, the country had to foot the bill. In 1 Kings v, 2-3 (English Bible, iv, 22-23), there is a precise account of the court's daily requirements of grain and meat. If one bears in mind that the consumption of meat among the simple rural population was always limited to special events and festive occasions, it is easy to realise that life at Solomon's court, with its daily consumption of great quantities of cattle, was far removed from the everyday life of the ordinary people. To guarantee the regular arrival of supplies from the country, Solomon introduced a comprehensive system of taxation. He divided the whole kingdom of Israel[2] for this purpose into twelve districts, each of which had to be responsible for supplying the royal court for one month of the year (1 Kings iv, 7). At the head of each district there was an 'overseer' (נִצָּב) who no doubt had to divide responsibility for maintaining supplies among the various landowners and to see that deliveries were made on time, collected in the 'store-cities' mentioned above, and delivered to Jerusalem in the appointed month. The head of the whole organisation was a supreme official who was called 'chief of the overseers' (עַל־הַנִּצָּבִים), whose office had not existed under David and who first appears among the leading officials in Solomon's reign (1 Kings iv, 5a). Presumably

---

[1] The brief account in 1 Kings ix, 10-13, according to which Hiram eventually had twenty cities in western Galilee ceded to him for his deliveries to Solomon, may not belong to this context since its explicit intention is an aetiological explanation of the name of the city Cabul (the modern *kābūl*), and its basis is simply the fact that at the time of the origin of the tradition the district of Cabul, which was really situated in Israelite Galilee, belonged to the territory of Tyre. It may then, subsequently and secondarily, have related this connection of the area with Tyre to the traditionally well-known connections of Solomon with Hiram of Tyre; but cf. below, p. 213, note 3.

[2] It is remarkable that we have no information about any corresponding division of the kingdom of Judah into districts by Solomon. It is evident that the division of the kingdom of Judah into twelve districts, on which the lists of places in Joshua xv, xviii, xix, is based, derives from a considerably later period (cf. A. Alt, 'Judas Gaue unter Josia', PJB, 21 [1925], pp. 100-117 = *Kleine Schriften zur Geschichte des Volkes Israel,* II [1953], pp. 276-288) and even the basis of it is clearly post-Solomonic (cf. M. Noth, *Das Buch Josua* [² 1953], p. 14). It is therefore an open question whether Solomon did not impose taxation on Judah at all, possibly because this kingdom was too small and poor, or whether it is merely an accident that there is no reference in the traditional records to a similar measure in Judah, which was later made the basis of a new division into districts in Judah.

David had already been compelled to impose the duty of supplying the court with certain provisions on the kingdoms of Judah and Israel, thereby interfering with the freedom of the Israelite tribes to dispose of the produce of their agriculture and cattle-breeding in their own way; under Solomon, however, the system of payment of duty in kind was enormously extended and firmly organised. The classification of the districts which was introduced, the details of which are given in 1 Kings iv, 8-19, provides a clear picture of the total extent and internal organisation of the kingdom of Israel[1], particularly as it shows very clearly the juxtaposition and the administrative division of tribal areas and city territories within the one political system based on historically evolved groupings and boundaries. A whole series of districts was formed by Israelite tribal territories. Such are the districts of 'Benjamin' (verse 18), 'mount Ephraim' (verse 8) (with the tribal territories of Ephraim and Manasseh) and also the Galilean districts of Issachar (verse 17), Naphtali (verse 15) and Asher (verse 16). Issachar presumably included the territory of Zebulun, whilst the territory of Dan certainly formed part of 'Naphtali'. To these belong, lastly, in the land east of the Jordan, the districts of Mahanaim (verse 14) with the Ephraimite-Manassite colonial territory in the land of Gilead south and north of the Jabbok and 'Gad' (verse 19)[2] with the area to the south. The other five districts included city-state territories, the three districts referred to in verses 9, 10 and 11 covering the city-states in the coastal plain as far north as Carmel, the district mentioned in verse 12 covering the city-states in the plain of Jezreel and in the adjoining plain of Beth-shan and, lastly, the district of 'Ramoth-Gilead' in verse 13 covering the city-states on the north-eastern border of the *'ajlūn* (cf. above, p. 192)[3]. Solomon's subdivision of the districts and his organisation of the system of tribute were maintained after his death in the kingdom of Israel[4].

Presumably Solomon also extended the Crown property and controlled its administration. At any rate we find among his lead-

[1] Cf. A. Alt, *Israels Gaue unter Salomo* (BWAT, 13 [1913], pp. 1 ff.)= *Kleine Schriften zur Geschichte des Volkes Israel*, II (1953), pp. 76-89.
[2] In the text the name 'Gad' was later altered in error to 'Gilead'.
[3] It is noteworthy that the plain of Acco was not included in this division into districts. Under David it appears still to have belonged to the kingdom of Israel (cf. above, p. 192). Had a loss of territory taken place here too under Solomon, possibly by cession to Hiram of Tyre, of which the aetiological narrative contained in 1 Kings ix, 10-13 (cf. above, p. 212, note 1), contains a no longer completely accurate recollection?
[4] This is shown by the Samaria ostraca from the period probably of Jeroboam II in the 8th century. Cf. M. Noth, PJB, 28 (1932), pp. 58 f.

ing officials a 'chief of the household' (1 Kings iv, 6a) who had not existed under David and who no doubt controlled all the royal properties, including not only the palace and the buildings pertaining thereto in Jerusalem but also all kinds of landed property in the country. This consisted of land inherited by the royal family and all manner of estates which devolved on the king, such as the property of criminals condemned to death[1]. It was therefore distributed throughout the whole country and appears to have consisted mainly of vineyards and orchards from which the royal household met its great requirements of wine and oil, which, according to 1 Kings v, 2-3 (English Bible, iv, 22-23), were not covered by the tribute of the country population[2].

To judge from all this, Solomon devoted himself most earnestly to the development of the royal properties and prestige, thereby, as the heir to David's empire[3], striving to emulate the great kings of the ancient Orient in Egypt and Mesopotamia. All this occasioned great expenditure which it was difficult to raise in the territory of his own state, since it was not greatly blessed with a wealth of natural resources. Hence, Solomon tried to add to his wealth by means of a variety of profit-making undertakings, and in fact he managed to amass great riches in Jerusalem. The records refer admiringly to Solomon's immense wealth (1 Kings x, 14-22) and posterity spoke of his proverbial wealth and 'glory' (Matt. vi, 29; Luke xii, 27). The fact that he had access to the gulf of el-'akaba through the province of Edom, and hence to the Red Sea, led him to undertake profitable voyages through the Red Sea with a fleet which he built himself (1 Kings ix, 26-28; x, 11, 12). These voyages were evidently a royal monopoly. Hiram of Tyre put experienced naval craftsmen and mariners at his disposal and received in return a share in the profits of these royal trading enterprises; for, having few harbours in their country, the Israelites were no seamen. These royal voyages extended as far as the land

[1] We have an example of this from a later period in 1 Kings xxi. The king automatically acquires possession of the vineyard which he covets near the city of Jezreel when the owner is falsely condemned to death.
[2] This is also shown by the Samaria ostraca. On the whole question cf. M. Noth, 'Das Krongut der israelitischen Könige und seine Verwaltung', ZDPV, 50 (1927), pp. 211-244.
[3] A few details show that the example of the ancient oriental kingdoms, especially of the neighbouring Egyptian kingdom, was already influential in the development of the state under David. In PJB, 31 (1935], pp. 29-75, K. Elliger has shown very clearly that 'David's thirty heroes' correspond, as a royal escort, to an Egyptian institution known from the period of Ramessides; and J. Begrich, ZAW, N.F. 17 (1940–1941), pp. 1-19, has shown that it is very probable that Egyptian models were followed for the supreme offices of מַזְכִּיר and סוֹפֵר (2 Sam. viii, 16 f.; xx, 24 f.; 1 Kings iv, 3).

of Ophir from which gold[1], valuable timber and all kinds of exotic rarities and valuables were brought home (cf. also I Kings x, 11, 22). The exact position of Ophir is uncertain and it is not even known for sure whether it was on the Arabian or, what is more likely, the African side of the Red Sea. Nor is it known whether Ophir was the source of the treasures which the fleet brought home or merely a trading centre. We do not know what Solomon offered in exchange for these treasures. Presumably with part of them he engaged in successful trading as a middleman. As the home port for his mercantile navy, Solomon built the city of Ezion-geber on the northern shores of the gulf of *el-'aḳaba*. Its remains have been re-discovered in the modern *tell el-khlēfi* west of *el-'aḳaba*[2]; and the excavations[3] undertaken on the site have shown that Solomon's port was a new foundation based on very careful plans, and had been preceded at the most by a quite meagre fishing settlement of which all traces have vanished. At the same time, they have made it clear that the city of Ezion-geber also served another purpose to which there is no reference in the literary records of Solomon's activities. Extensive installations were used for smelting copper and iron, by making use of the wind from the gulf of *el-'aḳaba*. Copper and iron were obtained from the mines on the borders of the *wādi el-'araba* and manufactured in Ezion-geber into all kinds of hardware products, great quantities of which have been found in the *tell el-khlēfi*. As Ezion-geber was a royal establishment, presumably the mining and metal-working in the province of Edom was also a royal monopoly which doubtless brought Solomon abundant profits. Finally we learn from I Kings x, 28-29, that Solomon engaged in a brisk and no doubt lucrative trade in chariots and horses with which 'the kings merchants' (סֹחֲרֵי הַמֶּלֶךְ), *i.e.* Solomon's agents, were occupied. The chariots and horses came from Egypt, the horses also from Cilicia[4] and they were sold to 'the kings of the Hittites' and 'the kings of Aram', meaning, probably, the kings of the small states in central and northern Syria.

Solomon therefore maintained extensive connections in the ancient oriental world and his prestige was no doubt very great.

[1] 'Ophir gold' is mentioned in the inscription cut on a potsherd from the end of the period of the Israelite kings, which was found on the *tell kasīle* north of *yāfa* (cf. B. Maisler, IEJ, I [1951], pp. 209 f., Fig. 13 f., Pl. 38A). Unfortunately this brief inscription does not throw any more definite light on the term 'Ophir gold'.

[2] Cf. Fr. Frank, ZDPV, 57 (1934), p. 244.

[3] Cf. the reports by N. Glueck in BASOR, 71 (1938), pp. 3-17; 75 (1939), pp. 8-22; 79 (1940), pp. 2-18.

[4] In I Kings x, 28, the name Kue occurs twice—now in a distorted form in the text—which we know from Assyrian sources as the name of a Cilician land or state.

He had inherited a mighty empire from his father, and the lustre of his monarchy will have brought him admiration and esteem from far and wide. It was entirely in keeping with his position that he had numerous foreign wives in his harem. In 1 Kings xi, 1 ff., the Deuter-onomist criticised him for this and made out that these wives induced him to forsake his God and worship idols. This latter notion is specifically deuteronomistic, but it is no doubt a fact that he had a large and motley harem. It was thought especially noteworthy that his women included an Egyptian princess (1 Kings iii, 1; ix, 16[1]); she will have been a daughter from the harem of one of the unimpor-tant Pharaohs of the 21st Egyptian Dynasty. A particularly close relationship with Egypt need have been neither the precondition nor the result of her presence in Solomon's harem.

It is understandable that the lustre of the monarchy in Solo-mon's state was regarded with admiration and possibly also with pride, but it is clear that the people groaned under the burdens which it imposed and, above all, its entirely secular and political set-up made an unfavourable impression on the Israelite tribes. The trend that had begun under David increased rapidly and intensely under Solomon and it is not surprising that the basic re-jection of the monarchy was based henceforth on the conception created by the historical actuality of Solomon's reign[2]. In fact Solo-mon represented the decadent successor who has entered upon a great inheritance and administers it with an outward show of bril-liance but who in reality allows it to fall into decay because he fails to acquire afresh for himself through his own skill and efficiency what he has inherited from his fathers.

17. Israel's Intellectual and Cultural Life under David and Solomon

The historical events which took place in the reigns of David and Solomon occasioned extremely great changes in the Israelites' con-ditions of life. A strong monarchy had relieved them of concern for self-preservation in their particular historical setting and they

---

[1] The statement inserted between 1 Kings ix, 15 and 17, in 1 Kings ix, 16, that the Pharaoh had conquered the city of Gezer as a Canaanite city and given it to his daughter as a dowry is strange and inexplicable. How could Gezer (the modern *tell jezer* near *abu shushe*) have maintained itself as an independent Canaanite city on the border of David's empire? And how can the Palestine campaign of a Pharaoh of the 21st Dynasty be explained? Cf., however, A. Alt, *Israel und Ägypten* (BWAT, 6 [1909)], pp. 20 ff.

[2] Cf., above all, the formulation of the 'royal law' in 1 Sam. viii, 11-18, on the part of the Deuteronomist.

enjoyed the advantages of living in a state that was not merely powerful but also well governed. We are told almost nothing of the administrative measures of David's reign, and even for Solomon's we are merely told a few things connected with his buildings and the royal household. But there can hardly be any doubt that David was responsible for some fundamental changes. Evidence for this is supplied by the lists of his leading officials (2 Sam. viii, 16-18; xx, 23-26) each of whom had to administer a particular department and was no doubt assisted by a staff of lower officials. It is clear that this organisation gradually became more elaborate. For from the list contained in 2 Sam. viii, 16-18, which it is impossible to date precisely, to the list in 2 Sam. xx, 23-26, which belongs at any rate to David's later period, and to the Solomonic list in 1 Kings iv, 2-6, there is apparent a constant increase in the number of principal officials. Evidently these officials were responsible for the whole territory of David's and Solomon's empire, or at any rate for the kingdoms of Judah and Israel, which were therefore united not only by the person of the king but also by these chief royal officials[1]. The Israelite army was also probably raised without regard to the distribution of the tribes between the two kingdoms of Judah and Israel.

In these two kingdoms the tribes were now combined with numerous Canaanite city-states and this also brought about a change in their position. It is true that, as is shown by the division of the kingdom of Israel into districts under Solomon, the historically evolved frontiers between tribal territories were taken into account in the administrative subdivision of the two kingdoms; but as a result of being united in the compact kingdoms of Judah and Israel, tribes and cities inevitably came into closer touch with one another and this living together with the Canaanites was bound to affect the Israelites' way of life. Even though the feeling that the Canaanites were foreigners (cf. above, pp. 142 f.) continued to prevail among them, urban ways presumably began to exert a stronger influence on them. A large and permanent political structure demands an urban foundation, not merely one urban centre—David had already created that in the royal city of Jerusalem—but urban centres throughout the country, which are necessary for efficient administration and where the specialisation of life in industry and commerce can take place which is involved in living together in a kingdom. Hence, no doubt, phenomena of urban civilisation such

[1] Here, too, a comparison may readily be made with the union of Upper and Lower Egypt under *one* monarchy with its single civil service.

as a money economy[1] and the consequent development of the distinction between rich and poor[2] found their way into the life of the Israelite tribes. It is impossible to trace this process in any detail in the records that have come down to us. It was certainly not a sudden change but a process which developed from the age of David and Solomon onwards. The fact, however, that the distinctively urban way of life was still regarded as not authentically Israelite is shown by the decree according to which dwelling-houses in walled cities —it is therefore assumed that Israelites too lived in such houses— were not to be subject to the jubilee regulations which applied to landed property in the rural areas (Lev. xxv, 29, 30).

The closer association of Israelites and Canaanites could easily have had serious consequences in the religious sphere. If, ever since the tribes had settled in Palestine, the Israelite system of worship had been richly nourished by the indigenous traditions, it is possible that the Canaanite cult may now have really exerted its influence on the Israelite tribes. And when, later on, the prophets refer to such peculiarly Canaanite fertility rites as so-called religious prostitution, or the sacrifice of children as having established themselves here and there in the worship of Yahweh, and assert that the worship of Yahweh had become simply a Canaanite Baal-cult[3], the incorporation of the Canaanite cities in the kingdoms of Judah and Israel, and the consequent blurring of the differences between the Israelite and Canaanite way of life, will have contributed to this result.

On the other hand, however, the formation of the kingdoms and the consequent strengthening of the roots which Israel struck in the ancient cultural traditions of the land, and the opening up of contacts with the wider world of the ancient Orient, aroused new intellectual forces in Israel. This led to the beginnings of more general education. Probably the tradition of the 'wisdom of Solomon' (1 Kings v, 9-14 [English Bible, iv, 29-34])[4] should be seen in this context. From the earliest times in the ancient Orient the 'wisdom' literature had promoted the transmission of a body of knowledge and experience within a 'cultured' stratum represented, above all, by the 'learned' scribes in the great cultures of the ancient Orient. Solomon's 'wisdom' is explicitly related to the

---

[1] To begin with, weighed-off metal was used as money; as far as we know, stamped coins with an officially guaranteed weight were not introduced in the ancient Orient until the establishment of the kingdom of Lydia and the Persian Empire.

[2] The statements by later prophets (above all, Amos, Isaiah and Micah) show these matters in their full development.   [3] Cf., above all, Hosea and the young Jeremiah.

Cf. A. Alt, 'Die Weisheit Salomos', ThLZ, 76 (1951), cols. 139-144.

great 'wisdom' tradition of the ancient Orient (1 Kings v, 10, 11 = iv, 30, 31 in the English Bible). The fact that he is said to have spoken of trees and animals, birds, reptiles and fishes, suggests that his 'wisdom' was connected with the lists of natural pheno- mena which are well known from Egypt and Mesopotamia and in which an attempt was made to be as all-inclusive as possible.   The only difference is that Solomon is stated specifically to have formu- lated this knowledge in 'proverbs' and 'songs'. What is said with particular reference to Solomon in 1 Kings v (English Bible, chap. iv) may no doubt be applied more generally to his whole age. It may even be that the later tradition recapitulated in the person of the king something which was true of the Israel of the age of Solomon in general, in which an educated class developed at the royal court and among the royal officials who needed not only for their work of internal administration, but also for the tasks which resulted from the world-wide importance of the empire of David and Solomon, a culture which then spread among the broader masses of the population. At any rate, new forces were awakened in the intellectual sphere in David's and, above all, in Solomon's time. This is supremely true in the field of literature. Difficult though it is to compile a real history of Israelite literature, since most of the writings incorporated in the Old Testament are anony- mous and impossible to date precisely, and on the whole not extant in their original separate forms, it is, nevertheless, possible to make one or two fairly certain statements in the present context. Writings which it is possible to describe as literature, in the sense of having been the deliberate and considered work of a professional writer, have come down to us first from the age of David and Solomon. These are historical works, describing the events of the time. In the earlier period historical memories had been recorded in the form of popular and primarily oral legends. The creative stage of the legend appears to have come substantially to an end when the kingdom was formed. It belonged to the phase when the clans and tribes were still free and independent. Anyway, the legendary material preserved in the Old Testament, as it is found above all in the narratives of the Pentateuch, in the story of the occupation of the land in the Book of Joshua and in the stories contained in 'Judges', are older in origin than the formation of the kingdom[1]; and there followed the protracted and complicated process of recording this material in writing. In the age of David and Solomon the historical chronicle took its place beside the popular legends and replaced

[1] Cf. M. Noth, *Überlieferungsgeschichte des Pentateuch* (1948), pp. 47 f.

them. The great historical events of this period, in which the
Israelites had an active share, and such important historical figures
as above all David himself, who had emerged from Israel, provided
sufficient incentive for recording the events of the time. Added to
these incentives, however—and this is the novel and surprising
thing—there was the ability to perceive the fundamental elements
and underlying relationships within the events and to express them
objectively and at the same time with literary skill. The result is by no
means simply a register of historical events. Such reports were made,
it is true—and they were also an innovation at the time—in the form
of official royal annals which were no doubt kept by the 'scribe' who
was a leading royal official (cf. 2 Sam. viii, 17b; xx, 25a). The list of
David's conflicts with neighbouring peoples in 2 Sam. viii, 1-14, was
probably based on an extract from the royal annals; and under
Solomon, who had two chief 'scribes' (1 Kings iv, 3a), the royal
annals were probably kept with still greater thoroughness and provided the material for the 'Book of the Acts of Solomon' (1 Kings xi,
41). These historical works were, however, more than mere enumera-
tions of individual events. Based though they were on solid first-hand
knowledge, they were intended to expound the fundamental development and setting of a deliberately chosen segment of history.

The main examples of this new type of historical writing are the
account of the rise of David in 1 Sam. xvi, 14–2 Sam. v, 10, and the
treatment of the question of the succession to the Davidic throne in
2 Sam. vii-xx, and 1 Kings i-ii, the former deriving in all probability from the age of David itself and the latter fairly certainly
written before the death of Solomon. The anonymous writers of the
two works must have been in fairly·close touch with the court of
David and Solomon, as is clear, in particular, from the intimate
knowledge of events at court which is revealed in the story of the
succession to the throne. All the same, these works were obviously
not commissioned officially. It is true that the description of David's
rise to power is unlimited in its admiration for the great king's successful progress, but the other narrative clearly shows the shadows
in David's portrait, reporting as it does on David's adultery with
Bathsheba, the cruel injustice of which he was guilty towards his
follower Uriah, his weakness towards Absalom and his lack of
resolution in the matter of the succession to the throne. The great
personalities and events of the period inspired the minds of
brilliant men of literary talent and led them to describe important
phases of history. These writers did not, however, merely want to
describe the course of events: they discerned in the happenings of

the time the action of their God. They speak of this divine activity in quite a new way, unlike the old popular narratives. They no longer see God intervening directly in the course of events with isolated mighty actions. In the foreground they see men acting with their human desires, their wisdom and successes, their follies and wickedness; and the events of their age seemed to them to be completely determined by human actions and their varied motives. Yet God still remained the Lord of history inasmuch as—often almost imperceptibly and invisibly—he determined human actions and by means of this human activity led the course of history to the goal which he intended. The story of David's rise to power opens in 1 Sam. xvi, 14, with the remark that 'the spirit of Yahweh departed from Saul', and in 1 Sam. xvi, 18, David is introduced straight away with the comment that 'Yahweh was with him'. This is followed by the description of David's successful rise to power, just as if David himself was solely responsible for his success. At the end, however, there is the sentence in 2 Sam. v, 10, which illuminates all the previous story: 'And David went on, and grew great and Yahweh, the God of hosts was with him'. The same thought is expressed with even greater restraint in the story of the succession to the throne. When Absalom revolted, the whole future depended on David gaining time to gather his forces and, in fact, after his entry into Jerusalem, Absalom decided, against the advice of the shrewd Ahithophel, to wait and call up the whole militia. In 2 Sam. xvii, 14b, the writer comments: 'Yahweh had appointed it so to defeat the good counsel of Ahithophel, to the intent that Yahweh might bring evil upon Absalom'. The two historical works we have mentioned represent a completely new departure[1], and they are at the same time masterpieces of their kind. They are also completely unique in the whole world of the ancient Orient; for though the Orient has bequeathed to us a wealth of sporadic historical information, mainly in the form of royal annals or other annalistic compilations, it has left no single historical work deserving the name. The fact that the God of Israel had met and still met his people primarily in historical events made Israel attentive to the interrelatedness of historical events, because in the final analysis they were the product not of human but of divine activity. And so

---

[1] This may be compared with the brief account of Abimelech in Judges ix which summarises the sequence of events as follows in verses 56, 57: 'Thus God rendered the wickedness of Abimelech, which he did unto his father, in slaying his seventy brethren; And all the evil of the men of Shechem did God render upon their heads; and upon them came the curse of Jotham the son of Jerubbaal'. It is not certain, however, that Judges ix was written before the period of David.

in the age of David and Solomon historical expositions of inter-related events were produced in Israel long before there was any historical writing in Greece or anywhere else in the known world.

Other literary works in the Old Testament are less certainly to be ascribed to the age of David and Solomon. All the same, it is probable that the oldest large-scale literary recapitulation and formulation of the extensive and originally oral material of the Pentateuch tradition, the work of the so-called Yahwist, may be attributed to this period. Whilst this work is based on tradition, and establishes the traditional narrative form of the basic religious themes of Israel's prehistory, it is not merely a masterpiece of the art of literary narration but also a theological work, which sets the divine influence on Israel's life within the wide framework of the whole of human history. The placing at the beginning of the primeval history, con-structed from all kinds of traditional materials, which the Yahwist added to the older traditions, opens up a world-wide vista, and with its very grave and gloomy statements about the nature of man in this world it forms the background for an understanding of the history of Israel by means of which Yahweh desires to bestow his blessing on humanity (cf. especially Gen. xii, 1-3). This work therefore also repre-sents a great intellectual achievement and, if the above dating should prove to be correct, would be evidence of the spiritual excitement and of the widening horizons of the age of David and Solomon.

It may be taken for granted that the literary recording of earlier popular stories and, in particular, of series of stories, also began in this period and hence the gathering together of oral traditions which had hitherto been widely scattered. In the nature of things, it is possible to date this process only in the rarest cases. All the same, it is possible, for example, to assign the combination of old local aetiological narratives into a description of the occupation of the land, as seen from an all-Israel point of view, which is contained in the old material of Jos. i-xii, with a high degree of probability, not, admittedly, to the immediate age of David and Solomon but to the period directly following the death of Solomon[1]. The incentives which the period of David and Solomon provided for literary activity and, above all, for the writing of historical narratives and the collecting, editing and recording of traditional material naturally continued to operate beyond the period itself.

In all this a rationalising tendency was at work, aimed at the arrangement, collation and interpretation of the traditions which had come down from earlier ages. Whereas reference had been

[1] Cf. M. Noth, *Das Buch Josua* (² 1953), p. 13.

made in confessions of faith to the basic acts of salvation of the God of Israel, and Israel's historical experiences of God had been passed on from one generation to another in vividly related oral legends, these traditions were now recorded and interpreted theologically. Not without good reason G. v. Rad has called the Solomonic period a period of 'typical Enlightenment' and has referred to a 'Solomonic-post-Solomonic humanism'[1].

These great descriptions of episodes from the history of David[2] have also a special significance in so far as they have established once and for all the fact that the monarchy represented an institution on the soil of Israel which had emerged in history long after the Israelite tribes had settled in Palestine and consolidated their position, and that, after the episode of Saul, David was the first to establish and bequeath to his son the monarchies over Judah and Israel which continued to exist in the history of the people. It was therefore difficult for the idea to emerge in Israel that the institution of the monarchy as such and the actual monarchies in Judah and Israel were elements of an unalterable and everlasting world order. If it is also borne in mind that the problematical nature of monarchy in general was felt among the Israelite tribes possibly from the very beginning and with ever-increasing force as time went on (cf. above, pp. 164 f.), it will be realised that the monarchy was bound to appear in a very different light than was the case in the rest of the ancient Orient and, above all, in the ancient oriental empires where monarchy was regarded as an essential element in an everlasting, divine order of things. In Israel the monarchy was bound always to be regarded as an institution that had evolved in the process of history, and it was precisely under the influence of the historical emergence of the monarchy that the form of historical writing arose in Israel to which there is no counterpart in the world of the ancient Orient. It was the result of Israel's unique historical consciousness which was based on the special nature of its experience of God. It is therefore wrong to apply without question to the monarchy in Israel the ancient oriental ideas of a sacral divine monarchy, with the attendant religious observances.

This is not to suggest that the monarchy was considered a purely secular institution in Israel[3]. Yahweh had 'been with David' (cf.

[1] G. v. Rad, *Der heilige Krieg im alten Israel* (1951), pp. 39, 49.

[2] They were probably combined at a very early date with the collected and recorded stories of Saul into the great complex of the story of Saul and David.

[3] This is most clearly to be found in the fundamental rejection of the monarchy, as it is found in the Deuteronomist, who did indeed see this institution as containing something secular and 'heathen' (cf. 1 Sam. viii, 5).

above, p. 221), that is, he had led him invisibly on his path to power
and thereby not merely approved of the establishment of David's
empire but actually brought it about, just as previously he had summoned the charismatic leaders before the foundation of the kingdom and 'been with them' (Judges vi, 16) and led them to victory
by 'delivering their enemies into their hand' (Judges iii, 28; iv, 14;
xi, 32). The only way it was possible to understand the great events
in David's period was by assuming that Yahweh had played an
active part in them. Moreover, David's monarchy contained a
divine promise for the future. At the opening of the old story of the
succession to the throne there is recorded a word of the 'prophet'
Nathan spoken to David (2 Sam. vii, 8-16) which, though it was
later revised, was no doubt formulated in the main before the death
of Solomon and must therefore be regarded as historically authentic.
In the name of Yahweh Nathan promises David that his monarchy
will be permanent and his dynasty endure. In fact, the relationship
between Yahweh and David's heirs is described as a relationship
between father and son (verse 14). Though this recalls the ancient
oriental conception of divine kingship, it is characteristic that it
should appear in a fundamentally different form. Possibly as a
deliberate reaction to this ancient oriental conception, the formula
of adoption is used to describe the relationship; the God-king relationship has no automatic existence, and the king does not possess
divine being or nature, but he is declared to be a son—when he
ascends the throne—by a manifestation of the divine will.   Probably when the heirs of David acceded to power the formula of
adoption was solemnly pronounced (Ps. ii, 7, and perhaps also
Ps. cx, 3). This means that the relationship was confirmed, on
a historical basis, at each new accession: it was not regarded
as having an intrinsic and absolute existence. This shows that,
whilst the Davidic monarchy made just as great claims in Israel as
monarchy did elsewhere in the ancient Orient, it was different in
quality. Moreover, the content of Nathan's promise implied that
the God of Israel desired the kingship of David and would continue to desire it because it served his purposes—about which
nothing is said in this connection. The declaration by a particular group of prophets later on, that David's monarchy would
play a fundamental part in God's plan of salvation, linked up with
this. This conception of the significance of God's activity in history
was something quite different from the idea of the intrinsically
divine nature of kingship which was current in the rest of the
ancient Orient.

CHAPTER III

THE COEXISTENCE OF THE SEPARATE KINGDOMS OF JUDAH AND ISRAEL

18. *Judah and Israel after the Death of Solomon*

SOLOMON died during the year which ran from the autumn of 926 B.C. to the autumn of 925 B.C. His death is the earliest event in the history of Israel which it is possible to date precisely, with the possible error of merely a few years. For the death of Solomon marks the beginning of the uninterrupted chronological sequence of the history of the kings of Judah and Israel which the author of the deuteronomistic history was able to draw from the official annals of the two kingdoms available to him in the 'Chronicles of the Kings of Judah' or 'of Israel', which he used as sources. These chronological notes supply, in the first place, the duration of the reigns of the kings in both kingdoms and, then, the synchronisation between Judah and Israel in accordance with which every change of sovereign in one of the two kingdoms was dated according to the year of the king's reign in the other kingdom. The firm system of relative chronology of the reigns in Judah and Israel which was arrived at in this way may be linked up by various historical points of contact with the chronology of the Neo-Assyrian empire which in its turn may be fixed absolutely by means of astronomical calculations[1]. According to 1 Kings xi, 42, when he died Solomon had reigned for forty years, and in 2 Sam. v, 4, 5, David's reign is also stated to have lasted forty years—reckoning from his appointment as king of Judah. In both cases it is probably merely a matter of a round figure[2]; if the figure is more or less correct—and there is no reason to question that—the reigns of David and Solomon occupied roughly the first three-quarters of the 10th century B.C.

---

[1] Cf. the brief reference to this in WAT, pp. 211 f., and in detail in J. Begrich, *Die Chronologie der Könige von Israel und Juda* (Beiträge zur historischen Theologie, 3), 1929. In what follows I give the dates according to Begrich (cf. the summary of his results, *op. cit.* p. 155) without going into the details. The latest attempt at a chronology of the kings of Judah and Israel, which differs in some details from that of Begrich, is by W. F. Albright, BASOR, 100 (1945), pp. 16-22.

[2] The number 40 often occurs elsewhere in the old Testament as a round number for the space of time in which a generation of grown men usually dies out.

At his death Solomon left David's empire outwardly in a splendid condition but it was already in a state of decline owing to threats from some of the outlying provinces or their actual loss, at least in part. Above all, there was the bad feeling which had arisen among the Israelite tribes about the ostentation and pretentiousness of Solomon's reign. His successor was therefore faced with an unusually difficult task which only a man of special strength and wisdom could master. That it was Rehoboam among his sons, probably his eldest son, who was intended to succeed him does not seem to have been in doubt. And in the city-state of Jerusalem and the kingdom of Judah Rehoboam apparently succeeded his father on the throne without any trouble. In the Canaanite city-states succession by heredity had long been the normal custom, and the fact that an heir of David again became king in the 'city of David' did not raise any problems. But at that period and thereafter the kingdom of Judah also held fast to the Judaean dynasty of David and apparently recognised Rehoboam as the new king without any further ado[1]. In the kingdom of Israel, however, the situation was different. We learn something about the events which took place there from the narrative of the prophet Ahijah of Shiloh (1 Kings xi, 29-39; xii, 1-32; xiv, 1-18) in which it is claimed that Yahweh fulfilled the promise made to Jeroboam by Ahijah and then rejected Jeroboam after he had become an apostate[2]. After this the tribes of the kingdom of Israel gathered in Shechem, the recognised urban centre of the Israelite tribal territories and the oldest seat of the central federal shrine. Rehoboam repaired there and the assembled tribes wanted to 'make him king', that is, they wanted to discuss the appointment with him and to make their own conditions. Their elders—for we may assume that it was they who had gathered together in Shechem—thus did not recognise the automatic succession by inheritance which had occurred in the emergency which followed the fall of Saul, owing to the influence of the powerful Abner (2 Sam. ii, 8-9), and again after the death of David on the strength of his own great authority; as had already been the case when Saul was made king (1 Sam. xi, 15) and, above all, when David was chosen to be king of Israel (2 Sam. v, 3), they wanted to bestow the crown themselves and to 'make a covenant' with the new king. They gave prior consideration to Rehoboam as

---

[1] Perhaps this took place by means of a solemn act, possibly in the ancient Judaean royal city of Hebron.

[2] In this narrative, too, God is seen as acting in human decisions. It was a 'dispensation' (סבה) of Yahweh, that Rehoboam acted unwisely, because Yahweh wanted to fulfil his promise to Jeroboam (1 Kings xii, 15); cf. above, pp. 221 f.

Solomon's eldest son, but required an assurance that the burdens which had become so oppressive under Solomon, would be lightened. No doubt they had in mind, above all, the payment of tribute in kind and—as far as the former Canaanite cities were concerned—the compulsory forced labour. Contrary to the advice of his older, experienced counsellors, Rehoboam gave an abruptly negative reply, being evidently completely mistaken as to the true situation; and so the elders of the kingdom of Israel declared themselves separated from the dynasty of David. Once again the watchword issued in a dangerous situation in David's reign (2 Sam. xx, 1) was revived, that, 'Israel' had 'no part in' the Judaean dynasty of David (1 Kings, xii, 16). It is impossible to say for sure how far the Ephraimite Jeroboam played a part in the background in the negotiations with Rehoboam. He had once 'lifted his hand against Solomon', had then escaped to Egypt (cf. above, p. 206 f.) and had now swiftly returned on hearing the news of Solomon's death. Anyway, he was now made king of Israel by the elders in Shechem in place of the Davidite. He had been designated a future king of Israel by the prophet Ahijah of Shiloh in the name of Yahweh, probably at the time of his revolt against Solomon[1]; and, apart from his personal ambition, this was the main reason why the elders elected Jeroboam in Shechem.

This brought to an end the empire built up by David. Important outposts were now inevitably lost. The Aramaean province in the north-east, in which the new independent Aramaean province of Damascus had already come into being in Solomon's reign, was now impossible to hold. With its ancient cities it became the centre of the new kingdom, which was rapidly consolidated and became a formidable enemy of the kingdom of Israel. The rule of the Davidites in Ammon also inevitably came to an end now, that is, assuming Solomon had been able to hold it until his death. Whilst there is no first-hand evidence of the existence of an independent king of Ammon until three-quarters of a century later[2], it is nevertheless clear that the Davidites, who, with the secession of the kingdom of Israel, lost their territorial contact with Ammon, were no longer in a position to remain kings of Ammon. The new king of Israel had no contact of any kind with the Ammonite kingship which David had once assumed in his own person. Only the small kingdom of Moab still continued to pay tribute to the kingdom of Israel for

[1] This was at any rate the opinion of the redactor who inserted the beginning of the story of Ahijah (1 Kings xi, 29-39) between 1 Kings xi, 26-28 and xi, 40.

[2] In the monolithic inscription of king Shalmaneser III of Assyria, col. II, l. 95 (cf. Gressmann, AOT², pp. 340 f.; TGI, p. 46).

a bare century more; and despite the new monarchy that had emerged in Edom, the province of Edom remained at least to some extent linked with the kingdom of Judah, at any rate for a time.

Judah and Israel now had to establish themselves as separate minor kingdoms within the political world of Syria and Palestine. The kingdom of Judah, which was considerably the smaller of the two, had the advantage over Israel inasmuch as it could build more on the past and it therefore found it easier to set up a stable order. So long as it existed at all it held unflinchingly to the succession of the dynasty of David. As the house of David was Judaean, once the 'men of Judah had anointed David king over the house of Judah' (2 Sam. ii, 4a), and the monarchy had passed by David's will to his son Solomon, the kingdom of Judah remained faithful to the house of David even after the death of Solomon. This established the principle of succession by inheritance so firmly that on subsequent occasions the throne passed on the whole without difficulty to the king's eldest son. Occasionally troubles did occur for special reasons, but they took place within the dynasty of David itself. The kingdom of Judah had also had its royal city from the very beginning. Jerusalem as the 'City of David' remained with the Davidites after the death of Solomon and they resided there until the kingdom of Judah came to an end. It was, however, no longer the royal city of an empire, the position to which it had been raised by David and in which it had been brilliantly developed by Solomon; as a merely Judaean royal city it was bound to languish. All the same, however, it did remain *the* royal city. In the sanctuary of the royal palace it contained the ancient sacred Ark[1], and it therefore was and continued to be the real religious centre of the Israelite tribes to which the tribes in the kingdom of Israel as well as those in the kingdom of Judah looked as their spiritual home.

The whole situation was very different in the kingdom of Israel. The appointment of Jeroboam as king after the death of Solomon implied a return to the earlier mode of election that had been followed in the case of Saul and which originated in the ancient charismatic leadership of the period before the establishment of the monarchy. The man designated to be the future king had been proclaimed by a prophet in the name of Yahweh; when a man had thus

---

[1] We hear of the Ark for the last time on the occasion of its transfer to the Temple by Solomon (1 Kings viii, 1 ff.); it may have remained there until the destruction of Jerusalem in the year 587 B.C.

been designated he could expect to ascend the throne at the next opportunity. In the kingdom of Israel, therefore, the monarchy was a most unstable institution. It is not surprising that a man designated as king would take the opportunity of removing the reigning monarch and usurping the throne by violence, and that in the end an ambitious man who had not even been so designated could easily seize the power. Admittedly, however, in the struggle against the system of charismatic leadership, the monarchy tended to become a more firmly established institution even in Israel and so led to the custom of succession by inheritance. The beginnings of this tendency had been apparent in the succession of Saul-Eshbaal and David-Solomon. This recurred again later and in the end real dynasties were established. Jeroboam was followed by his son Nadab. But the latter had hardly begun his reign[1] when there emerged in the year 906–905 B.C. an Issacharite named Baasha who was designated by a prophet (cf. 1 Kings xvi, 2) and seized the throne by murdering the king Nadab who was in camp with his militia. The new kingdom of Baasha did not fare any better, however; Baasha's son Elah, who succeeded his father, was not on the throne long[2] when he was murdered in the royal palace by one of his principal officials, Zimri, the captain of half the chariots (1 Kings xvi, 8 ff.): a case of assassination which led to the seizure of the throne by a high court official on his own responsibility. There is no reference to Zimri having been appointed by a prophet, and the omission is clearly no mere accident. The probability is that the sole reason for the murder was Zimri's personal ambition. And Zimri did not receive the recognition in Israel that would certainly have come to him if his appointment had been authorised by a word spoken in the name of Yahweh. He was only able to hold the throne for seven days (1 Kings xvi, 15). And as apparently no one had been designated as future king, a struggle for the succession broke out from which, in the end, as often happens in such cases, a military leader emerged triumphant. This was Omri, the head of the whole army, who ascended the throne in the year 878–877 B.C. These events show how a monarchy which was opposed to the formation and consolidation of a dynasty because of its basic association with the old system of charismatic leadership could easily become the plaything of ruthless and violent pretenders to the throne.

[1] Two years are ascribed to his reign (1 Kings xv, 25). According to the method of reckoning which was in use at this period, which counts parts of calendar years at the beginning and end as full years, this merely means that his reign covered one change of calendar year.

[2] The official reckoning again only gives him 'two years' (1 Kings xvi, 8).

After the disturbances Omri succeeded in maintaining his hold on the throne sufficiently for three of his descendants to sit on it and for the house of Omri to rule more than thirty years in the kingdom of Israel. Omri thereby became the founder of the first, albeit short-lived, dynasty in Israel. We know nothing about Omri's family background. That may be no mere accident. His name does not sound very Israelite nor does that of his son Ahab[1]. As leader of the militia Omri could quite easily have emerged from the ranks of the mercenaries, and a band of mercenaries usually contains elements of very varied origin. The dynasty of Omri was finally overthrown when a new king, designated by a prophet in the name of Yahweh, appeared once more. According to 2 Kings ix, 1 ff., Jehu, one of the officers of the militia who happened to be in the field at the time, was appointed and anointed by an emissary of the prophet Elisha[2]; and this Jehu proceeded brutally to wipe out the then reigning descendant of Omri and the whole family and to ascend the throne himself in the year 845–844 B.C. With this—a good three-quarters of a century after the death of Solomon—the custom of the designation of a king of Israel by a prophet became extinct, as far as we know. Jehu founded a dynasty which occupied the throne in the kingdom of Israel for about a century. And when Jehu's last descendant had been murdered after a short reign[3] (2 Kings xv, 10) for the last twenty years of its existence the throne in Israel was for the most part in the hands of swiftly changing usurpers who were unable to claim any kind of divine authorisation for themselves. In the name of his God the prophet Hosea could only say of them: 'They have set up kings but not by me' (viii, 4).

After the death of Solomon the kingdom of Israel still had, to begin with, no traditional royal city. Jeroboam had been proclaimed king in Shechem, the ancient and important urban centre of Mount Ephraim, which was favourably placed from the point of view of communications, and here in Shechem he resided to begin with. According to 1 Kings xii, 25 he 'built Shechem', that is, he organised it as his royal city. But then he left Shechem and 'built' Penuel as a residence, which lay in a remote part of the land east

---

[1] The root of the name Omri is common in Arabic names, and the name Ahab can also be explained on the basis of Arabic nomenclature; cf. M. Noth, *Die israelitischen Personennamen* (BWANT, III, 10 [1928], pp. 63, 222, note 7. Was the striking prohibition contained in the deuteronomistic 'royal law' against appointing a foreigner king (Deut. xvii, 15) based on the concrete case of Omri?

[2] In 1 Kings xix, 16, the anointing of Jehu is connected with the prophet Elijah, but probably on the basis of a secondary tradition.

[3] According to 2 Kings xv, 8, he only reigned for six months.

of the Jordan in the deep valley of the Jabbok (the modern *tulūl
ed̲-d̲ahab*)[1]. This strange transfer of the residence was no doubt
occasioned by some emergency, and the correct explanation is
probably that Jeroboam withdrew beyond the Jordan, with his
residence, in face of a warlike incursion of the Pharaoh Shishak
(Shoshenk) (cf. below, p. 239 f.). In the end he gave up Penuel again
as it was in such an unsuitable position, and returned to the land
west of the Jordan when Shishak had moved away and no further
threats were expected from that quarter. Curiously enough, he
did not return to Shechem[2] but chose the city of Tirzah, the precise
location of which has not yet been discovered but which was somewhere on Mount Ephraim[3]. In Tirzah the kings of Israel who
succeeded Jeroboam continued to reside for a time. It was in
Tirzah that Baasha ascended the throne (1 Kings xv, 33); it was
in Tirzah that Elah was murdered by Zimri (1 Kings xvi, 9) and in
Tirzah Zimri himself lost his life (1 Kings xvi, 18). Omri set himself
up as king in Tirzah (1 Kings xvi, 23), but afterwards he presented
the kingdom of Israel with a new royal city. Since, for some reason
or other, Tirzah was inadequate or unsuitable, Omri, in the process
of consolidating his monarchy, bought a hill in Mount Ephraim
about 6 miles north-west of Shechem in a beautiful and dominating
position overlooking a broad, fertile valley stretching away westwards, and here he built the royal city of Samaria (the modern
sebaṣtye) (1 Kings xvi, 24) which remained the residence of the
Israelite kings for a century and a half until the kingdom of Israel
came to an end. The excavations carried out on the site[4] have
disclosed the remains of the Israelite palace which was extended
by various kings after Omri, and they have revealed that there was
no previous urban settlement on this site and that Omri in fact
established a new city for the Israelite monarchy, thereby giving
the kingdom of Israel a permanent centre, which belonged to the
king in person.

[1] According to N. Glueck, *Explorations in Eastern Palestine*, III (AASOR, XVIII/
XIX [1939]), pp. 232 ff., the archaeological discoveries show that of the two hills of
tulūl ed̲-d̲ahab, only the eastern one, *tell ed̲-d̲ahab esh-sherḳi*, can have been the site
of ancient Penuel.

[2] It is not, apparently, to be assumed that Shechem had been too greatly destroyed
by Shishak, since Shechem was probably not mentioned at all in the hieroglyphic list of
the Israelite cities conquered by Shishak; cf. M. Noth, ZDPV, 61 (1938), p. 289.

[3] Cf. F.-M. Abel, *Géographie de la Palestine*, II (1938), pp. 485 f., who criticises the
earlier suggestions including the locating of Tirzah on the *tell el-fār'a* about 6 m. north-
east of Shechem; but his own suggestion has no assured basis either.

[4] Cf. Reisner-Fisher-Lyon, *Harvard Excavations at Samaria, 1908–1910*, I/II
(1924), and the report on the later continuation of the first excavation by J. W. Crowfoot,
K. M. Kenyon, E. L. Sukenik, *Samaria-Sebaste Publications*, I (1942).

It was more difficult to put the kingdom of Israel on its own feet in the sphere of worship. The royal Judaean sanctuary in Jerusalem continued to attract the tribes living in the kingdom of Israel with the Ark as the ancient common object of devotion, and there is hardly any doubt but that they made pilgrimages to Jerusalem. The story of Ahijah (cf. above, p. 226) shows that the religious tradition connected with Jerusalem was already so firmly established after the death of Solomon that it was possible to uphold the authority of the Temple as the central shrine of the tribes even though the authority of the Davidites was rejected. That Jeroboam already regarded this as most undesirable, since it meant that there was at least an indirect point of contact between all the Israelite tribes and the dynasty of David, was only natural, and it is stated in so many words in 1 Kings xii, 26 ff. Jeroboam therefore raised to the status of royal places of worship the two famous and ancient shrines of Bethel (the modern *burj bētīn* near *bētīn*) and Dan (the modern *tell el-ḳāḍi*) in the extreme south and north of the kingdom of Israel, which the Israelites had doubtless been frequenting for a long time[1]. He decked them sumptuously out, providing each with a so-called 'golden calf'. Later on, the residence of Samaria was no doubt given a royal shrine, and probably a 'golden calf' was erected there too; at any rate the prophet Hosea mentions the 'calf of Samaria' (viii, 5-6). Admittedly these royal Israelite centres of worship were unable to compete with the Ark in Jerusalem and its unique traditional place in the tribal life, even though the kings of Israel provided them with all the necessary equipment, with priests appointed by the king and a system of festivals which was an imitation of the one observed in Jerusalem. Later on, the Deuteronomist, assuming that Jerusalem had always been the one and only authorised religious centre in the country, saw in the establishment of these royal shrines in Israel the supreme sin committed by Jeroboam and all the subsequent kings of Israel. His assumption was not strictly applicable to the period of the Israelite kings, and the 'golden calves' were not intended as 'idols'. They were intended as part of the worship of the God of Israel who had done great things for Israel and 'brought Israel up out of the land of Egypt' (1 Kings xii, 28, cf. Exod. xxxii, 4); and they were probably not intended to be thought of as divine images, especially as theriomorphic images were unknown in the Near East—as opposed to Egypt. They were probably conceived as pedestals for the deity

---

[1] It is not clear what legal rights the Israelite king had to take possession of ancient local sanctuaries in places inhabited by Israelites.

who was imagined to be standing on them unseen[1]. The common folk may, however, have seen them as representations and materialisations of the deity; and even at that time it was probably clear that the Ark was the sole place where God was present for the whole of Israel: the one authentic and specifically Israelite shrine. Even in the pre-deuteronomistic narrative concerning the prophet Ahijah of Shiloh, Jeroboam was severely castigated for erecting royal shrines in Israel (1 Kings xii, 28-32). With its official religion the Israelite monarchy was to some extent opposed to the authentic and strict Israelite tradition from the very beginning; in this respect it was at a decided disadvantage compared with the Judaean monarchy of the Davidites.

To begin with, the relationship between the two kingdoms of Judah and Israel was anything but friendly. Our knowledge of the history of the two kingdoms after the death of Solomon is, admittedly, very incomplete. We have to rely very largely on the little that the Deuteronomist incorporated from the 'Chronicles of the Kings of Judah' or 'of Israel' and on the historical information which it is possible to gather from the various prophetic narratives which were embodied in the deuteronomistic history. In making extracts from the 'Chronicles' the Deuteronomist's aim was not in the least to provide a connected account of the history of the kingdoms of Judah and Israel. The 'Chronicles' themselves had presumably summarised the official annals of the two kingdoms from particular points of view, though we no longer know what these points of view were. The Deuteronomist extracted, in the first place, everything concerning the succession of the kings and the chronological sequence of events; as far as the kingdom of Israel was concerned he very largely left it at that. For the history of Judah, however, he also incorporated the details directly or indirectly concerned with the Temple in Jerusalem, since the house of David, with the promise given to it, and Jerusalem as the city of David and the city of Solomon's Temple, and, above all, the Temple itself as, according to deuteronomistic law, the sole legitimate shrine of Israel, were matters of importance to him. He judged the kings according to their attitude to the exclusive legitimacy of the Temple in Jerusalem. From this standpoint he was bound, with only a few exceptions, to pass a negative judgement on almost all the kings. The monotonous repetition of these condemnations only shows that

---

[1] In the Near East animals and anthropomorphically conceived deities were only connected in this way (cf. Gressmann, AOB², Nos. 331, 335, 338, 345, 354-356). For another interpretation of the 'golden calf' see O. Eissfeldt, ZAW, N.F. 17 (1940-41), pp. 199 ff.

he had no intention of describing the individual kings as persons in their own right or in the light of their historical importance. He aimed, rather, to represent the monarchy as a fundamental cause of Israel's defection from its God. It is clear, therefore, that he was unable to offer a history of the kingdoms of Judah and Israel. It should be remembered, however, that he did not consider that his task at all. This is obvious from the fact that he refers any who are interested to know what a particular king 'had done' to the 'Chronicles of the Kings of Judah' or 'of Israel' which he had used as sources himself. Nevertheless, the little that the Deuteronomist does transmit from his sources affords some insight into the course of the history of Judah and Israel after the death of Solomon.

After the death of Solomon enmity prevailed for a long time between Judah and Israel. It is true that Rehoboam's attempt to seize the throne in Israel by armed force, which is mentioned in the prophetic narrative in 1 Kings xii, 21-24, was soon abandoned. If in Judah the claim of the Davidites to the Israelite monarchy continued to be maintained for a time, and in Israel an attempt to regain control on the part of the Judaean Davidites was feared, it was probably soon accepted that the separation of the two kingdoms was inevitable. The dispute regarding the definition of the common frontier probably continued for a long time. Rehoboam succeeded in annexing for Judah part of the tribal territory of Benjamin, which had belonged to the kingdom of Israel under Eshbaal, David and Solomon. We do not know how this came about; presumably Rehoboam was able to seize this land by force of arms and keep it for Judah[1]. This was important for him, since his royal city of Jerusalem was situated precisely midway between the territories of Judah and Israel—that was just why David had chosen it (cf. above, p. 189 f.). After the separation of the two kingdoms it came to be on the border of Judah and in direct contact with Israel. The annexation of part of Benjaminite territory and the consequent shifting of the common frontier some distance northwards away from Jerusalem meant the acquisition of a defensive strip for the city over against the kingdom of Israel and hence a protection against sudden attacks and invasions. Evidently minor frontier warfare took place here continuously. When there is mention of constant war between Judah and Israel in the period

[1] Retrospectively the story of the prophet Ahijah describes this so as to suggest that Yahweh assigned the government of Israel to Jeroboam with the exception of a single tribe (*i.e.* Benjamin) (1 Kings xi, 31, 32, 36). Cf. also 1 Kings xii, 20, where 'tribe of Benjamin' originally stood in the place of 'tribe of Judah'. The kingdom of Judah which the Davidites naturally retained is not discussed at all in the story of Jeroboam.

of the kings Rehoboam and Jeroboam (1 Kings xiv, 30), and in that of the kings Asa and Baasha (1 Kings xv, 16), the reference is to this border warfare[1]. Probably Judah was able to maintain its hold on part of the Benjaminite territory as a defensive strip for Jerusalem against Israel which claimed, not unfairly, possession of the whole of Benjamin. The border conflicts, in which presumably both sides had some successes and reverses, probably took place entirely within the territory of Benjamin. This is suggested by the events which the Deuteronomist records in greater detail because the treasures of the Temple in Jerusalem played a part in them (1 Kings xv, 17-22). According to this account, the Israelite king Baasha (906–905 to 883–882 B.C.) succeeded in occupying the city of Ramah (the modern *er-rām*) which lies at the centre of Benjaminite territory on the main road leading to Jerusalem from the north, 5 miles away from Jerusalem, and began to develop it as an Israelite stronghold. In this difficult situation the Judaean king Asa persuaded the Aramaean king of Damascus to attack the kingdom of Israel from the north, by making him a rich present from the treasures of the Temple and palace in Jerusalem. Baasha had therefore to withdraw from his southern border to defend his northern frontier. Asa exploited the difficulties of his Israelite enemy not only by himself occupying Ramah but by moving the frontier of Judah and Israel still farther northwards. By using the materials that Baasha had assembled for fortifications in Ramah, he fortified the cities of Geba and Mizpah as Judaean frontier strongholds. Geba (the modern *jeba'*) lay 2 miles east of Ramah, south of the deep *wādi eṣ-ṣuwēnīṭ* which ran south-eastwards and which became the frontier between the two kingdoms in this area; Mizpah was probably situated on the modern *tell en-naṣbe*, 3 miles north of Ramah on the above-mentioned main road[2]. The frontier that was established in this way apparently became a permanency since, under the Judaean king Josiah (639–609 B.C.), Geba still appears as the northern frontier city of Judah in the phrase 'from Geba to Beersheba' (2 Kings xxiii, 8). Anyway, soon afterwards a change occurred in the relationship between Judah and Israel which brought the initial frontier disputes to an end. On the hills

[1] The basis of the story of a war of king Abijah of Judah with Jeroboam, which the Chronicler elaborated in 2 Chron. xiii, 3-20, belongs to this context.

[2] The situation of Mizpah has long been, and still is, in dispute. But the results of the excavations on the *tell en-naṣbe* (cf. C. C. McCown and J. C. Wampler, *Tell en-Nasbeh excavated under the Direction of the late William Frederic Badè*, I/II [1947]) fit in various respects so well with what we know about the history of Mizpah that it is at any rate highly probable that Mizpah was on the *tell en-naṣbe*. Cf. the detailed discussion of the question in A. Alt, ZDPV, 69 (1953), pp. 1 ff.

in the area of the main road which runs parallel with the watershed, Judah remained in possession of a considerable part of Benjaminite territory for the protection of the royal city of Jerusalem[1].

As part of a deliberate policy the Israelite kings of the dynasty of Omri buried their minor disputes with their Judaean neighbours (cf. below, p. 240f.) and tried to come to an understanding with them. The existing balance of power resulted in the smaller kingdom of Judah following behind the kingdom of Israel, which was led by able kings. The Israelite kings were able to maintain the upper hand over their obviously less important Judaean colleagues. The prophetic narrative in 1 Kings xxii, 2-38, reveals the Judaean king as the confederate of the king of Israel[2] in a military enterprise aimed at the possession of the city of Ramoth in Gilead which was directly important only for the kingdom of Israel; and in 2 Kings ix, 16 ff., we again find king Ahaziah of Judah in the entourage of the Israelite king Joram. The prophetic narrative in 2 Kings iii, 4-27, which is very obscure historically and difficult to elucidate, also refers to the Judaean king acting in unison with the Israelite king[3] in a war against Moab, which was primarily the concern of the kingdom of Israel, since Moab was the immediate neighbour and had previously been the vassal of the kingdom of Israel. The two royal houses were even united by marriage; the Judaean king Joram (852–851 to 845–844 B.C.) married, probably while still crown prince, Athaliah, a daughter of king Ahab of Israel (2 Kings viii, 26)[4], and this marriage naturally had a political background.

With the fall of the dynasty of Omri in Israel, Judah's political tie with Israel was destroyed again. In fact, to begin with, the rule of the family of Omri, which had just been eliminated in Israel, was revived in Judah. After the Judaeán king Ahaziah had lost his life in Jehu's rising against the house of Omri as a confederate of the last of the dynasty of Omri (2 Kings ix, 27 f.), his mother, the above-

---

[1] No considerable shift of the frontier took place in the Jordan Valley; at any rate the territory of the old city-state of Jericho was retained by the kingdom of Israel (cf. 1 Kings xvi, 34). But in the western hill country Judah was able to obtain some land at the expense of Israel. Rehoboam was able to develop the city of Aijalon (the modern *yālo*), which once belonged to one of the districts of the kingdom of Israel (1 Kings iv, 9), into a Judaean stronghold (2 Chron. xi, 10).

[2] The names of these kings were not mentioned in the original form of the narrative; and it is not quite certain whether the Deuteronomist's historical arrangement of the reigns of the kings Jehoshaphat and Ahab is factually correct.

[3] Here, too, the names of the kings Jehoram and Jehoshaphat obviously do not belong to the original contents of the narrative.

[4] In this passage she is called a 'daughter of Omri'. But it is clear from the following verse that this merely indicates her membership of the dynasty of Omri and that she was in fact a daughter of Ahab.

mentioned Athaliah, evidently a very ambitious woman, seized the throne and had all the surviving members of the house of David killed. She then ruled, probably very despotically, for six years (845-844 to 839-838 B.C.), though no details of her reign have come down to us. In the end she was overthrown and killed by a clever trick perpetrated by the high priest of Jerusalem, Jehoiada (cf. the detailed account in 2 Kings xi). A son of the last king Ahaziah, who was still quite a small child at the time when he was rescued from Athaliah's lust for blood, had all this time been hidden from her. This small Davidite, Jehoash by name, was now set on the throne of his fathers and the lawful succession of the Davidites was continued. Henceforth, as far as we can judge, there were no close ties between the kingdoms of Judah and Israel, nor was there any enmity between them. Only once did there occur a strange incident. According to 2 Kings xiv, 8-14, the Judaean king Amaziah (800-799 to 785-784 B.C.) one day challenged king Jehoash of Israel (802-801 to 787-786 B.C.), the grandson of Jehu, the founder of the dynasty, to a military trial of strength. The result was a battle at Beth-shemesh (the modern *tell er-rumēle* near *'ēn shems*) in which Amaziah was soundly defeated. As a result, the victorious Israelites were even able to occupy Jerusalem, plunder the Temple and the palace treasury (that is the reason why the Deuteronomist tells the story) and pull down part of the city wall. The real background of the event is not clear, but it does not seem to have had any lasting repercussions.

The dynasty of Jehu which was, to begin with, gravely troubled by foreign enemies, was able, in the end, to give the kingdom of Israel a period of relative peace and security. The long reign of king Jeroboam II (787-786 to 747-746 B.C.) was a comparatively good period for Israel[1]. The equally long reign of the almost contemporary king Uzziah brought a period of similar calm to Judah. This was the state of affairs shortly before new and tremendous events completely altered the situation for both Judah and Israel.

[1] The ostraca which have been found in the royal palace of Samaria throw a little light on the internal organisation of Israel. They are the oldest known written documents from Israel and probably belong to the period of Jeroboam II (cf. W. F. Albright, *Archaeology and the Religion of Israel* [2 1946], p. 214, note 41). They belong to the royal administration of the crown lands and were published by Reisner-Fisher-Lyon, *Harvard Excavations at Samaria* (1924), I, pp. 227-246, II, Pl. 55; cf. also WAT, p. 174 and III, 10 and TGI, p. 50. Cf. ANET, p. 321, DOTT, pp. 204-208.

19. *Struggles with neighbouring States*

The disintegration of the empire of David and Solomon turned Judah and Israel into minor kingdoms within the political world of Syria and Palestine. They were forced to fight for their survival in repeated conflicts with the other powers in this area.

It is not surprising that the change in the situation caused the Philistines in the south-west to bestir themselves again. Admittedly the earlier power of the Philistines had been broken by David once and for all, and all that ensued now was border warfare with no far-reaching effects[1]. Rehoboam had already protected the little kingdom of Judah by means of a complete system of fortified strongholds (2 Chron. xi, 5-10) and in this system the particularly powerful fortification of the western border of Judah is especially remarkable[2]. It is surprising to find the city of Gath among these fortified strongholds; this must be the famous one-time Philistine city whose king had played a leading part in David's time among the Philistine rulers and which still enjoyed political independence when Solomon came to the throne (cf. 1 Kings ii, 39, 40). We do not know when and how this most inland of the Philistine cities[3] had come into the possession of Judah. Did Solomon really take it by force of arms? Or did Rehoboam succeed in annexing this neighbouring Philistine city in his attempt to consolidate Judah as an independent state? In any case, it is not surprising that the Philistines henceforth tried to regain Gath. According to 2 Kings xii, 18 f., however, Gath was still in the hands of Judah at the time of the Judaean king Jehoash (839–838 to 800–799 B.C.). At that time the Aramaean king Hazael—evidently as an ally of the Philistines, who were no match for Judah on their own—conquered the city of Gath and even threatened Jerusalem, so that the king of Judah had to pay dearly to persuade Hazael to retreat by rendering tribute from the Temple and palace treasury in Jerusalem. Possibly Judah lost Gath once more at that time[4]; anyway, about a century later we find Gath in Philistine hands again.

---

[1] On the following, cf. O. Eissfeldt, 'Israelitisch-philistäische Grenzverschiebungen von David bis auf die Assyrerzeit', ZDPV, 66 (1943), pp. 115-128.

[2] Cf. G. Beyer, 'Das Festungssystem Rehabeams', ZDPV, 54 (1931), pp. 113-134, and especially the sketch-map on p. 116.

[3] It is impossible to ascertain its exact position. Most probably it was on the *tell es-ṣāfi* (as suggested most recently by K. Elliger, ZDPV, 57 [1934], pp. 148 ff., and O. Eissfeldt, *op. cit.* p. 119). *The Westminster Historical Atlas to the Bible* (1945), p. 109, represents a different view.

[4] The note in 2 Chron. xxvi, 6, according to which the Judaean king Uzziah pulled

The kingdom of Israel waged repeated border warfare with the Philistines near the city of Gibbethon. On two occasions we learn accidentally that the whole of the Israelite militia was encamped at Gibbethon (1 Kings xv, 27; xvi, 15-17). This place Gibbethon is probably identical with the modern *tell el-melāt*[1], and if so, it lay about 3 miles west of the city of Gezer (*tell jezer*) and also about 3 miles east of the Philistine city of Ekron (*'āķir*). The real struggle was therefore obviously for one of these two cities; the only question is whether the kingdom of Israel was trying to annex the neighbouring city of Ekron, just as Judah had annexed the neighbouring Philistine city of Gath, or whether the Philistines were threatening Gezer, which belonged to Israel. Apparently neither side was successful, and the Philistine wars had no great effect. The Philistines became dangerous for Judah and for Israel at this period only in so far as they worked hand in hand with the far stronger Aramaeans of Damascus. Just as, for Judah, this probably led to the loss of Gath, it also seems, according to the Septuagintal addition in 2 Kings xiii, 22, to have injured Israel. In the latter case, too, it was king Hazael of Aram who helped the Philistines to achieve their successes (cf. also Isa. ix, 11).

On one occasion a greater power from the south-west intervened for a time in the history of Israel and Judah. In the fifth year of king Rehoboam, that is, in the year 922–921 B.C., the Pharaoh Shishak I, a Libyan mercenary leader, who had founded the 22nd Dynasty in Egypt, undertook an expedition to Palestine, evidently in order to renew the tradition of the great Pharaohs of the New Kingdom who had for a time possessed the whole of Syria and Palestine. In 1 Kings xiv, 25-28, it is recorded that Rehoboam assembled all the treasures of the Temple and palace in Jerusalem to pay tribute to the Pharaoh. This was the price he had to pay for the sparing of Judah and Jerusalem. This is clear, too, from the list of cities which were conquered in Palestine, which Shishak compiled in imitation of similar lists which various Pharaohs of the New Kingdom had affixed to a wall of the great Amun temple of Karnak in Upper Egypt, in commemoration of his expedition[2]. There is no mention of any Judaean cities in this list. On the other hand, however, Shishak not only overran the Negeb in the south of Palestine and the district of Edom, but, above all, he sent his

down the walls of Gath, Jabneh and Ashdod on a campaign against the Philistines, is of uncertain origin and significance.
[1] G. v. Rad has suggested and argued this in PJB, 29 (1933), pp. 38 ff.
[2] More details of this list in M. Noth, ZDPV, 61 (1938), pp. 277-304.

troops to march through the territory of the kingdom of Israel. He marched into the plain of Jezreel and sent his troops on from there in various directions. In Megiddo, which is mentioned explicitly as No. 27 in his list, he even left documentary evidence of his presence; during the excavations a small fragment of a stele was found which bears his name[1]. This campaign of Shishak did not have any serious consequences, however; it was probably quickly over, and nothing of a similar nature occurred in subsequent years. It was intended as a demonstration and a plundering expedition. That is why Rehoboam's payment of tribute was sufficient for the Pharaoh to desist from plundering the kingdom of Judah. It is quite unlikely that Shishak wanted to intervene in the internal relations between the kingdom of Judah and Israel and take sides with one or the other. The aim of his expedition was simply to plunder the land in Western Asia nearest to Egypt.

The dangers which loomed from the north-east were far more menacing for Judah and, in particular, for Israel than the military troubles from the south-west. In the north-east the Aramaean monarchy of Damascus, which had been founded in Solomon's time, quickly became a dangerous enemy, and soon the strongest power of all, in the area of Syria and Palestine. From Damascus it dominated in the first place the ancient city-state territory of the northern land east of the Jordan and was therefore Israel's neighbour along the north-eastern border of the *ajlūn* and the eastern border of the upper Jordan Valley. It ruled over the *beḳā'* between the Lebanon and Anti-Lebanon which abounded in minerals and over which the Aramaean king, Hadadezer of Zobah, had once ruled (cf. above, p. 196), and no doubt included under its rule the Aramaeans who had settled in the interior of Syria. The surprising discovery of a stele of the king Benhadad I dedicated to the Tyrian god Melkart, and containing a brief inscription in Aramaic, in the district of Aleppo in northern Syria[2] illustrates the extent and varied nature of the contacts of the Damascus monarchy. This Benhadad, who describes himself[3] as a son of one Tabrimmon and grandson of one Hadyan in the inscription which is, however, very damaged at this point, and who was therefore a member of a

[1] Published in Cl. S. Fisher, *The Excavation of Armageddon*, Oriental Institute Communications, No. 4 (1929), Figs. 7 A, 7 B, 9.
[2] Published by M. Dunand, *Bulletin du Musée de Beyrouth*, 8 (1941), pp. 65 ff.; cf. also W. F. Albright, BASOR, 87, (1942), pp. 23 ff. Cf. also ANEP, No. 499, ANET, p. 501, DOTT, pp. 239-241 and Pl. 15.
[3] Cf. 1 Kings xv, 18. 'Benhadad' is the usual Hebraisation in the Old Testament of the name which appears as 'Barhadad' in Aramaic.

dynasty of 'kings of Aram' which had already reigned for several generations, must have had connections of a friendly character with the Phoenician coastal cities[1] and must, moreover, have been ruler of the Aramaeans as far as northern Syria. It is this same Benhadad I whom we meet as the first dangerous military enemy of the kingdom of Israel. He was the Aramaean king whom king Asa of Judah persuaded to attack Israel in the reign of Baasha by making him a lavish present (cf. above, p. 235). He gave orders for his troops to invade the uppermost valley of the Jordan from the *jōlān*, which was under his rule, and to occupy the Israelite cities of Ijon (the modern *tell dibbīn* on the *merj ʿeyyūn*), Dan (the modern *tell el-ḳādi*), Abel-beth-maacah (the modern *tell ābil*) and the western section of the hills of Galilee (1 Kings xv, 20). We are told nothing about the result of this undertaking which forced king Baasha to look to the defence of his northern frontier. Probably Benhadad did not seriously intend to take permanent possession of this Israelite territory which he had invaded, and he may have withdrawn of his own accord.

The situation was different in the land east of the Jordan which appears soon afterwards as the main battleground between Israel and Aram. Here David had incorporated part of the city-state territory north-east of the *ʿajlūn* in the kingdom of Israel (cf. above, p. 192), and Solomon had then joined it to the province of Ramoth (cf. above, p. 213). The Aramaeans evidently claimed possession of these city-states, since the rest of the city-states in the northern land east of the Jordan belonged to them. At any rate, in the period that followed, the Solomonic capital of Ramoth in Gilead (the modern *tell rāmīt* 4 miles south of *er-remṭe*)[2] was repeatedly contested by Israelites and Aramaeans.

The Israelite kings of the dynasty of Omri made the warding-off of this threat the main aim of their policy. They brought to an end the frontier disputes with the neighbouring kingdom of Judah, and the Judaean kings now appear as their allies in the struggles against the Aramaeans (cf. above, p. 236). They sought to establish contacts with the Phoenician coastal cities which were beginning at this period to embark on extensive and successful colonization in the Mediterranean area[3]. The marriage of the crown prince Ahab, the son and successor of Omri, to Jezebel, the daughter of the

---

[1] It is impossible to ascertain the basis of Benhadad's relations to the god Melkart of Tyre, to which the inscription testifies.

[2] Cf. N. Glueck, AASOR, 25-28 (1951), pp. 96 ff.

[3] Cf. W. F. Albright in *Studies in the History of Culture* (1942), pp. 40 ff.

'king of the Sidonians', Ethbaal of Tyre[1], is connected with this. Since the Aramaean king Benhadad was also developing his connections with the Phoenician cities (see above) it is very easy to see that, through his son's marriage, Omri was trying to establish a firm bond with the rich and powerful maritime and mercantile cities. Ahab's marriage with Jezebel aroused strong opposition in Israel itself, however, and in the tradition this was personified in Elijah the prophet. No doubt Jezebel, with her Tyrian retinue, practised her own Tyrian religion in a sanctuary built specially in the royal city of Samaria, just as Solomon had had shrines built for the cults of his foreign wives on the Mount of Olives east of Jerusalem (cf. 2 Kings xxiii, 13). These religions were not official state cults, and Yahweh no doubt remained *the* God of Israel for king Ahab and the kingdom of Israel[2]. But the very existence of this foreign religion and its attendant cult personnel[3] in Samaria evoked the resistance of the ancient strict tradition of the Israelite tribes, for whom the completely exclusive service of Yahweh was an absolute requirement. A terrible drought which resulted from a complete lack of rain in one year[4] was interpreted as a divine punishment for the worship of Baal[5] in Israel[6]. The despotic impulses of king Ahab were also attributed to the influence of the foreign queen[7]. It again became clear that the monarchy was bound to

[1] In 1 Kings xvi, 31, there is a reference to 'Ethbaal king of the Sidonians', whereas according to the quotation preserved in Josephus, *Antiqu. Iud.* VIII, 13, 2, § 324 Niese, Menander of Ephesus, the historian of the Phoenicians, speaks of the 'Tyrian king' 'Ιθώβαλος. To judge from this, the king's name was wrongly vocalised in the Old Testament and was really Ittobaal. The connection between 'Sidonians' and 'Tyrians' was probably that 'Sidonians' was used to describe the Phoenicians in general, and Ittobaal was a Phoenician king residing in Tyre about whose dominions we have no precise details.

[2] Attention has rightly been drawn to the fact that all the children of Ahab known to us have names which are compounds of the divine name Yahweh.

[3] In this context the Old Testament often refers to 'the prophets of Baal' ([1 Kings xviii, 19, 40;] 2 Kings x, 19).

[4] Menander of Ephesus also reported on a great ἀβροχία at the time of the king Ittobaal of Tyre (in Josephus, *loc. cit.*) which had obviously been a great and noteworthy catastrophe for Palestine-Syria. He states that it lasted precisely *one* year. According to 1 Kings xviii, 1, the drought came to an end 'in the third year', but in fact this comes to the same thing because, in accordance with the then customary method of pre-dating, the dry summer of the previous normal year was reckoned as the first year.

[5] In the stories of Elijah the god of the foreign cultus is simply called 'Baal'; in fact this was the state god of Tyre who was named Melkart.

[6] The divine judgement on Mount Carmel (1 Kings xviii, 17-46) originally had nothing to do with the struggle that arose from the worship of Baal in Samaria, but was concerned with the taking over of a local sanctuary for the worship of Yahweh; for further details see A. Alt, *Festschrift Georg Beer* (1935), pp. 1-18= *Kleine Schriften zur Geschichte des Volkes Israel*, II (1953), pp. 135-149.

[7] Cf. the story of Naboth's vineyard in 1 Kings xxi. It takes place in the city of

of the Dead Sea and in conquering the Israelite settlements and the cities subject to Israel on the table-land in a triumphant campaign. The Mesha inscription mentions the name of king Omri, who had 'oppressed Moab for a long time' (l. 5) and speaks of his sons who had succeeded him as kings and reckons 'the reign of Omri and half the reign of his sons' at 'forty years' (l. 8). This is clearly very much a round figure. But it implies that Mesha's victorious campaign came at the very end of the dynasty of Omri. Apparently the last members of the family of Omri suffered serious defeat in the battles east of the Jordan.

The first serious encroachment of the new Assyrian empire on Syria-Palestine also occurred in the period of the dynasty of Omri. This heralded a great change in the history of Syria-Palestine, though this first incident marked only a temporary phase. In the 9th century B.C. the power of the Assyrians began to rise again. They advanced beyond the Euphrates to the Mediterranean coast. The Assyrian king Ashurnasirpal II (884–859 B.C.) had already made a thrust into northern Syria and had reached the coast and received tribute from a number of Phoenician cities on the coast. In a number of expeditions his son and successor, Shalmaneser III (859–824 B.C.) advanced farther towards central and southern Syria. The small states of Syria and Palestine were in no sense a match for this great power and could at best only try to resist the dangerous enemy by joining their combined forces. In fact, on Shalmaneser's first appearance in central Syria, they shelved their quarrels and joined together for common defence. In the 6th year of Shalmaneser, in 853 B.C., a battle took place between Shalmaneser and a coalition of Syrian and Palestinian rulers. Among his enemies Shalmaneser mentions, in addition to Hadadezer[1] of Damascus and king Irhuleni of Hamath[2], 'the Israelite Ahab'

---

[1] The name which is given in cuneiform script as ᵈAdad-idri can only be the well-known Aramaic king's name Hadadezer which is familiar from 2 Sam. viii, 3 ff. and elsewhere. Usually this ᵈAdad-idri is identified with the Benhadad who is often mentioned in the Old Testament. But there is no sufficient reason for this, particularly as the prophetic narratives containing the name Benhadad are impossible to date precisely (cf. Jepsen, *op. cit.* pp. 155, 158 f.). If, according to an inscription of Shalmaneser (cf. below, p. 247) this ᵈAdad-idri was murdered by Hazael, whilst in 2 Kings viii, 7-15 the king murdered by Hazael is called Benhadad, this is not important since the name Benhadad in 2 Kings viii, 7, 9, is probably an addition to the original expression 'the king of Aram'. In the later transmission of the prophetic narratives Benhadad was regarded as denoting an Aramaic king in general. The Benhadad I who is known from the stele of Aleppo and from the annalistic record in 1 Kings xv, 18, 20, had died meanwhile, and Hadadezer (ᵈAdad-idri) was king of Aram about the middle of the 9th century B.C.

[2] Hamath (the modern *ḥama*) was at that time the centre of a fairly large political organisation in northern Syria.

(^1a-ha-ab-bu ^{mât}sir-'-la-ai) who participated with 2000 chariots and 10,000 soldiers[1]. The battle took place near the city of Karkar (*karkara*) in the province of Hamath (the modern *khirbet kerkūr* in the valley of the Orontes east of the *jebel ansariye*) in northern Syria, where the allies had gone to meet with Shalmaneser[2]. Shalmaneser boasted of a great victory. But, as far as one can see, the victory led to no tangible results, and, in the following years, his 10th, 11th and 14th year, Shalmaneser attacked Syria again to fight 'the 12 kings of the land of *Hatti*' among whom kings Hadadezer of Damascus and Irhuleni of Hamath were still occasionally mentioned as the most important. By their combined efforts the allies in Syria and Palestine still succeeded in resisting the Assyrian, and at any rate delaying his advance. The battle of Karkar took place at the end of Ahab's reign (871–870 to 852–851 B.C.). He took part in it as the ally of the king of Aram. In view of the great impending danger, the disputes between Israelites and Aramaeans, which, compared with the problem of resisting the Assyrians, were merely border disputes, were put on one side, though they revived no doubt once Shalmaneser had withdrawn again. We are not told to what extent Ahab's successors took part in the combined resistance to Shalmaneser's subsequent Syrian expeditions[3]. It is conceivable that only Ahab was magnanimous enough to shelve the internal disputes in Syria and Palestine and join the king of Aram against Shalmaneser, but that his successors turned their entire attention to holding their own position *vis-à-vis* their immediate neighbours. During an interval between Shalmaneser's various campaigns and at the time of a war with the Aramaeans, the house of Omri finally came to a somewhat inglorious end with the emergence of Jehu who had been designated king (845–844 B.C.).

Jehu rebelled against the house of Omri and its worship of Baal in Samaria in the name of the ancient Israelite tradition. He acted as champion of the unsullied worship of Yahweh. According to

[1] This is stated in Shalmaneser's annalistic report in his monolithic inscription, col. II, ll. 87 ff. (German translation in H. Gressmann, AOT², pp. 340 f., and also TGI, pp. 45 f., ANET, pp. 276–280, DOTT, pp. 46–50.) According to this, Israel represented, with Damascus and Hamath, the largest contingent in the combined force. The other confederates were represented by much smaller contingents; the Israelite chariot force was far and away the largest, even compared with that of Damascus and Hamath.

[2] Cf. the passage mentioned in the previous note. In other inscriptions, too, Shalmaneser refers to the battle of Karkar, without enumerating the confederate enemies in detail (apart from Hadadezer of Damascus and occasionally Irhuleni of Hamath).

[3] If Shalmaneser constantly speaks in a stereotyped manner of 'twelve' Syrian-Palestinian kings, this is a conventional expression and does not prove that he was always confronted in every campaign with the same coalition of enemies.

2 Kings x, 15 ff., he was, when he appeared, in league with Jonadab the leader of the order of Rechabites who personified the 'nomadic ideal' in their way of life (cf. Jer. xxxv, 1-19), thereby protesting against life in Palestine with its foreign religious influences. They thought Israel's task was to maintain its original, authentic way of life. In his 'zeal for Yahweh' (2 Kings x, 16) Jehu destroyed the shrine of Baal in Samaria (2 Kings x, 18-28). In spite of all this, however, Jehu's monarchy was also a secular institution and he, too, had to act in accordance with secular policies. For all his 'zeal for Yahweh' Jehu had usurped the monarchy, and a century later the prophet Hosea declared that Jehu's extermination of the house of Omri had laden the dynasty of Jehu with a guilt which Yahweh would yet avenge (Hos. i, 4). In accordance with the watchword with which Jehu had emerged, he was bound to abandon the political line of the Omri era. He gave up the connections with the Phoenician cities which had led to the worship of Baal in Samaria. He also dropped the special relationship with the kingdom of Judah, since the kingdom of Israel was now no longer strong enough to hold Judah in a state of vassalage. Apparently he gave up all foreign involvements whatsoever. When in his 18th year (841 B.C.) Shalmaneser appeared in Syria for the fourth time, Jehu evidently made no attempt at resistance but paid tribute to the Assyrian monarch like the Phoenician cities. On the basalt obelisk of Shalmaneser (the so-called Black Obelisk)[1] which was discovered in the Assyrian royal city of Calah (Kalaḫ, the modern *tell nimrūd*) the payment of Jehu's tribute is portrayed, and in the description his name is mentioned explicitly (*ia-u-a mâr ḫu-um-ri-i*)[2].

Israel's isolation exposed it all the more to the attacks of the Aramaeans; and in Damascus Hazael, who soon became a particularly dangerous enemy of Israel, now sat on the throne. At the outset he was still preoccupied with the necessity of resisting the Assyrians. Shalmaneser mentions *ᵈAdad-idri*[3] for the last time in his 14th year (845 B.C.) and *Ḥaza'-ilu* (Hazael) for the first time in his 18th year (841 B.C.)[4]. Jehu and Hazael may therefore have

[1] Cf. the illustrations in H. Gressmann, AOB², Nos. 121-125, ANEP, Nos. 351-355, DOTT, Pl. 3.
[2] This means literally 'Jehu of the house of Omri'. By 'house of Omri' Shalmaneser means the kingdom of Israel, since Israel had opposed him for the first time (853 B.C.) under the Omri dynasty. The Assyrians apparently did not know that Jehu had overthrown the house of Omri and founded a new dynasty. An annalistic extract of Shalmaneser's also mentions Jehu's tribute in Shalmaneser's 18th year (cf. Gressmann, AOT², p. 343, and TGI, p. 47).
[3] Bull inscription of Shalmaneser l. 100 (Gressmann, *op. cit.* p. 342).
[4] Obelisk inscription ll. 97 f. amongst others (Gressmann, *op. cit.* p. 343).

come to the throne about the same time, both of them as usurpers[1]. According to 2 Kings viii, 7-15, Hazael murdered the 'king of Syria' in Damascus and set himself on the throne; Shalmaneser also provides the information in the inscription on his great basalt statue[2] which was found in the city of Ashur, that *dAdad-idri* was murdered and 'Hazael, the son of a nobody'[3] had set himself on the throne (front, ll. 25-27)[4]. Shalmaneser's Syrian campaigns, which took place in his 18th and 21st years (841 and 838 B.C.), were aimed primarily against Damascus. In 841 B.C. Shalmaneser advanced on the city of Damascus itself, and encircled it for a time, though he did not conquer it. He then moved on through the city-state territory of the northern land east of the Jordan as far as the Hauran mountains (*šadu* ^{mât} *ḫa-ú-ra-ni*), the modern *jebel ed-drūz*, that is, through the heart of the Aramaean kingdom. He then proceeded to the mountain of *Ba'lira'si* 'which lies on the shore of the sea'[5]. These are the foothills on the *nahr el-kelb* north-east of *bērūt*; and here he set up alongside the old reliefs of the Pharaoh Rameses II his own portrait in relief on the rock above the coast-road, where it can still be seen today, as a token of the growing power of Assyria, which now claimed possession of Syria and Palestine, of which the Pharaohs of the New Kingdom had once been so proud[6]. The pressure which Shalmaneser put on king Hazael in the opening years of Jehu's reign undoubtedly resulted in a slackening of the Aramaean menace. And from this time on the situation in Syria and Palestine was very largely determined by the behaviour of the Assyrians.

As far as we know, Shalmaneser proceeded against Syria for the last time in the year 838 B.C. and captured several cities in the 'land of Damascus'[7]. He then withdrew from all further interference with Syria without having really gained any serious footing

[1] Hazael and Jehu are thus described side by side and parallel with one another in I Kings xix, 15-17.

[2] Cf. the publication of this inscription by E. Michel, WO, I, 2 (1947), pp. 57-63.

[3] This expression is intended to mean that he was a usurper, perhaps even by descent a slave. According to 2 Kings viii, 13, the prophet Elisha had promised him his future kingdom in the name of Yahweh (in I Kings xix, 15, the task was entrusted to Elijah) and thereby induced him to murder his predecessor.

[4] There is a German translation of the relevant section from the inscription of the basalt statue in H. Gressmann, AOT², p. 344. English translation, ANET, p. 280.

[5] Cf. the annalistic extract for the 18th year of Shalmaneser (E. Michel, WO, 14 [1949], pp. 265 ff.; Gressmann, *op. cit.* p. 343), ll. 14-23, ANET, p. 280.

[6] Cf. the illustrations in H. Gressmann, AOB², Nos. 146, 147, ANEP, No. 335. The Assyrian king on the relief of the *nahr el-kelb* is probably not Esarhaddon, as was formerly assumed, but Shalmaneser, who states explicitly, *loc. cit.*, that he had set up a royal portrait of himself on the mountain of *Ba'lira'si*.

[7] Cf. obelisk inscription ll. 102 ff. (Gressmann, *op. cit.* p. 343), ANET, p. 280.

in central and southern Syria as a result of his various campaigns. After him, Assyria did not at first intervene actively in Syria again. This made it possible for Hazael to consolidate and extend the power of Aram again and to bring home to the kingdom of Israel the superior might of Aram. The period of the first kings of the house of Jehu seems to have involved Israel in the most serious pressure from the Aramaeans. In the tradition of the Old Testament, Hazael is considered a particularly dangerous, dreaded and successful enemy (cf. 2 Kings viii, 11-12). Unfortunately no details about these battles have been preserved[1]. When, however, the prophet Amos, looking back on this, mentions that the Aramaeans cruelly devastated the land of Gilead, that is, the Ephraimite-Manassite settlement east of the Jordan (Amos i, 3), he can only be thinking of this last third of the 9th century B.C. The Aramaeans' successes encouraged other enemies to renewed attacks. Hazael supported the Philistines in their conflicts with the kingdoms of Israel and Judah (cf. above, p. 238). Amos's allusions to military successes of the Philistines (Amos i, 6) also probably refer to the period of Hazael. The Ammonites also took advantage of Israel's difficulties to invade the land of Gilead. According to Amos i, 13, they perpetrated some extremely brutal murders among the population. The land in question will have been the Gilead south of the Jabbok to which they had laid claim from an early period and in which they now wanted to 'enlarge their border' (Amos i, 13).

A change in this situation was finally brought about by the Assyrians. In his 5th year (800 B.C.) the Assyrian king Adadnirari III marched against Damascus, thus reviving the tradition established by Shalmaneser III. He encircled the Aramaean king[2] in Damascus and forced him to submit and to pay tribute[3]. This attack appears to have broken the power of the kingdom of Aram. In central Syria we note in the 8th century B.C. a more intense development of the power of the monarchy of Hamath (ḥama) at the expense of the authority of Damascus[4]; and there now came a

---

[1] Unless some of the prophetic narratives originally referred to this period (cf. above, p. 242, note 1). In 2 Kings x, 32, 33; xiii, 3 ff. the Deuteronomist only makes a few general observations.

[2] Adadnirari calls this king *ma-ri-'*; this is, however, probably not a name but the Aramaic word 'lord' which was used to address the king. It is doubtful if Hazael was still king at this time.

[3] Cf. the inscription on a relief stele of Adadnirari III, of which there is a German translation in Gressmann, *op. cit.* p. 345. English translation, ANET, p. 281, DOTT, p. 51.

[4] Cf. M. Noth, PJB, 33 (1937), pp. 47 ff.

period of revival for the kingdom of Israel[1]. The decline of Damascus was the necessary precondition for the successes of Jeroboam II (787–786 to 747–746 B.C.) of whom it is briefly recorded in 2 Kings xiv, 25, that he 'restored the frontier of Israel from Lebo-Hamath as far as the sea of the plain' (=the Dead Sea). This is a reference to the restoration of the whole length of the Israelites' eastern frontier from north to south. As a result of this Jeroboam II was probably able to enforce again the Israelites' territorial claims on the Aramaeans and renew the frontier as it was in the age of David and Solomon, which included a strip of the city-state territory in the northern land east of the Jordan with Ramoth in Gilead. Perhaps he was also able to turn back the Ammonites to their frontiers, if they had gained a footing in the land of Gilead. It is not clear what is meant by the expression, 'the sea of the plain', in 2 Kings xiv, 25. In this context the reference is to the frontier with Moab. Was Jeroboam able to revive the Israelite-Moabite frontier as it was in the age of Mesha in the latitude of the northern end of the Dead Sea[2] even if the Moabites had exploited Israel's difficult position in order to make further annexations? Or did he even succeed in reoccupying the land as far as the Arnon?

Since the Assyrians, once they had broken the power of Damascus, made no further inroads of any consequence for the time being, the kingdom of Israel enjoyed a kind of Golden Age in the first half of the 8th century B.C. in which the kingdom of Judah also shared. In the last resort they owed this Golden Age to the intervention of the Assyrians against Damascus. The great power of Assyria loomed sinisterly in the background, even though Israel and Judah rejoiced at the change of fortune which occurred in their affairs *circa* 800 B.C. and believed they were living in a period of renewed prosperity.

[1] There is a reference to this turn of affairs in 2 Kings xiii, 22-25 (cf. 2 Kings xiii, 4, 5); it is only connected here, however, with the transfer of the monarchy from Hazael to his son (the latter took the traditional Aramaean royal name Benhadad and was, so far as we know, the second with this name).

[2] The wording of 2 Kings xiv, 25 perhaps supports this assumption.

PART THREE

ISRAEL UNDER THE RULE OF THE GREAT
POWERS OF THE ANCIENT ORIENT

CHAPTER I

THE AGE OF ASSYRIAN AND
NEO-BABYLONIAN POWER

20. *The New Situation and its Meaning for Israel*

IN the year 745 B.C., at about the time when the long and happy reigns of kings Uzziah and Jeroboam II came to an end in Judah and Israel with the deaths of these monarchs[1], Tiglath-pileser III came to the throne in Assyria. He was not only himself an indefatigable and successful commander and conqueror, but he was the first of an uninterrupted series of great soldiers on the throne of Assyria who quickly brought the Neo-Assyrian empire to the zenith of its power and created an empire in the ancient Orient which for the first time united almost the whole of the ancient Orient under one strong ruler. To be assured of the possession of Syria-Palestine was an essential condition for success, since, for a power in Mesopotamia, Syria-Palestine was not only a valuable object in itself because of its wealth in timber, which was so rare in the Orient, and its minerals, and its long coast-line to the Mediterranean and its rich commerce, but at the same time it was the gateway to south-east Asia Minor on the one hand and to Egypt on the other. Thus Tiglath-pileser immediately took firm steps to incorporate substantial parts of Syria-Palestine in the Assyrian empire and to establish Assyrian sovereignty over the whole of Syria and Palestine. In so doing he went substantially further than the Assyrian kings in the 9th century who were, in the main, content with the payment of tribute by the Syrian and Palestinian kings they conquered. The Assyrians entered the land from the north, and thus northern Syria was the first to be affected. But the conquerors rapidly moved farther southwards into Syria-Palestine, which, from the Assyrians' point of view, was of no great size, and even Tiglath-pileser already included central and southern Syria-Palestine in his campaigns. With these tremendous events the whole of Syria-Palestine

---

[1] According to Begrich, *op. cit.* p. 155, both kings died in the year 747–746 B.C. It is not certain that this was the exact year, but it is correct to within a few years.

suffered a fundamentally similar fate. A great power whose centre lay outside the land had all the threads of this fate in its hands, and once the Assyrians had taken possession of the land, its history was henceforth determined very largely by the interplay of foreign powers, following one upon another, fighting among themselves and conquering one another. These powers were too overwhelming for serious resistance to their purpose to be feasible anywhere in Syria-Palestine for any length of time.

Israel in both the kingdoms of Judah and Israel was also affected by this fate, particularly as the formation of the kingdoms had drawn Israel closely into the history of the small states of Syria-Palestine. Israel's period of political independence now came to an end; and to the very end of its history Israel remained dependent on foreign powers—except for one brief interlude. Fundamentally the situation was not a new one, for Israel's previous history had been determined all the time by the general historical situation and had been constantly and completely dependent on the historical conditions prevailing over a wide area. Nevertheless Israel had gone its own way in this environment, and in the age of David and Solomon had attained a zenith of intrinsic importance. Even though it had become entangled in the conflicts raging in Syria-Palestine in which other, and to some extent more powerful, forces appeared, it had still been possible for the kingdoms which had arisen on Israel's soil to hold their own with greater or less success. Now, however, Israel was the victim of an overwhelming process in which all attempts at resistance were soon seen to be hopeless, and the scale of which was so great that the whole of Syria-Palestine was forced to submit to it. In fact, the whole of the ancient Orient was affected by it and it soon proved to be not a mere passing storm but a historical turning-point of lasting significance. Along with the other states of Syria-Palestine Israel now came to know the meaning of world history—within its own limited horizons—and all it could do was to endure its pressure. But this very endurance was instrumental in giving Israel an experience of the nature of world history. The naïve idea that world history is simply an extension on a vast scale of a nation's own history, and revolves around that history, now became inconceivable. In concrete and extremely brutal events, world history proved to be a movement that exceeds the range of a people's own life and an overwhelming process in which a people's life represents but a tiny force.

One has to try and realise what that meant for Israel's faith in God. It was an old idea that the God of Israel displayed his power in the guidance and preservation of his people. He had once caused the tribes to settle in Palestine with his active aid and had stood by them in their struggles to hold their own. He had been 'with David' in his establishment of a brilliant empire and had promised that his monarchy and dynasty would endure. It had long since been declared that he created and ruled over the whole world and that he had special plans for Israel[1] within the world of nations, of which it had been possible to form some idea since the age of David and Solomon with its extensive contacts. According to the traditional and widespread conception the only possible interpretation of the process that was now beginning was that, like the gods of neighbouring peoples and states, the God of Israel was now succumbing to the gods of the victorious Assyrians who appeared to be proving themselves even stronger, and in whose name and at whose behest the conquering Assyrian kings, as they solemnly aver in their inscriptions, were taking the field. There will have been many people in Israel who thought thus and who expected that their God must still 'save' them by a miracle[2], and who were then disillusioned again and again by the actual course of events.

In this situation there arose one voice in Israel that gave a different interpretation of these events. We refer to the unique historical phenomenon of the so-called 'classical prophecy' of the Old Testament which began about the middle of the 8th century B.C., just at the time when this change in the history of Israel and of the world to which it belonged was taking place, and which pronounced judgement on the historical events. Like the Hebrew word נביא which was applied to begin with to ecstatics, and then to men of God endowed with 'power', who were also a common phenomenon among other peoples, the term 'prophet', which in Greek means one who proclaims divine oracles (a common type in the history of religion), merely serves as a makeshift to describe the manifestation of classical 'prophecy'. Here were men who came forward as messengers of God[3] and claimed a hearing as preachers of a divine message which they presented in the form of oracular messages. The content of their message was that the events in world history which were now occurring and which would continue, were a great divine

---

[1] This is more or less what the Yahwist (cf. above, p. 222) had said.

[2] Such expectations have also come down to us in the Old Testament; cf. Jer. xxviii, 1 ff., and elsewhere.

[3] The figure of a messenger of God who has to convey divine instructions appears in the sphere of the Mari texts (cf. above, p. 18) (cf. M. Noth, *Geschichte und Gotteswort im Alten Testament* [Bonner Akademische Reden, 3 (1949)], pp. 9 ff.; W. v. Soden, WO, I, 5 [1950], pp. 397 ff.); but the content of these divine messages was not concerned with the great events of history.

judgement, a judgement by the very God in whose name they spoke, the God of Israel. Inasmuch as Israel was being forced to experience and endure these events, the God of Israel was proving himself to be the God not of a tribal confederation or a single people or state, beside whom the gods of other tribal associations could and must exist, but the Lord of the world, standing above the whole of human history. From this standpoint history appeared no longer merely as the history of a single nation or state, but as the history of the world in which God's action is concerned with the whole of mankind, no matter how far that world is thought to extend in a particular time and situation. The prophets were the first to interpret the events of their time from this universal and divine point of view, not explaining the past retrospectively or making a vague forecast of the general trend of future events, but discerning in the events of their own age the beginnings of the operation of a divine plan.

There is no real parallel to this manifestation of 'prophecy' anywhere else in human history. Above all, we can find nothing resembling it among Israel's neighbours, though the events in question affected not merely Israel but the whole area of Syria-Palestine in the same way and led to the same results, as the 'prophets' themselves said more than once (cf. Amos i, 3 ff., and elsewhere). The voice of the prophets was heard only in Israel. It was heard in the middle of the 8th century B.C. and thereafter in every time of great historical movement and change. Moreover, the 'prophets' explained quite clearly that everything that was happening was aimed in the first place at little Israel; they proclaimed this in Israel that Israel might know where it stood. It was God's purpose to execute an annihilating judgement on the present condition of this people because of its unforgivable faithlessness and disobedience. The prophets dared to declare that God was using the whole history of the ancient Orient for this one purpose. For this end the mighty king of Assyria became an instrument in the hand of God (Isa. x, 5), and later on the Neo-Babylonian king Nebuchadnezzar became a 'servant' of God (Jer. xxvii, 6) and the Persian king Cyrus an 'anointed' of God (Isa. xlv, 1). They dared to declare that, despite its historical insignificance, Israel was nevertheless the centre of world history in the events of their age, not, it is true, in the role of a leading power, but as the object of God's judgement, of a God who is the Lord of the world, not the visible pivot of historical movements but the secret centre of events. The 'unhistorical' was thus working in the midst of human history.

They were able to say all this solely on the basis of the presupposition that God had from time immemorial encountered Israel in history and that Israel's duty was to serve God in the future in the realisation of His universal purpose.

In the period that followed, what the 'prophets' had been proclaiming from the middle of the 8th century B.C., that Israel's traditional make-up was to be shattered by historical events, was quite soon translated into reality.

21. Subjection to the Assyrians

For Tiglath - pileser (Assyrian: *Tukulti - apil - Ešarra*) III, who reigned in Assyria from 745–727 B.C., the subjugation of Syria and Palestine was one of his principal aims. Unfortunately the annals of this king are badly preserved and incomplete so that it is impossible to get a clear view of all the details of his campaigns. But we know the main events. In the year 740 B.C. he began with the conquest of northern Syria and the establishment of Assyrian royal provinces on Syrian soil. In the year 738 B.C. he subjugated the northern and central Syrian state of Hamath (*hama*) which had increased its power since the decline of Damascus; he turned large parts of it into Assyrian provinces and left only a remnant as a small dependent state. At this time most of the other Syrian states, including various Phoenician coastal cities and a number of states in Asia Minor, paid tribute to him as a result of his victory[1]. Among the tribute-paying kings he mentions 'Rezon of Damascus' (*Raṣunnu* ᵐᵃᵗ*Dimaškai*)[2] and 'Menahem of Samaria' (*Miniḫimme* ᵃˡᵘ*Samerinai*)[3]. In the kingdom of Israel the dynasty of Jehu had meanwhile been overthrown. After the murder of the last king of the house of Jehu (2 Kings xv, 10), disturbances had occurred in

[1] *Annals*, ll. 150 ff., German in H. Gressmann, AOT², p. 346; for an English translation of the relevant sections of the Assyrian royal inscriptions see ANET, pp. 282 ff., DOTT, pp. 53-58.

[2] This is the Rezin mentioned in 2 Kings xv, 37; xvi, 5 f.; Isa. vii, 1 ff. and elsewhere, whose name is not quite correctly vocalised in the Old Testament. The correct reading Rezon is also presupposed in the Septuagint transliteration.

[3] The kingdom of Judah appears to have still held aloof from events. All the same Tiglath-pileser reports in *Annals*, ll. 103 ff., that in 738 B.C. he subjugated an *Azriyau* of *Yaudi* and forced him to pay tribute. The annalistic text, which is very fragmentary at this point, seems to indicate that this Azriyau was at the time the heart and soul of the opposition to Tiglath-pileser. It is difficult not to identify this Azriyau of Yaudi with Azariah = Uzziah of Judah. It is stated explicitly in 2 Kings xv, 17, 23 that (against the chronology of Begrich) Azariah of Judah was contemporary with Menahem of Israel. It is admittedly very difficult to explain historically how small Judah, lying wholly in the south, could have played such a part in the events of 738 B.C.

connection with the succession to the throne, from which Menahem finally emerged as a usurper, and he was able to hold the throne of Israel for a number of years. There is a reference to his payment of tribute to Tiglath-pileser in 2 Kings xv, 19 f.[1]. According to this he paid a thousand talents of silver and collected this sum from the free landowners in his kingdom who were liable to military service[2]. According to verse 19b he expected, as a result of this payment, a consolidation of the monarchy which he had usurped and which he was no doubt only able to maintain with difficulty in this age of regicide and disputes about the throne; Tiglath-pileser may indeed have desired that the kings who had surrendered to him of their own free will should remain on their thrones. But Tiglath-pileser did not rest content for long with the success he had achieved in 738 B.C. For the year 734 B.C. the Assyrian list of Eponyms[3] records as the most important event of the year an expedition 'to Philistia'[4]. Tiglath-pileser had therefore advanced as far as the remotest south-west corner of Syria-Palestine. We learn a few details about this campaign from a fragment of the Annals of Tiglath-pileser which has recently been discovered during the excavations in the royal Assyrian city of Calah (Kalaḫ, *tell nimrūd*)[5]. According to this, the Assyrian king, after he had secured a victory on the coast of central Syria, first of all forced his way through the territory of the kingdom of Israel, the western parts of which extended as far as the coastal plain of Palestine, through which the Assyrians moved to the south. In view of its importance for communications they may, in fact, have occupied this part of the kingdom of Israel[6]; he then effected the subjugation of the Philistine kingdom of Gaza, which is dealt with in Tiglath-pileser's 'Small Inscription' No. 1[7] in line 8 ff., after king Hanun of Gaza had escaped to Egypt to avoid having to surrender, and had abandoned his city to the Assyrians.

[1] Tiglath-pileser III is referred to here by his Babylonian throne name of Pul.

[2] The figures mentioned here add up to a total of 60,000 such landowners in Israel.

[3] This list, which has been preserved in many parts and copies, enumerates in chrono-logical order the high officials of the Empire, after whom it was customary to name the years within each reign in a definite sequence, and from the middle of the 9th century it makes brief references to the campaigns and other events of the individual years; cf. A. Ungnad, Eponymen, *Reallexicon der Assyriologie*, II [1938], pp. 412 ff.

[4] Cf. A. Ungnad, *op. cit.* p. 431 and D. D. Luckenbill, *Ancient Records of Assyria and Babylonia*, II (1927), pp. 427 ff., especially p. 436.

[5] Published by D. J. Wiseman, *Iraq*, 13 (1951), pp. 21 ff., Pl. xi., cf. ANET, p. 282, DOTT, pp. 55 f.

[6] On this interpretation of the badly preserved lines 10 ff. of the fragment cf. A. Alt. Tiglathpilesers III erster Feldzug nach Palästina, *Kleine Schriften zur Geschichte des Volkes Israel*, II [1953], pp. 150-162.

[7] German translation in Gressmann, *op. cit.* pp. 347 f.; TGI, pp. 52 f. English trans-lation, cf. ANET, pp. 283 f., DOTT, p. 55.

Finally he established a base on the 'river of Egypt' (the modern *wādi el-'arīsh*), that is, on the extreme south-western border of Asia. In this way he intended to make it quite impossible for the small states in Syria-Palestine to have any connection with Egypt. Probably the small states in the southern part of Syria-Palestine which were not yet directly affected by these events—and these must have included the kingdom of Judah—had to recognise Assyrian sovereignty by the payment of tribute. Within a few years, therefore, Tiglath-pileser had invaded the whole of Syria-Palestine, had spread fear of Assyria's overwhelming power everywhere, and where he did not convert the conquered territories into Assyrian provinces he had made the kings pay tribute to him.

In view of this, another attempt at combined resistance seems to have been planned for the following year, 733 B.C., in central and southern Syria-Palestine; in this Damascus played a leading part for the last time. Probably the so-called Syro-Ephraimite war[1] of which we hear in the Old Testament, belongs in this connection. According to 2 Kings xv, 37; xvi, 5 and Isa. vii, 1 ff., Jerusalem was attacked by the combined forces of the Aramaean kingdom of Damascus and the kingdom of Israel and subjected to the beginnings of a siege. According to Isa. vii, 6 the object of this undertaking was to overthrow the dynasty of David in Jerusalem and to install a king over Judah in its place, who, to judge from the name of his father, mentioned in Isa. vii, 6, was an Aramaean. The Davidic king affected was king Ahaz, a grandson of king Uzziah, who had meanwhile ascended the throne of David after the brief reign of his father Jotham[2]. In the kingdom of Israel a usurper named Pekah, son of Remaliah[3] had lately occupied the throne. The background of this Syro-Ephraimite war was obviously the fact that Aram and Israel wanted to attempt resistance to Tiglath-pileser but king Ahaz of Judah, frightened perhaps by Tiglath-pileser's campaign against near-by Philistia in the previous year, refused to join in. The two others intended to depose him, therefore, and replace him by an Aramaean who would bring the kingdom of Judah into the anti-Assyrian coalition. The attack by the two superior enemies on Jerusalem made good progress to begin with

[1] This traditional description is due to the fact that the English Bible always renders the name Aram as 'Syria' and that the kingdom of Israel was often called 'Ephraim' by the contemporary prophets (cf. especially Isa. vii, 1 ff.) after its central district.

[2] The chronology of the Judaean kings is very uncertain in this period; probably Ahaz had only been king for a short time (this is contrary to Begrich's view).

[3] In Isa. vii, 4 ff. he is disdainfully called 'the son of Remaliah', without his own name, to denote his non-royal descent.

(cf. Hos. v, 8-11)[1] and Ahaz was extremely hard-pressed and anxious in Jerusalem (cf. Isa. vii, 2). In this situation Ahaz decided —against the urgent insistence of the prophet Isaiah that he should trust quietly in his God (Isa. vii, 1-17)—to call in help from a greater power and he sent a 'present' from the Temple and palace treasuries in Jerusalem to no less a personage than Tiglath-pileser himself, with an offer of submission and a request for help against his enemies Aram and Israel (2 Kings xvi, 7-9). Unfortunately we are not told where Tiglath-pileser was at this time. Probably he was already with his army somewhere in Syria. Apparently events now moved rapidly. Thanks to the immediate intervention of the Assyrians, Ahaz was freed from his difficult situation even before Jerusalem fell into the hands of the attacking Aramaeans and Israelites; and so the Syro-Ephraimite war came to a premature end. It is also clear from this that Tiglath-pileser had not needed Ahaz's request for help as an incentive for his campaigns in Syria-Palestine. At that period his aim anyway was the complete sub-jugation of Syria-Palestine. He had already appeared in Philistia in 734 B.C. and after Hamath had been disposed of in 738 B.C. he found that the most important powers in Syria-Palestine were, firstly, the Aramaean kingdom of Damascus and, secondly, the kingdom of Israel. For the years 733 and 732 B.C. the above-mentioned list of Eponyms has the note 'to Damascus'. He seems indeed first to have crushed the kingdom of Israel in the year 733 B.C., probably in order to isolate Damascus and keep in check the small states of southern Palestine. At any rate, he notes in his Annals, after he has discussed the conquest of Damascus in detail, that he had already settled accounts with Israel in an 'earlier campaign' (ll. 227 ff.)[2]. According to 2 Kings xv, 29 he invaded the uppermost part of the Jordan Valley in 733 B.C.—coming probably through the *beḳāʿ* between the Lebanon and Anti-Lebanon—and from there he conquered Gilead on the one hand and Galilee on the other, and in the Annals ll. 227 ff. he himself recorded that he had annexed 'all the cities' of the land and only left Samaria (*Samerina*). It follows from this and from the lists of Assyrian provinces that have been preserved, that Tiglath-pileser only left king Pekah of Israel Mount Ephraim with the royal city of Samaria but, for the rest, in-

---

[1] Cf. the historical interpretation of this prophetic saying by A. Alt, 'Hosea v, 8–vi, 6', NKZ, 30 [1919], pp. 537-568 = *Kleine Schriften zur Geschichte des Volkes Israel*, II [1953], pp. 163-187.

[2] A German translation of the—unfortunately again very fragmentary—section of the annals on the events of 733–732 B.C. will be found in Gressmann, *op. cit.* pp. 346 f., TGI, pp. 51 f. English translation, ANET, p. 283.

corporated the territory of the kingdom of Israel in the Assyrian system of provinces. He divided it among three different provinces, which, according to the general Assyrian custom, were named after the provincial capitals. Galilee was amalgamated with the adjacent plain of Jezreel in the province of 'Megiddo'. The province of 'Dor' (the city of Dor is the modern *el-burj* near *eṭ-ṭanṭūra*) included the Israelite portion of the coastal plain of Palestine from Carmel in the north roughly to the *nahr el-'ōja* in the south. The Israelite land east of the Jordan became the province of 'Gilead'[1]. Whilst the indigenous Israelite peasant population in the new provinces was in general left where it was as a subject people, the urban upper class was deported in accordance with a custom that had arisen in the Neo-Assyrian empire. As is stated, rather vaguely, in 2 Kings xv, 29, they were taken 'to Assyria'; they were sent, that is to say, to some province or other in Mesopotamia or further to the eastern part of the Assyrian empire. In exchange for them, Assyrian governors and officials and a new upper class from other parts of the Empire were sent to the new provinces in their place. King Pekah (Assyrian *Pa-ka-ḫa*), however, was overthrown by his own people after his defeat (Ann. l. 228; Small Inscription No. 1, l. 17) and according to 2 Kings xv, 30 he was murdered by a certain Hoshea who now made himself king in Samaria over what little remained of Israel, and paid tribute to Tiglath-pileser and was then confirmed by Tiglath-pileser as a dependent vassal-king (Small Inscription No. 1, l. 17 f.)[2]. After Tiglath-pileser had conquered Damascus in the year 732 B.C. and terribly devastated the kingdom of Damascus and turned the whole of it into a series of Assyrian provinces, he was able to consider most of Syria-Palestine subject to his rule, since even the kings who still existed outside the Assyrian provinces administered by Assyrian governors, were tribute-paying vassals[3]. And so the situation continued until his death in 727 B.C.

Some years later king Hoshea of Israel was unwise enough to cease paying tribute to the Assyrian emperor—after the death of Tiglath-pileser the new emperor was Shalmaneser V—and to establish relations with Egypt, evidently with the object of escaping

---

[1] For the details see E. Forrer, *Die Provinzeinteilung des assyrischen Reiches* (1921), pp. 59 ff., 69 and above all A. Alt, 'Das System der assyrischen Provinzen auf dem Boden des Reiches Israel', ZDPV, 52 [1929], pp. 220-242 = *Kleine Schriften zur Geschichte des Volkes Israel*, II [1953], pp. 188-205.

[2] Tiglath-pileser says in this passage that he had appointed Hoshea (*A-u-si '*); he means that he confirmed the usurper. Cf. ANET, pp. 283 f.

[3] Cf. the list of the vassals in Gressmann, *op. cit.* p. 348.

from Assyrian sovereignty (2 Kings xvii, 4). It is not to be assumed that the tiny remnant of the kingdom of Israel was acting independently and on its own in this matter. Several states in southern Palestine must have co-operated, but we have no details. This was in the year 724 B.C. An Assyrian force succeeded in seizing king Hoshea in some way or other and in occupying the land. Only the fortified city of Samaria was able to resist for another three years. Shalmaneser will scarcely have employed all his forces to besiege Samaria. Samaria finally fell in the year 722–721 B.C. at the beginning of the reign of the Assyrian king Sargon, Shalmaneser V having died a short time previously[1]. And now even the remnant of the kingdom of Israel was abolished and turned into the Assyrian province of 'Samaria' (Assyrian: *Samerina*). The kingdom of Israel thereby ceased to exist, once and for all. Once again the upper class was deported, this time to Mesopotamia and Media, as is stated in 2 Kings xvii, 6; and there it no doubt suffered the fate of most of the deported upper classes, of being gradually absorbed into the numerically much greater indigenous population. A foreign upper class was introduced into the new province of Samaria, which, according to 2 Kings xvii, 24, came partly from Babylon, from the city of Babylon itself and the Babylonian city of Cuthah, and partly from Hamath in northern Syria[2], partly from places unknown to us. These foreign elements brought their own way of life and above all their own religions with them (cf. 2 Kings xvii, 29-31), but with the passage of time they too were absorbed in the Israelite population left behind.

To begin with, we hear little about the further fate of the four Assyrian provinces which arose on the territory of the kingdom of Israel. In the year 720 B.C. risings took place in Syria-Palestine in which the inhabitants of various provinces, including Damascus and Samaria, participated. What was left of the kingdom of Hamath rebelled against the Assyrians, but the rising was suppressed and the kingdom was turned into the Assyrian province of 'Hamath'. In addition, king Hanun of Gaza bestirred himself again at this period in combination with the rather vague figure of *Sib'u*, the 'supreme commander' of the land of Egypt[3], or, at any rate,

---

[1] Sargon often makes a brief reference in his texts to the conquest of Samaria; cf. Gressmann, *op. cit.* pp. 348 f.; TGI, pp. 53 f.; ANET, pp. 284 f., DOTT, pp. 58-63.

[2] Probably those from Hamath only came after the elimination of the remnant of the kingdom of Hamath in the year 720 B.C. See below.

[3] This *Sib'u* is no doubt identical with the 'king of Egypt' (named סוא 2 Kings xvii, 4) with whom king Hoshea of Israel established relations, when he ceased paying tribute to the Assyrians in 724 B.C.

with Egyptian help. A battle between Assyrians on the one hand and Hanun and *Sib'u* on the other took place near Rapiḫu (the modern *refaḥ*) on the extreme south-western border of Palestine, about 16 miles south-west of Gaza. Hanun fell into the hands of the Assyrians and *Sib'u* was forced to withdraw into Egypt. This not especially important encounter, which brought the kingdom of Gaza back into dependence on the Assyrians, is noteworthy as the first hostile encounter of the Assyrians, who had achieved supremacy in Syria-Palestine, with Egypt, the power that was henceforth to be behind all the anti-Assyrian undertakings in Syria-Palestine. The rebellious provinces were doubtless crushed with no great difficulty[1]. For the subsequent century there is only very scanty information available about the provinces in the former kingdom of Israel. A number of governors of the provinces of Samaria and Megiddo appear as Assyrian Eponyms in the course of the 7th century B.C.[2]. A few cuneiform documents from the province of Samaria throw some light on life in the provinces. The governors themselves, and presumably also their immediate subordinates, were no doubt Assyrians. A cuneiform text found in the ruins of the city of Samaria informs us of the title of one such official: the '*rab ālāni*', the 'head of the cities', who presumably had charge of the cities in the province and, above all, the crown properties, which were given to the members of the new upper class which had been transplanted to the provinces[3]. The personal names which occur in two cuneiform legal documents from the middle of the 7th century B.C. which were found during the excavations in Gezer (*tell jezer*) throw some light on the ethnic structure of the foreign upper class; they entirely confirm the information about their origin which is contained in 2 Kings xvii, 24[4]. It is noteworthy that in one of the Gezer documents the 'mayor' of this city appears with an Egyptian name. He was evidently the head of the old-established population in which, since Gezer was formerly a Canaanite city, Egyptian names may have occurred from early times. For the rest, it is not surprising that we hear hardly anything of the indigenous Israelite, and to some extent Canaanite, subject population in the provinces[5].

[1] Cf. especially the annals of Sargon for the second year of his reign (ll. 23-31), in German in Gressmann, *op. cit.* pp. 348 f., and also the Sargon texts, *op. cit.* pp. 349 f. (cf. TGI, pp. 54 f., ANET, p. 285, DOTT, p. 61).

[2] Cf. Forrer, *op. cit.* p. 69 and above all, A. Alt, ZDPV, 52 (1929), p. 226, note 3; p. 229, note 1.

[3] More details will be found in A. Alt, PJB, 37 (1941), pp. 102-104.

[4] The details in K. Galling, PJB, 31 (1935), pp. 81 ff.

[5] It is possible that in the Galilean province the city of Acco (the modern *'akka*) replaced

If the kingdom of Israel had been completely eliminated because of its anti-Assyrian activities in 733 and 722 B.C., for the time being the kingdom of Judah continued to exist as a dependent vassal State. King Ahaz had submitted of his own free will to Tiglath-pileser in 733 B.C. (cf. above p. 260). He continued to pay tribute to the Assyrian emperor. He is mentioned by Tiglath-pileser in a list of the tributary vassal kings[1]. He appears to have continued to resist the temptation to take part in the attempts at rebellion in Syria-Palestine. At least, we do not hear that Judah was implicated in the defection of king Hoshea of Israel and the movement of the year 720 B.C. in which the neighbouring province of Samaria in the north and near-by Gaza in the south-west were involved. Unfortunately, we do not know for certain if Ahaz was still king at this period, since the year of his death cannot be precisely ascertained[2]. He was followed by his son Hezekiah; and under Hezekiah anti-Assyrian activities took place in Judah too. It need not be assumed that Hezekiah's attitude to Assyria was fundamentally different from his father's. But in his time favourable opportunities seemed to occur for getting rid of Assyrian suzerainty. In the years 713–711 B.C. anti-Assyrian risings started in the Philistine kingdom of Ashdod. Sargon mentions them in various inscriptions, though the information cannot be interpreted with complete certainty historically, since the chronological sequence of events is not exactly stated. It is possible, all the same, to discern the main course of events. According to a fragment of a prism of Sargon[3], a revolt against Assyria took place in the ninth year of his reign (713 B.C.) arising from disturbances concerning the succession to the throne in Ashdod, in which Sargon had intervened after a cessation of tributary payments. The neighbours were also drawn into this revolt. Sargon reports that, in addition to the Philistines, the 'land of Judah (^{mât}ya-u-di), the land of Edom and the land of Moab' took part in the fighting, and that a combined effort was made to secure the aid of the 'Pharaoh, the king of the land of Egypt' (pi-ir-$'$-u $šar$ ^{mât} mu-$uṣ$-ri). In Egypt, probably in 714 B.C., the 25th Ethiopian dynasty had come to power with the accession

---

Megiddo as the provincial capital already in the Assyrian period, cf. A. Alt, PJB, 33 1937, pp. 67 ff.= *Kleine Schriften zur Geschichte des Volkes Israel*, II (1953), pp. 376 ff.

[1] Gressmann, *op. cit.* p. 348. King Ahaz is mentioned here with the full form of his name *Jauhazi* = Jehoahaz.

[2] Begrich, *loc. cit.*, places the death of Ahaz in the year 725–724 B.C. According to 2 Kings xviii, 1 it took place even earlier. According to the dates of the reigns of the Judaean kings given in the Old Testament and according to 2 Kings xviii, 13, it seems likely, however, that it took place later; W. F. Albright, BASOR, 100 (1945), p. 22, note 28, suggests the year 715 B.C. [3] Gressmann, *op. cit.* p. 351.

of the pharaoh Shabaka; and Shabaka seems to have taken an immediate interest in this activity in southern Palestine. At any rate various negotiations took place and Hezekiah of Judah also participated in them. According to Isa. xviii, 1-6, it was at this period that the foreign-looking Ethiopian legates of the Ethiopian Pharaoh appeared in Jerusalem. Sargon, who was preoccupied in the north and north-west at the time[1], did not intervene with armed force until the third year[2]. He then sent the Assyrian supreme commander, the *turtānu*, to Ashdod with an army[3]. During these three years the prophet Isaiah warned against trusting in Egyptian-Ethiopian help by means of a sensational and symbolical action in Jerusalem (Isa. xx, 1-6). And in fact the help did not come, when in the 11th year of Sargon's reign (711 B.C.) the rising in Ashdod was put down by the Assyrians. The Pharaoh even handed over to the Assyrians the rebellious king of Ashdod who had escaped to Egypt from the Assyrians. The territory of Ashdod, which included the former Philistine city of Gath at this period[4], which had then become Judaean and was later lost to the kingdom of Judah (cf. above, p. 238) was turned into an Assyrian province. Its neighbours in southern Palestine, including the kingdom of Judah, seem to have withdrawn from the undertaking in good time and to have paid their tribute to Sargon. At any rate they seem to have escaped with impunity.

The anti-Assyrian risings which were occasioned by the death of king Sargon in 705 B.C. were on a larger scale. In the first years of his reign, his successor, Sennacherib, was preoccupied in various parts of his great empire, in enforcing his rule in the face of various rebellions. The South Palestinian states also used the opportunity to throw off Assyrian suzerainty, and this time Judah under Hezekiah did not play a purely marginal role, but was very active and took the lead. Payment of tribute was stopped, and the relationship of dependence on the emperor thereby abandoned, and all the tokens of foreign suzerainty removed. The so-called religious reforms of king Hezekiah to which a brief reference is made in 2 Kings xviii, 4, and for which Hezekiah was praised unreservedly by the

---

[1] Cf. the annals of Sargon on the years 9-11 of his reign.

[2] He reports on this in his annals for the eleventh year of his reign (ll. 215 ff.) and also in the so-called display inscription ll. 90 ff. (Gressmann, *op. cit.* pp. 350 f.; TGI, pp. 55 f., ANET, pp. 286 f.).

[3] Sargon worded his reports to suggest that he himself went to Ashdod. But Isa. xx, 1 contains the obviously more accurate statement that he sent the *tartan*. Sargon was only able to deal with the south Palestinian rising incidentally. In his 11th year he was also busy in the north-west of Asia Minor.

[4] Sargon's texts give the name of Gath in the form *Gimtu*.

Deuteronomist (2 Kings xviii, 3) belong in this context. In the ancient Orient political suzerainty required the adoption of the official religion of the ruling power, not in place of, but alongside, the native hereditary religions. In the Assyrian provinces the Assyrian cultus was no doubt introduced in the provincial capitals and practised by the governors. In the provinces in the territory of the former kingdom of Israel, there existed alongside the traditional religion of the local Israelite population, which naturally persisted (cf. also 2 Kings xvii, 25-28, 32-34), not only the religions which the foreign upper class had brought with them from their own land, so long as they maintained their own separate character (2 Kings xvii, 29-31), but also the official Assyrian religion, especially that of the imperial god Ashur. This was also true of the dependent vassal states. When king Ahaz of Judah surrendered to Tiglath-pileser, he had to make room for the Assyrian religion in the official sanctuary in Jerusalem. 2 Kings xvi, 10-18 contains a detailed account of how Ahaz had to appear before Tiglath-pileser in Damascus—after the fall of Damascus in 732 B.C.—and had an altar erected in Jerusalem by the high priest of Jerusalem Uriah, in place of Solomon's old burnt-offering altar, in a central position in front of the Temple building, modelled no doubt on an Assyrian altar which stood in the new provincial capital of Damascus. The previous burnt offering altar was set aside and other furnishings of the traditional religion were modified; above all, the special 'king's entry' into the shrine—a symbol of royal authority over the sanctuary—was removed, and all this was done 'for the king of Assyria' (verse 18). So long as Judah was a tribute-paying Assyrian vassal, that is to say, far into the reign of king Hezekiah, the official Assyrian religion had a place alongside the traditional worship of Yahweh in the state sanctuary in Jerusalem. When Hezekiah abandoned his dependence on Assyria in 705 B.C., he quite consistently abolished this Assyrian religion and thereby 'reformed' public worship in Jerusalem[1].

Hezekiah had allies in his activities, above all among the neighbouring Philistines. It is true that the Philistine states of Gaza and Ashdod[2], which had rebelled against Assyria in 734 and 720 or 713–711 B.C. and had been severely punished, did not join in this

---

[1] Incidentally, non-Assyrian elements also fell victim to this 'Reform', such as the old brazen serpent of Nehushtan (2 Kings xviii, 4) which had probably stood in the Temple, since Hezekiah's measures will have referred specifically to the state sanctuary.

[2] A king of Ashdod again appears before Sennacherib, although Ashdod had become an Assyrian province in 711 B.C. We do not know whether a native king was left under the governor or whether the province had been given up again for unknown reasons.

time, but king *Ṣidḳa* of Ashkelon probably co-operated, as did the
people of Ekron[1], and their king *Padi*, who remained loyal to
Assyria, was delivered by them in chains to Hezekiah of Judah.
Judging from this, Hezekiah was evidently playing a leading part
at this time in southern Palestine. The assurance of Egyptian aid
was also sought again—the Ethiopian Shabaka was still on the
throne of the Pharaohs—and help was promised. At this time, too,
the prophet Isaiah often warned against trusting in the power of
Egypt (Isa. xxx, 1-5; xxxi, 1-3 etc.); he alludes to the fact that
envoys, no doubt Judaean envoys, 'went down into Egypt' to
negotiate for military aid[2]. Hezekiah's connections extended as far
as Mesopotamia. After Sargon's death Babylon, under Merodach-
baladan (Babylonian: *Marduk-apla-iddin*), had renounced Assyrian suzerainty, and one of the Isaiah narratives (2 Kings xx,
12-19) records that this Merodach-baladan sent envoys to Hezekiah
with letters and gifts, and that these envoys were shown the treasures, and, above all, the armoury in Jerusalem; this suggests that
the main purpose of the mission was to discuss joint military action
against Assyria.

The defection from Assyria had spread so far that for a time it
was possible to hope that at last the effort to destroy the suzerainty
of the emperor would be successful. And in fact Sennacherib did
require a number of years to suppress all the risings. First of all, he
enforced his rule in Mesopotamia and in the east of his empire,
subjugating Babylon again and banishing Merodach-baladan. It
was not until 701 B.C., four years after his accession, that he undertook the famous campaign against Syria-Palestine to restore the
old order there as well. He himself reported on the campaign in
detail[3]. He had no difficulty in marching through northern and
central Syria-Palestine; these provinces had apparently remained
peaceful. Then he marched along the Phoenician coast, where his
only task was to crush king Luli of Sidon[4], whilst the other coastal

[1] Sennacherib calls the name of this city *Amḳarruna*; its real name was therefore *'Aḳḳaron*. The traditional form of the name is based on a secondary erroneous
vocalisation.
[2] There is no doubt that the expressions in xxx, 2; xxxi, 1 must be understood thus.
It is uncertain whether xxx, 4 also refers to Judaean legates.
[3] This report is on two clay prisms, the so-called 'Taylor-cylinder' (German translation of the relevant section, II, 34–III, 41 in Gressmann, *op. cit.* pp. 352 ff. and TGI,
pp. 56 ff.) and a clay cylinder now in Chicago (cf. D. D. Luckenbill, *The Annals of
Sennacherib*, Oriental Institute Publications, II [1924], ANET, pp. 287 f., DOTT,
pp. 64-69 and Pl. 4). On Sennacherib's campaign cf. W. Rudolph, PJB, 25 (1929),
pp. 59-80; H. Haag, RB, 58 (1951), pp. 348-359.
[4] This Luli is identical with the Ἐλουλαῖος to whom Menander of Ephesus refers
in a quotation to be found in Josephus, *Antiqu. Iud.* IX, 14, 2, §§ 284-287 Niese.

towns hastened to pay tribute to him as swiftly as did the king of Ashdod and the kings of Ammon, Moab and Edom. He then turned
his attention to the subjugation of the rebellious Philistine states
of Ashkelon and Ekron. Whilst he was engaged on this, an Egyptian
force appeared in south-western Palestine. Near *Altaķū*, that is,
the Eltekeh mentioned in Joshua xix, 44 (the modern *khirbet el-
muķanna'*), a clash occurred between Assyrians and Egyptians
which ended with a victory for the Assyrians. It is not likely that
the Egyptians used a very formidable force. Sennacherib describes
his opponents as 'the kings of Egypt', that is, city rulers probably
from the Delta, and also the archers and charioteers of the 'king
of Ethiopia', that is, of the Ethiopian Pharaoh. The reference in
one of the Isaiah narratives to the intervention of 'king Tirhakah
of Ethiopia' against Sennacherib (2 Kings xix, 9) is evidently due
to a mistake, since in the year 701 B.C. Shabaka was still Pharaoh
and Tirhakah, his nephew, did not ascend the throne of the
Pharaohs as his second successor until 689 B.C. After the defeat
at *Altaķū*, the remnants of the Egyptian force withdrew from the
scene and the rebellious states in south-western Palestine were now
completely at the mercy of the overwhelming forces of the Assyrian
emperor, who quickly vanquished the Philistines. At the same time
he had the land of Judah occupied by his troops. 'Forty-six of the
fortified walled cities and the small towns were occupied.' In other
words, the whole land fell into the hands of the Assyrians. Hezekiah
was only able to hold out in Jerusalem, which was encircled by the
Assyrian troops[1]. One or two of the strongholds on the western
frontier also continued to offer resistance, including, for example,
the city of Lachish (the modern *tell ed-duwēr*), which was besieged
by Sennacherib himself[2]. In this situation there was nothing for
king Hezekiah to do but submit to the emperor and pay him a
heavy tribute. And he did so, as is recorded in 2 Kings xviii, 13-16,
in accordance with the Royal Annals of Judah, and also in Sennacherib's report[3]. Sennacherib accepted this surrender and allowed
Hezekiah to stay on his throne once again as a tributary vassal.
Admittedly, he inflicted a severe punishment on him. He restricted

[1] This situation is presupposed by the prophet's sayings in Isa. i, 4-9.
[2] Sennacherib had his siege and conquest of Lachish represented on relief pictures
in Nineveh (cf. Gressmann, AOB², Nos. 138, 140, 141, ANEP, Nos. 371-4, cf. DOTT,
pp. 69-70). According to 2 Kings xix, 8 he had to besiege the city of Libnah (probably
= *tell bornāṭ*) as well as Lachish. He did not himself appear outside Jerusalem but,
according to 2 Kings xviii, 17, sent his commander-in-chief (*turtānu*).
[3] From the fact that thereafter Jerusalem did not have to be conquered again by
force, the later Isaiah narratives in 2 Kings xviii, 17-xix, 9a; 36, 37 and 2 Kings xix,
9b-35 derived the idea of the city's miraculous deliverance.

his authority to the small city-state of Jerusalem, the city of David, and took the whole land of Judah away from him and gave it to the loyal Philistine kings, king *Mitinti* of Ashdod, king *Ṣilbēl* of Gaza and king *Padi* of Ekron who was restored to his former position of authority[1].

Later on the land of Judah was restored to the Davidites for some reason and on some occasion unknown to us. Possibly this took place under Hezekiah or his son and heir Manasseh. But from 701 B.C. for about three-quarters of a century until the downfall of the Assyrian empire the Davidites continued to be politically dependent on the Assyrian emperor. No doubt Hezekiah had once again to make room for the official Assyrian state religion in the royal sanctuary in Jerusalem, thereby opening the door to foreign modes of religion, for the practice of which his son Manasseh, who reigned for such an astonishingly long period, was severely criticised in the traditional records (2 Kings xxi, 1-18). Probably, in the course of time, all kinds of other foreign religious customs infiltrated into Jerusalem and other parts of Judah with the foreign state religion (cf. Zeph. i, 4-6, 8, 9; 2 Kings xxiii, 4 ff.). All this was the result of political dependence.

The great events in the last third of the 8th century had deprived Israel of the possibility of the free and independent development of her own historical life. The greater part of Israel now lived in a state of subjection in a number of Assyrian provinces, robbed of its upper class which had been deported to other parts of the empire; and the smaller part lived in the politically dependent vassal state of Judah. From 701 B.C. there was neither the opportunity nor the desire for political activity. The great events of world history, above all the Assyrian conquest of a great part of Egypt under Sennacherib's son Esarhaddon, which brought the Neo-Assyrian empire to the zenith of its power, took place near at hand but no longer had a direct influence on Israel.

22. *The End of Assyria and the Restoration under Josiah*

The great and dreaded supremacy of the Neo-Assyrian empire collapsed with surprising speed, only a short time after it had attained the summit of its power. The strength of the great empire suddenly flagged, it seems, and it fell a prey to various new enemies.

---

[1] Further details on this in A. Alt, PJB, 25 (1929), pp. 80-88= *Kleine Schriften zur Geschichte des Volkes Israel*, II (1953), pp. 242-249.

King Esarhaddon had been succeeded by his son Ashurbanipal
in 669 B.C.; and Ashurbanipal did not pursue any warlike activities.
His interests were mostly of a different kind; the library of cuneiform tablets which he assembled in his residence at Nineveh and
for which he had the works of Accadian literature copied, is famous.
In the years 650–648 B.C. his authority was seriously disturbed by
internal troubles. The brother of the king, who was called *Šamaš-
šum-ukīn* and had been appointed viceroy in Babylon, rebelled
against Ashurbanipal. Ashurbanipal managed to suppress this revolt, but, thereafter, the power of the Neo-Assyrian empire declined
rapidly. We have scarcely any information about the last years of
Ashurbanipal's reign. But when Ashurbanipal died in about 632 B.C.
and left the Assyrian throne first to his son *Aššur-etil-ilāni* and
later to the latter's brother *Sin-šar-iškun*, the empire was already
in decline. Babylon made itself independent under a monarchy of
its own as early as 625 B.C. Chaldean tribes whose home had been
on the borders of the Fertile Crescent, in the land south of the
mouth of the Euphrates, had meanwhile established themselves
there and seized the reins of government. A Chaldean named Nabopolassar (*Nabū-apal-uṣur*) now made himself king of Babylon and
became the founder of the Neo-Babylonian monarchy. Behind his
monarchy lay the ancient enmity of the Babylonians towards the
Assyrians. From the Iranian mountains the Medes began to thrust
forward westwards towards the land of the Tigris and threatened
from that side too the very centre of Assyrian power. Under a king
whose foreign-sounding name is rendered as *Umakištar* in Accadian
and *Cyaxares* in Greek, they became an important power and
began to play an active part in the history of the ancient Orient.
Finally, there appeared at this very same moment the bands of
Ummān-manda, evidently a marauding Scythian people from the
steppes of southern Russia, who did not apparently carry out any
consistent plan, but constituted a danger, nevertheless, on the
borders of Mesopotamia and drove the Assyrians into a tight
corner. To these three powers Assyria succumbed.

A fragment of the so-called 'Babylonian Chronicle' in which the
most important events of the years 616–609 B.C. are briefly summarised from the Babylonian angle, throws some light on the way
in which Assyria came to its end[1]. The document illuminates the
eventful conflicts of those years. Already by 616 B.C. the battles

[1] This piece was discovered by G. J. Gadd in the British Museum and published in
1923 under the title *The Fall of Nineveh*. German translation in H. Gressmann, AOT²,
pp. 362-365 and TGI, pp. 59-63, ANET, pp. 303-305, DOTT, pp. 75 f. Cf. also D. J.
Wiseman, *Chronicles of Chaldaean Kings* (1956).

were chiefly taking place simply around the central land of Assyria and Mesopotamia which adjoined it on the west; the other parts of the empire that had known such greatness until recently no longer played any part at all. These battles led to the royal Assyrian city of Nineveh falling into the joint hands of the Babylonians, Medes and *Ummān-manda* in 612 B.C. The king *Sin-šar-iškun* lost his life in the process. Thereupon, a certain *Aššur-uballit* made himself 'king of Assyria' in the city of Haran in western Mesopotamia, to maintain a residue of the old empire. But in 610 B.C. the Babylonians and *Ummān-manda* also conquered Haran and expelled *Aššur-uballit*; an attempt which *Aššur-uballit* made in the following year, from the direction of Syria and with Egyptian help, to seize the city of Haran was a failure. This marked the end of the Assyrian empire. Even Egyptian help was no longer able to save it. Egypt, which two generations ago had been the last great target of Assyrian conquest, was now Assyria's sole ally in its death-agony. Egypt had, in the period from 663 B.C. onwards, under the 26th, Saitic, Dynasty, regained its independence and consolidated its position. Though it had emerged in opposition to the Assyrian invaders, in the end it may have thought it worth while to preserve a weakened and reduced Assyria as a protection against the dangerous powers in the east, which were now threatening Assyria in the first place, but might soon encroach on the whole of the ancient Orient. So, at the very outset of his reign (609–593 B.C.) the Pharaoh Necho hastened to the aid of *Aššur-uballit*, albeit in vain. Nevertheless, he had for this purpose to march through the whole of Syria-Palestine, thus laying his hands on this land after Assyrian rule had come to an end.

As a result of these stirring and momentous events, the history of Israel also took a new turn. It is not surprising that the peoples subjugated and enslaved by the Assyrians in their far-flung empire began to stir when they saw that the dreaded power was showing signs of decline. In Israel the fall of the tyrant who, according to the 8th-century prophets, had been the instrument of divine judgement on the people of Israel, was awaited with intense longing[1]. In the political field however, the new situation was assessed quite realistically. In the four provinces on the soil of the former kingdom of Israel there was, for the time being, as far as we know, no reaction. Presumably the Assyrian administrative machine continued to function automatically for a time, even without the power

---

[1] This expectation is given lively expression above all by the prophet Nahum shortly before the fall of Nineveh.

of the empire behind it. The situation was different in the vassal kingdom of Judah. Here king Josiah drew the logical conclusions from the changed position.

King Manasseh, who had sat on the throne of David for more than half a century as the faithful vassal of the Assyrians[1], had been succeeded by his son Amon, who, after quite a short reign, succumbed to a conspiracy in his palace by members of his entourage[2]. The conspirators do not, however, appear to have achieved their aim; the old-established inhabitants of Judah rose against them straight away[3], killed the conspirators and installed Josiah, the eight-year-old son of the murdered king, to preserve the traditional succession in the House of David (2 Kings xxi, 23, 24; xxii, 1). We are not told why the conspirators murdered Amon. It is possible that it was simply an act of personal vengeance or due to a court intrigue. But it is not impossible—it took place in the year 639–638 B.C.—that it is connected with the decline of Assyria, and that the conflict between a pro-Assyrian and an anti-Assyrian attitude was partly responsible. It is not possible to be certain about this. The new king Josiah soon followed a line quite consistent with the general historical situation. During the first years of his reign, when he was still under age[4], nothing of decisive significance took place. But as soon as the time for independent action was ripe, he succeeded by degrees in breaking free from his dependence on Assyria.

In 2 Kings xxiii, 4-20 there is an extract, in chronological order, from the Royal Annals which concentrates on the king's activities in the sphere of public worship, but these also throw some light on the king's political line. As part of his so-called 'reform of public worship', he first of all removed the elements of the Assyrian state religion from the royal sanctuary (this is clearly implied in 2 Kings xxiii, 4). This meant the complete revocation of the vassal relationship, and it may be assumed that he also ceased the payment of tribute. Assyria did not take any counter-measures, for it obviously no longer had the power to enforce its sovereignty among its refractory vassals. We do not know exactly when Josiah took this

---

[1] In an enumeration of his vassals in the west of the Empire, Esarhaddon also mentioned king Manasseh of Judah (Gressmann *op. cit.* pp. 357 f.).

[2] It is possible that עַבְדֵי אָמוֹן means primarily leading royal officials.

[3] This is what is meant by עַם־הָאָרֶץ.

[4] We do not know precisely at what age a king could begin to reign independently or whether perhaps a particular age for this was customary. From Zeph. i, 8, where the 'king's sons' are mentioned alongside the supreme officials, but not the king, it is usually inferred that Josiah was under age at this time, and not yet personally responsible.

step; it may well have been during the last years of Ashurbanipal. Josiah continued to remove from the city-state of Jerusalem and from the whole kingdom of Judah all the other Assyrian forms of worship which had infiltrated, especially the worship of astral deities (2 Kings xxiii, 5).

The decline of Assyrian power allowed him to envisage as a further goal the restoration of the rule of the house of David in the former kingdom of Israel, which was now divided among four Assyrian provinces. In the absence of a king in Israel, the way was clear for an attempt to enforce the old claim of the house of David to rule once more over the kingdom of Israel and thereby to restore the former dual monarchy of David and Solomon in Judah and Israel. No serious opposition was to be feared from the Assyrians, since the Assyrian provinces in Syria-Palestine, with their own administrative organisation, were more or less autonomous. Josiah pursued this goal only very gradually. To begin with, he seized the adjacent southern part of the province of 'Samaria'. According to 2 Kings xxiii, 15, he demolished the ancient and famous shrine of Bethel which had formerly belonged to the Israelite kings. This presupposes that he had meanwhile brought under his rule Bethel, which was in the province of Samaria, (cf. 2 Kings xvii, 28) and the whole of the southern part of this province. This stage of affairs is reflected in a document to be found in Jos. xv, xviii, xix. On closer examination the list of places contained in these chapters turns out to be a list of the twelve districts of the kingdom of Judah, the present form of which can only derive from the period of king Josiah[1]. The twelfth of these districts (Jos. xv, 61b, 62a; xviii, 21b-24a), which originally embraced the eastern part of Benjaminite territory, in so far as it had fallen to the kingdom of Judah after the death of Solomon, included, according to this list, Bethel and Ophrah in the hills west of the Jordan (the modern *eṭ-ṭaiyibe* north-east of Bethel) and the city of Jericho in the Jordan Valley, that is, what was formerly Israelite territory and then an Assyrian province. The same list also shows that the fifth district, which had originally embraced only the most northerly part of the hill country west of Jerusalem, was astonishingly wide in extent (Jos. xv, 45 and xix, 41-46). The formerly Philistine city of Ekron and at least part of its territory as far as the hinterland of the port of Joppa (Japho, the modern *yāfa*)[2] now formed part of this district. Josiah had therefore

[1] Cf. A. Alt, 'Judas Gaue unter Josia', PJB, 21 [1925], pp. 100-116 = *Kleine Schriften zur Geschichte des Volkes Israel*, II [1953], pp. 276-288.

[2] Cf. the sketch map in M. Noth, *Das Buch Josua* (² 1953), p. 91 and the description on pp. 92 ff.

already widened his sphere of influence considerably to the north-west also and had even occupied Philistine territory which had not even belonged to the kingdom of David and Solomon. In addition, Jos. xiii also contains a list of places in a new, thirteenth district[1] which shows that in the southern land east of the Jordan too, Josiah began by seizing the territory of the former kingdom of Israel which had presumably been assigned meanwhile to the Assyrian province of 'Gilead', in so far as the neighbouring Moabites or Ammonites had not acquired the land south of the Jabbok when the kingdom of Israel fell. We can thus see that Josiah was extending his authority in various directions, towards the territory of the former kingdom of Israel; it is clear that he was making a systematic attempt to bring this area under his control. He aspired thus to restore the empire of David. At the same time, however, it is evident that he pursued this goal with all possible care and caution and only advanced towards it by degrees as far as the means at his command allowed him. Presumably, the governors of the provinces affected put up as much resistance as they could, with the help of the newly established foreign upper classes. The list of the districts of Judah under Josiah illuminates the initial stage in Josiah's undertaking which lingered on for sufficient time for a new demarcation of the northern districts to be undertaken.

That this was merely an entirely provisional situation is shown by the fact that the accession of territory was added, to begin with, to the kingdom of Judah which was divided into districts, and that it was not yet sufficient to form the basis constituent of a newly constituted kingdom of Israel. Later on, Josiah went far beyond this early provisional stage. According to 2 Kings xxiii, 19, he later enforced his religious policy in 'all the cities of Samaria'—this is the first time the name 'Samaria' appears in the Old Testament no longer as the name of a city but, in accordance with the Assyrian practice, as the name of a province or country—so he now possessed the whole territory of the Assyrian province of Samaria and therefore the central area of the old kingdom of Israel. Finally, he even encroached on the province of Galilee. In 2 Kings xxiii, 29, we hear of him with his army at Megiddo, the former capital of this Assyrian province. He had then come already fairly near his goal of reviving the kingdom of Israel under his rule. In Megiddo, however, his life and reign came to a sudden end before he had attained his goal.

But Josiah did not merely attempt to restore these external

[1] Cf. most recently, M. Noth, ZAW, N.F. 19 (1944), pp. 49 ff.

features of the old legitimate order, but also its inner nature, as it appeared to him in accordance with the conceptions of his own time. In reality, he did not merely return to an old order but, as usually happens in such attempts at restoration, created something new. In the 18th year of his reign (621–620 B.C.) a 'Book of the Law' was discovered during building operations in the state sanctuary in Jerusalem and was laid before the king by the high priest of the sanctuary (2 Kings xxii, 3–xxiii, 3). This 'Book of the Law' proved to be what was apparently an ancient formulation of the divine law. It claimed to be authoritative and its ordinances were being very largely flouted at this time. The king decided to enforce this 'Book of the Law'. The gradual elimination of the Assyrian State religion from the royal sanctuary was probably already under way as part of the process of breaking free from Assyrian suzerainty, when the 'Book of the Law' was discovered; Josiah now incorporated in his religious programme the observance of the ordinances of the 'Book of the Law'. He solemnly accorded official recognition to it, not by bestowing on it the status of a national law by dint of his royal authority, but by assembling the elders of Judah and Jerusalem in the Temple, and, reverting to the old tradition of Sinai, causing a covenant to be made in which the partners were Yahweh on the one side and the people, represented by the elders, on the other, whilst he himself, by virtue of his secular position as the ruler of the sanctuary in Jerusalem, which still ranked as the central shrine of the tribes of Israel, took part as leader of the ceremony. This led to a vague amalgamation of the religious order and the state which was also to determine the future course of events[1].

In all probability, this 'Book of the Law' was identical with the original form of the deuteronomic law which is preserved in the Old Testament. It was presumably compiled in the course of the 7th century B.C. and was based on various older collections of laws, and provided with homiletic and parenetic elaborations, the intention of the compilation being to reformulate the ancient divine law for the present age and to gain recognition for it[2]. It was presented as an interpretation of the law deriving from Moses and, because of this law and the literature connected with it, Moses became traditionally the specific mediator of the law. In fact it contains not merely some individually very ancient statutes, but its whole

---

[1] Cf. M. Noth, *Die Gesetze im Pentateuch* (1940), pp. 34 ff.
[2] Cf. G. v. Rad, *Deuteronomium-Studien* (1947), pp. 11 ff. English translation, *Studies in Deuteronomy* (1953), pp. 17 ff.

tendency of underlining the purity of the Israelite worship of God especially as against the local Canaanite religion, was based on an ancient Israelite attitude of mind. Whilst the initial demand for a single place of worship represents a new element and something not demanded in this way before, it does link up with the old system of the one central place of worship for the sacral confederation of the Israelite tribes. We do not know exactly in what circles in the 7th century this 'Book of the Law' was written on the basis of ancient tradition; nor do we know how it came to the Temple in Jerusalem and remained unnoticed to begin with[1]. Its historical influence only began when it was discovered in the reign of Josiah.

The king was not only responsible for mediating the covenant but used his royal authority further to enforce the statutes of the 'Book of the Law'. In this way, though with the best of intentions, he again exceeded his authority by allowing the power of the state to encroach on the realm of the ancient sacral institutions of the pre-monarchical period. As far as it was a matter of purifying the cult in the royal sanctuary in Jerusalem from foreign elements, he had authority to enforce the law and was even committed to doing so according to the covenant for which he was responsible, simply as a member of the Israelite people. But he went further. He singled out, no doubt somewhat one-sidedly, the requirement for a unified place of worship which stood at the head of the legal material proper, and defiled and made cultically unusable the local places of sacrifice in the land (2 Kings xxiii, 8a) which had been held sacred from very early times and had then been taken over by the Israelite tribes. He abolished them all in favour of the shrine in Jerusalem which was in fact intended by the law to be the one lawful place of worship within his sphere of government. In the areas which he subjugated anew during the course of his reign he also proceeded to destroy the local places of worship (2 Kings xxiii, 15, 19). He no doubt did so on his own royal authority although his secular powers did not entitle him to. The only obligation he had assumed as a member of Israel and as a result of the covenant was to share in the enforcement of the statutes of the 'Book of the Law'. The abolition of the local sanctuaries was an exceedingly violent infringement of the traditional religious life of the people. The limitation of all cultic activity to the one and only holy place in Jerusalem reduced the number of cultic observances to an extra-

[1] The formerly widely accepted idea, that the alleged discovery was simply a 'pious deception' staged by the Jerusalem priests, is hardly tenable.

ordinary degree and inevitably brought about a separation between everyday life and religious activity between which there had hitherto been a very close bond. A particular problem was what was to become of the priests who had been serving the shrines which were now abolished. The 'Book of the Law' in which this question had been carefully considered, had decreed that the priests were to be entitled to sacrifice in Jerusalem and perform their priestly functions there (Deut. xviii, 7). It was not possible, however, to realize this entirely (2 Kings xxiii, 9), probably owing to the opposition of the priests already in Jerusalem. There now came into being in Jerusalem, therefore, a second class of priests, in so far as the country priests received the traditional share of religious taxes to which they were entitled, though they were not allowed to sacrifice. It was only later that the position of this inferior class of priests was defined and established more precisely (cf. below, p. 339).

Josiah's religious policy had a powerful influence in the following period, since the 'Book of the Law' on which it was based, continued to be recognised as authoritative. The centralisation of worship was quickly realised and was soon taken so much for granted that it was no longer necessary to enforce it specifically. The fate which befell the king's political enterprises and successes was different. The restoration of the independence of the throne of David and the initially successful attempt to revive the old kingdom of Israel alongside the kingdom of Judah, were possible only thanks to the decline of the Assyrian empire which had the result that, to begin with, Syria-Palestine was left to itself, just as David's development of an empire had been based on the fact that in the 10th century none of the powers of the ancient Orient had been in a position to lay hands on Syria-Palestine. At the end of the 7th century, however, the revival of Israel was merely a brief episode which lasted only until power relationships in the Near East had settled into a new pattern after the tremendous events of the Assyrian collapse, and a new great power had appeared in place of the old. For from the middle of the 8th century there had come upon the ancient Orient the rule of great powers one after another, one power declining only because another was already in the ascendant. The great Assyrian empire had succumbed in this way to powers which were now making ready to take over the reins of power. The age of Josiah, which appeared to open up the prospect of a restoration of the old order, was therefore bound to remain a mere episode; and after Josiah had enjoyed a free hand for a time he was finally drawn once more into the interplay of the great powers which led to the end of his monarchy and his work.

In the year 609 B.C. a conflict occurred between Josiah and the Pharaoh Necho. At the time Necho was on the way to bring back the Assyrian king *Aššur-uballiṭ* to Haran (cf. above, p. 271) hoping in this way to save at any rate a residue of Assyrian power[1] and at the same time to regain possession of Syria-Palestine that had once been controlled by Egypt and which he hardly intended to give back to Assyria. By this action he became in every respect the enemy of Josiah. Josiah's work was based on his disengagement from Assyria and therefore on an anti-Assyrian policy; in fact Josiah was on the side of the powers who were preparing the way for Assyria's downfall, and hence, on the opposite side to Necho. At the same time, he was bound to be opposed to the Egyptian seizure of Syria-Palestine, since the independence of Syria-Palestine was necessary for the achievement of his aims and he could have no desire to see Assyrian sovereignty being replaced by Egyptian, just as, on the other hand, Necho could not allow a stronger power to arise in Palestine if he intended to subjugate Syria-Palestine. It therefore came about that Josiah resisted Necho when the latter invaded Syria-Palestine to bring *Aššuruballiṭ* back across the Euphrates. The clash occurred near Megiddo (2 Kings xxiii, 29) where the great road through Syria-Palestine which Necho evidently used, struck out from the coastal plain of Palestine into the plain of Jezreel after traversing the hill country in the rear of Mount Carmel, to lead then to northern Syria by way of Damascus. At the time Josiah was apparently already in possession of a part of the province of Galilee to which Megiddo belonged, and at this strategically favourable spot[2] he tried to hold up the Pharaoh. The

---

[1] From the 'Gadd Chronicle' (cf. above, p. 270, note 1) it is clear that the statement about Necho in 2 Kings xxiii, 29 is materially incorrect. It is stated in this passage that Necho had 'gone up *against* the king of Assyria'. Possibly the preposition was later altered accidentally or—owing to a misconception—intentionally (על instead of אל; it would also be better to read אל instead of the following על [אֶל נְהַר־פְּרָת]). The Chronicler's parallel account is worded with striking differences and in much more general terms (2 Chron. xxxv, 20: 'came up to fight at Carchemish on the Euphrates') and does not thereby contradict what actually took place, probably, however, not as a result of better knowledge of the facts, but in reference to Jer. xlvi, 2, though it is not certain that this passage refers to the events of 609 B.C. A correct tradition has been preserved, however, alongside 2 Kings xxiii, 29 (or is it perhaps based on an earlier version of 2 Kings xxiii, 29?); in *Ant. Iud.* X, 5, 1, § Niese Josephus states the Pharaoh's goal quite correctly in the words: Μήδους πολεμήσων καὶ τοὺς Βαβυλωνίους, οἳ τὴν Ἀσσυρίων κατέλυσαν ἀρχήν· τῆς γὰρ Ἀσίας βασιλεῦσαι πόθον εἶχεν.

[2] The issue of the great road into the plain near Megiddo had already played a part in a similar way on one occasion under Thothmes III (cf. A. Alt, PJB, 10 [1914], pp. 53 ff.).

attempt was a failure. In 2 Kings xxiii, 29 there is a remarkably brief and allusive reference to the event: 'He [the Pharaoh] slew him at (or 'in') Megiddo, when he had seen him'. We may conclude from this that a battle between the two sides did not in fact take place at Megiddo[1] but that Necho succeeded in some way or other in seizing the person of Josiah and that the Israelite forces gave up the fight after the king had been killed.

With this Josiah's political work was destroyed, not so much because it had been too much bound up with the personality of this obviously very shrewd and energetic monarch, who found no successor of equal quality, but because the victorious Necho used his superior power to destroy the political structure that Josiah had built up. After his success at Megiddo, Necho moved on first of all to northern Syria to make a vain last attempt to help Assyria, which was already in a state of collapse. Meanwhile the body of Josiah was taken to Jerusalem and Jehoahaz, who was presumably his eldest son, was raised to the throne of David in his stead. This was done by the עַם־הָאָרֶץ, the free inhabitants of the land of Judah, who once again championed the traditional system of hereditary succession in the House of David (2 Kings xxiii, 30). Jehoahaz, however, was only king for three months (2 Kings xxiii, 31), that is, only so long as Necho was preoccupied in the north. According to the Babylonian Chronicle, ll. 66 ff. the battles around Haran, in which the Egyptians took part, lasted from the month of *Du'uz* (June/July) to the month of *Ulul* (August/September). Then Necho returned across the Euphrates without having achieved his purpose and acted as if he was master of Syria-Palestine. He pitched his headquarters in Riblah (the modern *rable* in the northern part of the *beḳā'* south of the Lake of *ḥomṣ*). He ordered Jehoahaz to come there and punished him severely (2 Kings xxiii, 33 f.). He not only deposed him, but had him imprisoned and later taken to Egypt, where he died. Probably Jehoahaz had begun to continue his father's policy; Necho would not tolerate this but considered it a rebellion against himself as ruler of Syria-Palestine. He imposed a heavy fine on the country, which, 'according to the commandment of Pharaoh' the inhabitants had to pay each according to his income (2 Kings xxiii, 35). Of his own accord Necho made another son of Josiah, named Eliakim, king, changing his name to Jehoiakim. This change of name was no doubt intended as a demonstration of sovereignty, to show that the new king was subject to

[1] The Chronicler was the first to think of a battle and to describe one (2 Chron. xxxv, 23 f.).

Pharaoh. There can be no doubt but that Necho reduced the dominions of the Davidites to the frontiers of the pre-Josiah period, limiting them to the city-state of Jerusalem and the old kingdom of Judah. He demanded recognition of his sovereignty and had the provinces on the territory of the former kingdom of Israel administered as Egyptian provinces. He no doubt proceeded similarly in the rest of Syria-Palestine. Thus, Syria-Palestine was relegated to its former state of dependence on an imperial power; and the prospects which the decline of Assyrian power had seemed to open up, were gone.

23. *Nebuchadnezzar and the End of the Kingdom of Judah*

Egyptian rule in the land did not last long. After the fall of Assyria the victorious Medes and Babylonians—the *Ummān-manda* had now disappeared from the scene—shared the Assyrian booty. The Medes took possession of the north-west and north of the empire, that is, the Assyrian mother country and the Iranian-Armenian hill country as far as eastern Asia Minor, whilst the new Babylonian government seized the rest of Mesopotamia and also claimed Syria-Palestine. To gain control of Syria-Palestine, it still had to contend with Egypt, which had meanwhile seized this part of the Assyrian empire. This conflict followed quite soon. Unfortunately we have hardly any reliable information about this event, the important results of which are so evident[1]. Unlike their Assyrian predecessors, the Neo-Babylonian kings, from whom one would expect to have had some information, left behind no annalistic inscriptions and referred to their historical actions only in general terms in inscriptions on their buildings. We are therefore dependent on the information in Jer. xlvi, 2 and the extract from the 3rd Book of Χαλδαϊκά of Berossus[2] which has survived in Josephus, *Ant. Iud.* X, 11, 1, §§ 219 ff. Niese. According to Jer. xlvi, 2, the Egyptian Pharaoh Necho, was defeated by 'king' Nebuchadnezzar[3] of Babylon in the fourth year of the Judaean king Jehoiakim—*i.e.* in 605 B.C. To this Berossus adds more precisely that Nebuchadnezzar

---

[1] Cf. now D. J. Wiseman, *op. cit.* and DOTT, pp. 78-80.

[2] In the 3rd century B.C. Berossus compiled in his Χαλδαϊκά a history of Babylon with the materials available to him.

[3] We use this form of the name which has become conventional and which derives from the inaccurate rendering in many passages in the Old Testament (especially in the Book of Daniel). The form Nebuchadrezzar, which occurs above all in the book of Jeremiah, is better (in Babylonian the name is *Nabū-kudurri-uṣur*).

was not yet king at that time, that he was entrusted with the command of the Babylonian forces by his father Nabopolassar, who was already a sick man, and he was therefore still only crown prince when he obtained the victory over Necho which had such an important influence on the consolidation of the Neo-Babylonian empire. He had to return quickly to Babylon after the victory and the subsequent subjugation of Syria-Palestine, to succeed his father who had died meanwhile (in 604 B.C.). According to Jer. xlvi, 2, a battle took place on the Euphrates near Carchemish (the modern *jerāblus* which lies at an important crossing of the Euphrates from Mesopotamia to northern Syria); on the face of it, it is not unlikely that a battle ensued at the spot where the two former powers had abutted on one another. It has been doubted, however, whether the reference to Carchemish in Jer. xlvi, 2[1] was originally part of the report on the defeat of Necho[2]; and so the question as to the exact site of the battle must be left undecided. Of greater importance is the fact that the Neo-Babylonian power obtained possession of Syria-Palestine as a result of its victory over Egypt. This is stated explicitly in 2 Kings xxiv, 7 in the words: 'And the king of Egypt came not again any more out of his land: for the king of Babylon had taken from the river of Egypt (*wādi el-'arīsh*) unto the river Euphrates all that pertained to the king of Egypt'.

Syria-Palestine thus had a new overlord once again, this time apparently without any further incident: at least we do not hear of any. The still existing independent political organisations, especially in southern Palestine, including the kingdom of Judah, had to recognise the sovereignty of Nebuchadnezzar. Unfortunately, we have no details about how the subject and dependent peoples were treated in the short-lived Neo-Babylonian empire in which the most important of the kings was Nebuchadnezzar (604–562 B.C.). It is therefore uncertain whether king Jehoiakim of Judah—like the other vassal kings—now had to provide a place for the Babylonian state religion in the royal sanctuary in Jerusalem. No doubt, the vassals had to pay regular tribute to Babylon. Furthermore, the Old Testament passes a very unfavourable judgement on Jehoiakim. According to 2 Kings xxiv, 4, he was a tyrant who shed much blood in Jerusalem, and the prophet Jeremiah also describes him as an unjust and brutal despot whose chief interest was in the

---

[1] Josephus, *Ant. Iud.* X, 6, 1, §§ 84 ff. Niese, already connects it with the statement about Nebuchadnezzar's victory.

[2] Cf. B. Alfrink, *Biblica*, 8 (1927), pp. 395 ff.; W. Rudolph, *Jeremia* (HAT, I, 12, 1947), p. 231.

sumptuous enlargement of the royal palace in Jerusalem (Jer. xxii, 13-19). He was not a worthy successor of his father Josiah[1].

Moreover, Jehoiakim was unwise enough to try and escape from Babylonian sovereignty. According to 2 Kings xxiv, 1 he only remained loyal to Nebuchadnezzar for three years[2]; when he rebelled, Nebuchadnezzar sent Babylonian troops against him and also gave orders for troops from the neighbouring states of 'Edom', Moab and Ammon to proceed against him. According to the period mentioned in 2 Kings xxiv, 1 this must have occurred around 602 B.C. Either Jehoiakim was able to withstand this not particularly strong attack for a time, or he reverted on this attack to his former acknowledgment of Neo-Babylonian sovereignty, only to secede again after three or four years. At any rate it was not until the year 598 B.C. that Nebuchadnezzar punished Jehoiakim vigorously, by besieging Jerusalem[3]. It is true that the punishment no longer affected Jehoiakim personally, since he died in that year and left the kingdom of Judah and the royal city of Jerusalem to his son and successor, Jehoiachin, in an extremely precarious position. According to 2 Kings xxiv, 8, Jehoiachin, who was only 18 years old at the time, was only king for three months and it is possible that he came to the throne when Jerusalem was already being besieged and unable to hold on much longer. The city was occupied[4] and the king was deported with his family and retinue and his leading officials to Babylon. The treasures of the Temple and the palace and other precious things in Jerusalem were seized as booty. The craftsmen in Jerusalem and the military ruling class who had probably been called up to defend the royal city, were removed to Babylonia (2 Kings xxiv, 12-16). Jehoiachin continued to live for a long time in Babylon as deposed king. Four cuneiform documents found in Babylon from the period of Nebuchadnezzar mention his name (*Ya-'-u-kīnu* or *Ya-ku-ú-ki-nu*) and even describe him as 'King of (the land of) Judah' (*Ya-ú-du* or *Ya-a-hu-du* or *Ya-ku-du*); they mention that certain quantities of sesame oil were given to him and 'the five sons of the king of Judah'—as Jehoiachin was very

[1] In Jer. xxvi and xxxvi Jehoiakim appears as a scorner of the prophet's words.

[2] The statement in Dan. i, 1 that in the third year of the reign of Jehoiakim Nebuchadnezzar besieged and captured Jerusalem is derived from this chronological reference, the beginning of which must be the Neo-Babylonian occupation of Syria-Palestine or Nebuchadnezzar's accession, and from a faulty combination of 2 Kings xxiv, 1 f. with 2 Kings xxiv, 10 (but cf. Alfrink, *op. cit.* pp. 396 ff.).

[3] Probably he was not present himself. In 2 Kings xxiv, 10 ff. the subject is partly the 'subordinate (officers)', partly Nebuchadnezzar himself (verse 11 tries to smooth out this inconsistency).

[4] The reference to the year in 2 Kings xxiv, 12b ('eighth year of' Nebuchadnezzar's reign) is not entirely correct.

young when he was deported to Babylon, this probably refers to princes of the royal house in the wider sense—and to 'eight people of the land of Judah'. These documents were discovered in the royal palace of Babylon. It appears from this that Jehoiachin lived in this palace as a deposed king with members of his family and retinue in a household of his own[1]. The Judaeans who were deported to Babylonia dated their years from 'the exile of king Jehoiachin' (Ezek. i, 2)[2] and probably regarded Jehoiachin as the last and still rightful king of Judah and hoped for his return and reinstatement (cf. Jer. xxviii, 1 ff.)[3]. When, after the death of Nebuchadnezzar in the year 562 B.C., *Amēl-Marduk* (in the Old Testament his name appears in the form Evil-merodach) became king of the Neo-Babylonian empire, Jehoiachin was brought to the royal court and treated with honour, probably as part of an act of amnesty (2 Kings xxv, 27-30); this did not, admittedly, imply a restoration of his royal prerogatives but was simply a friendly, purely personal gesture.

After the conquest of Jerusalem Nebuchadnezzar had affairs in Judah reorganised. He allowed Judah to continue as a vassal kingdom under its own king and still refrained from making it a Babylonian province. As king he installed an uncle of Jehoiachin, a younger son of Josiah (cf. 1 Chron. iii, 15) named Mattaniah, and he changed his name to Zedekiah (2 Kings xxiv, 17), probably, again, to mark the fact that the king and his kingdom were subject to him. In addition, he probably reduced the territory of the kingdom of Judah. At any rate, the prophetic saying in Jer. xiii, 18-19 referring to the catastrophe of the year 598 B.C., notes that 'the cities of the Negeb shall be shut up, and none shall open them'. It may be inferred from this[4] that the Negeb was lost to the kingdom of Judah at this time and the southern frontier running north to the latitude of Hebron established, which is well known to us as the southern frontier of the later province of Judah in Persian times. The southern part of the territory of the kingdom of Judah which was separated off in this way was presumably allocated to the Edomites, who had long since encroached on the southern borders

---

[1] Cf. E. F. Weidner in *Mélanges syriens offerts à R. Dussaud*, II (1939), pp. 923 ff. Cf. ANET, p. 308, DOTT, pp. 84-86. During the excavations at *tell bēt mirsim* in Palestine the seal of a certain 'Eliakim, servant of *Ywkn*' was found, that probably belonged to a vassal of the deported king Jehoiachin; cf. W. F. Albright, JBL, 51 (1932), pp. 77 ff.

[2] The Book of Ezekiel continues to date events from this era.

[3] Cf. A. Malamat, *Journal of Near Eastern Studies*, 9 (1950), pp. 223 f.; *Palestine Exploration Quarterly*, 83 (1951), pp. 81 ff.; M. Noth, *Revue d'histoire et de philosophie religieuses*, 33 (1953), pp. 81 ff.   [4] Cf. A. Alt, PJB, 21 (1925), p. 108.

of the land west of the Jordan from their original home, having come westwards across the *wādi el-'araba*, and were advancing in a northerly direction towards the mountains west of the Jordan. The defeat of the kingdom of Judah in 598 B.C. brought them a substantial gain in this direction.

In the reduced vassal state of Judah the people found it difficult to acquiesce in the new situation. In spite of the historical experiences forced on them during about a hundred and fifty years, there were still voices among them proclaiming the early restoration of what had just been lost (cf. Jer. xxviii, 1-4). They were able to gain a hearing and to stir up the people, and were successful in their attempt to influence the obviously weak and undecided king Zedekiah. At this period the prophet Jeremiah issued urgent and repeated warnings and demanded obedience to the sovereign will of Nebuchadnezzar as to the will of God who had for the time being transferred world rule into his hands (Jer. xxvii-xxix). But the people were loath to listen to the prophet and distrusted him as a traitor because of his words (cf. Jer. xxxvii, 11-16). It is true that the king himself, who owed his throne to the Babylonian overlord, was not, in his perplexity, entirely unreceptive to the prophet's warnings. To the very end, he sometimes summoned him in secret —for fear of public opinion—and asked him for his advice (Jer. xxxvii, 17-21; xxxviii, 14-27). In the end, however, he allowed himself to be persuaded by his leading officials and the clamour of the people to take the insane step of renouncing his allegiance to Nebuchadnezzar. As a consequence, in the 9th year of his reign (589 B.C.) a Babylonian army appeared in his land (2 Kings xxv, 1). His defection must therefore have occurred shortly before this. Probably Zedekiah did not make his move entirely without some preparation. It is true that we hear nothing of one or other of the vassal states in southern Palestine joining in the enterprise, but we have to remember that Neo-Babylonian sources contain nothing about events in Judah in the years 589–587 B.C. and that the extracts from the royal Judaean annals concentrate specifically on the fate of the city of Jerusalem. It may be inferred, however, from the course of events that Zedekiah attempted to establish contact at any rate with Egypt, and probably received a promise of aid from that quarter.

At first the kingdom of Judah alone was, apparently, the object of the Neo-Babylonian attack and there was clearly no question of Egyptian help at the outset. Almost the whole territory of Judah probably fell quite rapidly into the hands of the Neo-

Babylonian troops and only a few strongholds were able to hold out against them. In Jer. xxxiv, 7 there is a reference to a situation in which, except for Jerusalem, only the two fortresses of Lachish (the modern *tell ed-duwēr*) and Azekah (the modern *tell ez-zakarīye*) in the hill country on the western border of the kingdom of Judah, held out, whilst all the other strongholds and, naturally, all the open country had already fallen to the enemy. This may have taken place in the course of the year 588 B.C. The so-called Ostraca of Lachish, inscribed potsherds which were found during excavations on the *tell ed-duwēr* on the site of the great gateway to this city[1], contain brief reports in letter form, obviously addressed to the commander of the fortress of Lachish. They come from various outposts which maintained communications between the besieged cities in enemy-occupied territory. At the same time they record all kinds of observations. The ostraca reveal very clearly the desperate situation in the kingdom of Judah. They probably include a reference to the fall of the fortress of Azekah which took place at the time. At any rate, in IV, 10 ff. it is stated that 'we give heed to the signals of Lachish . . . we can no longer see the (signals) of Azekah'. On the situation in Jerusalem it is recorded that there were people there 'who weaken the hands of the land and the city' (VI, 6 ff.). According to Jer. xxxviii, 4, this reproach was made in the same words to the king by the supreme officials in Jerusalem in reference to Jeremiah; and if the comment of the writer of the ostracon does not expressly mention the prophet Jeremiah, it does refer to the influence which proceeded from him and from those who shared his views. The statement in III, 13 ff., according to which the leader of the Jewish militia named Kebaryahu, *i.e.* the supreme commander, 'went down to Egypt', and supplied himself with provisions *en route*, is of great historical importance. The encirclement of Jerusalem where Kebaryahu must, after all, have had his real headquarters, and the enemy occupation of the land, do not seem to have been too severe to make that impossible. We do not learn what commission Kebaryahu had in Egypt, but it must have been concerned with obtaining Egyptian help.

In fact an Egyptian army did appear in the land at this time and forced the Babylonians to suspend the siege of Jerusalem for a time (Jer. xxxvii, 5; cf. Jer. xxxiv, 21). The Babylonians had first to ward off the Egyptian attack. They probably managed to do that

---

[1] Cf. H. Torczyner, *The Lachish Letters* (Lachish, I), 1938. The text of these ostraca is also given in J. Hempel, ZAW, N.F. 15 (1938), pp. 126 ff., and the text of the six most important ostraca in TGI, pp. 63-65. Cf. ANET, pp. 321 f., DOTT, pp. 212-217.

very quickly; the Egyptian army will not have been very strong.
Jeremiah proved to be right with his prophecy (Jer. xxxvii, 7-9)
that the Egyptians would return to their country and the Babylonians would renew the siege of Jerusalem. Once again faith in
Egyptian help was disappointed; and the fate of the kingdom of
Judah was thereby sealed once and for all. After Azekah, the fortress of Lachish also fell and was burned to ashes by the conquerors,
as the excavations have shown. And, finally, Jerusalem was over-
taken by its fate.

2 Kings xxv only contains a description of the fate of Jerusalem at
and after its fall, on the basis of the details contained in Jer. xxxix.
This is the only episode in the whole final struggle of the kingdom
of Judah which is mentioned. According to this, Jerusalem was
besieged from the 10th day of the 10th month of the 9th year of
Zedekiah to the 9th day of the 4th month of the 11th year. With
the short interruption caused by the Egyptian attack, the city thus
defied the enemy for well over one and a half years. By then it was
starved out and on that 9th day of the 4th month, that is, in the
August of the year 587 B.C., the besiegers succeeded in making a
breach in the city wall and entering the city through it. King
Zedekiah tried to escape with his retinue to the east through the
'wilderness of Judah' and then into the land east of the Jordan,
but was captured by Babylonian troops as he crossed the Jordan
Valley near Jericho and was taken captive before Nebuchadnezzar.
Nebuchadnezzar himself was not present at the conquest of
Jerusalem, but had his headquarters in Riblah in central Syria like
Pharaoh Necho in the year 609 B.C. It might be inferred from this
that at the time he was having to enforce his authority elsewhere
in Syria-Palestine and that Zedekiah's defection took place in connection with other attempts at rebellion in Syria-Palestine. But we
have no definite information on this point[1]. In Riblah he inflicted
a stern punishment on the faithless Zedekiah. Zedekiah had to
watch his sons being 'slaughtered'; he himself was then blinded
and led off to Babylon in chains, where he probably died soon
after. We hear nothing more of him. But conquered Jerusalem
was plundered by the conquerors and set on fire, with the royal
palace and the Temple. According to 2 Kings xxv, 8 this took place
on the 7th day of the 5th month of that same year, about a month
after the occupation and probably on the express instructions of

---

[1] An inscription of Nebuchadnezzar from the *wādi brīsa* (translated in AOT[2],
p. 365 f., ANET, p. 307) reports on battles waged by Nebuchadnezzar in the region of
the Lebanon. Unfortunately we are not told when these took place.

Nebuchadnezzar, who had first to be fetched from his headquarters in Riblah. The Temple of Solomon went up in flames, and with it presumably the ancient tribal relic of the Ark, about which tradition is silent after the statement of its transfer to the Temple built by Solomon; it had since stood in the adyton of this Temple as a reverently guarded traditional cult-object though it may not have played any considerable part in public worship[1]. As we know of no earlier plundering of the Temple to which it might have fallen victim, it was probably destroyed after 587 B.C. with the rest of the Temple, since the Babylonians are reported to have taken the treasures of the Temple in 598 B.C. but not to have taken or destroyed the Ark (2 Kings xxiv, 13). The city wall of Jerusalem was pulled down and the population were no doubt subjected to cruel treatment.

Nebuchadnezzar now made an end of Judaean autonomy. The Neo-Babylonians were apparently more hesitant in introducing new political systems than the Assyrians. But Nebuchadnezzar now did what he had failed to do in the year 598 B.C.; he incorporated Judah in the provincial organisation of the Neo-Babylonian empire and eliminated the Davidic monarchy which had ruled in Jerusalem for about four centuries. Following the Assyrian custom, he removed the ruling upper class from the land. A few men from king Zedekiah's immediate entourage as well as a number of especially prominent people in Jerusalem and the land of Judah who had not been taken prisoner with the king, were now arrested in Jerusalem and taken to Nebuchadnezzar's headquarters in Riblah, where they were put to death (2 Kings xxv, 18-21). For the rest, after the old upper class in Jerusalem and Judah had been taken away in 598 B.C., mainly the urban population of Jerusalem was deported, presumably again to Babylonia[2]. The peasant population, on the other hand, remained where they were. Inasmuch as he did not transplant any foreign upper class to Judah and did not set up any new independent organisation in the little territory, Nebuchadnezzar left the reorganisation of the population unfinished. In this respect the situation in Judah was quite different from that in the provinces established by the Assyrians on the

---

[1] From various allusions in cultic psalms it is indeed often assumed that the Ark was fetched from its adyton on the occasion of particular devotional festivals during the period of the kings and carried around in public processions (cf. Gunkel-Begrich, *Einleitung in die Psalmen* [1933], pp. 411 f.), but there is no absolute proof of this.

[2] Probably the prophet Ezekiel was not deported until this time (cf. on this—though with differences on certain details—Bertholet, *Hesekiel* [1936], pp. xiii ff.), and was taken to Babylonia.

territory of the former kingdom of Israel; and this was important for the future course of events. It also shows that the Babylonians acted less consistently than the Assyrians had done before them. Subjugated Judah was even given a Judaean as its supreme administrator. He was a certain Gedaliah, the son of a high Judaean official who is well known from the period of the kings Josiah (2 Kings xxii, 12, 14) and Jehoiakim (Jer. xxvi, 24). We do not know what it was that commended him to Nebuchadnezzar for the new post. To begin with, his official residence was not in Jerusalem. The reason for this was probably not so much the intention of degrading the rebellious royal city since the Assyrians had also had no scruples about installing their governors in the conquered royal cities. The reason was probably that Jerusalem had been destroyed so thoroughly that for the time being it was impossible to use it as an administrative centre. Gedaliah resided in Mizpah (probably the modern *tell en-naṣbe*) which was situated rather away from the centre of Judah, being on its northern border. Perhaps the reason why this city was chosen was that it had not suffered so badly as other Judaean cities in the battles of the years 589–587[1].

Gedaliah's period of office did not last very long. He was soon murdered by a few Judaean officials or officers who had escaped from the catastrophe and fled to the Ammonites in the land east of the Jordan. The motive behind their action is unknown and is not made any clearer by the statement in Jer. xl, 14 that they acted at the instance of the king of the Ammonites. The only reason why we have any details about these events is that the prophet Jeremiah was involved in them because the former retinue of Gedaliah and many other Judaeans in Mizpah and elsewhere in the land decided to flee to Egypt for fear of Nebuchadnezzar's vengeance for the murder of his deputy and the escape of the murderers, and took the prophet with them against his will. We lose sight of him once he has arrived in Egypt. We have the fairly detailed report in Jer. xl, 7–xliii, 7 (there is an extract from it in 2 Kings xxv, 22-26), but we have no information at all concerning the further course of events. It is possible that Judaeans were appointed as administrative officials even after the murder of Gedaliah. Tiny Judah was probably not established at all as an independent province; it was probably incorporated in the neighbouring province of Samaria,

---

[1] The archaeological findings at *tell en-naṣbe* which should throw a more exact light on this, are not entirely clear (cf. *Tell en-Naṣbeh*, I [1947], pp. 50 ff.); but they do show that the settlement on this site lasted beyond the beginning of the 6th century until the Persian period; and traces of a great catastrophe in the year 587 B.C. have apparently not been found.

so that the Judaean at its head was only a subordinate of the governor of Samaria, a deputy-governor with limited rights; this might explain the situation which we find very much later in the middle of the 5th century B.C.[1] In time Mizpah was also abandoned as an administrative centre, and, in the Persian period, the deputy-governor resided in Jerusalem again. The frontiers of the administrative area of Judah were identical with the area of the kingdom in its last period, if the separation of the southern part of Judah had taken place already in 598 B.C. (cf. above, p. 283). It embraced the actual ancient tribal territory of Judah in the mountains west of the Jordan, beginning only north of the city of Hebron, and also the former city-state territory of Jerusalem with the larger southern part of the old tribal territory of Benjamin.

24. *The Situation after the Fall of Jerusalem*

What happened in the year 587 B.C. was merely the conclusion of a long historical process, which had begun already in the middle of the 8th century B.C. It did not signify in any way a sudden change in the historical situation for Israel. The overwhelming intervention of a great foreign power in Israel's history had long been a factor which had constantly to be reckoned with. But it is obvious that the fall and destruction of Jerusalem first revealed the whole truth about its real situation to Israel and that Israel regarded this event as a great and decisive turning-point in its history. Under the impact of this event the deuteronomistic historian described the history of his people, on the basis of the sources available to him, as a history of constantly repeated and increasing disobedience, leading to this culminating event[2]. The threatening prophecies of the 8th and 7th centuries seemed to be fulfilled in this event; the divine judgement that had been foretold had now come to pass.

In fact, whilst the end of the kingdom of Judah was no epoch-making event of world-historical importance—in Nebuchadnezzar's inscriptions it is not even considered worth mentioning at all—it was important for Israel from several points of view. It meant the end of the last remnant of political independence on the soil of Israel. Admittedly, for one and a half centuries, apart from a few brief intervals, Judah had merely been a dependent vassal state

---

[1] Cf. A. Alt in *Festschrift Otto Procksch* (1934), pp. 5 ff.= *Kleine Schriften zur Geschichte des Volkes Israel*, II (1953), pp. 316 ff.

[2] Cf. M. Noth, *Überlieferungsgeschichtliche Studien*, I (1943), pp. 100 ff.

within the dominions of various oriental powers, and it had included only a small part of the Israelite tribes. But it had at any rate had its own king and its own administrative system, and therefore a political life of its own, albeit somewhat restricted; with various opportunities of cultivating and safeguarding its life and existence with its own resources. It was still possible to hope that this small and limited residue of independence might some time become the basis of a restoration of Israelite independence; and the successes of king Josiah not so long ago had shown that the hope was not entirely groundless. This hope had now vanished completely. Above all, the Davidic monarchy had now disappeared in Jerusalem, with the promise and the hope that had been attached to it. It is true that the deported Davidite Jehoiachin lived for a time, though only as a prisoner of the emperor in Babylon; and it is highly probable that all kinds of hopes of revival were connected with his person, both among the Israelites remaining in the old Palestinian homeland and among the scattered exiles. But in the end Jehoiachin died, as the Deuteronomist specifically reports at the end of his work (2 Kings xxv, 27-30), without any of the hopes that had been placed in him having been fulfilled. The Israelite tribes now merely formed a subject population in various provinces, which were governed by the king's representatives; and even though the deputy-governor of the province of Judah may have continued to be a Judaean, he was, all the same, an official of the emperor and as such responsible in every respect to the emperor.

The institution of the monarchy had now come to an end on the soil of Israel. Viewed from the standpoint of the whole of Israel's history, it had merely been an episode. It had only emerged when the Israelite tribes had already lived united in a sacral confederation for more than two hundred years on the soil of Palestine; and as an independent institution it had not lasted longer than a mere two and a half centuries in the two kingdoms of Judah and Israel; for one and a half centuries all that remained was the vassal monarchy in the kingdom of Judah. For more than four centuries Israel then continued without a king and without a political life of its own. After its rapid and extraordinary rise in the age of David and Solomon, the monarchy had soon become a factor leading to decay and had involved Israel in the quarrels of the minor states of Syria-Palestine and drawn her into mostly unhappy altercations with the great powers which intervened. Its disappearance did not mean the end of Israel, just as its emergence had not represented the beginning of the history of Israel. But a return to the state of affairs before the formation of the kingdom was no longer possible in Israel.

It is true that the Israelite tribes continued together in their basic stock on the soil of Palestine. But they were no longer free tribes, as they once had been, with the task and opportunity of consolidation in their own hands. They had become absorbed in the great and varied company of subject-peoples of a foreign power. What held them together and marked them off from others, was their faith which they clearly still had the opportunity of practising in religious observances. Admittedly, the ancient tribal relic of the Ark, which had formed the sacred centre of the tribal confederation, had been destroyed. But the Ark had probably long since receded into the background in public worship and become merely a relic guarded in the sanctuary. The holy place in Jerusalem which the Ark had once made into the religious centre of the tribes, and which had meanwhile acquired an importance of its own, had become more significant. It had become the place where 'Yahweh of hosts dwelt' (Isa. viii, 18) where Yahweh 'caused his name to dwell' (Deut. xii, 11 and elsewhere). It is true that the Temple which Solomon had built on this site had gone up in flames. But the sacredness of the place was not tied to the Temple building. As a ruin it still remained a holy place, it still remained the 'house of Yahweh'. According to Jer. xli, 5, even after the destruction of Jerusalem by the Babylonians, people came from Shechem, Shiloh and Samaria, in other words, from the territory of the tribes that had never belonged to the kingdom of Judah. Without regard to political frontiers, they made their pilgrimage to the sanctuary in Jerusalem as the central sanctuary of the tribes, to make their sacrifice to the 'house of Yahweh'. Religious ceremonies no doubt continued to take place in Jerusalem's holy place, and the tribes remained linked with this place in worship.

The tribes had not, however, remained completely intact. Their upper classes had been deported by the victors. Even though these upper classes had only formed a tiny part of the tribal stock numerically, they had provided the political and intellectual leaders; and that was the very reason why the victors wanted to take and uproot this section. A foreign upper class had been introduced in the four provinces on the soil of the former kingdom of Israel which had brought with it its own intellectual and religious traditions. It is true that in time it became assimilated to the indigenous country population, just as the inhabitants of the

Canaanite city-states which had been incorporated in the kingdoms of Israel and Judah under David had been absorbed by the local population. This meant, however, that the greater part of the Israelite tribes became mixed with a foreign element, and only the tribes in the area of the former kingdom of Judah continued without this foreign element of a new upper class. Their own leading groups had, however, been taken off to more or less remote parts of the empire. Those who had been deported by the Assyrians in the 8th century had long since vanished completely; and only the recently deported Judaean upper class lived together in Babylonia and probably kept up the connection with those who remained behind in their own homeland. The same no doubt applied to the Judaeans who had migrated to neighbouring Lower Egypt after the murder of Gedaliah.

Although the old way of life and the old traditions were maintained to some extent both in Babylonia and Lower Egypt, nevertheless the tribes left behind in the old country continued to be the centre of Israelite history and Israelite life. For them the events of 587 B.C. did not in any way signify the end. The links with Israel's past were preserved here, just as was the worship in the holy place in Jerusalem. The probability is that the deuteronomistic history was written in Palestine[1], where all the sources for the history of Israel contained in literary notes, which the author used in his work, were available. Here, above all, the deuteronomic law continued to be known and applied. The tribes had committed themselves to it in the covenant established by king Josiah, and it played an important part in the Deuteronomist's work as the authoritative formulation of the divine will. It is true that we have no direct information about the Israelite tribes in Palestine for the half century following the fall of Jerusalem, either concerning the outward circumstances and the course of their existence or concerning their inner life. This is an unfortunate gap in our knowledge; for no doubt the reorganisation which took place at the beginning of the Persian period is linked to the situation as it had developed in the interim. Our sources fail us here completely. The only continuous source which we have for the history of Israel up to the end of the monarchs is the deuteronomistic history with the older traditions which it worked over. But this work comes to an end with the fall of Jerusalem; and the very much later historical compilation of the Chronicler, which, in its final section (Ezra/Nehemiah), provides a continuation of the deuteronomistic history in a certain direction,

[1] Cf. M. Noth, *op. cit.* p. 110, note 1.

was able to make use of a few sources for the Persian period but completely ignored the final fifty years of Neo-Babylonian rule because of lack of information and lack of interest. There are no sources outside the Old Testament available for the situation of the tribes in Palestine during the period in question, not only because the Neo-Babylonian monarchy, which was ruling in Syria-Palestine at the time, left behind very few historical records anyway, but also because hardly any events of any importance or any substantial changes took place in the western provinces of the empire which could have had any significance for the empire as a whole. The only question is whether the vassal states of southern Palestine, which were neighbours of the former kingdom of Judah, did not themselves lose their political independence in the Neo-Babylonian period, so that, except for a few Phoenician towns on the coast, the whole of Syria-Palestine was incorporated in the provincial organisation of the empire. Round about the time of the fall of Jerusalem, the states of Ammon, Moab and Edom were still in existence. According to Jer. xl, 14, the then king of Ammon had had a hand in the murder of the Judaean deputy Gedaliah; and Jer. xxvii, 3 provides evidence of the existence of kings in Ammon, Moab and Edom alongside the kings of the Phoenician cities of Tyre and Sidon, at any rate in the 4th year of Zedekiah[1]. These eastern states, however, were evidently not affected by the catastrophe which fell upon the kingdom of Judah. In the first place we do not hear of anything to this effect and, secondly, it is expressly stated in Jer. xl, 11 that in the year 587 B.C. many Judaeans fled to Moab, Ammon and Edom, no doubt because there they were able to escape from the direct clutches of the Babylonians. In the course of time, however, these states too were brought to an end. Unfortunately we have no certain information. All the same a statement by Josephus[2] deserves attention in this connection, according to which, five years after the conquest of Jerusalem (582 B.C.) and in the 23rd year of his reign, Nebuchadnezzar made war on and subjugated the Ammonites and Moabites during a campaign against Coele-Syria[3], following this up with a campaign against Egypt. It is quite impossible to check this information and ascertain precisely where its contents belong historically. But we cannot regard it as impossible and it may mean that the independence of

---

[1] The date given in the present text of Jer. xxvii, 1 has been corrupted and should be altered in accordance with the original text of xxviii, 1.

[2] *Antiq. Iud.* X, 9, 7, §§ 181 f. Niese.

[3] The inscription of Nebuchadnezzar from the *wâdi brîsa* mentioned above on p. 286, note 1 may perhaps be regarded as confirming this.

these states was destroyed presumably because of a revolt against Babylonian sovereignty. In this case only the final fate of the Edomite kingdom remains completely shrouded in darkness. For Israel these events in Ammon, Moab, and possibly in Edom too, meant that she was completely encircled by the dominions of the foreign empire, that Israel now lived in the world of Syria-Palestine inside a complete and coherent provincial system, and that any attempt therefore to change its political situation was unthinkable until such time as the existing order was overthrown by great historical events.

Important though the tribes living in Palestine continued to be for the history of Israel, the fact that parts of Israel were living in other lands far from the homeland also acquired significance. The lands in question were above all Egypt and Babylonia; self-contained groups lived there, keeping together and adhering to the old traditions. Stray individuals who had emigrated for one reason or another or had been driven somewhere or other by the catastrophic historical events, soon became lost; and all the time individuals were no doubt leaving the larger self-contained groups and soon becoming absorbed in the foreign environment. For obvious reasons we rarely hear any more of them[1]. As far as Egypt is concerned, we know hardly anything about the life and fate, in the immediately following period, of those who migrated to Lower Egypt in connection with the catastrophe in Judah. The Lower Egyptian group does not emerge as an important and significant factor until the Hellenistic period. The only reason we refer to them at all in this context is that they had their origin in that migration of a numerically far from large band of Judaeans who did probably keep together. On the other hand, we are comparatively well-informed about the so-called 'Judaean military colony' of Elephantine owing to the discovery of papyri[2] from the island of Elephantine at the lower end of the first cataract of the Nile. The colony consisted of Israelites who had been settled on this island in the Nile by the Pharaohs, with their families, and who

---

[1] In cuneiform documents, especially of the 5th century B.C. (cf. above all *The Babylonian Expedition of the University of Pennsylvania*, Ser. A. Cuneiform Texts, ed. by H. V. Hilprecht, Vols. IX, X, and the University of Pennsylvania, The Museum, *Publications of the Babylonian Section*, Vol. II), we meet numerous Judaean names, particularly in the documents of the great business house of the 'sons of *Murašu*'. These Judaeans had evidently become absorbed in Babylonian life and felt they were part of the Babylonian world.

[2] Edition of the text and (English) translation in A. E. Cowley, *Aramaic Papyri of the Fifth Century B.C.* (1923). German translation of a few important pieces in AOT², pp. 450 ff. Cf. also ANET, pp. 491 f., DOTT, pp. 256-269.

were maintained there as a border force to guard the southern frontier of Egypt. Contrary to the deuteronomic requirement of a single place of worship, they had a temple in Elephantine in which, besides Yahu, two other deities were worshipped, evidently a female deity and apparently a young god—in other words, a triad of deities, like other similar groups of deities known in the ancient Near East[1]. The colonists thus practised a considerably paganised cult of Yahweh, but celebrated the festivals of the ancient Israelite tradition[2] and maintained their connection with Jerusalem[3]. The papyri of Elephantine derive from the 5th century B.C., that is, from the period of Persian rule. But the colony originated in a considerably earlier period, at least as far back as the Neo-Babylonian period. In one of the papyri the colonists say explicitly that their fathers built the temple in Elephantine and that the Persian king Cambyses found this temple already completed when he came to Egypt and subjugated the land to Persian rule[4]. Unfortunately it has not been possible to ascertain the exact date and the circumstances of the foundation of this military colony, and the origin of the curious cult of the three deities, which certainly did not begin in Egypt, but was introduced from somewhere in Syria-Palestine, is still somewhat obscure. In the Neo-Babylonian, and also the Persian period, the military colony of Elephantine was one of the self-contained groups which lived as Israelite outposts far from the homeland, and that is why we have mentioned it in this context. Unlike the Lower Egyptian group about which we know so little, this Upper Egyptian colony did not apparently last very long. We hear nothing more about it after the 5th century. Probably it was scattered and dispersed in the end[5] and disappeared.

The Judaeans who were deported in 598 and 587 B.C. lived in Babylonia; and this Babylonian group played a not unimportant role at the beginning of the Persian era. As was probably also the case in Lower Egypt, the group kept together and so maintained the traditions of their own past, except for a few individuals who

---

[1] Cf. especially the *Pap. Cowley*, No. 22, which provides a list of the taxes for the temple of Elephantine for the year 419 B.C. (brief extract from this in AOT², pp. 453 f., ANET, p. 491). The three deities are named here as יהו, ענתביתאל and אשמביתאל.

[2] According to *Pap. Cowley*, No. 21 (AOT², p. 453; TIG, p. 73, ANET, p. 491, DOTT, pp. 258-260) at any rate the feast of Passover and unleavened bread was celebrated from the 14th (15th) to the 21st of the month of Nisan.

[3] Cf. above all the letter sent by the colony to the governor of Judah in Jerusalem in the year 408 B.C. (*Pap. Cowley*. No. 30 [AOT², pp. 450 ff., ANET, p. 492, DOTT, pp. 260-265.])

[4] Thus *Pap. Cowley*, No. 30, ll. 13 f. (AOT², p. 451).

[5] *Pap. Cowley*, No. 30, ll. 4 ff., already reports on the attacks by the neighbouring Egyptians on the colony and the destruction of its temple.

gradually became absorbed in the new environment. We have all kinds of information about the Babylonian groups which shows that they cultivated and continued the traditions of their fathers. Admittedly, the importance of this group must not be exaggerated. The Chronicler, basing himself on a conception of legitimacy which is understandable in the context of his own age, and in very marked antithesis to the Samaritan schism[1], so portrayed the course of events as to suggest that the real history of Israel after the fall of Jerusalem may be traced by way of the 'Babylonian exile' of the Judaeans and the later return of these 'exiles' to the province of Judah. This view of things, which has become traditional under the influence of the Chronicler, is one-sided. Certain though it is that very important developments in life and thought took place among those deported to Babylon, which were to influence the whole later history of Israel, nevertheless even the Babylonian group represented a mere outpost, whereas Palestine was and remained the central arena of Israel's history, and the descendants of the old tribes who remained in the land, with the holy place of Jerusalem, constituted not only numerically the great mass but also the real nucleus of Israel.

There is some information about the life of the exiles in Babylonia in the early period in the book of Ezekiel. Even if, contrary to the later tradition, the prophet's warnings from the period before the fall of Jerusalem were probably spoken in Jerusalem, he was presumably one of those deported to Babylonia in 587 B.C. In any case, the book of Ezekiel was edited in Babylonia from the standpoint of conditions there; and so it is a source of information on the mode of life of the exiles. It shows very clearly that the exiles were not 'prisoners' but represented a compulsorily transplanted subject population who were able to move about freely in their daily life, but were presumably compelled to render compulsory labour service. The exiles had villages where they 'dwelt' (Ezek. iii, 15); they were able to build houses and plant gardens there and enjoy their produce. They were able to marry and give in marriage (Jer. xxix, 5 f.). The book of Ezekiel is familiar with the exiles mainly in the region of the 'river Chebar' (Ezek. i, 1, 3 and elsewhere), the *nāru kabaru*, one of the canals which traversed the deep alluvial land of the lower Euphrates and Tigris and irrigated its fertile soil[2]. One of the places inhabited by the deportees was

---

[1] Cf. M. Noth, *Überlieferungsgeschichtliche Studien*, I (1943), pp. 174 ff.

[2] These are the 'waters of Babylon' which are referred to in Ps. cxxxvii, 1 as a typical feature of the Babylonian landscape.

Tel-abib (Ezek. iii, 15)[1]; a few other names of settlements of exiles in Babylonia are mentioned in Ezra ii, 59 = Neh. vii, 61. The exiles were able to meet together, and they gladly met whenever someone wanted to sing or speak to them (cf. Ezek. xxxiii, 30-33). They felt strangers in this new land. For them it was a 'strange land' (Ps. cxxxvii, 4), an 'impure' land (cf. Ezek. iv, 13), in other words, a land where it was impossible for them to practise their cult. Their cult was bound up with their old homeland and, according to the deuteronomic requirement, linked specifically with the holy place of Jerusalem; and so they yearned for Jerusalem which they could not forget (Ps. cxxxvii, 5 f.).

The result of this separation from religious observances was that certain traditional customs acquired importance as tokens of their unity with their own past and with the tribes in their old homeland and at the same time as signs of their belonging together. These customs were not necessarily connected with the actual cult and had been practised hitherto without having any particular weight attached to them. First of all there was the custom of Sabbath rest on every seventh day, a very old custom, the origin and original meaning of which cannot now be discovered with any certainty. Among the exiles the observance of the Sabbath now became an expression of the old faith and a mark of separation from the foreign environment; for fundamentally the Sabbath was not in itself really a festival-day to be marked by cultic observances, but a kind of 'tabu day' which could be observed without religious ceremonial. The book of Ezekiel refers repeatedly to the 'sabbaths of Yahweh' as a 'sign (of unity) between Yahweh and his faithful' which is to be 'kept holy' and not 'profaned' (xx, 12 ff.; xxii, 8, 26; xxiii, 38). Presumably the custom of circumcision acquired a similar importance in the same situation. On the other hand, it is not mentioned in the book of Ezekiel and it may therefore only have become important later on. It had been generally practised in the Syrian-Palestinian area in which Israel had lived hitherto, as it was also in Egypt. Only the Philistines, the 'uncircumcised' had seemed foreigners among Israel's neighbours. It could not therefore be a distinguishing mark in this region. From very ancient times, however, this custom appears to have been unknown in Mesopotamia, and in this *milieu* it could and was bound to become a 'sign', a 'token of the covenant betwixt me (God) and you' (Gen. xvii, 11). It is therefore probable, though it is impossible to prove,

[1] The name Tel-abib is probably a native place-name which the exiles altered to suit their own pronunciation.

that the custom of circumcision which was not religious in the narrower sense and was not in any case tied to one particular place of worship, acquired the significance among the exiles in Babylonia which it later assumed beyond their immediate sphere. In the course of time the influence of this group became important inasmuch as the customs which had become significant in their special situation acquired great weight for the whole of Israel. The latest stratum of the great Pentateuch tradition, the so-called Priestly Code, connects the Sabbath with the creation of the world (Gen. ii, 3) and makes circumcision a 'token' of the 'covenant' between God and Abraham which was fundamental for the history of Israel (Gen. xvii, 11). It is hardly possible to prove, or even to do more than indicate as probable, that the Priestly Code was written in the midst of the exiles in Babylonia. The strong emphasis on the observances of the Sabbath and circumcision presupposes that these customs had acquired fundamental importance throughout Israel; and, on the other hand, owing to the Priestly Code and the Pentateuch which was based on it, they assumed great prominence throughout Israel.

Altogether Israel's situation had become more and more difficult in every respect since the intervention of the Assyrians in the middle of the 8th century B.C.; and after the loss of the last remnant of political independence in the year 587 B.C., the external situation was well nigh hopeless. Israel was now completely at the mercy of world historical events, bereft of almost all chance of independent action in the maintenance and safeguarding of its life; and this was true of the tribes remaining in Palestine as well as the groups living in Egypt and Babylonia. Fundamentally, Israel now lived on the traditions of the past. The backward glance to its previous history and traditions filled its whole life; it held on to whatever things it was possible to hold on to, and it was these things which now assumed particular significance. These traditions were, however, so rich in content that they were able to survive and keep the separated parts connected with the whole. Israel had shared with all the peoples in Syria-Palestine the fate of losing its political independence, and the partial dispersal and deportation of its upper class. But so far as we know, none of these peoples was able to preserve the idiosyncrasy of its character and way of life as did Israel, whose uniqueness now led to this historically concrete result. The traditions to which Israel looked back, also contained, however, a reference to the future. In the midst of the annihilating events of the past one and a half centuries, the prophets of the 8th and 7th centuries had not only spoken their warning of the judgement of God—imminent and indeed already in operation—but at the same time they had occasionally spoken of God's further plans for Israel. It may be that, under the immediate impact of the final catastrophe, it was difficult to keep alive any hope in a future restoration, and that very many were unable to believe in it any longer. And yet this hope did not die even when outward circumstances were most oppressive. Perhaps these very circumstances revived it more and more. And the hope in a new future which had been promised, no doubt helped to keep Israel together and maintain its awareness of its particularity among the many peoples of the great world empire. It needed the reasonable prospect of a fundamental change in the world historical situation to fan the glimmering fire of hope into life again.

CHAPTER II

THE RULE OF THE PERSIANS AND MACEDONIANS

25. *The Re-establishment of the Sanctuary and the Cultus in Jerusalem*

THE Neo-Babylonian empire did not last long. It declined rapidly after the death of Nebuchadnezzar in the year 562 B.C. Its last king Nabonidus (*Nabū-nā'id*), who came to the throne in 555 B.C., was a strange character who allowed the political organisation to decay, and fell out with the priests of the imperial god Marduk in Babylon. But meanwhile events were taking place in the near-by Iranian highlands which were soon to have a decisive influence on the history of the whole ancient Orient. The power of the Medes had earlier contributed in a decisive manner to the collapse of the Assyrian empire; and as the fruit of their victory they had acquired the northern part of the Assyrian realm as an addition to their Median motherland, and had extended their rule over Armenia and the mountains of Asia Minor westwards as far as the river Halys. In the south-east they had subjugated the Persian rulers of the house of Achaemenes, who ruled over ancient Elam[1]. The latter were responsible for the fall of the Medes about the middle of the 6th century B.C. In alliance with the Neo-Babylonian king Nabonidus, who feared the military strength of the Median empire in his vicinity, the Achaemenid Cyrus overthrew the Median king Astyages, with the support of certain circles among the Median nobility who rebelled against the despotic rule of their own king. Cyrus allowed himself to be made king of the Medes and Persians by the Median and Persian nobility and assumed the government of the great Iranian empire in the Median capital of Ecbatana. Babylonia now saw the still more dangerous Persian monarchy arising in its vicinity in place of the dreaded Median monarchy. To begin with, it is true, Cyrus extended his power farther to the west and east. His western neighbour was the Lydian kingdom in the western

[1] Cf. P. J. Junge, *Dareios I, König der Perser* (1944), pp. 14 ff.

part of Asia Minor which arose at the beginning of the 7th century B.C., the first power of any size to emerge on the soil of Asia Minor since the collapse of the Hittite empire. The proverbially rich king Croesus of Lydia was a contemporary of Cyrus. When the overthrow of the Median monarchy at the hands of Cyrus had upset the stability of Iran, Croesus attacked the kingdom of the Medes and Persians, but was utterly defeated by Cyrus in 546 B.C. and lost his kingdom to the king of the Persians, whose power extended henceforward as far as the western coast of Asia Minor. When Cyrus had subjugated the broad territories to the east of Iran he held an extraordinary wealth of power in his hands.

It was inevitable that these events should be followed with very great anxiety in the Neo-Babylonian empire. But the subject peoples had good reason to hope for the imminent collapse of Neo-Babylonian power. The Judaeans who had been deported to Babylonia looked with great expectation to the victorious and powerful Cyrus. It is therefore not surprising that the prophet whose name is unknown and who is called 'Deutero-Isaiah' (Isa. xl-lv), who at this time foretold a new and imminent intervention of the God of Israel as the one divine Lord of all history, thus continuing the older prophecy of the 8th and 7th centuries, incorporated Cyrus in his prophecy as the king empowered by God with government as the instrument of God, and even occasionally mentioned him by name (Isa. xliv, 28; xlv, 1), and that he foretold the imminent fall of Babylon quite plainly (Isa. xlvii). It is unfortunately impossible to decide whether Deutero-Isaiah, who was no doubt one of those deported to Babylonia, based his prophetic words on the historical events in near-by Iran or whether, on the basis of the prophetic tradition, he proceeded from eschatological expectations of the coming of the kingdom of God and a revival of Israel and then incorporated the person of the victorious Cyrus in these expectations[1]. It may be taken for granted, anyway, that his words were gladly listened to by the exiles in Babylonia and powerfully kindled their hopes for a change in their affairs.

In fact Cyrus's expected attack on the Neo-Babylonian empire followed quite soon. After Cyrus had extended his power in various directions to the limits of his horizon, the only power left for him to subjugate was the Neo-Babylonian empire with its dominion over Mesopotamia and Syria-Palestine. He no doubt knew that he was far superior to this power and that he only needed to attack it to overthrow it quickly. He turned against Nabonidus in the year

[1] Cf. J. Begrich, *Studien zu Deuterojesaja* (1938).

539 B.C. He gave orders to one of his high officials, Gobryas, to attack him. Nabonidus was defeated in a pitched battle, and, soon after, the victors occupied the city of Babylon, which Nebuchadnezzar had developed brilliantly and on a grand scale as the royal seat of the Neo-Babylonian empire. Cyrus then entered the ancient and famous city, welcomed as liberator by the priests of Marduk and by many Babylonians who were dissatisfied with the government of Nabonidus. The Neo-Babylonian empire thereby devolved upon him. Mesopotamia will have submitted to him without difficulty and Syria-Palestine will also have recognised the mighty victor without any further ado, even though, as far as we know, he did not appear there with his army. After his son and successor, Cambyses, had subjugated Egypt to Persian rule in the year 525 B.C., the whole area of the ancient Orient was combined in one empire, which far exceeded the size of even the Neo-Assyrian empire, which at the time of its greatest power in the first half of the 7th century had represented the hitherto most far-reaching power in the whole history of the ancient Orient. Israel, both the part which remained in the old homeland and the groups living far away from home, was now in the hands of one emperor.

But the foundation of the Persian Empire signified more than a mere change of sovereign and a further concentration of power. In contrast to their Assyrian and Babylonian predecessors, the Persian kings adopted a fundamentally different policy in their treatment of the numerous subject-peoples in the empire—and this was to become important for Israel too. Their predecessors had tried to secure their authority as far as possible by uprooting and putting under tutelage the indigenous peoples in the subjugated areas, and, by deporting the upper classes, forming a uniform mass of subjects within the empire, over which in the provinces the authority of the ruling people was organised with the emperor at its head. Above all, they introduced the official religion—at any rate in the provincial capitals—alongside the local religions, though they continued to tolerate these. The Persian kings, however, respected the traditions and character of the subject-peoples, but certainly not out of benevolent tolerance. Needless to say, they kept the real power in their own hands. It remained concentrated in the person of the king; and the leading officials of the empire—after the division into satrapies, introduced by Darius I, they were satraps with great authority—were Persians in every part of the far-flung empire. Nevertheless, it was a principle of official Persian policy, adopted no doubt in their own interest, not only to allow but even to com-

mand their subjects to develop their own life within the limits
dictated by the necessities of imperial politics. This is shown by the
official regulation of the language question in an empire which
embraced so many peoples. The great monumental inscriptions
which have survived from the first Achaemenian kings, are in three
languages; they are written in a Babylonian version as well as in
ancient Persian and in Elamite[1], and all three are in the cuneiform
script which derives from Mesopotamia[2]. Hitherto the emperors of
the ancient Orient had only had their inscriptions written in their
own language, the language of the nation in power at the time.
The fact that the Achaemenian inscriptions were in three languages
put the subjugated peoples on a level with the victors, at any rate
in this respect. In official correspondence within the empire, however, even more official languages were permitted according to
local conditions, and these were also used in correspondence with
the central government. Thus Aramaic was regarded as the official
language throughout Syria-Palestine and in Egypt. Aramaic had
been fairly widespread as a spoken language in central and northern
Syria, and along the middle course of the Euphrates, since the
Aramaean tribes had occupied the land towards the end of the 2nd
millennium B.C., and had also come to be written more and more
in the alphabetic script deriving from the Canaanite world. In the
final period of the Neo-Assyrian empire, it had penetrated into
originally non-Aramaean regions in Mesopotamia and also in
Syria-Palestine and Egypt as a commercial language, not, to begin
with, as a spoken vernacular, but at any rate as an international
language which was understood by royal officials and scribes, and
by merchants, and which could be written and read by reason of
the simple alphabetic script[3]. By the very nature of things it was

[1] Elam had been subject to their dominion even before the great rise of Persian power.

[2] Cf. F. H. Weissbach, *Die Keilinschriften der Achämeniden* (1911).

[3] Cf. above all 2 Kings xviii, 26, according to which already at the end of the 8th
century B.C.—provided that the prophetic legend in question has not anachronistically
in mind the conditions of a period about a century later—whilst the people in Jerusalem
could not yet speak Aramaic, the ministers of the Judaean kings as well as the high
Assyrian officer and official who was besieging Jerusalem at the time were able to. As
far as the latter is concerned, we may leave it aside—the narrative presupposes somewhat naïvely that he was also able to speak 'Judaean'—but this passage is certainly
typical of the situation in Syria-Palestine towards the end of the Assyrian period. In this
connection the letter of a south Palestinian ruler found in *saḳḳāra* in Egypt in 1942—
his name and the name of his residence have unfortunately not been preserved in the
fragmentary text—is very significant. It is addressed to the Egyptian Pharaoh in the
period of Neo-Babylonian rule, and is written in Aramaic, which was not the mother-
tongue either of the writer or, still less, of the addressee. (The text in H. L. Ginsberg,
BASOR, 111 [1948], p. 25.) Aramaic written in alphabetic script was used at this period
for international correspondence, like the Babylonian which was written in cuneiform
script in the Amarna period.

the only language that could be used as an official language in a major part of the Persian empire and Syria-Palestine and Egypt because it was already so widespread. The official use of Aramaic in the south-western parts of the Persian Empire had an important influence on the development of this language. It not only promoted the further advance of Aramaic as a spoken vernacular—in Syria-Palestine it almost completely drove out the older Canaanite dialects in the course of time—but at the same time a particular form of language was developed in official correspondence, and a particular orthography, the so-called 'Imperial Aramaic'[1] which was the basis of the further development of the Aramaic dialects.

Even more important, however, than this consideration for the national life of the many peoples living in the empire in the matter of language, was the attitude of the Persian government to traditional local religions. This was a sphere which the subject peoples inevitably felt to be particularly closely bound up with their very being, and the importance of which was only enhanced by their political tutelage. The Persian kings treated this matter with particular care, no doubt with the intention of thereby reconciling their subjects to their sovereignty. By means of this wise policy they strove, certainly not without success, to strengthen their empire. We have some remarkable evidence from various sources on this point. After his entry into Babylon, Cyrus revived the local religions in Mesopotamia, restoring to their traditional places the divine images which the last Neo-Babylonian king Nabonidus had arbitrarily moved to the city of Babylon, thereby presenting himself in marked contrast to Nabonidus, as protector of the ancient religious traditions[2]. Cambyses too, the son and successor of Cyrus (529–522 B.C.) who succeeded in bringing Egypt into subjection to Persian rule, and who made himself hated on account of his despotic and brutal nature, followed basically the same line; and from Egypt itself, the conquest of which was accompanied by all kinds of cruelty and senseless destruction, we have evidence that Cambyses respected the religious traditions, and, where necessary, restored them. He not only added an Egyptian throne name to his own as king of Egypt, in accordance with the traditions of the land, he also turned his attention to the ancient cult of the goddess Neith in the Delta city of Sais—which had been the home of the

---

[1] On this concept cf. H. H. Schaeder, *Iranische Beiträge*, I (Schriften der Königsberger Gelehrten Gesellschaft, geisteswiss. Kl. VI, 5 [1930]), pp. 27 ff.; the same, *Esra der Schreiber* (1930), p. 41.

[2] Cf. the so-called Cyrus-cylinder (Weissbach, *op. cit.* pp. 2 ff.; AOT², pp. 368 ff.; TGI, pp. 70 ff.; ANET, pp. 315 f., DOTT, pp. 92-94, Pl. 6), ll. 33 ff.

last Egyptian dynasty abolished by him—and which he probably considered the capital. According to the inscription of Uzahor[1], in response to the latter's representations, he removed the foreign elements which had meanwhile infiltrated into the shrine of Neith, saw 'that the Temple was purified', 'that the property of the deity was given to the great mother goddess, Neith, and to the great gods in Sais, as of old', and 'that all festivals and processions were celebrated as of old'. The Israelite colonists on the isle of Elephantine reported, however, that when Cambyses entered Egypt not the slightest damage was done to their temple, whereas the temples of the Egyptian gods were pulled down[2]. Darius endeavoured all the more to preserve and promote the religious traditions of the subject-peoples. The most important evidence of this is the decree which he issued to Gadatas, the Persian administrator of crown lands in the district of Magnesia on the Meander in western Asia Minor, which was cut in stone later, in Roman times, and has therefore come down to us[3]. It is written in Greek, which was probably the official language of the Persian administration in western Asia Minor. This decree is important above all because it speaks of the royal 'attitude to the gods', thereby explicitly characterising the content of the decree as the result of a fundamental attitude to religious institutions and customs. It declares further that this attitude had been handed down by the royal 'forefathers'. Gadatas is threatened with the king's wrath if he does not forthwith cease to disregard this fundamental attitude of the king in that he has imposed a tax on the 'sacred gardeners of Apollo' and compelled them to do secular forced labour; in other words, he has violated the evidently traditional privileges of certain persons connected with the cultus. For the later Achaemenids we have only the evidence of the Passover ordinance of Darius II of the year 419 B.C. which has been found among the papyri of Elephantine[4]. The text, which is unfortunately in a bad state of preservation, contains a decree by the king which was sent to the Persian satrap of Egypt, and orders that the feast of the Passover and unleavened bread shall be celebrated in Elephantine in exact conformity with current regulations. Unfortunately it is not known precisely what occasioned this decree. It is difficult to believe that the Persian govern-

---

[1] Cf. the translation in R. Kittel, *Geschichte des Volkes Israel*, III (1927/29), p. 291, note 1.

[2] *Pap, Cowley*, No. 30 (AOT², pp. 450 ff., ANET, p. 492, DOTT, pp. 262 f.), ll. 13 f.

[3] The Greek text in Ed. Meyer, *Die Entstehung des Judentums* (1896), pp. 19 f.

[4] *Pap. Cowley*, No. 21; cf. AOT², p. 453 and TGI, p. 73, ANET, p. 491, DOTT, pp. 258-260.

ment bothered itself with all the details of the innumerable religions in its great empire. Wherever—as in this latter case and the case of the decree sent to Gadatas—definite abuses were brought to its knowledge in reports or complaints, it will have intervened with very definite official regulations designed to preserve or restore ancient local religious institutions.

In this broad context there belongs also the important decree of Cyrus concerning the rebuilding of the Temple, a decree which was to have such significant consequences. The official Imperial Aramaic text of this decree has come down to us in Ezra vi, 3-5, as part of an official correspondence from the time of Darius I, between the satrap of the great satrapy of 'Beyond the Rivers' which embraced most of Syria-Palestine[1]—this satrap may have resided in Damascus—and the royal court. This correspondence, which is concerned with the question of permission to rebuild the Temple in Jerusalem, consists of the satrap's question as to whether the rebuilding is permissible, and a reply in which Cyrus's basic decree is referred to and quoted verbatim (Ezra v, 6–vi, 12). This correspondence, which was so eminently important for the religious community in Jerusalem, became known by some means or other in Jerusalem and a copy of it was preserved there. Considerably later it was put, with another correspondence referring to the rebuilding of the city of Jerusalem, in a collection of Aramaic documents, provided with a narrative framework. This collection is now to be found in Ezra iv, 6–vi, 18, and was available to the Chronicler as the main source of his presentation of the events in Ezra i-vi[2]. Cyrus's decree dates from the 'first year of king Cyrus'—meaning the first year of his rule over the formerly Neo-Babylonian empire, in other words, the year 538 B.C.—and ordains that 'the house of God in Jerusalem be [re-]built in the place where it is the custom to kill the sacrifices and offer "fire sacrifices" (?)', that is, on the site of the former sanctuary where religious ceremonies had continued to be maintained. The expenditure for the reconstruction was to be met 'from the king's house', that is, from public funds. Finally, the decree ordains the surrender and return to the rebuilt Temple of the valuable fittings of the former royal sanctuary which Nebuchad-

---

[1] The official Aramaic description of the satrapy was עבר נהרא 'Beyond the River (Euphrates)' (as seen from Mesopotamia).

[2] The authenticity of these documents, which has often been doubted and still is occasionally doubted even today, has been very clearly substantiated in detail above all by Ed. Meyer, *Die Entstehung des Judentums* (1896), pp. 8 ff. On the problem of the literary origins of the Aramaic section Ezra iv, (6), 7-vi, 18 and its parts cf. M. Noth, *Überlieferungsgeschichtliche Studien*, I (1943), pp. 151 ff.

nezzar had seized as booty and which had been taken to Babylon and were evidently still there. Cyrus's decree therefore represents an act of reparation, and clearly belongs with the other examples of the restoring of ancient religious institutions in accordance with the policy of the Persian kings.

It may be asked how Cyrus came to bother himself about what he can scarcely have regarded as a very significant local cult on the very confines of his great empire so soon after taking over control of the Neo-Babylonian dominions, in a land which, though it came to him as part of the Neo-Babylonian empire, he never even entered himself. The action was certainly not due to his own initiative. But it is easily conceivable that some of the Judaeans who had been deported to Babylonia and who watched Cyrus's restoration of the ancient religions in Mesopotamia, drew the attention of the Persian court to the fact that a Neo-Babylonian ruler had also destroyed a sanctuary in Jerusalem which ought now to be restored, and that, to prove this, it should still be possible to find the sacred objects which had been stolen as booty from this holy shrine. It was not difficult to discover this evidence in Babylon. But for the exiles, as well as for the tribes who had remained in the land and for other scattered groups of ancient Israel, the restoration of the Temple was a matter of basic importance, for the central federal cult which had been located in Jerusalem for so long was still the centre of an Israel which held fast to its traditions. It is true that the fact that Cyrus did give official instructions for the restoration of the Temple in Jerusalem did not, by any means, signify the fulfilment of the expectations which Deutero-Isaiah had linked to the person of Cyrus as the instrument of God, who was to effect the final decisive change in history, but it showed, nevertheless, that the hope of a fundamental change and improvement in the situation which had been connected with the emergence and approach of Cyrus had not been unwarranted. Some have found it particularly difficult to believe that Cyrus made available public funds for the rebuilding of the Temple, and have used this as an argument against the authenticity of the decree quoted in Ezra vi, 3-5. But it was in line with the policy of promoting the local religions to give state financial aid where necessary. In the present case there was a special reason to do so; Nebuchadnezzar had destroyed and robbed the Temple, and so Cyrus, as the heir of Neo-Babylonian rule, who was deliberately adopting a different policy in religious matters, had good cause to make amends for the wrong done by Nebuchadnezzar, and, in addition, the Temple was a former royal sanctuary, the care of which now devolved on the Persian emperor as the legal successor of the former Judaean kings. But if Cyrus made himself responsible for the cost of restoring the Temple, it was only fitting that he should also give some general directives on the style of the new building (Ezra vi, 4a).

Cyrus's decree refers exclusively to the restoration of the sanctuary. Later on, in his story of the new beginning after the 'exile', the Chronicler gave a paraphrase of his own in Hebrew (Ezra i, 2-4), on the basis of the text with which he was familiar, connecting with the order for the restoration of the Temple a granting of freedom of return to the exiles. Since he thought of the ancient homeland, and, in particular, the city of Jerusalem as an almost uninhabited ruin, he was probably bound to conclude that Cyrus made available the forces needed for the restoration work and allowed those exiles to return home who offered their services for the work. His view was that only a tiny residue of country folk (cf. 2 Kings xxv, 12) had stayed in Palestine and that only the foreign upper class had remained in the provinces of the former kingdom of Israel. According to him, however, none of these elements took part in the sacred work of rebuilding the Temple. For him the legitimate line of Israel's history was represented by the Judaeans who had been deported to Babylonia, many of whom had to return to the homeland if a restoration of the Temple was to be feasible. He therefore supplemented the original text of Cyrus's decree in the way that seemed to him objectively necessary and historically appropriate. In fact there is no mention in Cyrus's decree of a repatriation of the exiles. It was not necessitated by the rebuilding of the Temple, since the main body of the tribes had remained in the land and had continued to hold religious services in the holy place even after Nebuchadnezzar's destruction of the Temple. They could now undertake the restoration. It may be that some of the exiles did then return to Jerusalem and the land of Judah, and that the Persians did not put any obstacles in their way; but the number who returned was presumably not very large, particularly as conditions in the land, with so many towns and villages destroyed and not yet rebuilt, and the city of Jerusalem itself still very largely in ruins, can hardly have been very inviting[1].

How far from encouraging the situation actually was, in spite of

[1] In Ezra ii, 1-67 (69) = Neh. vii, 6-69 (71) we have a long list, of which it is uncertain whether the Chronicler himself used it as traditional source material or whether it was inserted at a later date. It is introduced as a list of exiles returning home; but it is impossible to decide whether that is what it really represents or when the return of the people listed took place. On this list cf. now K. Galling, JBL, 70 (1951), pp. 149 ff.

Cyrus's decree, is shown by the pathetically slow progress of the work itself. Cyrus had to issue a special order to get his decree enforced. According to the information of the elders in Jerusalem and Judah, which was used in the above-mentioned communication from the satrap of 'Beyond the River' to Darius I, Cyrus had commissioned a certain Sheshbazzar[1] to take the restored treasures of the Temple back to Jerusalem and to take charge of the rebuilding, and this Sheshbazzar had at any rate had the foundations of the new building laid (Ezra v, 14-16). Sheshbazzar is described as a 'governor'[2] installed by Cyrus (Ezra v, 14). Yet it is not easy to say what official position he held. Was he governor of the province of Judah, which had existed as an independent province or had been reconstituted; or was he subordinate governor of the special district of Judah which came under the provincial administration of Samaria? Or was he perhaps not the holder of a normal office of governor at all, but merely a special agent charged with returning the Temple fittings and the restoration of the Temple in accordance with the instructions described in Ezra v, 15?[3] It is impossible to give a decisive answer. All that is known for certain is that Cyrus in fact gave a definite commission for the execution of his decree. Nor do we know who Sheshbazzar was. His Babylonian name shows that he was not a Persian official. As it is not clear why a Babylonian should be given the commission, it is usual to think—and probably rightly—that he was a deported Judaean who, like others of his kind in Babylonia, had been given a Babylonian name[4] and for some reason or other seemed to the Persian government to be a suitable person for this task. It is idle to attempt to identify him with any other known personality[5], such as the Shenazzar mentioned in 1 Chron. iii, 18, who appears fourth in the list of sons of the exiled Judaean king Jehoiachin[6]. Conceivable though it is that a Davidite was entrusted by the Persians with the execution of the royal decree concerning the rebuilding of the

[1] This form reproduces the Babylonian name *Šamaššapla-uṣur*. The Chronicler mentions Sheshbazzar in Ezra i, 7-11 in connection with the list—authentic or invented—of the restored treasures of the Temple which he includes (cf. on Ezra i, 7-11 K. Galling, ZDPV, 60 [1937], pp. 177-183) and of his own accord he gives him the title 'Prince of Judah'.

[2] The Hebrew-Aramaic פחה is not entirely clear, and could describe a Persian satrap or a provincial governor. [3] On the latter sense see Galling, *op. cit.* p. 179.

[4] Cf. for example Zerubbabel who will be mentioned later, and also Dan. i, 7, and M. Noth, *Die israelitischen Personennamen* (1928), p. 63.

[5] The Chronicler does not appear to distinguish him from Zerubbabel, since he tacitly has Sheshbazzar's instructions carried out by Zerubbabel (Ezra iii, 1 ff.).

[6] Thus, above all, Ed. Meyer, *op. cit.* pp. 75 ff., and latterly E. Sellin, *Geschichte des israelitisch-jüdischen Volkes*, II (1932), pp. 83 f.

Temple, there is no real case for identifying Sheshbazzar with Shenazzar[1]. It is better to accept the fact that all we know about the person of Sheshbazzar is the little contained in Ezra v, 14-16.

The foundations of the new Temple were laid without delay. But then the work came to a standstill. The reasons may be inferred from the prophetic sayings in Hag. i, 1-11. The situation in Jerusalem and in the surrounding country was so bad, and therefore so discouraging, that no one could muster any enthusiasm for the work of rebuilding the sanctuary, and even the royal ordinance that the work was to be paid for out of public funds did not suffice as an incentive to start operations. It was said: 'The time has not come that Yahweh's house should be built' (Hag. i, 2). People were still far too preoccupied with their own troubles and worries and 'every man was busy only with his own house' (Hag. i, 9). There were, it is true, people who were already living in 'panelled houses' (Hag. i, 4), but probably they were few in number and Jerusalem was still very largely a ruined city where many people were pitifully housed, and in the villages of the countryside things were no better. On top of all this there was a drought (Hag. i, 10 f.) and in its train bad harvests (Hag. i, 6) to make the inhabitants concentrate all the more on their own personal afflictions. Thus the foundations remained untouched and the work presumably soon came to a complete standstill.

A new impulse was needed to bring about a change. It was provided once again from great historical events. Sixteen years after the Cyrus decree and after the first start at rebuilding the Temple, the Persian king Cambyses died (522 B.C.) without leaving a son to succeed him. The monarchy thereby devolved on another line of the house of Achaemenes, on Darius, the son of Hystaspes, who had been a member of Cambyses' immediate entourage until the latter's death in Syria. But before Darius was able to take over, he had first of all to overcome numerous dangerous risings which broke out in many parts of the empire after the death of Cambyses. Cambyses had had a younger brother named Bardiya, who, unlike Cambyses, had not been born until after Cyrus's accession to the throne and thus, as a royal prince, enjoyed wide esteem. Before embarking on the conquest of Egypt, Cambyses had secretly had this brother killed as a dangerous rival. After the death of Cambyses a man called Gaumata passed himself off as this brother,

[1] If manuscripts of the Septuagint seem to suggest the likelihood of this identity of names, what has happened is either that the names have inadvertently been distorted or, possibly, the two names have been intentionally approximated to one another.

who had allegedly not been killed at all, assumed the name Bardiya and usurped the Persian throne. He found many supporters, above all in the central parts of the empire, in Media-Persia as well as in Mesopotamia, and at the same time various parts of the empire took the opportunity of regaining their former independence. For a whole year Darius overcame his enemies in unremitting, intense, but on the whole successful, battles, and subjugated the rebellious areas, until in the end, towards the end of the year 521 B.C., he was able to regard his position as sole ruler as fundamentally secure[1].

The shock that went through the great empire in that year revived in Israel the expectation of the last decisive crisis in history which the prophets had foretold. Even though Syria-Palestine was not directly involved in the disturbances of the time, the course of events was watched with excitement, and the excitement continued even after the situation in the Persian empire had become stable again. In the second half of the year 520 B.C. the prophet Haggai spoke in Jerusalem, and at the beginning of the year 519 B.C. the prophet Zechariah had the nocturnal visions recorded in Zech. i, 7–vi, 15.[2] Both prophets were awaiting the coming of God's reign which was heralded by the historical confusions of the time. For both of them it was important in this connection that, in view of the impending events, the Temple in Jerusalem should at last be rebuilt and completed. They were unable to conceive the presence of God except in relation to a holy place—in this cultic interest they were unlike the earlier prophets of the 8th and 7th centuries. Therefore Haggai in particular urged the resumption of work on the Temple. The difficulties of the time—he argued, as against the general opinion—did not in any way prohibit the work of restoration: on the contrary, these very troubles were themselves the divine punishment for the delay in resuming the work (Hag. i, 1-11). And if the shabbiness of the new building—compared with the splendour of the former royal shrine of David, which old people in Jerusalem had seen with their own eyes in their youth—took all pleasure from the work of reconstruction, it should be remembered that every nation would soon be bringing its treasures to this house of God, once the Kingdom of God had dawned (Hag. i, 15b and ii, 1-9). In fact, by his insistence, Haggai brought about the resumption of work on the Temple towards the end of the year 520

---

[1] Cf. now P. J. Junge, *Dareios I König der Perser* (1944), pp. 43 ff., which is based on the great Darius inscription on the rock of Behistun (illustrated in the *Westminster Historical Atlas to the Bible* [1945], p. 9).

[2] For a different chronological estimate and historical interpretation of Zechariah's night-visions see now K. Galling, *Vetus Testamentum*, 2 (1952), pp. 18-36.

B.C. (Hag. i, 12-14). In one of his visions Zechariah saw the high priest being purged and dedicated to the service of the new sanctuary (Zech. iii, 1 ff.).

At the time the Davidite Zerubbabel was 'governor' in Jerusalem. He was a grandson of the king Jehoiachin, a son of the latter's first-born son Shealtiel[1]. He was appointed as a Persian official and acted as provincial governor in Judah or as subordinate governor under the governor of the province of Samaria. According to Hag. i, 1 ff., it was Zerubbabel in particular whom the prophet reminded of the need for the rebuilding of the Temple, and according to Hag. i, 12 he did in fact take up the work. But very much more far-reaching hopes were associated with him. Should not he, the scion of the House of David, presumably even in the line of the first-born, and at the moment the leading man in Jerusalem and Judah, albeit for the time being only an official of the Empire, be the future king in a renewed Davidic empire as occasionally foretold by the prophets of the 8th and 7th centuries? In fact Haggai and Zechariah saw the figure of Zerubbabel more or less clearly in this light. In face of the imminent shaking of the whole world, Haggai addresses him as the signet chosen by Yahweh (ii, 20-23), meaning probably that in the Kingdom of God Zerubbabel would be God's representative on earth. In vi, 9-14, however, Zechariah speaks of a divine commission which came to him to prepare a crown and to set it on the head of Zerubbabel as the future king[2]. This is a unique case of prophets referring the expectation of a future 'Messiah' to an already existing historical figure, and it is clear from this with what feverish excitement men were looking for an impending and final change in the historical situation. We do not learn the extent of the influence exerted by the prophetic vision expressed by Haggai and Zechariah and the hope centred in Zerubbabel, but it is easy to imagine that impatience and excitement were great in Jerusalem itself and probably among the tribes in the countryside too.

We know nothing about the outcome of this affair. When Haggai and Zechariah were speaking, Darius I had the empire firmly in his hands again; and it was soon bound to become clear that the disturbances that followed the death of Cambyses had not been 'the beginning of the sufferings' (Mark xiii, 8) of the eschatological

---

In Haggai (and also in Ezra) Shealtiel is always referred to as father. This is probably correct in contrast to the statement in 1 Chron. iii, 19, according to which Zerubbabel was the son of a younger son of Jehoiachin. The name Zerubbabel is Babylonian (*Zêr-Babili*).

[2] Subsequently the name Zerubbabel was replaced by the name of the priest Joshua in Zech. vi. 11 in view of the historical outcome.

end of time, but only a temporary crisis, that the empire was again rapidly consolidated in the hands of a strong and shrewd ruler and that the course of history resumed its progress on the same line as before. So the hopes that had moved men's minds for a time soon had to be abandoned as false. Outwardly this movement probably did not make much impact or find expression in concrete action. It is possible that the Persian power, now firmly re-established, did not have to intervene. There had been no open revolt against their sovereignty. Possibly, too, nothing further happened to Zerubbabel in spite of the hopes that had centred in him. At any rate, we do not hear of anything happening to him, though it must be remembered that, apart from the fairly late commentary on the Aramaic documents in the book of Ezra, there is no Old Testament tradition from which one might have expected any information on the matter. Perhaps Zerubbabel continued as governor or subordinate governor in Judah. Perhaps, on the other hand, if the internal happenings in Jerusalem and Judah had become known to the governor of Samaria and the satrap of Beyond the River and hence to the Persian court, he was recalled as a somewhat dangerous official and replaced with a successor. The whole affair was clearly of no great importance to the Persian authorities.

This is clear from the fact that Darius gave express permission for work on the completion of the Temple in Jerusalem to be continued. The most important historical result of the eschatological hopes of the first years of Darius's reign had been the resumption of work on the rebuilding of the sanctuary. Admittedly, this work, and this only, was contested by the satrap of Beyond the River; he had enquiries made in Jerusalem and sent in a report·to Darius with a request for further instructions, and he received a reply from the Persian court. This official correspondence has been preserved in Ezra v, 6–vi, 12. Unfortunately it is not precisely dated, but it undoubtedly derives from the period after the appearance of the prophets Haggai and Zechariah as described in the later framework in Ezra v, 1-5. After all, it was these prophets, and Haggai in particular, who succeeded in getting work on the Temple resumed; and the satrap could not have obtained a report on it until it had been resumed. It is striking that in his report the satrap only passes on the information given by the elders in Jerusalem, in which reference was made above all to Cyrus's decree about the rebuilding of the Temple, without any mention of the movement which proceeded from Haggai and Zechariah and the figure of the governor, Zerubbabel. The Persian authorities took no official cognisance at all of the movement and possibly they never even heard of it. But Darius's reply explicitly confirmed Cyrus's decree on the basis of official investigations, and repeated the instruction contained in the decree that the costs of rebuilding were to be borne by the state, and that even the requirements of the sacrificial cult in this former royal sanctuary, which had earlier been the concern of the Judaean king, were to be provided from state resources (Ezra vi, 8, 9), and that, in return, prayers were to be offered in the new sanctuary 'for the life of the king' (Ezra vi, 10). The ancient character of the building as a state shrine—the elders in Jerusalem had expressly mentioned that 'a great king of Israel' had built the Temple (Ezra v, 11)—was therefore to that extent preserved; and this was entirely in line with the policy of restoring the ancient religious customs, the only difference being that the rights and duties of the earlier kings of the now subject peoples had now been transferred to the Persian monarchy and its great administrative machine.

The impulse that had proceeded from Haggai and Zechariah continued, even though the eschatological hopes behind it inevitably died away for the time being; and so, after Darius had confirmed the Cyrus decree, within a few years the rebuilding of the Temple was completed. According to a statement in Ezra vi, 15 which, belonging to the framework of the Aramaic documents, may be regarded as quite reliable and based on a firm tradition, the rebuilt sanctuary was solemnly consecrated on the third day of the month Adar in the 6th year of Darius's reign, *i.e.* in the spring of the year 515 B.C. Thus Israel again had a religious centre where the traditions of Solomon's Temple could be resumed, and the event was of decisive importance for Israel's future life precisely because it had lost its political independence and many of its people were living away from the homeland. Even if the old sacral confederation of the twelve tribes had continued to exist, not merely as an idea but also expressed in actual forms, during the period of the kings, with Jerusalem, the place of the sacred Ark, as its religious centre[1], nevertheless, as an outward form of Israel's life, it had inevitably been pushed into the background by the various and varied political organisations; and in this period the central sanctuary had been in the first place a royal sanctuary. Political independence and the institution of an independent monarchy had now ceased to exist and the Temple, whose character as a state sanctuary was now

[1] Cf. M. Noth, *Die Gesetze im Pentateuch* (1940), pp. 23 ff.

only apparent in the fact that its restoration had been ordained in a decree issued by the far-off Persian emperor and that in it prayers were offered for this emperor, and that the requirements above all of sacrificial animals for the official rites were met from public resources, had again become the real centre of Israelite life. Israel was now the great religious community centred on this shrine. Among the many peoples embraced by the empire which extended over most of the known world, Israel was marked out and held together by the tradition of the deeds which God had performed on its behalf, by a number of special customs, and, above all, by a common allegiance to the Temple in Jerusalem. This did not mean a return to the former amphictyonic organisation. The tribal system had been, at any rate, greatly relaxed. It is true that substantial parts of the old tribes still lived in their old tribal areas. But in addition to them there were now strong and important groups in Babylonia and Lower Egypt, among whom membership of a particular tribe was soon preserved only as a fiction; and to these groups were added, in the course of time, further larger and smaller groups of scattered Israelites in the wide realms of the Persian empire and even beyond its frontiers. It was impossible to revive the functions of a tribal confederation, which, already limited in many respects since the formation of the monarchy, were bound gradually to decay as a result of the events which took place after the middle of the 8th century. The tribal relic of the Ark no longer existed; all that remained was the holy place which it had formerly occupied and which retained its unique significance as a place of worship. Israel remained gathered round it as a religious community, in the narrower circle of those who had remained in the homeland or had returned thither, and in the wider circle of the Diaspora.

This led to the priestly element in Israel acquiring an importance which it had not had hitherto. The first priest of the Temple in Jerusalem now became the head of all Israel: he became the 'High Priest'. Israel had not had a priestly hierarchy before. We do not know whether the former tribal confederation had maintained an amphictyonic priesthood at the central sanctuary. In any case, numerous local sanctuaries had existed alongside the central cult, and these, or at any rate the more important of them, had had their own bodies of priests. And so it had continued in the period of the kings, when the priests at the central sanctuary in Jerusalem had been royal officials of the house of David, whose authority only extended, however, to this central sanctuary, and who were quite unconnected with the other priests in the country. It was king Josiah's fulfilment of the deuteronomic requirement of a single place of worship that had made the High Priest of Jerusalem the priestly head of all Israel. But he still remained a royal official. The end of the house of David effected a change. We do not know who saw to the continuance of worship on the site of the ruined Temple of Solomon. The rebuilding of the Temple which resulted from Cyrus's decree, and the reorganisation of public worship in Jerusalem which this made possible, also led to a reorganisation of the priesthood in this sanctuary. How this happened, we do not know. As royal officials and members of the upper class in Jerusalem the Zadokites, who had held priestly office in Jerusalem by heredity since the reigns of David and Solomon, had been deported by Nebuchadnezzar. It may be that members of the Zadokite family had remained behind in Jerusalem, that they continued to act as priests and that they formed the basis of the reorganisation of the priesthood. It may also be that, as a result of Cyrus's decree, some deported Zadokites returned to Jerusalem[1]. In any case it is highly probable that the Zadokites formed the priesthood in the new sanctuary too, with a new and far more important role at the head of Israel. In Haggai and Zechariah, and thereafter in the framework of the Aramaic collection of documents and in the Chronicler's narrative in Ezra i-vi, we meet Jeshua the son of Jozadak as 'High Priest'. He is the first holder known to us, and presumably the actual first holder of this office, which played such a great part from now until the end of Israel's history. After the decline of the old amphictyonic organisation and the elimination of the independent state as the basic vehicles of Israelite life, cult and priesthood came into the foreground.

26. *The Reorganisation of Life under Persian Influence*

For the next half-century after the dedication of the new Temple we have practically no information about the history of Israel. The restoration of the sanctuary and the reorganisation of the priesthood did not lead to the complete renewal of the decayed organisations of the old Israel or their replacement by new organisations. There was a plan for reorganisation, which probably arose among

---

[1] In this case the statement in 1 Chron. v, 41 may be historically correct. According to this the father of the Joshua who is mentioned immediately afterwards was a Zadokite deported by Nebuchadnezzar.

the exiles in Babylonia, since it was appended to the book of the prophet Ezekiel which was compiled in this circle (Ezek. xl-xlviii). This plan reckons, however, with an eschatological order of things and disregards historical facts. It was therefore only of limited use as the basis of a practical order which was bound to take into account the actual historical situation.

Thus life in Israel continued for the time being without a new organisation. In principle the deuteronomic law continued to be valid; it had not been introduced as a state law, so that it did not necessarily cease to have validity when the state organisation was dissolved. As it had received its authority from a covenant between God and people it was independent of political changes. In fact the deuteronomic requirement of a unified place of worship appears to have been strictly adhered to; and, so far as we know, no other sanctuaries, such as had flourished a generation previously, emerged again, even in the period when the sanctuary in Jerusalem was in ruins. After its restoration, however, the Temple of Jerusalem was regarded all the more as the only legitimate shrine. In other respects, however, the deuteronomic law which Josiah had already regarded in a one-sided manner from the point of view of its demand for unity in worship, was probably little observed. How far from satisfactory conditions were after the restoration of the Temple is shown by the collection of prophetic words which has been preserved under the name 'Malachi'—not a real name—and which is usually assigned, probably correctly, to the period between the completion of the Temple and the appearance of Ezra and Nehemiah. In this collection there is a reference to the carelessness with which the priests carried out their functions, inasmuch as they disregarded the regulation that the animals intended for sacrifice should be without blemish, and neglected their duty of religious teaching (i, 6–ii, 9). There is also mention of their dishonesty in the delivery of tithes for the sanctuary (iii, 6-12), of their failure to take the worship of God and the fear of God seriously enough (iii, 13-21), and of the readiness with which marriages were dissolved (ii, 10-16). Marriages were often made with foreign women from neighbouring peoples, and such foreign marriages even occurred in the families of the priests themselves (cf. Neh. xiii, 23-28). Strict observance of the Sabbath was no longer carried out (cf. Neh. xiii, 15-22).

The impulse for a new order of life proceeded in the end from the exiles in Babylonia, who, in their foreign environment, probably kept more strictly to their fathers' traditions and ordinances than did the tribes who had remained in Palestine. They managed to interest the Persian government in the need for reorganisation in Palestine. Certainly the Persians themselves had no personal knowledge of the nature of the regulations which were important for Israel. But they were probably able to understand the importance of consolidating the situation in Palestine and particularly in the land of Judah. It is true that this was only a small and peripheral part of their great empire, but it was of some importance. The rebellion of the satrap Megabyzos of Beyond the River about the middle of the 5th century B.C. made Syria-Palestine a delicate spot for them, and they were inevitably concerned to create as calm an atmosphere as possible in this area; the more so as in the second half of the 5th century Persian rule had to be enforced in Egypt against all kinds of attempts at independence. The land of Judah was near the military route to Egypt, not far from the final halting-places on Asiatic soil before the passage through the Sinaitic desert into the land of the Nile. The foundations of a warehouse from the 5th-4th century have been found near the province of Judah, south of the frontier stronghold of Gaza, in the ruin mound of *tell jemme* which lies on the *wādi ghazze*; this store was evidently intended for the supply of the Persian troops who were sent to Egypt[1]. Still further south on the *wādi ghazze* the tomb of a Persian from the last third of the 5th century has been discovered, evidently that of a Persian officer who was stationed there[2]. In a word, it is clear that the Persians were interested in restoring stability in the land of Judah and in Palestine in general, and that they were therefore open to suggestions which seemed likely to appease the population in this area, especially if these proposals seemed likely to result in the restoration of the traditions of one of the subject peoples, such as they had always promoted. This is the wider context in which the official sending of Ezra and Nehemiah to Jerusalem is to be understood.

It is not easy to unravel the traditional records concerning Ezra and Nehemiah, nor is it possible to be quite sure of their chronological relationship. We hear of both of them only within the framework of the Chronicler's historical work which was not written till very much later, though in this section it was able to turn to account certain literary sources. The tradition concerning Nehemiah is much more certain and fruitful than that concerning Ezra. For

---

[1] Cf. Fl. Petrie, *Gerar* (1928), Pl. xiii.
[2] Cf. Fl. Petrie, *Beth-Pelet*, I (1930), Pls. xliv-xlvi and also J. H. Iliffe, *Quart. of the Departm. of Antiqu. in Palestine*, 4 (1935), pp. 182 ff.

Nehemiah, the Chronicler had at his disposal Nehemiah's own statement, the so-called 'Memoirs of Nehemiah', and he incorporated this statement verbatim and perhaps in its entirety. According to Neh. i, 1; ii, 1, Nehemiah was sent to Jerusalem for the first time in the 20th year of Artaxerxes. This must refer to Artaxerxes I Longimanus, since in a papyrus of Elephantine of the year 408 B.C. there is mention of the sons of the governor Sanballat of Samaria[1], who is no doubt identical with the Sanballat whom Nehemiah repeatedly refers to as his opponent. This rules out all possibility of a later Artaxerxes having been Nehemiah's royal master. Nehemiah therefore went to Jerusalem for the first time in the year 445 B.C. The traditional sources regarding Ezra are very much more meagre. The Chronicler had at his disposal the official document commissioning Ezra, of which he gave the Imperial Aramaic text in Ezra vii, 12-26. Everything else that is told about Ezra is contained in the later Chronicler's own account as is proved by a linguistic scrutiny of the whole story of Ezra[2]. The content of the Ezra narrative is based entirely on the information in the above-mentioned document and the Chronicler's own combination of Ezra and Nehemiah[3]. Now this document also mentions an Artaxerxes as having commissioned Ezra (vii, 12). To take this also as a reference to Artaxerxes I is to begin with merely the opinion of the chronicler, whose work was probably only composed in the course of the 3rd century B.C. and of which it is impossible to be certain that he had at his disposal a trustworthy tradition of the Ezra-Nehemiah period based on oral transmission. He described the story of Ezra and Nehemiah on the assumption that their activities were more or less contemporaneous and very largely overlapping. The authentic sources, the Ezra document and the Nehemiah memoirs, make no reference to any such co-operation. All the same, it is probable that Ezra's Artaxerxes was also Artaxerxes I Longimanus (465–424) and not Artaxerxes II Mnemon (404–358)[4] or even Artaxerxes III Ochus (358–337), since the reorganisation of life in the religious community in Jerusalem with which

[1] *Pap. Cowley*, No. 30, l. 29 (cf. AOT², p. 452, ANET, p. 492, DOTT, pp. 260-265).
[2] Cf. A. S. Kapelrud, *The Question of Authorship in the Ezra-Narrative* (1944). There is not sufficient evidence for the opinion expressed here that at any rate an oral Ezra-tradition was transmitted in 'circles connected with the Chronicler', until it was finally fixed in writing.
[3] Cf. M. Noth, *Überlieferungsgeschichtliche Studien*, I (1943), pp. 145 ff.
[4] The thesis that Ezra did not come to Jerusalem until after Nehemiah and under Artaxerxes II was first argued in detail by A. van Hoonacker, 'Néhémie et Esdras, une nouvelle hypothèse sur la chronologie de l'époque de la restauration', *Le Muséon*, 9 [1890], pp. 151-184; 317-351; 389-401.

both Ezra and Nehemiah were particularly concerned, emerged as an urgent problem about the middle of the 5th century and was also recognised as such by the Persians. All the same, the assignment of Ezra to the reign of Artaxerxes I is merely very probable, not absolutely certain; and even then the exact dating of Ezra is problematical. It is true that it is stated in Ezra vii, 7-9 that Ezra was sent to Jerusalem in the 7th year of Artaxerxes—the year 458 B.C. if one accepts that this was Artaxerxes I. But not only is Ezra vii, 7 a post-chronistic addition, but presumably the passage Ezra vii, 8, 9 too was only subsequently inserted in the Chronicler's work[1], since it plainly interrupts the flow of the narrative. It is not known why Ezra's mission was later placed in the 7th year of Artaxerxes' reign. But if the Aramaic Ezra document and the Chronicler's narrative place Ezra in the age of Artaxerxes (I) only in a general way, the question of his chronological relationship to Nehemiah still remains unsolved. It is true that we have the Chronicler's opinion that Ezra came to Jerusalem before Nehemiah; but again it can hardly be assumed that this opinion was based on a real tradition. It might well be the case that the Chronicler only put Ezra first and made him work simultaneously with Nehemiah because Ezra's special task seemed to him more urgent and important. The question would then be whether it is possible to reach some conclusion on objective grounds about the chronological relationship between Ezra and Nehemiah. It may then be said that Nehemiah found cause, in Jerusalem and the land of Judah, to create order in a chaotic situation in religious and everyday affairs, and this would not suggest that Ezra had already brought to Jerusalem that law whose task was to provide the foundation for a unifying organisation of the whole of the community's life[2]. For this reason Nehemiah will be put before Ezra in what follows here, and it will be assumed that Ezra only came to Jerusalem in the latter years of Artaxerxes' reign[3]. It must be stressed, however, that it is impossible to reach an absolutely firm decision on this point because there is a lack of reliable and unambiguous evidence, and that all we can hope to attain is a limited degree of probability.

---

[1] Cf. M. Noth, *op. cit.* pp. 125 ff.

[2] The Chronicler's account makes Ezra wait for the appearance of Nehemiah before proclaiming and enforcing his law (Neh. viii, 9). This is highly unlikely. Nehemiah is then said to have carried through various reforms without any reference to this law (Neh. xiii, 4 ff.).

[3] W. F. Albright also places Ezra chronologically after Nehemiah in the final period of Artaxerxes I (*The Biblical Archaeologist*, 9 [1946], p. 13); cf. also H. H. Rowley, 'The Chronological Order of Ezra and Nehemiah', *Ignace Goldziher Memorial Volume*, I [1948], pp. 117 ff. = *The Servant of the Lord* (1952), pp. 129-159.

Nehemiah was descended from the group of exiles in Babylonia. He had reached the position of a royal cup-bearer in Susa, one of the Persian royal cities. This gave him the opportunity of direct access to the king's person. He is the sole concrete example known to us of the way in which it was possible to obtain the Persian king's interest in Jerusalem's affairs. He was perhaps not the only exile to obtain some kind of post at court. At the outset of his own account of himself (Neh. i, 1–ii, 8) he tells how once some people who had to come to Susa from Judah reported to him on the hopeless conditions that still prevailed in Jerusalem, with its walls and gates and a good part of its houses in ruins. He used the good-will which he evidently enjoyed with his king to have himself sent on an official mission to Jerusalem to restore the walls of Jerusalem. To safeguard his journey, he asked for official letters to the provincial governors of the satrapy of Beyond the River and also instructions to a controller of a royal estate—his official district is unfortunately not mentioned—to provide the timber necessary for the building in view of Palestine's lack of timber. He finally arrived in Jerusalem with a military escort of horsemen and their officers (Neh. ii, 9). He appeared in Jerusalem not only with a special mission, but also with an official position which the king had conferred on him. He became governor of the province of Judah (Neh. v, 14)[1], and he remained in Jerusalem long after his special mission of building the walls had been fulfilled. According to Neh. v, 14 he was in Jerusalem from the 20th to the 32nd years of Artaxerxes' reign (445–433) and, according to Neh. xiii, 6 f., he had himself sent to Jerusalem again, no doubt with the same position. Nehemiah's appointment as governor, granted to him by the king's good-will, probably signified at the same time the constitution of Judah as an independent province. If Judah had hitherto been merely a district of the old province of Samaria with a subordinate governor, it was now separated from Samaria and raised to the status of an independent province[2]. Not surprisingly, this brought Nehemiah the enmity of the governor Sanballat of Samaria from the very outset[3]. Sanballat was associated in this enmity with 'Tobiah, the Ammonite slave'—as Nehemiah likes to call him—who was probably the governor of the neighbouring province east of the Jordan (Neh. ii,

---

[1] The word התרשׁתא, which is used to describe Nehemiah in Neh. (viii, 9), x, 2 seems to be a (Persian) title; cf. Ed. Meyer, *op. cit.* p. 194.

[2] Cf. A. Alt, *Festschrift Otto Procksch* (1934), pp. 5 ff.

[3] That Sanballat was governor of Samaria we learn explicitly for the first time from the Papyri of Elephantine (*Pap. Cowley*, No. 30, l. 29; AOT², p. 452, ANET, p. 492, DOTT, p. 264); Nehemiah himself disdained to call him by his official title.

10). Nehemiah had presumably made the king agree to the restoration of Judah's independence because it was a necessary condition for the proposed work of rebuilding the walls of Jerusalem.

This work had had a previous history in which officials of the province of Samaria had played a part. A correspondence about the rebuilding of the city of Jerusalem and its walls which derives from the period of Artaxerxes has been preserved in the framework of the collection of Aramaic documents in the book of Ezra (Ezra iv, 7-22). Later, because of the narrative framework of the documents, it was wrongly put with the correspondence about the building of the Temple, but the text of the documents shows quite plainly that the matter under discussion in this correspondence is the rebuilding of the city, which was quite separate from the restoration of the sanctuary. The Artaxerxes who is named as the recipient of the first document quoted can only have been Artaxerxes I. The correspondence must have taken place in the period before Nehemiah's mission which finally settled the question of the rebuilding of the walls. The documents in question do not bear any more exact date; all we can say is that they come from some time during the first twenty years of Artaxerxes I's reign. They show that officials of the provincial government of Samaria[1] were in Jerusalem, which was presumably still subject to the governor of Samaria, along with the district of Judah, and ascertained that it was intended to rebuild the city and its walls and that a start had already been made. They sent a report on the matter to the king, probably through official channels via the satrap of Beyond the River[2], pointing out that Jerusalem which, as they say, had been a rebellious city from of old, would become a menace to the security and safety of the empire once it felt safe again within the protection of its walls. In this connection we hear for the first time from an authentic traditional record that Judaeans had come to Jerusalem from Babylonia (iv, 12). Meanwhile various exiles had in fact returned to the homeland, probably not in one big movement, but in smaller groups; and it may have been they who provided the initial impulse that led to the attempt at restoring the ruined city. The people who had remained in the country had hardly been able to summon up

---

[1] Apart from the two provincial officials mentioned by name who conducted the correspondence, a whole series of Persian official titles, some of which are unintelligible, and various ancestral titles also, are listed in iv, 9. All these probably refer to members of the foreign upper class which was deported to Samaria.

[2] The rather obscure introductory formulae in iv, 7, 8 may perhaps be understood in this sense. The satrapy 'Beyond the River' is mentioned in the introductions to the report and to the king's answer (iv, 10, 17).

enough strength at one time even for the task of merely rebuilding
the sanctuary, and had left the city lying in ruins, so that the returning exiles were the first to take on the task of reviving the city
of which they had thought with such longing in far-away Babylonia
(cf. Ps. cxxxvii, 5-6). In Samaria, the governor's residence, however, and the former royal city of Israel, the revival of the ancient
royal Judaean city was looked on with disfavour. Because of its
sanctuary it played a special part among the Israelite tribes, and
once the city was rebuilt it could become an undesirable rival. As
a result of the report which was sent to Artaxerxes, further work
on the rebuilding of Jerusalem was expressly forbidden until further
notice (iv, 21) in a decree which the king sent to Samaria (iv, 17-22).

Nehemiah's appearance on the scene was probably more or less
closely connected with this incident. Sooner or later after the issue
of the prohibition the exiles who had returned home used their
connection with the exiles in Mesopotamia to secure the king's
permission to continue the rebuilding. Nehemiah's position in the
king's personal entourage offered a welcome opportunity for an
approach to the king. Resistance to the rebuilding had started in
Samaria. If the restoration was to succeed, Jerusalem and Judah
would have to become as independent as possible of this province
and its government. Nehemiah knew this, or the people who had
come from Judah made a point of telling him so. He therefore
obtained the king's sanction for the separation of Judah from the
province of Samaria, and its constitution as a separate unit. As
governor of the newly constituted province of Judah, he was in a
position to embark on the restoration of Jerusalem without having
to consult officially with the province of Samaria.

Nevertheless, after his arrival in Jerusalem, Nehemiah had to
proceed with all the caution and shrewdness at his command in
order to attain his goal. It was only to be expected that the governor,
Sanballat of Samaria, would do all he could to hinder the rebuilding
of Jerusalem. To begin with, therefore, Nehemiah kept his plans
secret and three days after his arrival he inspected the whole extent
of the walls by night, on horseback and with only a few men with
him (Neh. ii, 11-15)[1]. Only then did he announce his plans in Jerusalem and he found willing hearers. It was now a matter of acting
as swiftly as possible before the opposition of the neighbours could
hinder the work. Nehemiah therefore divided the whole wall into

---

[1] On the topography of this nocturnal ride along the city wall cf. A. Alt, PJB, 24
(1928), pp. 91 ff. For a different account see J. Simons, *Jerusalem in the Old Testament*
(1952), pp. 437 ff.

sections, all of which were taken in hand simultaneously; and at the same time, as the population of Jerusalem was still numerically rather small, he summoned labourers to work on the walls of the city from the whole province, bringing in the heads of the districts into which the province was divided, with their people. The families in Jerusalem, and these district administrators, were each allotted a section of the wall to rebuild (Neh. iii, 1-32). To begin with, this somewhat improvised undertaking merely aroused the scorn of the neighbours in Samaria and the east Jordan province of Ammon (Neh. iii, 33 ff. [English Bible, iv, 1 ff.]). But when the wall had already been half built and the workers were working with enthusiasm and joy, the neighbours attempted to interrupt the work by force (Neh. iv, 1 ff. [English Bible, v, 7 ff.]). The governors of Samaria and Ammon gave orders for an attack on Jerusalem—no doubt unofficially, keeping themselves in the background—in which people from the south and west also took part[1]. The plot did not remain secret, however. People living on the borders of the province brought the news to Jerusalem so that Nehemiah was able to take defensive measures in time. When this became known, the attack which was intended to be a surprise, was called off. All the same, the incident showed that it was necessary to be on guard in Jerusalem. Nehemiah therefore organised a permanent watch and made arrangements for rapid warning to be given to all the workers on the wall. The work now had to be done under these more difficult conditions; but nevertheless the wall was finally completed. It is true that Nehemiah's enemies[2] still tried to intimidate him by imputing to him rebellious intentions, or attempted to seize his person by cunning, in order to remove him (Neh. vi, 1-14). But Nehemiah was wise enough not to get involved in anything, and so in spite of all opposition he finally attained his goal. The work was completed in the astonishingly short period of 52 days (Neh. vi, 15). Nehemiah made arrangements for the newly walled city to be carefully guarded under a 'captain of the fortress' and gave orders for the opening of the city gates in the morning and their closing at night (Neh. vii, 1-3). Thus the province of Judah again had a safe and sure centre and seat of government.

[1] In Neh. iv, 1 [English Bible, v, 7] Arabians and Ashdodites are mentioned in addition to the Ammonites. The Ashdodites were no doubt people from the neighbouring province in the west which was officially called Ashdod, whereas the Arabians were probably neighbours in the south who had infiltrated into the west Jordan part of the province from the southern desert.

[2] Among them there appears in this context as well as Sanballat and Tobiah, the Arabian Geshem (Neh. ii, 19; vi, 1 ff.), who may have been no more than a tribal chieftain.

But the city which had been for so long in ruins and unprotected was still only sparsely inhabited. Nehemiah therefore filled it up by a process of synoecism, *i.e.* by settling in Jerusalem a tenth part, chosen by lot, of the inhabitants from all the provinces (Neh. vii, 4, 5a and xi, 1, 2)[1]. When this had been carried through, the solemn dedication of the new city wall took place (Neh. xii, 27 ff.). It is clear from all this that, to begin with, this new Jerusalem had no greater need of space than the original city of David. The Jerusalem of the period of the kings had in general consisted of the old Jebusite and Davidic city on the small 'south-east hill' by the Kidron Valley above the spring of Gihon, and the city of Solomon immediately to the north, together with the royal palace buildings, and had only been extended on the western side of Solomon's city by a not very extensive 'new city' (2 Kings xxii, 14; Zeph. i, 10). Nehemiah's Jerusalem was similarly confined to these narrow limits at first, and, even in the period that followed, the city hardly needed any enlargement. This accords with the fact that archaeological research has produced no evidence that Jerusalem extended in pre-Hellenistic times to the broad hill on the west. It was only Hellenistic Jerusalem's need for more space that extended the city beyond its former narrow limits.

After the completion of the wall Nehemiah continued as governor to attend to the ordering of life in Jerusalem and in the province of Judah wherever opportunity offered. This was no doubt part of the mission with which he had been entrusted when he was sent to Jerusalem. He found the province divided into a number of districts. We learn this from the reference to the allocating of the various sections of the wall to the heads of these districts and their people in Neh. iii, 1-32. We do not know from what period this division of the province into districts actually dates. As the districts are described by the Accadian word *pilku > pelek*, they may already have been instituted in the Neo-Babylonian period. These districts were named after their chief place, though there were some double districts which shared a capital because the country had been denuded of cities[2]. So we have a double district of Jerusalem, a double district of Beth-zur (the modern *khirbet eṭ-ṭubēka*) in the southern part of the province, as well as a double district of Keilah (the modern *khirbet ḳīla*) in the hill country extending to the west of the Judaean mountains. The district of Beth-haccherem is probably

---

[1] This connected passage in the Nehemiah memoirs was subsequently interrupted by the Chronicler's insertion of Nehemiah (vii) viii-x.

[2] Cf. the cartographical description in H. Guthe, *Bibelatlas* ([2] 1926), No. 7 III.

to be sought west of Jerusalem, if this place is identical with the modern *ēn kārim*. The district of Mizpah (the modern *tell en-naṣbe*) occupied the northern part of the province. From these names we can obtain a rough idea of the total extent of the province, which had apparently not been altered in extent since Nebuchadnezzar's institution of the district of Judah. A few details contained in the report on the building of the wall in Neh. iii about isolated communities which took part in the building as special groups, round off the picture. According to this the province extended in the mountains southwards to a line between Beth-zur and Hebron, which already, since the occupation of the land, had formed the boundary between the actual tribal area of Judah, and the areas of the Calebites and other small tribes that had settled in the most southerly parts of the mountains. The land south of this line had probably been separated from the kingdom of Judah as early as 598 B.C. and ceded to the Edomites, and had since become part of the province of Edom which lay on both sides of the Dead Sea and the *wādi el-'araba*. With its extension into the western hill country the province reached, north of the latitude of Beth-zur, approximately the western frontier which the kingdom of Judah had normally had. The same applies, generally speaking, to the northern border, which ran north of Mizpah. The only striking feature is the extension of the province to the north-east as far as the lowest part of the Jordan Valley including Jericho. According to Neh. iii, 2, 22, the 'men of Jericho' and the 'men of the (Jordan) plain' took part in the building of the wall. The western half of the lowest part of the Jordan valley had once been part of the kingdom of Israel and then belonged to the province of Samaria. Apparently a small part of Josiah's annexations had survived here (cf. above, p. 273), since this area presumably continued to be in the kingdom of Judah even after the collapse of Josiah's work, and then belonged first of all to the sub-province and finally to the independent province of Judah.

As governor, Nehemiah introduced in this very small province one or two innovations which had an important stabilising influence. In his memoirs, in the middle of his description of the building of the wall, he reports on a general remission of debts which he ordered. As the memoirs are obviously arranged chronologically, this remission of debts was probably one of Nehemiah's first measures (Neh. v, 1-13). It was occasioned by an obvious abuse. After the Judaean upper class had been deported by Nebuchadnezzar, a new contrast, like that which had already characterised the economic and social situation in the latter period of the kings, had developed between rich and poor within the population that remained behind. It is impossible to say how far the return of the exiles who claimed their family property again had contributed to this. In any case Nehemiah was confronted with an impoverished and debt-ridden section of the population which had in the end to sell its property and even became enslaved because of debt. This restless and discontented element constituted a danger. Nehemiah therefore made the creditors solemnly promise in the sanctuary to agree to a general remission of debt and to a restoration of mort-gaged or alienated property. How poor the province was as a whole, is clear from the fact that Nehemiah voluntarily refused the revenues due to the governor which were normally raised by the province, and contented himself with modest taxes in kind (Neh. v, 14-19).

At the end of his statement (Neh. xiii), Nehemiah has collected various regulations which he made to introduce order into the situation in the province, and above all, in Jerusalem. It is clear from Neh. xiii, 6 f. that these regulations were made partly or perhaps even entirely in the second part of his governorship, when, after twelve years in office, he had returned to Babylonia in the 32nd year of Artaxerxes' reign (433 B.C.) and then returned to Jerusalem as governor after a longer or shorter absence. We are not told the reason for his second mission. It may be that new abuses which had arisen in the province necessitated his return, and that the regulations listed in Neh. xiii were intended to redress them. In particular, the behaviour of the high priest Eliashib, who had taken part in the building of the wall (Neh. iii, 1), necessitated the intervention of a restraining hand. He had taken advantage of Nehemiah's departure from his post in Jerusalem to follow his own political line, which was based on maintaining good connections with the governors and upper classes of the neighbouring provinces, whereas Nehemiah—following tendencies which were active, above all, among the exiles in Mesopotamia—had worked for the inde-pendence and isolation of the province of Judah. This is the first evidence we have of the high-priestly Zadokites adopting towards the neighbouring, and partly foreign, surrounding provinces that friendly attitude which they showed repeatedly in later periods. It is also the first sign of that contrast between openness towards the surrounding world and an attitude of strict isolationism in view of the peculiar nature of the community's life, which permeated the whole spiritual history of Israel after the loss of political inde-pendence. The particular case here was that Eliashib, one of whose grandsons was the son-in-law of the Samaritan governor Sanballat (Neh. xiii, 28), had for some unknown purpose put at the disposal of the 'Ammonite Tobiah' a room in the Temple in Jerusalem, which was really intended to serve the cultic needs of the sanctuary (Neh. xiii, 4 ff.), because he was in some unspecified way related to this Tobiah[1]. After his return to Jerusalem Nehemiah put a stop to this wrong use of a Temple room in no uncertain manner. Furthermore—before or after this—he proceeded against the numerous marriages between Judaeans and members of foreign neighbouring peoples, not actually dissolving them, however—at any rate there is no explicit statement to that effect—but making the Judaeans swear not to allow their children to contract such marriages (Neh. xiii, 23 ff.)[2]. Nehemiah then took action against the negligence in the payment of the tithes due to the sanctuary which was already complained of in the book of 'Malachi'. He pledged the 'rulers' of the people[3] to see that the payment of the tithes was punctually fulfilled and appointed reliable inspectors in the sanctuary to check the incoming tithes (Neh. xiii, 10 ff.). He also regulated the delivery to the sanctuary of the timber that was needed for the sacrificial fires (Neh. xiii, 31). The fact that these measures were necessary shows how little, almost a century after the rebuilding of the Temple, public worship was being really seriously observed in Jerusalem, by people in the province of Judah, and by the Israelite tribes in the land who remained loyal to the sanctuary in Jerusalem. Finally, Nehemiah had to take measures to see that the Sabbath rest was properly observed. On this matter Nehemiah probably championed the strict views of the Babylonian exiles. It is true that the Sabbath had already been observed in the period of the Judaean-Israelite kings as a day when work in the fields (2 Kings iv, 23), and buying and selling in the cities (Amos viii, 5), had to cease. Among the exiles, however, the observance of the Sabbath had acquired a special importance (cf. above, pp. 297 f.), whereas in Jerusalem and elsewhere in the land the Sabbath rest was very carelessly observed. In Jerusalem, the chief market of the land, people came in from the countryside on the Sabbath

---

[1] It is not certain that the priest Eliashib who was 'appointed over the chambers of the house of our God' (Neh. xiii, 4 ff.) was identical with the high priest Eliashib (Neh. iii, 1; xiii, 28); but he was at any rate a member of the priestly Zadokite family.

[2] The reference to the 'law of strangers' of Deut. xxiii, 4-6 in Neh. xiii, 1-3 is a later addition.

[3] These 'rulers' are mentioned fairly often in the Nehemiah Memoirs and are described with an Accadian word as סגנים. Their functions appear to have corresponded roughly to those of the earlier 'elders' of the tribal associations that had meanwhile decayed; they may have been the heads of the local associations. Cf. also Ed. Meyer, *op. cit.* pp. 132 ff.

with their donkeys, to offer their produce for sale; and the Tyrian merchants who had settled in Jerusalem to sell the fish caught on the Mediterranean coast and other goods, took no notice whatsoever of the Sabbath. In view of these conditions Nehemiah enforced the keeping of the Sabbath, at any rate in Jerusalem, by closing the market on the Sabbath, and by not permitting the city gates to be opened throughout the Sabbath (Neh. xiii, 15 ff.).

A document preserved in Neh. x is related in a strikingly direct fashion to Nehemiah's measures as reported in Neh. xiii. It contains an 'agreement' in which, in the form of a solemn declaration in the first person plural, the obligation is undertaken conscientiously to fulfil certain requirements, and these correspond more or less exactly to the above-mentioned instructions issued by Nehemiah. According to verse 1 the agreement was contained in a document signed by representatives of the whole community and attested with their seals[1]. This document was obviously not included in Nehemiah's Memoirs; it forms part of the great chronistic interpolation in the Nehemiah Memoirs. The Chronicler appended it to the story of Ezra's proclamation of the law, because for him Ezra was the one primarily responsible for the introduction of the law; but in fact it obviously has nothing to do with Ezra. If it is an authentic document—and there is no good reason to doubt that— it may be regarded as a traditional document that came down to the Chronicler but which he inserted in a historically inappropriate place. Its connections with Neh. xiii would suggest that Nehemiah ultimately pledged the responsible men in the province of Judah to carry out his instructions by means of a written declaration; and this declaration was preserved in Jerusalem and finally came to the notice of the later Chronicler.

Nehemiah's work had been concentrated in the main on the external organisation of the province of Judah; no doubt the wording of the instructions he received from the Persian government was along these lines. He had rebuilt and repopulated the urban centre and seat of government; he had rectified certain abuses in public worship at the central sanctuary, which had been restored on official instructions and out of public resources, and introduced the most urgent social reforms in the province. In addition, however, he had taken a personal interest in some special concerns of the Babylonian group of exiles such as the separation of the population in the province from the neighbouring

---

[1] The list of signatories inserted in Neh. x, 2-28 is certainly apocryphal and was only later inserted in this inappropriate position.

peoples, and the strict observance of the Sabbath. Apart from these particularly obvious matters he had not concerned himself with the inner life of the religious community in Jerusalem. The conditions that he found when he arrived showed, however, that reform was urgently needed in this sphere too. Nehemiah had worked in the main in accordance with a political commission using political methods and with political aims in view, and he regarded the cultus in Jerusalem as one of the province's public institutions. If the 'agreement' recorded in Neh. x is based on a genuine tradition and if it was really due to Nehemiah's initiative, it provides us with a very typical example of Nehemiah's methods. It represents a legal act, the signing of a binding document by the responsible representatives of the whole community, and there is no mention of the act being solemnly consecrated. The content of the 'agreement' ensued from the abuses which it was intended to rectify, and from a number of special concerns which probably derived from the Babylonian group of exiles. There is an occasional reference to 'the Law'; and if the 'law' in question is one that has come down to us, it appears to refer most probably to the deuteronomic law which had continued to be in force since the making of the covenant under Josiah, and the introductory formula of the 'agreement' (verse 30) does suggest a markedly deuteronomic style.

The time now seemed to have come to give the religious community in Jerusalem, which was not in the least identical with the population of the province of Judah, a new and binding organisation. The old tribal federation and its organisations had dissolved, and its place had been taken by an 'Israel' that was to some extent dispersed in the Diaspora, which maintained the old traditions in various ways and still found its unity in the worship in Jerusalem, but which had not yet really found a new form. This is obviously where Ezra's mission came in. We are much less well-informed about Ezra's than about Nehemiah's work, as the only authentic traditional material we have about him is his official instructions which are recorded in Ezra vii, 12-26. For the rest, since the story of Ezra is the work of the Chronicler, it cannot be used as a historical document, since it can hardly be assumed that the Chronicler was able to draw on a direct oral tradition concerning Ezra. On the other hand, we learn from these official instructions that Ezra had in his hand 'a law of the God of heaven'—in the Persian period this was the normal official term for the God of Israel—which it was evidently his task to enforce. Such a mission would fit very well into the period directly following Nehemiah, however, and so the possibility which we considered above on p. 320, that Ezra appeared in the latter years of Artaxerxes I, may be assumed to be correct for the purposes of our discussion.

Ezra was a priest (Ezra vii, 12); and as he was sent to Jerusalem from the 'province of Babylon' (Ezra vii, 16) and evidently came from the Babylonian group of exiles, he probably belonged to a family of the Zadokites who had formerly been deported from Jerusalem. His official mission may have been instigated by himself or by influential people in his circle. In view of the confused situation in Jerusalem and Judah and the opposition to be expected, it was important for him to arrive with official instructions from the Persian government. If Artaxerxes had already agreed to instal Nehemiah as governor of the province of Judah recently made independent, he may now have agreed to give Ezra instructions, the content and range of which were no doubt suggested to him by members of the group of exiles. Perhaps Ezra's mission can be connected with Nehemiah's second mission and ought indeed to be linked with it. Both episodes must have been very close chronologically if Ezra really followed Nehemiah, yet still went to Jerusalem during the reign of Artaxeres; for only the last nine years of Artaxerxes' reign were available for Nehemiah's return to Babylonia, his second mission and Ezra's mission. What probably happened was that the news of the unsettled conditions in Jerusalem and Judah which made Nehemiah ask for his second appointment as governor, induced the exiles in Babylonia to think beyond the possibilities open to Nehemiah, who could, in his position, merely remove a few crying abuses, and so to prepare a comprehensive plan of reform and to urge that Ezra should be entrusted with the execution of the plan, the political importance of which they were probably able to explain to the Persian authorities. At any rate Ezra ultimately received a special commission, which did not burden him with the administration of a particular office, like Nehemiah, but merely assigned to him a special and single mission. This is clear even from the official title which, according to Ezra vii, 12, he received for the fulfilment of his task. Apart from the description of 'priest' which concerned his position in the Jerusalem religious community, he also bore the official title of 'a scribe of the law of the God of heaven'. The Chronicler later tried to paraphrase this title in Hebrew in Ezra vii, 6 in the words 'a scribe skilled in the law of Moses, which Yahweh, the God of Israel had given', and also in Ezra vii, 11; in Neh. viii, 1 ff., however, he chose the abbreviation, 'Ezra the scribe'[1]. The development in the meaning of the word *sōfer* then led to the idea of 'Ezra the learned exegete'. In reality, however, Ezra's official title was a technical term in the Imperial Aramaic official language of the Persian empire, which was not intended to describe Ezra either as the writer of the 'law of the God of heaven', or a learned expert in or interpreter of this 'law'. In this official language the Aramaic word 'scribe' was a common expression for an official with a particular official sphere which was described with the dependent genitive. Ezra was therefore an 'official for the law of the God of Heaven' or—as his mission was not to be repeated—'state commissioner for the law of the God of Heaven'[2].

To judge from this title, his mission to Jerusalem must primarily have included the task of enforcing a particular sacral law. There is no explicit mention of this, however, in the official instructions to him recorded in Ezra vii, 12-26; it was taken for granted that that was the real purpose of his mission. Only at the end, in verse 25 f., is it ordained that in the area of the satrapy Beyond the River 'the people'—which can only mean 'Israel', which lived not only in the province of Judah but as compact groups in several provinces of this satrapy, and also dispersed in other areas as well[3]—was to be judged according to the new law which, as a sacral law, necessarily embraced certain spheres of everyday life as well—and that the law was to be made known to and binding on the whole 'people'. This could hardly mean that all the surviving descendants of ancient Israel were to be forcibly subjected to the law of Ezra, since it would hardly have accorded with the Persian practice to apply compulsion in this way. But it probably was intended to mean that all those who still desired to be considered members of the community of 'Israel' and to belong to the Jerusalem religious community, had to submit to this law. For them Ezra was to appoint judges, who were to judge according to the new law. It may seem surprising that a Persian ordinance should have gone so far in support of a strict legal reform within Israel, but it must be remembered that it is possible that the influence of the Babylonian exiles on Artaxerxes may have been so great that he gave his official consent to a pro-

[1] The passage Ezra vii, 11b looks like an addition to vii, 11a; in the latter verse the Aramaic title is rendered with the circumlocution 'a scribe of the words of the commandments and of the statutes of Yahweh to Israel'.

[2] On the meaning of the word *sāfar/sōfer* cf., above all, H. H. Schaeder, *Esra der Schreiber* (1930), pp. 39 ff.

[3] 'Dispersed' Israel also existed outside this satrapy, above all in Mesopotamia and in Egypt. This fact is not taken into account, since Ezra's mission was limited to the satrapy of Beyond the River.

posal put to him from this quarter—perhaps the whole text of Ezra's official instructions was drafted by exiles—and gave the 'divine law' submitted to him the binding force of a 'royal law', so that it was possible to mention the 'divine law' and the 'royal law' in one and the same breath (verse 26).

The enforcement of the 'law of God' throughout Israel with the support of Persian authority had a far-reaching effect. Submission to this law became the decisive token of membership of Israel and of the Jerusalem religious community. The organic unity of the old Israel was replaced by the circle of those who acknowledged the law; and this circle was, on the one hand, narrower than the descendants of the old Israel, since many of the dispersed left were no doubt the old community in course of time, and, on the other hand, it was wider, since in principle and in practice there was nothing to stop non-Israelites joining the ranks of those who acknowledged the law and therefore entering the religious community. All the same, the circle no doubt continued to consist on the whole of descendants of the former tribes who had remained in the old homeland, and the dispersed Israelites who held fast to the old traditions. In this way, however, after the dissolution of the old tribal confederation and after the interim period of a formless gathering around the old traditions and the Temple worship in Jerusalem, Israel found a new form, and one which was indeed authorised by the state, as a community subject to a special law of God, for which this law was binding, but which had at the same time a claim, recognised by the state, to be judged according to this law. It is obvious that the meaning which the divine law thereby acquired for Israel was bound to become extraordinarily important, not only for its outward form but also for its inner life.

We have no certain information as to how Ezra carried out his task. On the occasion of his mission to Jerusalem he obtained a few extra rights which are listed in his official instructions. As he was inevitably concerned to strengthen the influence of the Babylonian group of exiles, who stood behind his mission, he was anxious to take with him a group of repatriates from this group; and so the king gave permission for any who wished voluntarily to return home to do so (verse 13), and Ezra probably recruited volunteers in Babylonia for such a return. No doubt he did go to Jerusalem with a larger or smaller body of repatriates. Then, in view of the difficult economic conditions in the impoverished province of Judah, as they are clearly described in the Nehemiah Memoirs, he wanted to take money with him to Jerusalem. He therefore obtained from the king and his leading advisers a special oblation for 'the God of Israel, whose habitation is in Jerusalem' (verse 15), as well as permission to collect free-will offerings in the province of Babylonia (verse 16), which were intended in the first place for the purposes of public worship in Jerusalem, and also to receive vessels for the service of the sanctuary in Jerusalem (verse 19). In addition he obtained the renewal of the privilege already given by Darius by which the needs for sacrificial purposes of the sanctuary in Jerusalem were to be partly met from public funds, within limits which were now exactly defined (verses 20-22). Finally he secured official confirmation of the general exemption from taxation for the whole staff of the sanctuary, which it is possible already existed (verse 24). With these official concessions Ezra finally went to Jerusalem with his attendants.

On Ezra's activities in Jerusalem all we have is the Chronicler's account. According to him, the first matter which Ezra tackled on his arrival in Jerusalem was the question of mixed marriages (Ezra ix, x). The Chronicler knew from the Nehemiah Memoirs that there had been numerous marriages between Israelites and members of neighbouring peoples at that period, and could probably not help concluding that Ezra, whom he placed before Nehemiah chronologically, was bound to have removed this stumbling-block which must have been particularly serious to him. According to his account it was only considerably later, after Nehemiah had arrived in Jerusalem, that Ezra proclaimed the law he had brought with him in a solemn assembly, that it was explained by the Levites, and that a Feast of Tabernacles was celebrated in exact conformity with the ordinances of the law (Neh. viii). It is impossible to say whether Ezra had reason to concern himself with the question of mixed marriages after Nehemiah, who presumably preceded him, had dealt with it. In any case he did not, as the Chronicler would have it, wait for years before fulfilling his main task, the proclamation of the law. There is no authentic record of the manner in which this took place. No doubt it can only have occurred within the framework of a sacral act. Probably a covenant was concluded in accordance with the Israelite traditions which Josiah had followed when he introduced the deuteronomic law. This making of a covenant committed the whole of 'Israel' to the new law. It was not a matter of concluding a new covenant between God and the people. On the contrary, even after the dissolution of the old tribal confederation—and in spite of the threats of the prophets of the 8th and 7th centuries—the conviction was upheld that the covenant still continued in force. Just as in former times the 'renewal of the covenant' had been celebrated (cf. Deut. xxxi, 10-13) and Josiah had instigated a reform of the covenant by means of the deutero-nomic law, so now once again the law between God and the 'people' was re-defined by means of a new law. The only difference was that now the covenant relationship increasingly became merely an element in an old tradition, which was now affirmed again in an act of covenant-making organised by Ezra, while it was the law now assumed the foremost place as an absolute revelation of the divine will[1].

There still remains the important and difficult question as to where this 'law of the God of heaven', which 'was in the hand of Ezra' had come from, and what were its contents. There is no reference to this either in Ezra's official instructions or in the later narrative of the Chronicler. In all probability this law had been compiled or elaborated among the Babylonian group of exiles and was then made binding on the whole of Israel with the authority of the Persian state. Apart from the prophecy of Deutero-Isaiah, this was the most important and momentous example of the influence of the Babylonian group on the life of Israel as a whole. If Ezra's law gave the Israel of the Jerusalem religious community its permanent form after the interim period following the loss of political independence—and we have every reason to assume that this was so, as we hear of no other occasion which could have given rise to the reform which can be clearly discerned in the following period—the law must necessarily have come down to us as part of the Old Testament tradition, the canonising of which began not so long after Ezra. In the past it has occasionally been assumed that it was the Priestly Code stratum of the Pentateuch narrative (P) that Ezra brought to Jerusalem and introduced as the 'law'. This is not very likely since P was a narrative work, and much more exclusively so than was thought when numerous legal sections were assigned to it which in fact did not belong to it originally or even secondarily[2]. P was no 'law' and could hardly be described as such even figuratively. We should rather think of various of the collections of regulations which were subsequently incorporated in the great Pentateuch narrative, for example the corpus of the so-called Law of Holiness in Lev. xvii-xxvi or certain collections of cultic regulations such as may now be found in Lev. i-vii and Lev. xi-xv, or perhaps as a collation of various pieces of

[1] Cf. M. Noth, *Die Gesetze im Pentateuch* (1940), pp. 70 ff.
[2] Cf. M. Noth, *Überlieferungsgeschichte des Pentateuch* (1948), pp. 7 ff.

that kind. This possibility must be taken seriously into account, though this would make it impossible to define with any precision the extent and content of Ezra's law. Probably the most widespread idea is that it was the more or less completed Pentateuch that Ezra brought with him to Jerusalem[1]. In that case Ezra's 'Law' would have rested on a broad narrative foundation and would have been presented within the framework of the whole tradition of Israel's prehistory which was basically very old. The reformation of the Jerusalem religious community would then have proceeded in the closest connection with a renewed remembrance of the great historical acts of God which had befallen Israel, and given it its special position among the nations. It is clear that it would have been very important if this remembrance had been behind the reform of life in the Jerusalem religious community. Unfortunately the thesis that Ezra brought with him the whole of the Pentateuch and made it a binding document of the 'law' for the Jerusalem religious community, cannot be proved. It is indeed not even probable since there are important reasons against its acceptance. Above all, there is no cogent reason why the Pentateuch should have been compiled in Babylonia rather than in Palestine. Even the Priestly Code was more probably written in Palestine and the older sources of the narrative came into being and were transmitted in Palestine in any case. It is therefore probable that the whole of the Pentateuch was not brought to Jerusalem from Babylonia and that it was not 'the law in the hand of Ezra'; it was compiled rather in Palestine itself. Admittedly, this must have taken place very soon after Ezra, unless the Pentateuch *narrative* existed before Ezra, since about a century later the Samaritan community which separated itself from Jerusalem retained the complete Pentateuch as a holy book that had already been firmly accepted. In this case, however, 'the law' of Ezra is probably embedded in the legal sections that were subsequently interpolated in the Pentateuch narrative, since it became, at any rate, part of the document of the Pentateuch that was soon canonised as the valid basis of the life of the Jerusalem religious community. Unfortunately it is quite impossible to define this law of Ezra exactly.

With the consolidation of the province of Judah, which resulted from Nehemiah's governorship, and the reform of the life of the Jerusalem religious community which resulted from Ezra's special

---

[1] Thus J. Wellhausen, *Geschichte Israels*, I (1878), p. 421, and, in recent times, H. H. Schaeder, *op. cit.* pp. 63 f., O. Eissfeldt, *Einleitung in das A.T.* ([2]1956), p. 699, and probably also A. Weiser, *Einleitung in das A.T.* ([2] 1949), p. 247.

mission, presumably some degree of stability was established after the collapse of the old order, producing conditions in which Israel was again able to live.

27. *The Life of the Jerusalem Religious Community*[1] *in the Persian Period*

For two centuries Israel, together with the whole of the Near East' lived under Persian rule. Apart from what we learn from the material handed down about the reform of public worship in Jerusalem resulting from Cyrus's decree, and about Nehemiah's governorship in the province of Judah in the third quarter of the 5th century, and finally about Ezra's mission in the period immediately after Nehemiah, we know almost nothing about the history of Israel in this long period. And even what we do know is, generally speaking, limited to the narrow confines of the small province of Judah with Jerusalem as its centre. But Israel extended far beyond the province of Judah, apart from those parts which were scattered in the Diaspora. In the neighbouring provinces of Samaria and Acco assuming that was the name of the Galilean province at the time (cf. above, p. 263, note 5)—and to some extent also in the provinces of Ammon and Ashdod there lived descendants of the old Israelite tribes who, as is evident from the history of the following period, still regarded themselves as belonging to the community of Israel and the Jerusalem religious community, and took part in public worship in Jerusalem. Ezra's introduction of the law naturally had them in mind too (cf. above p. 332); for Ezra's work was not merely an affair of the province of Judah, but concerned 'Israel' as a whole, and Ezra carried out his task in Jerusalem not as the capital of the province of Judah but as the centre of the Israelite religion. But we know practically nothing about the history of the Israelites in the other Palestinian provinces during the Persian period. Israel was excluded from taking independent historical action at this time, and so, as long as Persian rule persisted, historical events such as the constantly recurring struggles to maintain Persian sovereignty in Egypt, which were waged with varying success, or the military conflicts with rebellious Phoenician coastal cities which

---

[1] The phrase 'Jerusalem religious community' has been adopted to convey the meaning of the German 'Jerusalemer Kultgemeinde'. It denotes a people the focus of whose religious life was the cult in Jerusalem, though its members were not necessarily all living in the one place.

were waged repeatedly during the 4th century, passed Israel by on the whole, and did not affect it very materially, despite their proximity.

We know even less about the fate in this period of the more important groups in the Diaspora, not to mention the smaller groups of scattered Israelites. From the story of Nehemiah and Ezra we learn a little of the interest of the Babylonian group in the cultus in Jerusalem and the whole organisation of the religious community, and how they managed from time to time to influence the Persian court; but these are only isolated details in the history of this group which it is impossible to set in a wider context. We have no knowledge at all of the life of the Lower Egyptian group in this period. This is the more regrettable, as this group played a very important part in the subsequent Hellenistic period, and there can therefore hardly be any doubt that it already played a part in the Persian period. On the other hand, the above-mentioned papyri of Elephantine from the 5th century B.C. throw some light on the life of the Israelite military colony on the Upper Egyptian border. But although they still occasionally turned with their problems to the governor in Jerusalem[1], in the course of time these colonists no doubt abandoned their connection with the Jerusalem religious community as they had a strange Temple cultus of their own, and in this way they were lost to Israel; after the 5th century all trace of them is lost.

The period of Persian rule was, however, of quite fundamental importance for Israel inasmuch as reforms took place in the most varied spheres and had a decisive influence on its later history. Whilst it is possible to discern, at any rate the main outlines of the new form of its life, lack of source-material makes it impossible to trace the development of this, except where particular details of the process come to light, more or less accidentally, during Nehemiah's governorship and are therefore mentioned in his report on his activities.

It was during the Persian period that the Jerusalem cultus acquired the form which persisted in its essentials until the end of its existence. After Cyrus had given instructions for the rebuilding of the sanctuary, Jerusalem became the religious centre not only for the Israelites living in the vicinity but for those scattered throughout the world; and any local cult that still survived or was brought into being was therefore branded as illegal and heterodox. In Jerusalem there ruled a priestly hierarchy with the 'High Priest'

---

[1] Cf. *Pap. Cowley*, No. 30 (AOT², pp. 450 ff., ANET, p. 492, DOTT, pp. 262 f.).

(cf. above p. 316) at its head and a closed priesthood who derived from the Zadokite families of the Davidic period and now traced their origin even further back to Moses' brother Aaron, who was now assigned great prominence in the tradition[1]. The connection with the Zadokites of the period of the kings certainly existed, although after the rather long and chaotic transition period some families' claim to membership of this family was doubtful and disputed[2] and the precise delimitation of the 'Zadokite' priesthood was only achieved after all kinds of internal conflicts. In the course of the Persian period the *clerus minor* of the now so-called 'Levites' developed alongside this priesthood in what was presumably a fairly long process. In the programme for the future in the book of Ezekiel the priests of the local sanctuaries that had been abolished by Josiah, to whom the deuteronomic law had granted sacerdotal rights in Jerusalem (Deut. xviii, 6 f.) but who had presumably been excluded by the Jerusalem priests from the right to sacrifice (2 Kings xxiii, 9), were considered eligible to carry out inferior services in the sanctuary and above all to prepare the sacrificial rites (Ezek. xliv, 9-14) from which the lay element was now wholly excluded. In fact a body of Temple servants consisting of 'Levites' was formed after the restoration of the sanctuary. In this may have been included, from Josiah's time onwards, a section consisting of the priestly families from the former local sanctuaries[3]; but in time they were joined by all kinds of groups of non-priestly personnel, all of whom were finally gathered together into the body of 'Levites' as it came to be more closely integrated[4].

Not surprisingly, priests and Levites were concentrated in Jerusalem around the sanctuary; but they also lived outside Jerusalem and only came to the sanctuary at their strictly appointed times of service (cf. Luke i, 39 f.). The far-reaching organisation of the cult personnel, particularly on the level of the 'Levites', made precise distribution of the various official functions essential. This took place no doubt step by step over a fairly long period. But its foundations were certainly laid in the Persian period.

Public worship itself also assumed new forms during the Persian

---

[1] Cf., above all, the presentation in the Priestly Code in Lev. viii, ix and also the list in 1 Chron. v, 27-41.

[2] Cf. Ezra ii, 61-63= Neh. vii, 63-65. Disputes about the rights of the priests have also been recorded in a few later sections of the Pentateuch narrative such as Num. xvi, P.

[3] Cf. the lists of Levites in P (Num. iii, 5 ff. and elsewhere) and K. Möhlenbrink, ZAW, N.F. 11 (1934), pp. 184 ff.

[4] The work of the Chronicler especially contains in its secondary additions numerous lists of various groups of Levites, and mentions, above all, Levitical Temple singers (cf. especially 1 Chron. xxiii [2b], 3–xxvii, 34).

period. The Temple in Jerusalem was no longer, as in the Davidic period, a royal shrine, in which the king arranged for sacrifices to be offered by his official priests according to the customs traditional in the land and particularly in the place itself, and for the other usual religious rites to be observed. In the programme for the future in the book of Ezekiel the king's place, now vacated, is occupied by the person of a 'prince' who merely has to carry out in the main the former king's religious functions (Ezek. xlv, 7 ff.)[1]. But the 'prince' whom Ezekiel envisaged failed to become a historical reality. On the contrary, after the restoration of the Temple, and, above all, after the reform which Ezra presumably introduced, the whole religious community became responsible for public worship in Jerusalem. The old institution of the state sanctuary only survived in so far as the Persian kings granted special privileges to the sanctuary by meeting the cost of part of the materials needed for sacrifice and by causing prayers to be made in the sanctuary 'for their life' (cf. above p. 315). But they can hardly have exerted any direct influence on the actual conduct of public worship. They probably left it to the religious community itself to organise its worship in accordance with tradition. The Jerusalem religious community naturally adhered to the form of worship traditional in Jerusalem; but the changed situation led inevitably to all kinds of innovations. Whilst the three traditional pilgrim feasts, which were originally harvest festivals rooted in Palestinian tradition, but had meanwhile become to some extent festivals celebrating the great fundamental acts of God, continued to be celebrated, there was now in addition a particularly important 'Day of Atonement' which was observed five days before the beginning of the great autumn festival on the 10th day of the 7th month (Lev. xxiii, 27-32), and this now took the place of the autumn festival as the real beginning of the religious year (cf. Lev. xxv, 9 f.). An earlier ritual of the cleansing of the sanctuary was further developed (Lev. xvi). This introduction of the 'Day of Atonement' was connected with the increasing importance that was now attached to expiation in general in public worship; the divine judgement with its consequences in the present situation had aroused great fear of transgressing the divine commandments and a demand for repeated cultic purification. The worship itself was increasingly based on the punctilious fulfilment of existing regulations—the 'law of the God of Heaven' which Ezra had brought

[1] Cf. also elsewhere the maintenance of the king's religious functions after the removal of the monarchy, e.g. the ἄρχων βασιλεύς in Athens.

with him had no doubt included provisions for regulating public worship—and it thereby lost something of the unselfconscious 'rejoicing before Yahweh' of which the deuteronomic law had still spoken in stereotyped terms.

Above all, however, the Persian period was important because it saw the beginnings of the canonisation of a particular literature. It is certain that it was in this period that the Pentateuch not only acquired essentially its definitive form but also became a holy book which was binding on the whole Jerusalem religious community. It is true that the literary history of this great work goes much further back. But the older constituents had never played as great a part as was now played by the whole work. It had provided brief creed-like summaries of the basic acts of God, which it was the custom to recite on certain religious occasions; and the wealth of narrative material which had gathered around the individual themes of these creeds had been expressed in fixed forms in theological works which were read and passed on, without apparently having acquired any official sanction. Probably the summarising formulations of the valid divine law had been binding on the old tribal society, and these may have been set down in writing at quite an early period. It is impossible to trace their history in any detail. We are better informed about the fate of the deuteronomic law which represents, however, in its paraenetically more diffuse form, a comparatively late stage in the formulation of the law, and included and developed earlier compilations[1]. This deuteronomic law was made binding on the tribal association, which still existed at least in theory, by the covenant instigated by Josiah. This was, as far as we know, the first time that a more extensive document was recognised as valid for the whole of 'Israel'; and whilst it contained at its centre a collection of ordinances of the divine law, it constantly referred to the historical basis of God's special relationship to Israel in the homiletic elements in which it was set and with which it was interspersed. In Josiah's time there still existed at least the remnants of Israel's old traditional institutions. But with the loss of independence they soon collapsed completely, and, despite the fact that it now lacked the background of an existing institution, the document of the deuteronomist law now acquired a special weight as a record of traditional observances. The further development which took place in the Persian period followed on from this point. Though the deuteronomic law had still continued

---

[1] Cf. G. v. Rad, *Deuteronomium Studien* (1947), pp. 7 ff. English translation *Studies in Deuteronomy* (1953), pp. 11 ff.

in force at first, Ezra had ultimately secured recognition for the 'law of the God of Heaven' which he had brought with him, probably by means similar to those earlier used to enforce the deuteronomic law. Once again a document, a book, had become the foundation of life and action. Even if this 'law' of Ezra's was a compilation of ordinances of which we have now no detailed knowledge and not the complete Pentateuch itself (cf. p. 335 f.) it was soon followed by the final redaction of the great Pentateuch which pursued the same line and included Ezra's 'law'. This represented the culmination of a long process of editing, and summarised all the basic traditions concerning Israel's pre-history with the most important earlier and later formulations of the divine law[1]; and this great work was no doubt quickly acknowledged as authoritative, perhaps even without a special ceremony to give it official status. Thereafter it became the canonical holy book of the Jerusalem religious community, and as such it became the basis of the collection of writings now included in the Old Testament. The reading and knowledge of this holy book which, characteristically, was later simply called 'the law', in spite of its basic narrative, thereby became an essential task of the pious community and the pious individual; and this provided the impulse for a particular form of divine service alongside the central sacrificial rite in Jerusalem, a form which it was possible to cultivate outside Jerusalem as well, above all in the Diaspora, and which consisted in the reading aloud and interpretation of sections of 'the law'. It also led to the development of a technique of expounding this holy book, every detail of which was becoming important and which was not always immediately intelligible owing to its complicated background. Synagogue worship and scribal exegesis do not emerge into the clear light of history until the later Hellenistic period. The beginnings of this important process are obscure. We cannot be certain that it was already developing in the Persian period. But the canonising of the Pentateuch as sacred scripture was the first step that was bound to lead to the synagogue and to scribal exegesis.

The traditional records of the prophets' sayings also continued to be read and collected in the Persian period. Once the Pentateuch had conferred importance on the study and collection of the literary records of the past, this study was extended to the prophetic

[1] Only the deuteronomic law was not contained in the Pentateuch to begin with. But the combination of the Pentateuch with the deuteronomistic history which finally resulted in the incorporation of the deuteronomic law in the Pentateuch (cf. M. Noth, *Überlieferungsgeschichtliche Studien*, I [1943], pp. 211 ff.) certainly took place during the Persian period.

writings which contained the threats so clearly confirmed by the judgement of God which had been experienced, and also the promises which directed men's eyes away from the afflictions of the present to hope in what God might do in the future. The existing collections of words of the prophets were supplemented with expressions of hope for the future by means of a whole variety of reformulations of promises in accordance with the contemporary standpoint. It can hardly be doubted that a fairly large part of the secondary material in the books of the prophets as they have come down to us derives from the Persian period, though it is naturally impossible to trace this process in detail. It continued into the subsequent Hellenistic period, until the tradition of the prophets also finally became fixed some time in the course of the first century of the Hellenistic period, and further development was brought to an end when the existing books of the prophets were combined with the main part of the deuteronomistic history, which was now regarded as prophetic, to form the prophetic canon as the second part of the authoritative holy writings. A number of other writings which were finally included in the third part of the Old Testament canon doubtless came into being in the Persian period, though it is impossible to be certain about the details.

Thus the Persian period clearly had, in many respects, a decisive influence on the later course of Israelite history and Israelite life. After the decline and fall of the old order in the historical events of the Assyrian and Neo-Babylonian period, a new beginning and a re-ordering took place in the Jerusalem religious community as a consequence of the instructions for the reconstruction of the sanctuary in Jerusalem which Cyrus issued in his very first year, and, as a result of the pressure which was repeatedly brought to bear on the Persian state authorities by the Babylonian group of exiles, who obviously made a not unimportant contribution at this time to the life of the whole community. The things that were developed and prepared in this period had an important effect on the whole further course of Israel's history right up to its very end.

We have no continuous historical record of this period, as we have for the period of the Judaean-Israelite kings. Only isolated, though important, happenings are clearly illuminated in some parts of the tradition. There is also only a little information available outside the Old Testament. As a subject-people forming part of a large empire, Israel had even less influence on the outward course of history in the Near East than hitherto. It is not surprising, therefore, that archaeological excavation has yielded remarkably little from this period of Israel's history. The miserable and oppressive conditions under which the Israelite tribes lived in Palestine at the time did not permit them to develop their ability in the fields of building and the crafts generally in such a way as to be revealed significantly by archaeological excavation. The only noteworthy building of this period of which there is literary evidence, the new sanctuary in Jerusalem, which was built with difficulty over a fairly long period, cannot be studied archaeologically since the site is still occupied by a famous Muslim shrine and is not available to archaeological research. Up till now, therefore, there have been hardly any results worth mentioning in this field of research[1]. The only point of note is that coins have been found from the Persian period with the inscription yhd ='Judah'. Coins, the value of which was officially guaranteed by having their denomination stamped on them were not in circulation throughout the ancient Orient until the Persian period, after they had been introduced in the kingdom of Lydia. These coins with the inscription yhd[2] show that in this sphere too the province of Judah was granted autonomy by the Persians; and it may be that this was done in consideration for the Jerusalem religious community which the Persians promoted and which had its centre in the province of Judah, just as other important sanctuaries were given the right by the Persians[3] to mint their own coins. The yhd coins appear to have come into use in the course of the 4th century. Numerous jar handles stamped with the letters yhd or $yršlm$ (Jerusalem) have also been found. The clay vessels which had their handles stamped in this way were presumably used in the cultic taxation system. The most remarkable point is that the coins, which were made of silver, were minted on the model of Attic drachmas, some with the image of Zeus, some with a picture of the Athenian owl[4]. The ceramics of this period also included all kinds of Greek-Aegean ware. Greek influence and these Greek imports, which thus made their appearance a long time before the Macedonian conquest of the Orient, and naturally also appear outside the province of Judah, came through the Phoenician coastal cities, which enjoyed considerable independence under Persian rule and were developing their maritime trade on a large scale. The description of the Mediterranean coasts which appears under the name of

---

[1] The section on this period in W. F. Albright, *The Archaeology of Palestine* (1949), pp. 142-145, is characteristically brief and deals mainly with things which do not appertain directly to the history of Israel but only to Israel's neighbours.

[2] Cf. K. Galling, PJB, 34 (1938), pp. 57 ff.   [3] Cf. Albright, *op. cit.* p. 143.

[4] Cf. figs. 4 and 5 in Galling, *op. cit.* p. 77, ANEP, Nos. 226-227, DOTT, p. 233 and Pl. 14.

Scylax, an admiral of the time of Darius I, but which was probably written in the last years of the Persian era, shows that substantial parts of the coastal plain of Palestine were subject to various of these Phoenician cities at this time[1]. Phoenician maritime trade had many contacts with Greek commerce; and the Attic drachma had been common currency since the time of the Attic maritime alliance and through the influence of the Phoenicians it came into Syria-Palestine and was imitated there, and with it there came other products of the Greek world. Such indirect contacts with this world, however, scarcely had much influence on the inner life of the Jerusalem religious community.

Persian rule has left some archaeological traces at least in the immediate vicinity of the province of Judah. Apart from the Persian installations in the extreme south-west of Palestine, on the border of the Sinaitic desert, already mentioned on p. 318, a remarkable legacy of this period has been found at *tell ed-duwēr*, the site of ancient Lachish, namely, the remains of an imposing Persian palace from the end of the 5th or the beginning of the 4th century[2]. This suggests that Lachish must have been an important centre of Persian government; it is conceivable that this was the seat of the Persian governor of the province of Edom, which embraced the district on both sides of the southern end of the Dead Sea[3] and was the Province of Judah's southerly neighbour. If the centre of the provincial government was in fact Lachish, the choice of this peripheral situation far to north-west was probably due to the fact that the main approach to the province was from this side. Here lay the area, so important for the Persian rulers, from which the road led to Egypt, always insecure. In Gezer (*tell jezer*), not so far north of this area, which occupied the south-west corner of the province of Samaria and was quite close to the north-west frontier of the province of Judah, tombs have been discovered belonging to the Persian period[4], in which, in all probability, Persians, or at any rate officials in Persian employ, were buried. This also suggests that here was a minor centre of Persian government.

With this we have mentioned substantially all the certain archaeological finds which the soil of Palestine has yielded from the Persian period.

---

[1] The details will be found in K. Galling, ZDPV, 61 (1938), pp. 66 ff., especially pp. 78 ff.

[2] For the ground-plan of this palace see Albright, *op. cit.* p. 144, fig. 47.

[3] Cf. M. Noth, ZDPV, 67 (1944–1945), pp. 62 f.

[4] On the condition and correct dating of these tombs which were originally thought to be 'Philistine', cf. K. Galling, PJB, 31 (1935), pp. 88 ff.

28. *The Macedonian Conquest of the Orient and the Samaritan Schism*

After his victory over Darius III Codomannus at Issus in the year 333 B.C., Syria-Palestine fell into the hands of Alexander the Great who had already conquered Asia Minor. In 332 B.C. he moved from the north—Issus was situated near the modern North Syrian port of Alexandretta—southwards along the coast of Syria-Palestine, to reach and occupy Egypt as quickly as possible. For seven months he was forced to stay outside the ancient island stronghold of Tyre, which he finally overcame with the aid of a mole constructed from the near-by mainland to the island, and he had to spend another two months besieging the city of Gaza in south-west Palestine, before he was finally able, through the Sinaitic desert, to reach Egypt in order to occupy its rich land. He could not spare the time in this to conquer the interior of Syria-Palestine; he left it to his commander-in-chief, Parmenio, who gained control of this area without difficulty. In Palestine the only place that had to be conquered by force was the governor's seat in the province of Samaria, the former Israelite royal city of Samaria; thereupon a Macedonian colony was established there by the Macedonian Perdiccas. Jerusalem and the province of Judah, and so probably too the other Palestinian provinces inhabited by Israelites, yielded without resistance to the new power that appeared so suddenly and with such great military strength; and in the province of Samaria the Macedonians probably met little resistance apart from the city of Samaria itself. In the year 331 B.C. Alexander proceeded once again from Egypt through Syria-Palestine into Mesopotamia, where he dealt the decisive blow at the Persian empire in the great battle of Gaugamela near Arbela, and set about building his Greek-Oriental empire. These were events which affected the whole course of world history; they brought the history of the ancient Orient to an end and marked the beginning of the Hellenistic period in the eastern Mediterranean area. The progress of Alexander's campaign in 332–331 B.C. brought the main Macedonian force in direct proximity to the area inhabited by the Israelite tribes and must have made a powerful impression on them. Nevertheless there is no definite reference to this event in the Old Testament. The historical writings in the Old Testament do not go any further than the end of the old kingdoms of Israel and Judah and—in the Chronicler's narrative—the restoration in the Persian period; and the later historical writings (the books of Maccabees, Josephus) do not go back so far with any definite information. Perhaps one might expect some references to the age of Alexander in very late parts of the prophetic canon, which was only closed in the course of the 3rd century. Attempts have in fact been made to see in Alexander's campaign the historical background of the prophet's words in the book of Habakkuk (Hab. i, ii) in which a tyrannical and audacious conqueror is threatened with the judgement of God[1]; this is not improbable, but we have no certain proof; and the words of the prophet in Zech. ix, 1-8 have also been thought to refer to Alexander's march through Syria-Palestine in the year 332 B.C.[2]. But these are mere possibilities that call for consideration; apart from the impression made by Alexander's overwhelming and rapid incursion, the passages we have mentioned throw no detailed light on the fate of the Jerusalem religious community in this period. Presumably the transition from one sovereign power to another took place without any great external upheavals.

The struggles of the Diadochi for power after the death of Alexander in the year 323 B.C. again took place partly in Syria-Palestine, the centre of so many trade routes, and occasionally in direct proximity to the Jerusalem religious community. First of all Ptolemy, Alexander's governor in Egypt, had near-by Palestine and Phoenicia occupied from Egypt. In the battles against Antigonus and his son Demetrius Poliorketes, who claimed the inheritance of Alexander and therefore had most of Alexander's other governors against them, Demetrius Poliorketes was defeated in 312 B.C. in a battle near Gaza, and Ptolemy proceeded to take renewed possession of Palestine and Phoenicia. After Antigonus had lost the battle and his life at Ipsus in Phrygia in 301 B.C., the dominions of the Diadochi, who had meanwhile adopted the style of kings, were gradually consolidated. Egypt formed the nucleus of the Ptolemaic state with the 'City of Alexander' in the western delta of the Nile (Alexandria) as the royal seat. The centre of gravity of the Seleucid state lay in northern and central Syria. This state acquired its royal centre in the new foundation of Antioch on the lower Orontes and to the east it embraced Mesopotamia. To begin with, the Ptolemies were able to hold Palestine and Phoenicia against the Seleucids who, not surprisingly, were interested in acquiring this neighbouring country. The area which was the focus

[1] Thus, above all, B. Duhm, *Das Buch Habakuk* (1906).
[2] Thus in recent times K. Elliger, *Das Alte Testament Deutsch*, 25 (1950), pp. 135 ff., and ZAW, 62 (1949-1950), pp. 63-115.

of the Jerusalem religious community therefore belonged for the time being to the Ptolemies.

We know very little about the fortunes of the Jerusalem religious community in the period of Ptolemaic rule. It is hardly likely that this new power intervened in its inner life, and so the change of government that took place after the collapse of the Persian empire may at first not have had much effect on it. We learn a little about the Ptolemaic period in Palestine from the Zeno papyri which were found in 1915 in the ruins of the military colony of Philadelpheia in the oasis of *faiyum*, south-west of the delta of the Nile[1]. These papyri contain the correspondence of a certain Zeno who was the land agent of the Ptolemaic minister of finance Apollonius (261–246 B.C.). Apollonius owned all kinds of estates, some in Palestine and also in the area east of the Jordan, which he had probably received in fief from his king Ptolemy II Philadelphus. These estates were presumably crown lands, which may well already have long been in royal possession. The kings of Israel and Judah had already had their crown lands (cf. above, pp. 213 f.); and after the abolition of the independent state this crown land had passed into the direct ownership of the then reigning power, which was able to use it for the benefit of its officials and for military installations. We have no detailed information about the nature and extent of this crown land. But parts of it no doubt appear in Apollonius' property in Palestine. The Ptolemies certainly will not have encroached on the property rights of the Israelites any more than did the Persians before them.

A considerable group of members of the Jerusalem religious community probably gathered in the Ptolemaic royal city of Alexandria already in the 3rd century, some of whom were descendants of those who had earlier migrated to Lower Egypt and others of whom were new-comers attracted by the rapidly flourishing city. This group adopted the Greek language which prevailed in Alexandria instead of Aramaic; and Alexandria soon became one of the most important centres of a Greek-speaking Hellenistic Diaspora which was to be found also in other Hellenistic cities in the eastern Mediterranean. Earlier groups of scattered Israelites were joined in these by a variety of new elements who were attracted by the worship and faith of the Jerusalem religious community and submitted to its 'law'; they were called Proselytes ($\pi\rho o\sigma\acute{\eta}\lambda\upsilon\tau o\iota$), *i.e.* 'new-comers'. In these groups, which no longer understood the Hebrew of the Old Testament and the Aramaic vernacular of the

[1] Cf. J. Herz, PJB, 24 (1928), pp. 105 ff. (cf. p. 106, note 1 ff. for bibliography).

Israelites resident in Palestine or had never understood them at all, there arose the need for a Greek translation of the holy book of the Jerusalem religious community, which for the time being consisted merely in 'the Law' (Pentateuch). And so, in the course of the 3rd century, the sections of the 'Law' appointed to be read aloud and interpreted, were translated into Greek, to begin with probably orally in the synagogue service, and from this there developed in Alexandria, and possibly elsewhere as well, a Greek translation of the Pentateuch, at first lacking uniformity. This was later followed by translations of the other parts of the Old Testament as they were canonised[1]. This was a very important step. In the Greek-speaking Diaspora the holy book of the Jerusalem religious community was thus cut loose from its original Hebrew, which by then was already restricted to public worship and learned exegesis, and thereby it came to be exposed to the possibility of the influence of Greek thought which, already simply in the use of the Greek language and mode of expression, exercised an influence on this translation. All this followed inevitably from the process which had started with Alexander's appearance in the Orient, though one does not have to assume that the Ptolemies, as the rulers of Palestine and Phoenicia during the 3rd century, instigated the Hellenisation of the Jerusalem religious community or that they helped to shift its centre of gravity to the Hellenistic or Hellenised Diaspora. They no doubt allowed the traditional religious rites to continue unimpeded in Palestine and Phoenicia as they did in Egypt.

In the end, however, the Ptolemies lost Palestine and Phoenicia to the Seleucids. In the Seleucid state the reign of Antiochus III (223–187 B.C.) marked the zenith of its power. In combination with Philip of Macedonia he was able to extend his rule into Asia Minor and make his influence felt as far as Greece. Before he came at a later stage into conflict with the Romans on this account, he was able to realise the ancient claim of the Seleucids to Phoenicia and Palestine. It is true that a first attempt at this failed. In the year

[1] The pseudepigraphon, the so-called Letter of Aristeas which has been preserved in numerous manuscripts (German translation in F. Kautzsch, *Die Apokryphen und Pseudepigraphen des A.T.s* [1900], II, pp. 1 ff. English translation in R. H. Charles, *Apocrypha and Pseudepigrapha of the Old Testament* II (1913), pp. 83-122) provides a legend describing the translation of the 'law' into Greek at the instigation of Ptolemy II Philadelphus (285–246 B.C.). It was not written until the end of the 2nd century B.C. and was intended to proclaim as possessing exclusive authority a particular translation of the Old Testament into Greek which existed in Alexandria at the time (cf. P. Kahle, *The Cairo Geniza* [1947], pp. 132 ff.). It claims that this translation was prepared in the 3rd century by seventy-two scholars (hence the name 'Septuagint') on official instructions. Probably there is truth in this legend in so far as it places the beginnings of the Greek translation in 3rd century Alexandria.

217 B.C. he was defeated by Ptolemy IV Philopator in a battle at Raphia (the modern *refaḥ*) in the extreme south-western corner of Palestine on the coast road to Egypt, and had to give up Palestine and Phoenicia which he had conquered. But in 198 B.C. he finally succeeded in defeating Ptolemy V Epiphanes—who had meanwhile come to the throne—so decisively in the district of the sources of the Jordan near the city of Paneion (the modern *bānyās*), that he obtained possession of Phoenicia and Palestine once and for all, and Ptolemy was forced to make peace with them on this basis. Once again, therefore, the Israelites in Jerusalem and Palestine had a change of sovereign. They do not appear to have disliked the change. At any rate we learn from a document which we are about to discuss that, evidently after the battle of Paneion, they captured the Ptolemaic occupation forces in Jerusalem and gave a 'splendid' welcome to the Seleucid troops with their war elephants, and provided them with abundant supplies. Perhaps there was nothing more behind this than the discontent which a foreign power always evokes among its subjects in the end and the understandable intention of commending themselves to the new sovereign once he had clearly shown himself as such. For his part, Antiochus at once showed his good-will to the Jerusalem religious community in order to win them over to his side, which he regarded as important, especially in view of the far-reaching connections they had as a result of their widespread Diaspora. In *Ant. Iud.* XII, 3, 3 (§§ 138-144 Niese) Josephus has recorded the text of a decree issued by Antiochus III to a certain Ptolemy, who may have been the state commissioner for the newly conquered regions. This decree contains a number of regulations benefiting Jerusalem and the Jerusalem religious community, and, as a document preserved in Jerusalem, it may presumably be considered authentic[1]. By this decree the city of Jerusalem, as a reward for the attitude of its people at the change of sovereignty from the Ptolemies to the Seleucids, was granted the return of the inhabitants who had been dispersed in the course of the wars of the preceding period and the release of those who had fallen into slavery as well as a general exemption from taxation and the reduction of payments in kind by a third for

---

[1] The authenticity of this decree has often been doubted (cf. most recently H. Willrich, *Urkundenfälschung in der hellenistisch-jüdischen Literatur* [1924], pp. 21 f.). For its authenticity cf. Ed. Meyer, *Ursprung und Anfänge des Christentums*, II (1921), pp. 126 f., and latterly E. Bickermann, *Revue des études juives*, 100 (1935), pp. 4-35 (with detailed historical interpretation) and A. Alt, ZAW, N.F. 16 (1939), pp. 283 ff. (here there is an analysis of the complicated structure of this decree). For the Greek text of the decree see TGI, pp. 76 f.

a period of three years with a view to assisting its rebuilding and the improvement of its economic position (§§ 138, 139, 143, 144). In this connection alone do we learn incidentally that Jerusalem had probably suffered considerably in the fighting between the Ptolemies and the Seleucids; few details about these battles have come down to us. At any rate, the new ruling power tried to repair the damage that had been caused. Furthermore, Antiochus' decree granted certain privileges to the sanctuary in Jerusalem; above all, the supply of sacrificial materials and other requirements for the cultus up to a certain limit from state resources, probably from the produce of the crown lands, and also the right to live in accordance with 'the laws handed down by their fathers', and finally permanent exemption from taxation for the cult personnel (§ 140-142). These privileges had already existed in the Persian period (cf. above, p. 334) and may not have been infringed by Alexander and the Ptolemies, so that Antiochus, as the new sovereign, may merely have been confirming the old rights rather than giving new privileges. Only in some of the details may there have been further extensions. For example, state aid was promised for more or less essential extensions of the sanctuary (§ 141) and the supply of wood for the sacrificial fires which Nehemiah had had to pledge the members of the religious community themselves to supply (Neh. x, 35), was made duty-free (§ 141). Finally, the exemption from taxation accorded to the cult personnel was extended to the 'council of elders' (γερουσία) and the 'scribes' (γραμματεῖς), who here make their first appearance in history.

The friendly relationship between the new ruling power and the Jerusalem religious community which this created did not indeed last for long. Antiochus III was soon afterwards involved in conflicts with the Romans, who intervened in the eastern Mediterranean area immediately after the Second Punic War, because the power of Antiochus III, who was allied with Philip of Macedonia and to whom Hannibal had fled after his defeat, seemed to them to be becoming dangerous. At the battle of Magnesia on the Meander in Asia Minor, Antiochus was defeated by the Romans in 190 B.C. and was forced in the following year to agree to the humiliating Peace of Apamea. This was the beginning of the decline of Seleucid power; and in the course of this decline there took place, under Antiochus IV Epiphanes, the great conflict with the Jerusalem religious community which initiated a new phase in Israelite history.

Meanwhile, however, an event had taken place which had an

important effect on the inner history of this community, namely the separation of the Samaritan community from Jerusalem and the establishment of an independent Samaritan cultus on the ancient holy mountain of Gerizim near Shechem. It is impossible to assign an exact date to the carrying through of this separation; but it merely marks the completion of a long development, the beginnings of which went back a long way. The process had its ultimate roots in the age-old division between the southern group of tribes and the rest of the tribes, which had their main representatives in the Central Palestinian group. David had brought the southern tribes into prominence historically, and after the death of Solomon the southern kingdom of Judah had kept within its sphere of influence in its royal city of Jerusalem the ancient tribal relic of the Ark which formed the religious centre of the whole tribal confederation. This sanctuary, no doubt, continued to be visited by members of all the Israelite tribes. But the kings of Israel tried to compete with the Jerusalem shrine with state shrines of their own (cf. 1 Kings xii, 26 ff.); and Jerusalem as the central shrine can hardly have been acknowledged wholeheartedly among the tribes of the kingdom of Israel, particularly as they still remembered that the new dignity of Jerusalem was due to the Judaean David and that it entirely lacked the authority of great age. The Ark and hence the religious centre had always previously been set among the central group of tribes, first in Shechem, then possibly for a time in Bethel and Gilgal and certainly finally in Shiloh, and religious observances had continued to take place on the ancient sacred site of Shechem, which pointed to Shechem's original role as the central place of worship. In view of the tenacity with which religious institutions and ideas are usually preserved, this memory will hardly have faded completely when the kingdom of Israel came to an end and its shrines lost their previous importance and a foreign ruling class came into the country with its own cults. It is unlikely that the cults of these foreigners had any considerable influence on those parts of the tribes that stayed behind in the former kingdom of Israel or on their religious traditions. Then came Josiah, who abolished the local places of worship even in the province of Samaria which he had annexed, including the ancient and celebrated shrine of Bethel, and who centralised the whole religious system in Jerusalem on the basis of the deuteronomic demand for unity of worship. For a time the old local shrines may have continued among the Galilean and East Jordanic tribes, *i.e.* in the Assyrian provinces of Megiddo and Gilead, which Josiah had not yet subjugated when he met his sudden death[1]; we have no definite information on this point, however, and Jerusalem may well have established itself quickly as the one legitimate place of worship attended by members of all the tribes that had remained in the land. This probably continued to be the case after the Temple had been destroyed in the year 587 B.C. and only the holy place as such remained. It was now no longer a royal Judaean shrine and could therefore be recognised more readily as the one central shrine common to all. But the old antithesis between north and south still continued below the surface and broke out again when plans were made for the rebuilding of the sanctuary in Jerusalem following Cyrus' decree. This time the resistance came from the Judaean side. The inhabitants of the land of Judah regarded the Temple as their own sanctuary and its rebuilding as their task, and did not want the Israelites from the neighbouring provinces to take part, while the latter not unjustly claimed a share in the work of restoration since the building in question was the ancient central shrine. The inhabitants of the neighbouring provinces, in which the foreign upper classes had gradually been absorbed or were in process of being absorbed by the local Israelite population, were regarded by the Judaeans, who had had no foreign upper class imposed on them, as cultically unclean. At any rate this is how the prophet Haggai appears to have looked at the matter, if the symbolical action of questioning the priests about the effect of 'clean' and 'unclean' which is reported in Hag. ii, 10-14, and which implies that 'this people and this nation' as infected with contaminating cultic uncleanness, really refers to the inhabitants of the neighbouring provinces who were not to be allowed to defile the purity of the work of restoring the Temple[2]. It may be that the Judaeans who were deported to Babylonia, and who influenced the course of events in Judah in this period by reason of their access to the Persian court, also wanted to have the restoration of the cultus in Jerusalem regarded as a purely Judaean concern.

Perhaps the old political conflict between Judaeans and Israelites still played a part at this period. But the religious and cultic aspect appears to have been more to the fore, the more so since Judah was

---

[1] Josiah only seems to have been able to gain control of the small southern part of the land east of the Jordan (cf. above, p. 274).

[2] Thus W. Rothstein, *Juden und Samaritaner* (1908). Later, in Ezra iv, 1-5, the Chronicler assumed that there was a conflict between the repatriated exiles and the population that had remained in the homeland over the rebuilding of the Temple and thereby introduced a slightly false emphasis. At the time of the rebuilding of the Temple hardly any of the exiles had returned home.

probably still subject to the governor of Samaria and the restoration of the Temple took place under the jurisdiction of the provincial government in Samaria. The situation changed when Judah was constituted as an independent province under Nehemiah and a marked antithesis arose again between Samaria and Jerusalem, to which Nehemiah refers repeatedly in his Memoirs[1]. This political rivalry, in which the old claim of the Central Palestinian tribes to represent the real core of Israel was revived in a new form, inevitably had an effect in the religious sphere. It was only with reluctance that the Israelites in the province of Samaria—the Galileans and East Jordanians were no doubt less interested in this political antithesis—recognised Jerusalem as the only legitimate centre of worship. But, to begin with, they apparently acquiesced in the situation as it had evolved, particularly as the Persian government was singling out the Jerusalem sanctuary for special treatment and was granting it all kinds of privileges. But they were moving towards separation from the sanctuary in Jerusalem and towards the establishment of their own cultus based on the age-old religious traditions of their area; the only question is when the time arrived for them to realise this intention.

In *Ant. Iud.* XI, 8, 3-7 Josephus tells of Alexander the Great's progress through Syria-Palestine, and in this connection he makes the high priest in Jerusalem defy Alexander out of loyalty to the Persian emperor, whilst, according to him, the governor of the province of Samaria submitted straight away to the conqueror and asked for permission to erect a shrine of his own, which permission Alexander granted at once (§§ 321-324 Niese). The whole story is full of legendary details and introduces all kinds of figures, such as the governor of Samaria Sanballat, who do not belong to this historical context. The story of how Alexander finally came to Jerusalem himself, and how, in spite of the initial attitude of the high priest, the city was saved in a miraculous fashion (§§ 325-339 Niese), is obviously completely lacking in any real foundation. But it is possible that the story of the difference between the attitude to Alexander's appearance which was adopted in Jerusalem and Samaria does contain an accurate tradition. It is so likely historically that the appearance of a new sovereign was welcomed in Samaria, as opposed to Jerusalem which had obtained so many privileges from the Persians, and that the change of government

---

[1] This conflict appears to have been unknown to the colonists in Elephantine; as late as 408 B.C. they wrote on one and the same matter simultaneously to the governor Bagoas in Jerusalem and to the sons of the governor Sanballat of Samaria (*Pap. Cowley*, No. 30; cf. AOT², pp. 450 ff., ANET, p. 492, DOTT, pp. 262 f.

was used by the Samaritans to realise the desire of establishing a
cultus of their own and one independent of Jerusalem, that one
might be inclined, even without Josephus's story, to place the
establishment of the Samaritan cultus on Gerizim at the beginning of the Hellenistic period. It is not very likely that the goal was
attained during the Persian period in Samaria. The Persian attitude
to the Jerusalem cultus militated against this. And it was also
necessary for the Pentateuch to have become so firmly accepted as
the holy book in the Jerusalem religious community as to leave
the Samaritans no option but to adopt it as the foundation of their
cultus too. This would bring us, at the earliest, to the end of the
Persian period. On the other hand, however, it would be wrong
to go too far into the Hellenistic period. It is true that the first
explicit evidence of the existence of the Samaritan sanctuary on
Gerizim dates from the period of Antiochus IV Epiphanes (2 Macc.
vi, 2); but it here appears alongside Jerusalem as an important
shrine, already distinguished presumably by a certain tradition.
Needless to say, Josephus' story of Alexander's having given
immediate permission for the erection of a Samaritan sanctuary on
his first arrival in Syria-Palestine can lay no claim to historical
truth; but it is probable, nevertheless, that during the period of
Alexander's rule, or during the conflicts of the Diadochi, Samaria
found an opportunity of obtaining official permission to establish
the cultus of her own for which she had striven for so long.

Leaving out of account as less important the Israelites who were
still living in Galilee and in the land east of the Jordan, the cultus on
Gerizim was no doubt intended for the whole population of the
province of Samaria, who were thereby to be given their own
religious centre, just as the province of Judah had for so long had
its centre in Jerusalem. This goal was not, it is true, completely
achieved. The new cultus no doubt attracted most of the Samaritans.
But the old tradition of Jerusalem which had been for so long the
religious centre even for the inhabitants of the province of Samaria
as well, maintained its hold on many of them. At any rate the
Israelites in the southern districts of the province of Samaria apparently maintained a fairly solid attachment to Jerusalem owing to
their proximity to Judah and Jerusalem, and this ultimately led,
about the middle of the 2nd century B.C., to the separation of these
districts from the province of Samaria and their assignment to the
province of Judah[1].

[1] Cf. below, p. 378, and the detailed remarks by A. Alt in PJB, 31 (1935), pp. 94 ff.,
especially pp. 100 ff.

Not surprisingly, people in Jerusalem always regarded the cultus on Gerizim as illegitimate. The Samaritans were considered apostates and religiously unclean. The whole of the Chronicler's history was compiled—about 300 B.C.—with the purpose of proving the unique legitimacy of the Jerusalem tradition historically, as opposed to the Samaritan cultus. With this in view, prominence was given from the very outset to David and his activity, well-pleasing to God, of preparing for the building of the Temple. The history of the kings of Judah was then traced as the real history of Israel, and finally, as the bearers of the authentic tradition, the group of deported and later repatriated Judaeans was connected with the work of restoring the Temple and reorganising the religious community[1]. We have no information as to how the Samaritans regarded things. Probably they answered the question whether men 'ought to worship in this mountain (*i.e.* on Gerizim) or in Jerusalem' (John iv, 20), by pointing out that Shechem had the older tradition as an Israelite shrine, and that the transfer of the Ark into the royal Judaean city of Jerusalem by the Judaean David was an arbitrary and illegitimate action.

The Samaritan religious community managed to survive through the vicissitudes of history. Josephus, adopting the Judaean point of view, criticises the Samaritans for a contemptible lack of principle, as a result of which they had steered their way through the twists and turns of history, stressing, as seemed most opportune at the time, either their relationship to the larger unity of Israel and their connection with the Jerusalemites, or their separateness and special position (*op. cit.* §§ 340 ff.). In the end, however, the Samaritans shared the fate of all those who, though appealing perhaps to age-old traditions, rebel against a situation that has evolved over a long period of time, and try to base their life on historical conditions which have long since disappeared. They gradually degenerated and became almost completely uncreative. Today there is a tiny remnant of Samaritans in the city of *nāblus* (Shechem)[2]; they celebrate their Passover on Gerizim[3] but have otherwise become a mere historical curiosity.

[1] Cf. M. Noth, *Überlieferungsgeschichtliche Studien*, I (1943), pp. 174 ff.

[2] P. Kahle gives a survey of the Samaritan population in the year 1909 in PJB, 26 (1930), pp. 89 ff.

[3] Cf. J. Jeremias, *Die Passahfeier der Samaritaner* (1932).

PART FOUR

RESTORATION, DECLINE AND FALL

CHAPTER I

THE MACCABEAN RISING AND THE REVIVAL OF THE MONARCHY

29. *The Conflict under Antiochus IV and its Consequences*

THE Seleucid dominion in Palestine did not last very long. After only one generation there broke out the great conflict between this power and the Jerusalem religious community which was ultimately connected with the decline and fall of the Seleucid state, and which finally led to the emancipation of the religious community from political domination, and to the establishment of its own monarchy. About the events of this period we are comparatively well informed, thanks to the literary records, above all, to the two books of Maccabees, which were included in the Greek form of the Old Testament, the Septuagint, and thus preserved. The first book of Maccabees, which was probably originally written in Hebrew, but which only survives in Greek translation, relates the events of the period from 175 to 134 B.C. and is a valuable historical source in which it is possible that notes made at the time were used. It portrays things from the point of view of a strict reverence for the law and attempts, above all, to emphasise the merits of the Maccabean-Hasmonaean leaders. The second book of Maccabees only deals with the period from 175 to 161 B.C. and forms, in accordance with its own statement (2 Macc. ii, 23 ff.), an extract from the history of one Jason of Cyrene, who is otherwise quite unknown to us, but who evidently wrote a work on the history of the period in five books which the writer of the second book of Maccabees made it his task to summarise in one book. Jason of Cyrene evidently came from the Hellenistic Diaspora and probably wrote in Greek, and so Greek is also the original language of the second book of Maccabees. The second book of Maccabees provides more detailed information on the prehistory and beginnings of the Maccabean rebellion than the first book of Maccabees, but does not equal the latter in historical value, since obviously legendary elements are represented more strongly in it. There are all kinds of discrepancies between the two books in their description of events; and one is inclined to give more credence to the first book in such cases, though it should be remembered that this first book also sees and summarises events from its own special and subjective point of view[1].

The conflict broke out because the Seleucid authorities made serious encroachments on the property, rights and regulations of the sanctuary in Jerusalem and the Jerusalem religious community. The reason for these infringements is not quite clear. They did not accord with the fundamental attitude of the Hellenistic rulers to subject peoples and their religions. The fact that Antiochus III had explicitly confirmed the privileges of the Jerusalem religious community, after the conquest of Palestine, and had also shown his good-will in other ways, had been nothing out of the ordinary. In the interim, however, the situation of the Seleucid state had considerably deteriorated. Antiochus III had already been defeated by the Romans and had been forced to conclude the Peace of Apamea with them in 189 B.C. He had been followed after his death in 187 B.C. by his son Seleucus IV Philopator, whose brother Antiochus had to live in Rome as a hostage. Seleucus managed to secure his return by sending his own son Demetrius to Rome as a hostage in his stead. When Seleucus was murdered by his minister Heliodorus in 175 B.C., this brother of his, Antiochus, seized power as Antiochus IV Epiphanes by passing over the real heir to the throne, Demetrius, who was living in Rome. This initiated the period of disputes about the throne in the Seleucid dynasty which prevented the state from attaining any calm and stability, and which contributed to its decline. In addition the Romans were reaching out more and more powerfully into the eastern Mediterranean area and the Seleucid state was no match for them when it came to a real conflict. Danger also threatened from Ptolemaic Egypt, which had until quite recently been in possession of Palestine and Phoenicia, and the danger was the greater since at this period Rome was supporting the Ptolemies against the Seleucids; Antiochus IV was compelled to fight several campaigns against Ptolemy VI Philometor. In a word, the power of the Seleucids had become very shaky, and they became increasingly touchy about the internal life

---

[1] The question not merely of the relationship between the contents of the two books of Maccabees but of their literary relationship is very complicated. There are grounds for presuming that they both drew from a common source, but the nature and origin of this common source still remain an open question, cf. W. Kolbe, *Beiträge zur syrischen und jüdischen Geschichte* (1926), pp. 124 ff., who assumes that Jason of Cyrene was also the source of the first book of Maccabees, and, on the other side, F.-M. Abel, *Les Livres des Maccabées* (1949), pp. xxxviii ff., who disputes the existence of any common literary source at all.

of the subject peoples and sensitive to any signs of unrest among them. The disastrous wars and their new military tasks, also landed them in great financial straits which made them covet the possessions of the subject peoples[1].

On the other hand, conflicts had also arisen within the Jerusalem religious community itself which could not be welcome to the Seleucid state and which gave it reason to intervene. This was the real source of the conflicts which broke out under Antiochus IV. In the first place it was a question of the conflict between the traditional character of the Jerusalem community and the character of Hellenism. The Hellenisation of the Orient which was initiated by the Macedonian conquest of the whole of the Persian empire, was bound to have an effect on the Jerusalem religious community, especially as this community had itself a Greek-speaking Diaspora in the Eastern Mediterranean area which, though not perhaps very large numerically, had many ramifications. For the sake of the Diaspora, part at least of its holy book had been translated into the Hellenistic vernacular from the original Hebrew already regarded as sacred. No doubt the central place of worship in Jerusalem was regularly visited by members of the Diaspora, who thus made Jerusalem familiar with Hellenistic ways. Hellenistic life had, however, also entered Palestine itself and hence into the immediate vicinity of the centre of the Jerusalem religious community, even in the period of Ptolemaic rule. The centres of this life were in Hellenistic cities which were founded in place of earlier urban settlements and which were no longer crowded, unplanned agglomerations of dwellings within a city wall, but more spacious, well-planned sites based on the so-called Hippodamic system, which was named after the architect Hippodamus[2]. In the period of Alexander, Perdiccas had replaced the former Israelite royal city of Samaria with a Macedonian military colony. Under Ptolemaic rule there arose Hellenistic cities which their very names sometimes prove to have been Ptolemaic foundations, like Philadelphia, which was named after Ptolemy II Philadelphus and which was built on the site of the ancient Ammonite capital of Rabbath-bene-Ammon (the modern 'ammān), and Ptolemais which was laid out on the site of the former city of Acco (the modern 'akka), and Philoteria

---

[1] On the whole complex of problems cf. H. L. Jansen, *Die Politik Antiochos' des IV* (1943), especially pp. 17 ff.

[2] Cf. C. Watzinger, *Denkmäler Palästinas*, II (1933), p. 11. Only few archaeological traces have survived of these Hellenistic cities, since they were usually extended in Roman and Byzantine times and the Hellenistic stratum has disappeared under the later strata.

(the modern *khirbet el-kerak*) which was situated at the southern
end of the Sea of Tiberias. In the Ptolemaic or at the beginning of
the Seleucid period there arose the Hellenistic city of Nysa Scythopolis (the modern *bēsān*) which took the place of the former city of
Beth-shan[1]. It was inevitable that the Hellenistic life that developed
in these cities, with its freedom and glamour, should make an impression on the Israelites and stimulate them to copy it. No
doubt very many were attracted by it. The establishment, recorded
in 2 Macc. iv, 12 ff. *circa* 175 B.C. by a high priest in Jerusalem of
a *gymnasion* to form the centre of a community living in the Hellenistic style within the ancient holy city, where discus throwing and
the like was carried on and attracted enthusiastic spectators, was
not the peculiar idea of one particular scoundrel, but the result of a
movement in Israelite circles which, as participants or spectators,
fervently joined in the activities of the new *gymnasion*. 2 Macc. iv,
14 f. notes explicitly that even some of the priests in Jerusalem
were carried away by the attractions of this new way of life. On the
other hand, there were no doubt large groups which rejected the
foreign ways more or less vigorously and consistently for the sake
of their own venerable traditions, and who saw in the departure
from ancestral customs an act of disloyalty to the traditional faith
in God, and nothing less than disguised or even open idolatry. In so
far as there was in fact an ancient and intimate connection between
the Greek-Hellenistic games and the Greek worship of the gods,
they had good reason for their view. The conflict first becomes
evident in the books of the Maccabees for the period *circa* 175 B.C.;
there can be no doubt that it did not suddenly appear at that
time, but had gradually developed, perhaps more or less latently, in
the course of the 3rd century, as part of the process of the advancing
Hellenisation of the Orient under the rule of the Diadochi. It confronted the Jerusalem religious community with the serious and
fundamental question as to what its attitude ought to be to the
foreign Hellenistic customs and ways of life. The solution of this
question could only be found over a period of time, but the problem
threatened, unless a solution was achieved in time, to result in a
violent explosion in view of the increasing force and bitterness of the
conflict. It only needed some incident to touch off such an explosion.
At the beginning of the 2nd century B.C. the internal situation of
the Jerusalem religious community was certainly very strained,
and the unrest that this might lead to in Palestine in the vicinity

---

[1] On these Hellenistic urban foundations cf. A. H. M. Jones, *The Cities of the
Eastern Roman Provinces* (1937), pp. 238 ff., 447 ff.

of a hostile Egypt could not be a matter of indifference to the Seleucid government, and was bound to stimulate it to try to force a decision and so, as far as possible, to bring about a stabilisation of conditions.

Disturbance was also caused in Jerusalem about this time by all kinds of struggles around the office of high priest. The conflict between the traditional and the Hellenistic way of life only played an incidental part in these contentions. In general, the priests appear to have welcomed Hellenism, and at any rate they tried to establish good relations with the Seleucid ruler. But various priestly families and persons were probably contending for the political power of the supreme priestly office. We have no information about any previous history of these disputes, as there are no reliable records about the history of the office of high priest in the 3rd century and the beginning of the 2nd century. Under Seleucus IV we meet with a high priest named Onias; he was regarded by the circle who remained faithful to the law as a pious and worthy representative of the office (2 Macc. iii, 1 ff.; iv, 1 ff.), but he had enemies among his fellow priests who tried to get him removed by conveying slanderous reports on him to the king (2 Macc. iii, 4 ff.; iv, 1 ff.). Seleucus, who, according to 2 Macc. iii, 3, once more explicitly confirmed the privileges of the Jerusalem religious community, does not seem to have yielded to their demands. But when Antiochus IV seized power in 175 B.C. after the murder of Seleucus, a certain Jason, who, according to 2 Macc. iv, 7, was the brother of Onias, succeeded in getting Onias removed from office by royal command and having himself made high priest by promising the new king rich gifts of money and a vigorous promotion of Hellenisation in Jerusalem (2 Macc. iv, 7 ff.)[1]. This was a monstrous intervention of the royal power in an internal concern of the religious community of Jerusalem, but it was not due to the king's own initiative. It was brought about by certain circles of the Jerusalem priesthood itself, which tried to obtain the king's support in their struggle for power, thereby inciting the king to intervene now and in the future in the appointment of the high priest and in the religious affairs of Jerusalem in general. And this is what happened henceforward. When, three years later, a certain Menelaus[2] offered the king still larger sums, Jason was removed by command of the king and Menelaus appointed high priest in his

[1] According to Josephus, *Ant. Iud.* XII, 5, 1, § 239 Niese, this Jason's original name was Joshua, but characteristically he assumed the Greek name of Jason.

[2] According to Josephus, *loc. cit.*, Menelaus' original name was Onias, which he too exchanged for a Greek name.

stead (2 Macc. iv, 23 ff.). When, in the year 169 B.C., the rumour spread that Antiochus had lost his life in a campaign in Egypt, Jason seized the city of Jerusalem and the office of high priest again by force of arms and banished Menelaus and his supporters, who went to Antiochus. The latter restored Menelaus by force, so that Jason had to flee once more to the land east of the Jordan, where he had retired after his first deposition (2 Macc. v, 5 ff.).

These events, which involved Antiochus in the quarrels in Jerusalem, made him take a further step. His financial anxieties made him covetous, anyway, for the treasures and valuables of the shrines within his sphere of government. Polybius comments on one occasion (XXX, 26 fin. Büttner-Wobst) that Antiochus IV had 'sacreligiously despoiled most of the temples', though it is not clear from the context whether this remark is intended to be taken generally or refers to a particular district. Moreover, we know from a brief note in Granus Licinianus[1], that he plundered the Temple of 'Diana' in Hierapolis and robbed it of its treasures, and Polybius (XXXI, 9 Büttner-Wobst) reports that immediately before his death he made a vain attempt to acquire the riches of a temple of 'Artemis' in the country of Elymais (Elam), where he had come on a campaign against the Parthians. These are pieces of information that happen to have survived and it is not unlikely that in order to get money Antiochus pursued this policy elsewhere. It is therefore intelligible that the sanctuary in Jerusalem, in whose affairs he was repeatedly involved, should also have interested him from this point of view. It is reported in 2 Macc. iii, 6 ff. that Seleucus IV had already had his attention drawn to the riches of the Temple by a Jerusalemite enemy of the then high priest Onias, and had tried to seize these treasures through the agency of his minister Heliodorus, but, by a miracle, the attempt had failed. The whole story may be legendary, but it does show that the hankering of the Seleucid rulers of that period after the treasures of the sanctuaries had to be taken into account. So Antiochus IV also took advantage of the restoration of Menelaus to the office of high priest in 169 B.C. to take with him the valuables of the Temple in Jerusalem and to this end he himself even entered the sanctuary (1 Macc. i, 17-28; 2 Macc. v, 15 ff.). This violation of their sanctuary naturally made the strict law-abiding Israelite circles extremely angry. They were now compelled to regard Antiochus as a determined enemy of their faith, even if the king's interference in the appointment of the high priest had not already made them see him in this

[1] Cf. Jansen, *op. cit.* p. 34.

light. It was now hardly possible to conceal a feeling of hostility towards the king.

Perhaps the incident even led immediately to a regular insurrection in Jerusalem which would help to explain the measures which the king proceeded to take[1]. When on a renewed campaign against Egypt in the year 168 B.C., Antiochus had been forced by a decree of the Roman Senate, delivered by Popilius Laenas, to leave Egypt and to abandon all his designs on Egypt, he gave orders for his leading tax-official—according to 2 Macc. v, 24 this was the 'mysarch' named Apollonius—to make a surprise attack on Jerusalem, and for the city to be pillaged and burnt down, and its houses, and above all its walls, pulled down; many inhabitants of Jerusalem lost their lives. Women and children were taken as slaves and Jerusalem was treated as an enemy city (1 Macc. i, 29 ff.). Above all, the fortified position was then established which is often referred to by the Greek name of 'Akra' in the first book of Maccabees and by Josephus, and which played a considerable part in the history of the following years. According to 1 Macc. i, 33 ff. 'godless people' were established inside this area which was protected by a strong circular wall furnished with towers. These 'godless people' were probably primarily the Hellenistically minded section of the Jerusalem population, whereas the law-abiding Jerusalemites fled from the city in great numbers. Weapons and provisions were stored in this area to make it capable of being defended against attack; and it also received a Seleucid garrison. This 'Akra' therefore took the place of the former city of Jerusalem which was now robbed of its enclosing wall and partially depopulated, the new community probably being organised on Hellenistic lines. It is impossible to define its position exactly. It has been located on the so-called 'west hill' of the city territory of Jerusalem, in the west opposite the sanctuary and separated from it by the so-called 'city valley'[2]. But, as it is stated in 1 Macc. i, 33 that it was built on the site of the 'city of David', and as the author of 1 Macc. may, unlike Josephus, who came later, have known the exact position of the historical 'city of David', the probability is that the 'Akra' was situated on the south-east hill, *i.e.* on the mountain-ridge south of the sanctuary and this is supported by archaeological discoveries and topographical considerations[3].

[1] Cf. on the following above all E. Bickermann, *Der Gott der Makkabäer* (1937), pp. 69 ff.

[2] Thus most recently F.-M. Abel, *Histoire de la Palestine*, I (1952), p. 122.

[3] Cf. most recently, with detailed evidence, J. Simons, *Jerusalem in the Old Testament* (1952), pp. 144 ff.

This interference with the status of the city of Jerusalem was extraordinarily violent. But Antiochus IV soon took a further decisive step. As part of his hostile policy he decided to eliminate altogether the Jerusalem religious community which to him appeared to be rebellious. In a decree (1 Macc. i, 41) he prohibited all important religious observances; he forbade the offering of the traditional sacrifices, the observance of the Sabbath, and the custom of circumcision, and he had the holy books destroyed. He made the breaking of these prohibitions punishable by death. He even introduced a foreign system of worship into the sanctuary in Jerusalem and dealt with the Samaritan sanctuary on Gerizim in the same way[1]. According to 2 Macc. vi, 2 a cult of Zeus Olympius was established in Jerusalem and a cult of Zeus Xenius on Gerizim; and the king required everyone to take part in these new cults. The king's officials had to try to enforce the king's instructions throughout the land. On the 15th day of the month Kislev in the 145th year of the Seleucid era (1 Macc. i, 54) i.e. in December of the year 167 B.C., the 'abomination of desolation' was set up in the Temple in Jerusalem. This probably means that the new cult was begun. In the towns in the countryside altars were set up at which everyone now had to sacrifice. The privileges which had been granted to the Jerusalem religious community from the beginning of the Persian period by the reigning emperors, and which had been repeatedly confirmed right up to the reigns of Antiochus III and Seleucus IV, and which guaranteed the community the right to live according to its own religious laws, were thereby abolished.

Antiochus may have thought that the Jerusalem religious community would submit to these ordinances, even though under protest, just as many other subject peoples under his rule had in time accepted Hellenistic or Hellenising cults. But this was impossible for the Jerusalem religious community; they served a God who could not be compared with the traditional deities of the surrounding peoples. On this basis a bitter war of religion against the secular power was inevitable. The most prominent part in this religious war was taken by those resolute circles which had always rejected the Hellenistic way of life. They had perhaps not hitherto played a very active part, but the moment had now come to defend their faith. The Hellenising elements were paralysed in their resistance because they had already taken a step in the new direction;

---

[1] We do not hear anything about the Samaritan attitude to Antiochus, presumably they kept as far away as possible from the disputes which took place in Jerusalem, but were treated by Antiochus, who probably saw no fundamental difference between them, in a similar way to the Jerusalemites.

and some of them had already departed so far from the old traditions that they did not want to offer any resistance at all. The high priest Menelaus who was appointed by Antiochus probably acquiesced, and with him a great many of the Hellenistically inclined priests. Many others, who were horrified by the things that were happening, submitted out of fear and joined in the pagan sacrifices when this became necessary. The little company of those who 'would rather have been killed than be desecrated by unclean foods and profane the sacred covenant' (1 Macc. i, 63), was probably not very large to begin with. Many of them no doubt escaped persecution by fleeing from their homes. For the immediate future action depended on the resolution of the determined minority, and for them the fight against the king's violent measures became at the same time a fight against the Hellenistic way of life in general.

The struggle was aided by the situation of the Seleucid state which was burdened with all manner of internal difficulties and conflicts in the royal house. But it would, all the same, hardly have attained its goal if it had not soon found determined and resolute leaders. In the small town of Modein (the modern *el-midye*) on the western border of the mountains east of Lydda there lived a priestly family which traced its descent (1 Macc. ii, 1) from the priestly house of Joiarib (Neh. xii, 6, 19; 1 Chron. xxiv, 7). Its more recent ancestor was a certain Hasmon (Josephus, *Bell. Iud.* 1, 3, § 36; *Ant. Iud.* XII, 6, 1, § 265 Niese)[1], and they called themselves 'Hasmonaeans' after him. At this time the senior member of the family was Mattathias, who had a number of sons. When a Seleucid official appeared in Modein, to require the pagan sacrifice from all the people there, Mattathias not only refused to comply with the order, but he killed with his own hand an Israelite who made the required sacrifice, and the royal official as well (1 Macc. ii, 15-28). This was the signal for open resistance and the news of Mattathias' action was no doubt swiftly spread abroad. It was impossible for Mattathias and his family to stay in Modein. He called on his fellow-inhabitants to follow him and escape with him, and went with his supporters to the mountains in the inaccessible wilderness of Judah. There, in the course of time, like-minded followers gathered around him. All this took place in the course of the year 166 B.C. To begin with, it merely led to minor engagements between this steadfast band and the Israelites who had submitted

---

[1] Josephus gives the name in the form 'Ασαμων(αῖος), the later Judaean tradition probably in the form (·)ןומשח; cf. G. Dalman, *Aramäisch-neuhebräisches Handwörterbuch* (³1938), p. 163.

to the royal commands, and who for the sake of their own peace and security wanted to avoid having an insurrection in the land. Mattathias' supporters made surprise attacks, destroyed pagan altars, killed apostates who agreed to take part in the pagan sacrifices, used force to circumcise children who, in accordance with the royal command, had not been circumcised. Their enemies in their turn attacked them in their hiding-places and tried to eliminate them; they took advantage of the pious observance of the Sabbath which made resistance on the holy day impossible, so that the adherents of the law had to resolve to defend themselves on the Sabbath during the period of the emergency (1 Macc. ii, 29-48). The aged Mattathias died during these minor conflicts, probably in the course of the year 166 B.C. His place was taken by his third eldest son Judas. According to 1 Macc. ii, 4 he was nick-named Μακκαβαῖος[1], i.e. 'the hammer', or better perhaps, 'the hammer-like (man)'; this nickname, which was intended to mark him out as a dreaded and ready warrior, was given to him no doubt because of his military achievements. Because of this nickname, we call the struggles of the faithful in which Judas won the decisive victories, the 'Maccabean' rising and the period which it marked, the 'Maccabean' period. Judas was indeed a bold warrior, 'resembling the lion in his deeds and like a young lion pouncing with a roar on its prey' (1 Macc. iii, 4). But above all he was a bold, far-sighted leader, who took events beyond the stage of minor battles and sudden attacks, and envisaged a general conflict between law-abiding Israel and the enemy forces. To that extent the episode is rightly called by his nickname; and it is not surprising that he acquired numerous new supporters, especially after he had won his first clear-cut victories.

Under his leadership the first conflicts with the Seleucid power took place. The Seleucids could not look on idly at events in Palestine for long but were bound to take up arms against the rebels. According to 1 Macc. iii, 10-12, Judas succeeded, first of all, in defeating a Seleucid division under the leadership of a certain Apollonius[2] at a place which is unfortunately not specified, and Apollonius was killed in this engagement. After this he defeated Seron, the military commander of 'Syria'[3], at Beth-horon

---

[1] The basis is an Aramaic מַקָּבָא or מַקְּבַי (cf. Hebrew מַקֶּבֶת).

[2] This was perhaps the same Apollonius who, according to 2 Macc. v, 24, had carried out the conquest and pillaging of the city of Jerusalem in the year 168 B.C. on behalf of Antiochus (in 1 Macc. i, 29 the name of this 'supreme tax official' is unfortunately not mentioned).

[3] 'Syria' is obviously not intended to mean the whole Seleucid state but only a part of it, possibly the so-called 'Coele-Syria' which probably embraced the southern part of the land of Syria.

(the modern *bēt ʿūr*), in the north-west of the province of Judah, where an army division approaching the coastal plain from the north first reached the province of Judah, and he pursued the defeated enemy into the coastal plain (1 Macc. iii, 13 ff.). Thereupon king Antiochus was forced to take more energetic measures. As he was himself having to fight the Parthians in the east, he left the fighting in Palestine to Lysias, who had been left behind as regent, and the latter sent out the three generals Ptolemy, Nicanor and Gorgias with a considerable army against Judas and his followers in the 147th year of the Seleucid era (in the summer of 165 B.C.). A battle took place at Emmaus (the modern *ʿamwās*) on the western border of the mountains south of Beth-horon in which Judas was able, by skilful manœuvring, to defeat his enemies once again (1 Macc. iii, 27–iv, 25). Lysias now took charge himself. This time he approached Judaea, not from the west, but from the south through the province of Idumaea, and a battle took place on the southern frontier of the province of Judah near Beth-zur (the modern *khirbet et-ṭubēḳa*). Judas was able to secure a victory in this case too (1 Macc. iv, 26-35). These amazing successes led to Judas and his supporters being masters of the province of Judah, except for the 'Akra' in Jerusalem with its Seleucid garrison. It may be asked how these victories were possible. No doubt the Seleucid state, which was involved in fighting the Parthians in the east, was unable to muster any very large armies against Judas[1]. All the same, their forces were certainly superior in numbers and equipment. On the other hand, Judas and his supporters had the advantage of detailed local knowledge of their own homeland, the mountainous character of which provided them with all kinds of opportunities for skilful operations, and above all they had the conviction that they were waging an urgent war for the cause of their own faith, and the readiness to stake everything for this cause regardless of their personal safety.

The successes which they had achieved encouraged the faithful to hope that their cause would triumph in spite of the forces opposed to it; and they no doubt brought Judas many new followers and fellow-combatants, who had previously held back for fear. But these successes also made it plain to the devout that God was on their side, since only his help against the secular power could have made the victories possible. In fact it appeared that the final issue between the rule of God and the secular rule of man was being

[1] The numbers of the enemy armies mentioned in the books of the Maccabees are probably exaggerated, as was often the case in old traditions.

decided in these battles, which were concerned to save the foundations of the faith. It was during the period of these successes that
the visions recorded in the second half of the book of Daniel were
written in their final form (Dan. vii-xii). In them the events of the
time were interpreted as the ultimate phase of history before the
imminent irruption of the visible rule of God on earth which would
be realised in the 'royal power of the saints of the most High' (Dan.
vii, 18). The brutal and bloody suppression of the Jerusalem religious community by Antiochus IV, which was without precedent
in Israelite history, and the life and death struggle which its loyal
adherents were forced to wage against this abolition of privileges
which had existed for centuries, and against the oppression which
followed, awakened the conviction that an ultimate and final
decision was now at hand. Following up a series of stories which
had arisen in the course of the 3rd century, and which were intended
to demonstrate by examples God's help for the faithful who held
out against the pressure of the world (Dan. i-vi), the visions of
Daniel interpreted the events of the time as the beginning of the
end of the worldly power which had appeared in the course of time
in a series of successive world empires, and as the preparation for
the coming of the rule of God, for which the successes of Judas and
his followers could indeed only be a provisional 'little help' (Dan.
xi, 34), and which would be rather a mighty act of God. And so
there developed in the midst of the troubles and excitements of the
time the so-called Apocalyptic, which, continuing the prophecy of
the earlier period, explained the world and its history as leading to an
end brought about by God. It is probable that this vision gave Judas
and his struggle a great stimulus and brought him supporters.
Judas himself and many of his fellow-combatants presumably
did not, however, entirely share the conception of the apocalyptic visions of Daniel, and did not think of their actions as merely
a 'little help', but will have seen the waging of this war against
the power of the state as an essential task. When it is stated in
Dan. xi, 34 that 'many shall cleave' to the fighters for freedom
'with flatteries', what the writer had in mind was possibly the expectation of winning a secular victory by force of arms, instead of
expecting everything to come from the acts of God himself. This is
the first evidence of a dissension at the heart of the Maccabean
rising and it was soon to come into the open.

The task which Judas envisaged after his initial successes was the
liberation of Jerusalem and the restoration of the sanctuary. After
the desecration of the Temple in 167 B.C., the faithful had erected a

kind of substitute sanctuary at Mizpah (*tell en-naṣbe*) north of Jerusalem. In accordance with the law it was not permissible to offer sacrifices there; but meetings were held there, and the tithes required by the law were brought there, and such of the priestly garments and the holy books as it had been possible to save were taken there (1 Macc. iii, 46-49). But the real holy place was still Jerusalem, now desecrated, and this was Judas' present goal. In the second half of the year 164 B.C. Judas and his followers advanced to Jerusalem. He had the Seleucid garrison and the disloyal population shut up in the 'Akra' to prevent them causing any trouble; and he then turned his attention to the restoration of the sanctuary. He appointed priests who had remained loyal to the ancestral traditions; he had the elements of the worship of Zeus Olympius removed and the burnt-offering altar, which had been desecrated by the foreign cultus, pulled down; he had a new one built in its place and prepared new cultic equipment as necessary. On the 25th Kislev of the 148th Seleucid year, *i.e.* in the December of the year 164 B.C., that is three years after its desecration, the Temple was restored for the legitimate worship of God with an eight-day festival with sacrifices, prayer and singing. To ensure its safety the area in which it stood was fortified and garrisoned, just as Beth-zur on the southern border of the province of Judah was fortified and garrisoned (1 Macc. iv, 36-61).

A most important step had thus been taken. In the following spring the arch-enemy Antiochus IV Epiphanes died during a campaign against the Parthians, and he was succeeded by his eight-year-old son Antiochus V Eupator, who was entirely dependent on his guardian, the regent Lysias. But the urgent struggle was not yet ended. The 'Akra' with its garrison still existed alongside the site of the Temple in Jerusalem and the ordinances of Antiochus IV, which had prohibited the whole worship of the Jerusalem religious community, had not yet been rescinded. Outside the province of Judah Seleucid rule was undisputed and its representatives were able to insist on the members of the Jerusalem religious community, who lived outside the province of Judah, carrying out these orders. So in the year 163 B.C. Judas undertook campaigns which led far beyond the frontiers of the province of Judah, above all to Galilee and into the land east of the Jordan where Israelites were living who were faithful to the Jerusalem religious community. They were in a difficult position, since they were living away from Jerusalem on the periphery in districts with a mixed population and in the vicinity of foreign peoples and Hellenistic cities. They were

hard pressed in the period of persecution by Antiochus IV. So
Judas sent his next eldest brother Simon, who now appears in
history for the first time, to Galilee, and he himself went to 'Gilead',
i.e. into the land east of the Jordan, with his youngest brother
Jonathan. Both of them had military successes; but as their power
was not great enough to maintain these old Israelite areas permanently, they took the whole of the Israelite population that wanted
to remain members of the Jerusalem religious community with
them to Judaea. Judas then undertook another expedition to
Idumaea, where he besieged and destroyed Hebron, and to Philistia,
where he made a surprise attack on Ashdod, probably only to in-
spire the neighbour of the province of Judah with fear and respect
(1 Macc. v, 1-68)[1]. Then Judas began to besiege the 'Akra' in
Jerusalem with its garrison. The garrison appealed for help to
Antiochus V, and other pro-Hellenistic Israelites also took the
opportunity of trying once again to persuade the king to intervene
on their behalf. This time Antiochus V, with Lysias, did make a
serious effort to crush the rebels (163–162 B.C.). An attack with a
strong force was made from the south. Beth-zur, which Judas had
fortified, was hard pressed and Judas withdrew from this fortress
to the north. Afterwards Beth-zur was forced to surrender to the
aggressors. But meanwhile the Seleucid's main force pursued Judas
northwards. A battle took place near Beth-zechariah (the modern
bēt iskārye), about 6 miles south-west of Bethlehem, in which the
Syrians, who had elephants to put into the attack, were victorious,
so that it was now possible to besiege the fortified sanctuary of
Jerusalem to which Judas and his men had withdrawn and to reduce
it to the direst straits by starvation (1 Macc. vi, 17-54). The cause
of Judas and his supporters now seemed lost. But unexpectedly an
internal dissension in the Seleucid state came to their aid; and as a
result of the rapidly advancing degeneration and decay of the
Seleucid monarchy one of the surprising changes took place which
were often to occur in the following period. A rival of the regent
Lysias, whom Antiochus IV had appointed guardian of his young
son and heir before his death on the Parthian campaign, was preparing to seize power, so that Lysias suddenly found it urgently
necessary to bring the campaign in Judaea to a rapid end. He
therefore induced the young king to offer peace to the besieged, on
the basis of an assurance of freedom to worship in accordance
with the traditional law. When this assurance was confirmed by
an oath, Judas accepted the offer and surrendered the fortified area

[1] On these military campaigns of 163 B.C., cf. K. Galling. PJB, 36 (1940), pp. 43 ff.

of the Temple. It is true that, contrary to the agreement, the fortifications of the Temple area were subsequently demolished; but the Syrian army withdrew, and above all, the orders issued by Antiochus IV in the year 167 B.C., which had led to the outbreak of the military conflict, were now officially rescinded and the Jerusalem religious community was thereby restored to its old position.

The goal of the Maccabean rising thereby seemed to have been attained; and there was no apparent reason for continuing the struggle, particularly as the Seleucids now evidently had peaceful intentions too. In the year 162 B.C. Demetrius, the son of Seleucus IV, who had been the real heir to the throne after his father's death but had been living as a hostage in Rome at the time, had appeared in Antioch, and, after he had instigated the murder of Antiochus V and Lysias at the hands of the military, he had ascended the throne as Demetrius I Soter. In Jerusalem, after the last high priest Menelaus had been removed by Antiochus V, probably in connection with the agreed re-organisation of the cultus (cf. 2 Macc. xiii, 1-8), a certain Alcimus[1], who appears to have been a legitimate member of the high-priestly family (so 1 Macc. vii, 14), was officially appointed high priest. The evident purpose of this appointment was to serve the cause of peace within the Jerusalem religious community, and a message was sent to Judas and his followers inviting them to make peace. At the time many of the devout in Israel, including those who had taken part in the urgent struggle against violence and oppression, believed that the time had come to rest content with what had been achieved. The right freely to conduct public worship and daily life in accordance with the traditional law had been officially recognised, and a legitimate high priest was once again in office, and even though there was still a Seleucid garrison in the 'Akra' in Jerusalem and Seleucid officials and troops were still present in the land, this was merely due to the fact that the land was under foreign rule and the Jerusalem religious community had lived for centuries under foreign rule. But Judas and his followers were of a different mind and their view is clearly expressed in the description of the events and personalities we have just mentioned, which is given in 1 Macc. vii, 1-25. They had no confidence in the peace. In fact they considered it obnoxious that, for all his legitimacy, the new high priest had been appointed by the king with the aid of political and military resources in the same way as his immediate predecessors had been appointed by hostile kings. The events that followed also showed that there

---

[1] His name is probably a Greek form of the native name Eliakim.

was some justification for fearing that further attempts would be made to interfere in the internal affairs of the Jerusalem religious community. But, above all, Judas and his followers were aiming at complete political independence and the complete elimination of foreign rule. This purpose now emerged quite clearly. If the struggle had begun as a fight against the king's destructive acts of despotism and as a fight for freedom, in time the leaders of the struggle came to envisage a goal leading far beyond the restoration of the previous state of affairs. But this led to a disastrous and momentous cleavage in the ranks of those who had hitherto worked together. On the one side were the 'Hasmonaeans' with their followers, who were forced by this cleavage more and more on to the purely political line, and on the other side were those groups who were really concerned only with the freedom to practise their worship unhindered and with the right to live strictly in accordance with the law. These latter formed a group on their own and simply called themselves 'the pious'[1]. There were, in addition, Hellenising groups, particularly, it seems, among the priestly families, the 'Sadducees'[2], and the high priest Alcimus probably had leanings in this direction too.

The uncompromising attitude of Judas and his followers made the intended peace impossible. According to 1 Macc. viii, 1-32, Judas had tried to establish contact with Rome by sending a deputation there and in this way he had made his fight for freedom a part of the great historical conflicts of the time, another indication that his aims were now primarily political. Alcimus, on the other hand, who had been brought to Jerusalem with a military escort, was unable to maintain his position. He soon had to ask Demetrius for help. The latter sent Nicanor to Jerusalem with an army to quell the rebels. The attempt to induce Judas into submission by negotiation came to nothing; hostilities therefore broke out. Judas was victorious in an engagement at Caphar salama, which may have been identical with the modern *khirbet selma*, half a mile north-west of *ed-jīb*, that is, about 6 miles north-west of Jerusalem. After Nicanor had summoned further reinforcements, a battle

---

[1] In Hebrew they described themselves as חֲסִידִים, and from that was derived the Greek Ἀσιδαῖοι (1 Macc. vii, 3 and elsewhere). Later on the term 'the separated', *פְּרִישִׁים, Φαρισαῖοι, 'Pharisees', emerged for the same groups (cf. Josephus, *Ant. Iud.* XIII, 5, 9, §§ 171 f. Niese and elsewhere).

[2] According to an interpretation by A. Geiger (*Urschrift und Übersetzungen der Bibel* [1857], p. 102), which has been vigorously contested but is still not unlikely, the 'Sadducees' were the 'Zadokites', *i.e.* members of the old priestly family in Jerusalem which was still the legitimate priestly family. It became a party in the conflicts of the 2nd century.

ensued on the 13th Adar, *i.e.* in the March of the year 161, near Adasa (the modern *khirbet 'adāse*), 4 miles north of Jerusalem. Nicanor was defeated and lost his life in the battle; Judas was able to pursue the defeated enemy right down into the coastal plain (1 Macc. vii, 26-50). Thereupon Demetrius entrusted Bacchides, who occupied the high position of 'friend of the king', with the task of crushing the rebels. His retinue included the high priest Alcimus, who had evidently again made representations to the king. This time, in the first month of the 152nd Seleucid year, *i.e.* in the April of 160 B.C., a very imposing force was evidently summoned to obtain the desired victory once and for all. As it is unfortunately impossible to interpret the references to places in 1 Macc. ix, 2 ff., we have no exact information about Bacchides' route of march and it is also impossible to locate the place called Elasa, which is mentioned as the scene of the decisive battle. Confronted with such overwhelming forces Judas was in a very difficult position, particularly as many of his supporters refused to venture on the seemingly hopeless engagement. Nevertheless Judas plunged into the battle with a small band of faithful followers. He was defeated and himself fell in the battle (1 Macc. ix, 1-22). Bacchides now tried, with the help of the high priest, to restore peace and order in the land. Freedom of worship and the validity of the law were not restricted; but wherever it was possible to get hold of them, Judas' adherents were put to death. Some of them were able to save their lives only by escaping to hide-outs in the desert of Judah. They were now in a similar position to the one in which Mattathias and his followers had found themselves at the beginning of the Maccabean rising. In the place of Judas they chose his youngest brother Jonathan to be their leader. They now seemed to have hardly any prospect of success, for the majority of those who were faithful to the law now acquiesced in the new situation and refused to have anything more to do with these intransigent fighters. Bacchides had established a number of strongholds and occupied them with garrisons to secure the Seleucid rule in the land. All that Jonathan could do with his followers was repeatedly to disturb the peace in the land. If occasional collisions with royal troops such as the engagement on the Jordan recorded in 1 Macc. ix, 43-49, or the struggle for Beth-basi (probably the modern *khirbet bēt baṣṣa*) east-south-east of Bethlehem on the edge of the wilderness of Judah, which Jonathan had lightly fortified (1 Macc. ix, 62-69), turned out successfully, they were only minor engagements and the results were unimportant; they had little effect on the general situation. Nor did the connection which Jonathan sought to establish with the Nabataeans who had settled towards the end of the 4th century on the eastern side of the Dead Sea and of the *wādi el-'araba* in the ancient land of the Edomites, and were the natural enemies of Seleucid rule in neighbouring Palestine, have any important consequences. John, the eldest brother of Jonathan, had been killed on a mission to the Nabataeans (1 Macc. ix, 35 ff.); and probably the attempt to establish contact with the Nabataeans was abandoned after that.

Once again internal difficulties in the Seleucid state unexpectedly came to the aid of Jonathan's purposes. This is the only possible explanation of the fact that after the engagement at Beth-basi Bacchides suddenly agreed to negotiate with Jonathan. At Jonathan's request he handed over the prisoners and the booty and desisted from further hostilities. Obviously as a result of an understanding with Bacchides, Jonathan now established his residence in Michmash (the modern *mukhmās*), 8 miles north-north-east of Jerusalem, and from there he 'judged the people' as if he was one of the old 'judges of Israel' (1 Macc. ix, 70-73). This was in the year 157 B.C. For the present the war now really had come to an end. The high priest Alcimus had died two years previously (1 Macc. ix, 54-56) and his position had not yet been filled again. But in Jerusalem the 'Sadducean' priesthood held sway and for the time being Jonathan evidently did not wish to enter their area. He therefore ruled from Michmash. Subsequently Jonathan turned the disputes about the throne in the Seleucid house very cleverly, but also most unscrupulously, to his own account, in order to come nearer his goal, which was fairly obviously political, secular power. In the year 153 B.C. a certain Alexander Balas, who passed himself off as a son of Antiochus IV Epiphanes, and as such claimed the Seleucid throne, rebelled against the king Demetrius. Under these circumstances Demetrius considered it a good thing to have friends, and he therefore tried, by offering amazing concessions, to win over Jonathan. He gave him official permission to maintain an armed unit and to make other warlike preparations; he also handed over the hostages who had been held in the 'Akra' in Jerusalem. Armed with these concessions, Jonathan moved to Jerusalem, refortified the area of the Temple and kept the anxious garrison and occupants of the 'Akra' in check. The only other garrison which the Seleucids still maintained was the one in the fortress of Beth-zur (1 Macc. x, 1-14). But at the same time the pretender Alexander Balas was also seeking Jonathan's favour, and Jonathan accepted his benefactions too without the slightest hesitation. Alexander entrusted him with the office of high priest which had not been filled since the death of Alcimus; and Jonathan solemnly entered upon this office at the great autumn festival in the year 152 B.C. And so the supreme and leading office in the Jerusalem religious community had been conferred in due form—by a sovereign act of the foreign Seleucid king—on a member of the non-'Zadokite', non-'Aaronite', priestly family of the Hasmonaeans; and Hasmonaeans occupied this office until the reign of Herod. Alexander even sent Jonathan a purple mantle and a golden crown, the tokens of secular power, and thus Jonathan was given the position of a subject king under the Seleucid government (1 Macc. x, 15-21). All these things were the gifts of a pretender to the throne, who made himself out to be the son of the former arch-enemy Antiochus IV Epiphanes! For a time Jonathan must have steered a middle course, as far as possible, between Demetrius and Alexander. But in the end he declined as insincere a further offer by Demetrius, which included universal exemption from taxation and rich donations to the Jerusalem religious community, as well as the inclusion of a contingent of Judaean troops under their own officers in the Seleucid army (1 Macc. x, 22 ff.), and so went over to Alexander's side. He was fortunate, for in time Alexander made his way against Demetrius and, finally, in the year 150 B.C., Demetrius was killed in battle against Alexander. Jonathan was rewarded for his support. He was invited to Ptolemais (Acco) where Alexander Balas celebrated his marriage with Cleopatra, the daughter of Ptolemy VI Philometor, and there Alexander honoured him highly and made him a 'general' and 'joint-ruler' in the Selecucid state (1 Macc. x, 59-66). It is not surprising that, under these circumstances, Jonathan's position in the province of Judah became more and more uncontested. His old adherents had triumphed with him and no doubt new followers rallied round the successful leader, whilst his enemies were forced to be silent (cf. 1 Macc. x, 61-64).

Alexander Balas continued to need Jonathan's support, since, in the year 147 B.C., the son of Demetrius I, who was also called Demetrius, rebelled against his position as king. To begin with, Jonathan stood by Alexander and undertook a few expeditions in the region of the Philistine cities against the troops of the young Demetrius, and as a reward he received the city of Ekron (the modern *ākir*) and its adjoining territory. But, for the rest, he took advantage of the disturbances of the time, in which Ptolemy VI also intervened, to besiege the Seleucid garrison in the 'Akra' of Jerusalem. Alexander Balas was finally defeated in the year 145

B.C. and, shortly after, Ptolemy VI died on his Palestinian-Syrian campaign. The young Demetrius was therefore able to ascend the throne as Demetrius II Nicator (1 Macc. x, 67-xi, 19). The new king immediately summoned Jonathan to Ptolemais to call him to account. Jonathan succeeded in assuaging the king's wrath and even winning his favour by rich gifts; and instead of being punished for his behaviour he returned to Jerusalem with new concessions from the king. Demetrius not only explicitly confirmed him in his offices and also confirmed the privileges of the Jerusalem religious community but, in return for a rich present, he handed over to him the three southern districts of the province of Samaria, whose inhabitants had remained loyal to the cultus of near-by Jerusalem and did not take part in the Samaritan cultus on Gerizim (cf. above, p. 355). These were joined to the province of Judah. The districts in question were Aphaerema (the modern *et-ṭaiyibe* northeast of Bethel) on the eastern slope of the mountain, Ramathaim (the modern *rentīs*, about 16 miles east of *yāfa*) on the western side of the mountain, and Lydda (the modern *lidd*) on the inner edge of the coastal plain. In this way the province of Judah was enlarged by a wide strip of land northwards and north-westwards. Demetrius also granted exemption from taxes to this enlarged province (1 Macc. x, 20-37).

In the end, however, Jonathan's political changeability became his own downfall. Demetrius II was not prepared to make further concessions—Jonathan wanted the withdrawal of the Seleucid garrison from the 'Akra' in Jerusalem and from Beth-zur—not even after Jonathan had sent troops to help him to suppress a rebellion in Antioch (1 Macc. xi, 41-53). Jonathan therefore parted from Demetrius. When a certain Diodotus Tryphon appeared in the year 145 B.C. to win the Seleucid throne for the son of Alexander Balas, who was called Antiochus and still under age, he allowed himself to be won over by this agitator and was, with his brother, given the task of subjugating the whole of the southern part of Syria-Palestine 'from the Tyrian ladder to the Egyptian frontier' (1 Macc. xi, 59) for the young aspirant to the throne. Jonathan and Simon undertook this task in a series of successful campaigns which extended from the southern coastal plain as far as Galilee and the region of Damascus (1 Macc. xi, 60-74; xii, 24-38). But this made Jonathan's position dangerously strong. Once again he established contact with Rome and also with Sparta (1 Macc. xii, 1-23). Furthermore, he built strongholds in the province of Judah, strengthened and raised the wall of Jerusalem and built a high wall between the Syrian occupied 'Akra' of Jerusalem and the rest of the city to make interference from the 'Akra' impossible. Diodotus Tryphon, who had merely used the young Antiochus as a pretext and was striving after the throne himself, could not let this go unpunished. He treacherously lured Jonathan with only a small retinue to Ptolemais and had him imprisoned there. In Jerusalem his brother Simon, Mattathias' second eldest son, was put in Jonathan's place. Simon was able successfully to defend the province of Judah which Tryphon tried to attack from various sides. Tryphon took the captive Jonathan with him on his expeditions and finally had him killed in the land east of the Jordan at a place called Bascama whose location is not now known to us (1 Macc. xii, 39-xiii, 32). This happened in the year 143 B.C.

After the connection with Tryphon had had such evil consequences, Simon now turned to Demetrius II who, since he was having difficulty in maintaining his throne against Tryphon, was very anxious to come to a good understanding with Simon and was prepared to make concessions to this end. He granted the Judaeans freedom from taxation and also an amnesty, and sanctioned retrospectively the fortifications which Simon had meanwhile taken in hand in the province of Judah. Simon behaved more and more as an independent ruler and at this period the Seleucid state was hardly in a position to enforce its authority effectively. With the consent of the people Simon gave himself the official title of 'great high priest, general and leader of the Judaeans' (1 Macc. xiii, 42), and had official matters dated according to the years of his reign; he reckoned the 170th Seleucid year (142–141 B.C.) as his '1st year' (1 Macc. xiii, 41 f.). He kept up the connections with Rome and Sparta which Jonathan had begun (1 Macc. xiv, 16-24). Above all, he succeeded in forcing the 'Akra' of Jerusalem to surrender, and its inhabitants to withdraw, by laying siege to it, and the king was unable to intervene. The traditional records have assigned a precise date to this important event; on the 23rd day of the 171st Seleucid year, that is, in the middle of the year 141 B.C., there was celebrated in Jerusalem the entry into the 'Akra' which had for so long been occupied by a disloyal population and protected by a foreign garrison, and once again Simon strengthened the defences of the Temple precincts (1 Macc. xiii, 49-52). He had the site of the former 'Akra' resettled with '(faithful) Judaeans' and probably had it included within the city wall which he had improved (1 Macc. xiv, 37). He also enlarged the province of Judah as a result of a number of successful campaigns, and once again the king was unable to check him. He conquered the city of Gazara, the ancient Gezer (the modern *tell jezer*) on the coastal plain south-east of *yāfa*; he annexed it for the province of Judah and assigned Gazara as a garrison-town to his son John (1 Macc. xiii, 43-48, 53), whom he had made commander of the military forces in the province. But, above all, he conquered the port of Joppa (*yāfa*) and thereby acquired direct access to the Mediterranean for the province (1 Macc. xiv, 5). The fact that in 1 Macc. xiv, 6, it is stated in this connection that he 'extended the frontiers of the people' suggests that he may also have been responsible for the extension of Judaea to the north-east at the expense of the province of Samaria, which is first explicitly attested by Josephus[1] and Pliny[2], but which had no doubt taken place considerably earlier. This extension covered, in addition to the three areas of Samaria, Aphaerema, Ramathaim and Lydda which had been made over to Jonathan in 145 B.C., the further district of 'Akrabattine', *i.e.* the district of Acrabetta (the modern *'akrabe*) about 8 miles south-east of *nāblus* (Shechem)[3] which had also previously belonged to Samaria. As a result of this expansion the province of Judah extended north of the district of Aphaerema in the highlands and on the eastern side of the mountains of Samaria fairly near to Shechem, the ancient capital of the Central Palestinian mountains; and on the north to south road on the mountain heights between Jerusalem and Shechem, the place called Anuath Borcaeus now became, as Josephus explicitly notes later[4], the boundary between the provinces of Judah and Samaria. Its name survives in the name of the spring *'ēn berķīt* which is only about 10 miles from Shechem, but over 22 miles north of Jerusalem. So Simon was able to round off and secure his territories and reign fairly undisturbed in the province of Judah. Simon is described as a just and benevolent ruler, and, after the troubles that had preceded it, his reign was regarded as a time of peace and prosperity (1 Macc. xiv, 4, 8 ff.). On the whole, Simon was able to consider his achievements complete and secure, and in a great assembly of the people it was resolved, at his instigation, to record his *res gestae* and publish them on bronze tablets on the Temple Mount in Jerusalem; his father and his brothers, above all Jonathan, were briefly commemorated too, but the main reference was to his own successes and merits (1 Macc. xiv, 25-49).

Finally Simon was affected once again by the conflicts in the Seleucid house; but his position was no longer seriously endangered

[1] *Bell. Iud.* III. 3, 4, 5, §§ 48, 55 Niese.   [2] *Hist. Nat.* V, 14, 70.
[3] Cf. A. Alt, PJB, 31 (1935), pp. 97 f.   [4] *Bell. Iud.* III, 3, 5, § 51 Niese.

by them. Probably in 140 B.C. Demetrius II Nicator undertook an expedition against the Parthians in the east, in which he was taken prisoner by the Parthians. Thereupon his brother, Antiochus VII Sidetes, set himself on the throne in Antioch. The latter took up the struggle against Diodotus Tryphon, who was still alive, and for this reason he was most anxious for a good understanding with Simon (1 Macc. xv, 1-14). But he soon managed to overcome Tryphon who finally gave up the struggle and took his own life, and he now attempted to proceed against Simon's very independent position. He called on Simon to surrender the conquered territories, above all Gazara, Joppa and the 'Akra' of Jerusalem. When Simon refused, he sent his general Cendebaeus against the province of Judah (1 Macc. xv, 25-41). Simon instructed his two sons Judas and John to ward off the attack of the enemy, who, advancing from Jamnia (the modern *yebna*), had already begun to lay waste parts of the province of Judah. In the vicinity of Modein, the ancient home of their family, the two sons of Simon succeeded in defeating Cendebaeus and pursuing the enemy troops far out into the plain (1 Macc. xvi, 1-10). Thus the safety of the province of Judah was again assured, and apparently no further effort against Simon was undertaken.

At the beginning of the year 134 B.C. Simon, now advanced in years, succumbed to an attempt on his life by his son-in-law Ptolemy. The latter was commander in the district of Jericho and had a residence called Dok by the spring which is still called ʿēn dūk, west-north-west of Jericho. On a visit to Dok, Simon with his two sons Mattathias and Judas were treacherously murdered by Ptolemy, who was striving for power himself. Ptolemy now sought to establish relations with the king and to obtain his support, and meanwhile he prepared to occupy the whole province with his troops and, above all, to remove Simon's son John, whom Simon had installed in Gazara and who resided there. John was warned in time, however, and was able to meet the attack and, before Ptolemy was really under way, he had himself installed as successor in his father's offices in Jerusalem (1 Macc. xvi, 11-22). As a grandson of Mattathias and son of Simon he probably soon received the approbation and support of the Judaeans. He locked up the murderer Ptolemy in his residence Dok, but did not dare to attack him in any strength, since his mother was in Ptolemy's hands. In the end he gave up the siege, but Ptolemy murdered his mother all the same and escaped[1].

[1] Josephus, *Ant. Iud.* XIII, 8, 1, §§ 230 ff.; *Bell. Iud.* I, 2, 3, 4, §§ 54 ff. The first book of Maccabees closes with the story of the murder of Simon. From that point

As John Hyrcanus I, John then reigned in the province of Judah in the offices and with the titles of his father. In his very first year, however, he landed into most serious trouble. After the defeat of his general Cendebaeus, Antiochus VII Sidetes made a renewed attempt to destroy the independence of the province of Judah. This time he succeeded in occupying the province and shutting up John Hyrcanus in Jerusalem and besieging the city, which in time came into the direst straits owing to starvation. In the end, however, an agreement was reached. In view of the general situation in his state, Antiochus was probably unable to afford to spend a long time on the siege of Jerusalem and had presumably hoped to finish it off more quickly. John had to make a considerable payment for the districts conquered by his father, above all Joppa; but that it belonged to the province was now at any rate officially recognised. He had to hand over his weapons and furnish hostages (*Ant. Iud.* XIII, 8, 2, 3, §§ 236 ff.). Finally Antiochus VII undertook a campaign against the Parthians and met his death on this campaign in the year 128 B.C. During the campaign Demetrius II had been released by the Parthians, and, as the rival of his brother Antiochus, he ascended the throne again, attacking his brother in the rear. After the death of Antiochus, Demetrius became king again for a few years. But from now on quarrels about the succession to the throne went on all the time among unimportant and weak members of the Seleucid house, and to all intents and purposes this meant independence for the province of Judah. In the year 128 B.C. there came to an end the long and difficult conflict of the Jerusalem religious community with the Seleucid power, which had entered a critical stage with the violent interference of Antiochus IV Epiphanes with the Temple worship in Jerusalem.

30. *The Rise and Fall of the Hasmonaean Monarchy*

After the Maccabean rising had achieved freedom of worship for the Jerusalem religious community in quite a short time, the sons

onwards we are primarily dependent on Josephus, who only provides scanty information on the following period to begin with, but more and more detail as he proceeds, very largely on the basis of good traditions available to him, as, for example, that of Nicolaus of Damascus, who lived at the court of Herod and had also written history himself. In the introduction to the *Bellum Iudaicum* Josephus made a fairly brief summary of his sources—beginning with Antiochus Epiphanes—for the period up to the intervention of the Romans. He reports in greater detail on this period in the *Antiquitates Iudaicae*, a work which was written later, and which will therefore be the main source of our subsequent quotations.

of the priest Mattathias strove more and more clearly and confidently for the political independence of, to begin with, the province of Judah. Judas already envisaged this goal and Jonathan and Simon even more so, and Simon's son John Hyrcanus went further in the same direction. This striving after secular independence and power did not meet with the undivided approval of the Jerusalem religious community. The large groups of the 'pious' rejected it or, at any rate, reserved judgement. They were satisfied with the assurance of freedom of worship and freedom to lead a life in accordance with the law, and for the rest they awaited liberation from the troubles and afflictions of the time, not from human actions but from a future glorious act of God which would remove the powers of this world. Nor did the 'pious' approve of the not always particularly straight paths which the Maccabean leaders, especially Jonathan, took to approach their goal by means of secular methods of bargaining in these tumultuous times. On the other side there were the friends of the Hellenists, probably including some of the 'Sadducean' priesthood, who could hardly have any inclination to fight the Hellenistic ruling power. All the same, the Maccabean leaders must have had a great band of supporters which increased with their successes, otherwise they would not have been able constantly to hold their position through all the vicissitudes of events and in spite of what were, to begin with, great difficulties. In these circles their actions were felt to be of historical significance; and, in fact, after centuries of dependence on one empire after another, the Maccabean rising signified a renewal of Israel's active intervention in the development of its own history. It is therefore not surprising that the deeds of Mattathias and his descendants found historians ready to record them and to describe the way that they had trodden as right and pleasing to God, just as David had once stimulated the writing of the first important Israelite history. So far as we can tell from the traditional records that have survived, this was the first time since the age of David and Solomon that historical writing was composed under the more or less immediate impact of the events and persons described. The oldest document of which we have certain evidence is the 'Chronicle of the Office of High Priest' by John Hyrcanus mentioned in 1 Macc. xvi, 24, which was probably finished soon after his death, *i.e. circa* 100 B.C. As it has not survived, it is impossible to say whether it was an actual historical work or not rather simply an annalistic compilation. The first book of Maccabees, which quotes from this 'Chronicle', was probably written soon afterwards. No doubt on the basis of traditional records, it gives a connected account of the deeds of the 'Maccabeans' up to Simon with a marked bias in their favour. The five-volume work of Jason of Cyrene on 'the Maccabean Judas and his brothers' (2 Macc. ii, 19), which was subsequently summarised in the second book of Maccabees, adopted a similar attitude. Unfortunately it is impossible to fix the time and place of its origin. The events of the 2nd century also gave a new stimulus to other literary activity[1]. We have already mentioned the book of Daniel (cf. above, pp. 369 f.), the only one of these literary productions to be included in the Hebrew canon of the Old Testament. According to the preface to the Greek translation of the book of Jesus ben Sira, the original Hebrew version of this beautiful and significant book of wisdom must have been written about the beginning of the Maccabean period. The revival of the Hebrew language for literary works instead of the everyday Aramaic—except among the Greek-speaking and writing Hellenistic Diaspora—was a sign of the newly awakened interest in the venerable traditions and values of the past. The Daniel narratives (Dan. i-vi) had probably been written down in Aramaic in the 3rd century, but whereas, in the period of persecution between 167 and 164 B.C., the vision of Daniel vii was still composed in Aramaic, Hebrew was used for the later visions (Dan. viii-xii). The Book of Wisdom of Jesus ben Sira was written in the Hebrew language, as stated in the preface to the Greek edition, and confirmed by the original text, which has been discovered. Probably the first book of Maccabees, of which only the Greek translation is extant, was originally written in Hebrew rather than Aramaic.

In spite of everything, the events which took place in connection with the Maccabean rising could not lead to a real rebirth of Israel, and the eventual revival of the monarchy and the restoration of political independence cannot really be compared with the emergence of the monarchy under Saul and David. The foundations of the Hasmonaean monarchy were shaky from the very beginning. Only favourable circumstances, the fact that the Seleucid state was in a condition of increasing decline but still sufficiently powerful to prevent other powers laying hands directly on its territory,

---

[1] Apparently at this time people again studied the subjects of the ancient Pentateuch tradition and particularly in the circles of the Hellenistic Diaspora in which the traditional stories were reinterpreted mythologically and rationalistically in a clearly derivative manner. The adaptations of the traditional narratives by Artapanus and Eupolemus, of which we have only indirect and quite fragmentary knowledge, may have originated about the beginning of the 1st century B.C.; cf. A. Schlatter, *Geschichte Israels von Alexander dem Grossen bis Hadrian* ([3]1925), pp. 187 ff.

led to adroit leaders on the periphery of this state in southern Palestine founding a state of their own which was really independent though it had not broken away formally from Seleucid sovereignty. This state of affairs did not last very long. As soon as a stronger hand seized the Seleucid state the independence of the Hasmonaean monarchy came to an end. For this monarchy lacked a really firm basis. David's monarchy had been sustained by the consent of the free Israelite tribes in the two kingdoms of Judah and Israel, whereas, to begin with, the Hasmonaean monarchy relied very largely on the support of a particular party in the little province of Judah; and even though it did reach out quite far beyond these narrow confines, the make-up of the people on which it must base itself had become far too disunited after centuries of foreign rule and many vicissitudes of fate to form the basis of a permanent political structure. The Jerusalem religious community had become something different from what the ancient people of Israel had been. With their supporters, the Hasmonaeans established and maintained their power primarily by military means. From the outset they had to reckon on numerous, albeit not over-active, enemies among the Israelites and they were, therefore, never able to attain a healthy, integrated political system. It is not that they were mere adventurers. The goal they had in mind was a monarchy over Israel, and David's formation of a kingdom will have served as their model. Judas had already concerned himself with the Israelites in Galilee and the land east of the Jordan, and later on the Hasmonaeans were able to extend their rule over roughly the whole territory of the old Israelite tribes. But the conditions needed for a restoration of the Davidic monarchy never really existed in their time.

The Hasmonaeans left few visible traces of their rule behind. We know a little about the building activities of the Hasmonaean rulers, but more from literary records than archaeological discoveries. They helped to change the face of the royal city of Jerusalem. According to Josephus (*Bell. Iud.* V, 4, 1, § 139) the Hasmonaeans eventually levelled the site of the one-time 'Akra'[1], thereby probably beginning the end of the settlement on the 'southeastern hill' of Jerusalem which to this day has never again been fully occupied. On the other hand, they built a royal palace in Jerusalem, though unfortunately no information about the building has come down to us; but Josephus, who mentions a 'Hasmonaean

---

[1] Later on, Josephus specifically attributed this work to Simon (*Ant. Iud.* XIII, 6, 7, §§ 215 ff.) but probably erroneously.

house' in Jerusalem (*Bell. Iud.* II, 16, 3, § 344) and a 'royal fort' in Jerusalem which derived from the Hasmonaeans (*Ant. Iud.* XX, 8, 11, §§ 189 f.), testifies to its existence. This Hasmonaean palace is to be sought on a part of the west hill of Jerusalem which projects opposite the southern part of the Temple area[1]. In addition to this, the Hasmonaeans also established on a hill north-west of the Temple area a fortress which was evidently intended to dominate the sanctuary and which was called 'Baris' (*Ant. Iud.* XV, 11, 4, § 403). As a result, the centre of gravity of the city of Jerusalem was gradually shifted westwards and northwards. Herod's later building activities intensified this tendency still more. The Hasmonaean rulers also erected forts in the country outside Jerusalem. To judge from its name, the fort of Hyrcania was established by John Hyrcanus; it lay east-south-east of Jerusalem in the Judaean desert on the site of the modern *khirbet mird*, and more than once played an important part in the subsequent period. The fort of Alexandrium which lay on the summit of the *karn sartabe* which jutted out into the lower valley of the Jordan from the west Jordan hills, and which derived its name from Alexander Jannaeus, played an important part in the fighting of the late Hasmonaean period. The same Alexander Jannaeus also extended the fort of Machaerus (the modern *khirbet el-mukāwer*) in the southern land east of the Jordan. However, all these Hasmonaean installations were put in shade the by the later buildings of Herod.

After the death of Antiochus VII Sidetes in the year 128 B.C. had given him more or less a free hand, John Hyrcanus I, as high priest and ethnarch, extended his power in various directions as a result of military campaigns. For this purpose he primarily used mercenaries which he had recruited, just as David had done. But whereas David, who had himself been a professional soldier, used this method because it was part and parcel of the strategy with which he was familiar, with John Hyrcanus it was a sign of his lack of popular support. With these mercenaries he marched into the southern land east of the Jordan, and after a six months' siege he captured the city of Medeba and then a few other places, laying his hands on the country of *el-belka* which under David had been part of the kingdom of Israel. He also undertook a campaign against the province of Samaria, seized the city of Shechem, occupied Mount Gerizim and destroyed the Samaritan Temple built on it. Furthermore, he invaded the province of Idumaea ('Edom') which adjoined Judaea in the south and the territory of which had

[1] Cf. J. Simons, *Jerusalem in the Old Testament* (1952), pp. 152 f.

been Judaean until the year 598 B.C., seized the cities of Adora (*dūra*) west-south-west of Hebron, and Marisa (*tell sandaḥanne*) near the modern *bēt jibrīn*, and forced the inhabitants of Idumaea to accept the custom of circumcision and the whole law of the Jerusalem religious community, and so incorporated them by force into this religious community (*Ant. Iud.* XIII, 9, 1, §§ 254 ff.). Later on he attacked the province of Samaria once again, including the provincial capital of Samaria itself. It had to be besieged for a long time and John Hyrcanus left this task to his two sons Aristobulus and Antigonus[1]. As the inhabitants of this provincial capital summoned Seleucid help in their distress, the besiegers were for a time in serious difficulties. They finally succeeded in capturing the city in the year 107 B.C. after besieging it for about a year, and Samaria was completely destroyed by its conquerors (*Ant. Iud.* XIII, 10, 2, 3, §§ 275 ff.).

Thus John Hyrcanus' successes were great. Nevertheless he had internal difficulties. In *Ant. Iud.* XIII, 10, 5, 6, §§ 288 ff., Josephus tells as an anecdote, but probably with a basis of truth, of a disagreement between him and the Pharisees, who can indeed scarcely have approved of his political and military activities. This led to Mattathias' grandson approaching the Sadducees, who, with their mainly pro-Hellenistic attitude, found it easier to reconcile themselves to his activities. For the rest he behaved like an independent ruler. He had coins minted with the inscription: 'The high priest Johannes and the community of the Judaeans' or 'The high priest Johannes, the head of the community of the Judaeans'. On these coins double cornucopias appear as on Seleucid copper coins and also a poppyhead, symbols of fertility, which were no doubt intended to refer to the benefactions of the government of John Hyrcanus[2].

In the year 104 B.C. John Hyrcanus died. He intended his wife to succeed him. But his eldest son, Aristobulus, seized power, had his mother taken to prison and starved. He also imprisoned three of his brothers and allowed only his brother Antigonus to share the government with him. Intrigues were now started against Antigonus by members of Aristobulus' entourage, which caused the latter to distrust his brother and finally to have him treacherously

---

[1] The Greek names (or nicknames) of the two are noteworthy.

[2] Cf. C. Watzinger, *Denkmäler Palästinas*, II (1933), p. 23; A. Reifenberg, *Ancient Jewish Coins* (² 1947), pp. 13 f., 40 f., Pl. II. A coin found during the excavations at Beth-zur with the name probably of a high priest comes from the pre-Maccabean Hellenistic period (cf. W. F. Albright, BASOR, 53 [1934], p. 22). Cf. DOTT, p. 234, Pl. 14.

murdered (*Ant. Iud.* III, ii, 1, 2, § 301 ff.). This fratricide clearly reveals the degeneration of the Hasmonaean dynasty which was soon to assume even worse forms. Aristobulus took advantage of the situation and assumed the title of king and conferred a royal diadem on himself. On the coins which derive from him, however, he does not bear the title of king. Their inscription runs : 'High priest Judas[1] and the community of the Judaeans'[2]. According to Josephus, *Ant. Iud.* XIII, 2, 3, §§ 318 f., he waged war in the extreme north of the country and forced the Ituraeans in the north of Galilee to introduce circumcision and accept the law of the Jerusalem religious community. He therefore appears at any rate partly to have subjugated Galilee. He died in the year 103 B.C. after he had reigned only for a year.

Aristobulus' wife, Salome[3] Alexandra, now released the three imprisoned brothers of the dead king from prison and appointed one of them king. His native name was Jonathan but he was called by his pet name Jannai and only used his native name as a surname to a Greek name, so that he became known as Alexander Jannaeus[4]. The degeneration of the Hasmonaean dynasty was clearly revealed in him, the great-grandson of Mattathias. It is no longer possible to decide exactly what role was played by Salome Alexandra who put him on the throne. At any rate, she married him[5] and took on the government after his death; this suggests that she will already have had a strong influence during his lifetime. Of his two surviving brothers he had one murdered—evidently to safeguard his own authority—but the other one, who had no political ambitions, he left alone (*Ant. Iud.* XIII, 12, 1, §§ 323). For the rest, he constantly made war, with changing fortune, but with the result, nevertheless, that in the end he controlled practically the whole of Palestine. An attack on the port of Ptolemais (Acco) at the beginning of his reign involved him in an armed conflict with Ptolemy Lathyrus who, banished from Egypt, was ruling in Cyprus at this time and had been called to their aid by the inhabitants of Ptolemais. Ptolemy Lathyrus invaded the land and defeated Alexander Jan-

---

[1] According to Josephus, *Ant. Iud.* XX, 10, 3, § 240, Judas was the original name and Aristobulus the Greek nickname.

[2] Cf. A. Reifenberg, *op. cit.* pp. 14, 41, Pl. ii.

[3] In *Ant. Iud.* XIII, 12, 1, § 320 this name appears miswritten as Salina.

[4] On his coins (cf. also C. Watzinger, *op. cit.* p. 23; A. Reifenberg, *loc. cit.* pp. 14 f., 41, Pl. ii) so far as they followed the previous type of high priest coins, he used his native name in the inscription: 'The high priest Jonathan and the community of the Judaeans'. In addition he then had new royal coins minted with the bilingual inscription: 'King Jonathan (Hebrew)—King Alexander (Greek)'.

[5] There is no explicit evidence of this; but probably the name Salome Alexandra nevertheless always refers to one and the same person at this period.

naeus so thoroughly in a battle on the middle Jordan near Asaphon[1] that he was able to regard himself as master in the land. Only the opposition which Ptolemy Lathyrus encountered from Egypt, especially from his mother Cleopatra, forced him to withdraw to Cyprus and freed Alexander Jannaeus from his distress (*Ant. Iud.* XIII, 12, 2-13, 2, §§ 324 ff.). Once he had a free hand again, Alexander Jannaeus marched first of all into the land east of the Jordan, captured, after a long siege, the city of Gadara (the modern *umkēs*) which lay on the south side of the Yarmuk, and then the city of Amathus (the modern *'ammata*) on the eastern edge of the central valley of the Jordan, thereby laying his hands on the central land east of the Jordan. He then turned his attention to the southern coastal plain and occupied the cities of Raphia (the modern *refaḥ*) and Anthedon (north-west of Gaza) and finally overcame the important city of Gaza by treachery, and had it sacked and set on fire (*Ant. Iud* XIII, 13, 3, §§ 356 ff.). Later on he invaded the land east of the Jordan again, subjugated the inhabitants of Moabitis and Galaaditis, *i.e.* of the southern and central land east of the Jordan again and captured the city of Amathus once more; his rule, which was based on purely military resources —he too waged his wars with mercenaries—was nowhere very permanent and always began to crumble once he was making war in another area. After the conquest of Amathus he penetrated as far as Gaulanitis, the present region of *jōlān* north of the Yarmuk. An engagement took place here with Obedas, the 'King of the Arabs', *i.e.* Obodath, the king of the Nabataeans, who was preparing to subjugate the land east of the Jordan as far as Damascus. He fell into an ambush and only just managed to save his life, escape and flee to Jerusalem. The episode showed how strong the opposition to him was among his own people. They tried at this moment to rid themselves of his rule and even appealed for the help of the Seleucid Demetrius III Eukairus who was in control of part of Syria *circa* 90 B.C. His forces did in fact defeat Alexander Jannaeus at Shechem, though he was already in a very tight corner. He had to flee to somewhere in the mountains. In this situation enough supporters who did not want their own monarchy to be defeated rallied around him, however, and, according to Josephus, he was joined by 6000 Judaeans; and with them Alexander Jannaeus was able to establish his rule again. Demetrius III withdrew and Alexander Jannaeus took a terrible and cruel ven-

---

[1] On the precise situation of Asaphon or Asophon cf. F. V. Filson, BASOR, 91 (1943), pp. 27 f., and, on the other hand, N. Glueck, AASOR, 25/28 (1951), pp. 354 f.

geance on his Judaean enemies (*Ant. Iud.* XIII, 13, 5-14, 2, § 372 ff.). He maintained authority by terror and thereby succeeded in ridding himself henceforth of all internal difficulties. But he still had to go through struggles with his external enemies, above all with the Nabataeans, whose growing power and lust for expansion was endangering near-by Palestine. From their ancient dwellings in the mountains south-east of the Dead Sea they not only pressed forward to the far north on the eastern border of the land east of the Jordan, but they also tried to reach the Mediterranean by way of the *wādi el-'araba* on the southern border of Palestine; and everywhere their nearest important neighbour was the land ruled by Alexander Jannaeus. The latter was then involved in the struggles between the Seleucid state and the Nabataeans. When one of the last of the Seleucids, Antiochus XII Dionysus, a younger brother of the above-mentioned Demetrius, tried to proceed against the Nabataeans through the coastal plain of Palestine and hence through Alexander Jannaeus' territory, the latter attempted to block the Seleucid's way by means of a ditch and a wall which he set up between Chabarsaba (the modern *kefr sāba*) and Joppa (*yāfa*); the Seleucid burnt and destroyed this work, but soon afterwards he was killed on the Nabataean campaign (*Ant. Iud.* XIII, 15, 1, §§ 387 ff.).

This was followed by direct and serious conflicts between the Nabataeans and Alexander Jannaeus. Aretas, who had meanwhile become king of the Nabataeans, advanced far into Judaea, and at Adida (probably *el-ḥadīte* east of Lydda) he inflicted a severe defeat on Alexander Jannaeus, so that the latter was forced to make concessions to obtain the withdrawal of the enemy (*Ant. Iud.* XIII, 15, 2, § 392). Finally, he carried out a number of successful expeditions in the land east of the Jordan. He occupied the cities of Pella (the modern *khirbet faḥil*) on the eastern border of the central valley of the Jordan and Gerasa (*jerash*) in the 'ajlūn, and also, north of the Yarmuk, the cities of Golan, the capital of Gaulanitis (exact position unknown)[1], Seleucia (the modern *selūkye*) and Dion (the modern *tell ash'ari*) as well as the citadel of Gamala[2]. In the land east of the Jordan his life came to an end. Weakened by a dissolute life, he died in his 51st year during the siege of the citadel of Ragaba (the modern *rājib*) in the southern 'ajlūn. Besides many military successes he had also suffered a number of

---

[1] This city is often identified with the modern *saḥem ed-jōlān*.
[2] The names given in *Ant. Iud.* XIII, 15, 3, §§ 393 f. and *Bell. Iud.* I, 4, 8, §§ 104 f. differ somewhat. Both lists have been collated with one another above.

serious defeats. Apart from ancient Judaea he had also inherited Samaria and Galilee from his predecessors and had made conquests himself in the southern coastal plain and then, above all, he extended his dominion in the land east of the Jordan and managed to maintain his power to some extent against the increasingly powerful Nabataeans. In *Ant. Iud.* XIII, 15, 4, §§ 395-397 Josephus describes the dominions of the 'Judaeans' towards the end of the reign of Alexander Jannaeus; according to this, they more or less embraced the territories of the old kingdoms of Judah and Israel over which David and Solomon had ruled, and also the former land of the Philistines and the coast road to Egypt as far as and including Rhinokorura (*el-ʿarīsh*). Though his successes did win him some support, he had had to contend with the enmity of the 'pious', the 'Pharisees' who hated this secular and already extremely degenerate monarchy. Josephus relates in *Ant. Iud.* XIII, 15, 5, §§ 399 ff. that before his death he advised his wife, Salome Alexandra, to allow the Pharisees a certain influence in the future, *i.e.* to try to reconcile them to the Hasmonaean monarchy, which could not in fact stand this internal discord in the long run.

After the death of Alexander Jannaeus in the year 76 B.C. his energetic and shrewd wife, Salome Alexandra, reigned for nine years. She presumably seized the throne on her own responsibility, particularly as her elder son, Hyrcanus (II), who should have succeeded his father, was very indolent and irresolute. She allowed him to succeed his father in the office of high priest which the existing law prevented her from assuming, but kept the monarchy for herself. She held back her younger son, Aristobulus (II) who, unlike his brother, was very bold and enterprising. Above all she now established contact with the Pharisees and complied to a very large extent with their wishes and demands. Hence her reign was subsequently regarded as a favourable period. There was also the fact that she managed, without waging wars, to keep the Hasmonaean state together and steer it through all kinds of difficulties (*Ant. Iud.* XIII, 16, 1-6, § 405 ff.). The only person she failed to manage was her son Aristobulus. The Sadducee priesthood had more reason for dissatisfaction than anyone else because of the influence which the Pharisees had suddenly acquired. This discontent was turned to account by the restlessly ambitious Aristobulus, who had been kept under and who was striving for power. But before it came to open rebellion the queen died in the year 67 B.C. at the age of 73 and left the Hasmonaean dominions to the dissensions of her two sons.

To begin with, Hyrcanus II, who was entitled to the throne as the elder of the brothers, did in fact take up the royal office; he had already been high priest since the beginning of his mother's reign. But Aristobulus, who was the stronger character, refused to acquiesce in this state of affairs. With his followers he defeated Hyrcanus' forces at Jericho and large numbers of the latter went over to the enemy. He then shut up Hyrcanus in the fortress[1] of Jerusalem and forced him to surrender. Hyrcanus ceded his office as king and high priest to his brother and in return he was promised enjoyment of his income (*Ant. Iud.* XIV, 1, 2, § 4 ff.). This appeared to have brought the dispute to an end. But a new figure now appeared on the scene, who was soon to play a great part in the history of Israel. Under Alexander Jannaeus and Salome Alexandra a certain Antipater (Antipas for short) had been governor in Idumaea[2]. His son of the same name, whose official position is not definitely known, but who may also have been governor in Idumaea, now espoused the cause of the defeated Hyrcanus. Probably he did not much like the government of the ambitious and energetic Aristobulus. He assembled associates who were sympathetic in Judaea and also got in touch with the Nabataean king Aretas and managed to persuade Hyrcanus to leave Jerusalem for security reasons and put himself under the protection of the Nabataean king. Hyrcanus left the city by night with Antipater and went to the royal Nabataean city of Petra. The Nabataean king promised to take him back to Jerusalem with a military escort and install him as king there in return for the surrender of a number of cities on the eastern side of the Dead Sea, in the old land of the Moabites, which Alexander Jannaeus had taken away from the Nabataeans; and Hyrcanus promised to fulfil this condition (*Ant. Iud.* XIV, 1, 3, 4, §§ 8 ff.). Thereupon Aretas proceeded to Judaea with an army and defeated Aristobulus' forces in a battle, the place of which is not mentioned by Josephus. The result was that a major part of Aristobulus' troops went over to the victor and Aristobulus, who was thus left in the lurch, was forced to withdraw to Jerusalem to defend himself in the fortified Temple area, where the priesthood still stood by him. But Aretas besieged him in the sanctuary, and the people in Jerusalem and probably elsewhere as well supported the party that was for the moment in the ascendant. The prospects

---

[1] This fort was not the former 'Akra' which had played such a great part in the Maccabean fighting, but the fortification laid out by the Hasmonaeans on an elevation north-west of the Temple enclosure which was called 'Baris' at the time.

[2] That Antipater was himself an 'Idumaean' is stated by Josephus, *Ant. Iud.* XIV, 1, 3, § 8 and elsewhere.

for Aristobulus were far from favourable and it appears that Hyrcanus might soon have attained the goal desired by Antipater if another and much stronger power had not intervened at this moment, which gave the course of events a completely new twist. The situation in which this happened revealed once again the wretched state to which the Hasmonaean monarchy had sunk. Two brothers were quarrelling about the throne. The driving force behind the dispute was a leading royal official, possibly the governor of Idumaea, who wanted to see the king who was functioning at the moment removed. The dispute was conducted with the military aid of the Nabataean king whom this official had enlisted for the purpose. The price which had to be paid to the foreign king, who was a natural enemy of the Hasmonaean kingdom, consisted in the surrender of a large area which had been acquired in the process of restoring the Israelite kingdom, more or less, on the model of David's kingdom. Now this foreign king, who had been summoned to help by the Judaeans themselves, was encamped with his troops outside the sanctuary in Jerusalem which was being used as a fortress; and the Judaean troops and the people were on his side because he was the superior and obviously victorious party. It was clear that the Hasmonaean monarchy was historically already played out. Forty years had not yet passed since a Hasmonaean had first called himself 'king' and already the complete decay of this institution was evident.

31. *Israel's Inner Life in the Hellenistic Period*

The struggles that began in the Maccabean period not only greatly agitated the Jerusalem religious community externally, but also stirred up its internal life intensely. The traditional records about this period reveal very varied religious and intellectual tendencies. Needless to say, this differentiation of the community's inner life was not brought about in the first place by the conflict with the Seleucid power; it merely became intensified in the course of these events, but had its roots in earlier periods about which we are unfortunately much less well-informed. We have to reckon with the fact that life in Israel had been becoming more and more individualised for a long time. Even though the old Israel of the twelve tribes, living as a self-contained unit in its homeland, was certainly not a shapeless collective entity in which the individual was no more than a mere member of a larger whole, and even though such a thing as 'Solomonic-post-Solomonic humanism' (cf. above, p. 223) had existed, nevertheless it was inevitable that the gradual undermining of the organism of the original Israel, resulting from the catastrophes of the divine judgement which destroyed Israel's political independence, should lead to a further dissolution of traditional ties and an ever-increasing prominence being given to the individual with his personal inclinations and decisions. It is true that the events of the Persian period had reunited Israel as a great community gathered around the Temple cultus in Jerusalem linked with the ancient traditions, and had given all Israelites a binding rule for daily life in the 'law of the God of heaven'; but this very law had confronted the individual with the question of his personal acceptance and therefore of his membership of 'Israel' and also made it possible for individual non-Israelites to share this acceptance. It may be assumed that the process of individualisation was further promoted by involvement in the intellectual atmosphere of the Hellenistic world, though it is impossible to prove the point in detail. Above all, in the widespread Diaspora the individual was dependent on his own resources in a foreign environment and had, if necessary, himself to prove his loyalty to the traditions of Israel. The Daniel narratives in Dan. i-vi which probably originated and were put together in the course of the first century of Hellenistic rule, reveal the typical situation of the Diaspora Israelite who could easily find himself in a position where he was forced to maintain his obedience to God and his law by the strength of his own faith. And in view of the constant intercourse between the Diaspora and the homeland, the situation in the Diaspora no doubt had a lasting effect on the intellectual outlook of the Israelites who were still living together in Palestine. Even before the outbreak of the Maccabean conflicts, Israel's life is therefore likely to have been in many respects individualised; and it is not surprising that the reaction which the events of the period of Antiochus IV Epiphanes evoked in the Jerusalem religious community was by no means uniform. The crisis that occurred in this period did, however, no doubt make clear and precise the existing differences and bring about particular groupings within the Jerusalem religious community which continued to be of great importance right into the Roman period.

There were certain Hellenising circles which, in so far as they were not simply absorbed by the pagan world, and thereby separated from the history of Israel, but adhered more or less deliberately to their membership of the Jerusalem religious community, were devoted to the Hellenistic life which surrounded this community on every side in the homeland and in the Diaspora, especially the Egyptian Diaspora. These groups began to play an important part under Antiochus IV and probably had a considerable share in the outbreak of the conflict in Jerusalem (cf. above, p. 361 f.). No doubt they evolved an intellectual life of their own both before this, and also afterwards, in which an attempt was made to combine Israel's traditions with Hellenistic thought in some way or other. But hardly any products of this intellectual life have survived. The fact is that these groups succumbed in the fighting of the 2nd century, at least in Palestine; and when, after the end of Israel, the Synagogue withdrew into itself and rejected all elements which appeared to be alien, works which had arisen in these circles, even if they were still read in the Diaspora of the Mediterranean world, were not transmitted further. All that we possess of this Israelite-Hellenistic literature are the meagre fragments which found a place in the works of early Christian writers by way of the great collector Alexander Polyhistor (first half of the 1st century B.C.) or by other routes. All the same, these fragments do show that this type of literature did exist. Thus, about the middle of the 2nd century, the philosopher Aristobulus in Alexandria attempted to show that the Old Testament law, when its basic content is analysed out, agrees with the various schools of Greek philosophy, in fact that Greek philosophy had, from of old, drawn on the Mosaic law[1]. This was an attempt to interpret and justify the traditions of Israel before the forum of Hellenistic thought. The method used was that of allegorical exegesis. Philosophers of the type of Aristobulus were joined, as mentioned above on p. 384, note 1, by historians such as Artapanus and Eupolemus[2]. Later on we find the same approach in the allegorical and mystical philosophy of Philo of Alexandria on the one hand and in the historical writing of Josephus on the other, as far as the latter is a description of Israel's ancient history for the Hellenistic and Roman world, and not contemporary history.

In the Maccabean-Hasmonaean period the Sadducees sympathised with this Hellenising tendency. They were the group of priests in Jerusalem, and, as such, the representatives of a legitimist approach

[1] A German translation of the fragments of Aristobulus will be found in P. Riessler, *Altjüdisches Schrifttum ausserhalb der Bibel* (1928), pp. 179 ff. Cf. also on Aristobulus A. Schlatter, *Geschichte Israels* (3 1925), pp. 81 ff. Cf. also W. N. Stearns, *Fragments from Graeco-Jewish Writers* (1908), pp. 75 ff.

[2] For the fragments of Artapanus and Eupolemus see Riessler, *op. cit.* pp. 186 ff., 328 ff. Cf. also Stearns, *op. cit.* pp. 42 ff., 29 ff.

in public worship, though this only in a predominantly formal sense, so that they were not averse in principle to the adoption of Hellenistic modes of life. Thanks to the conservatism of religious traditions they were able to endure the whole crisis of the conflict with Hellenism and survive right up to the end of Israel's history.

Admittedly, the anti-Hellenistic forces won the victory in the struggles of the 2nd century. The division which occurred in their midst and which we have discussed above on p. 374, came about when the leaders of the struggle against the Seleucid attacks set out for and attained the goal of political independence and secular power, in the end to find their successors in the rebels against Roman supremacy, who helped to bring about the end of Israel's history. Even in an early stage of the struggles against the Seleucids, the 'pious' who had, to begin with, contributed to the movement of resistance against the attacks on the very life of the Jerusalem religious community, but later no longer approved of continuing the line of military and political action, parted company with these political activists. The important thing for them was the unhindered continuation of the Jerusalem cultus and the freedom to live their lives in accordance with their ancestral traditions. They formed themselves into the group of Pharisees, and as such they continued to exert a determining influence on the inner life of the Jerusalem religious community to the very end of Israel's history, and even after its end they left a decisive mark on the face of the Judaism that then arose. From the 2nd century, the most important evidence of their attitude is the series of visions of Daniel in Dan. vii-xii. These visions are based on a very clearly pronounced conception of world history as a succession of rule by world powers which will one day be brought to an end by the breaking in of the rule of God. This conception of the course of history had an even earlier beginning. The collection of Daniel narratives in Dan. i-vi already contained that vision (Dan. ii, 29 ff.) which, using Israelite theories of world ages and patterns of world history, had formulated the contrast between secular and divine rule in the sense of a succession in time, no doubt on the basis of earlier prophetic announcements in the Old Testament of an expected kingdom of God. In the period of persecution by Antiochus IV this vision of history was actualised in the conviction that the age of world powers had run its course and the coming of the rule of God was imminent (cf. especially Dan. vii). World history is conceived here as a great unity, not only in the sense that it can be represented simply as a succession of empires replacing one another, but also that fundamentally it has emerged from chaos opposed to God (cf. Dan. vii, 2b, 3a) and must be regarded, at least in its tendency, as hostile to God. This conception prepared the way for a dualistic view of the world, a view not found in the Old Testament prophets, in spite of all their recognition of the human presumption and guilt which prevail in history. It is possible that this dualistic tendency had its source in a rationalisation of the content of the faith which went hand in hand with individualisation, and and that it was not uninfluenced by the Iranian dualism with which this kind of rationalisation had much in common. Behind the rationalising historical view of history of the visions of Daniel, lay the experience of the centuries of the life of the Jerusalem religious community within various empires, whose protection it enjoyed, and whose magnanimity in the allotment of privileges to the Jerusalem cultus it experienced, but to whose dominion and power and, in some cases, tyranny, it was exposed, and which followed a system of worship which the Jerusalem religious community condemned as 'pagan'. But at the same time the hope for an end of the historical process which had been determined by the godless world-powers was still alive. It was a development of the Messianic proclamations of the pre-exilic prophets and the eschatological expectations of the post-exilic period, which looked forward to the people of God, oppressed in present world conditions, being gathered and liberated, and also glorified. There was a rational element in this hope too in so far as it was considered possible to determine and even to calculate the moment of the great change over from secular to divine rule. The conviction that the period of persecution under Antiochus IV represented the ultimate stage of the present course of the world, had probably developed spontaneously to begin with under the impact of extreme affliction such as had never been actually experienced in previous history; but an attempt was made at the same time to prove the accuracy of this conviction, not only by believing that they were living in the fourth age of world power, in accordance with the traditional schema, and hence the final and irrevocable stage, but also by trying to estimate by a complicated reckoning in 'year-weeks', as put forward in Dan. ix, 24-27, how short the time would be until the coming of the rule of God.

Apocalyptic, which was to play a great part in the circles of the 'pious', arose with the visions of Daniel, on the basis of a comprehensive view of history and the expectation of a final and imminent crisis, and on the assumption that it was possible to calculate the position of the present age within the course of events. The expectation was that everything would come from an act of God, who would make an end to the hitherto existing course of history without human assistance. The sole concern of the Jerusalem religious community was to remain faithful to their God in obedience to the 'covenant' (cf. Dan. ix, 27), by which they were bound, in order to receive a share of the blessings of the coming reign of God. How far the 'Israel' which still existed in the form of the Jerusalem religious community would occupy a special position in the future rule of God was a question that was answered differently according to circumstances. If 'the saints of the most High' who, according to Dan. vii, 18, are to be given the government after the end of world history, originally meant, as seems likely, heavenly beings, who will reign on God's behalf, nevertheless they were interpreted from a very early period as referring to the Israelites, in fact already in the secondary additions to the visions of Daniel (cf. Dan. vii, 21). They will not bring about the rule of God but receive the gift of 'power' from God, though no precise indications are given of the character and scope of this 'power'. Those already dead may also share in the life of this future time. In Dan. xii, 2, 3 there is a reference to the 'awakening' of those who 'sleep in the dust of the earth', *i.e.* in the world of the dead, of an awakening either 'to everlasting life' or 'to everlasting contempt'. 'Many' of the dead, it is said, will share this awakening and receive differing fates, evidently as reward or punishment for their deeds in the time of their earthly life. It is possible that these 'many', who can obviously only represent a part of the total number of the dead, refer primarily to those who fell or lost their lives in other ways in the Maccabean fighting, and who, according to whether they stood for obedience or disobedience to the ancestral traditions, have to expect divine reward or punishment after death. In any case this is the first explicit reference—already a very general one—to a resurrection of the dead and a divine judgement after this resurrection, though there had already been expressions, within the Old Testament faith, of the conviction that even the death of the body would not bring to an end union with God (cf. Ps. lxxiii, 24). Individual expectation of a life after the death of the body thus took its place alongside the expectation of the ending of history by the coming of the kingdom of God, though for the time being no attempt was made to establish a closer connection between them.

In the following period a fairly richly elaborated apocalyptic literature was developed from these beginnings[1]. Its products were not included later in the selection of 'canonical' writings made by the Synagogue after the fall of Jerusalem at the end of the 1st century A.D. In so far as they did not vanish altogether, they only survived for a time in various forms of the Greek translation of the Old Testament used in the early Christian Church, and from there they reached the Oriental national churches, where they were included in various Oriental translations of the Old Testament[2]. It is therefore difficult to ascertain their original Hebrew-Aramaic form and the time when they were written. In general, however, they derive from the 2nd/1st century B.C. To the element of eschatological expectation for the individual, for Israel and for humanity, they add a gradually developing angelology, of which the beginnings appear already in the book of Daniel, as well as a strong cosmological interest. Alongside the development of apocalyptic literature there was a further preoccupation with the old narrative tradition of the Old Testament. The 'book of Jubilees' in which the material of the book of Genesis is presented in a new priestly-Pharisaic version, probably derives from the 2nd century B.C. This book was also not included at a later stage in the Old Testament canon, although it was certainly composed in Hebrew (or Aramaic) in Palestine.

The fact that they were not included in the canon later stamped these literary works deriving from the 'pious' of the 2nd/1st century as illegitimate, apocryphal and sectarian. Originally this blemish was certainly not attached to them amidst the various religious and intellectual movements of this period. It may be asked, however, whether, once the 'Pharisees' had taken the path of 'separation' (cf. above, p. 374, note 1) from the tendencies prevailing at the time of their emergence, though they later became a very influential group within the Jerusalem religious community, the tendency to this kind of separation did not soon extend beyond the Pharisees, in the direction of an absorption in apocalyptic-gnostic speculations, and above all in the direction of a rigorism surpassing the legalism of the Pharisees in matters of ritual purity and ascetic abstinence. This latter tendency in particular was bound to lead to the formation of parties and sects. The later Rabbinic tradition and Josephus and Philo have made us familiar with

[1] Cf. P. Volz, *Die Eschatalogie der jüdischen Gemeinde im neutestamentlichen Zeitalter* ([2] 1934).

[2] In German translation in E. Kautzsch, *Die Apokryphen und Pseudepigraphen des Alten Testaments*, II (1900), English translation in R. H. Charles, *Apocrypha and Pseudepigrapha of the Old Testament*, II (1913).

baptising sects and, above all, with the 'Essenes' in the 1st century B.C. and especially the 1st century A.D.[1]. The concept of the 'Essenes', whom Josephus places as a third group alongside the Sadducees and Pharisees, probably embraces a whole wealth of slightly differing sectarian organisations. It is highly probable that these separatist movements originated in the external and internal upheavals of the 2nd century. They are at the same time an indication that the inner life of the Jerusalem religious community had become sterile. The persecution under Antiochus IV had once again aroused lively and vigorous forces of resistance in an atmosphere which was perhaps not, generally speaking, unfavourable to Hellenism. But the victory of these forces had not given any really new content to the community as a whole. The victors pursued the path of outward power; those, such as the Pharisees, who did not go this way, turned increasingly to a legalistic moralism, which led to an increasingly subtle casuistic treatment of the traditional laws of God, and in the face of this even the apocalyptic expectations of the end, as they had been expressed in the visions of the book of Daniel, receded into the background. It is not surprising that many sought the fulfilment of their hopes in small groups, some of which united their members by means of a common life. It is not unlikely that the community which has become known as a result of the discovery of its writings in some caves in the neighbourhood of the *khirbet kumrān* on the north-western edge of the Dead Sea[2], originated in the 2nd century B.C. According to the evidence of the archaeological discoveries at *khirbet kumrān*, this community lived in the first century A.D. until the great rebellion of the years A.D. 66–70 in a monastery-like settlement in the otherwise almost uninhabited area on the Dead Sea south of Jericho, and probably carefully preserved its writings in these caves to prevent their destruction in the chaos of the insurrection, and was later unable to retrieve them from this hiding-place. It is very difficult to date the manuscripts palaeographically; they may have been in use for a good time before they were put in the caves. In so far as they are not Biblical books such as the book of Isaiah, which is extant in two copies, the writings themselves contain compilations of regulations for the life of the community, liturgical pieces and apocalyptic material, the latter also in the form of the interpretation of traditional books of the Old Testament (*e.g.* 'Commentary on Habak-

---

[1] Cf. above all A. Schlatter, *Geschichte Israels* ([3] 1925), pp. 170 ff., 173 ff.

[2] On this sensational manuscript discovery which was made in the spring of 1947 see a brief report in WAT, pp. 246 ff.

kuk'). It is not yet possible to assign an exact date to these writings which contain various allusions to contemporary history; some of the contents suggest the period when the Seleucid Empire was still in existence, *i.e.* the century following Antiochus IV[1]. It is also possible that the various writings were composed at different times. However this question is ultimately solved, it remains probable at any rate that the community of *khirbet ḳumrān* derived from the separatist tendencies of the agitated period of the 2nd century; and the manuscript discoveries by the Dead Sea throw a surprising light on the parties and sectarian organisations in the very heart of the Jerusalem religious community of which no trace can be found in earlier times, and which, as far as we can see, only developed from the Maccabean period onwards. Even if they did not play a very important part in the foreground of historical events, they did have an important influence on Israel's internal life in the final phase of its history[2].

[1] Cf. H. H. Rowley, *The Zadokite Fragments and the Dead Sea Scrolls* (1952)— which includes a detailed account of the scholarly investigations into the meaning of the manuscripts that have been made so far and a complete bibliography of the literature that has appeared on them up to 1952.

[2] For more recent developments and publications, reference may be made to Millar Burrows, *The Dead Sea Scrolls* (1955) and *More Light on the Dead Sea Scrolls* (1958), and to C. Burchard, *Bibliographie zu den Handschriften vom Toten Meer* (BZAW 76, 1957).

CHAPTER II

THE ROMAN PERIOD

32. *The Intervention of the Roman Power*

I N the year 65 B.C. the Roman power appeared in Syria-Palestine. Israelite history thereby acquired a new background. From now on its course was decisively affected by this new power. It thereby entered into its final phase. It is true that, indirectly, Rome had already influenced it for a long time; the decline and decay of the Seleucid state which had made possible the events of the Maccabean-Hasmonaean period had, since the defeat of Antiochus III at Magnesia in 190 B.C., been an indirect result of the expansion of Roman power in the eastern Mediterranean; and the Maccabeans had already established relations with Rome from time to time. But, practically speaking, this had meant little; hitherto Rome had remained in the distance, whereas now the military might of Rome appeared in Syria-Palestine itself.

After Pompey had conquered the Pontic kingdom of Mithridates and the Armenian king Tigranes had agreed to surrender, under the impact of the Roman victories, Pompey prepared to impose a new order in the Roman style on western Asia and to liquidate the Seleucid state, which was already in a state of complete decay. In this connection he sent his legate M. Aemilius Scaurus to Syria in 65 B.C. The latter heard in Damascus of the conflict in Judaea and went there straight away. Not surprisingly, both the hard-pressed Aristobulus in Jerusalem and the successful Hyrcanus turned to him. Both offered him an equally large bribe to obtain his favour and support. Scaurus decided to help Aristobulus because, despite his present position, he thought his chances better from a long-term point of view. By means of threats he forced Aretas to raise the siege and to withdraw, and he confirmed Aristobulus in his previous offices (*Ant. Iud.* XIV, 2, 3, §§ 29 ff.). Thus the situation came about in which the course of events was determined by the insight or the arbitrariness of Roman decisions. Henceforth, to be successful it was necessary to obtain the good-will of whatever Roman authority happened to be most important in the particular situation; and this gave rise to the undignified striving for the favour of Roman overlords, which played an important part in the following period. How varied this was to make the course of events was to be shown very quickly in the present case. At this time Rome was entering the period of great internal conflicts and civil wars; and the disturbances of this period were bound constantly to affect the history of Israel.

Pompey himself soon appeared in Syria, where he spent the winter of 64/63 B.C. in winter quarters. In the spring he moved on to Damascus where deputations from all parts of the country appeared very soon with requests and entreaties. Aristobulus had already tried to influence him with a large bribe. He had also sent his legate to Pompey, whilst at the same time Antipater appeared before Pompey as Hyrcanus' representative, as did envoys of the people, evidently from Pharisaic circles, who wanted to see Hasmonaean rule completely abolished and the former position of the priesthood restored. Aristobulus and Hyrcanus appeared in Damascus in person. Pompey took Aristobulus' violent manner amiss, but postponed a definite decision and promised to reorganise Judaean affairs once he had completed the intended campaign against the Nabataeans (*Ant. Iud.* XIV, 3, 1-3, §§ 34 ff.). As Aristobulus refused to wait for this, and quickly returned to Judaea, probably to take measures to safeguard his power, Pompey deferred the Nabataean campaign and also went with his army to Judaea. He went via Pella (*khirbet faḥil*) and Scythopolis (*bēsān*) to Korea (the modern *ḳarāwe* in the lower *wādi fār'a*), where the territory of the real province of Judah, with its four extensions into south and south-east Samaria, at this time began. In the vicinity, west of the issue of the *wādi fār'a* into the Jordan Valley, on the impressive rounded mountain top dominating the Jordan Valley, which now bears the name *ḳarn ṣarṭabe*, was the fort Alexandrium which Alexander Jannaeus had extended (cf. above, p. 386). Aristobulus had proceeded to this fort. After some hesitation Aristobulus surrendered the fort on Pompey's orders, but then went in haste to Jerusalem to organise resistance against Pompey. Pompey followed him through Jericho into the vicinity of Jerusalem. But then Aristobulus gave up his cause for lost. He went to Pompey's camp and promised to hand over the city of Jerusalem. Pompey held on to him and sent Gabinius to Jerusalem with troops. The inhabitants refused to admit him into the city, however. Enraged by this, Pompey had Aristobulus imprisoned and moved on Jerusalem with the whole of his armed forces. At this, most of the inhabitants gave up the fight and opened the gates of the city to the Romans; only a minority, who were determined to continue to defend the city at all costs, went on resisting fiercely in the fortified Temple area. Pompey was forced to proceed to a regular siege with siege-machinery and only after three months could he make a breach in the wall and occupy the Temple area. A terrible massacre took place among the defenders. Pompey himself and other Romans entered the Temple and even the Holy of Holies to see it for themselves: an action which outraged all the faithful. The Temple was not plundered, however, and on the following day Pompey gave orders for the resumption of the traditional sacrificial rites. Hyrcanus was reinstalled as high priest (*Ant. Iud.* XIV, 4, 1-4, §§ 54 ff.). Aristobulus was taken to Rome as a prisoner and likewise his two sons Alexander and Antigonus, though the first of them escaped. When Pompey celebrated his triumph in Rome in the year 61 B.C., the Hasmonaean king Aristobulus was forced to show himself to the Roman people in the triumphal procession along with the other prisoners, whilst at the same moment his brother was, by Roman dispensation, high priest in Jerusalem.

In 63 B.C., after the end of Seleucid rule, Pompey introduced a fundamental reorganisation in Syria, also rearranging the territorial dispositions of the previous Hasmonaean kingdom. Syria-Palestine, *i.e.* the western part of the former Seleucid state, became the Roman province of Syria and M. Aemilius Scaurus its first governor. New political arrangements were made within this province under the rule of its governor. In Palestine the Hasmonaean conquests were for the most part separated from Judaea again. The coastal cities were constituted as independent urban communities and placed directly under the province. The same thing happened with a number of cities in the central and northern land east of the Jordan, including Pella and Scythopolis in the Jordan Valley, which combined to form the community of the 'ten cities' ('Decapolis'). These were for the most part Hellenistic foundations or re-established cities which had then been subjugated by the Hasmonaeans. They were now 'liberated' again and rightly regarded this liberation as the beginning of a new chapter in their history, counting their years henceforth from the beginning of the 'Pompeian' era. Samaria was also separated from Judaea again. The city of Samaria, formerly a Macedonian military colony, was constituted as an independent urban community, but for the rest the land of Samaria was put directly under the province of Syria, as the Samaritan religious community's own area, like the area of the Jerusalem religious community. If the cultus on Gerizim had been stopped under Hasmonaean rule, a point about which we have no definite information, it was at any rate restarted now. The territory of the Jerusalem religious community under the high priest, who was subject to the provincial governor, was now restricted once again to the old province of Judah, with the addition of Peraea and Galilee. Judaea retained the four southern and south-eastern districts of Samaria, which Jonathan and probably Simon had acquired, and also Idumaea which had been conquered by John Hyrcanus I, but was now separated again from the sea coast by the 'liberated' coastal cities. A strip of the southern and central land east of the Jordan connected with Judaea, remained under the control of the high priest; this strip was now called 'Peraea' and was bordered in its southern half by the still independent state of the Nabataeans and in its northern half by the territories of the cities of the 'Decapolis'. The Galilean interior was also left to the Jerusalem religious community under the high priest but was now separated geographically from Judaea and Peraea. On the whole, Pompey appears to have placed those areas under the high priest whose inhabitants almost all took part in the Jerusalem cultus; these were the old Israelite territories in Judaea including Idumaea, in the western part of the southern and central land east of the Jordan and in the interior of Galilee. With the establishment of a cultus of its own on Gerizim, Samaria had separated itself from Jerusalem and was accordingly granted independence within the framework of the Syrian province. One is bound to admit that the arrangement introduced by Pompey was a fitting one and on the whole took into account the actual membership of the Jerusalem religious community. The Hasmonaean kingdom and its conquests was thereby liquidated and once again there remained the Jerusalem religious community with its actual high priest at the head and with the people who actually took part in the Jerusalem cultus. The Hasmonaean family only continued to play a part in the person of the high priest Hyrcanus.

In the year 57 B.C. the Syrian governor A. Gabinius reorganised the affairs of the Jerusalem religious community once again. As proconsul and Pompey's favourite he had been entrusted in 57 B.C. with the administration of the province of Syria, which was important on account of its position on the eastern frontier. Pompey had deprived Hyrcanus of the title of king; Gabinius now took away from him all the political authority which he had had as head of the areas of Palestine which belonged to the Jerusalem religious community, and confined him entirely to his religious office. He divided the territory of the 'people' who made up the Jerusalem religious community into five independent districts, which were placed directly under the provincial governor. The real Judaea was thereby broken up into the districts of Jerusalem, Gazara[1] and Jericho. The district of Jerusalem embraced substantially the Judaean-Idumaean mountains; the district of Gazara covered parts of the western hill country, and that of Jericho the eastern slope of the mountain with Aphaerema and the Akrabattine, whilst Peraea was constituted as the district of Amathus (*'ammata*) and the interior of Galilee as the district of Sepphoris (the modern *ṣaffūrye*) (*Ant. Iud.* XIV, 8, 5, §§ 169 f.)[2].

The arrangements introduced by Pompey and Gabinius were reasonable enough to have settled the conflicts in Palestine and above all to have stabilised the position of the Jerusalem religious community and brought peace to the country. But the passions of the former antagonists were still so inflamed that they continued to create unrest, and the situation in Rome was so unstable that affairs in the Syrian province were constantly being influenced by the great political movements of the time. There now ensued a very unpleasant interplay of disputes and intrigues in which Aristobulus, who was still imprisoned in Rome with his son Antigonus, and also his son Alexander, who had escaped from the Romans, as well as Antipater and his increasingly prominent sons Phasael and Herod, and finally, in the background, Pompey and Caesar, Antonius and Octavian and the Roman governors and generals in Syria all played their part. Josephus gave a detailed account of these events in *Ant. Iud.* XIV, 5-16, and *Bell. Iud.* I, 8-18. It is not worth while going into them in detail and it will suffice briefly to mention the main operative factors.

First of all, Aristobulus and his two sons Alexander and Antigonus tried to regain the position of which they had been deprived by Pompey, at the expense of Hyrcanus who had been installed by the Romans. In this they were widely supported by members of the Jerusalem religious community itself, who were dissatisfied with the weak Hyrcanus and with the reorganisation of their affairs. To begin with, only Aristobulus' elder son Alexander was free to act, as he had succeeded in escaping from Pompey and had not been taken to Rome. Soon after Pompey had departed he tried to proceed

---

[1] In *Ant. Iud.* and *Bell. Iud.* the manuscripts give, in error, Gadara instead of Gazara.   [2] Cf. H. Guthe, *Bibelatlas* (² 1926), No. 10.

against his uncle Hyrcanus by force of arms. When A. Gabinius came to Syria in the year 57 B.C., he forced Alexander to surrender in the fortress of Alexandrium (*karn ṣarṭabe*) which was his base. Soon afterwards Aristobulus himself succeeded in escaping from Rome with his younger son Antigonus. They arrived in the land and, with their supporters, took up arms against Hyrcanus, but were seized by Gabinius in the fortress of Machaerus (the modern *khirbet el-mukāwer*) on the southern border of Peraea on the eastern side of the Dead Sea and taken to Rome again. Gabinius had hardly embarked on an expedition to Egypt when Alexander took up arms again. But as soon as Gabinius returned to Syria, Alexander was soundly defeated by him in the region of Mount Tabor on the southern border of Galilee. Gabinius, who was defending the order established by Pompey, now thought it his duty to strengthen the position of the high priest Hyrcanus against which the machinations of Aristobulus and his son had been directed. He therefore cancelled the division of the territory of the Jerusalem religious community into five independent districts that he himself had introduced in 57 B.C. and placed the whole area under the high priest again. In the year 54 B.C. M. Licinius Crassus, one of the triumvirs of the year 60 B.C., took over the province of Syria to conduct the war against the Parthians. He pillaged the province very thoroughly and also plundered the treasures and valuables of the Temple in Jerusalem. In the following year he was attacked and murdered by Parthian soldiers after an ill-starred campaign against the Parthians. The province of Syria was now administered from 53 to 51 B.C. by his quaestor C. Cassius Longinus. The latter was again forced to suppress a revolt against the existing organisation in the Jerusalem religious community.

In the year 49 B.C. Caesar crossed the Rubicon and Pompey and his supporters withdrew to the eastern half of the Empire. Caesar wanted to send Aristobulus, who was still a captive in Rome, to Syria to fight Pompey's partisans. Since it was Pompey who had deprived Aristobulus of his offices of king and high priest in Jerusalem, he no doubt gladly accepted this task. Before he departed, however, he was poisoned in Rome by supporters of Pompey, and his son Alexander, who had presumably been involved in his father's intended mission, was murdered soon afterwards in Antioch on Pompey's instructions. No doubt Hyrcanus and Antipater continued on Pompey's side for the time being. But when Pompey was defeated at Pharsalus on the 9th of August 48 and soon afterwards murdered on the coast of the Nile Delta, Hyrcanus and Antipater quickly attempted to win the favour of the victorious Caesar. When Caesar was faced with difficulties in Alexandria, Antipater managed to put him under an obligation by sending troops to his assistance which, together with those sent by Mithridates of Pergamon, conquered the important frontier-fortress of Pelusium on the eastern side of the Delta for Caesar and performed other services for him in Egypt; and Hyrcanus, as high priest, persuaded the members of the Jerusalem religious community in Egypt to side with Caesar. In the following year, 47 B.C., Caesar came to Syria. Antigonus, Aristobulus' surviving son, did, it is true, try to plead his allegedly better right to the office of high priest with Caesar and to put Antipater, who had been valuable to Caesar, in the wrong. But Caesar obviously did not really trust Antigonus, although only a short while previously he himself had tried to use Aristobulus and his sons against the supporters of Pompey in Syria. He bestowed his favours more on Hyrcanus and Antipater. He not only left them in their old positions and thereby rejected Antigonus' claims; Antipater and his master, Hyrcanus, had succeeded so well in coming over rapidly to the victorious side and obtaining Caesar's good-will, that Caesar richly rewarded them both for their assistance. Hyrcanus was expressly confirmed in the hereditary office of high priest, and he was also appointed to the hereditary office of 'ethnarch'. The Jerusalem religious community was granted the power of jurisdiction in its own affairs. Hyrcanus, with his descendants, was declared the 'confederate' of the Romans and his territory exempted from military contributions and from the duty of billeting Roman troops in the winter. Permission was also given for Jerusalem to be fortified again. Roman citizenship was conferred on Antipater, however, and he was appointed Roman procurator (principal administrative official) of Judaea. The territory of Judaea was extended. Above all, the important port of Joppa (*yāfa*) was restored to Judaea and also the villages on the great plain, *i.e.* the plain of Jezreel, evidently the area outside the already existing city territories[1]. Elsewhere, in the Diaspora, in the region of the eastern Mediterranean, Caesar also granted privileges to the members of the Jerusalem religious community and promised them, above all, freedom to conduct their worship with all its attendant rites[2]. These were astonishing concessions, which it is impossible to explain merely as a reward for the military help

[1] These important arrangements are given in *Ant. Iud.* XIV, 8, 5, §§ 177 ff. They were apparently subsequently confirmed by decree of the Senate. Cf. the collection of documents in *Ant. Iud.* XIV, 10.

[2] Cf. the documents in *Ant. Iud.* XIV, 10, of which the authenticity is admittedly not uncontested.

in Egypt. Caesar, who was deeply interested in the eastern parts of the great empire, wanted to conciliate the subject peoples in order to give his power a firm foundation.

Caesar's reorganisations had, above all, greatly strengthened the position of Antipater, who now brought his two sons Phasael and Herod to the fore. The elder son Phasael was given the administration of Judaea and Peraea and the younger son Herod that of Galilee, both with the title of '*strategos*'. It is not surprising that the power of Antipater and his sons aroused the displeasure of many members of the Jerusalem religious community, above all of the priesthood and the aristocracy. They tried to act on the weak Hyrcanus and to incite him to take action against Antipater and his sons. Under their pressure Hyrcanus did in fact make an effort to rouse himself to action. In Galilee Herod had put an end to the banditry that flourished there and had the leader of a band of robbers and many of his followers executed. This gave his enemies an opportunity to accuse him since he had thereby overridden the jurisdiction of the Sanhedrin, the 'Supreme Council', the assembly in which the priestly aristocracy and with them the Pharisaic scribes dealt with the basic internal affairs of the Jerusalem religious community; and Hyrcanus dared to summons Herod to appear before the Sanhedrin. Herod, who had strong support behind him in the then Syrian governor Sextus Caesar, put on such a dictatorial air that the Sanhedrin did not dare to sentence him. Herod departed secretly from Jerusalem soon to appear again outside the city with troops. This was too much even for his father Antipater. With difficulty he restrained Herod, who wanted to take bloody vengeance on the Sanhedrin, from brute violence and Herod returned again to Galilee after he had at any rate shown what it was to be up against him.

In the year 44 B.C., on the Ides of March, Caesar was murdered. The murderers then made for the eastern parts of the empire; and one of them, C. Cassius Longinus, who had already administered the province of Syria in the years 53–51 B.C. for the Crassus who had been murdered by the Parthians, became governor of Syria from 44 to 42 B.C. He exploited the province intensively and thereby made himself very unpopular. Antipater, however, who always tried to be on good terms with whoever was in power, served him zealously. This could only damage his reputation still further in the eyes of the Jerusalem religious community. In the end he fell victim to a conspiracy in which purely personal antagonism played a part. Hyrcanus was also drawn into the plot. Antipater was poisoned. But it was already too late. The position of his sons

Phasael and above all Herod was already too strong for the murder of Antipater to make any essential difference to the situation. Herod had the real instigator of his father's murder, an Arab named Malichus, who was himself attempting to attain an influential position in Judaea, treacherously murdered, thereby intimidating Antipater's enemies. In addition, the power of the governor Cassius was behind Phasael and Herod.

Antigonus, the son of Aristobulus, now bestirred himself again. He invaded Galilee with his army but was defeated by Herod and expelled from Galilee. This victory even brought Herod the goodwill of Hyrcanus, who normally mistrusted the superior power of Antipater and his sons, although they were responsible for keeping him in his position. All the same, his nephew Antigonus was his real enemy since he coveted his position and Hyrcanus was therefore grateful to Herod for driving Antigonus away and persuaded him to become engaged to his grand-niece Mariamne[1], a Hasmonaean, a granddaughter of his brother Aristobulus and a daughter of the latter's son Alexander. Antigonus then sought for further opportunities to realise his intentions. When in the year 42 B.C. Caesar's murderers had been defeated by M. Antonius and C. Julius Caesar Octavianus in the battle of Philippi, the government of the east devolved on Antony. Various deputations from the Jerusalem religious community tried to prejudice him against the brothers Phasael and Herod but without success, although the attempt was made to play off Hyrcanus against the two of them. By appearing before him in person Herod was able to win over Antony; and when Hyrcanus himself also visited Antony, when he came to Antioch, and declared himself for Phasael and Herod, their position was again secure for the time being, particularly as Antony had been the guest of their father Antipater during his earlier stay in Syria under A. Gabinius[2]. For the moment, therefore, Antigonus had no prospects of success. It is true that Antony made himself very unpopular in Syria owing to the great sums which he extorted in taxation, but nothing could be done against the powerful position he occupied. Finally, however, Antigonus reached his goal owing to a quite unforseen event. When Antony was staying with queen Cleopatra in Alexandria and was also very much preoccupied with events in Italy, the Parthians invaded the Roman provinces in the Near East and also occupied Syria. This was in the year 40 B.C. By

[1] Strangely enough Josephus does not mention this name in *Ant. Iud.* XIV, 12, 1, § 300, but only in the parallel passage in *Bell. Iud.* I, 12, 3, § 241.

[2] Phasael and Herod were appointed tetrarchs and entrusted with political leadership, and Hyrcanus was thereby limited again to his office of high priest.

making them substantial promises Antigonus succeeded in enlisting their support. While the Parthians were still in northern Syria he hastened to Judaea, collected supporters and forced his way into Jerusalem, where he became involved in fighting with Phasael and Herod. The Parthian forces then came to Jerusalem, and, under pretext of wanting to settle the quarrel, they summoned Phasael to the Parthian headquarters in Ekdippa (the modern *ez-zīb* north of Acco). In spite of the warnings of his brother Herod, who saw through the deceit, Phasael went with Hyrcanus and both were immediately imprisoned. The Parthians then installed Antigonus as king and high priest in Jerusalem and for three years he occupied the position he had desired. A small Parthian garrison stayed behind in Jerusalem; Hyrcanus and Phasael were handed over to Antigonus by the Parthians. Phasael killed himself; Antigonus had Hyrcanus' ears cut off, thereby incapacitating him for the office of high priest, and then handed him back to the Parthians, who took him with them to Babylon as a prisoner. There are in existence coins from the reign of Antigonus (40–37 B.C.) which, like the coins of Alexander Jannaeus, bear a Hebrew-Greek inscription and also refer to the native name of Antigonus, Mattathias, whom otherwise we know only by his Greek name; the inscription reads: 'The high priest Mattathias (Hebrew) —King Antigonus (Greek)'[1]. Otherwise we know nothing about his reign.

The only opponent of Antigonus now left was Herod. When Hyrcanus and Phasael were captured by the Parthians, he rescued his family and that of his brothers and took them to the almost inaccessible steep rock of Masada (the modern *es-sebbe*) on the western shore of the Dead Sea and left them in the care of his younger brother Joseph. He himself wanted to go to Petra to secure the help of the Nabataean king but he was not allowed in. He therefore decided to try and obtain the strongest possible support for his own cause and went personally on an adventurous journey to Rome. It was clear anyway that Rome did not approve of the monarchy of Antigonus who had been installed by the Parthians and that Antigonus would not be left in office after the expected reconquest of Syria; and Rome would welcome assistance in the reconquest of Syria from one who was acting in his own interest too. By skilful negotiation and bribes Herod succeeded in winning over Antony in Rome, and, through Antony, Octavian was also won over. At the end of the year 40 B.C. the Senate decided to appoint

[1] Cf. A. Reifenberg, *Ancient Jewish Coins* (² 1947), pp. 17 f., 42, Pl. III.

Herod king of Judaea. Admittedly, Herod had first to conquer his kingdom. He went straight from Rome to Syria and landed at Ptolemais. In Syria the Roman governor P. Ventidius had meanwhile driven out the Parthians. It is true that they made another attack in the year 38 B.C. but this time they were repelled once and for all by P. Ventidius. For the time being Ventidius had left Antigonus undisturbed in Jerusalem. With the support of the Roman governor, Herod made his first progress in 39 B.C. He occupied Joppa and was able to relieve the members of his family who had been besieged in Masada on instructions from Antigonus. But then there began to be difficulties. A siege of Jerusalem was a failure since the Roman general who was second in command did not support him or, possibly, was unable to support him owing to the feeling among his troops. Herod therefore went to Galilee. In the year 38 B.C. the Romans had to deal with the renewed invasion by the Parthians. Herod therefore made little progress. At the time Antony was occupied with the siege of Samosata on the upper Euphrates. Herod did not miss the opportunity of calling on him personally and reassuring himself of Roman support. During his absence with Antony, his brother Joseph, who was acting as his deputy in Judaea, was defeated by Antigonus and fell in the battle himself. When Herod returned, he embarked anew on the conquest of his kingdom—this time with the real support of the new Syrian governor C. Sosius. First of all he obtained possession of Galilee; then, still in the year 37 B.C., the rest of the territory except for the city of Jerusalem fell into his hands as a result of various successful battles against Antigonus and his forces. In the year 37 B.C. Jerusalem was then occupied by Sosius.and the Roman troops after a fairly long siege and assault. The Roman victors wrought great havoc in the fallen city so that Herod had to persuade Sosius to withdraw the Roman troops, by offering him bribes. Herod was now able to take up his royal office in Jerusalem. Antigonus was taken away as a prisoner by the Romans and, at Herod's request, executed in Antioch.

33. *The Reign of Herod and his Descendants*

From 37 B.C. onwards Herod was in uncontested possession of his kingdom. For this he had entirely to thank the Romans with whom his father Antipater had been constantly in touch and with whom he himself sought the closest possible relations. He was obviously unusually clever and successful in getting the support of the most important men of the time. He spared no pains in securing personal audiences with them at the right moments and he achieved a good deal in this way. On one further occasion his position was gravely threatened. Since the battle of Philippi his patron had been Antony. When the inevitable conflict between Antony and Octavian broke out and Antony was defeated by Octavian in the decisive battle of Actium on the 2nd September 31 B.C. and took his own life soon afterwards in Alexandria, Herod as Antony's supporter was threatened with the victor's vengeance. In the year 30 B.C., therefore, Herod—and this was typical of his whole mode of behaviour —went to see Octavian in person while the latter was staying in Rhodes and with a theatrical gesture he voluntarily laid his crown at Octavian's feet. His action did not fail to have the desired effect; he received his crown back from Octavian and was further rewarded with an extension of his territory. In his own interest he remained deliberately subservient to Octavian-Augustus for the rest of his life.

We have detailed information about the reign of Herod (37–4 B.C.), above all from Josephus, who describes it extensively and in great detail in *Ant. Iud.* XV, 1-XVII, 8, and in *Bell. Iud.* I, 18-33, drawing mainly on the history of Nicolaus of Damascus who had himself lived in his time at the court of Herod. Considerable and imposing remains of Herod's numerous buildings in the land have also survived, and even today they convey an impression of the outward splendour and luxury of this monarchy[1].

Herod held the position of a 'confederate king' within the Roman system of government. As such he did not come under the governor of the province of Syria, but was directly responsible to the princeps and received from him or from the Senate all important directives on foreign policy. He had to provide auxiliary troops and to protect the Imperial frontier in his area, which was bounded on the east and south by the kingdom of the Nabataeans with Petra as its capital. In the internal administration of his kingdom, Herod was independent and he was also free from the payment of tribute.

Herod was able to round off the frontiers of his kingdom under very favourable conditions. When he entered office in the year 37 B.C. the territory he had under him was more or less the area that Pompey had left to the Jerusalem religious community after

---

[1] On Herod and his descendants, cf. W. Otto, *Herodes*, 1913 (separate publication of the articles on the subject in Pauly-Wissowa's *Realencyklopädie*).Cf. also S. Perowne, *The Life and Times of Herod the Great* (1956), and *The Later Herods* (1958).

the elimination of the Hasmonaean kingdom, in other words, Judaea with Idumaea, and also Peraea and the interior of Galilee. To these had been added the port of Joppa and the villages of the plain of Jezreel which Caesar had ceded to Hyrcanus. To begin with, this territory was threatened by the ambitious and tyrannical queen Cleopatra who was friendly with Antony, and wanted to see the old Ptolemaic claim to Palestine and Phoenicia realised by Antony who was ruling in the east at this period. In fact Antony gave her all the coastal cities of Palestine, which meant that Herod lost Joppa again, and he also gave her the area of the tropically fertile oasis of Jericho (34 B.C.). Probably Cleopatra, who once visited Jerusalem herself, wanted still more. Her own death and that of Antony after the battle of Actium left her wishes unfulfilled. When in 30 B.C. Herod had obtained the favour of Augustus and visited him once again in Alexandria after the death of Antony and Cleopatra, the Palestinian areas which had been presented to Cleopatra were transferred to him, so that Herod now became master of the whole of the coastal plain of Palestine, and he was also given the city and province of Samaria as well as the cities of Gadara (*umkēs*) and Hippos (*ḳal'at el-ḥuṣn*) in the northern land east of the Jordan. Finally Herod was given the areas of Trachonitis, Batanaea and Auranitis in the land east of the Jordan north of the Yarmuk, eastwards as far as the great mountain of *jebel ed-drūz* (23 B.C.). Herod thereby came into possession of practically the whole of Palestine with the exception of the territories of the free cities of the 'Decapolis'; and he ruled over all this territory until his death.

Herod honoured Augustus most zealously. Even before his visit to Rhodes he hastened to take part in fighting Antony's supporters in Syria to make his change of position immediately clear. When Augustus marched through Syria on the way to Egypt in 30 B.C., he received him with ceremony in Ptolemais; and after he had visited Augustus in Alexandria after the death of Antony and Cleopatra, he accompanied him on his return journey through Syria as far as Antioch. When Augustus came to Syria again in the year 20 B.C. he gave Herod a few more districts in the uppermost part of the Jordan Valley. In the year 12 B.C. Herod himself travelled to Italy and met Augustus in Aquileia, to get him to settle a quarrel with two of his sons; and soon afterwards he was in Italy and Rome once again. Only once, about the year 9 B.C., Herod temporarily incurred the Emperor's displeasure on account of his methods of fighting the Nabataeans; but the good understanding between Augustus and Herod was restored through the mediation of

Nicolaus of Damascus. Herod also tried to be on the best of terms with the Emperor's influential friend, M. Vipsanius Agrippa. About the year 22 B.C. he visited Agrippa in Mytilene on Lesbos, and in the year 15 B.C. Agrippa himself came to Jerusalem at Herod's invitation and was received with great pomp and ceremony. On this occasion Herod showed him in particular his magnificent buildings all over the country. Later on Herod visited Agrippa again in Asia Minor. Herod honoured Augustus by naming his rebuilt cities after him. The first work of this kind was the extension of the old city of Samaria. Gabinius had already begun to build a city in the Hellenistic-Roman style on the beautiful hill in the mountains of central Palestine which had once borne the royal city of the former kingdom of Israel and which afforded the space for a more extensive city[1]. Herod, who had received Samaria from Augustus in the year 30 B.C., began a few years later magnificently to extend this city and to erect an imposing temple of Augustus, the outside staircase of which is still in existence *in situ* today. To this city which he made into a strong fortress with a city wall and gateways with towers, he gave the name 'Sebaste'[2] in honour of Augustus. Herod's greatest achievement in city building was the new port on the Mediterranean coast. About 22 miles south of the Carmel salient there was a fairly old, quite small place called 'Strato's-Tower'. This place had been made over to Herod in the year 30 B.C. with the whole coastal area. On its site Herod had a magnificent city built at great expense over a period of twelve years, with artificial harbour installations and with all the public buildings such as a theatre, amphitheatre and hippodrome which formed part of a complete Hellenistic-Roman city. In the year 10 B.C. it was ceremoniously opened with magnificent games for which Augustus and Livia gave a considerable sum. This too was given a name in honour of the Emperor: Herod called the city 'Caesarea' (the modern *ḳēṣārye*) and its harbour 'Sebastos-harbour'.

Apart from these urban foundations in honour of Augustus, Herod did an extraordinary amount of other building in the land[3]. No period in the history of the country ever saw so many splendid buildings arise in such a short time as the period of Herod. He changed the face of his royal city of Jerusalem with the massive buildings he had erected and so determined its pattern for the future.

[1] Cf. C. Watzinger, *Denkmäler Palästinas*, II (1933), pp. 25 f.

[2] The Greek translation of the word '*augustus*' is σεβαστός; hence the settlement on the site of the old city of Samaria is still called *sebaṣṭye*.

[3] The best detailed description of Herod's building activities, on the basis of the archaeological findings, is in C. Watzinger, *op. cit.* pp. 31 ff.

In the north-western corner of the city, in the area of the modern Jaffa Gate, he had a new strongly fortified royal castle built with massive towers. In the year 20 B.C. he began work on the renewal of the Temple building. By means of great embankments and an imposing outer wall, wide stretches of which still stand today and may be seen reaching a considerable height, for example at the so-called 'Wailing Wall', he extended the Temple area and thereby created that great holy area which is still by far the most impressive memorial of the old city of Jerusalem. He had gates and market-halls built in the Temple area and began to rebuild the actual sanctuary on the model of the Solomonic Temple. In the north-west corner of the Temple area he had already had a citadel built on the site of the Hasmonaean 'Baris' (cf. above, p. 386), which had been named 'Antonia' after his friend of that period. Outside Jerusalem he surrounded the site of the tombs of the patriarchs in Hebron with a tremendous outer wall—like the outer wall of the Temple in Jerusalem—and he likewise enclosed the venerable shrine of Abraham at Mamre north of Hebron (the modern *ḥaram rāmet el-khalīl*) in a rectangular wall. On the other hand, he also provided the shrine of the pagan god Pan at the source of the Jordan right up in the north near the modern *bānyās*, with a temple for the worship of Augustus.

For himself he built a series of fortresses, above all in the inaccessible areas of the wilderness of Judah and the Dead Sea. The development of the enormously high and steep rock of Masada (the modern *es-sebbe*) on the western edge of the Dead Sea roughly opposite the peninsula of *el-lisān* is particularly worthy of note. On the flat surface of this rock he had a great palace and extensive storerooms built[1]. North-east of this, on the other side of the Dead Sea, was the castle of Machaerus, which had already been fortified by Alexander Jannaeus and which Herod rebuilt on a bigger scale as a strong fortress. Three miles south-east of Bethlehem, on the edge of the wilderness of Judah, on a mountain, the summit of which he had levelled down for the purpose, he built a great castle with a settlement at the foot of the mountain, and he called this castle, in which he had his own tomb built, 'Herodium' (the modern *jebel ferdēs*). Above Jericho he built a castle which he called 'Cypros' after his mother's name[2]. In building these castles, which were in-

---

[1] Cf., on the basis of detailed archaeological investigations, A. Schulten, 'Masada. Die Burg des Herodes und die romischen Lager', ZDPV, 56 [1933], pp. 1 ff.; with numerous illustrations and plans.

[2] Cf. A. Alt, PJB, 21 (1925), pp. 23 f., who locates this citadel on the modern *tell el-'akabe*.

tended as places of refuge in time of emergency, he was concerned for the safety of himself and his family.

Apart from the great cities of Sebaste and Caesarea which we have already mentioned, he had other places built or developed in the Hellenistic-Roman style. South of the ancient site of Jericho the existing remains still testify to Herod's building activities which gave a new appearance to this oasis settlement[1]. To the south, below the Hasmonaean fortress of Alexandrium (*karn ṣarṭabe*), which was probably also further developed by Herod, he built a new settlement in the Jordan Valley and called it Phasaelis (the modern *khirbet faṣā'il*) after his dead elder brother Phasael, after whom he had also named one of the massive towers of the royal castle in Jerusalem. He named after his father the city of Antipatris which he either founded or revived on the inner edge of the coastal plain near the sources of the *nahr el-'auja*, which reaches the Mediterranean north of Jaffa.

The great number and—for Palestine—the unusual size of all these buildings clearly shows what an imperious ruler Herod was. For it is obvious that all this building required an enormous amount of money and labour which had to be supplied by the realm over which he ruled, which was by no means very large. Outside his own land, too, he presented Hellenistic cities with gifts and buildings to increase his fame and prestige, thus imitating the great and rich Hellenistic kings. That he was able to extract all this from a country that had been exhausted by the almost endless wars and conflicts of the last century and a half, shows how firmly he ruled. On the other hand, however, he also succeeded in increasing the prosperity of his land in the peaceful period which began with his accession. Admittedly he used cruelty and brutality to overcome his real or supposed enemies. His path to the power which he finally obtained had already been marked by cunning and violence; and as king he continued on this path. In love and hate, particularly in the latter, he apparently brooked no restraints. The outstanding qualities of his character were passion, egotism and suspicion. As king he was a cruel tyrant, above all in his own house. The details of these domestic incidents, which are reported extensively by Josephus, need not detain us. The best known of them is the execution

---

[1] On the recently begun American excavations on the site of Herodian Jericho which now bears the name *tell abu el-'alāyik* cf. the preliminary accounts by J. L. Kelso, BASOR, 120 (1950), pp. 11-22 and J. B. Pritchard, BASOR, 123 (1951), pp. 8-17. Traces of Hellenistic building have been found among the Herodian remains, and the Hasmonaeans had evidently erected some building or other there, apparently at least a fortified tower.

of his second wife, the Hasmonaean Mariamne, against whom his jealousy had been aroused by slander, and the later execution of the two sons of his marriage with Mariamne, Alexander and Aristobulus. For a time his son Antipater played a large part. He was a child of his father's first marriage with the Jerusalemite Doris and was Herod's first-born son. It was he above all who had instigated the removal of his two half-brothers Alexander and Aristobulus. In his first will his father had appointed him his successor. But in the end he fell victim to his own cunning, and only a few days before his own death Herod had him executed.

It is not surprising that the rule of Herod was abominated by very many members of the Jerusalem religious community. Perhaps there was less concern here about the quarrels and intrigues in the royal house. They were merely a symptom of the objectionableness of this monarchy in general. Above all, Herod was rightly regarded as a friend of Rome and was unpopular as such, since the Roman authorities had already repeatedly interfered high-handedly in the affairs of the Jerusalem religious community and, in spite of all the occasional favours that they had bestowed, through Caesar for example, they were felt increasingly to represent an oppressive foreign dictatorship. And whatever his descent may in fact have been, Herod himself was considered a foreigner. Neither his splendid rebuilding of the sanctuary in Jerusalem nor his interest in the patriarchal sites in Hebron was able to reconcile the Jerusalem religious community to his rule. In spite of his formal membership of the Jerusalem religious community Herod was in fact fundamentally a Hellenistic pagan ruler, who was far more interested in the building of large-scale cities in the Hellenistic-Roman style and the erection of places of worship for his imperial master Augustus than in the concerns of the Jerusalem religious community and the law recognised in it as valid. Under his wilful rule the Sadducee priesthood in Jerusalem was unable to play any part, and his character and actions were even more an abomination to the pious and especially to the strict Pharisees. He disposed of the office of priest in the most objectionable way and made it the object of political moves. At the beginning of his reign he had appointed a certain Ananel as high priest, since, not being of priestly descent himself he could hardly combine the office with the monarchy, as the members of the old priestly family of the Hasmonaeans had been able to do. Ananel had come from Babylonia and from a priestly family. It is true that the old Hyrcanus, who had been high priest until 40 B.C., had meanwhile returned from Babylonia. But the mutilation that

Antigonus had inflicted on him made it impossible for him to take the office on again. In the year 30 B.C. Herod found a pretext to have him executed, at the age of 80, as a possible rival. But the ambitious Alexandra, a daughter of Hyrcanus and wife of her cousin Alexander, who had been put to death by order of Pompey (cf. above, p. 407) was working against Ananel. She was the mother of Mariamne and thus Herod's mother-in-law. She wanted the office of high priest for her son Aristobulus, Herod's brother-in-law, as being actually the rightful hereditary successor. This was the period when Antony and Cleopatra were still ruling in the east; and Alexandra was in touch with Cleopatra. Under these circumstances Herod thought it advisable not to annoy the two dangerous women, and he therefore deposed Ananel again and made Aristobulus high priest. After one year, however, he found an excuse, because of treacherous intrigues, to have the high priest drowned while swimming at Jericho (35 B.C.); and after he had come to an understanding with Cleopatra he also had Alexandra imprisoned and later had her killed. This treatment of the high priest's office, which went as far as the murder by the king of a high priest while in office, inevitably aroused the utmost displeasure of the Jerusalem religious community, among the Sadducee priests as well as the strict Pharisees.

Herod's rule was founded on terror and violence; but he managed by these means to remain in undisputed possession of the monarchy. His position was never seriously threatened during his reign, and the main reason was that he succeeded in retaining the recognition of the great Roman power. Outwardly his monarchy was brilliant, and in this respect a final climax in the history of Israel; and after the long period of endless armed conflicts, it was certainly a blessing for the land to be without warlike disputes internally and serious battles externally for a generation and more. This was also a result of Augustus' pacification of the Roman world. Nevertheless this monarchy could not possibly endure for long. The Hasmonaean monarchy, in spite of the fact that it had resulted from a lively reaction to oppression by a foreign power, had had no firm foundation, as it was impossible even for those sections of the Jerusalem religious community that still existed in Palestine to be a nation; and Herod's tyranny, based upon Roman support, was all the more lacking in any healthy and organic basis. It was only to be expected that it would not last long after his death. Revolts had occasionally occurred even during his rule, but he had managed to crush them quickly and ruthlessly; but they showed that he would not be able to leave his monarchy in a very firmly established condition, particularly as, owing to the continuous troubles in his own house, he had not been able to solve the problem of the succession clearly or for very far ahead.

In the year 4 B.C. he died in Jericho after a long and painful illness, from which he had sought healing or relief at the thermal springs of Callirrhoe on the eastern shore of the Dead Sea. His death was scarcely lamented. His body was brought from Jericho to the Herodium in a magnificent funeral procession and buried there. Shortly before his death he had made a new will. In it he had made provision for his younger sons, namely Archelaus and (Herod) Antipas, the two sons of his marriage with the Samaritan Malthake, and Philip, the son of his marriage with the Jerusalemite Cleopatra. Archelaus was to inherit the actual monarchy, whilst Antipas and Philip were to become more or less independent tetrarchs, the one of Galilee and Peraea, the other of the most northerly area of the land east of the Jordan. This will had to be confirmed by Augustus, and so Archelaus and Antipas went one after the other to Rome to press their claims and to get as much as they could for themselves. In this, Antipas wanted the whole succession for himself in accordance with an earlier will his father had made. Other members of Herod's family also went to Rome to plead their cause; and the leading circles of the Jerusalem religious community also sent a deputation to Augustus to ask him to put an end to the rule of the family of Herod altogether and to restore the former independence of the Jerusalem religious community. Faced with these various requests, Augustus made his decision in the main according to Herod's last will. Archelaus was given Judaea with Idumaea and Samaria, without the title of king, but with the title of ethnarch. He also had to give up the city of Gaza as well as the Decapolis cities of Gadara and Hippos which Augustus had made over to Herod; they were placed directly under the province of Syria as self-governing urban communities. In accordance with the terms of the will, Herod's sister Salome was given the cities of Ashdod and Jamnia in the southern coastal plain as well as a palace in Ashkelon and also the new Herodian foundation of Phasaelis in the Jordan Valley. Antipas and Philip both became tetrarchs; the first was given the geographically separated territories of Galilee and Peraea, and the latter Trachonitis, Batanaea and Auranitis with a part of the uppermost Jordan Valley (*Ant. Iud.* XVII, 9-12; *Bell. Iud.* II, 1-6). The result was that Herod's kingdom was divided up; and that was probably what the emperor had intended.

The history of these states ruled by Herod's descendants was anything but glorious. Once again Josephus has recorded the details in *Ant. Iud.* XVII, 13– XIX, 9 and *Bell. Iud.* II, 7-12. Immediately after the death of Herod, and all the more during the absence in Rome of the aspirants to the throne, riots had broken out in various parts of the country, directed against the rule of the family of Herod but also against the Roman power. P. Quintilius Varus, well known for his later unfortunate campaign in Germania, governor of the province of Syria from 6 to 4 B.C., had to intervene, as did the procurator Sabinus whom Augustus had sent to Palestine to settle the question of the succession to the throne. Varus occupied Jerusalem by force of arms and had the rebels sought out and punished throughout the country. The severity with which the Roman troops proceeded could not help but increase the anti-Roman feeling. When Herod's successors returned, the country remained unsettled. The power of Archelaus, on whom had devolved the greatest part of his father's inheritance, was the first to come to an end. His severe and despotic government soon made him so hated that a deputation of his subjects went to Augustus to complain about him; and Augustus found cause to depose him and to banish him to Vienne in Gaul (A.D. 6). Barely ten years after the death of Herod the land governed by Archelaus, that is, the central and southern part of the land west of the Jordan, was deprived of its independence and constituted as a procuratorial province. This situation was only interrupted temporarily in the years A.D. 41–44. As a minor province of inferior status[1] this territory was given a special administration under a procurator (governor) who resided in the port of Caesarea founded by Herod. This procurator had military command over the troops which were raised from the land itself. Garrisons were maintained in various places, including the fortress of Antonia in Jerusalem. The procurator also exercised the supreme judicial powers. The jurisdiction exercised by the Sanhedrin was indeed recognised, but the procurator reserved the right to pass sentence of death. He was responsible for gathering in the taxes which were collected by the native authorities. The territory under the procurator was divided, for administrative purposes, into eleven so-called toparchies, on the basis of older divisions. The toparchies were Jerusalem, Gophna (the modern *jīfna*) north of Jerusalem, Acrabetta (the modern *'akrabe*) north-

---

[1] On the legal status and the organisation of such procuratorial provinces, of which there were several in the Roman Empire at this time, cf. F.-M. Abel, *Histoire de la Palestine*, I (1952), pp. 424 ff.

east of Gophna, Thamna (the modern *tibne*) west of Gophna, Lydda (the modern *lidd*), Emmaus (the modern *'amwās*) southeast of Lydda, Bethleptepha (the modern *bēt nettīf*) south of Emmaus, Idumaea (embracing the southern part of the mountains and the hill country), Engaddi (the modern *'ēn jidi* on the western shore of the Dead Sea), Herodium (the modern *jebel ferdēs*) on the edge of the desert of Judah south of Jerusalem, and, finally, Jericho in the lower Jordan Valley[1]. The special characteristics of the Jerusalem religious community were respected as far as possible. It is true that its members were required to take the oath of allegiance to the emperor, but they were not required to take part in worship of the emperor. The Roman garrison on the Antonia in the immediate vicinity of the Temple also supervised the proceedings in the Temple, but as a rule the troops did not bring their effigies of the emperor with them to Jerusalem.

In spite of all the careful consideration which the Romans showed, opposition to the presence of Roman power in the land was strong. In the period of the first procurator the governor of the Syrian province, P. Sulpicius Quirinius, carried out the Roman census in 'Judaea'—that was the official name of the territory under the procurator's jurisdiction—in order to reorganise the system of taxation. This measure caused great unrest and led to the rise of a radical anti-Roman movement which was soon to make itself felt with disastrous effects. To begin with, it is true, there was some outward acquiescence in the strong Roman government. The procurators frequently did not behave very carefully, and often gave cause for not unjustified indignation. The best known of them was Pontius Pilate, who held the office of procurator from A.D. 26–36. He had scant regard for the scruples of the Jerusalem religious community and also acted cruelly towards the Samaritans. In the end he was deposed at the suggestion of the Syrian governor, L. Vitellius, who himself treated the Jerusalem cultus with particular respect.

Whilst Jerusalem and the whole of the central and southern part of the land west of the Jordan were already under direct Roman administration, Herod Antipas ruled as tetrarch under Roman suzerainty in Galilee and Peraea during a fairly long reign (4 B.C.–A.D. 39). To begin with, the capital of his territory was Sepphoris (the modern *ṣaffūrye*) in the hills of Lower Galilee, which Gabinius had made the centre of the district and which Antipas now raised

---

[1] Cf. the list in *Bell. Iud.* III 3, 5, §§ 54 f. On Bethleptepha cf. *Bell. Iud.* IV, 8, 1, § 445 (the other passage gives instead, probably inadvertently, the name 'Pelle').

to the status of a city. Later on, *circa* A.D. 20, Antipas built himself a magnificent new residence on the western shore of Lake Gennesaret, calling it Tiberias after the reigning emperor Tiberius. To the present day it has remained the most important settlement on the shores of the lake. He had a royal palace built there. Previously he had already developed Betharamphtha (the modern *tell er-rāme*) in Peraea in the Jordan Valley north-east of the northern end of the Dead Sea, as a fortress over against the neighbouring Nabataeans and gave it the name of Julias or, later, Livias. These names show how deliberately he courted the favour of the Roman Imperial house. It is true that Antipas was somewhat more careful than his elder brother Archelaus, and was therefore able to continue longer in power; but in his personal life he was probably not much less lacking in restraint than his father. The story of his marriage to the ambitious Herodias, a daughter of the Aristobulus who was the son of Herod's marriage to the Hasmonaean Mariamne, is well known. He himself had first been married to the daughter of the Nabataean king, and Herodias had had as husband an otherwise undistinguished son of Herod who was also called Herod and was a stepbrother of Antipas. Herodias thought she would be able to attain greater distinction as wife of the tetrarch Antipas. At Herodias' instigation Antipas therefore cast off his Nabataean wife and married Herodias. This marriage produced a daughter, Salome[1], who, with her mother, played a part in the beheading of John the Baptist. John had appeared on the Jordan in Antipas' territory of Peraea and Antipas had had the inconvenient and dreaded preacher of repentance arrested and imprisoned in the fortress of Machaerus[2], and finally had him executed. The marriage to Herodias only brought disaster to Antipas. The repudiation of his Nabataean wife, which had taken place at her instigation, involved him in a war with his Nabataean neighbour in which he was defeated (A.D. 36) so that the emperor Tiberias had to send the governor L. Vitellius of Syria against the Nabataeans. The restlessly ambitious Herodias also persuaded Antipas to apply to the emperor—now C. Caligula—for the title of king. This was his final ruin, for he thereby incurred the opposition of the Herod Agrippa of whom we shall be speaking in a moment. He had Antipas charged before the emperor, and in A.D. 39 Caligula deposed him after a long reign and banished him to Lugdunum in Gaul.

[1] We only know this name from Josephus, *Ant. Iud.* XVIII, 5, 4, §§ 136 ff.
[2] Only Josephus mentions Machaerus as the place of imprisonment in his section on John the Baptist, *Ant. Iud.* XVIII, 5, 2, §§ 116 ff.

After Herod's death in 4 B.C. his son Philip had inherited as tetrarch the territories in the most northerly part of the land east of the Jordan. Josephus praises him as a good ruler. Admittedly, we know little about his period of office. In the year 2/1 B.C. he established a residence for himself in the vicinity of the shrine of Pan by the easternmost source of the Jordan at the south-western foot of Mount Hermon, and called it Caesarea (Caesarea Philippi) in honour of the emperor. Lake Gennesaret and the course of the Jordan north of this lake formed the boundary between the tetrarchies of Antipas and Philip. In the borderland east of the Jordan, near where it flows into Lake Gennesaret, Philip attempted to raise Beth-saida to the status of a city with the name Julias, but apparently he abandoned the attempt[1]. He finally married Salome, the daughter of Antipas and Herodias, but died childless in the year A.D. 34. Thereupon his territory was added to the province of Syria.

Eventually a member of the family of Herod once again had the good fortune to rule for a short time as king over almost the whole of Herod's dominion. He was a son of Herod's son Aristobulus, whose mother was the Hasmonaean Mariamne, and who was therefore a full brother of Herodias. He was called Agrippa, so named after M. Vipsanius Agrippa, the friend of Augustus. Herod Agrippa lived in Rome and had succeeded in obtaining the favour of the emperor C. Caligula, even before the latter ascended the throne. Immediately on his accession Caligula gave his favourite the tetrarchy of Philip, which had fallen three years previously to the province of Syria, as his own domain, and at the same time he conferred on him the title of king. He also gave him Abilene, *i.e.* the district of Abila (the modern *sūķ wādi barada*) north-west of Damascus in the region of the Anti-Lebanon, which had hitherto formed a separate tetrarchy adjoining that of Philip in the north. It was this success which had given his sister Herodias no peace. When Agrippa, who had, to begin with, remained for a time in Rome, arrived in Palestine during the year A.D. 38, ranking now as king, she persuaded her husband Antipas to ask the emperor to give him the royal title too. But, as the emperor's favourite, Agrippa managed to get Antipas deposed instead and himself assigned Antipas' tetrarchy, in other words, Galilee and Peraea (A.D. 39).

Eventually, Agrippa, who had returned to Rome in the year A.D. 40, was also given Judaea with Idumaea and Samaria. Meanwhile very grave incidents had taken place there. When, in the year A.D. 38, Agrippa had been in Alexandria on his journey from

[1] Cf. A. Alt, PJB, 33 (1937), p. 85, note 4.

Rome to Palestine, the presence of the king had given rise to serious excesses against the members of the Jerusalem religious community in that place. Soon after his accession, Caligula, who considered himself a god, had proceeded to require his subjects throughout the empire to participate in the worship of the emperor. The demand was fulfilled with greater or less zeal. Only the members of the Jerusalem religious community would not and could not take part in the worship of the emperor. For adopting this attitude they were hated by the others. Not only was king Agrippa publicly derided in Alexandria, but the people of Alexandria also demanded that effigies of the emperor should be placed in the synagogues of the city; and the Roman governor of Egypt, A. Avilius Flaccus, to whom Caligula was not very favourably inclined, and who therefore strove in every way to obtain the emperor's good-will, complied with these demands without any demur. So some of the synagogues in Alexandria were desecrated by the setting up of effigies of the emperor and some were destroyed altogether, and intense and bloody persecution befell the members of the Jerusalem religious community in Alexandria. It is true that Flaccus was recalled in the autumn of the year A.D. 38, but there was, to begin with, no fundamental change under his successor. In the year A.D. 40 a deputation from both of the contending parties went to Rome from Alexandria to see the emperor, and the leader of the synagogue deputation was the well-known writer Philo. The emperor treated the synagogue deputation very ill-humouredly and with marked discourtesy and conceded nothing at all[1]. It was not until the following year that the emperor Claudius put an end to the persecution in Alexandria shortly after his accession by restoring the privileges of the Jerusalem religious community and promising it unhampered freedom of worship. But meanwhile the incidents had spread to Palestine. Probably during the year A.D. 39 the pagan inhabitants of the city of Jamnia (the modern *yebna*) had set up an imperial altar, which was destroyed by members of the Jerusalem religious community. When this was reported to the emperor, he commanded his effigy to be set up in the Temple in Jerusalem; and the Syrian governor P. Petronius himself, whose duty was to enforce the emperor's intentions in Jerusalem, was given instructions to carry out this monstrous order. Petronius was prudent enough to desist from the use of force for the time being. First of all he sent for the heads of the community while he was in Sidon, where he was staying on his march from Antioch and tried to persuade them to comply; need-

[1] Cf. the treatise of Philo, *Legatio ad Gaium*.

less to say, in vain. The news of this threatened action led to very great unrest in the Jerusalem religious community. When Petronius had moved on to Ptolemais he was stormed by a great crowd of people who besought him not to carry out the order. He thereupon wrote to the emperor to ask him to postpone the order; but in vain. He then went to Tiberias, and once again he was surrounded for forty days by a great crowd imploring him not to carry out the order. He then decided on his own responsibility not to fulfil his commission; he took his troops back to Antioch and wrote to the emperor to ask him to cancel his instructions. At the same time king Agrippa tried to get his friend the emperor to revoke his order. But the emperor was no longer favourably disposed to him, although in response to a letter from Agrippa he did make one concession, but rescinded it straight away. The sudden murder of the emperor Caligula in January A.D. 41 saved the Jerusalem religious community from the threat of further violent persecution and the governor Petronius from the punishment intended for his disobedience. Fortunately the emperor's letter which commanded him to take his own life did not reach him until after the news of the emperor's murder. The new emperor Claudius desisted, however, from enforcing the worship of the emperor in the Jerusalem religious community.

Agrippa, who was still in Rome, had supported the accession of Claudius, whom the soldiers had chosen as their leader after the murder of Caligula. To thank him for this service, Claudius gave him, in addition to the areas which he had already received by favour of Caligula, the parts of Judaea (*i.e.* the real area of Judaea with Idumaea and Samaria) which had previously been administered by procurators. Agrippa now combined under his royal sceptre the whole territory ruled by his grandfather Herod with the exception of the south-western coastal plain around Gaza and the territories of the cities of Gadara and Hippos in the northern area east of the Jordan; furthermore, in the far north he possessed Abilene in the Anti-Lebanon. Soon after his success in Rome Agrippa returned to Palestine (A.D. 41). He was then about 50 years old. He had already led an eventful and frivolous life, had often been for long periods in Rome since his childhood and had there acquired a thorough knowledge of, and himself practised, the hazardous game of adventure and intrigue. Fortunate circumstances had now placed an imposing kingdom in his hands. There is little to be said in praise of his short reign. He passed himself off in Jerusalem as a man of exemplary piety, made a show of observing the ordinances of the strict Pharisees, spent money on the Jerusalem cultus, gave a golden chain, which had been presented to him by the emperor Caligula, to the Temple treasure and championed the external interests of the Jerusalem religious community. This attitude was based on political motives, not on personal conviction. In Caesarea he organised games, and outside his own dominions he acted like a rich Hellenistic ruler, made great donations, for example, to the city of Berytus (*bērūt*), arranged for gladiatorial games to be held there and made a great display of his wealth. His conduct in Jerusalem nevertheless—and this was his intention—attracted much sympathy from the Jerusalem religious community, whereas the Hellenistic cities such as Sebaste which came under his rule were less satisfied with his regime. All the same, the country enjoyed a few years of peace under him. He tried to extend and refortify the city of Jerusalem. On the north side of the city he began, north of the previous wall, the building of a very strong section of wall with towers, which was intended to give the city more space on this side. This is the so-called 'third wall'[1]. This work was not finished, however, not merely because the king's short reign was not sufficient but also because the Syrian governor, C. Vibius Marsus, was instructed by the emperor to protest against its continuation. In other ways, too, Agrippa occasionally behaved like an independent ruler with great political plans. He invited to Tiberias five other Roman vassal rulers from Syria and Asia Minor. It is difficult to say what the intention of this meeting was. It was probably more in the nature of a boastful undertaking on the part of Agrippa. The meeting actually took place, but no sooner had it started than the Syrian governor Marsus appeared and the gathering was dispersed.

Agrippa was not an important ruler: even if he had lived longer, his reign would probably not have acquired any real significance. He died suddenly in the year A.D. 44 in Caesarea during festive games that were being held there in honour of the emperor, after he had appeared in public with great regal splendour and the people had greeted him as an incarnate god. Shortly after, he was attacked with violent pains, had to be carried away, and within a few days

---

[1] Whether this 'third wall' of Agrippa (Josephus, *Bell. Iud.* V, 4, 2, §§ 147 ff.) is to be identified with the stretch of wall in the northern outer district of modern Jerusalem, impressive remains of which survive and have been preserved (cf. E. L. Sukenik and L. A. Mayer, *The Third Wall of Jerusalem* [1930]), or whether it was not rather on the line of the later Turkish north wall, which still shuts off the old city of Jerusalem on the northern side (cf. J. Simons, *Jerusalem in the Old Testament* [1952], p. 459), is a question that has not yet been solved with certainty.

he was dead (cf. Acts xii, 21-24). Apart from several daughters, he left a son aged 17, who was also called Agrippa. The emperor Claudius did not, however, allow this son to succeed his father, but turned the whole territory into a Roman province and put it under procurators who again resided in Caesarea. The whole of the territory under these procurators was officially called Judaea. The legal and actual position in this Judaea was now the same as in that smaller Judaea which had been formed after the deposition of Archelaus in the year A.D. 6 and which had lasted until A.D. 41. The tensions between the Roman power and administration and the Jerusalem religious community soon appeared again; and the agitation among wide circles of the Jerusalem religious community became more and more menacing.

34. *The Rejection of Christ*

Whilst people in Jerusalem and elsewhere in the country resented the Roman power and complained about the behaviour of the Roman procurators who resided in Caesarea, and whilst the anything but worthy Antipas was ruling as tetrarch in Galilee and Peraea, events of decisive importance were taking place at the centre of the Jerusalem religious community. Jesus of Nazareth was living and working at this period. World history took no notice of him at the time. Not even Josephus, who records so many details about the movements and forces of the period, found any reason to spare a word to refer to his appearance[1]. Only when his followers had emerged as a historically concrete fact did his name begin to be mentioned[2]. In the history of Israel the important concerns of the time seemed to be the consolidation of the Jerusalem religious community against the constantly threatening encroachments of superior secular forces, the safeguarding of the threatened freedom of worship, the preservation of the right to live in accordance with the strict requirements of the traditional law. They did not include the attitude to be adopted to an itinerant preacher who had gathered a band of followers around him and finally appeared in Jerusalem with high-flown claims. He seemed an insignificant figure in the history of Israel, which was so full of striking or strange

[1] It is generally agreed that the section on Jesus in *Ant. Iud.* XVIII, 3, 3, §§ 63 f. is a later Christian insertion.

[2] Josephus also finally mentioned 'Jesus the so-called Christ' in *Ant. Iud.* XX, 9, 1, § 200, in the context of a remark about the early Christian community in Jerusalem. Cf. the well-known statements by Suetonius, *Claudius*, ch. 25 and Tacitus, Ann. XV, 44.

personalities. For a brief moment his appearance had caused a flutter of excitement in Jerusalem; then the episode belonged to the past and there were other affairs, seemingly more important, to worry about. Yet here an ultimate and final decision had been made in the history of Israel.

The story of Jesus' human life had been, in the first instance, simple and straightforward. He had worked in the circles of the still surviving Israelite tribes in the interior of Galilee[1]. Nazareth (the modern *en-nāṣira*), his home, was a village in the hills of Lower Galilee north of the plain of Jezreel of which there are no records from earlier times and which was perhaps still a recent settlement in Jesus' time. It lay only four miles south of Sepphoris (*ṣaffūrye*), Antipas' first residence, which he had made a city, but it did not belong to the territory of this Hellenistic-Roman city, but to a group of villages in the old territory of the tribe Zebulun and was no doubt inhabited by Israelites. Jesus had gone from there to the north-western shores of Lake Gennesaret, but not to the magnificent royal city of Tiberias which had just been re-established by Antipas, but into the region of the no doubt Israelite villages such as Capernaum (the modern *tell ḥūm*) and Chorazin (the modern *khirbet kerāze*) north-east of Tiberias. This area was near the frontier which divided the tetrarchies of Antipas and Philip. A few miles north-east of Capernaum the Jordan flowed into Lake Gennesaret and on the other side of the Jordan the village of Beth-saida was already inside the tetrarchy of Philip. But a basically Israelite population lived on both sides of the Jordan and the fishermen on the lake plied freely from one shore to the other in spite of the tetrarchy boundary in between. All the same, there were custom-houses and also a Roman garrison in this frontier area. It was here that Jesus preached among the simple Israelite people around the lake and found men who followed him and crowds who listened attentively to his words. Travels farther afield occasionally took him as far as the area of Caesarea Philippi (the modern *bānyās*), the residence of the tetrarch which had been newly established by Philip right up in the north of the old Israelite settlement, or into the region of Tyre and Sidon, *i.e.* probably to the territory of the city of Tyre, which extended through the whole of Upper Galilee to the western edge of the uppermost Jordan Valley and therefore also included part of the territory settled by the ancient Israelites. This wandering and

---

[1] On the following, cf. above all A. Alt, *Die Stätten des Wirkens Jesu in Galiläa territorialgeschichtlich betrachtet* (BBLAK, 68, 1 [1949], pp. 51 ff.).

preaching therefore took place in the first instance on the periphery of the Palestinian areas of the Jerusalem religious community and will hardly have been noticed in Jerusalem where people were more concerned about the central sanctuary and its integrity. We learn all this only from the stories which were passed on orally, to begin with, among Jesus' followers.

Finally, however—and this too, is only recorded in the early Christian tradition itself—Jesus went to Jerusalem to bring about a decision between his claim to be the revelation of the living God and the traditions of the Jerusalem religious community. It is not possible to ascertain the exact year in which that took place. It was shortly before the day of the Passover. Jesus made a Messianic entry into the city of Jerusalem, riding on a donkey; and then he appeared in the holy precincts of the Temple, preaching with authority. On his entry he had been hailed by an enthusiastic crowd as the long-awaited Messianic king, and they gathered round to hear him. But the official leaders of the Jerusalem religious community did not submit to his claim; and they soon used their influence to turn the crowd against him. They could not see the promised Messiah in this Jesus of Nazareth from Galilee. In the long period of foreign rule the old Judaean prophets' expectation of a future Messianic king had developed into the hope for a political liberator; and the greater the resentment in the land had become at the Roman regime, the more the idea of a Messianic victor over the odious foreign power had become fixed. In the light of this conception Jesus of Nazareth could not be the expected Messiah. And this dichotomy gave the leading men in Jerusalem a convenient reason for rejecting Jesus' claim. For the human guardians of a sacred tradition are always inclined to defend the tradition against a vital innovation. But if Jesus of Nazareth was not the Messiah, the 'Christ', then he must be a seducer and a deceiver. And if he was a dangerous seducer and deceiver then he must be removed for the sake of the safety and peace of the Jeusalem religious community. Therefore the Sanhedrin which was responsible for the religious community took action against Jesus. One night he was arrested by trickery and immediately brought before the Sanhedrin, the supreme court in the internal affairs of the Jerusalem religious community. The fact that Jesus acknowledged at the hearing that he was the Messiah and therefore, in accordance with Old Testament statements, the Son of God, sufficed to condemn him to death for terrible blasphemy. According to the existing law, this sentence needed to be confirmed and carried out by the Roman procurator.

At the time this office was held by Pontius Pilate (A.D. 26–36) who was hated on account of his infringements of the laws of the Jerusalem religious community. He had just come up to Jerusalem from Caesarea for the impending Feast of the Passover, to supervise in person the proceedings which would be attended by a great multitude of people, and he resided, presumably, in the royal palace in the north-west of the city built by Herod. The captive Jesus was presented to him by the men of the Sanhedrin and at the same time a crowd was raised which noisily demanded the death sentence from the procurator. The procurator agreed, after pains had been taken to explain clearly to him the danger to the state the prisoner was alleged to constitute. He had practically no idea what the case was really about, but it gave him an opportunity to do the people of Jerusalem a favour and so later he could perhaps manage further to infringe their rights. In Judaea the *ius gladii* belonged to the procurator alone; and he therefore arranged for Roman soldiers to carry out the sentence of death on Jesus of Nazareth. At this time the Romans often used the shameful and agonising method of execution by crucifixion, above all for rebellious subjects in the provinces. It was chosen this time, especially as the accusing multitude had expressly clamoured for this method. Outside the walled city Jesus was crucified with a few other condemned men by soldiers appointed for the task. A small band of followers was left, which stayed together in Jerusalem and soon began to spread the gospel by their preaching. Their enterprise did not appear to have much significance. But it was frowned on by the leaders of the Jerusalem religious community who had intended the condemnation of Jesus of Nazareth to settle the whole affair. As occasion offered, therefore, attempts were made to suppress Jesus' followers and their activities. King Agrippa in Jerusalem with his ostentatious Pharisaic piety, also tried to make himself popular by persecuting Jesus' followers. He had one of the leaders of this band, James by name, killed for some unknown reason, and another, Simon Peter, he had put in prison (Acts xii, 1 ff.). Later on, a high priest took advantage of a short vacancy in the procuratorial office, the new procurator not yet having arrived, and, exceeding his authority, since executions could only be authorised by the procurator, had a brother of Jesus who was also called James, stoned with a few other followers of Jesus (A.D. 62)[1]. For the rest, however, Jesus' followers, who sent out representatives into the

---

[1] Cf. Josephus, *Ant. Iud.* XX, 9, I, §§ 200 ff.; in this connection Josephus mentions the name of 'Jesus the so-called Christ'.

country and began also to preach in the Greek-speaking Diaspora and in the whole Mediterranean world, did not attract very much attention at first. This is roughly how things must have appeared to the Jerusalem religious community. Jesus himself, with his words and his work, no longer formed part of the history of Israel. In him the history of Israel had come, rather, to its real end. What did belong to the history of Israel was the process of his rejection and condemnation by the Jerusalem religious community. It had not discerned in him the goal to which the history of Israel had secretly been leading; it rejected him as the promised Messiah. Only a few had joined him, and from them something new proceeded. The Jerusalem religious community imagined it had more important concerns, and kept aloof from this new movement. Hereafter the history of Israel moved quickly to its end.

35. *The Insurrections against Rome and the End of Israel*

Dangerous conflicts soon occurred in the procuratorial province of Judaea which had been newly constituted in the year A.D. 44. Feeling in the land was becoming increasingly sensitive on the subject of Roman rule and irritated by it. Already after the removal of Archelaus, when Roman procurators for the central and southern part of west Jordan had come to Caesarea, a party had been formed whose aim was to resist and abolish foreign rule. These people called themselves 'Zealots'. They drew concrete political conclusions from the demand that the one God should be worshipped exclusively, and interpreted the traditional promises in a nationalistic sense. They refused to pay taxes to a foreign power and intended to take up arms to fight for the freedom of the people of God, just as Mattathias had done with his sons and followers under the Seleucid regime. They considered the Pharisees, from whose ranks the movement had proceeded, as inconsistent and weak because, in spite of their faithful adherence to tradition and the law, they put up with the foreign power as a necessary evil; and the attitude of the Sadducees, who had always been inclined to live on good terms with the ruling secular power, was, in their sight, even more reprehensible. They regarded violence as essential, though to begin with they acted not on a large scale but in innumerable minor engagements, and so kept the land in a state of constant unrest. The more the Roman procurators indulged in provocative or merely careless interventions in the affairs of the Jerusalem religious community, the more the followers of the movement naturally increased, though the great mass of the population no doubt kept aloof from these radical elements. No major incidents occurred in the first third of the century, and the situation remained fairly calm on the whole under the existing relationship between rulers and ruled. But the excesses of the year A.D. 39 and the emperor Caligula's threatened interference with the Jerusalem cultus seemed likely to lead to a serious crisis; and only the good sense of the Syrian governor, Petronius, prevented the worst from happening (cf. above, p. 425 f.). The three years of the reign of king Agrippa (A.D. 41–44), who, though he owed his kingship to the emperor's favour, did exert a power of his own and behaved towards the Jerusalem religious community as if he was one of it, brought a brief period of appeasement. But after his death the previous situation recurred.

Josephus has recorded at length the details of what followed in *Bell. Iud.* from the second book onwards. His account is our main source for this period too. The land was administered by the Roman procurators from Caesarea. The younger Agrippa, the son of king Agrippa, occupied a curious position. To begin with, he lived, as his father had done, in Rome. After his father's death the emperor Claudius had not given him his father's kingdom, on the pretext that he was too young. But as he had good connections in Rome he was ultimately compensated for this loss. In the year A.D. 50 he received the small kingdom of Chalcis (the modern '*anjar*) in the *beḳā'* between Lebanon and Anti-Lebanon, after the death of his uncle, Herod, a brother of his father, who had previously held this kingdom. Presumably he nevertheless remained in Rome for the time being. Soon afterwards this small territory was exchanged for a rather larger kingdom, which embraced Philip's former tetrarchy in the northernmost area east of the Jordan together with Abilene in the Anti-Lebanon north-west of Damascus. Above all, however, with the kingdom of Chalcis he had received the right to supervise the Temple in Jerusalem and to nominate the high priest in Jerusalem; and he exercised this right up to the outbreak of the insurrection in the year A.D. 66. This represented a final remnant of independent royal suzerainty within the Jerusalem religious community, and the emperor no doubt intended the arrangement as a concession to the community which would at least keep the Roman procurator to some extent away from the sanctuary in Jerusalem. The younger Agrippa also championed the interests of the Jerusalem religious community on various occasions. The strict adherents of the law could not, however, really reconcile themselves to a Herod deposing and appointing high priests at his own discretion. Nor was he a particularly worthy administrator of the Temple. Moreover, the fact that he lived with his sister Berenice (cf. Acts xxv, 13), the widow of his uncle Herod of Chalcis, gave rise to the worst possible gossip.

The first two procurators after A.D. 44 still managed to treat the Jerusalem religious community with the necessary discretion, and their period of office was therefore comparatively peaceful. It is true that they were unable to prevent a variety of agitators in the Jerusalem religious community from stirring up trouble. Under the third procurator, Ventidius Cumanus (A.D. 48–52), however, very serious incidents occurred. A Roman soldier's derision of the crowd which had assembled for the feast of the Passover led justifiably to great indignation, against which the procurator proceeded with armed force. Above all, a band of Galilean pilgrims to the festival were attacked and murdered by Samaritans on their journey through Samaria; since the procurator, who had been bribed by the Samaritans, did not intervene, a group of Zealots undertook a cruel campaign of vengeance against Samaria, and the procurator used military force against these Zealots. The waves of excitement in the Jerusalem religious community, which seemed likely to have the direst consequences, were assuaged only because the younger Agrippa, who happened to be in Rome at the time, succeeded in persuading the emperor Claudius to have the leading Samaritans executed and the procurator Cumanus deposed. His successor was Antonius Felix (cf. Acts xxiii, 24 ff.), one of the emperor's favourites, who was in office from A.D. 52–60. He quickly made himself hated. His personal life was obnoxious; he was married three times, one of his wives being a sister of the younger Agrippa named Drusilla (cf. Acts xxiv, 24) whom he had taken adulterously while she was still married to someone else. In the exercise of his office he indulged in every possible form of despotism. Anti-Roman agitation therefore increased enormously under him. Groups of so-called Sicarii were formed, who made a habit of carrying a dagger (*sica*) hidden on their persons, and who filled the land with murders. Even Porcius Festus, a fair and just man (cf. Acts xxiv, 27 ff.) was unable to alter this situation in his short term of office (A.D. 60–62) not least because he was followed by the shamelessly corrupt Albinus (A.D. 62–64) under whom the general corruption and maladministration in the land only increased still more. If further deterioration in the situation was possible, it was brought about by the next procurator

Gessius Florus (A.D. 64–66). He plundered the land quite openly and without restraint, and wherever there was a chance of deriving personal advantage from it he gave full scope to disorder and robbery.

Things were moving towards an open outbreak of hostilities between the Roman power and the population of the land, and in the end only some small incident or other was needed to kindle the flame of a great and general insurrection. The Roman procurators with their corrupt and violent administration no doubt bore an abundant measure of responsibility for this development. But it must be remembered that we owe our knowledge of these events very largely to Josephus, who, particularly as he himself played an active part in the insurrection, was concerned to show that the representatives of the Roman power were primarily to blame for the outbreak of hostilities, and selected the details which he included accordingly. All the same, it is also evident from his statements that the struggle against Roman power had already been in progress for some long time in the Jerusalem religious community, on grounds of principle and not merely as a reaction to Roman interference. The Zealots too had been using violence for a long time and by small incidents had kept the country in a state of constant unrest. There is no doubt at all that they had constantly been challenging and attacking the representatives of the Roman administration and giving them cause for counter-measures and reprisals. The conflict, therefore, became more and more critical, and despotism on the part of the Roman procurators was one more factor making the situation intolerable. The Jerusalem religious community, which had lived comparatively peacefully for centuries under one secular power after another, had proceeded, after resisting the persecution which it suffered at the hands of Antiochus IV Epiphanes and which had struck at its very existence, to seek the way of political and national freedom for Israel. This way had led to the fragile Hasmonaean monarchy and then to the hated regime of Herod, the protégé of Rome. The intransigent group now demanded a struggle against the superior power of Rome. This was the logical culmination of the path they had been treading, but this struggle led to the end of Israel.

A prelude to the great struggle took place in Caesarea during the year A.D. 66. In this outwardly brilliant foundation of Herod's, in which the Roman procurators resided, there had always been friction between the pagan sections of the population and the members of the Jerusalem religious community who lived there. In the end, the latter were only able to escape from public molestation and derision by leaving the city with their holy books. This incident inevitably added a powerful stimulus to the agitation which was already intense. Soon afterwards, in the May of A.D. 66, the procurator Florus ventured on an act of violation in Jerusalem which brought the insurrection to explosion point. He had seventeen talents taken away from the Temple treasury; to this the people in Jerusalem replied with public derision of the procurator. Thereupon, in great wrath, Florus allowed his soldiers freely to pillage a part of the city, and in spite of the expostulations of queen Berenice who happened to be in Jerusalem, the Roman troops raged with the utmost brutality. Florus then ordered the population of the city to give a ceremonial welcome to two Roman cohorts which were marching in from Caesarea. The high priest, who, with many other prudent members of the community, was trying to preserve the peace, tried to persuade the people to comply; and once again he managed to get the people to accept the humiliation required of them. But when the Roman soldiers did not return the people's greetings, the people gave vent to their displeasure in abuse of the procurator and the soldiers took up arms. The enraged Jerusalemites occupied the area of the Temple and pulled down the porticoes between the Temple area and the fortress of Antonia which was in Roman hands, to break the link between them. At the moment Florus was not strong enough to overcome the rebellious mob; he therefore withdrew to Caesarea and only left one cohort behind in Jerusalem. Meanwhile, king Agrippa had arrived in Jerusalem, and, in a public speech, he tried to persuade the people to abandon their resistance, which was hopeless from a long-term point of view. The people would have been prepared to make some concessions; but they were no longer willing to obey the procurator Florus, and so Agrippa left the city without having achieved his purpose. The rebels were now masters of the situation; at their head stood Eleazar, a son of the high priest. They had succeeded in overcoming the Herodian fortress of Masada (*es-sebbe*) on the Dead Sea, and in Jerusalem, at the instigation of Eleazar, they decided to stop the daily sacrifices for the emperor and not to accept any further sacrifices from foreigners. This meant a complete break with the Roman power, going far beyond the various lesser or more serious conflicts in the country, and all that remained now was a struggle to the death. It is true that the high priest made one more attempt, with the majority of the other priests and the more level-headed leaders of the Pharisees, to overcome the rebellious mob, this time by force. At his request Agrippa sent 3000 horsemen to occupy part of the city. But even this force proved too weak. After long and bitter struggles in the city and around the Temple area which was the rebels' main base, they had to retire to Herod's palace, and in the end they had to be content to make a free and honourable withdrawal. The rebels even succeeded in occupying the fortress of Antonia. The Roman cohort took refuge in the three fortified towers on the north side of Herod's palace; in the end they too were allowed to withdraw, but were then treacherously slaughtered. The high priest was murdered, his palace and also the Hasmonaean palace which Agrippa and Berenice had latterly used as a residence, had already been set on fire, and also a part of Herod's palace. The rebels were now sole masters of Jerusalem. Bloody conflicts had also taken place in many other parts of the country, success in which was determined by the relative local strength of the pagan population and the rebels.

The procurator Florus was no longer able to control the situation. In the autumn of the year A.D. 66, therefore, the governor of the province of Syria, C. Cestius Gallus, approached from Antioch with a Roman legion and numerous auxiliary troops to suppress the rebellion. He marched by way of Ptolemais and Caesarea in the coastal plain southwards as far as Lydda, then went up the mountains and approached the city of Jerusalem from the north. He pitched his camp on the so-called Mount Scopus (the modern *rās el-meshārif*), a hill on the northern edge of the hollow of Jerusalem across which the main road from the north enters into this hollow. He occupied the northern suburb of Jerusalem, but an attack on the Temple area failed. As Cestius realised that Jerusalem was being defended with enormous determination, and that his forces were not sufficient to overcome the city, he beat a retreat. As he was climbing down the mountain on the old road of Beth-horon (the modern *bēt 'ūr*) he was suddenly attacked on all sides by the rebels; his troops suffered serious losses and lost most of their baggage and arms to the rebels, and Cestius had to consider himself lucky to escape with a nucleus of his troops and return to Antioch. The rebels had won the day and were now masters of the situation throughout the land. Jerusalem was filled with jubilation.

All this, however, had only been a beginning. As so often, the rebellion that had been started with such lively enthusiasm had met with an initial success, before the enemy had had a chance to gather his forces. It was only now that preparations for a real war began to be made. The leaders of the rebels in Jerusalem, who refused to brook any opposition to their attitude, particularly as it was now impossible to turn back, tried to organise resistance throughout the land to the expected counter-attack. There could only be partial success in forming a serviceable army from the entirely heterogeneous population, among whom lack of discipline had become widespread by the activities of the Zealots. Besides, there was a complete lack of experience and of the necessary war materials. The land was divided into districts, each of which was allotted a military commander. Apart from Jerusalem and its environs, Galilee was above all bound to become an important battle area, since it had a relatively compact population which still adhered to the Jerusalem religious community. Joseph, the son of Matthias, was sent there as commander-in-chief. This was the later historian, Josephus. He belonged to the moderate wing which did not want to carry things to extremes and perhaps still hoped for an eventual agreement with the Roman power. He was therefore opposed by the Zealots in Galilee, whose stronghold was Gischala (the modern *ed-jish*) in Upper Galilee, and who were led by a certain John of Gischala. This John distrusted Josephus as a traitor in the struggle against Rome and made several attempts to remove him, in which Josephus only barely escaped being murdered. This quarrel was symptomatic of the internal situation in the Jerusalem religious community. The rebels were not united among themselves—and this was soon to become evident in Jerusalem too. The rather more cautious people still had the leadership in their hands; but they had behind them the utterly impetuous elements of the Zealot party, who, as was only natural, were to get the upper hand as the difficulties and failures increased. Recognising perfectly correctly that his forces would not be a match for the Roman legions in the open field, Josephus quickly had the most important cities in Galilee fortified, and formed a not inconsiderable army which he quickly had trained as a makeshift force. He also set up a special administrative organisation for Galilee, so that in an emergency Galilee would have been able to live in tolerable order independently of, and separated from, Jerusalem. Similar preparations were made in Jerusalem and the other areas belonging to the Jerusalem religious community.

Meanwhile, however, the emperor Nero had commissioned one of his best-tried generals, T. Flavius Vespasianus, to suppress the rebellion, seeing that the Syrian governor had failed so badly and, incidentally, had died soon after. Vespasian made his preparations in the winter of A.D. 66–67; he gathered a great army of Roman troops and numerous auxiliaries in Antioch, and at

the same time sent his son Titus to Alexandria to fetch further
Roman troops from there. The combined forces were to meet in
Ptolemais. When Vespasian arrived there in the spring of A.D. 67
he at once received from the city of Sepphoris (*ṣaffūrye*) which, as
a foundation of Antipas', had a predominantly non-Israelite
population, a request for a Roman garrison, and Vespasian was
therefore able to occupy this important lower Galilean place
straight away. As soon as Titus had arrived in Ptolemais and
Vespasian had three Roman legions (the 5th, 10th and 15th)
as well as the auxiliary troops, at his disposal, he began his
attack first on Galilee from Ptolemais. Josephus' forces made off
merely on hearing that the Roman troops were approaching and
withdrew to the fortified cities, so that the open land fell into the
Romans' hands without a single blow. The mass of the rebels had
taken refuge in the fortified Jotapata (the modern *khirbet jefāt*),
north of the plain of *sahl el-baṭṭōf*, and so Josephus went there from
Tiberias, where he had stayed to begin with, to lead the defence.
Vespasian therefore also concentrated first of all on the conquest of
this city. It had to be besieged, and Josephus describes its desperate
defence from first-hand knowledge. The first attacks failed, and only
after a struggle lasting forty-seven days did the Romans succeed in
invading the city in the July of A.D. 67. Josephus himself escaped
to a cave; he rejected his companions' demand that he should take
his own life, and surrendered instead to Vespasian, who treated
him leniently, had him taken prisoner, and received him into
his headquarters. After this victory Vespasian allowed his troops
in Caesarea a short peace. Then he had the cities of Tiberias and
Tarichaea (the modern *el-mejdel*)[1] on Lake Gennesaret occupied
by Titus; the first surrendered at once, and the latter was taken by
a bold *coup de main*. In October, the strongly fortified city of
Gamala (the modern *tell el-ehdēb*), in the north of the land east
of the Jordan, was successfully occupied, although it had been
boldly and stubbornly defended, and Vespasian himself took part
in the attack, whilst a Roman detachment occupied Mount Tabor
on the plain of Jezreel simultaneously. Finally, Titus was able
quickly to take the Zealot base of Gischala (*ed-jish*) after John of
Gischala had fled from the city at the last minute with a band of
followers. The whole of Galilee had now fallen into the hands of the
Romans and for the winter of A.D. 67–68 Vespasian was able to move

[1] The original and local name of this place, which lay 3 m. north-west of Tiberias on
the shore of the lake, was Magdala; this has survived in the modern name and is well
known from the New Testament, above all from the name of Mary Magdalene, the
second part of which refers to her place of origin

his troops into winter quarters. The 5th and 15th legions took up their winter quarters in Caesarea and the 10th legion in Scythopolis (*bēsān*). The main struggle was now bound to be concentrated more and more on Jerusalem.

In Jerusalem senseless internal disputes were taking place. The defeat in Galilee weakened the position of the leaders who had been in command up to now and gave the extreme elements the upper hand. John of Gischala, who had fled from Titus, went to Jerusalem with his followers and agitated against the Sanhedrin. The Zealots occupied the Temple area but were hard pressed then by the inhabitants who did not want to put themselves in the hands of these wild fanatics, who had already spread murder among their opponents. The Zealots therefore sent for help to Idumaea; and with the aid of the advancing Idumaeans they succeeded in overwhelming their enemies in Jerusalem and killing many of them, and obtaining absolute power in the city. The Idumaeans, who had not wanted this at all and had been fetched on false pretences, marched off again. Elsewhere in the country too the Zealots generally won the upper hand over the moderates. It was probably about this time that the original Christian community left Jerusalem and went to the territory of the city of Pella (*khirbet faḥil*) in the Decapolis on the eastern side of the central valley of the Jordan, which lay outside the area affected by the insurrection.

Vespasian could afford calmly to watch the weakening effect that the internal disputes were having in Jerusalem. In the spring of A.D. 68 he had the rebellious areas around Jerusalem brought into subjection. Peraea was occupied, except for the strong fortress of Machaerus (*khirbet el-mukāwer*) in the far south of the area. He himself moved southwards from Caesarea on the coastal plain, occupied the rebellious areas on the coastal plain and in the Judaean hill country, and then went to Idumaea. He returned northwards through the coastal plain and approached the Jordan Valley through Samaria and occupied Jericho. This meant that all the country within a wide radius of Jerusalem was conquered, and Vespasian was now able to concentrate on the struggle against Jerusalem itself. Whilst he was occupied with preparations for this, the news of the death of the emperor Nero (9th June A.D. 68) reached him in Caesarea. Vespasian now decided to await developments in Rome and a pause therefore took place in the war against the rebels. The latter were still further exhausting their strength in a senseless fratricidal war. A leader of a gang called Simon bar Giora marched through such of the land as was not yet occupied by the Romans, plundering it as he went, and he finally attacked the Zealots in Jerusalem intending to take over the control of the city himself. The Jerusalemites were tired of John of Gischala's tyrannical rule and let Simon bar Giora into the city. The Zealots, with John of Gischala, retired to the Temple area and Simon bar Giora ruled over the rest of the city (the spring of A.D. 69).

Finally, in June A.D. 69, Vespasian prepared anew to attack Jerusalem, now that the situation in Rome seemed to have been clarified. In Rome, Galba had ascended the imperial throne after the death of Nero, but had been murdered on the 15th January 69. Otho, who now seemed to have the supreme power in his hands, had become emperor. The Judaean undertaking was thus delayed once again by events in Rome. The German legions had proclaimed the governor of Lower Germania, A. Vitellius, as rival emperor. Otho had taken his own life and Vitellius had marched into Rome. When news of this reached the Orient, the legions stationed in the Orient also thought it incumbent on them to act. On the 1st July A.D. 69 Vespasian was proclaimed emperor in Egypt and shortly afterwards in Palestine and Syria too, and within a short time he was acknowledged as such throughout the Orient. From now on Vespasian, whose cause finally triumphed in Rome too, and who, after Vitellius had been murdered in Rome on the 20th December 69, finally went to Rome himself in the summer of A.D. 70, was preoccupied with the question of the imperial throne. He left the continuation and completion of the fight against the rebels in Palestine to his son Titus. So the year A.D. 69 passed without any further action.

Titus opened his attack on Jerusalem in the spring of A.D. 70. He had at his disposal no less than four legions and numerous auxiliary troops. Apart from his father's three legions, the 5th, 10th and 15th, he also had the 12th under him. The 5th legion came up from Emmaus ('amwās), the 10th from Jericho. He himself moved up with the 12th and 15th legions from Caesarea and appeared outside the city shortly before the Passover, approaching from the north. He set up his headquarters on Mount Scopus north of Jerusalem. The northern side of the city was the best to attack from, since on all the other sides the city walls towered above the more or less steep slopes of the valley. The northern side was nevertheless particularly strongly fortified by no less than three walls, about which Josephus gives some information. One wall ran westwards from the then particularly well fortified Temple area in the north-eastern corner, north of which the fort of Antonia extended, to the palace of Herod; it may have originated in the

Hasmonaean period and have been built after the residential part of the city had spread from the narrow eastern hill south of the Temple enclosure to the more spacious western hill. In front of it there extended a second wall which adjoined the fort Antonia and ran from there to a point in the first-mentioned northern wall which it is no longer possible to define exactly; it is not known for certain when this second wall was built. Still farther to the north lay the great wall which king Agrippa I had begun to build but had left unfinished; it enclosed the new, most northerly part of the city, and had been quickly fitted up for defence purposes in the emergency. In spite of his strong army Titus therefore found himself faced with a difficult task. It is true that, confronted with the approach of the Roman troops, bloody conflicts had broken out in the city during the Passover between the various parties. But when the Roman attack began, all the parties decided to combine in defence of the city. On the northern front the defence was led in the western sector by Simon bar Giora, and in the eastern sector near the Temple and fort Antonia by John of Gischala. The city was defended with all possible gallantry and determination. The call for voluntary surrender was flatly rejected; and, to begin with, the Romans suffered some painful reverses in sudden sallies by the enemy. But then a regular assault on the city began with all the technical resources which the Romans had at their disposal as a result of long experience in siege warfare. They were forced, nevertheless, to overcome one wall and occupy one part of the city at a time. They managed comparatively quickly to make a breach with their siege-machinery in the most northerly wall and to invade the most northerly part of the city; and soon afterwards the second wall was taken and after one set-back finally held. But only then did the struggle for the real city with fort Antonia and the Temple area begin and the aggressors now failed to advance so rapidly. Both sides fought with great tenacity. In spite of starvation and epidemics the leaders in the city refused to contemplate surrender, and they exercised a harsh and severe rule over the inhabitants, whose numbers had been increased by the Passover pilgrims, who had just arrived when the attack began. Titus had the city surrounded with a solid siege-rampart (*circumvallatio*), making all connection between the city and the outside world impossible. He had deserters mutilated or crucified in sight of the city. He now began an attack on the strong fortress of Antonia, by having assault-ramparts built against it. After a few untoward incidents, he finally succeeded in penetrating and occupying Antonia in July of the year A.D. 70. He had the forti-

fications of the fort demolished and now stood on the very edge
of the Temple area. He intended to spare the Temple itself, where
the daily sacrifice now had to be stopped; but an invitation to
surrender it without a fight was rejected. Titus therefore had to
begin an assault on the sacred area. When the first attempts
failed owing to the strong fortifications, Titus set fire to the gates.
Contrary to his intention, this led to the immediate surroundings
of the Temple-building catching fire. In the wild excitement that
followed, the Roman soldiers invaded the sacred area and wrought
a frightful massacre. Titus himself quickly entered the famous
sanctuary and the holy of holies; then the building that Herod had
erected went up in flames. This occurred in August of the year
A.D. 70. With the destruction of its central sanctuary the Jerusalem
religious community lost its real centre. The Romans set up their
standards and sacrificed before them. The whole city was not
yet conquered however. John of Gischala was able to escape with
a band of Zealots from the Temple area into the part of the city
which lay on the western hill, the so-called 'Upper City'. The last
defenders took refuge in Herod's palace with its strong towers, and
here Titus had to proceed to another regular siege. When the
Romans had finally broken through the walls by the use of their siege
technique and had penetrated into this last bulwark, resistance came
to an absolute end (September A.D. 70). The last defenders tried
to escape or go into hiding. The victors murdered and plundered
in the city which had withstood them so tenaciously. The city was
completely destroyed. Only a part of the city wall in the west by
Herod's palace and the three strong towers of Herod's palace were
left standing. The Roman garrison took up its quarters there. The
lives of the leaders, John of Gischala and Simon bar Giora, who had
fallen into the victors' hands as prisoners, were spared, and they
were taken to Rome for the triumphal procession, together with a
group of other specially chosen prisoners. In the following year
Titus, as Imperator, displayed the greatness of his victory over
Jerusalem to the Romans in a triumphal procession. The Titus
arch in Rome still testifies to his pride in having conquered
Jerusalem. From the illustrations of this arch[1] it is clear that he
had fetched the precious sacred objects from the burning Temple to
display them as the victor's spoils.

With the conquest of Jerusalem the issue was decided, but the
insurrection had not been completely overcome. Three strongholds
were still in the rebels' hands: the Herodian forts of Herodium

Cf. the illustrations, AOB,[2] No. 509.

(*iebel ferdēs*), Masada (*es-sebbe*) and Machaerus (*khirbet el-mukāwer*.) Titus left them to be dealt with by the governor of Judaea, who had the 10th legion as garrison troops. During the struggle for Jerusalem the governor, S. Vettulenus Cerialis, had been the commander of the 5th legion. After the fall of Jerusalem he was followed by Lucilius Bassus. He undertook the conquest of the still existing strongholds. The Herodium appears to have fallen into his hands without any fighting worth mentioning. He had to lay siege for a time to the fort of Machaerus east of the Dead Sea in the southern part of Peraea; in the end the defenders surrendered when assured that they would be allowed to make a free withdrawal, which was in fact granted to them. There remained Masada. This lofty fort built on a rock had been occupied at the very beginning of the rebellion in A.D. 66 by a group of Zealots under the leadership of a Galilean named Eleazar, who from there made marauding expeditions in the surrounding countryside. Masada was the most difficult fort to overcome. Lucilius Bassus, who probably died in the year A.D. 72, failed to occupy it as he had planned to do. The task devolved on his successor in the governorship, L. Flavius Silva, who had to employ all the resources of Roman skill in siege warfare to overcome the precipitous stronghold. He surrounded it with a complete *circumvallatio*. He then had a gigantic rampart built to enable the siege-engines to be brought to the wall surrounding the fort high up on the rock. The remains of these works of Roman siege warfare have been preserved in very good condition to the present day in the uninhabited district of Masada on the southern part of the western shore of the Dead Sea. The stone wall of the *circumvallatio* can still be followed almost continuously, and the enclosures and stone foundations of the internal structures of the eight Roman camps around the *circumvallatio* are still in existence over a wide area, two big camps for half a legion each and six small camps for various auxiliary troops; and the astonishing construction of the great rampart can still be clearly discerned[1]. The planning of these installations required a considerable time. Silva seems to have begun the attack on Masada in the summer of A.D. 72; but it was only in the spring of A.D. 73 that it was possible to bring the siege-engines to the wall with the aid of the rampart. Meanwhile, the defenders had had time to erect a second wall on the site of the rampart behind the original wall; and

---

[1] All these remains have been accurately recorded by A. Schulten, 'Masada, die Burg des Herodes und die römischen Lager', ZDPV, 56 [1933], pp. 1-185 with Plates 1-14 and Plans I-XXVIII.

when the original wall had yielded to the blows of the battering-ram, the second wall was able to resist. The besiegers then succeeded in setting fire to it. The attack on the fort was to follow the next day. When the defenders realised from the sight of their burning wall that they were lost, they all committed suicide in Herod's palace in the fort, after setting fire to the palace. Only two women with five small children had hidden themselves and survived this gruesome tragedy. When the Roman soldiers penetrated the fort the next day they met with no resistance but only a mass of corpses in the ruins of the once proud palace of king Herod. That was the end of a revolt against Roman suzerainty which had been carried on for a long period.

At an earlier stage Vespasian had already reorganised affairs in the country. Nero had transferred the procuratorial province of Judaea to him and Vespasian now had it administered as an imperial province under the official name of Judaea, which was retained. As before, the procurators resided in Caesarea and were simultaneously commanders (*legates*) of the *Legio X Fretensis*, which stayed in the land as a garrison and was stationed among the ruins of Jerusalem and in its environs. Remnants of the old population lived alongside the Roman soldiers in the destroyed city. In time new inhabitants joined them, including, presumably, Jewish Christian groups. In place of the old city of Shechem a Roman colony was established with the imperial name of Flavia Neapolis (the modern *nāblus*) which had a predominantly pagan population. In Emmaus (*'amwās*) Vespasian settled 800 veterans with landed property. The members of the Jerusalem religious community now had to pay the previous Temple tax to the *fiscus Judaicus* for the benefit of Jupiter Capitolinus.

For the rest, there was no substantial official interference in the internal affairs of the Jerusalem religious community. It continued to enjoy the protection of a *religio licita* in the Roman empire. What had taken place, however, was in fact of ultimate and decisive significance. The central sanctuary had been destroyed and the possibility of rebuilding it was out of the question. The holy place had been desecrated, and no sacrificial rite could take place there any more. The priestly office could no longer be exercised. Even in the motherland it was impossible to conduct public worship and cultivate the traditions of the past except on the limited scale in which it had still been possible in the Diaspora. All the same, this much was still possible; for a long time now certain forms of synagogue worship and observance of the law had been developed in the Diaspora, and also in the motherland, apart from and independently of the central sanctuary. This it was possible to preserve, even after the loss of the Temple in Jerusalem. For a long time there had been a certain contrast between the legalistic piety of the Pharisees and the religion of the Sadducee priesthood which was bound up with the sanctuary. Leadership now devolved on the Pharisees and after the great catastrophe they gathered the remnants of the Jerusalem religious community around the Law in the motherland as well. The city of Jamnia (the modern *yebna*) on the coastal plain south of *yāfa* took the place of Jerusalem as a meeting-place. A new supreme council was formed there. The former Sanhedrin in Jerusalem, in which the priestly aristocracy and, later on, leading Pharisees had been represented, had still given something of a lead in political affairs. That was ended now. The supreme council in Jamnia consisted of 72 'Elders', who were Pharisaic scribes. Its task was the authoritative interpretation and application of the Law. It also acted as a court of law and made decisions in internal matters and probably passed sentence in criminal cases. The Roman power apparently left this court of law alone; and the court no doubt took care not to encroach on the judicial powers of the Roman officials. The reputation of this supreme council grew rapidly and its decisions were also accepted in the Diaspora. Its chairman bore the title of 'ruler'[1], which had come down from the Old Testament, especially from the programme for the future in the book of Ezekiel (Ezek. xl-xlviii). He soon enjoyed great prestige. Thus began the learned Rabbinic tradition which came to be represented in the course of time by a number of famous and influential men. The first name is that of Jochanan ben Zakkai; after the catastrophe in Jerusalem he had a decisive influence on the new development. He was soon followed by other celebrated rabbis, especially Gamaliel II.

After the cessation of the cultus in Jerusalem, the traditional holy scripture became the exclusive foundation even more than previously. The rabbis devoted their main work to it. The synagogue canon was now established definitively in its traditional three parts, everything that was not considered genuine and authoritative being rejected. Special care was devoted to the meticulous conservation and study of the established text of the canonical holy scriptures. For the Greek-speaking Diaspora new Greek translations were made to replace the older Greek translation of the Septuagint, which the Christians in the Graeco-Roman world used as their holy book,

---

[1] Hebrew נשיא.

and which did not accord either in its extent or its text with the strict requirements of the rabbis. These new translations sometimes followed the authoritative Hebrew canon slavishly. The rabbis' exegetical work, which was based on tradition and also on new decisions, was recorded in writing in new compilations.

There is no need to do more than hint at all this, since it no longer forms part of the history of Israel. In these happenings the new manifestation of Judaism was being constituted, which was no doubt a continuation of developments that had already begun long since in the Diaspora, but which acquired a special and permanent form of its own in the new situation. The Jerusalem religious community had ceased to exist. It had originated as the form in which Israel continued to exist after the loss of political independence. In the first instance it had united those parts of the Israelite tribes that had remained behind in the homeland. Scattered groups had existed on the periphery which gave rise in time to the increasingly important Diaspora. But the old Israel in Palestine had continued to form the real heart of this Jerusalem religious community. This nucleus was, it is true, undermined more and more intensely. But Israel still existed and Jerusalem the city of David had been its centre. Anyone who had wantonly violated the sanctuary had been resisted throughout the territory of the ancient Israelite tribes. Antiochus IV Epiphanes had learnt that to his cost; and the Hasmonaean monarchy, that had evolved from the opposition to Antiochus, had been able to make at least an attempt, albeit in an unsatisfactory manner and without permanent success, to lead Israel to political independence after the model of the period of the former kings. Even in the insurrection of A.D. 66–70, though in a tremendously distorted form, this same Israel had once again appeared, fighting for its sanctuary after it had been violated by the Roman procurator. Jerusalem was now the garrison of a Roman legion; and there was no further point in taking up arms for it. A centre in the old sense no longer existed. Jamnia with its supreme council could not really take the place of Jerusalem. The supreme council might just as well have met anywhere else. Its authority was not tied to a particular place, but only to the weight of the personalities, who as rabbis made the necessary decisions. Thus the difference between the motherland and the Diaspora, which had hitherto turned on Jerusalem, fell to the ground. To all intents and purposes life in Palestine had already for a long time been lived to a large extent 'in the Dispersion', and this was all the more so after the terrible losses of life that occurred in the years A.D. 66–70 (73). Even Jerusalem had now ceased to be the vital symbol of the 'homeland'. There was nothing but Diaspora, and even in the motherland life could only be lived as it had been lived hitherto in the Diaspora. Israel thereby ceased to exist and the history of Israel came to an end.

All the same, it was some time before all those involved came to realise this. It is not surprising that the hope for a 'restoration of Israel' remained alive. Had not the situation after the catastrophe of 587 B.C. been similar? And had not the Temple then been rebuilt, and had not the Jerusalem religious community reassembled round it? Was it not permissible to hope that this might happen again? Did not the Old Testament contain promises of God's final and glorious intervention, which would bring the power of this world to an end? There is no doubt that at the time the prophecies were interpreted in the sense of just such a restoration of the historical Israel. Though decimated and dispersed, there were still in the country enough descendants of members of the former Jerusalem religious community to form the basis of such a restoration. A sequel did in fact take place which was concerned with a restoration of this kind; and this sequel therefore forms an appendix to the history of Israel, which had really already come to an end[1].

There are only a few details available about the events which took place after the year A.D. 73, because Josephus' account, which is the main source up to that year, stops at that point. The Roman emperors concerned themselves at various times with the Judaism which had already become an entity in their empire. In general the Flavians were not amicably disposed to Judaism, which is not surprising in view of the great insurrection in Judaea which had cost so many Roman lives. We have no definite information, however, about the details. Presumably the emperor Trajan (A.D. 98–117) also made various moves against Judaism; at any rate, great Jewish insurrections broke out under him, above all in the Diaspora[2]. When, towards the end of his reign in A.D. 115, he had set out for the east to wage war against the Parthians in Mesopotamia, the Jews in Cyrene and Egypt, in Cyprus and even behind the front in Mesopotamia rebelled against him. Especially in Cyrene the Jews wrought cruel havoc for a time among the heathen population, and a great deal of blood was shed in Cyprus

---

[1] On the following cf. H. Bietenhard, 'Die Freiheitskriege der Juden unter den Kaisern Trajan und Hadrian und der messianische Tempelbau', *Judaica*, 4 [1948], pp. 57-77, 81-108, 161-185.

[2] All that we know about this is the little contained in Dio Cassius (LXVIII, 32) and, later, Eusebius (*Hist. eccl.* IV, 2), apart from the scattered allusions in the Rabbinic literature.

too. Trajan overcame these risings and no doubt acted brutally against the rebels. In this connection the most interesting question about these disturbances, which really belong to the history of Judaism, is whether there were not simultaneous disturbances in Palestine which might be regarded as a prelude to what happened soon afterwards under Hadrian. This possibility is suggested by the fact that Trajan appointed his general, Lusius Quietus, a Mauretanian cavalry leader, governor of Judaea as soon as he had ruthlessly suppressed the Jewish rebels in Mesopotamia, perhaps in order to restore order in Judaea too. But we have no definite information on this point[1].

A last great rising took place under Hadrian (A.D. 117–138). From all that can be ascertained, this was an episode on a scale comparable to that of the events of A.D. 66–70. But whereas Josephus has left a detailed account of the latter, all that we have about the rising under Hadrian are the rather laconic statements in Dio Cassius (LXIX, 12–14) and Eusebius (*Hist. eccl.* LV, 6), and a few other sporadic details. The sources even differ about the cause of this tremendous insurrection, which spread very widely and went on for several years, so we cannot be certain why it broke out[2]. Dio Cassius says that the foundation of the Roman city of Aelia Capitolina on the site of the ruins of Jerusalem, and the erection of a shrine of Jupiter on the site of the former Temple, made the Jews, who now saw heathen life and even heathen worship arising on the site that was still holy to them, so intensely furious that they took up arms. According to Dio Cassius, the foundation of Aelia Capitolina was connected with the journey to the Orient which the emperor Hadrian undertook in the year A.D. 129. Hadrian was first of all in Syria and the province of Arabia, which had been reorganised under Trajan in the year A.D. 106; he then went to Egypt for the winter of 130–131 and came back to Syria in the year 131. So long as the emperor was in their own country or in its vicinity the Jews had kept their peace and only made preparations; but then the storm broke. A statement made by Spartianus (*Hadr.* 14), however, implies that the Jews had become rebellious because of a prohibition of circumcision issued by the emperor. This may be connected with the fact that Hadrian did renew a prohibition of castration already issued by

[1] On the Rabbinic allusions to a 'war of Quietus' which may well have taken place in Palestine, cf. E. Schürer, *Geschichte des jüdischen Volkes*, I (4, 3 1901), pp. 667 f. (E.T.T² (1898), p. 286) ; H. Bietenhard, *op. cit.* pp. 69 ff.
[2] Cf. the detailed discussions in H. Bietenhard, *op. cit.* pp. 85 ff., and also F.-M. Abel, *Histoire de la Palestine*, II (1952), pp. 83 ff.

Domitian and made it more severe, and that he evidently regarded circumcision as being the same as castration. This may be inferred from the fact that a decree of the emperor Antoninus Pius (A.D. 138–161), which allowed the Jews to practise circumcision again, is so worded as to imply that Jewish circumcision was to be excepted from the general prohibition of castration which was still in force[1]. The problem is how to assess these differing accounts. Some scholars have taken the view that neither of them can be right, since these measures taken by the emperor can only be understood as arising from the struggle against the rebellious Jews, or as a punishment for their revolt[2]. In that case, the real cause of the revolt, in which the Jews' political and nationalistic expectations were to be realised once again, must remain unknown. The prohibition of circumcision is difficult to understand as a special measure against the Jews, particularly as it was merely considered a special case of castration, since circumcision was practised by many other peoples in the Orient over which Rome ruled. It is likely, therefore, that the prohibition was a general one and not specially directed against the Jews, but that it met with particularly stubborn resistance from the Jews, because they had long attached special importance to circumcision as an act of acknowledgement of adherence to the ancestral traditions. Unfortunately it is quite unknown when this prohibition of castration and circumcision was issued; and it is therefore uncertain whether it played a part in the beginnings of the Jewish insurrection. On the other hand, it is not unlikely that the plan for establishing a pagan Roman city with a shrine of Jupiter on the site of the old Jerusalem originated in the period immediately preceding the rebellion. It fits in very intelligibly, as Dio Cassius makes plain, with the emperor's oriental journey in the years A.D. 130–131, since Hadrian gave instructions on other such journeys for the establishment of many new cities and monumental buildings. There is also evidence to this effect in the Orient. We do not know whether Hadrian visited Jerusalem himself. In the spring of A.D. 130 he was, at all events, in the city of Gerasa (the modern *jerash*) in the land east of the Jordan[3]; and it is not unlikely that he took the opportunity of inspecting the garrison of the *Legio X Fretensis*. But

[1] The text of this decree is given in Schürer, *op. cit.* p. 677, note 80 (E.T.*T*[2] (1898), p. 292, n. 68a).

[2] Thus A. Schlatter, *Geschichte Israels von Alexander dem Grossen bis Hadrian* ([3] 1925), pp. 373 f.

[3] Cf. the dedicatory inscription of the triumphal arch in Gerasa erected on the occasion of the emperor's visit, dated in the 192nd year of the Pompeian era of the city, which was found in 1934, and is reproduced in W. F. Stinespring, BASOR, 56 (1934), pp. 15 f.

even if that was not the case, it is easy to imagine that his attention was drawn on this occasion to the city of Jerusalem, with its famous past, and that he then gave orders for the ruined site of Jerusalem to be rebuilt as a Roman city. Whatever may be the truth about the prohibition of circumcision, it is probable that this intention to establish a new city on the site of Jerusalem, even if nothing was done to realise it at first, drove the still unsettled, and still expectant Jews, to a desperate use of force. Furthermore, according to Dio Cassius' credible report, the Jews in the Diaspora took a lively interest in what was happening in Palestine. They did all they could to support the rising in Palestine, and partly in secret and partly openly, they also rebelled against the Roman authorities. Indeed the movement spread to other dissatisfied elements in the Roman empire.

It is impossible to trace the course of events in detail. A man named Simon became the leader of the rising. According to Christian writers, he was given the honorary name of 'Bar-Cocheba', 'son of the star'. The famous scribe Rabbi Akiba is said, according to Rabbinic sources, to have suggested this name for Simon as a Messianic description based on Num. xxiv, 17, and therefore to have conceived its bearer as the embodiment of the Messianic hope. Rabbinic sources give the name in the form Bar-Koziba, which was interpreted, after the failure of the enterprise, as meaning 'son of lies'. Probably 'Ben-Kosba'[1] was originally a term denoting descent which was secondarily altered and its meaning reinterpreted. The real revolt broke out in the year A.D. 132 after the emperor's return from the Orient. As the Romans failed at first to take the matter really seriously, the rebels were able at first to attain their goal. 'Israel', with Simon at its head, achieved its independence; Jerusalem was 'liberated' and Simon ruled the country, no doubt from Jerusalem. Evidence for

---

[1] A sensational discovery made very recently appears to throw light on the question of the name. In the winter of 1951–52 the fragments of numerous documents were found near the Dead Sea about 15 m. south-east of Jerusalem in a very inaccessible cave on the *wādi murabba'āt*. They include a proclamation and two letters from a 'Simon ben Koseba', whom one is greatly tempted to identify with the leader of the Jewish insurrection under Hadrian, particularly as the cave yielded other discoveries from the same period (*e.g.* so-called insurrection coins). In this case we should have not only original documents in the hand of this 'Messianic' leader but also evidence of the authentic form of his name; his name would then be 'Simon ben Kos(e)ba' (with ס), and if this is the case the later Rabbinic 'Bar Koziba' (with ז) was a deliberate distortion of the name ('son of lies'). On the discovery, cf. the note by L. Rost, ThLZ, 77, (1952), coll. 317 ff., and the preliminary report by G. L. Harding, *Palestine Exploration Quarterly*, 84 (1952), pp. 105-109. A facsimile reproduction of one of the two letters of Simeon will be found in RB, 60 (1953), Pl. xiv and *Biblica*, 34 (1953), opposite p. 420.

this is provided above all by the so-called 'Insurrection Coins'[1]. Special coins were minted with Hebrew inscriptions. The years were re-numbered on these coins on the assumption that a new era had begun. Coins from the 'year 1' and the 'year 2' have survived. To judge from this, the rebels did, in fact, rule for a considerable time. These coins bear the inscription 'Simon, the Prince of Israel'. The coins also celebrate the 'liberation of Israel'; the new era is dated from the 'liberation of Israel'. There are also coins bearing the name of the city of Jerusalem or which refer to the 'liberation of Jerusalem'. It is unfortunate that we have no more exact knowledge about what took place in Jerusalem at this time. No doubt the cultus was revived. There are coins from the year 1 of the new era which bear the inscription 'the priest Eleazar'[2]. Apparently, therefore, the priesthood resumed its functions; and that can only mean that sacrifices were begun again. One would like to suppose that a beginning was made with the rebuilding of the Temple but there are no definite records on this point. Anyway, an amazing revival took place, and it is easy to imagine that for a time enthusiasm and hope were intense. It seemed that 'Israel' was to rise again as a religious community and also as an independent people.

Once again, however, whilst the revolt was successful to begin with, it was crushed in the end by the superiority of the Roman forces. When the revolt began, Tineius Rufus was the Roman governor of Judaea. He could not overcome the rising. The rebels avoided an open encounter with Roman troops. They concentrated their forces on many strongholds and in inaccessible areas and waged a constant guerrilla warfare which wore the enemy down, Even when the governor of the neighbouring province of Syria, Publicius Marcellus, was ordered to Judaea to help suppress the revolt, the Romans still did not obtain a decisive victory over the Jews. How unsuccessful the Roman efforts were to begin with is shown above all by the fact that the rebels were able to remain in power for a considerable time, not only in remote parts of the land, but even in Jerusalem. In the end, Hadrian commissioned one of his most efficient generals, Julius Severus, who had already proved his worth in Britannia and was governor of Britannia at the time, to lead the war against the Jews; and with the help of an unusually big levy

[1] Cf. A. Reifenberg, *Ancient Jewish Coins* ([2] 1947), pp. 33 ff., Pll. xii-xv.

[2] The relationship of this priest with his own coins to the 'prince Simon' is not very clear. As no priest-coins from the 2nd year have come to light so far, it may be that internal tensions and disputes took place which were finally resolved in favour of the 'prince'.

of Roman legions and auxiliary troops he succeeded in suppressing
the revolt. Bearing in mind the desperate courage of the rebels, he
did not proceed to open battles but chose, as Dio Cassius records,
the more protracted but less costly method of starving them into
surrender, *i.e.* he had to encircle innumerable bases and hiding-
places until they were ready to surrender. There is no specific
record of the fact, but Jerusalem probably fell in the same way It
was therefore a slow and agonising death in which the newly
revived 'Israel' perished. The last act of the tragedy was again the
struggle for a fortified position, in which the 'prince' Simon was
offering ultimately hopeless resistance with the surviving remnants
of the rebel forces. High above the southern border of the valley
through which the railway now runs from Jaffa to Jerusalem,
there lies a dominating rounded hill-top called *khirbet el-yehūd*
('ruin of the Jews'), about six miles west of Jerusalem near the
present-day village of *bittīr*. In ancient times this hill-top was the
site of Bethter[1], the name of which has survived in that of the
present village. Simon entrenched himself here with his few
surviving followers, probably after escaping from Jerusalem when
it was occupied by the Romans[2]; and here a last stubborn fight was
put up. Julius Severus was forced to lay a regular siege to the place.
The surviving remains of the Roman *circumvallatio* which can still
be seen on the site provide tangible evidence of this final struggle[3].
In the end this place also fell, either because of hunger and thirst
—the only spring in the neighbourhood of the present village
of *bittīr* had been taken by the besiegers—or by the ultimately
successful use of the normal methods of assault. Here too Julius
Severus had had to use a powerful force. An inscription found in
the village of *bittīr* which no doubt derives from the time of the
siege refers to detachments of the *Legio V Macedonia* and the
Legio XI Claudia which were employed at the time. Simon Bar-
Cocheba lost his life in the struggle, but we are not told exactly
how this happened. This was the end of the insurrection that had
been intended to 'liberate Israel'. It probably took place in the
year A.D. 135.

During the stubborn and protracted fighting the country had

[1] The Old Testament mentions it in Joshua xv, 59 LXX. It is doubtful whether it
still existed on this site in the 2nd century A.D.
[2] Eusebius reports on this final struggle for Bethter (*Hist. eccl.* IV, 6).
[3] On the archaeological discoveries cf. A. Alt, PJB, 23 (1927), pp. 10 ff. (with sketch
map) and also A. Schulten, ZDPV, 56 (1933), pp. 180 ff. For the story of the struggle
for Bethter and the whole Bar-Cocheba insurrection see H. Strathmann, PJB, 23
(1927), pp. 92 ff.

been terribly devastated. Large numbers of the population had lost their lives. The captured rebels were sold in the market by Abraham's terebinth in Mamre and in the slave market in Gaza or were deported to Egypt. The number of these prisoners, men and women, old and young, was so great that they could only be sold for the lowest prices. The remnants of the old Israelite population which had already suffered innumerable losses in the rising of A.D. 66–70 were decimated once again in a fearful manner. The land now really became a Roman province. On the site of Jerusalem there arose the Roman colony with the official name of Colonia Aelia Capitolina, so called in honour of the victorious emperor. The plan for this new foundation, which had presumably given rise to the rebellion, was now executed magnificently as a token of the victory. The city was given a temple of Jupiter Capitolinus on the site of its holy place and an equestrian statue of the emperor Hadrian, and also a temple of Venus, roughly on the site of the later church of the Holy Sepulchre. As a Roman provincial city it was given a well-designed system of streets and adorned with the usual representative buildings[1]. The Jews were forbidden to enter it on pain of death; it was inhabited by a heathen population. The Jews were therefore excluded from their own ancient holy city, which had for so long formed the centre of their ancestors' lives. The province now probably exchanged its former name of Judaea for the new name of Palestine, which it bore henceforth and which derived from the older description of the coastal area as 'the land of the Philistines'; not even the province's name should suggest that it was still a 'land of the Jews'[2]. And so the descendants of the Israel of old had become strangers in their own former homeland just as they were in the Diaspora; and their holy city was prohibited to them. Thus ended the ghastly epilogue of Israel's history.

[1] On the archaeological remains of Hadrian's Aelia Capitolina cf. C. Watzinger, *Denkmäler Palästinas*, II (1935), pp. 79 ff. and also F.-M. Abel, *loc. cit.* pp. 98 ff.
[2] For the details see M. Noth, ZDPV, 62 (1939), pp. 125 ff.

SELECT BIBLIOGRAPHY

ABEL, F.-M., Géographie de la Palestine, I (1933), II (1938).
Histoire de la Palestine depuis la conquête d'Alexandre jusqu'à l'invasion arabe, I, II (1952).
ALBRIGHT, W. F., The Archaeology of Palestine and the Bible ([3] 1935).
From the Stone Age to Christianity ([2] 1946).
Archaeology and the Religion of Israel ([2] 1946).
The Archaeology of Palestine ([2] 1951).
ALT, A., Israel und Ägypten (BWAT, 6) (1909).
Die Landnahme der Israeliten in Palästina (Reformationsprogramm der Universität Leipzig 1925).
Die Staatenbildung der Israeliten in Palästina (Reformationsprogramm der Universität Leipzig 1930).
Der Gott der Väter (BWANT, III, 12) (1929).
Die Ursprünge des israelitischen Rechts (Berichte üb. d. Verh. d. Sächs. Ak. d. Wiss. zu Leipzig, phil.-hist. Kl. 86, 1 [1934]).
Israels Gaue unter Salomo (BWAT, 13, pp. 1-19) (1913).
Judas Gaue unter Josia (PJB, 21 [1925], pp. 100-117).
Das System der Stammesgrenzen im Buche Josua (Sellin-Festschrift [1927], pp. 13-24).
Die Rolle Samarias bei der Entstehung des Judentums (Festschrift Otto Procksch [1934], pp. 5-28).
Kleine Schriften zur Geschichte des Volkes Israel, I, II (1953).
AMARNA LETTERS : J. A. Knudtzon, Die El-Amarna-Tafeln (Vorderasiatische Bibliothek, 2) (1915).
AUERBACH, E., Wüste und Gelobtes Land, I (1932), II (1936).
BEGRICH, J., Die Chronologie der Könige von Israel und Juda (1929).
BERTHOLET, A., Kulturgeschichte Israels (1919).
BICKERMANN, E., Der Gott der Makkabäer. Untersuchungen über Sinn und Ursprung der makkabäischen Erhebung (1937).
BREASTED, J. H., Ancient Records of Egypt, I-V (1906/7).
CASPARI, W., Die Gottesgemeinde vom Sinai und das nachmalige Volk Israel (1922).
CHABAS, M., Mélanges Égyptologiennes, I (1862).
DALMAN, G., Arbeit und Sitte in Palästina, I-VII (1928-1942).
Aramäisch-neuhebräisches Handwörterbuch ([3] 1938).
DUSSAUD, R., Les Origines cananéennes du sacrifice israélite ([2] 1941).
EISSFELDT, O., Einleitung in das Alte Testament ([2] 1956).
Baal Zaphon, Zeus Kasios und der Durchzug der Israeliten durchs Meer (Beiträge zur Religionsgeschichte des Altertums, Heft 1) (1932).
EUSEBIUS, Historia ecclesiastica : Eusebius Kirchengeschichte hrsg. von E. Schwartz. Kleine Ausgabe ([2] 1914).
Das Onomastikon, ed. E. Klostermann. Die griechischen christlichen Schriftsteller : Eusebius' Werke, III, 1 (1904).
FISHER, C. S., The Excavation of Armageddon (The University of Chicago Oriental Institute Communications No. 4) (1929).
FORRER, E., Die Provinzeinteilung des Assyrischen Reiches (1921).

456 BIBLIOGRAPHY

GADD, G. J., The Fall of Nineveh (1923).

GALLING, K., Biblisches Reallexikon (HAT, I, 1) (1937).

Textbuch zur Geschichte Israels (1950).

GLUECK, N., Explorations in Eastern Palestine I, II, III, IV (AASOR, XIV, XV, XVIII/XIX, XXV/XXVIII) (1934, 1935, 1939, 1951).

GRESSMANN, H., Altorientalische Texte und Bilder zum Alten Testament (² 1926/27).

GROLLENBERG, L. H., Atlas of the Bible (1956).

GUTHE, H., Geschichte des Volkes Israel (³ 1914).

Bibelatlas (² 1926).

Palästina (Monographien zur Erdkunde, 21) (² 1927).

GUY, P. L. O., New Light from Armageddon (The University of Chicago Oriental Institute Communications, No. 9) (1931).

INGHOLT, H., Rapport préliminaire sur sept campagnes de fouilles à Hama en Syrie 1932–1938 (1940).

JANSEN, H. L., Die Politik Antiochos' des IV (1943).

JEPSEN, A., Untersuchungen zum Bundesbuch (BWANT, III, 5) (1927).

JEREMIAS, J., Die Passahfeier der Samaritaner (BZAW, 59) (1932).

JIRKU, A., Geschichte des Volkes Israel (1931).

Die Wanderungen der Hebräer im 3. und 2. Jahrtausend v. Chr. (AO, 24, 2) (1924).

JOSEPHUS : Flavii Josephi opera recogn. B. Niese, I–VI (1888–1895). (Also in Loeb Classical Library (1926 ff.)).

JUNGE, P. J., Dareios I König der Perser (1944).

KAPELRUD, A. S., The Question of Authorship in the Ezra-Narrative (1944).

KITTEL, R., Geschichte des Volkes Israel, I (⁵, ⁶ 1923), II (⁶ 1925), III 1/2 (1927/ 1929). (English translation of earlier edition: A History of the Hebrews (1895)).

KLOSTERMANN, A., Der Pentateuch (1893). Neue Folge (1907).

KOLBE, W., Beiträge zur syrischen und jüdischen Geschichte (BWANT, II, 10) (1926).

LIDZBARSKI, M., Altsemitische Texte I : Kanaanäische Inschriften (1907).

LODS, A., Israël des origines au milieu du VIIIᵉ siècle (1930). English translation: Israel (1932).

LUCKENBILL, D. D., Ancient Records of Assyria and Babylonia I/II (1927).

McCOWN, C. C., and J. C. WAMPLER, Tell en-Naṣbeh, I/II (1947).

MARI-TEXTS : Archives royales de Mari I–V (Musée du Louvre. Département des Antiquités Orientales. Textes cunéiformes XXII–XXVI (1946, 1941, 1948, 1951) et Archives royales de Mari publiées sous la direction de A. Parrot et G. Dossin, I–V (1950–1952).

MEYER, E., Die Entstehung des Judentums (1896).

Die Israeliten und ihre Nachbarstämme (1906).

Ursprung und Anfänge des Christentums, II (1921).

Geschichte des Altertums, II, 1 (² 1928), II, 2 (² 1931).

MÖHLENBRINK, K., Der Tempel Salomos (BWANT, IV, 7) (1932).

MORITZ, B., Der Sinaikult in heidnischer Zeit (Abh. d. Gött. Ges. d. Wiss., N.F. 16, 2) (1916).

MULLER, M. W., Die Palästinaliste Thutmosis' III (MVAG, XII, 1) (1907).

NOTH, M., Das System der zwölf Stämme Israels (BWANT, III, 10) (1930).

Das Buch Josua (HAT, I, 7) (² 1953).

Die Gesetze im Pentateuch (Schriften d. Königsb. Gel. Ges., geisteswiss. Kl. XVII, 2) (1940).
Die Welt des Alten Testaments (² 1953).
Überlieferungsgeschichtliche Studien, I (Schriften d. Königsb. Gel. Ges., geisteswiss. Kl. XVIII, 2) (1943).
Überlieferungsgeschichte des Pentateuch (1948).
OPPENHEIM, M. v., Die Beduinen, I/II/III (1939/43/52).
OTTLI, S., Geschichte Israels bis auf Alexander den Grossen (1905).
OTTO, W., Herodes (1913).
PETRIE, FLINDERS, Researches in Sinai (1906).
POSENER, G., Princes et pays d'Asie et de Nubie. Textes hiératiques sur des figurines d'envoûtement du Moyen Empire (1940).
PRITCHARD, J. B. (editor), Ancient Near Eastern Texts Relating to the Old Testament (1950, ² 1956), The Ancient Near East in Pictures Relating to the Old Testament (1954).
RAD, G. v., Das formgeschichtliche Problem des Hexateuchs (BWANT, IV, 26) (1938).
RAS SHAMRA TEXTS : C. H. Gordon, Ugaritic Literature. A comprehensive Translation of the poetic and prose Texts (1949).
REISNER-FISHER-LYON, Harvard Excavations at Samaria 1908–1910, I/II (1924).
ROBINSON, T. H., and W. O. E. OESTERLEY, A History of Israel, I/II (1932).
ROST, L., Die Überlieferung von der Thronnachfolge Davids (BWANT, III, 6) (1926).
ROTHSTEIN, J. W., Juden und Samaritaner (BWAT, 3) (1908).
SCHAEDER, H. H., Esra der Schreiber (1930).
SCHLATTER, A., Geschichte Israels von Alexander dem Grossen bis Hadrian (³ 1925).
SCHÜRER, E., Geschichte des jüdischen Volkes im Zeitalter Jesu Christi, I (³, ⁴ 1901), II (⁴ 1907), III (⁴ 1909). (English translation of 2nd edition : A History of the Jewish People (1897-98)).
SELLIN, E., Geschichte des israelitisch-jüdischen Volkes, I (1924), II (1932).
SETHE, K., Die Ächtung feindlicher Fürsten, Völker und Dinge auf altägyptischen Tongefässscherben des Mittleren Reiches (Abh. d. Preuss. Ak. d. Wiss., phil.-hist. Kl. 1926, Nr. 5).
SIMONS, J., Jerusalem in the Old Testament. Researches and Theories (1952).
STURM, J., Der Hettiterkrieg Ramses' II (Beihefte zur Wiener Zeitschrift für die Kunde des Morgenlandes, 4) (1939).
THOMSEN, P., Die Palästina-Literatur. Eine internationale Bibliographie, I (1908), II (1911), III (1916), IV (1927), V (1938), VI (1954).
Palästina und seine Kultur in fünf Jahrtausenden (AO, 30) (³ 1932).
TORCZYNER, H., Lachish I : The Lachish Letters (1938).
UNGNAD, Eponymen (Reallexikon der Assyriologie, II [1938], pp. 412-457).
WATZINGER, C., Denkmäler Palästinas. Eine Einführung in die Archäologie des Heiligen Landes, I (1933), II (1935).
WEBER, W., Das antike Judentum (Gesammelte Aufsätze zur Religionssoziologie, III) (1923).
WEISER, A., Einleitung in das Alte Testament (² 1949).
WELLHAUSEN, J., Geschichte Israels, I (1878).

WILLRICH, H., Urkundenfälschung in der hellenistisch-jüdischen Literatur
  (Forsch. z. Rel. u. Lit. d. A. und N. Test., N.F. 21) (1924).
WRIGHT, G. E., and F. V. FILSON, The Westminster Historical Atlas to the
  Bible (1945, ² 1958).

INDEX OF BIBLICAL REFERENCES

The Hebrew enumeration is followed where this differs from the English

INDEX OF NAMES AND SUBJECTS

The page references under the five entries Egypt; Jerusalem; Jezreel, plain of; Josephus; *and* Mesopotamia *are arranged in two groups of which the second, within brackets, are the minor references.*